THE SECRET FILE OF
JOSEPH STALIN

THE SECRET FILE OF
JOSEPH STALIN

―――

A HIDDEN LIFE

―――

ROMAN BRACKMAN

FRANK CASS
LONDON · PORTLAND, OR

First published in 2001 in Great Britain by
FRANK CASS PUBLISHERS
Newbury House, 900 Eastern Avenue
London, IG2 7HH

and in the United States of America by
FRANK CASS PUBLISHERS
c/o ISBS, 5824 N.E. Hassalo Street
Portland, Oregon, 97213-3644

Website: www.frankcass.com

British Library Cataloguing in Publication Data

Brackman, Roman
The secret file of Joseph Stalin: a hidden life
1. Stalin, I. (Iosif), 1879–1953   2. Heads of state – Soviet
Union – Biography   3. Secret service – Soviet Union – History
4. Soviet Union – Politics and government – 1936–1953
I. Title
947′.0842′092

ISBN 0-7146-5050-1 (cloth)

Library of Congress Cataloging-in-Publication Data

Brackman, Roman, 1931–
    The Secret file of Joseph Stalin: a hidden life / Roman Brackman.
      p.   cm
    Includes bibliographical references and index.
    ISBN   0-7146-5050-1 (cloth)
    1. Stalin, Joseph, 1879–1953.   2. Heads of state–Soviet
Union–Biography.   3. Soviet Union–Politics and government–
      1917–1936.
4. Soviet Union–Politics and government–1936–1953.
5. Russia–History–Nicholas II, 1894–1917.   6. Russia. Okhrannyia
otdieleniia.   7. Soviet Union. Narodnyi komissariat vnutrennikh del.
I. Title.
    DK268.S8   B69 2000
    947.084–dc21

00-050861

Typeset by Regent Typesetting, London
Printed in Great Britain by
Creative Print and Design (Wales) Ebbw Vale

Contents

List of Illustrations

Between pages 172 and 173

1. House of the Dzhugashvili family, where Stalin was born.
2. Stalin's mother, Ekaterina Georgievna Dzhugashvili (née Geladze).
3. Kamo being delivered from Germany in shackles to the Tiflis prison in 1909.
4. Prison photographs of Stalin at the time of his last arrest in 1913.
5. The 'Eremin Letter'.
6. Copy of the original Okhrana document, dated 31 March 1911.
7. Ekaterina Svanidze, first wife of Stalin.
8. Fabricated photograph of Lenin sitting next to Stalin.
9. Roman Malinovsky.
10. Nadezhda Allilueva, Stalin's second wife, shortly before her suicide in 1932.
11. Marshal Mikhail Tukhachevsky.
12. Prison camp inmates building the White Sea–Baltic Canal.
13. Stalin with Yezhov, Molotov and Voroshilov at the opening of the White Sea–Baltic Canal.
14. People's demonstration in Red Square in 1938.
15. Chief prosecutor Andrey Vyshinsky at the Moscow show trial.
16. Stalin's son Yakov Dzhugashvili, captured by the Nazis.
17. Stalin and Ribbentrop watch as Molotov signs the Nazi–Soviet Pact in August 1939.
18. Lev Trotsky and his wife Natalia Sedova arrive in Mexico in 1937.
19. A Mexican policeman holds up the axe that killed Trotsky.
20. Funeral procession in March 1953 with the coffin of Stalin.

Acknowledgements: Figures 1, 4, 8, 10, 11, 12, 13, 14, 15, 16, 17, 18, 19, 20 reproduced by permission of David King. Figure 5 reproduced by permission of *Life* magazine. Figure 6 reproduced by permission of the Hoover Institution, Stanford University. While attempts have been made to obtain permissions from all other copyright holders, the publisher apologizes for any omissions; these can be rectified in later editions.

Foreword

Of all the dictators the world endured in the twentieth century, Joseph Stalin was unquestionably the mightiest. His image acquired superhuman proportions, and any serious study of Soviet history must take full account of his personality, his personal attitudes and his personal involvement in all spheres of activity during the period of his rule. In this book, Roman Brackman focuses on the most intensely personal aspects of Stalin's character, and connects them with events in his life that have never before been so comprehensively examined.

Succeeding Lenin in 1924, Stalin took over a state that was still recovering from the ravages of the First World War, three years of civil war and six of communist depredations. In a country populated overwhelmingly by peasants, the Soviet leaders saw the future in terms of a state founded on industrial power. But they also had to find a way to feed the expanding workforce and to do it with the help of a resentful agrarian population. Yet by the late 1930s, only some 15 years after Stalin had become the new leader, the Soviet Union was an industrial power on an international scale. On vast construction sites, armies of workers had been mobilized to fulfil Stalin's ambitious Five-Year Plans, straining every sinew to build and set in motion giant steel works, power stations, arms and ammunition plants, aircraft and tank factories. Schools and universities had multiplied, and a large technical and cultural intelligentsia had been created. Science and technology had made great strides, and Soviet military and strategic science was highly regarded in the West. By the time Stalin died in 1953, he could claim that within one generation he had overseen the development of the USSR from a backward state into nuclear 'superpower' status.

In the 1930s, moreover, the Soviet Union was widely perceived in the West – especially by industrial workers and intellectuals – as a country that had saved the working class from the jungle law of the capitalist system, from unemployment and exploitation, and to have done so by getting rid of the owners as a class, by introducing public ownership throughout, and, in particular, by organizing national output on the basis of rational planning. While the industrialized countries of the West were languishing in mass unemployment and widespread social distress and were drifting rudderless towards an unknown future, they saw a USSR that was in full production and being guided towards the bright future of communism by the intelligent, far-seeing and above all the rational leadership of Joseph Stalin. To many people in the West, to say nothing of his own country, Stalin represented a force for good – for the greater good of mankind as a whole, indeed. Although his public appearances were extremely rare, his image was to be seen everywhere throughout the country. Like a Colossus, he stood astride the pinnacle of the Soviet state, a symbol of its might and a beacon to the world.

This image, and the enthusiasm of the 'fellow-travellers' who supported Soviet aims, were somewhat dented by the Pact Stalin made with Hitler in 1939, according to which neither would attack the other. But then in June 1941 Stalin's progressive credentials were restored when the Soviet Union was invaded by Nazi forces and it was brought, willy-nilly, into the war against Germany. After recovering from the shock of the initial attack and the massive defeats inflicted on the Red Army, Stalin began to educate himself in the art of modern warfare and in due course was able to make a constructive and effective contribution to the Soviet war effort and the great victory of 1945. The war greatly enhanced Stalin's standing in the world. Half of Europe was under his control, and the USSR emerged from the war no longer the pariah state it had been before 1941. After the war, while the Soviet people were still traumatized from its horrors and their huge losses, in every sense, Stalin roused them again to make a supreme effort in the reconstruction of the country and its economy. When he died, hundreds of thousands of people packed into the streets near the Kremlin, there was widespread weeping and many people have testified that they thought it was the end of the world as they had known it.

This picture of Soviet achievement had an reverse side, however. The feelings of mastery that workers had experienced from the victory of a revolution carried out in their name would barely outlast the Civil War, as the new regime took over the trade unions and introduced its own brand of coercion into the industrial scene. The peasants were given a brief period of free trade in order to revive the agrarian economy, but by the end of the 1920s Stalin had decided that they must be brought under state control, and, using the most savage means, had driven them into collective farms. At least five million of the most 'recalcitrant' – among them the most successful farmers, condemned as 'kulaks' – died in the process, either exterminated by Red Army units, or starved to death in the northern wastes to which they had been forcibly deported. The rapidly expanding intelligentsia soon found that intellectual and cultural freedom were not communist goals, and from the late 1920s both artists and academics found themselves mobilized into state service to promote the Communist Party's propaganda slogans or to rewrite the country's history to conform to a new pattern. Failure to conform or obey resulted in disastrous consequences.

Although Marxist aims had always been expressed in terms of the impersonal forces of history and the laws of economics, the Russian Revolution – and other communist revolutions that followed it, for that matter, for example in China, North Korea, Cuba – erected monumental personalities before the people as the embodiment of its ideals. From 1917 until his death in 1924, it was Lenin who fulfilled this role, and indeed, until the end of the system itself in 1991 it was Lenin who, as an embalmed relic in the Kremlin Mausoleum or a name to be uttered whenever ideological authority was needed, was the acknowledged guide to a brilliant future.

Stalin had set about securing his position as Lenin's chosen heir and successor as soon as Lenin departed the scene. As a first step it was necessary to rewrite the history of the revolution in a way that would highlight and magnify Stalin's role, diminishing that of others with a better claim in the process. Throughout the 1920s and 1930s, books and articles were written and revised in numerous editions by Bolshevik memoirists and official historians with this aim in mind. By the mid-1930s, when it seemed the Soviet Union was not only secure economically, but also entering a phase of social stability, Stalin had become virtually a demi-god, an ubiquitous icon, and an omnipotent dictator with more power than ever.

In some respects, the Stalinist approach to social mobilization worked. The economy was re-energized and the country was made strong again. But alongside industrial and agrarian coercion and constantly raised targets, under Stalin the propaganda machine completely blurred the distinction between political exhortation and outright lies. Objective criteria were virtually extinguished and only 'the Party line', i.e. Stalin's word, was acceptable currency. He operated a system of fear and terror in which the entire population were made to inform on each other. A word out of turn, uttering an opinion that was politically correct only yesterday but not today, a moment's hesitation in carrying out an order, let alone questioning it – any such 'misdemeanour' could result in the dreaded knock on the door in the small hours. Literally millions were arrested and taken away, to face execution, decades in prison or concentration camp or harsh exile in homicidal conditions. Trials on the whole were reserved for those whose testimony – invariably false and extracted under torture – could be used by Stalin's henchmen to arrest further echelons of 'enemies of the people'.

Since its inception, the regime had been characterized by repressive and coercive practices. Political opponents were deported abroad, executed or sent into camps and exile from 1918, and persecution in various forms continued right through the Stalin era and after, uninterrupted even by the war. Stalin did not maintain a lofty distance between himself and the penal process: he personally scrutinized lists of those who had been arrested – hundreds of thousands of them – and he personally scrawled the sentence they were to receive beside their names, all too frequently writing 'death penalty'. Like Lenin, who had established the terror state, Stalin was personally vengeful. But if repression was one of the main hallmarks of the entire Stalin period, it was the year 1937 that sharpened that image to the point of extremism. The country was convulsed by a series of show trials and a terror campaign that led to the deaths and incarceration of millions of innocent people. Those affected included half a million Communist Party functionaries, ranging from Stalin's closest and Lenin's oldest comrades down to lowly clerks, 45,000 senior officers of the Red Army – 15,000 of whom were shot – factory and farm managers, leading scholars, writers, heads of research institutes and often their entire staffs, educationists and their students, simple workers and peasants, and even swathes of the penal service, the NKVD, itself. The gamut of society was traumatized by this assault. Show trials of the Bolshevik Old Guard 'proved' that virtually all the top layers of Party and state administration had been engaged in various conspiracies to eliminate Stalin, and all allegedly on the orders of the disgraced, absent, hunted, and best-known hero of the revolution, Trotsky.

The country was pervaded by a climate of distrust and betrayal. The 'long night' of 1937 was revisited in the post-war 1940s in a series of psychopathic campaigns that might have gone even further, had not Stalin died when he did. Stalin suffered from pathological suspiciousness, as his successor Nikita Khrushchev – no saint himself – put it. Always guarded and defensive, he had never been as convivial as his comrades. His rewriting of Party history exposed obvious insecurity about his revolutionary credentials, and his resort to harsh methods, even if it was a development of Lenin's approach, never appeared to be out of character. Nevertheless, the precise cause of the scale and savagery of the violence of the mid-1930s has never been definitively explained.

Was the permanent climate of fear manufactured by Stalin precisely in order to create a submissive and obedient system, one that was deemed essential if the country was to become strong enough to resist a surrounding world that was hostile to its very existence? It is difficult to reconcile that idea with the fact that large numbers of his most loyal executives, his closest aides and even their families were among the victims. Did he sacrifice them as a constant reminder to others that no one, however exalted, was safe from the Leader's long reach?

Was this the 'normal' behaviour of a dictator, who, by virtue of his omnipotence, must expect to be surrounded by potential enemies who wish to diminish his power? It would have been surprising if Stalin could *not* have pointed to real potential enemies. But he so dominated the Party organization and its rank-and-file membership that his word came to represent the Party line, and all opposition to it was therefore doomed. Similarly, the country as a whole accepted the propaganda, adoring their omnipotent leader, as the populations of other dictatorships were doing elsewhere in Europe. Under these circumstances, it is natural to suppose that real opposition no longer existed.

Were Stalin's political actions a reflection of his personality? Had he become lethally affected by the power he inherited when he succeeded Lenin? Did his pathological outlook originate in the taciturn young provincial of limited culture, who had watched as more brilliant intellectuals dominated Party debate and ideological argument, and shone as orators on the streets of Petrograd in 1917 and later in the Civil War as tribunes to the front-line troops? Stalin had always been more of a 'backroom boy', rather than one for the grandstand. But, though limited, he was not ignorant of Marxist scripture; indeed, he was probably a better Marxist scholar than any of his successors.

It is Roman Brackman's view, demonstrated throughout this book, that Stalin harboured so dark a secret about himself, one that was so compromising, that his need to prevent its disclosure in the mid-1930s drove him to his homicidal excesses. The canon of personal morality in the revolutionary underground knew no more heinous crime against the sacred cause of revolution than betrayal of one's comrades to the Okhrana, the tsarist secret police. Suspicion that Stalin had indeed been a police spy was aroused as early as 1899, when he was an underground revolutionary in Georgia, but it was his subsequent impressive record of arrests and escapes that prompted a belief in wider party circles that he must have police protection. Had he been exposed when the police archives were partly opened after the February Revolution of 1917 he would have been shot or committed suicide, like many other secret agents, and the world would never have heard of him. Various attempts to establish Stalin's collaboration with the St Petersburg Okhrana in the years just before the First World War were made at intervals throughout the Soviet era by Western researchers and Soviet defectors, largely based on inside knowledge of Soviet intelligence circles. Since the late 1980s, when writers began to fill the 'blank pages' of Soviet history, researchers have dug deeper, survivors have surfaced and their memories recorded, and the Party archives have yielded significant new material.

This fascinating book is Roman Brackman's carefully researched account of the question. Focusing his attention on the obscure fate of a 'Stalin File' that was held by the St Petersburg Okhrana and unearthed in the mid-1920s, he penetrates the most secret part of a system that was itself obsessed with secrecy – the world of the NKVD. He has re-assessed all the known material and fitted it together with new archival and other unpublished sources, shedding light on many hitherto obscure aspects of the explosive story and explaining their significance with valuable insight. The result is a compelling account of one of the most intriguing mysteries of Soviet history.

Professor Harold Shukman
St Antony's College, Oxford

Preface

'Strange fact: in none of Stalin's biographies does he come to life!' the historian Bertram D. Wolfe observed some years ago.[1] In his recent biography Robert Conquest refers to Stalin as 'unreal'.[2] But Stalin was real enough to the millions he sent to their deaths and to the generations he forced to live in terror and abject misery. Yet it is also true that Stalin emerges from his previously published biographies as unreal indeed. They describe someone quite mousy who gives birth to a colossal mountain of horrors, leaving the reader with the sensation of an almost palpable disparity between cause and effect. The torrent of revelations in the era of *glasnost* has done little to dispel the mystery of Stalin the man and to fill in the blanks in his life and in Soviet history.

Stalin's secrets have remained hidden because during his rule, lasting more than a quarter of a century, he was able to destroy or distort much of the evidence about his past, and to cover up many of his crimes. He almost succeeded in his drive to hide his real self. Stalin was obsessed with the destruction of archival documents and bent on murdering witnesses; he forged documents to replace truth with fraud; he habitually lied and practiced the precise opposite of what he preached. A gigantic propaganda machine worked for decades to glorify him.

All of this has made the task of Stalin's biographers extremely difficult. At best, they have made a modest attempt to explore the almost barren terrain of his early years. None of them mentions the bitter family conflict caused by the belief that Stalin was the child of an adulterous affair, a belief that poisoned the lives of his parents and led to the family's breakup. No biographer mentions the severe beatings by Stalin's father Vissarion, which left the 10-year-old boy's arm crippled for life. These traumas left Stalin's soul crippled as well. And none delves into the murders instigated by Stalin as a young man, including that of his own father. But it is only in the light of Stalin's childhood traumas and the early murders that the carnage of his rule will begin to become comprehensible. He turned into a brutal and cunning 'serial killer' long before the Revolution furnished him with the opportunity to gratify his craving for blood on a giant scale.

Only one, early, biography mentions in passing that Stalin was an agent of the tsarist secret police, the Okhrana.[3] Yet the story of Stalin's Okhrana career is crucial, even central, to an understanding of his psychological makeup and character, of the course of Soviet history and the very nature of the Soviet police state that inflicted deep psychological damage on generations of people. But, however important the story of Stalin's Okhrana career might be on its own merit, it pales into insignificance in comparison with the horrors that Stalin's fear of revelation of his Okhrana past burdened Soviet history.

None of Stalin's biographies reveals that Stalin's Okhrana file survived the Revolution and was discovered in the old archives by high Soviet officials, who plotted to depose and execute him. Fragmentary early accounts of Stalin's Okhrana career do exist but have frequently been dismissed as unsubstantiated rumors or mere sensationalism. But the evidence I have assembled argues overwhelmingly that the 'rumors' were based on truth and that the revelations that emerge from the evidence – although indeed sensational – have nothing to do with sensationalism. Stalin's paranoia, which his biographers often cite, had roots in reality, and the history of Stalin's Okhrana file makes comprehensible, if no less horrible, the bloody convulsions of Stalin's era.

This book is the result of historical detective work to recover the truth. In this salvage operation, I neglected no piece of information, however minute, and left unexplained no omission or displacement of data. I closely scrutinized Russian secret police archives, old publications, newspaper reports, memoirs, recent revelations in Soviet archives and the press, even old movies Stalin had sponsored. I also interviewed scores of witnesses and their descendants. The process was akin to the slow and painstaking restoration of a portrait that had been torn to pieces. Its often tiny, warped and widely scattered fragments had to be collected and placed in the proper relationship with respect to each other. The result makes intelligible many baffling and seemingly inexplicable events that took place during Stalin's rule and occurred even decades after his death. The reader will discover the real Stalin, the great imposter, hiding behind the mask of a revolutionary zealot; the deranged despot, haunted by fear of exposure of his crimes and duplicity; a mass-murderer without a conscience, who himself was poisoned. A man who, having climbed to the pinnacle of power, plunged into the abyss of insanity. Stalin's true story is more dreadful and bizarre than any fiction, but he emerges from it as quite real.

Ironically, Stalin himself often unintentionally helped salvage the truth about himself. The records of the macabre show trials he staged during his rule reveal one of his peculiar passions – his irresistible craving to force his victims to confess to the selfsame crimes he himself had committed. These confessions, like the play within Shakespeare's *Hamlet*, contained fragments of events that indeed had taken place – not in the lives of the show trial defendants but in Stalin's own life. Thus the show trial confessions are criminal evidence that is unique in history.

Another peculiarity of Stalin also provides a rich mine of information about his hidden past: he was victim to a compulsive urge to use political and social issues, individual people, and whole ethnic groups as props and surrogates on which to project and act out his personal emotional conflicts, re-enacting over and over the traumatic events of his life.

Yet another of Stalin's obsessions was helpful in recovering the truth: he inundated Soviet archives with fake documents in order to hide the record of his Okhrana service and to glorify his past as a revolutionary. But he did it in a peculiar way: he 'doctored' many real Okhrana documents, inserting fraudulent information and erasing some statements, thus changing the documents' true meaning, but leaving some of the text intact. Fortunately, these fabrications are crude and easily detectable. Many particles of truth that Stalin failed to erase from these documents proved to be extremely valuable in the reconstruction of his career.

During the many years of my research, I had the feeling that if I failed to unearth Stalin's story, it might remain buried forever, and the numerous bits and pieces of evidence I had gathered would disappear with the passage of time, unnoticed or neglected by others. With the information that emerged from decades of inquiry, I gained a unique insight into Stalin's personality, the 'method in his madness'. Rightly or wrongly, I also felt that the circumstances of my own life had conspired to burden me with the task of unearthing Stalin's story.

I was born and grew up in Moscow, on Arbat Street, the usual route taken by Stalin and his entourage speeding in their limousines to and from the Kremlin. During my childhood, I often stayed with my grandparents. I loved and respected my grandfather, whom I remember well: a tall scholarly man with a full gray beard, who, in referring to Stalin, would often mutter, 'The bandit!' in a low voice meant only for my grandmother's ears. But I heard him. As a child, my classmates and I had to attend the parades in Red Square. As the columns moved past the Kremlin, I would look at Stalin, standing on top of the Lenin mausoleum, waving his hand from time to time. I thought of my grandfather and wondered why all these people around me were shouting hysterically, 'Long live Stalin!'

In 1950 two of my classmates and I, 19-year-old students at the time, were arrested for attempting to escape across the Soviet–Turkish border and for 'anti-Soviet propaganda'. Five years later, in the amnesty of the post-Stalin thaw, my friends and I were released, like millions of other prisoners. During the five years I spent in the gulag, I met many people, and their stories left a deep impression on me. Many of them could not explain why they had been arrested. They kept asking: 'Why?'

Perhaps my research started then, in the gulag, with my repeatedly encountering that 'Why?' Or maybe it was prompted even earlier by my grandfather's derogatory muttering and my puzzlement as to why a man he called a bandit was adulated by vast crowds. In any case, Stalin's story emerged after many years of hunting down sources, following leads, and piecing together fragments of information. The result is this book. It is never too late to uncover the truth and to explain why historical events happened the way they did. The end of the calamity that Stalin left behind is not yet in sight. The truth about the greatest criminal and tyrant in modern history may help to explain his legacy, which is at the roots of the turmoil and violence that threaten to flare up in the former Soviet empire. Russian people today, almost half a century after the dictator's death, are still in the process of freeing themselves from the consequences of Stalin's rule. People who have been denied the knowledge of their past tend to repeat it. The purpose of this study is to recover the truth and make this process irreversible.

NOTES

1. Bertram D. Wolfe, *Three Who Made a Revolution*, vol. 2, New York, 1964, p. 89.
2. Robert Conquest, *Stalin: Breaker of Nations*, New York, 1991, p. 323.
3. Edward Ellis Smith, *The Young Stalin – The Early Years of an Elusive Revolutionary*, London, 1968.

Acknowledgements

No book can be the effort of only one person. My gratitude therefore goes to many people who contributed to this book in various ways, first of all to my family, to my wife Nadine, to my sons Alexander and Peter, and to my daughter Yvette for their encouragement, support and endurance during many years of my research and writing.

A very small group of pioneers dared to venture into the murky and forbidden terrain of Stalin's Okhrana (Tsarist Secret Police) career. They blazed the trail of his top-secret Okhrana file, the story that makes intelligible many unexplained and baffling events and atrocities during Stalin's long and brutal reign.

I am most thankful to Ambassador George F. Kennan, Professor Emeritus at the Institute for Advanced Study, School of Historical Studies at Princeton, who has been deeply involved in the study of Stalin's Okhrana career and has greatly contributed to my research by advice, information and encouragement.

I also owe a great deal to the late Isaac Don Levine, who pioneered the first biography of Stalin (1931) and published the book *Stalin's Great Secret*. I am especially grateful to him for sharing with me his insights and important documents in his archive on Stalin.

My gratitude goes also to the late Edward Ellis Smith, a CIA expert on Russia, for initiating research (1956) in the Okhrana Collection at the Hoover Institution on War, Revolution and Peace at Stanford University and also for providing me with many important documents on Stalin that he had collected in his archive. His book *The Young Stalin* (1967) was an important contribution to the search for the real Stalin. He signed his book: 'To Roman Brackman. With high regards and all best wishes in the murky world of Stalin. Best of luck. Edward Ellis Smith.'

I want to express my great appreciation to Dr John J. Dziak, a 31-year veteran expert on Russia with the United States Department of Defence military intelligence, currently professor at universities in Washington, for his advice, trust in me, and for his encouragement.

I also want to express my deep gratitude to the late Raymond Rocca, a specialist on Russia and a veteran of many years of US intelligence service and its expert on Russia, for being a staunch advocate for publication of my manuscript on Stalin.

I am also grateful to my old friend Michael Steinhardt for his support, unwavering trust in me and his strong belief in the historical importance of my book on Stalin.

I am deeply indebted to Professor Peter Reddaway for his help in bringing the manuscript to the attention of Frank Cass Publishers.

My gratitude goes to all people whom I mention in the source references. They preserved widely scattered particles of truth that were helpful in bringing to light Stalin's story.

I hasten to state my gratitude to the Okhrana Collection at the Hoover Institution on War, Revolution and Peace at Stanford University, to the Boris Nikolaevsky Collection at the Hoover Institution and to the Bakhmetieff Collection at Columbia University for allowing me to do extensive research in their archives.

I bear sole responsibility for collecting, evaluating and citing the evidence and for the contents of the narrative. Finally, I must add that without the exceptional forbearance and help of my wife Nadine and my children this effort would not have succeeded.

I

THE ROOTS OF EVIL

Early in 1874, a tall, broad-shouldered stranger with a full black beard arrived at Gori, a small provincial town located in the heart of Georgia, then a southern province of the Great Russian Empire. In appearance he seemed one of the recently freed serfs who had left their native villages to escape poverty and find employment in the cities and towns. His name was Vissarion Dzhugashvili, and his arrival at Gori was in a way a return to the land where his peasant ancestors, all serfs, had once lived.

Vissarion's knowledge of his ancestors was limited to a few stories about his grandfather Zaza Dzhugashvili, a serf born in about 1800 in a village near Gori, shortly before Georgia was absorbed into the Russian empire. Zaza took part in several peasant uprisings suppressed by Russian troops. He was captured twice, but managed to escape and hide in a remote mountain hamlet, where he herded sheep. Later he settled in the village of Didi-Lilo and got married and had children.[1] (A number of his descendants still lived in Didi-Lilo in the 1930s.[2])

One of Zaza's sons, Vano, had a vineyard. Children in Didi-Lilo started early helping their parents in the fields, or else they learned a trade. Vano's son, Vissarion, left Didi-Lilo at the age of 14, after the abolition of serfdom in 1864. Vissarion went to work at the shoe factory of an Armenian businessman Adelkhanov in Tiflis, the capital of Georgia. Ten years later, he moved to Gori to work at another shoe factory, where he was offered more money.[3]

The inhabitants of Gori assumed that Vissarion Dzhugashvili came from Ossetia, which borders Georgia in the north, since his name had the same root as the common Ossetic name Dzhukaev. They were wrong. Ossets often migrated to Georgia and became assimilated there, but Vissarion was not one of them. The name Dzhugashvili consists of two words, *shvili*, which means 'son of,' and *dzhuga*, which is not used in contemporary Georgian but existed in Old Georgian and meant 'yoke for oxen'. The word was absorbed into Old Georgian from a language of one of the Indo-European tribes that in ancient times dwelt in the area. Words of the same root and similar meaning, such as the Russian word *igo* (yoke), are common to all Indo-European languages, to which Georgian however does not belong.[4] One of Vissarion's remote Georgian ancestors was probably a craftsman who made yokes for oxen, devices in great demand then. The Dzhugashvili family name dates back to that time.

Having settled in Gori, Vissarion soon gained the reputation of being an excellent shoemaker. This encouraged him to open his own shop. His business prospered, and he bought a small house. Vissarion became friendly with a local priest, Koba Egnatashvili, and two brothers by the name of Geladze, who had a sister, Katerina, or Keke, as everyone called her. She and her brothers had been born to a family of serfs in a village near Gori. After the abolition of serfdom, the family had moved to Gori, where the father died soon afterwards. In Gori, the family stayed together in the same house. Keke helped her mother while her brothers opened a pottery shop.[5]

Vissarion was 24 when he proposed to Keke, who was then 16. The register of marriages for the year 1874 states: 'Joined in wedlock on 17 May [1874] Vissarion Dzhugashvili, peasant, temporary resident of Gori, Orthodox Christian, age of bridegroom 24, and Ekaterina, daughter of Glakh Geladze, peasant, formerly resident of Gori, deceased. Orthodox Christian, her first marriage, age 16.'[6] The couple had a splendid Georgian Orthodox ceremony in a Gori church, conducted by the priest Koba Egnatashvili.[7]

But happiness was not to be the couple's lot. In the first three years of marriage, Keke gave birth to three children who either died in early infancy or were stillborn. In later years she once mentioned that she had two sons, and another time she spoke of three babies, which suggests that one of them was a girl.[8] The causes of their deaths and even their names remain unknown.

The fourth child, a boy, was born a month before the Eastern Orthodox Christmas, 1878. A photocopy of the entry in the records of the *Uspensky Sobor* (the Cathedral of the Assumption) in Gori states: 'Iosif Dzugashvili born 6 December 1878. Christened 17 December [1878], parents Vissarion Ivanovich Dzugashvili, peasant, and his lawful wedded wife, Ekaterina Georgievna, residents of the township of Gori. Godfather – Tsikhatrishvili, peasant, resident of Gori.'[9] This boy survived. Everyone called him Soso, the Georgian diminutive of Iosif. He was to become known to the world as Iosif Vissarionovich Stalin. Contrary to the church birth record, Stalin's official biography, starting from 1922, began to claim that he was born a year later, on 21 December 1879. For decades to come this invented date was celebrated as Stalin's birthday. This was one of the earliest and perhaps the least significant of Stalin's fabrications.

The one-room house where Soso was born stands today as the only remaining Stalin museum. All buildings in the neighborhood were destroyed in 1937 to turn the area into a park. The house became a shrine, protected from nature by an imposing marble enclosure. In Stalin's youth this house was considered a typical modest dwelling. A creaking plank front door led into a single room, whose floor comprised broken bricks stamped into the ground. Two small glass windows left the room in constant semi-darkness; its muggy air, dank from rain, wet clothes and cooking, never circulated. A huge Georgian-style ancestral bed, the resting place for the entire family, took up half the available space. The other half was filled with a few pieces of simple furniture: a four-drawer commode with a round mirror, a small table with tripod stools, a small cupboard and a wardrobe. In one corner stood clay pots for storing drinking water, and a wooden basin caught the rain that leaked through the roof. A small square patch of backyard with an outhouse was surrounded by a high wooden fence.[10]

In Stalin's youth, Gori's population was some 8,000, mostly Georgians. There was also a sizable number of Armenian Christians who had fled to Georgia from Turkey and Persia to escape Muslim persecution. Other inhabitants were Ossets, Tartars, and a few families of Georgian Jews. Maxim Gorky visited Gori at the turn of the century and recorded his impressions:

Along the slopes and also sprawled at the bottom of the hill are small huts and tiny houses, scattered wide, all built of limestone. Over the whole area lies an aura of nonconformity and wild originality. A white-hot sky hangs over the town . . . not far away stand mountains with evenly distributed caverns – this is a cave-town. Motionless white clouds are always suspended upon the horizon: these are the mountains of the main chain, covered with silver, everlasting snow.[11]

To the relatives and neighbors, the newborn Soso appeared normal except for a slight deformity in his left foot: the second and third toes were fused.[12] The deformity attracted attention and started gossip, which with the passage of time was distorted and turned into a rumor, still alive in Georgia today, that Stalin had six fingers.[13] In ancient times, and as late as the Middle Ages, it was common to kill babies with physical abnormalities. To superstitious minds, they signified the mystical intervention of diabolical forces, evil spirits, dragons and so on. Such superstitions have survived in the mythology of our time. Grigory, one of the characters in Dostoyevsky's *The Brothers Karamazov*, believes that his six-fingered son is a 'dragon' and is glad when the baby dies.

There is no evidence to suggest that Vissarion thought Soso was a dragon, but his behavior toward Soso suggests that he hated his son for another reason. The family's neighbors believed that Vissarion suspected

Keke of infidelity and doubted that Soso was his son. The rumor was that Vissarion hated Soso because he suspected him of being a bastard child. The neighbors long remembered Vissarion's brutal beatings of the boy.[14] One of them recalled that Soso once had asked Vissarion for money to buy paint, for he liked to paint pictures. Vissarion was drinking wine with friends, and he angrily flung a coin at him. When Soso asked for more, Vissarion, unable to control his rage, threw a hammer at the boy, barely missing him. Soso ran away, pursued by Vissarion, who cursed and called him *nabichuari* ('bastard' in Georgian).[15] Hints at Stalin's illegitimacy appear early in his biographies. Trotsky mentions in passing that some Georgians cited 'ticklish facts'.[16] Boris Souvarine refers to Georgian Bolsheviks who 'adduce rather unpleasant facts by way of proof'.[17] Roy Medvedev makes the claim that 'in Georgia, even today, there are rumors which attempt to give Stalin higher status, as the illegitimate son of an aristocrat or high-placed clergyman'.[18] But such rumors would hardly have been created out of nothing in order to elevate Stalin's status in Georgia – illegitimacy has long been considered a disgrace and the ultimate insult among Georgians with their traditions of family ties, kinship and honor. The name that invariably comes up in rumors identifying Stalin's 'true' father is Koba (Yakobi) Egnatashvili, the Gori priest who officiated at Vissarion's and Keke's wedding.[19]

The Egnatashvili family belonged to the *aznauri*, the numerous and proud Georgian gentry, whose members traditionally went into military or civil service or took the cloth. Egnatashvili was married and had a large family, but of all his children only two sons survived the smallpox epidemic of the winter of 1887. This epidemic almost claimed Soso's life as well, leaving his face extensively pockmarked.[20] During Stalin's rule, Egnatashvili's two sons for many years enjoyed Stalin's protection. Alexander Yakovlevich Egnatashvili was promoted by Stalin into the Georgian Secret Police and then transferred to Moscow, where he became a general in Stalin's personal bodyguard. He was known among the officers there as Stalin's half-brother.[21] He was also known among them as 'rabbit', because his main responsibility was to taste all the food that was served at the table of his 'brother', to ensure that it contained no poison.[22] (General Egnatashvili disappeared at the time of Stalin's death. He was probably shot either on Stalin's orders or on the orders of the chief of the Soviet security police, Beria.[23])

Egnatashvili's other son, Vasily Yakovlevich Egnatashvili, was the editor of the Georgian Communist Party paper *Zaria vostoka* ('Dawn of the East') and later a secretary of the Georgian Supreme Soviet. A vain and ignorant man, he could not resist the temptation to brag, often hinting that he was Stalin's brother. Once he told the prominent Georgian movie director David Rondeli, 'You know, my brother liked your movie', uttering the words 'my brother' with special emphasis. 'Who is your brother?' asked Rondeli. 'Don't you know that Koba is my brother?' exclaimed Vasily with an air of surprise, adding in a low voice: 'Koba Stalin is my brother.' (Koba was Stalin's nickname, widely known in Georgia.) When he learned of Vasily's indiscretions, Stalin was annoyed by this threat to the aura of adoration he had created around his name, and ordered Vasily's arrest. After Stalin's death, Vasily was released from prison. His wife, Maria, was prone to complain: 'Stalin was my husband's half-brother. Our family suffered because of Stalin. All Georgia suffered.' In 1955 Vasily's son Koba Egnatashvili got into a fist fight with a classmate, Zviat Gamsakhurdia (who many years later became a leading Georgian dissident and in 1989 was elected president of Georgia). Gamsakhurdia shouted, '*Stalinis deda bozi ikho*' ('Stalin's mother was a whore').[24]

Clearly, the rumor of Stalin's illegitimacy was widespread. Egnatashvili and Soso's mother, Keke – the only people who could have definitively answered the question of his paternity – died a long time ago. If Soso was their child, they could hardly have revealed this. Such a confession would have started a bloody feud among the Dzhugashvili, Egnatashvili and Geladze families. The ancient tradition of *siskhus akheba*, or bloody revenge for a man's injured pride and soiled honor, exists in Georgia even today. The question of whether Soso was Egnatashvili's son may never be answered. But far more important than whether or not the rumor was based on reality is the fact that the belief in the adultery did exist, and that it probably destroyed Soso's family. Georgians do not use the word *nabichuari* lightly. Vissarion would not have called his son a bastard had he not suspected Keke of having been unfaithful to him. The suspicion that his wife had given birth to a bastard profoundly affected Vissarion. He turned from an outgoing, cheerful man, an engaging storyteller and a fine singer, into a bully and a drunkard who spent all his earnings on alcohol, and was feared and avoided by Soso.[25]

In 1884, when Soso was 5, Vissarion left Gori for Tiflis, where he again began to work at the Adelkhanov shoe factory. Keke and Soso remained in Gori.[26] For the next five years, Vissarion lived in Tiflis alone, not visiting them even once. In September 1888 Soso was enrolled in the first grade of Gori's Preparatory Ecclesiastic School, where usually only the sons of the gentry and clergy were accepted. A neighbor pointed out years later that 'it was at that time highly unusual for a boy with a peasant background and a peasant name like Dzhugashvili to be accepted at an Ecclesiastic School. Soso was given a stipend: he was to receive three rubles a month. His mother worked for the teachers and school, earning up to ten rubles a month. They lived on these funds.'[27] The stipend and Keke's job had been arranged by Egnatashvili.[28]

Some two years after he started school, 10-year-old Soso was almost killed during a Christmas celebration. He was standing in a group of schoolboys, when a fast-moving horse-drawn carriage knocked him off his feet, the wheels rolling over his legs. Soso lost consciousness. But when he was brought home, he told his mother not to worry. She immediately called a doctor, who stopped the bleeding and told her that no internal organs were injured. Soso stayed in bed for two weeks and then went back to school. He convinced himself later that a miracle had saved him from death, heralding a special destiny.[29]

Soon after this accident, Vissarion wrote to Keke that he intended to take Soso to Tiflis to teach him the shoe-making trade. He came to Gori sometime in early spring of 1890. Soso was attending the second preparatory grade at that time. Despite Keke's objections, Vissarion was determined to take Soso out of school and force him to come to work with him in Tiflis. Keke, knowing that Vissarion loathed Soso, feared that he would abuse the boy. Besides, she had always wanted her son to become a priest. Vissarion was enraged by her objections. 'You want my son to become a priest?' he shouted at her. 'You'll never live to see that happen! I'm a shoemaker. My son must also be a shoemaker. No matter what, he'll be a shoemaker.'[30]

Egnatashvili was on Keke's side. He argued with Vissarion that it would be absurd to take Soso out of school. Vissarion did not budge. Soso's attending the Ecclesiastical School as well as Egnatashvili's intervention on the boy's behalf, may well have been for Vissarion the final proof of Keke's adultery. To take Soso with him may have been his revenge for the insult to his honor. That Soso was afraid of him and did not want to leave Gori further enraged him. 'Look at this *nabichuari*!', he shouted. 'He doesn't want to be a shoemaker like me!'[31]

Soso was to remember for the rest of his life his father's fights with his mother during that visit. Stalin told his daughter Svetlana how, while defending his mother, he threw a knife at Vissarion, who ran after him screaming.[32] A neighbor recalled another fight in which Vissarion called Keke a whore and knocked her down and began to strangle her. Soso ran to the neighbors and pleaded with them, 'Help! Come quick, he is killing my mother!' Vissarion resisted the neighbors' attempts to restrain him;

they had to club him and tie him up.³³ Keke gave a decorous account of these fights years later when she stated,

Soso studied excellently, but his father – my late husband, Vissarion – took it into his head to remove the boy from school so that he could teach Soso the shoe-making trade. I did oppose it and argued as much as I could, I even quarreled with my husband, but to no avail: my husband insisted, and his wish prevailed. After some time, I nevertheless succeeded once again in enrolling Soso in school.³⁴

Keke's oddly redundant reference to Soso's father as 'my late husband, Vissarion' suggests that she wanted to dispel any doubts about who Soso's father was. In the statement 'after some time, I nevertheless succeeded once again in enrolling Soso in school', Keke glossed over a series of dramatic events that took place in Tiflis in the summer of 1890.

Vissarion and Soso lived in a small rented room in Avlabar, a slum section of Tiflis populated mostly by laborers and craftsmen.³⁵ Vissarion made Soso work at the Adelkhanov shoe factory, where he helped the workers wind thread and served as an errand boy.³⁶ Meanwhile, Keke and Egnatashvili petitioned His Eminence, the Exarch of Georgia, the head of the Georgian Orthodox Church, who had great influence in administrative and educational matters, to intervene in the conflict in the Dzhugashvili family, to protect 10-year-old Soso from Vissarion's beatings and to return him to his mother, thus giving the boy the opportunity to continue his religious education. Koba Egnatashvili, as a priest and a member of the Georgian gentry, had comparatively easy access to the court of the Exarch, under whose jurisdiction the Gori Ecclesiastical School was. The Exarch offered a compromise: leave Soso in Vissarion's custody, but allow him to attend a church school in Tiflis and sing in the choir instead of working at the factory. Teachers at the Gori Ecclesiastical School concurred and advised that Soso stay in Tiflis – as employees of the Department of Religious Affairs, however, they could hardly disagree with the Exarch's recommendation. The officials of the Exarch's court gave Keke the same advice, but her mind was unchanged. She was determined to bring her son back to Gori.³⁷

The Exarch's attempt at a compromise failed. Vissarion refused to allow Soso to return to school, insisting that he alone had the right to decide on what to do with his son. Since his custody rights could be annulled only by the courts, he had the law on his side. Only fragments remain of the events that led to Soso's liberation. Keke's laconic 'after some time, I nevertheless succeeded again in enrolling Soso in school', is supported by a neighbor's account: 'After some time the mother, in her turn, went to Tiflis and took her son away from the factory.'[38] The 'in her turn' indicates that someone went to Tiflis before Keke did to help her free Soso from Vissarion. The only person likely to have gone to Tiflis in an attempt to retrieve Soso is Koba Egnatashvili, but the neighbor's account, as many other recollections quoted in Stalin's childhood biography, was truncated by Stalin, and the information is missing.

A clue as to what happened in Tiflis was provided by Stalin himself. Once, explaining how his left arm, which was shorter than his right by a couple of inches, was crippled, he, with unusual candor, told his wife's family that it was injured during his childhood when there was no one to help after blood poisoning developed. He said, 'I don't know what saved me then. Either it was my strong constitution or the ointment of the village quack, but my health improved.'[39] In his childhood, Soso was without his mother only during his sojourn with Vissarion in Tiflis in 1890. Stalin did, however, confide to his second wife's family that it was Vissarion who had injured his arm during one of his usual beatings, but this revelation remained the family's secret for many years.[40]

After injuring Soso, Vissarion did not call a doctor, possibly because he was indifferent to Soso's condition or feared that a doctor would notify the police about the injury. Keke and Egnatashvili learned about Soso's grave illness and rushed to the Exarch, pleading with him to take Soso away from Vissarion. This time the Exarch demanded that the police arrest Vissarion and the courts punish him for gravely injuring the boy. At the trial Soso testified about the numerous beatings he had suffered, including the one that had injured his arm. The court sentenced Vissarion to a prison term and voided his custody rights.[41] Crushed and humiliated after serving his term, Vissarion became a vagrant and a drunk.

Vissarion left his wife and son with a heavy burden of bitter memories, hatred and shame. Decades later, his son compulsively staged show trials in which the scene of boys testifying against their fathers and demanding severe punishment for them was re-enacted over and over again. During his rule Stalin also created a cult around Pavlik Morozov, a young peasant boy who testified in a Soviet court against his doomed father. In glorifying Pavlik Morozov, Stalin was glorifying himself. In this and many other cases, he re-enacted the traumatic events of his own life.

Soso returned to Gori at the end of September 1890, a few weeks after the beginning of the school year. He was admitted to the first regular grade of the Gori Ecclesiastical School. His injured left arm healed slowly. In time the arm regained its strength, but its growth was impaired by the damaged bone, developing osteomyelitis, a bone disease resulting from infection, which in Stalin's youth, before the discovery of antibiotics, was more often than not fatal. Soso's left arm became shorter by a couple of inches than his right one only later, as he grew. It was never a 'withered' arm. It looked normal in all respects other than its length. Soso told no one, not even his childhood friends, what he had lived through in Tiflis.[42] Keke and Egnatashvili, too, kept silent about what had happened there.

Soso fully recovered and became a strong boy, always eager to demonstrate his physical prowess and determined to assert his superiority by any means. He challenged a classmate to a wrestling match, which onlookers declared a tie. The wrestlers rearranged their clothing and started to walk away, but Soso suddenly seized his opponent from behind and slammed him to the ground, triumphantly driving his knee into the boy's chest. His followers clapped and cheered. The other boys protested vehemently, but Soso proclaimed himself the winner.[43]

Soon after returning to Gori, Soso adopted the nickname 'Koba'. His classmates probably assumed that he chose this name after the hero of the popular romantic story *Father Killers*, by the Georgian writer Prince Kazbegi. In this novel the hero Koba, the Georgian diminutive of Yakobi, or Jacob, a daring, fierce outlaw – a kind of Caucasian Robin Hood – avenges the death of his friends Yago and Yago's bride Nunu. The novel's bandit villain, Girgola, collaborates with the Russian invaders. He abducts Nunu and accuses her of murdering her own father. Yago is killed in a skirmish with Girgola's band and Nunu dies in prison. Koba escapes and later ambushes Girgola and mortally wounds him. When the dying Girgola hears Koba's triumphant shout, 'It's me, Koba!' he confesses to the murder of Nunu's father.[44]

Despite the popularity of Kazbegi's romantic novel, it is doubtful that Soso took the name Koba from its hero. There was a far more important Koba in Soso's life, his benefactor, Koba Egnatashvili. Children traumatized by the brutality of their fathers often reject them and postulate a new origin for themselves, which they symbolize by choosing a new name.[45] They tend to do this even when no logical choice for the newly appointed father presents itself. After the traumatic events in Tiflis, it would have been natural for Soso to reject Vissarion as his father and to assume Egnatashvili to be his father. But in Soso's case there was also a 'legitimate' basis for his rejection of Vissarion: he had heard Vissarion call his mother a whore and him a bastard. He may even have known of the rumor that Koba Egnatashvili was his true father.[46] Egnatashvili was an obvious choice for a

worthy father, and Koba became Stalin's first pseudonym. He never explained his choice, but once the young Stalin had decided on it, he insisted
on being called Koba.

Koba had learned early in life to keep his thoughts and feelings to
himself. Certain events had deep meaning for him. One such event took
place in February 1892, soon after his twelfth birthday. A description of the
event appeared in recollections of Koba's classmates that Stalin included in
his childhood biography and edited himself. On that day, Gori residents
gathered in a public square, where gallows had been erected for the public
hanging of two Georgian peasants sentenced to death for murder. Koba
stood in a group with his classmates, watching the execution. One of the
condemned, Dzhioshvili by name, was a tall man with broad shoulders and
a full black beard. His resemblance in appearance and name to Vissarion
could not have escaped Koba. A priest holding a cross appeared on the
scaffold to perform the last rites. Koba watched the hanging silently,
expressing no emotion. The two pages of recollections of this event in
Stalin's childhood biography contain no mention of his reaction to the
execution or of the name of the priest holding the cross, but they describe
other people's pity and sympathy for the condemned. The inclusion of the
hanging in the biography suggests that it affected Koba profoundly, possibly
by making him imagine that he was witnessing not the execution of two
strangers but the hanging of his enemy, Vissarion, who had been given the
last rites by Koba Egnatashvili.[47]

Stalin's daughter Svetlana stated that if her father felt any attachment to
people, it was only to those he associated with his mother.[48] Despite the fact
that he took pride in having been chosen to sing in a church trio because of
his voice and musical ear, Koba expressed heretical thoughts about God
that frequently shocked his classmates.[49] Koba felt free to approach his
teachers with suggestions to forgive the offenses and shortcomings of his
classmates and to advise them on how to help failing students.[50] In placing
himself in the position of benevolent intermediary between higher
authority and his fellow students, he practiced an ostensible altruism; in
fact, his behavior was self-serving, since it promoted him to a position of
superiority.

Duplicity had, however, already entered into the picture; while courting
authority, Koba was provoking confrontations with the teachers behind
their backs. The 1890 school year began with the introduction of a Russian
government decree ordering teachers and pupils to speak only Russian, and
specifically prohibiting use of the Georgian language. The new rule aroused
nationalist anger among pupils and parents, with Koba instigating a series

of assaults against school authorities. One morning a group of pupils
attacked a school inspector, a Russian, who freed himself, swinging his fists
wildly and calling his attackers 'savages'. Several pupils were punished, but
Koba was not one of them. His role as the instigator of the attack remained
unknown to the authorities.[51]

In the spring of 1894, Koba graduated from the Ecclesiastical School and
enrolled in the Tiflis Orthodox Seminary, where he got free tuition, room
and board, as well as an allowance.[52] All this was arranged by Egnatashvili.[53]
Until the beginning of his third year at the seminary, Koba was a good
student, and he was considered one of the best singers in the choir.[54] Then
the trouble began. At first it was minor disobedience; Koba was disciplined
for having been caught patronizing a city library and reading the works
of Victor Hugo, a subversive author according to school officials. Then
Koba began to insult the teachers; the record book reports that he was
'disrespectful and rude'.[55] In 1897 Koba and several of his classmates joined
a Young Socialists Circle for the study of Marxism. He demanded that the
circle members defend his 'opinions', which invariably ran counter to the
opinions of their lecturer. Although Koba did not tolerate criticism of his
views, his opinion often abruptly and drastically changed. 'The search for
truth did not interest him', recalls one of his classmates. 'He would often
dispute positions which he previously maintained, and defend views which
he previously condemned.' Some members of the circle 'became confused,
others became reticent and cautious, and avoided participation in the
political discussions – either out of fear or the realization of the futility of
any attempt to convince Koba, or even to persuade him to adopt a more
tolerant position'. The circle split into supporters and opponents of Koba.
'Only the intellectually shallow types, who were willing to toady up to
Koba, remained with him.'[56]

Toward the end of 1898, Koba's relations with seminary officials became
increasingly hostile. He refused to bow to the inspector, who complained
to the Board of Supervisors.[57] An entry in the Seminary's records states that
in the course of a search of the fifth-grade dormitories, 'Iosif Dzhugashvili
tried several times to enter into an argument with seminary officials,
expressing dissatisfaction with the repeated searches of students, and declaring that such searches were never made in other seminaries.'[58] What the
record book fails to mention is that Koba was directly responsible for the
search. Koba tried to induce some 45 of his fellow students to drop out
of the Seminary and join the revolutionary underground. They refused,
arguing that their parents would disapprove and terminate their financial
support. Koba responded with a brazen provocation aimed at ruining the

careers of these students, smuggling illegal pamphlets and inflammatory leaflets into their dormitory, and placing them under pillows and mattresses. He then denounced them to the rector, who ordered the dormitory searched.[59] Koba used the occasion to demonstrate his extreme indignation by loudly protesting about the searches in order to deflect any suspicion from himself of having provoked the incident. According to the record, 'Iosif Dzhugashvili was reprimanded and put for five hours in a punishment room by the order of the Father Rector.'[60] The rector, the monk Germogen, had no choice but to reprimand Koba: he had to hide the fact that it was Koba who had informed him about the illegal pamphlets. Germogen encouraged Koba to continue his studies, but he found him unwilling or unable to do so. Koba became the Seminary's worst student and his behavior became intolerable. He answered his teachers' criticism with 'malicious, scornful laughter'.[61] On 27 May 1899 Koba failed to take the exams he had to pass in order to be transferred to the fifth and last grade. He did not respond to Germogen's offer to take the exams at a later date and refused to provide an explanation, leaving Germogen with no choice but to expel him. On 29 May 1899 a laconic entry was made in the Seminary's record book: 'Iosif Dzhugashvili was expelled for not taking the examinations; reason unknown.'[62]

Soon thereafter some 45 students who had been implicated by Koba in the scandal of the illegal leaflets were also expelled from the Seminary. The expelled students found out that it was Koba who had planted the incriminating leaflets, and also informed on them. They accused him of causing their expulsion. Their parents besieged the rector with petitions to reinstate their sons, who, they complained, were innocent victims of Koba's provocation. Koba did not deny the charge, remarking blithely that his motive had been to give these students the opportunity to become 'good revolutionaries'.[63]

At the time of his expulsion from the Seminary, Koba looked bleary-eyed and ill.[64] His mother later stated: 'I took him home on account of his health. When he entered the Seminary, he was as strong as a boy could be. But overwork had weakened him by the time he was nineteen, and the doctors told me that he might develop tuberculosis. So I took him away from the school. He did not want to leave. But I took him anyway. He was my only son.'[65] Koba's deteriorating health, as well as his academic failure and hostility toward teachers and fellow students, suggest a profound emotional crisis had affected his ability to function. A hint at a traumatic event that may have contributed to or even caused this crisis is found in Stalin's childhood biography. A curious literary insertion hints that Koba may have encountered his father Vissarion at the end of 1897 or the beginning of 1898. Vissarion had by that time been released from jail. Inserted in the biography is the poem 'Musha' ('The Porter'), in which the great Georgian poet Prince Ilia Chavchavadze describes an encounter with a porter-vagrant, a man whose fate bears an unmistakable resemblance to that of Vissarion:

MUSHA

His life is spent in toil
But brings him no reward.
Hurrying from Middle Market in Tiflis, suddenly in the heat of noon I saw you, Musha lying against a wall under the cruel, burning sun, and your quiet song filled my heart with anguish. I sensed suffering in your plaintive song, I heard a tale of torment and inner sorrow. Wherefore did you come to the slums of this city? Did you flee your master, unable to bear the whip? You left behind your family, your hut and garden, your fields, your streams and free mountain vistas. Perhaps you sought shelter and work in this city, in your heart you were led by the hope of succor. What did your soul lose when you left your village? And what did you find in its stead in Tiflis, unlucky Musha?[66]

The image of this porter-vagrant was obviously associated in Koba's mind with something important to him, something Stalin did not want mentioned directly in his childhood biography but nevertheless felt compelled to hint at. Musha stood for Vissarion in Koba's mind. A sea of contradictory feelings must have rushed to the surface – hatred, disgust, guilt, memories of fear and pain – all producing a severe emotional strain, which found expression in rebellion against authorities and ill health. Stalin's relations with Vissarion left a deep imprint on his personality. A childhood friend of his wrote that Koba's 'heart was filled with the inexpressibly malicious hatred his merciless father had already begun to engender in him when he was still a child . . .'. When Koba left the Seminary, 'he took with him a grim, sullen hatred . . . it was a hatred for every form of authority . . . Everywhere and in everything he saw only the negative, the base, and he did not credit mankind with any lofty ideals or noble qualities.'[67]

NOTES

1. V. Kaminsky and I. Vereshchagin, *Detstvo i yunost' vozhdia: documenty, zapiski, rasskazy* [*Childhood and Adolescence of the Leader*, Stalin's childhood biography], Moscow, 1939, pp. 24ff.
2. H. R. Knickerbocker, 'Stalin Mystery Man Even to His Mother,' *New York Evening Post*, 1 December, 1930, p. 2.
3. Kaminsky and Vereshchagin, *Detstvo i yunost' vozhdia*, pp. 20–5.
4. See *Evreiskaya entsiklopediya* (Jewish Encyclopedia in Russian), vol. VI, St Petersburg, 1913,

pp. 808f, for the analysis of the Georgian language by the academic N. Ya. Marr, a prominent linguist, who at the turn of the century claimed that the Georgian language was of Semitic origin. Other linguists have argued that it is related to a group of Caucasian languages.

5. Kaminsky and Vereshchagin, *Detstvo i yunost' vozhdia*, pp. 25ff.
6. Edvard Radzinsky, *Stalin*, New York, 1996, p. 19 (quoting from Gori archive).
7. Kaminsky and Vereshchagin, *Detstvo i yunost' vozhdia*, p. 26.
8. Knickerbocker, 'Stalin Mystery Man'. See also Isaac Deutscher, *Stalin: A Political Biography*, New York and London, 1968, p. 2.
9. Radzinsky, *Stalin*, p. 12.
10. J. Iremaschwili, *Stalin und die Tragödie Georgiens*, Berlin, 1932, pp. 8–11.
11. Kaminsky and Vereshchagin, *Detstvo i yunost' vozhdia*, pp. 23ff.
12. Okhrana Report no. 5500, dated 1 May 1904, in Roy Medvedev's *New Pages from the Political Biography of Stalin*, in Robert C. Tucker (ed.), *Stalinism*, New York, 1977, pp. 200ff.
13. The historian Andrey Amalrik related this popular belief in an interview with the author in Chappaqua, New York, 1976.
14. Iremaschwili, *Stalin*, pp. 11ff.
15. Taped interview with Nugzar Sharia in Sag Harbor, Long Island, in 1971.
16. Lev Trotsky, *Stalin*, New York, 1941, p. 8.
17. Boris Souvarine, *Stalin: A Critical Survey of Bolshevism*, London, 1939, p. 3.
18. Roy Medvedev, *Let History Judge*, New York, 1971, p. 337.
19. Robert Conquest, *Stalin: Breaker of Nations*, pp. 4, 9, 12. Also *Kazakhstanskaya pravda*, 10 November 1988. See also L. Kafanova, 'O velikom druge i vozhde', *Novoe Russkoe slovo*, 23 and 24 March 1977.
20. Kaminsky and Vereshchagin, *Detstvo i yunost' vozhdia*, p. 38.
21. Related to Nugzar Sharia by Stalin's bodyguard Gogi Zautashvili. Taped interview with Nugzar Sharia.
22. Felix Svetlov, a former Soviet lawyer and son of a high-ranking Soviet Secret Police official, told the author about Stalin's 'rabbit' during an interview in New York in 1989.
23. Nugzar Sharia, taped interview.
24. Nugzar Sharia, taped interview.
25. Iremaschwili, *Stalin*, pp. 11ff.
26. Kaminsky and Vereshchagin, *Detstvo i yunost' vozhdia*, p. 28.
27. Ibid., p. 34.
28. Anatoly Rybakov, 'Deti arbata', *Druzhba narodov*, nos 4–5. See also L. Kafanova, 'O velikom druge i vozhde', *Novoe russkoe slovo*, 23 March 1977. Kafanova quotes the prominent Soviet composer Vano Muradeli, a native of Gori.
29. Kaminsky and Vereshchagin, *Detstvo i yunost' vozhdia*, p. 37.
30. Ibid., p. 43ff.
31. Interview with Nugzar Sharia.
32. Svetlana Allilueva, *Only One Year*, New York, 1969, p. 360.
33. Joseph Darvichewy, *Ah! Ce qu'on rigolait bien avec mon copain Staline*, p. 34. Quoted in Daniel Rancour-Laferriere, *The Mind of Stalin*, Ann Arbor, 1988, pp. 36ff.
34. Kaminsky and Vereshchagin, *Detstvo i yunost' vozhdia*, p. 44.
35. Ibid., p. 59. (Kaminsky and Vereshchagin quote Maxim Gorky's article in *Nizhegorodskii listok*, no. 174, 28 June 1898.)
36. Ibid. p. 45.
37. Ibid.
38. Ibid.
39. A. S. Allilueva, *Vospominaniya*, Moscow, 1946, p. 36.
40. F. D. Volkov, *Vzlet i padenie Stalina*, Moscow, 1992, p. 24. Volkov quotes from oral testimony by Anna Allilueva, Nadezhda Allilueva's sister-in-law.
41. Andrey Amalrik related the story of Vissarion's imprisonment in an interview with the author in Chappaqua, New York, in 1976.
42. Iremaschwili, *Stalin*, p. 5ff.
43. Ibid., p. 5.
44. A. Kazbegi, *Otseubiitsy, Izbrannye Sochineniya*, vol. I, Tbilisi, 1941.
45. For a discussion of Hitler's similar rejection of his father see Walter C. Langer, *The Mind of Adolf Hitler*, New York, 1972, pp. 146–60.

46. L. Kafanova, 'O velikom druge i vozhde', 23 March 1977. She quotes a prominent Soviet composer Vano Muradeli, a native of Gori, who recalled, 'Koba seemed to have learned the truth about how this kind and loving priest was related to him.' It is unlikely that, in all his years at Gori, Koba never once heard the rumor that Egnatashvili was his real father.
47. Kaminsky and Vereshchagin, *Detstvo i yunost' vozhdia*, pp. 48ff.
48. Allilueva, *Only One Year*, p. 361.
49. Iremaschwili, *Stalin*, p. 8.
50. Kaminsky and Vereshchagin, *Detstvo i yunost' vozhdia*, p. 41.
51. Ibid., p. 39. Also Iremaschwili, *Stalin*, p. 7ff.
52. Iremaschwili, *Stalin*, p. 16.
53. Anatoly Rybakov, 'Deti arbata', *Druzhba narodov*, no. 4–5, 1987.
54. Iremaschwili, *Stalin*, pp. 16–18.
55. Kaminsky and Vereshchagin, *Detstvo i yunost' vozhdia*, p. 71.
56. Iremaschwili, *Stalin*, pp. 19–22.
57. Kaminsky and Vereshchagin, *Detstvo i yunost' vozhdia*, p. 84.
58. Ibid., p. 84.
59. Andrey Amalrik interview. Also S. Vereshchak, 'Stalin v tur'me', *Dni*, 22 and 24 January 1928.
60. Kaminsky and Vereshchagin, *Detstvo i yunost' vozhdia*, p. 84.
61. Ibid.
62. Ibid., p. 86.
63. R. Arsenidze, 'Iz vospominanii o Staline', *Novy zhurnal*, no. 72, June 1963. Vereshchak, 'Stalin v tur'me', Andrey Amalrik interview.
64. Iremaschwili, *Stalin*, p. 20.
65. Knickerbocker, 'Stalin Mystery Man'.
66. Kaminsky and Vereshchagin, *Detstvo i yunost' vozhdia*, p. 59.
67. Iremaschwili, *Stalin*, p. 24.

2

'SAMEDOV DISEASE'

In December 1899 Koba started to work at the Tiflis Geophysical
Observatory as a record keeper, moving into a small room in the dormitory.
Lado Ketskhoveli, a close friend, helped him to get this job.[1] Lado was born
into the family of an impoverished nobleman, a priest in a village near Gori.
Like Koba, Lado had been abused by his father, who severely punished
him for bad behavior and poor grades. Lado had graduated from the Gori
Ecclesiastical School four years earlier than Koba and, like Koba, attended
the Tiflis Seminary. In 1893 – the year before Koba enrolled there – Lado
was expelled from the Seminary for 'Georgian nationalism' and was exiled
to Kiev. In the fall of 1897, he returned illegally to Tiflis. The newly
appointed chief of the Tiflis secret police, E. P. Debel, reported to St
Petersburg Lado's arrival but did not order his arrest.[2] In all probability,
Lado turned police informer at that time, in return for permission to live
in Tiflis. Lado went to work for a printer by the name of Kheladze.[3] It was
probably Lado who, toward the end of 1889, supplied Koba with the illegal
leaflets that provoked the expulsion of 45 students from the Tiflis Seminary.
Lado may well have involved Koba in other provocations sponsored by the
Tiflis secret police.[4]

In 1898, Lado introduced Koba to the Social Democratic group in Tiflis,
which sent him to two workers' circles as a propagandist. But the Tiflis
Social Democratic leaders Noi Zhordania and Silvester Dzhibladze soon
found out that Koba was conducting propaganda not against the government and capitalists but against them, charging them with a 'lack of mili-
tancy' and 'betrayal of the proletariat'. These leaders also learned of Koba's
planting of illegal leaflets at the Seminary, which was much discussed in
Tiflis at that time. Annoyed, they told Koba to stop smearing them and to
stay away from the workers' circles.[5]

Planting illegal leaflets was a typical method of provocation used by the
Russian secret police *Okhrannoe Otdelenie* (Security Section) of the Department of Police, but commonly referred to as Okhrana, which, at the turn
of the century, employed aggressive counterintelligence methods when
revolutionary agitation was on the rise. The Okhrana made extensive use
of *provokatsiya* (provocation), as part of its intelligence operations. Okhrana
agents and informers were usually called *agents provocateurs*, but the Okhrana

applied this term more narrowly. A. T. Vasiliev, the last director of the Department of Police, described the *agent provocateur* as a secret collaborator who 'himself sets on foot some revolutionary movement and then betrays to the authorities the people he has befouled'.[6]

The leading proponent of provocations was the chief of the Moscow Okhrana Section, Sergey Vasilievich Zubatov, a pioneer in the wide use of informers and agents. His influence extended far beyond Moscow. Zubatov advocated the theory of 'police socialism', meaning the infiltration of revolutionary parties and trade unions by Okhrana agents and informers. One of his methods was to set up an underground printing press and to print illegal leaflets to implicate revolutionaries, who could then be arrested and sent to Siberia. The vacancies thereby created allowed Okhrana agents to advance to leadership positions in the revolutionary organizations. Zubatov's career followed a pattern found time and again in the long history of the revolutionary movement. He was arrested in his youth as a member of a revolutionary student group. While in prison, he turned informer and betrayed his comrades. Then he became a 'secret collaborator', or agent. By betraying his friends he advanced his career and was promoted to the rank of officer. Eventually, he became chief of the Moscow Okhrana Section. His philosophy was reflected in the fact that Okhrana agents – either on being prodded by their case officers or on their own initiative – committed provocations, instigated violence and caused scandals that embarrassed the Okhrana. Zubatov's methods of using *agents provocateurs* became known in Russian history collectively as *Zubatovshchina*. They were so common and extreme that some Okhrana officers suspected Zubatov of being a 'hidden revolutionary' who had wormed his way into the Okhrana to subvert the government from within.[7]

In 1901, a scandal caused by a Zubatov-style provocation rocked the Tiflis Okhrana, prompting an investigation by top officials in the Department of Police and in the Ministry of the Interior. It was established that Iosif Dzhugashvili and Lado Ketskhoveli, both informers handled by an officer of the Tiflis Okhrana Samedov, had printed illegal leaflets. (In the investigation, Samedov claimed he had known nothing of Koba's and Lado's action.) These leaflets came from a 'secret press' made of a typesetting board against which sheets of paper could be pressed, allowing the production of some 700 leaflets in 24 hours. The press was located in the basement of a house on Lotkin Street in Tiflis.[8]

The printing was done by a young criminal known in the Tiflis underworld as Kamo Somekhi ('Kamo the Armenian'), whom Koba had met in Tiflis. In the years that followed, Kamo was to play a major role in Koba's schemes, rising from printer of provocative leaflets to murderer at Koba's instigation. Koba used him like a puppet, and Kamo was invariably deceived about the true reasons behind the acts that Koba made him commit. The deception began with the first job Kamo did for Koba. Kamo had no idea that in printing the leaflets he was taking part in an Okhrana provocation. He printed the leaflets on yellow paper, with large uneven letters, in Russian, Georgian and Armenian. The leaflets stated in part: 'We appeal to all of you to come to the First of May celebration to join in a unanimous and energetic protest against the present social and political system.'[9] Kamo distributed the leaflets in various public places in Tiflis. Their inflammatory message alarmed the chief of the Tiflis Okhrana, Captain Lavrov, who was ignorant of the fact that they had been produced by informers working for one of his officers, and started an investigation.

On 15 March 1901 Lavrov received a report by his officer, Samedov, stating that the leaflets had been issued by a Marxist 'secret circle' in Tiflis, headed by Victor Kurnatovsky, and that they had been printed at the press owned by Kheladze (the press owner for whom Lado worked). Samedov had received this information from Koba and Lado. Kurnatovsky was a revolutionary of long standing.[10] On 21 March 1902 all members of Kurnatovsky's secret circle and Kheladze were arrested.[11] Lado and Koba hurriedly planted the 'evidence' at Kheladze's press.

Kurnatovsky, the members of his circle, and the press owner Kheladze denied that they had anything to do with the illegal leaflets. Okhrana investigators analyzed the leaflets and determined that they had not been printed at Kheladze's press but somewhere else. A. T. Vasiliev wrote many years later about a provocation in one of the southern cities: an Okhrana informer, in order to implicate the owner of a print shop and divert attention from himself, 'quickly arranged typesetting to correspond to the leaflet, and if not for his little bit of carelessness in doing this, the scheme would probably have succeeded, and the absolutely innocent printer would have been sent to Siberia'. The printer was released, and the minister of the interior issued the order for the officer in charge of the section to quit his office at once, and for the commander of the gendarmerie to be informed without delay of his dismissal.[12] The printer, Kheladze, was released from prison. Somewhat later, Captain Lavrov was dismissed from his post. The members of Kurnatovsky's circle, however, remained behind bars to face charges of revolutionary activities, although the charge relating to the 1 May criminal leaflets was dropped. The case of the Okhrana officer Samedov and his informers Koba and Lado was turned into a 'special secret investigation' to avoid exposure of a scandal that might embarrass the Okhrana. In his defense, Samedov blamed Lado and Koba for acting without his knowledge. Learning of this and fearing arrest, Koba and Lado left Tiflis on 28 March 1901, seven days after the Okhrana dragnet. Koba returned to Gori, while Lado made his way to Baku, the Caspian Sea port and growing center of the oil industry. Kamo stayed in Tiflis. He knew nothing about the Okhrana scandal that the leaflets had caused. Moving from place to place with his primitive press, he continued to print leaflets, and the Okhrana's attention turned to him.

Kamo's real name was Simon Ter-Petrosian. His father, a well-to-do Gori Armenian merchant, at the age of 35 married a 16-year-old girl. His wife gave birth to 11 children, but only Simon and five sisters survived. The boy's history was one of abuse: his father often whipped him for being 'rebellious'. Kamo was expelled several times from school for bad behavior and poor grades. His father pleaded with school officials each time to readmit his son, sweetening his pleas with the traditional bribes of bleating lambs. When Kamo grew older, he threatened to kill his father.[13] When Kamo was 16, his mother fell ill and died soon afterwards. His father sent him to Tiflis to live with an aunt, who hired private tutors for him, one of whom was Koba. The aunt did not know that Kamo and his tutor frequented the town's criminal hangouts, where Kamo acquired his nickname from his mispronunciation of the Russian word *komu* (whom). He pronounced it *kamo*, with the accent on the 'o'. This amused his companions, who mocked him with the chant, '*Kamo! Kamo!*' and the nickname stuck.[14] (Years later, when Lenin was first told about Kamo, whose expertise at armed robbery he was to draw upon to procure funds, Lenin laughed and asked, 'Did I catch that correctly? The accent is on "o" – Kamo?') Kamo became a source of income for Koba, giving him money from armed robberies. Kamo had a secret hiding place in the cellar of the house at 2 Goncharnaya Street, a criminal hangout run by an ageing madam, where he kept his revolvers and bombs.[15]

Koba, too, was known in the underworld by a nickname not of his own choosing, nicknames among criminals usually reflecting physical defects, habits of speech or ethnic background. Koba's face suggested the Georgian nickname *Chopur*, or 'Pockmarked'. (At the Tiflis Okhrana, similarly, Koba was recorded as *Riaboy*, 'Pockmarked' in Russian.[16]) Koba, Kamo and Lado had come to Tiflis from Gori, which may well have contributed to their becoming friends. More importantly, they also shared similar childhoods of abuse at the hands of their fathers and the physical and emotional traumas of such abuse. All three had complex and ambivalent relationships with their fathers, and shared habits of thought and attitudes: they despised authority and its symbols, and were indifferent to accepted ideas about good and evil.

The leaflets printed by Kamo contributed to the violence that occurred when, on 1 May 1901, a large demonstration by Tiflis workers was dispersed by Cossack troops. Fourteen workers were killed, many more were wounded, and 50 were arrested. Koba came to Tiflis from Gori to watch the bloody confrontation from a safe distance. On his return to Gori, he gleefully told his childhood friend Iosif Iremashvili how Cossack sabers and whips had spilled the blood of 'proletarian workers'. Koba's excitement over the bloody violence disconcerted Iremashvili and left him with the impression that Koba was 'intoxicated by workers' blood'.[17] In his early articles, Koba repeatedly described 'proletarian workers' falling under the blows of Cossack sabers and whips. But in one of these articles, he drew a portrait of a 'typical proletarian worker'. He stated:

Imagine a shoemaker who had a tiny workshop but could not stand the competition of big business. That man closed his shop and hired himself out to, say, Adelkhanov at the Tiflis shoe factory. He went to Adelkhanov's factory not to remain a worker forever, but to save money, to lay aside a small capital, and to reopen his own shop. As you see, the position of this shoemaker is already that of a proletarian; his consciousness, however, is not yet proletarian, but petty-bourgeois through and through.[18]

This was to a large extent Vissarion's story, including such detail as the Adelkhanov factory, where Vissarion had worked and Koba had suffered abuse from him and been an errand boy for the 'proletarian workers'. The passage barely veils its author's contempt for the workers whose champion he sets himself up to be. Koba's vehement outburst and his vilifying of the Cossacks with their sabers and whips has the elements of a Freudian reaction formation: the opposite of the hidden impulse of relish.[19]

The Okhrana dragnet in March and May of 1901 left the Tiflis Social Democratic organization in a shambles. In October of 1901 Koba returned to Tiflis and attempted to promote himself into a leadership position during a meeting of workers gathered to elect new representatives to the Tiflis Committee of the Social Democratic Party. Koba addressed the gathering stating, 'Here they flatter workers. I ask you, are there among you even one or two workers fit to join the Committee? Tell the truth, with your hands on your hearts!' The workers voted against Koba. One of them depicted him as a man 'driven by personal caprice and striving for absolute power', a man who 'persisted in spreading slander, trying to discredit the popular and recognized leaders of the Social Democratic movement, thus attempting to capture a leadership position in the party organization'.[20]

On 11 November 1901 Koba was invited to a meeting of the committee members, who had investigated his statements slandering party leaders. One of the participants wrote, 'This was the first time in the history of Georgian Social Democracy for a party member to be tried by a party court. The committee voted unanimously to expel Koba from the Tiflis organization as a slanderer and intriguer.'[21] In late November 1901, Koba left Tiflis for Batum, a growing Black Sea port near the Turkish border. Kamo also moved there, taking his press with him. In a statement to Batum workers, Koba declared: 'Your revolutionary work is moving slowly; it must move more swiftly. The Tiflis workers sent me to you, comrades, to talk with you. The Tiflis workers, as you know, have awakened from their sleep and are preparing for struggle with their enemies. The Batum workers are still peacefully sleeping. I appeal to you to follow the example of the Tiflis workers.'[22] This was a shameless lie. No one had sent Koba to Batum; he had been expelled from the Tiflis party organization. Koba also accused the leaders of the Batum workers, Chkheidze and Ramishvili, of 'cowardice, lack of ability, and treason against the working class'.[23] They in turn called Koba a 'madman' and 'troublemaker'. Noi Zhordania, a leading Georgian Social Democrat, stated that Koba's behavior 'could not be called anything other than provocation'.[24]

Early in 1902, Koba left Batum for Baku to visit Lado.[25] The Okhrana investigation of the leaflets case was in progress, and Koba needed to plot a common strategy with Lado to place the blame for the provocation on their Okhrana handler, Samedov. While Koba was in Baku, almost all the members of the Batum Workers' Committee were arrested.[26] When Koba returned to Batum, there was a vacuum at the top of the workers' organization. Koba's intrigues, his absence when the mass arrests of prominent party leaders took place, and his return at a perfect time to move into a leadership position aroused the workers' suspicion that the arrests had resulted from his informing to the Okhrana on the Batum leaders, and that his brief absence had been timed to cloud his role in the arrests. The workers started to avoid Koba, accusing him of being an Okhrana informer.[27]

In early March 1903 a strike began at the Batum factories. Events moved swiftly. On 7 March 1902 the Okhrana arrested some 30 workers. In the following days prison guards and Cossack troops opened fire, killing 15 and wounding 54 workers. Over 500 people were arrested.[28] On 12 March 1903 during a funeral procession in honor of the dead workers, Kamo distributed a leaflet written by Koba who, among other things stated, 'All honor to your shades that hover over us and whisper in our ears, "Avenge our blood!"'[29] Inspired by violence and death, Koba was becoming an eloquent voice for further bloodshed.

The workers' suspicion of Koba's involvement with the Okhrana grew as these events unfolded, but his arrest some three weeks after the workers' funeral restored some of his prestige and kept him from being unmasked as an *agent provocateur*.[30] The workers did not know that Koba was arrested not by the Okhrana but by the Batum criminal police, who were conducting an investigation into a local criminal gang with which he was connected. Koba's involvement with the Batum underworld had begun when he moved into the house of the Darakhvelidze brothers, who ran a counterfeiting operation and were also involved in armed robberies, in which Kamo took part. Koba became the 'cashier' of the band and the 'arbiter' of disputes among its members. (He almost caused the murder of a band member, a young Georgian whom he accused of stealing the band's money. Koba sentenced the thief to death and assigned another member of the band to shoot him during a boat ride on the Black Sea. When the condemned man understood the danger, he dropped to his knees and pleaded for his life, swearing that he had not stolen the money. Unable to bring himself to pull the trigger, the would-be executioner ordered the man to swim to the nearby Turkish shore and never again return to Batum. A few days later, Koba said with apparent regret that the money had been found and the man been killed for nothing. One of the members of the band recalled that when Koba heard that the accused man had not been killed, he 'said nothing, only turned gloomy like a cloud'.[31])

The police raided the house of the Darakhvelidze brothers on the night of 5 April 1903 arresting them and two members of their band, Kostia Kandelaki and Koba. The arresting officer stated in his report: 'Iosif Dzhugashvili: expelled from the Theological Seminary; has been living without a passport and no definite address in Batum . . . '.[32] Finding himself behind bars for the first time in his life, Koba made an offer to his interrogators: he would give them information about the revolutionary underground in return for his release from prison. Colonel Shabelsky, the chief of the Batum Okhrana, responded: 'Free him, if he agrees to give the Gendarme Department information about the activity of the Social Democratic Party.'[33]

Back in his cell, Koba accused one of the prisoners of being a police informer and incited his fellow prisoners to attack the man. His body, covered with blood, was carried away by the guards.[34] The incident was symptomatic of Koba's lifelong psychological peculiarity: time and again throughout his life, Stalin accused innocent people of acts that he himself was guilty of and had them punished for those acts.

Colonel Shabelsky intended not to initiate criminal proceedings against Koba and to release him, but unforeseen developments tied his hands: on 17 June 1903 he received an Okhrana communication stating that the Tiflis gendarmerie was investigating I. V. Dzhugashvili and that he should be arrested 'in connection with the case of the Secret Circle in Tiflis'.[35] Shabelsky notified the Tiflis Okhrana of Koba's arrest and received the instruction to keep Koba in the Batum prison for further investigation. The Tiflis Okhrana made this decision in order to keep members of Kurnatovsky's circle, who were still under investigation in the Tiflis prison, from learning that Koba and Lado had provoked their arrest. More than two months after Koba's arrest, Colonel Shabelsky was forced to create a file on Koba. The first entry read: 'Iosif Vissarionov Dzhugashvili; Height: 2 arshina, 4.5 vershkov [5ft 4in]. Build: medium. Age: 23. Second and third toes on left foot fused together. Appearance: ordinary. Hair: dark brown. Beard and mustache: brown. Nose: straight and long. Forehead: straight and low. Face: long, swarthy and pockmarked.' Shabelsky also reported Koba's nick-name, *Riaboy* ('Pockmarked'), which earlier had been recorded by the Tiflis Okhrana.[36]

Koba, still in prison after two months, hoped to stay in Colonel Shabelsky's good graces by giving him Lado's address in Baku. Lado was arrested and taken to the Metekh prison in Tiflis, where he was placed in a solitary cell next to the section assigned to common criminals, in order to keep him isolated from the members of Kurnatovsky's circle and prevent them from determining who had provoked their arrest. The Okhrana was still unable to arrest Kamo, who kept moving from place to place, leaving a trail littered with leaflets. The 'secret case' of the provocation involving the Okhrana officer Samedov and his informers Koba and Lado was decided in midsummer 1903. Koba was charged 'in connection with the case of a secret circle of the RSDWP [the Russian Social Democratic Workers' Party] in the city of Tiflis' and was sentenced 'on the basis of the HIGHEST AUTHORITY decree of 9 June 1903, to be exiled administratively to eastern Siberia in the Balagan region of Irkutsk province under open police surveillance for the term of three years'.[37] A similar decision was reached in the case of Lado. Of the three perpetrators of the leaflets provocation, Kamo alone was still at large. Samedov was fired from the Okhrana and exiled to Siberia, but the memory of his role in the provoca-tion lingered for a long time among the Okhrana officers in Tiflis, and they wryly labeled provocations involving Okhrana officers and their informers 'Samedov disease'.[38]

The members of Kurnatovsky's secret circle were sentenced to various terms of exile. On 4 August 1904 16 of them were being marched off from the courtyard of the Tiflis prison to the railway station for a train to Siberia, when a strange event took place. Lado was watching them from the window of his solitary cell. Suddenly he began singing the 'Marseillaise' and shouting, 'Long live socialism!' He paid no attention to the guards ordering him to stop. An officer in charge told one of the guards to take aim. Instead of moving away from the window, Lado kept shouting slogans. The officer ordered the guard to fire, and he pulled the trigger, killing Lado.[39] What prompted Lado to this act of defiance is impossible to say. Perhaps he hoped to prove to the Kurnatovsky circle convicts and to himself that he was a true revolutionary. Perhaps the brooding loneliness of solitary confinement had made him susceptible to the excitement of the moment and feelings of guilt. In any case, his life glowed most brightly when he sacrificed it at that moment of glory. (Years later Stalin was to point to Lado's portrait in his Kremlin office, calling him his first mentor and claiming that Lado was a greater revolutionary than even Lenin himself.[40])

Two weeks after this incident, on 19 August 1903 Koba was transferred from the Batum to the Kutais prison with a group of prisoners who had been convicted for taking part in the Batum demonstration. He pretended to be one of them. (Later in his biographies, Stalin insisted that he had been sentenced in 1903 for leading the Batum demonstration.) At the beginning of September 1903 the Batum convicts were shipped to their places of exile, but Koba remained at the Kutais prison for another month. The reason for his detention was that the Kutais Okhrana hoped to use Koba to apprehend Kamo, who at that time was distributing leaflets in the city. Koba did not provide the Okhrana with Kamo's address or the names of Kamo's contacts – either because he did not know the Kutais underworld or because he saw no advantage in revealing the information. He probably offered to find Kamo, provided he was freed, but the Okhrana could not release a convict from prison in disregard of a 'HIGHEST AUTHORITY' decision to exile him. The alternative, to arrange a bogus 'escape' from prison – sometimes done in special cases – required permission from someone at the level of the director of the Department of Police. Such escapes were also risky because prison guards were liable to learn of them and expose the fraud, as had happened on occasion.[41] Exposure of the fraud naturally rendered the 'escapee' useless to the Okhrana, since it unmasked the agent. Usually, the Okhrana did not arrange prison escapes but would help collaborators to 'escape' from their places of exile, where there was only token police surveillance and actual escapes were common.

Toward the end of September 1903 Koba was sent under guard to the village of Novaya Uda, near Irkutsk, in eastern Siberia, but he did not stay there long. He was followed by a telegram addressed to the Irkutsk Okhrana by the Kutais Okhrana stating: 'I. V. Dzhugashvili plans to leave. Do not stop him. Render assistance.'[42] Toward the end of October, Koba left Novaya Uda carrying the identification document of an Okhrana agent he had obtained from the local Okhrana. At a railway station he showed this document to a gendarmerie officer, who allowed him to proceed to Batum where he told a story of how he had 'fabricated an identity document in the name of an agent of one of the Siberian policemen' and had shown it to a gendarmerie officer, who had helped him on his journey.[43] Koba did not explain how he, a young exile in a remote Siberian village, had managed to 'fabricate' the personal identification document of an Okhrana agent. Such documents were given only under extraordinary circumstances to convicts who entered into a secret agreement with the Okhrana.[44] Koba arrived at Batum in mid-November of 1903.[45] He managed to establish contact with Kamo and send him a message asking him to come. On 26 November 1903 Kamo stepped off the train at the Batum railway station and into the hands of an Okhrana officer waiting for him with a warrant for his arrest. Kamo offered the officer money to let him go, but to no avail.[46] This was Kamo's first but by no means his last arrest.

At the end of December 1903 Koba arrived at Tiflis and met there for the first time a young Social Democrat, Lev Kamenev, whom one of the party leaders, V. I. Lenin, had sent to Tiflis to take the place of the arrested Kurnatovsky. Kamenev had become Lenin's disciple at the Second Social Democratic Party Congress in London in the summer of 1903. At the congress, Lenin had advanced his program of 'democratic centralism', by which he meant the dictatorship of a small group of 'professional revolutionaries' under his leadership. Lenin's supporters were a very small minority in the Social Democratic Party. Lenin performed a propaganda sleight of hand by declaring his small group of supporters a 'majority'. At this point the party had split into the 'Bolsheviks', or the majority faction, and 'Menshevik', or minority, who opposed Lenin and demanded free discussion of all questions of party policy. Kamenev hoped that Koba, a young escapee from Siberian exile, would help him set up a Bolshevik organization in Tiflis. From Kamenev, Koba learned for the first time about Lenin and the split in the party. On 5 January 1904 shortly after meeting Koba, Kamenev was arrested.[47] On the same day, an officer in the Tiflis Okhrana made an entry in Koba's file: 'On 5 January 1904 Dzhugashvili disappeared from his place of exile.'[48] The date, 5 January 1904, of this entry and the same date of Kamenev's arrest strongly suggests that the Okhrana officer was compelled to report Koba's 'escape' because he used Koba's information to arrest Kamenev and felt the need to protect himself from any possible charge that he, while aware of Koba's presence in Tiflis, had not reported his escape from exile. An added incentive to protect himself must have been this officer's knowledge that Koba was connected with Kamo, whose case was being considered at the highest level in St Petersburg.

On 27 April 1904 the Minister of Justice, N. K. Muraviev, wrote to the Minister of the Interior, V. K. Plehve: 'I, on my part, would prefer to decide this case by administrative order and to exile Simon Ter-Petrosov (Kamo) to the Arkhangelsk *gubernia* [region] for four years under open police surveillance.' Muraviev recommended that the case of Kamo, the 21-year-old criminal, be decided in secret, to avoid revealing the scandal in the Tiflis Okhrana and to allow him to present this secret case for 'decision by the HIGHEST AUTHORITY'. In his petition to the Tsar, Muraviev stated that 'in the interest of the preservation of State order and public tranquility' the court proceedings should be held behind closed doors.[49]

The scandal in the Tiflis Okhrana was typical of that period. Another similar scandal led to Zubatov's downfall. In 1903 one of Zubatov's agents, Dr Shaevich, organized a strike by Jewish workers in Odessa that led to a serious confrontation with police. Prime Minister Plehve, already outraged by numerous acts of violence and disorder that had been provoked by Okhrana agents, summoned Zubatov to his office. After upbraiding him for the violence that Zubatov and his 'Jew Boy, Shaevich' had instigated, Plehve fired Zubatov.[50] (Zubatov was to commit suicide at the time of the 1917 February Revolution.)

Although Zubatov was fired and his network of Okhrana agents purged, Zubatovshchina survived and continued to spread. (Plehve himself was soon assassinated in a terrorist act directed by the top secret Okhrana agent Evno Azef.) What happened at the Tiflis Okhrana was similar to what happened everywhere: the Tiflis Okhrana was purged on orders from St Petersburg. Captain Lavrov was fired and replaced by Colonel N. A. Zasypkin, who purged the network of Okhrana agents and informers recruited by Lavrov. A new warrant, issued by the Department of Police on 1 May 1904, for the arrest of Iosif Dzhugashvili arrived at Tiflis.[51] Koba learned about it and immediately left for Gori.

Koba's mother was happy about his return. She hoped that her 25-

year-old son would marry and settle down. One of Koba's former Seminary classmates, Alexander Svanidze, introduced Koba to his 18-year-old sister, whose name, like that of Koba's mother, was Katerina, or Keke. Her name may have had some bearing on Koba's decision to marry her. People for whom he felt affection were invariably those he could in some way or other associate with his mother.[52] Despite Koba's frequent maligning of religion and church ritual, his mother insisted on a church wedding,[53] and Koba married Keke Svanidze on 21 June 1904 in one of Gori's eight churches. Koba Egnatashvili officiated at the wedding.[54] The young bride was deeply religious, having been brought up in the traditional Georgian ways. The young couple made their home in Didi-Lilo because Koba's wife wanted to stay close to her family. But Koba soon left for Tiflis, and in the years that followed, rarely visited his wife. 'She regarded him as a demigod and lived in fear for his safety, spending countless nights in ardent prayer, waiting for her husband to return from his secret trips, so displeasing to God, and would learn to lead a peaceful life of toil and contentment.'[55]

NOTES

1. V. Kaminsky and I. Vereshchagin, *Detstvo i yunost' vozhdia: documenty, zapisky, rasskazy*, Moscow, 1939, pp. 87–90.
2. Ibid., pp. 63 and 74. See also L. Beria, 'Lado Ketskhoveli', *Pravda*, no. 189, 11 July 1937.
3. Kaminsky and Vereshchagin, *Detstvo i yunost' vozhdia*, p. 83.
4. F. D. Volkov claims that documents stating that Stalin was recruited as an agent of the tsar's secret police are in the possession of Nikolay Stepanovich Shumsky, Dean of the Department of Philosophy of the Taganrog Teachers Institute. F. D. Volkov, *Vzlet i padenie Stalina*, Moscow, 1992, p. 16, n. 19.
5. N. Vakar, 'Stalin po vospominaniyam N. N. Zhordania', *Poslednie novosti*, Paris, 16 December 1936.
6. A. T. Vasiliev, *The Okhrana*, London, 1930, pp. 57ff.
7. B. P. Kozmin, *Zubatov i ego korespondenty*, Moscow, 1928. V. D. Novitsky, *Iz vospominanii zhandarma*, Leningrad, 1929. A. I. Sokolova, *Moskovskaya suysknaya politsiya*, Petrograd, 1916. Vasiliev, *The Okhrana*, pp. 57ff. Vasiliev praises Zubatov highly.
8. Kaminsky and Vereshchagin, *Detstvo i yunost' vozhdia*, pp. 91ff.
9. Ibid., p. 15.
10. G. Volchek and V. Voinov, *Viktor Kurnatovsky*, Moscow, 1961.
11. Ibid., pp. 95ff.
12. Vasiliev, *The Okhrana*, pp. 63ff.
13. Dubinsky-Mukhadze, *Kamo*, pp. 7–13.
14. Ibid., pp. 14f.
15. Ibid.
16. Okhrana Report, dated 17 June 1902, signed by the chief of the Batum Okhrana Section, Colonel S. P. Sabelsky. On file at the Hoover Institution, Stanford University. Copy in the author's archive. See also the reproduction of the report in Boris Souvarine, *Stalin: a Critical Survey of Bolshevism*, London, 1939, p. 46 and Edward Ellis Smith, *The Young Stalin – The Early Years of an Elusive Revolutionary*, London, 1968, p. 102.
17. J. Iremaschwili, *Stalin und die Tragödie Georgiens*, Berlin, 1932, pp. 27ff.
18. I. V. Stalin, *Sochineniya*, vol. I, Moscow, 1946–51, pp. 314ff.

19. For a discussion of reaction formation, see any elementary psychology textbook.
20. S. T. Arkhomed, *Rabochee dvizhenie i sotsial-demokratiya na Kavkaze*, Geneva, 1910, p. 74.
21. G. Uratadze, 'Moi vospominaniya'. Manuscript on file at the Hoover Institution, Stanford University, pp. 56ff.
22. *Batumskaya demonstratsiya 1902-go goda*, Moscow, 1937, p. 152.
23. N. Vakar, 'Stalin po vospominaniyam N. N. Zhordania,' *Poslednie novosti*, Paris, 16 December 1936, p. 2.
24. Ibid.
25. B. Souvarine, *Stalin: a Critical Survey of Bolshevism*, London, 1939, p. 46. Also R. Arsenidze, 'L. Beria: K Voprosu ob istorii bolshevitskikh organizatsii v Zakavkazie', *Caucasian Review*, no. 1, 1955.
26. R. Arsenidze, 'Iz vospominanii o Staline', Novy zhurnal, no. 72, 1972. Also 'L. Beria . . .', *Caucasian Review*, no. 1, 1955.
27. Vakar, 'Stalin', p. 2. Also E. E. Smith, *The Young Stalin*, London, 1968, p. 99.
28. *Batumskaya demonstratsiya 1902-go goda*, pp. 150–3.
29. Stalin, *Sochinenia*, vol. I, p. 419.
30. Vakar, 'Stalin', p. 2. Also Smith, *The Young Stalin*, p. 99.
31. Ludmila Kafanova, 'O velikom druge i vozhde', *Novoe russkoe slovo*, 23 and 24 March 1977. See also *Batumskaya demonstratsiya 102-go goda*, pp. 150–3 and S. Vereshchak, 'Stalin v tur'me: vospominaniya politicheskogo zakluchennogo', *Dni*, 22 and 24 January 1928. (Vereshchak describes the counterfeiting operation of the Darakhvelidze brothers.)
32. Lev Trotsky, *Stalin*, New York, 1941, pp. 34ff.
33. For a brief account of Colonel S. P. Shabelsky's career, see Smith, *The Young Stalin*, p. 103. Also see Roy Medvedev, *Let History Judge*, New York, 1971, pp. 319–23. Medvedev states that in the early 1930s the historian, Professor Sepp, author of *The October Revolution in Documents*, happened upon the file of a police agent, Iosif Dzhugashvili, and that the file contained Dzhugashvili's request to be released from prison. A note on the request stated: 'Free him, if he agrees to give the Gendarme Department information about the activity of the Social Democratic Party.' (Shabelsky did not know of Koba's work as an informer in Tiflis: Koba would not have mentioned it, having fled Tiflis to avoid arrest in connection with the leaflets provocation. Okhrana policy was to keep the identity of informers secret even within Okhrana departments. Communication between the Okhrana departments of different cities was always routed through the Special Section of the Department of Police in St Petersburg.)
34. *Batumskaya demonstratsiya 102-go goda*, pp. 120–2. See also Vereshchak for similar incidents of Koba accusing other prisoners of being Okhrana agents.
35. Okhrana Report no. 5500, dated 1 May 1904, on file at the Hoover Institution and published in Robert C. Tucker (ed.), *Stalinism*, New York, 1977, pp. 200ff.
36. Souvarine, *Stalin*, p. 44.
37. Okhrana report no. 53–c, dated 14 March 1911 and other Okhrana documents, including the circular letter attached to Okhrana report no. 97984, dated 19 April 1913, which states that I. V. Dzhugashvili was exiled by the 'HIGHEST AUTHORITY decree of 9 June 1903 for a state crime . . .'.
38. R. Bagratuni's letter to I. D. Levine, dated 8 May 1967. In I. D. Levine's archive. Copy in the author's archive.
39. S. Alliluev, *Proidennyi put'*, Moscow, 1946, pp. 63ff.
40. Nugzar Sharia, taped interview with the author, Sag Harbor, Long Island, New York, 1971. Nugzar Sharia related recollections of his uncle, Peter Sharia, Stalin's assistant. Starting in 1937, Stalin ordered publication of numerous articles and books glorifying Lado. One of the many authors was Lavrenty Beria – see, for instance, his *Lado Ketskhoveli*, Moscow, 1938.
41. Colonel A. Eremin, for example, released the *provocateur* Solomon Rys from a Kiev prison in 1906 after securing the permission of the director of the Department of Police, M. I. Trusevich. See Chapters 6 and 8.
42. Dr Norman Syrkin, in a letter, dated 4 January 1975, addressed to the author. Also Syrkin's interview with the author and Vitaly Svechinsky in Haifa, Israel, in January 1972. Syrkin's father, Zalman Syrkin, who worked for many years in the USSR Academy of Sciences, learned in 1964 that this telegram had been found in the Irkutsk Okhrana archive, but was not published because Khrushchev was deposed that year and his de-Stalinization campaign ended with Leonid Brezhnev's assumption of power.

43. *Batumskaya demonstratsiya 1902-go goda*, p. 140. See also *Batumskaya demonstratsiya 1902-go goda*, p. 140. See also M. A. Bulgakov, *Sobranie Sochinenii*, in 5 vols, Vol. 3, Moscow, 1990, 'Khudozhestvennaya Literatura', p. 697.

44. M. A. Bulgakov, *Sobranie sochinenii*, vol. III, Moscow, 1990, commentary on pp. 697ff. In 1937, Stalin commissioned Bulgakov to write a play (titled *Batum*) based on a hurriedly published book on the Batum Demonstration of 1902 (*Batumskaya demonstratsiya 1902-go goda*). Bulgakov underlined the book's recollections of how Stalin explained his escape from Novaya Uda. Stalin withdrew the commission for the play before it was completed by Bulgakov. The commentary to the play describes the 'personal identity' document of an Okhrana agent.

45. E. Yaroslavsky, *Vazhneishie vekhi zhizni i deyatelnosti tovarishcha Stalina*, Moscow, 1940/London, 1942, p. 31.

46. I. Dubinsky-Mukhadze, *Kamo*, Moscow, 1974, pp. 32ff.

47. Trotsky, *Stalin*, p. 46, fn. 9.

48. Okhrana Report no. 101145, dated 31 March 1911 signed by the vice director of the Department of Police, Vissarionov, and the chief of the Special Section, Colonel Eremin. On file at the Hoover Institution. Copy in the author's archive.

49. Dubinsky-Mukhadze, *Kamo*, p. 34.

50. I. V. Alekseev, *Provokator Anna Serebriakova*, Moscow, 1932.

51. Okhrana Report no. 5500, dated 1 May 1904.

52. Svetlana Allilueva, *Only One Year*, New York, 1969, p. 367. Svetlana states: 'Everyone to whom he [Stalin] had ever been attached, for whom he had ever felt any affection, had been connected in his consciousness with his mother. His first wife bore her name Catherine.'

53. Ibid., p. 367. Svetlana writes: 'This quiet pretty girl had pleased the mother, and at the mother's insistence the marriage had been solemnized in church.'

54. Budu Svanidze, *My Uncle Joe*, London, 1952, pp. 6 and 16. 'Budu Svanidze' was a pen name of the Soviet diplomat Bessedovsky, who knew Stalin personally and who, having defected in 1930, wrote several books under various pen names. Bertram Wolfe points out in his book *The Diary of Maxim Litvinov* that Bessedovsky did not invent anything but invariably wrote of what he actually knew.

55. Iremaschwili, *Stalin*, pp. 30–9.

3

MEETING THE 'MOUNTAIN EAGLE'

Kamo escaped from the Batum prison on 11 September 1904. On the same day, Colonel Tiapkin, the chief of the Kutais Okhrana, sent a telegram to St Petersburg, stating: 'Urgent. To the chief of the Special Section, Vasiliev. Simon Arshakov Ter-Petrosov (Kamo) escaped from the Batum prison . . . I have the honor of requesting an All-Empire search.'[1] Batum was under the jurisdiction of the Kutais Okhrana, which made Tiapkin responsible for the investigation of Kamo's case. Tiapkin summoned Koba to Kutais in the hope that he would help him locate Kamo. While in Kutais, Koba submitted several reports to the Okhrana providing information on local Social Democrats.[2] But this time, he was not inclined to turn Kamo in, probably fearing that he would arouse Kamo's suspicion if he once again delivered him into the Okhrana's hands. Besides, Kamo promised to be a great asset to him as a source of funds acquired from 'expropriations' – a euphemism for armed robberies of banks, post offices and wealthy individuals – activities that were growing in popularity among revolutionary groups and common criminals.

Toward the end of 1904, strikes, robberies and violence spread throughout the Russian Empire. The Russo-Japanese war, which had begun in January 1904, was going badly for Russia. Her army had lost over 400,000 soldiers, dead or wounded; her navy had lost most of its ships. On 20 December 1904, the Russian Pacific Naval Base Port Arthur was surrendered to the Japanese. The war was to drag on for nine more months. On 5 September 1905, President Theodore Roosevelt arranged the signing of the Russo-Japanese Peace Treaty at Portsmouth, New Hampshire. By that time, the revolution of 1905 was threatening to topple the tsarist regime. The military defeats and worsening economic conditions were the main causes of revolutionary upheaval. Okhrana agents added to the general turmoil by provoking confrontations with the authorities. An Okhrana agent, Father George Gapon, provoked a major revolutionary explosion that took place on 9 January 1905 and became known as 'Bloody Sunday'. On that day Gapon, an Orthodox priest and the leader of the 'Assembly of Russian Workers', led a large column of workers carrying icons and singing patriotic hymns to the Tsar's Winter Palace in St Petersburg. He intended to submit a petition to the Tsar demanding respect for civil rights, amnesty for political exiles, and an eight-hour working day. The troops guarding the palace tried to stop the marchers, but they continued to advance. The soldiers opened fire, and the workers fled, leaving behind hundreds of dead and wounded. The massacre might have been avoided had Nicholas II been there, but he was not in the palace that day. The Tsar wrote in his diary: 'A grim day! . . . Many were killed or wounded. God, how sad and grim!'[3]

News of the tragedy reached Lenin in Geneva. He predicted more bloodshed to come. If Russia was defeated in the war, this would, he hoped, lead to the overthrow of the tsarist government and to the establishment of the 'dictatorship of the proletariat' headed by him, the leader of the Bolsheviks. After Bloody Sunday, Father Gapon went to Geneva, where Lenin welcomed him with open arms as a hero and offered him membership in the Bolshevik organization. Gapon agreed, but mastering the intricacies of Marxist idiom proved to be too great a challenge for this confused and illiterate priest and Okhrana agent. Gapon parted company with Lenin and tried to re-establish his reputation as a workers' leader, but he was soon unmasked by members of the Social Revolutionary Party. One of them lured Gapon to a secret meeting place in Finland and hanged him there.[4]

Koba was far from these events. He was 26, but had not been drafted into the army because of his crippled left arm. Early in 1905, he joined a small Bolshevik group in Tiflis headed by Stepan Shaumian, who had met Lenin while studying abroad. Lenin had sent Shaumian to Tiflis to take the place of the arrested Kurnatovsky and Kamenev. The Tiflis Bolsheviks voted to send Shaumian to Lenin's Third Party Congress, scheduled to be held in April 1905 in London. But Shaumian was unable to attend: Koba denounced him to the Okhrana and he was arrested – the third Bolshevik leader to have been betrayed by Koba. Shortly before Shaumian's intended departure, the new chief of the Tiflis Okhrana, Colonel N. A. Zasypkin (who had replaced Captain Lavrov), had arrested Koba on a Tiflis street. According to the warrant issued by the Department of Police on 1 May 1904, ordering Koba's arrest and exile, Zasypkin was supposed to send Koba to Siberia. But Koba told the colonel that his 'escape' from Novaya Uda had been sanctioned by the Okhrana and that he had helped the Okhrana to apprehend Kamo. Koba informed Zasypkin of Shaumian's plans and promised to provide information about an underground Menshevik press in Tiflis that was printing subversive leaflets. Koba signed a pledge to collaborate with the Okhrana.[5] Zasypkin released him and arrested Shaumian. During Shaumian's interrogation, Zasypkin slipped up, mentioning the address of Shaumian's secret apartment in Tiflis. Shaumian at once recalled that the only person to whom he had told this address was Koba, and realized who had betrayed him.[6] Shaumian's arrest gave Koba the opportunity to make his first contact with Lenin. In lieu of Shaumian, Koba's close friend Mikha Tskhakaya went to London. He was about 30 and considered by the Tiflis Bolsheviks to be an 'old man'. He had a long prison record and was known in the criminal underworld by the nicknames 'Old Man Mikha', 'Gurgen' and 'Gambeta'.[7] Lenin introduced Tskhakaya to the Congress as the 'delegate from the Tiflis Bolsheviks'. Lenin told Tskhakaya about his idea of a secret, conspiratorial Bolshevik organization. He was impressed by what Tskhakaya told him about Koba and Kamo and their expertise in armed robberies. Lenin also liked a leaflet composed by Koba and printed by Kamo, in which they quoted a fraudulent report that they themselves had fabricated, supposedly by a high police official, General Lopukhin, that ran: 'It is necessary to inflame ethnic and racial hatred; it is necessary to organize "Black Hundreds" [Russian nationalistic vigilantes] . . .; it is necessary to transform the struggle between the police and the revolutionary circles into the struggle of one half of the people against the other half of the people. . . '.[8] The provocative leaflet was written using Koba's characteristic repetitive style. Lenin must have recognized the document as the obvious forgery it was, but he had thousands of copies of it printed for smuggling into Russia. The brief comment he added was: 'We, too, are for civil war . . . Long live the revolution. Long live the open civil war against the tsarist government and its supporters!'[9] That the 'Lopukhin report' was a crude fabrication apparently did not bother Lenin.

Tskhakaya also told Lenin about the leaflets with which Koba and Kamo had 'wrecked the career' of the chief of the Tiflis Okhrana, Captain Lavrov.[10] This information may have suggested to Lenin that Koba and Kamo had been involved in an Okhrana provocation and connected with the printing of the leaflets that had caused the arrest of Kurnatovsky and his secret circle. Tskhakaya, after his return to Tiflis, told Koba about Lenin's idea of a conspiratorial Bolshevik organization and his request for money from expropriations to finance party work. Lenin's concept of a highly secretive party organization led by a strong leader appealed to, and was in tune with, Koba's conspiratorial nature. He also realized that the more secretive such a party was, the more valuable to the Okhrana would be information about it. He sensed in Lenin a man with character traits similar to his own and resolved to meet him personally. The opportunity came when Lenin arranged the Bolshevik Conference in Tammerfors, Finland, in December 1905.

At the end of November, a Baku worker, Peter Montin, was elected to

represent Caucasian workers at Tammerfors, but on the eve of his departure for Finland he was assassinated. A stranger shot him in the head as
Montin was walking at night with his bride. The murderer was never
apprehended. Suspicion fell on Sergey Alliluev, Koba's friend (and future
father-in-law). But Alliluev presented an alibi in court that he was to recall
in great detail and with puzzling contradictions in his memoirs some three
decades later:

Montin returned to Baku on December 6, but I, without seeing him, went on
the same day to Tiflis, where after a five-year prohibition I again received
permission to work in the railroad shops. I was met at the Tiflis railroad station
by comrades holding a telegram, which stated that on the evening of
December 6, Peter Montin had been killed by a shot through the head . . . His
body lay on the street all night.[11]

Alliluev does not mention the names of the 'comrades holding a telegram',
and does not explain how he managed to go to Tiflis on 6 December, the
day Montin was killed, and to be met there by a telegram telling about the
murder and the fact that Montin's body had lain in the street all night. (The
distance between Baku and Tiflis is some 300 miles, and Alliluev should
have arrived at Tiflis no later than the night of Montin's murder.) Alliluev
adds that Montin's bride testified that 'the bullet hit Montin in the temple,
but he managed to take a pistol out of his pocket and fire a shot'.

    In her memoirs, Alliluev's daughter, Anna, repeats her father's earlier
story, but adds one peculiar detail: she states that Montin was murdered by
the Okhrana.[12] Anna published her memoirs in 1946, four decades after the
murder that took place when she was 7 years old. Alliluev himself makes
no such assertion. This assertion was suggested by Stalin, who habitually
accused others of crimes he himself had committed.

    Sergey Alliluev lost his mother early in life and never saw his father, a
wandering gypsy. He was raised by an uncle on his mother's side. He was
unable to keep a job and several times was fired after quarreling with his
employers. In May 1903, during the workers' unrest in Tiflis, he was
arrested and interrogated for taking part in the demonstration, but he was
soon released by the chief of the Tiflis Okhrana, Captain Lavrov (the same
Lavrov whose career had been wrecked by Koba, Lado and Kamo). In 1937
Stalin forced Alliluev to write his memoirs and provided him with documents found in Alliluev's file in the Tiflis Okhrana archive; Alliluev quotes
verbatim from his conversation with Captain Lavrov, who made him an
offer to become an informer. At this point, Alliluev stops quoting and
begins paraphrasing, stating that he indignantly refused the offer. Despite

his refusal, writes Alliluev, he was released while another man, Nikifor Beridze, became an informer, was exposed and then killed.[13] In fact, however, Alliluev was released after he had signed a pledge to collaborate with the Okhrana. A year later, when Lavrov was fired and the network of agents in the Tiflis Okhrana purged, Alliluev was exiled to Baku, with a 5-year prohibition against living in Tiflis. He received permission to move to Tiflis when he went there the day of Montin's murder.

Koba was a victim of the same purge. It was clear that Alliluev had been exiled to Baku as a dismissed Okhrana informer. There was also a connection between Alliluev and Kamo, whose biographer states that Alliluev was 'tied to Kamo by many deals'.[14] Whether the murder of Montin was one of those deals is unknown, as were the whereabouts of Kamo on 6 December 1905. But it is known that Kamo was arrested again two weeks later, on 18 December. On that day, his band was almost wiped out by Cossack troops in a skirmish in a Tiflis suburb. Kamo was wounded in the arm and captured. The Cossacks hanged him, but the rope snapped and Kamo's almost lifeless body fell to the ground. Frightened by this obviously divine intervention, the Cossacks decided to deliver their captive alive to the Tiflis prison. Alliluev saw Kamo, covered with blood and barely able to walk, being led to prison, and told Kamo's aunt what had happened.[15]

Koba left for Finland to attend the Tammerfors Conference in lieu of Montin the day after Montin's murder. This development makes Koba an obvious suspect in the murder, since he was the only clear beneficiary. But Koba had an alibi: he was in Tiflis at the time of the murder and had witnesses to prove it. Alibi or no, it would have been out of character for Koba personally to murder someone; bloodying his own hands was not Koba's style. All his life Stalin practiced blackmail and manipulated people to commit his crimes. (Dostoyevsky in *The Possessed* describes how Peter Verkhovensky instigates the murder of a student and then manipulates the murderers by threatening to expose them.) Alliluev devoted a large space in his memoir to the murder of Montin and to his own tortured alibi. His lifelong servility to Stalin suggests a similar type of relationship.

At the Tammerfors Conference, Koba met Lenin, a man he at first described as 'a most ordinary looking man, below average in height; in no way, literally in no way, distinguishable from ordinary mortals'.[16] Earlier he had imagined him as a 'mountain eagle'. Actually Lenin was a very short and bald man, with wide, protruding cheekbones and slightly slanted Kalmyk eyes. He helped Koba gain admittance to the conference, where Koba registered under the codename 'Ivanovich'. At the conference, Lenin first

advocated participation in the elections to the state Duma, the newly established Russian parliament, arguing that the revolution could be preached
from the Duma platform the same way it could be preached from a 'dung
heap' or in a 'pigsty', so why not do it in the 'pigsty of the Duma'? But he
soon changed his mind and called for a boycott of the Duma elections. He
stated that the time for preaching was over and called for armed insurrection. There were some 40 delegates at the conference. Anticipating a revolutionary uprising, they used the intervals between sessions to learn to shoot.

Lenin believed the revolution was gaining momentum, when in fact it
was about to collapse. The Tsar had been forced to make many concessions
to opposition groups and in October 1905 issued the 'Manifesto of the
Seventeenth of October', which virtually abolished autocracy: it proclaimed
that no law could be passed without the consent of the Duma. Count S. Y.
Witte, a liberal and farsighted statesman, was the driving force behind the
Manifesto and the reforms. He was appointed prime minister, but his
authority was challenged by the Soviets (Councils) of Workers' Deputies,
which sprang up in various industrial centers. The St Petersburg Soviet
aspired to the role of national government, issuing appeals that were obeyed
by the public while the Tsar's decrees were ignored. On 14 December
1905 the Soviet appealed to all citizens to stop paying taxes and to demand
that wages be paid in gold. It warned foreign powers that the future revolutionary government of Russia would honor no loans made to the tsarist
regime. Two days later, all the members of the St Petersburg Soviet were
arrested. One of those arrested was Lev Trotsky, who had been elected
President of the St Petersburg Soviet on 12 December 1905, the day the
Tammerfors Conference opened.[17] While at Tammerfors, Koba and Lenin
held secret meetings, discussing expropriations. Koba promised to provide
Lenin with money. The Conference closed on 17 December 1905, the day
after the arrests in St Petersburg. The Tammerfors delegates called for
insurrection.

After the conference, Lenin invited Koba to travel to St Petersburg with
him. There they visited the party headquarters and the offices of the party
newspaper, and attended a secret gathering, at which Lenin and other
party leaders discussed Bolshevik–Menshevik unity. The St Petersburg
Okhrana received a detailed report from an informer, codenamed
'Ivanov', describing this meeting and stating that 'the Social Democratic
Central Committee and a number of delegates, Menshevik and Bolshevik,
met at 9 Zagorodny Prospect in St Petersburg to discuss unity . . . '.
Informer 'Ivanov' listed the names of all the people who had attended the
meeting, including 'Ivanovich, the delegate from Tiflis'.[18] The informer

'Ivanov' and 'Ivanovich, the delegate from Tiflis', were one and the same person. 'Ivanovich' was still unidentified in the first party history published in 1926. Stalin was afraid that he could be exposed as the Okhrana informer 'Ivanov' if the identity of 'Ivanovich' were established.[19]

At the beginning of 1906, when Koba returned to Tiflis, he learned that Kamo had been arrested. He met with the survivors of Kamo's band in a Tiflis wine cellar and ordered them to murder General Griaznov, the Military Governor of the Caucasus, explaining that Griaznov was a symbol of oppression. In Griaznov, a figure of power and authority, his 'grim, sullen hatred . . . for every form of authority' found a ready target.[20] One of the members of the band drew the lot to carry out the assassination. It was the general's habit to take rides in an open carriage. The assassin threw a bomb, killing him. Koba watched the scene from a safe distance. A policeman rushing to the bloody site shouted at him, 'What are you loitering here for?' and pushed him aside. The assassin was caught and tried in a martial court, then hanged in a Tiflis square.[21]

During these events, Kamo was in prison, looking for a way to escape. His wounded arm healed. The prison authorities were unable to establish his identity. On 8 February 1906, he impersonated one of his cellmates, who had been called to be released from prison, and walked out a free man. He soon found Koba, who told him about Lenin's request to organize a major expropriation. For this endeavor, they needed more men. A large band operated in the town of Telavi in eastern Georgia; Koba and Kamo went there to recruit new members for Kamo's band.[22] Early in March, Kamo and his band hijacked money transports in Kutais and on the Kodzhor road near Tiflis. Kamo went to the Finnish resort village of Kuokkala, where Lenin and his wife were renting a *dacha*, to deliver the money. This was Kamo's first meeting with Lenin who watched intensely as Kamo unpacked a 'strange thing', which turned out to be a leather wine bag with a double bottom in which the money was hidden. Lenin initially seemed tense, sat sideways, covered his face with his hands as if trying to hide from the light of the lamp. But Kamo noticed his probing eyes, peeking through his loosely folded fingers.[23] Lenin took the money and thanked Kamo. Then he sent him to St Petersburg to join a band that was preparing further expropriations and assassinations.

NOTES

1. I. Dubinsky-Mukhadze, *Kamo*, Moscow, 1974, p. 36.
2. Roy Medvedev, *Let History Judge*, New York, 1971, p. 319.
3. *Dnevnik imperatora Nikolaya II*, Russkii revolutsionnyi arkhiv, Berlin, 1923, p. 194.
4. Sidney Harcave, *First Blood: The Russian Revolution of 1905*, New York, 1964, p. 69. See also Edward Ellis Smith, *The Young Stalin: The Early Years of an Elusive Revolutionary*, London, 1968, p. 133.
5. See Chapter 5. Also see Colonel N. A. Zasypkin's report in *Shkola fillerov*, *Byloe*, no. 3 (25), 1917, pp. 66ff. Quoted in Smith, pp. 165f.
6. N. Vakar, 'Stalin po vospominaniyam N. N. Zhordania', *Poslednie novosti*, Paris, 16 December 1936, p. 2.
7. See Chapter 5 below for Tskhakaya's role in the liquidation of the Avlabar underground press in Tiflis.
8. Dubinsky-Mukhadze, *Kamo*, pp. 37–42.
9. V. I. Lenin, *Polnoe sobranie sochinenii*, Moscow, 1958–65, vol. 9, p. 334.
10. Dubinsky-Mukhadze, *Kamo*, p. 39.
11. S. Alliluev, *Proidennyi put'*, Moscow, 1946, p. 157. Alliluev's recollections are riddled with inconsistencies.
12. Anna S. Allilueva, *Vospominaniya*, Moscow, 1946, p. 63.
13. Alliluev, *Proidennyi put'*, pp. 69–72. Photocopies of the Okhrana documents that Stalin provided for Alliluev are found in the appendix to Alliluev's memoirs.
14. Dubinsky-Mukhadze, *Kamo*, p. 52.
15. Ibid.
16. I. V. Stalin, *O Lenine*, Moscow, 1951, pp. 22f.
17. At this historic moment, Trotsky was already a prominent revolutionary leader. He had not yet met Koba, nor heard about this shadowy figure just emerging from the murky border where the criminal underworld and revolutionary movement met and often merged. See Joel Carmichael, *Trotsky*, London, 1975, pp. 68ff.
18. Isaac Deutscher, *Stalin: A Political Biography*, New York and London, 1968, p. 81. Also see F. Matasova, 'Nabludenie za V. I. Leninym', *Krasnaya letopis'*, no. 1 (12), 1925, pp. 123–5.
19. See Chapters 6 and 12 for additional information on the identity of the St Petersburg Okhrana informer 'Ivanov'.
20. J. Iremaschwili, *Stalin und die Tragödie Georgiens*, Berlin, 1932, p. 24.
21. H. Montgomery Hyde, *Stalin: the History of a Dictator*, New York, 1971, pp. 70ff., quoting Essad-Bey, *Stalin: the Career of A Fanatic*, New York and London, 1932, pp. 71–5. See also Boris Souvarine, *Stalin: a Critical Survey of Bolshevism*, London, 1939, p. 100, and Lev Trotsky, *Stalin*, New York, 1941, p. 101.
22. L. Beria, *K Voprosy ob istorii bolshevitskikh organizatsii v Zakavkazie*, Leningrad, 1936, p. 40. See also R. Arsenidze, interview, on file at the Radio Liberty Committee; copy in the author's archive.
23. Dubinsky-Mukhadze, *Kamo*, pp. 58–60.

4

THE MURDER OF VISSARION

All Stalin's biographers have insisted that his father, Vissarion Dzhugashvili, died in 1890. They refer to a statement by Koba's childhood friend, Iosif Iremashvili, who in his memoirs, published in 1932 in Berlin, mentioned in passing Vissarion's death in Tiflis in 1890.[1] Iremashvili did not know Vissarion personally. He met Koba for the first time at the end of September 1890 in the first grade of the Gori Ecclesiastical School, soon after Koba's return from Tiflis. They became friends and Iremashvili often visited Koba's home. Koba and his mother never mentioned Vissarion in Iremashvili's presence, but he heard stories from Gori residents about the brutal beatings to which Vissarion had subjected Koba and Keke. He thought that they had nothing good to say about Vissarion and interpreted their silence in the light of the old custom of not speaking ill of the dead. This deduction led him to surmise that Vissarion had died in Tiflis during Koba's sojourn there in the summer of 1890.

Actually, Vissarion was murdered 16 years later, in 1906. In his childhood biography, which Stalin edited in 1939, he inserted a footnote: 'Vissarion Ivanovich Dzhugashvili died in 1906.'[2] Stalin also told his daughter, Svetlana, that his father had 'died in a drunken brawl – somebody stabbed him with a knife'. Like Stalin, she provided this information in a footnote in her memoirs.[3] No police record of the murder has ever come to light, and the exact day when it took place remains unknown. It was Stalin's habit of gathering archival documents referring to him in his personal secretariat. It is possible that he destroyed this record during his rule.

But some clues survive, suggesting that by 8 March 1906 Koba already knew that Vissarion was dead. On that day, he published an article, 'The State Duma and the Tactics of Social Democracy', signed 'I. Besoshvili' ('Son of Beso'). Beso is a diminutive of Vissarion. A profound transformation had taken place in Koba's mind: he had suddenly become a loving son of Vissarion and his hatred had been swept away by an ardent desire for identification with him. This transformation suggests that Koba knew about the murder.[4] In his article, Koba criticized the new Russian parliament, the Duma, calling it 'a parliament–bastard', an echo of Vissarion's taunt of *nabichuari*.[5] Koba's verbal attack on the Duma was a description of a murder: he repeats the word 'blow' 14 times, mentioning a 'double blow', a 'blow from both sides', a 'blow from the top', a 'blow from below', a 'blow from outside', and a 'blow from inside'. Was he describing the murder, substituting the 'parliament–bastard' for Vissarion?

In this article, Koba for the first time used the expression 'enemies of the people', which years later became the slogan of Stalin's mass repressions.[6] The accusations fit a lifelong pattern: Stalin's ability to blot out the truth about his crimes by projecting them on to 'false targets', as he himself called this method in moments of insightful self-reference.[7] He was using the psychological defense mechanism of projection: attributing his own crimes to others, thereby freeing himself from guilt.[8]

During March 1906 Koba wrote three more articles, all entitled 'On the Agrarian Question', and all signed 'I. Besoshvili'.[9] Never again was he to use this pen name. In these articles Koba fervently championed the interests of the peasantry, advocating redistribution of land among it. On this issue he disagreed even with Lenin, who was for nationalization of land. Besoshvili wrote about the 'breaking of the old customs' and the 'rebellious village', about the peasantry, which 'only yesterday was beaten down and humiliated, but today gets on its feet and straightens its back . . . yesterday helpless, today, like a turbulent stream, it thrusts itself against the old order; get out of my way – otherwise I will knock you down'.[10] A confused mix of impulses was behind Koba's fervent declarations on behalf of the peasantry. Koba, the son of Beso, felt an ardent desire for identification with Vissarion, who in his mind was connected with the village and peasants. On the other hand, this passionate statement contained a figurative reference to himself: he, Koba, had been helpless, beaten down and humiliated by Vissarion, but was now on his feet, having swept his enemy from his path. Koba was feigning the role of a political journalist, but the issues he wrote about had meaning for him only as refections of his personal conflict, in which he used these issue as proxies.

The silence surrounding Vissarion's murder, Koba's sudden identification with Vissarion, and the projection of the murder scene on a 'false target' raises the question of Koba's involvement in this murder. Koba did not mention Vissarion's death when he was questioned by the Okhrana. Okhrana reports as late as 1909 and 1913 stated that Koba's father 'leads the life of a vagrant' and his 'whereabouts are unknown'.[11] This misleading information could have come only from Koba, who chose to conceal from the Okhrana the fact of his father's death in order to avoid questions about the time, place and circumstances of the murder, fearing, perhaps, that such questioning could lead to exposure of his involvement in the crime.

The question of where Vissarion was murdered was answered by one of

Stalin's grandsons, Evgeny Dzhugashvili, at the time a captain in the Soviet Rocket Forces. He learned of the location of Vissarion's grave on 30 August 1967, when he was invited to join in the commemoration of the sixtieth anniversary of the murder of Prince Ilia Chavchavadze, the great Georgian poet and public figure (whose poem 'Musha' was inserted in Stalin's childhood biography). Evgeny and other guests gathered in Chavchavadze's former estate near Telavi, the capital of Kakhetia, the eastern province of Georgia. One of the other guests, an elderly Telavi resident, offered to lead Evgeny to the grave of his great-grandfather Vissarion in the old Telavi cemetery. A fervent admirer of Stalin, Evgeny was glad to visit the forgotten grave.[12]

These fragments of information – Vissarion meeting a violent end sometime before 8 March 1906, not in Tiflis but in Telavi – only partly dispel the mystery that has surrounded Vissarion's death. To reconstruct the murder and the role Koba may have played in it requires other clues, which Stalin himself unwittingly provided by his actions in later years. He had the peculiar compulsion to 're-enact' the traumatic events of his life in order to appease his psychological need to externalize them by projecting his crimes on to other people. He frequently gave very detailed orders on how to murder his hated enemies. For example, in 1940 he instructed an assassin to murder Trotsky by striking him with an axe.[13] And in 1948 he ordered a squad of secret police assassins to murder a prominent public figure, Solomon Mikhoels, in a bizarre way: Mikhoels was to be struck 'with an axe wrapped in a wet quilted jacket'.[14] These peculiar instructions point to an obsession connected with a compulsive re-enactment of a murder by an axe, having roots in an earlier crime that was highly charged emotionally. There was no murder during Stalin's life that could have been more emotionally charged than that of his father. Trotsky's assassin had to carry a heavy coat in which he wrapped an axe on a hot August day in Mexico City, while Mikhoels was murdered with an axe wrapped in a wet quilted jacket on a freezing January night in Minsk. Stalin's bizarre orders begin to make sense only if we recognize them as the result of a fixation on an axe as a murder weapon. This fixation appeared elsewhere, too: Stalin suggested numerous scenes in the Sergei Eisenstein movie *Ivan the Terrible* – commissioned by Stalin to glorify his favorite Tsar – in which an axe in the hands of an executioner played a prominent role. He ordered that the following refrain be provided as a continuous choral background for major scenes: 'And the axes kept swinging, kept swinging . . .'. In many scenes, Tsar Ivan was shown hiding behind a Kremlin wall, watching his enemies being beheaded with an axe or assassinated with a knife. Stalin eventually ordered all copies of the film destroyed, realizing perhaps that this portrayal of Tsar Ivan bore too obvious a resemblance to him. But one of the copies was hidden away and preserved by a courageous studio worker. After Stalin's death the film was shown in Russia and abroad.

Although *Ivan the Terrible* portrays the Tsar as a mass murderer, it does not depict him murdering anyone with his own hands. In Stalin's record, similarly, nothing has been discovered implicating him personally in anyone's murder. Stalin instigated murders or ordered his henchmen to murder his enemies; he did not bloody his own hands. If Stalin was involved in the murder of Vissarion, he most probably remained behind the scenes. Stalin's fixation on murder with an axe offers an important clue to the identity of the actual murderer. This can be found in Stalin's instruction as to how to murder Solomon Mikhoels in 1948. In addition to ordering that Mikhoels be killed 'with an axe wrapped in a wet quilted jacket', Stalin instructed his agents to run the body over with a truck.[15] This instruction mirrors an earlier murder: in 1922, Kamo was killed on Stalin's orders – he was run over with a truck as he was cycling at night in Tiflis.[16] The two murders, one by axe, the other by a truck, merged in the case of Mikhoels. This merging of two murders suggests that there was a connection between them in Stalin's mind. The question is, what was this connection?

The truck in Mikhoels's murder points to Kamo as the murderer. This clue is reinforced by an argument that if Kamo murdered Vissarion at the instigation of Koba, then Stalin, playing his lifelong alternating roles of instigator and avenger, may well have had Kamo killed in revenge for the murder of Vissarion. This suggestion is further strengthened by a striking revelation: Stalin's hatred of Kamo did not stop with Kamo's murder in 1922, 16 years after Vissarion's murder, but erupted again much later, in 1938, 16 years after Kamo's own death, when Stalin ordered Kamo's grave and gravestone in the Tiflis cemetery to be destroyed in an explosion of hatred and revenge.[17]

Kamo's record indicates that he was a cold-blooded murderer, and axe was his favorite murder weapon. As a youth he once broke into his parents' bedroom and chased his own father with an axe in hand, trying to kill him.[18] In 1906, he murdered a certain 'Volodka', who was accused, most probably by Koba, of being an Okhrana informer.[19] The mere mention of the word 'informer' in Kamo's presence was enough to throw him into a blind rage. He swore to murder all informers, if he could only find them.[20] Like many of Stalin's accomplices, he accepted Stalin's assertions as divine revelations.[21] All it would have taken was for Koba to assert that Vissarion was a police informer to provoke Kamo to murder him.

As the first 'I. Besoshvili' article suggests, Vissarion was murdered shortly before 8 March 1906. On 8 February 1906, Kamo, who until then had been incarcerated in Tiflis prison, fooled the guards and escaped. He and Koba went to Telavi to recruit there members of a large band, whom they needed for the planned hijacking of money transports.[22] It was probably during this visit to Telavi that Koba encountered Vissarion, who lived there with his brother Glakh. The fateful encounter might have taken place anywhere, possibly in a Telavi wine cellar, one of the local *dukhans*, where drunkards, vagrants and criminals congregated, sipping Kakhetian wine to pass the time. Vissarion was 55 years old by then. Koba would still have recognized him, but it is doubtful that Vissarion would have recognized his 27-year-old son, whom he had last seen as a 10-year-old boy.

February and March are part of the rainy season in Georgia. It was, most likely, raining in Telavi the night of the murder and Kamo wore a quilted jacket that must have become soggy by the time he took it off and wrapped an axe in it to hide the weapon. He probably stalked Vissarion in a deserted Telavi street and struck him on the head with the axe still wrapped in the wet jacket and then killed his unconscious victim by stabbing him repeatedly with a knife. Stalin's later fixation on axes and multiple 'blows' (knife stabs) from all sides suggests that he watched the murder from a safe distance, hiding behind houses and fences. The police in this provincial town did not pay much attention to the murder of one of the local drunkards. It stated that Vissarion had been knifed to death in a drunken brawl. Stalin's daughter Svetlana heard this police version from her father many years later and mentioned it in her memoirs. He, of course, did not tell her about his role in this murder. But Koba's fear of being accused of the murder was not his only reason for hiding the truth from the police and his daughter. He was also hiding it from himself, blotting out the memory of the crime and projecting it on a false target, thereby purging himself of guilt and shame.

Freud called parricide the 'principal and primal crime of humanity as well as of the individual'. He recognized it as 'the main source of the sense of guilt . . . and the need for expiation . . .'. He wrote 'it can scarcely be owing to chance that three of the great masterpieces of literature of all time – *Oedipus Rex* of Sophocles, Shakespeare's *Hamlet* and Dostoyevsky's *The Brothers Karamazov* – all deal with the same subject, parricide'. Freud pointed out that in these masterpieces 'the motive for the deed, sexual rivalry for a woman, is laid bare'.[23]

To what extent Koba's hatred of Vissarion may have had roots in the Oedipal complex rather than in the abuse he suffered from his father is difficult to say. It may appear logical to suggest that Koba's motive for the murder was revenge for the beatings he had suffered as a child, for his crippled arm, and for the mistreatment of his mother. But what seems to be obvious often turns out to be quite misleading. Freud suggested that the main symptoms of neurosis in young men are sexual impotence and a ferocious hatred of their father, and that these symptoms are inter-related. A man exhibiting these symptoms cannot approach a woman sexually and usually finds a wife only after his father's death.[24] Koba does not seem to fit this description, since he got married two years before the murder of his father. But his relationship with his young wife was peculiar: he rarely visited her, and she was forever waiting for him to return home from his secret journeys. They had no children during the first two years of their marriage. It is perhaps significant that their first child was born two years after the murder of Vissarion. There is no evidence that prior to his marriage Koba ever fell in love, or that he had a tender relationship, or even a female companion. Sexual incapacity and the inability to form emotional attachments – common afflictions of fanatics and criminals – may have lurked behind his hectic life of expropriations, service in the Okhrana and party intrigues.

A person with a battered-child past, who was brutally abused by his father, usually manages later in life to blot out and psychologically exclude his father in order to function. Such exclusion is often possible when the hated father stays away, which creates the illusion of his death. But if a man with a battered-child past suddenly encounters his father, he no longer can exclude him psychologically, and in extreme cases he may 'exclude' him by homicide.[25] Such an extreme situation may have arisen when Koba encountered Vissarion in Telavi, and the murder may have become for him a matter of psychological and sexual survival.

Soon after the murder of Vissarion, Koba visited Gori to inspect a tunnel that Kamo's band had dug under the Gori state bank for a planned robbery.[26] While Koba was in Gori his benefactor, priest Koba Egnatashvili, was murdered. The priest's body was found in his home, lying in a pool of blood. Vano Muradeli, a prominent Soviet composer and a native of Gori, recalled years later that 'Suspicion concerning the murder fell upon Koba. He had come to Gori from Tiflis just for that day. There was talk among us in Gori that Koba seemed to have learned the truth about how this kind and loving priest was related to him.' (Like many other inhabitants of Gori, Muradeli believed that Egnatashvili was Koba's true father.[27]) The Gori police questioned Koba, but ruled out his involvement in the murder. To the policemen in this small provincial town it must have been inconceivable to suspect Koba of having anything to do with the murder of the priest – according to rumors his real father – who had treated him with kindness and love, and generously helped in his upbringing and education. For them to suspect Koba of this dreadful deed would have defied all common sense. They could not have realized that common sense had very little to do with the world in which Koba lived.

After the traumatic events in Tiflis in 1890 Koba rejected Vissarion as his abusive father and accepted Koba Egnatashvili as his true father. In postulating this new origin for himself Koba planted a psychological time bomb. All father–son relationships are ambivalent, but in Koba's case, the ambivalence ran very deep. Even though as a boy Soso may have chosen the nickname Koba as a symbolic act of denying that Vissarion was his father and accepting Koba Egnatashvili as his father substitute, in 1906 he suddenly assumed the pen name 'I. Besoshvili' (son of Beso). 'Son of Beso' felt a strong need to identify with his murdered father, which may have been complemented by an equally strong need to hate Egnatashvili, Vissarion's rival and a convenient false target on which to project guilt. Love transformed into hate is a not uncommon psychological phenomenon.[28] Such a transformation could have made it possible for Koba to cast Egnatashvili in the role of Vissarion's murderer. Koba, by instigating the murder of the priest, could fantasize avenging the murder of Vissarion, thus exculpating himself. Many of the crimes Koba was to engineer in later years show such a distortion of reality. In Stalin's mind, his crimes invariably underwent precisely this kind of transformation, and he played the alternating roles of the villain and the avenger of the crimes he himself had committed.

The murder of Egnatashvili attracted no more attention from the people of the Great Russian Empire than that of Vissarion. But on 30 August 1907 another murder shocked Georgia and the rest of the Russian Empire. Prince Ilia Chavchavadze, the great Georgian poet, writer and an advocate of liberal reforms, was murdered by Koba's close friends Sergo Ordzhonikidze, Filip Makharadze, and several other assassins, instigated by Koba. Chavchavadze was ambushed at the Black River crossing near Telavi, on the road to his ancestral estate. Koba, as usual, did not personally take part in the murder, but he ordered and directed it.[29] (Sixty years later Chavchavadze was canonized by the Georgian Orthodox Church, but the names of his assassins were revealed only in 1987; their graves subsequently were desecrated in a belated outburst of outrage over their crime.[30])

The assassins may have believed Koba's assertion that Prince Chavchavadze was a 'class enemy'. But Koba was driven by hidden motives and impulses rooted in traumas of his personal life. In Koba's mind, Chavchavadze was connected to Vissarion: Stalin inserted Chavchavadze's poem 'Musha' in his childhood biography which suggests that this poem had an important hidden meaning for him, reminding Koba of Vissarion's cruel fate, of the encounter with him in Tiflis in 1898, of Vissarion's murder, and prompting the projection of guilt on to the author of the poem, thus arousing the need to 'avenge' the murder by projecting it on this 'false target'.

NOTES

1. J. Iremaschwili, *Stalin und die Tragödie Georgiens*, Berlin, 1932, p. 12.
2. V. Kaminsky and I. Vereshchagin, *Detstvo i yunost' vozhdia: documenty, zapiski, rasskazy*, Moscow, 1939, p. 44.
3. Svetlana Allilueva, *Twenty Letters to a Friend*, New York, 1967, p. 158, fn.
4. I. V. Stalin, *Sochineniya*, vol. 1, Moscow, 1946–51, pp. 206–13. It is not clear whether the date, 8 March 1906, is Old Style or New Style. Stalin often changed dates to correspond to New Style. If he changed the date here to correspond to New Style, this would mean that Vissarion was murdered sometime in February 1906. If he did not change the date to New Style, this would mean that Vissarion was murdered either in February or early March 1906 Old Style.
5. This article is not available in its Georgian original, but the Russian word *ubliudok* with which Stalin refers to the Duma means 'bastard' (*nabichuari* in Georgian).
6. Stalin, *Sochineniya*, pp. 206–13.
7. I. V. Alekseev, *Provokator Anna Serebriakova*, Moscow, 1932, p. 160. Stalin, under the pen name I. V. Alekseev, wrote this chapter, as well as the foreword to this book, which is mostly a collection of Okhrana documents.
8. Sigmund Freud, *Freud: Dictionary of Psychoanalysis*, New York, 1969, p. 112; see also Walter C. Langer, *The Mind of Adolf Hitler*, New York, 1972, p. 183.
9. Stalin, *Sochinenia*, vol. 1, pp. 214–29.
10. Ibid., p. 214.
11. Department of Police Report no. 15179, dated 19 August 1909, and no. 97984, dated 19 April 1913, citing a copy of a Tver Okhrana report no. 245, dated 21 March 1913. On file at the Hoover Institution, Stanford University. All copies in the author's archive.
12. Interview with Nugzar Sharia, Sag Harbor, NY, 1972.
13. See Chapter 32 below for the murder of Trotsky.
14. Taped testimony of Vasily Rudich. See Chapter 36 below for the murder of Mikhoels.
15. See Chapter 36 below for the murder of Mikhoels.
16. See Chapter 15 below for the murder of Kamo.
17. Roy Medvedev, *Let History Judge*, New York, 1971, p. 202.
18. I. Dubinsky-Mukhadze, *Kamo*, Moscow, 1974, pp. 91f.
19. V. D. Bonch-Bruevich, quoted in Dubinsky-Mukhadze, *Kamo*, p. 62.
20. Dubinsky-Mukhadze, *Kamo*, pp. 126, 157, 165.
21. Alexander Orlov, *Tainaya istoria stalinskikh prestuplenii*, New York/Jerusalem/Paris, 1983, pp. 323–35. Orlov cites an example of what kind of people Stalin selected as his point men: they exhibited a doglike devotion to him and accepted his statements as divine revelations.
22. Lavrenty Beria, *K Voprosy ob istorii bolshevitskikh organizatsii v Zakavkazie*, Leningrad, 1936, p. 40. See also R. Arsenidze, interview, on file at the Radio Liberty Committee; copy in the author's archive.
23. Sigmund Freud, 'Dostoyevsky and Parricide', in *The Complete Psychological Works of Sigmund Freud*, vol. XXI, (1927–31), London, 1961, p. 183.
24. Sigmund Freud, *Moses and Monotheism*, New York, 1939, pp. 98–101.
25. See Thomas A. Harris, *I'm OK – You're OK*, New York, 1973, p. 128.

26. H. Montgomery Hyde, *Stalin: The History of a Dictator*, New York, 1971, pp. 71f., quoting Zhgenty and Zhordania.
27. Ludmila Kafanova, 'O velikom druge i vozhde', *Novoe russkoe slovo*, 23 March 1977.
28. See Freud, *Dictionary of Psychoanalysis*, p. 112.
29. J. Iremaschwili, *Stalin und die Tragödie Georgiens*, p. 37ff. The fact that Stalin's two close assistants Ordzhonikidze and Makharadze took part in the assassination of Chavchavadze confirms Stalin's complicity in this murder.
30. V. M. Gurgenidze (director of the Archive of the Georgian SSR), 'Ubiistvo Il'i Chavchavadze v arkhivnykh dannykh', in T. and E. Gudava's article in *Novoe russkoe slovo*, 1 April 1988, p. 9, and Boris Gass, 15 March 1988, p. 4.

5

THE BETRAYAL OF
THE AVLABAR PRESS

On 29 March 1906 Colonel Zasypkin, the new chief of the Tiflis Okhrana, arrested Koba on a Tiflis street. Several Social Democrats saw Koba being escorted to the Okhrana headquarters. They were surprised when he emerged from there a few hours later, explaining that Zasypkin had made him an offer to become an Okhrana agent but that he had refused. Sometime later Koba would claim that he had escaped from prison.[1]

A year earlier, in April 1905 when Zasypkin had for the first time arrested and released him, Koba had betrayed Stepan Shaumian and had promised to provide Zasypkin with information about the location of an underground press where Tiflis Mensheviks printed illegal leaflets.[2] Koba did not provide this information for almost a year. The press was producing a large amount of subversive literature, which alarmed Zasypkin and, having arrested Koba for the second time, he demanded the promised information. Koba had learned the location of the press shortly before that second arrest on 29 March 1906 when, following the unification of the Bolshevik and Menshevik factions, Koba's friend Mikha Tskhakaya had joined the entirely Menshevik Tiflis party organization, and was put in charge of a laboratory that produced explosive devices. Tskhakaya moved the laboratory to the location of the press, which was in the Avlabar section of Tiflis. Koba learned through Tskhakaya where the press was and bought his freedom by revealing its whereabouts to Zasypkin.

After receiving this information, Zasypkin promoted Koba to the status of agent of the Tiflis Okhrana.[3] Zasypkin also agreed to Koba's taking a trip to Stockholm, where the Fourth Party Congress was to open on 11 April 1906. Shortly after his release by Zasypkin, Koba left for St Petersburg and from there proceeded to Stockholm.

On 1 April 1906 Zasypkin sent a secret report to the director of the Department of Police in St Petersburg, stating that 'according to information received from an agent on 29 March 1906 the secret printing plant of the Caucasian Union of the Social Democratic Party . . . is located on the outskirts of the city, near the railway track . . .'. Zasypkin described 'vaulted underground quarters with a concealed entrance' and stated his intention 'to verify the above information by means of a search to be carried out after keeping the premises under a limited degree of observation'.[4] The fact that the Avlabar press was located near the railway track prevented Zasypkin from personally directing the raid, because the area along the track was under the jurisdiction of the Main Railroad Administration of the Separate Corps of Gendarmes. Captain P. D. Yulinetz, the chief of the Batum Gendarme Administration of the Transcaucasian Railways was to raid the press with his gendarmes and Cossacks, while Zasypkin with his officers was to conduct surveillance and to arrest suspects in other parts of Tiflis.[5]

Koba told Zasypkin that Mikha Tskhakaya maintained contact with the press and the laboratory through his mistress, Nina Aladzhalova.[6] Zasypkin arrested Aladzhalova and accused her of involvement in terrorist activities, which could mean the death penalty. She was frightened and agreed to become an Okhrana informer. Zasypkin in return promised her and her lover, Tskhakaya, immunity from prosecution. He ordered her to move to an apartment overlooking the Avlabar press and to help the Okhrana identify people visiting it. In his report to his superiors in St Petersburg, he stated that 'the most experienced surveillance agents were ordered to begin observation . . .'.[7] But Zasypkin had to admit to 'one unforeseen, meaningless occurrence . . . involving one of the surveillance agents who unexpectedly ran into a person under observation . . .'. The agent, not knowing how to take precautionary measures and, proceeding several steps, turned around and noticed the subject under surveillance staring intensely at him.'[8] Zasypkin added that the agent had reported this episode to him and that he had decided to act promptly.

On 15 April 1906 Captain Yulinetz and a detachment of gendarmes and Cossacks searched the small one-storey building and discovered a deep well with a side tunnel leading to 'vaulted underground quarters' with printing presses and a laboratory with explosives. In his report, Zasypkin talked of 'a fantastic conspiracy . . . on a grandiose scale, with bombs, infernal machines and forged documents . . .'.[9] He expressed regret that 'none of the residents of this printing plant had been apprehended. A day or two later the surveillance agent who had been identified by his subject was killed on the street by the revolutionaries.' In conclusion, Zasypkin stated that 'thanks to the surveillance, the entire Social Democratic organization and documents establishing the connection between the said printing plant and laboratory were seized' at the party meeting in the editorial offices of *Elva*, the Georgian Menshevik newspaper.[10]

The Russian press gave this operation front-page coverage, describing it as an important Okhrana coup and a serious blow to the revolutionary movement. The director of the Department of Police, A. T. Vasiliev, submitted a report to the interior minister, P. N. Durnovo, who in turn reported the event to the prime minister, Count Witte.[11]

In all, 26 people were arrested, including Tskhakaya and Aladzhalova. These two were kept in prison for a month and a half and then released. The other 24 Georgian Mensheviks were kept in prison for 20 months and on 24 December 1907 sentenced to various terms of exile. Shortly after his release from prison, Tskhakaya went abroad and joined Lenin in Geneva, where he remained until the February 1917 Revolution. Meanwhile Aladzhalova stayed in Tiflis.

Tskhakaya and Aladzhalova were the only comrades of Stalin whom he did not destroy during his rule. Tskhakaya suffered from severe megalomania and told everyone who cared to listen that he was the greatest revolutionary who had ever lived. Stalin allowed him the rare luxury of dying a natural death in a mental asylum. Trotsky was to wonder why Stalin spared Tskhakaya the fate of his other comrades – the firing squad or Siberian exile. 'Tskhakaya managed to outlive himself', Trotsky remarked.[12]

As for Aladzhalova, she managed to outlive even Stalin. After the February Revolution she was arrested by the Georgian Menshevik Government and accused of being an Okhrana agent. When Soviet troops occupied Georgia in 1921 she was released from prison. During Stalin's rule she served in many party and government positions in Georgia. In this respect, she shared the privilege of many former Okhrana agents whom Stalin patronized during his rule and 'kept on the hook', blackmailing them with documents from Okhrana archives. She retired with a lavish pension and a large, prestigious apartment in Tbilisi (the former Tiflis, renamed during Stalin's rule). After Stalin's death, she published a four-page recollection in which she presented her version of the Okhrana raid on the Avlabar press, explaining that shortly before the raid she had moved into an apartment overlooking the press. The gendarmes, she wrote, broke into this apartment, knocking on her door and announcing the delivery of a telegram. She stated that despite a thorough search they had found nothing incriminating, but had nevertheless arrested her. Her tale had a happy ending: 'After a month and a half I was free', she wrote.[13]

Three decades after the Okhrana raid on the Avlabar press, Stalin, too, presented his own fanciful version of the events: he started to claim that he had ordered the establishment of the Avlabar press in 1903 from his prison cell in Batum and that it had been operated under his leadership until its liquidation by the Okhrana.

NOTES

1. R. Arsenidze, 'Iz vospominanii o Staline', *Novy zhurnal*, no. 72, June 1963, p. 75. See also Lev Trotsky, *Stalin*, New York, 1941, p. 447.
2. 'Shkola Filerov', *Byloe*, no. 3 (25), pp. 66ff.; quoted in Edward Ellis Smith, *The Young Stalin: The Early Years of an Elusive Revolutionary*, London, 1986, pp. 165ff. Zasypkin recounted the events leading to the raid on the underground Avlabar press at the hearings, in November 1909, of the Department of Police special commission headed by Major-General A. V. Gerasimov, which was gathering information on ways to improve the Okhrana's effectiveness.
3. Zasypkin reported to St Petersburg that he received information about the Avlabar press from an 'agent'. See his report in 'Shkola Filerov', p. 66; quoted in Smith, *The Young Stalin*, pp. 119, 165.
4. *Istoricheskie mesta Tbilisi*, 1944, p. 119, quoted in H. Montgomery Hyde, *Stalin: the History of a Dictator*, New York, 1971, p. 72, fn.
5. See Smith, *The Young Stalin*, p. 395, fn. 343.
6. Okhrana Report no. 53-c, dated 14 March 1911, on file at the Hoover Institution, Stanford University.
7. 'Shkola Filerov', p. 66ff.
8. Ibid.
9. Ibid.
10. Ibid.
11. *Avlabarskaya nelegalnaya tipografiya*, Tbilisi, 1954, pp. 74ff.
12. Trotsky, *Stalin*, p. 60.
13. *Avlabarskaya nelegalnaya tipografiya*, pp. 60–3.

6

THE HOTEL BRISTOL

Before traveling to Stockholm in April 1906 to attend the Fourth Party Congress, Koba stopped briefly at St Petersburg. He went to the Okhrana headquarters and offered to provide information about the congress. In line with standard procedures, the St Petersburg Okhrana reported Koba's offer to the chief of the Okhrana Foreign Agency, Arkady Mikhailovich Garting, whose responsibility was to gather information on the activities of revolutionaries abroad. The Foreign Agency had very few personnel. It received support, in the form of agents sent from the St Petersburg or the Moscow Okhrana, only on important occasions, such as when the observation of a socialist congress or a conspiracy abroad required the strengthening of the services in western Europe.[1] The Okhrana knew about the departure of the Social Democratic delegates for the Stockholm congress. The St Petersburg Okhrana saw in Koba's offer the opportunity to send this informer to attend the congress and work with Garting.[2] At this moment, Garting was very interested in information about the Stockholm congress. He arranged for an Okhrana officer to travel to Stockholm to escort Koba to a rendezvous with him. The officer and Koba agreed to travel to Stockholm separately to avoid being seen together, to meet there in the lobby of the Hotel Bristol, and from there to proceed to meet Garting.[3]

Koba arrived in Sweden with a passport bearing the name 'Ivan Ivanovich Vissarionovich'.[4] This passport had been fabricated at the Avlabar press, which had facilities for such forgeries.[5] The Swedish border police recorded that 'Ivan Ivanovich Vissarionovich, a journalist' intended to reside at the Hotel Bristol during his stay in Stockholm. The Stockholm police, as was customary, followed up on this information by checking at the hotel and recorded that Vissarionovich had not registered there.[6] Koba indeed was not staying at this expensive hotel. He never went beyond the lobby, where he met, as planned, his Okhrana contact who led him to Garting.

Garting, né Avraam Gekkelman, was born around 1860 into a well-to-do Jewish family in the town of Pinsk, near the Russian–Polish border. He was admitted to a Russian gymnasium at Pinsk – one of the few Jews who managed to be included in the low quota allowed for Jewish students. After graduating, he enrolled at the Geological Institute in St Petersburg, where

he joined a student revolutionary group and was arrested. During his inter-
rogation, he agreed to turn informer and was released. In 1883, he became
an agent of the St Petersburg Okhrana, taking the codename 'Landezen'.
His fellow students soon began to suspect him of collaborating with the
Okhrana, and he left for Riga, where he enrolled at the Polytechnic
Institute. There, too, he was suspected of collaboration with the Okhrana,
and in 1884, he fled to Switzerland and enrolled at the Zurich Polytechnic
Institute. In May 1885, he became an agent of the chief of the Okhrana
Foreign Agency in Paris, P. I. Rachkovsky. In 1890, he was granted the title
of 'Honorary Citizen' for his betrayal of the 'People's Will' group in Paris
that planned to assassinate Tsar Alexander III. In 1892, he was baptized into
the Russian Orthodox Church in Wiesbaden, Germany, and adopted the
name Arkady Mikhailovich Garting. His godfather was the Secretary of
the Russian embassy in Berlin, Count N. K. Muraviev, later to become the
Russian foreign minister. Garting married Madeline Palot, a Catholic
woman from a prominent Belgian family. From 1900 to 1902, he was the
chief Okhrana resident in Berlin, where he recruited a number of agents,
among them Lenin's close friend Dr Yakov Zhitomirsky. In June 1905,
Garting was appointed chief of the Okhrana Foreign Agency.[7]

In April 1906 Garting recruited Koba. The Stockholm Fourth Party
(Unity) Congress opened on 11 April 1906. Koba claimed to represent the
'Burchalo Social Democratic organization', but the Congress's Credentials
Commission established that no such organization existed. Lenin asked the
Menshevik delegation 'not to object' to Koba's presence at the congress 'as
a participant with advisory status'. The Mensheviks, wishing to avoid
disagreements with the Bolsheviks, accepted the arrangement. Koba was
registered under the alias 'Ivanovich'.[8] (Again, he did not choose this name
by accident – it was Vissarion's patronymic.)

At the congress Lenin declared that the revolutionary tide was rising and
that therefore 'the party should recognize guerrilla raids by fighting squads
as party policy that is acceptable in principle'. The Mensheviks strongly
objected, stating in their resolution that 'classless layers of society, the
criminal elements, and the jetsam of the urban population have always used
revolutionary upheavals for their own antisocial goals, and the revolutionary
people have had to undertake extreme measures against the bacchanalia of
stealing and pillage'.[9] (The Georgian Mensheviks initially did not support
their Russian comrades on this point, and cooperated with the Bolsheviks
for some time.) The Menshevik resolution was approved by a vote of 68 to
4, one of the dissenting votes being Lenin's. Koba, as a non–delegate, did
not vote. During the debates on the agrarian question, Koba joined a small

group of delegates who advocated distribution of land among the peasants. As he had done shortly after Vissarion's murder in his articles on agrarian reform, Koba defended the social class of peasants, to which his father and he officially belonged. On the agrarian question, he disagreed even with Lenin, who advocated nationalization of the land. The Mensheviks were for 'municipalization' of the land, that is, ownership of the land by local municipalities.

Despite the resolution against guerrilla raids, Lenin set up a secret group consisting of L. B. Krasin, A. A. Bogdanov and himself to direct armed robberies as a 'simple way of replenishing the cash register'.[10] Lenin introduced Koba to Krasin and Bogdanov as a successful 'expropriator', who, together with Kamo, had provided him with money. Koba promised that he and Kamo would deliver more money. Lenin also told Koba that he had sent Kamo to St Petersburg to take part in a planned expropriation.[11]

In his Okhrana report to Garting, Koba described the debates at the congress and listed its participants.[12] He did not mention Lenin's plans for robberies and his own role in them. Returning from Stockholm, Koba stopped briefly in St Petersburg to see Kamo, who had joined the 'Maximalist' (extreme left-wing) faction of the Left Social Revolutionary Party. Kamo was involved in a scheme to expropriate money from banks and assassinate high government officials. Koba found Kamo learning to master a new bomb that had been invented by two of Lenin's friends, the engineer Leonid Krasin and Professor M. M. Tikhvinsky. Lenin had great hopes for this bomb, writing with his usual underscoring that it would become '*a necessary part of popular armaments*'.[13] Having learned from Kamo about the robberies and assassinations planned by the Maximalists and Bolsheviks, Koba reported this information to the St Petersburg Okhrana, signing his report with the codename 'Ivanov'. He had used the same codename at Tammerfors four-and-a-half months earlier.[14]

During Koba's brief presence in St Petersburg, Kamo murdered 'Volodka', one of the members of the Bolshevik–Maximalist group, claiming that Volodka was an Okhrana informer. After murdering him, Kamo threw his body into the Neva.[15] It was never established that Volodka was an Okhrana informer, however, and the facts that he was murdered while Koba was in St Petersburg and that Kamo was the murderer are suggestive. Koba was in the habit of accusing others of what he himself was guilty of, and Kamo hated informers and blindly believed everything Koba told him. The accusation against Volodka probably came to Koba's mind during his presence in St Petersburg, and the murder was his way of purging himself of the guilt he felt for providing information to the Okhrana.

When the chief of the St Petersburg Okhrana, General A. V. Gerasimov, received a report by the informer 'Ivanov' about the Maximalists' criminal plans, he attached great importance to this information and brought it to the attention of M. I. Trusevich, the director of the Department of Police.[16] Trusevich was alarmed and ordered the Okhrana to find a source confirming Ivanov's report. This order was received by, among others, Colonel A. M. Eremin, the acting chief of the Kiev Okhrana temporarily substituting for Colonel A. I. Spiridovich, who had been seriously wounded in a terrorist attempt on his life.[17] Eremin reported to Trusevich that he had arrested a member of the Maximalist group, a certain Solomon Ryss, who offered to become an informer and expose the assassinations and armed robbery schemes of the Maximalists if he were released. Trusevich ordered Eremin to arrange Ryss's bogus escape from a Kiev prison and to bring him to St Petersburg so he could personally interrogate him. In June 1906 Ryss 'escaped'. He left together with Eremin by train for St Petersburg. Trusevich hoped to use Ryss to check agent 'Ivanov's' report, but Ryss intended to mislead Trusevich and help his Maximalist friends to carry out their plans by, as he put it, 'wagging the Okhrana by the nose'.[18]

The summer of 1906 was a difficult period in the history of Russia. The country was in turmoil. An attempt to advance toward parliamentary democracy failed. The Constitutional Democrats Party (Kadets), the largest Duma faction, proposed legislation that was designed to break up large estates of nobles and to distribute the land among peasants, with nominal compensation to the landlords. They also demanded the formation of a cabinet responsible not to the Tsar but the Duma. The Menshevik faction supported this demand, while the tiny Bolshevik faction, on Lenin's insistence, opposed it. Lenin agitated against the participation of the Social Democrats in the proceedings of the Duma. To Lenin's delight, the Tsar dissolved the Duma, and its deputies issued an appeal to the Russian population to protest by refusing to pay taxes or serve in the army. To aggravate the crisis, the Social Revolutionary Party, the Esers (or SRs), issued their 'Manifesto to All Russian Peasants', calling for insurrection.

On 21 July 1906 the Tsar appointed P. A. Stolypin as prime minister. Kamo and his 'fighting squad' of Bolsheviks and Maximalists took note and set off a large explosion in Stolypin's *dacha*. Stolypin narrowly escaped death, but his son and daughter were maimed. The same fighting squad then attacked a money transport in Fanarny Lane in St Petersburg. Since Solomon Ryss had provided no information on either terrorist act, and since the report of the informer 'Ivanov' was at odds with Ryss's information, Director Trusevich began to suspect Ryss of double-dealing and ordered his arrest. Ryss fled to the small Ukrainian coal-mining town of Yuzovka. He was arrested there in April 1907 and hanged in January 1908.[19]

In September 1906, a month after the attempt on his life, Stolypin signed a decree ordering court-martial proceedings to punish terrorists severely for anti-government violence. Those condemned for armed attacks were to be executed by hanging. (The noose was quickly labeled 'Stolypin's necktie'.) This was the proverbial stick; but Stolypin also offered a carrot by introducing, in November 1906, his agrarian reform, designed to distribute parcels of land among peasants and thus stimulate the emergence of a large and prosperous class of small landowners with a vested interest in supporting the tsarist government. In a short while Stolypin's reforms began to pacify the country. The revolutionary tide began to ebb.

After the attempt on Stolypin's life, Kamo hurriedly left St Petersburg for Tiflis in August 1906. Koba was waiting there with a plan for creating a purely Bolshevik 'unit' for the expropriation of state funds.[20] Kamo's unit attacked a train at the Chiatura rail junction in Georgia, hijacking 21,000 rubles. Koba set aside 15,000 rubles for Lenin and kept the rest for himself and Kamo. Kamo again went to Finland to hand over the money to Lenin. Some months later, Lenin decided to use Kamo for shipments of arms to the Caucasus. He insisted on armed uprising and robberies and hoped that his call for it would be approved at the next party congress, which was scheduled for April 1907 in Copenhagen.

Late in March 1907, Koba left Tiflis for Copenhagen, where he again met Garting. He told Garting that he was not sure about his chances of being admitted to the congress, because, as in the previous year, he was not a delegate. On 24 April 1907 Garting wired a report to his superiors in St Petersburg, stating that he had applied all his efforts and 'undertaken all measures' to assure 'the presence of the Foreign Agency at the congress'. He added:

In connection with it I have issued 1,000 francs to an agent for his traveling expenses due to his efforts connected with the organization of the congress. Today I sent him another 500 francs, following his request for additional funds for travel to London, although there is no guarantee that he will be able to take part in the congress.[21]

Koba indeed had unforeseen expenses: the Danish king, in deference to his nephew, the Tsar, did not give the Russian Social Democrats permission to hold their congress in Denmark. The delegates went to Sweden, but the Swedish chief of police refused to allow them to stay. He remembered all too well that the previous year he had had to raise funds to buy return

tickets for poor Russian socialists. Chased out of Sweden, the hapless delegates proceeded to Oslo, but the Norwegian government was just as unwilling to allow them to hold their congress there. Koba went to Oslo
together with the rest of the delegates, and Garting followed them there.[22]
Finally, the British socialists secured permission for their Russian comrades
to hold their congress in London. For the trip there Garting gave Koba 500
rubles.

Among the participants at the London congress were two Okhrana
agents. One was Dr Yakov Zhitomirsky, a close friend of Lenin's, who
headed the Bolshevik émigré organization in Europe and had the status of
a fully accredited delegate. The other was one of the four non-delegates admitted to the congress at Lenin's insistence. Lenin made a proposal to
'adopt without discussion' a resolution granting these four non-delegates
'advisory status'. The Menshevik leader Martov shouted from his place in
the presidium, 'I would like to know who is being granted advisory status.
Who are these people, where do they come from, and so forth?' Lenin
replied evasively, 'I really don't know, but the congress may rely on the
unanimous opinion of the Credentials Commission.' The Mensheviks did
not want to quarrel over what seemed a minor point and granted Lenin's
request. They had no idea that Koba and the three other non-delegates,
L. B. Krasin, A. A. Bogdanov and Maxim Litvinov, were members of
Lenin's secret group, who, in defiance of the party resolution banning
armed robberies, were planning new expropriations. The London congress
again passed a Menshevik resolution against all types of violence. As at
Tammerfors and Stockholm, Koba registered under the alias 'Ivanovich'.[23]

Koba provided Garting with a report on the debates and the views of
delegates on various issues. Garting then sent Koba's report to St Petersburg,
describing his agent as a 'Social Democrat' who had performed 'quite valuable services' for the Okhrana, following the Okhrana's strict rule of never
mentioning the names of its agents. Garting recommended an award for his
agent of 1,500 rubles, a large sum at the time.[24] In London, Koba met for
the first time Maxim Litvinov, a man mentioned in Okhrana documents
by his real name, Meir Vallakh, and several aliases: 'Papasha' (Daddy),
'Finkelshtein', 'Felix'. His other alias, 'Maxim Litvinov', would be the
name he adopted for the rest of his life. After the London congress,
Litvinov, Krasin, Bogdanov and Koba went to Berlin for a secret meeting
with Lenin. They discussed a large expropriation to be carried out by
Kamo's band in Tiflis.[25]

NOTES

1. A. T. Vasiliev, *The Okhrana*, London, 1930, pp. 38ff.
2. For a similar example of the St Petersburg Okhrana providing such support for the Foreign Agency, see the report 'Absolutely Secret' of 13 May 1910, no. 125483. On file at the Hoover Institution. Copy in the author's archive. See also Vasiliev, *The Okhrana*, pp. 38ff.
3. See E. S. Holtzman's 'confession' at the Kamenev–Zinoviev trial (in Chapter 25 below and in H. Montgomery Hyde, *Stalin: the History of a Dictator*, New York, 1971, pp. 338ff).
4. The name is mentioned in a police record in the Stockholm City Police Archive. Copy in Edward Ellis Smith's archive; see *The Young Stalin: the Early Years of an Elusive Revolutionary*, London, 1968, pp. 176, 396, ref. no. 363.
5. The Okhrana seized several passports and passport blanks at the Avlabar press and in the offices of the Georgian Menshevik paper *Elva* during the raid on 15 April 1906. See S. Meglakelidze and A. Iovidze, 'Revolutsia 1905–1907 gg.', *Novoe vremia*, St Petersburg, 27 April 1906, p. 780. Also see *Novoe vremia*, St Petersburg, 22 April 1906, cited in Smith, pp. 164–7. Early in April 1905 Mikha Tskhakaya traveled to London to attend the Third (Bolshevik) Congress, carrying a passport manufactured, according to Kamo's biographer, 'by Kamo's own hands'. (I. M. Dubinsky-Mukhadze, *Kamo*, Moscow, 1974, p. 37.) But it is unlikely that the passport had been made by Kamo, since his forgeries tended to be crude. Tskhakaya was in close contact with the Tiflis Mensheviks and he probably obtained his passport from their Avlabar press and provided Koba with a passport from the same source. It is highly unlikely that the Okhrana would provide its obviously non-Russian agents with passports bearing a distinctly Russian name like 'Ivan Ivanovich Vissarionovich'.
6. Stockholm City Police Archive. A copy of the archive record is in Smith's archive; see Smith, *The Young Stalin*, London, 1968, p. 176 and fn. 363 on p. 396. See also H. M. Hyde, *Stalin*, p. 76, fn.
7. *Padenie tsarskogo rezhima*, vol. VII, Moscow/Leningrad, 1925, p. 322; also vol. I, p. 327, and vol. III, pp. 75 and 494.
8. G. I. Uratadze, 'Moi vospominaniya', p. 140, On file at the Hoover Institution, cited in Smith, p. 396, fn. 363a.
9. 'Chetvertyi (obyedinitelnyi) syezd RSDRP, April 1906 goda: protokoly', pp. 262–7 and 336f.
10. Lev Trotsky, *Stalin*, New York, 1941, p. 99, quoting G. Alexinsky and N. Krupskaya, Lenin's wife.
11. Dubinsky-Mukhadze, *Kamo*, pp. 61ff.
12. Garting received reports on the congress from two agents, Dr Yakov Zhitomirsky and Koba. Both reports were, as was usually the case, unsigned by the agents. On file at the Hoover Institution. See also Hyde, *Stalin*, p. 82, fn.
13. Lenin, *Polnoe sobranie sochinenii*, vol. XI, Moscow, 1958,–65, p. 269. Also Dubinsky-Mukhadze, *Kamo*, pp. 61f.
14. *Padenie tsarskogo rezhima*, Burtsev's testimony, vol. I, pp. 311f.
15. V. D. Bonch-Bruevich, quoted in Dubinsky-Mukhadze, *Kamo*, p. 62.
16. *Padenie tsarskogo rezhima*, Burtsev's testimony, vol. I, pp. 311f.
17. *Padenie tsarskogo rezhima*, vol. VII, p. 420.
18. Ibid, pp. 310-12.
19. Ibid.
20. Boris Souvarine, *Stalin: A Critical Survey of Bolshevism*, London, 1939, p. 99.
21. Garting's report no. 152 dated 24 April 1907 (Old Style) on file at the Hoover Institution; see also Smith, pp. 183 and 397, fn. 375b.
22. See Chapter 27 below for how the Oslo trip appeared in Piatakov's 'confession' at his show trial in January 1937.
23. Trotsky, *Stalin*, p. 90.
24. Garting's 'top secret' report no. 225, dated 26 May 1907 (Old Style) to the director of the Department of Police. On file at the Hoover Institution; see also Smith, pp. 186f and 397, fn. 387.
25. Trotsky, *Stalin*, p. 108.

7

THE GREAT TIFLIS BANK ROBBERY

After the London congress in April 1907 Lenin summoned Koba, Litvinov, Krasin and Bogdanov to Berlin because of extraordinary developments.[1] At the end of 1906 Kamo and Litvinov paid a large sum of money for arms but failed to smuggle them to the Caucasus. Their yacht *Zora* with the arms shipment had been swept into shallow waters and sank off the Rumanian coast of the Black Sea. Kamo was arrested by the Rumanian police. The director of the Department of Police, Trusevich, announced that the *Zora* had been carrying 'no less than 2,000 rapid-fire rifles, 650,000 rounds of ammunition, many boxes of bombs and grenades and a considerable quantity of illegal literature'.[2] The Russian government requested Kamo's extradition, but the Rumanian authorities released him. Litvinov urgently asked Lenin for money to buy a new shipment of arms, and this was the reason for the meeting in Berlin. The decision reached was for Koba and Kamo to stage a massive expropriation in Tiflis in the summer of 1907.

At the time of the meeting, the Central Committee was in the hands of the Mensheviks. They strongly objected to armed robberies, so much so that the Georgian Mensheviks decided to return to the Russian government 200,000 rubles that had been robbed from the State Bank in the Georgian town of Kvirili. Garting sent a report to St Petersburg stating, 'Litvinov is here [in Paris]. He has an argument with the Central Committee. It spent 40,000 rubles and does not want to give [the money] back to him.'[3] Koba and Kamo had been involved in the Kvirili raid.

Koba and Litvinov traveled to Tiflis. Kamo joined them there in June 1907 and worked on preparations for the planned raid. At that time, Koba was reporting information on underground activities to his handler, the Tiflis Okhrana officer Mukhtarov, who was responsible for a group of agents and reported their information to Colonel Zasypkin, the chief of the Tiflis Okhrana. Koba told Mukhtarov that revolutionaries were planning a robbery and promised to inform him of where and when it would take place. In fact, he had no intention of doing so.[4]

On the morning of 13 June 1907 Erevan Square in Tiflis was crowded with people. Two bank clerks with money satchels rode in a horse-drawn carriage to the Russian Imperial Bank, escorted by several mounted Cossacks. Suddenly, ordinary-looking pedestrians threw bombs at the

Cossack escort, turning the routine banking operation into an inferno. Three Cossacks were killed, 50 passers-by wounded. Frightened and bleeding horses galloped away with the carriage. Kamo, dressed in an army officer's uniform, rode after the carriage and caught up with it, swearing and shooting his revolver. He grabbed the two satchels, pitched them to one of his men and disappeared. Then the entire band vanished. For a few days, the money lay hidden under a couch in an office of the Geophysical Observatory, where seven years earlier Koba had been employed for the first and last time. Kamo then delivered the money to Lenin in Finland, and Litvinov smuggled it to Europe.[5] The total take was over 341,000 rubles, but out of this amount only 91,000 rubles were in small enough bills to be untraceable by the police. Krasin, Lenin's 'cashier', paid Bolshevik debts with part of this money and sent some of it to Koba.[6] The remaining 250,000 rubles were in 500-ruble notes and had serial numbers known to the police.

During the robbery Koba was seen standing in the doorway of a house, smoking and watching the bloody scene. Later in the day his Okhrana handler Mukhtarov and several other officers brought Koba to one of their secret apartments on the outskirts of Tiflis. Mukhtarov asked Koba why he had not warned him about the robbery. Koba insisted that he had told Mukhtarov about the plan for the holdup of the money transport in time to prevent it. Mukhtarov denied this and accused Koba of deliberately deceiving him and of diverting the Okhrana's attention. After a long argument with Koba, the outraged Mukhtarov lost control and struck Koba in the face. Not knowing whom to believe, the other Okhrana officers restrained Mukhtarov. The testimonies of Koba and Mukhtarov were recorded and given to Colonel Zasypkin who found it difficult to decide who was telling the truth. He sent the testimony of both men to St Petersburg.[7]

The Tiflis bank robbery was a front-page sensation. The serial numbers of the 500-ruble banknotes were sent to banks and police departments all over Europe. The Ministry of the Interior and the Department of Police sent a special commission to Tiflis to investigate the case. Several months later, the commission had still reached no decision. Mukhtarov was suspended from Okhrana employment, while Koba was ordered to leave Tiflis for Baku and wait there for the decision on his case. He left for Baku in July of 1907, taking with him his wife Keke and 20,000 rubles from the bank loot. Koba and Keke settled in a house belonging to a local Muslim.

Toward the end of the summer, Sergey Alliluev, who also had been ordered by the Okhrana to leave Tiflis, visited Koba in Baku. Some three decades later, he wrote in his memoirs, 'I told Koba about my decision to go to St Petersburg and the circumstances forcing me to take this step.'

Alliluev's leaving conveniently obscured these 'circumstances'. Koba brought a bundle of money from another room and gave it to Alliluev, saying, 'Yes, you have to go. Shubinsky will not leave you alone.'[8] Shubinsky, a Tiflis Okhrana officer, was in charge of purging the network of agents and informers in the Tiflis Okhrana, while the St Petersburg investigators were purging and reorganizing the Okhrana officers' staff.[9] Alliluev was one of the informers who became a victim of the purge. The Tiflis bank robbery, just like the scandal of the illegal leaflets planted by Koba and Lado in 1901, had implicated the Tiflis Okhrana in a scandal involving its agents, informers and officers. The Tiflis Okhrana was once again afflicted with 'Samedov disease'.

Following the robbery, many members of Kamo's band escaped abroad, among them Alexander Svanidze, Koba's brother-in-law. He was to live in Vienna until the revolution.[10] Kamo himself, after delivering the money to Lenin, stayed at Lenin's *dacha* in Finland during July and August 1907, 'the two happiest months of his life', according to his biographer.[11] At the beginning of September, he went to Paris and then, together with Litvinov, to Belgium to buy arms and ammunition for smuggling to Russia. Then he traveled to Bulgaria, where he bought 200 detonators. Early in October, he arrived in Berlin with an introductory letter from Lenin to Dr Yakov Zhitomirsky, the head of the Party Central Bureau in Europe and an Okhrana agent. In his letter, Lenin asked Zhitomirsky to find the best medical help to treat Kamo's eye, which had been injured in an accidental explosion while Kamo was manufacturing bombs. Zhitomirsky told his Okhrana handler, Garting, everything he was able to learn from Kamo. On 22 October 1907 Garting sent a coded telegram to Director Trusevich:

Kamo in Berlin. Keeps in his room suitcase with 200 bomb detonators for millions-of-rubles expropriation in Russia known only to Nikitich [Krasin] and Vallakh [Litvinov]. Because of extreme difficulty in tracing the suitcase, which is soon to be sent to Finland, the only solution is to search Kamo in Berlin, to arrest him and to demand extradition. I ask your urgent reply so that I have enough time to go there without delay for negotiations with officials.[12]

Trusevich replied: 'Go to Berlin. Enter agreement with police president. Immediately on arrival telegraph address.'[13] In a subsequent report to Trusevich, Garting described Kamo as a Georgian and stated that Kamo had a band of some 15 people ready to stage the largest bank robbery in history. Garting added that Kamo had 'found somewhere in Russia a bank with fifteen million rubles in government funds; part of it, about six million, is in gold'.[14]

Berlin's Police President von Yagov agreed to arrest Kamo. The Berlin police found a suitcase in his room with 200 bomb detonators and a passport in the name of an Austrian citizen, 'Dmitrius Mirsky'. When questioned, Kamo refused to reveal his real name. Zhitomirsky was of no help, since he didn't know it. In one of his reports Garting wrote: 'Kamo needed a good long range telescope for his gigantic expropriation, and it is possible to conclude on the basis of some indications that the target of this expropriation is located on a mountain, or that it is possible to observe it from some elevation.'[15] This was the only useful information that Kamo had related to Zhitomirsky. Trusevich reported it to Prime Minister Stolypin, who sent urgent messages to the finance minister, Count V. N. Kokovtsev, trying to determine which bank Kamo had in mind. It was imperative to determine the bank's location as soon as possible, since Kamo had told Zhitomirsky that his band was on its way there. Garting also sent a report stating that Kamo had been involved in the Tiflis bank robbery and knew where the stolen money was.[16] Trusevich ordered the chief of the Tiflis Okhrana, Colonel Zasypkin, to establish the identity of Kamo and the location of the stolen Tiflis bank money. Zasypkin summoned Koba from Baku to Tiflis in late November 1907.[17] As a result of his meeting with Zasypkin, Koba went to Europe with a passport, provided by the Okhrana, bearing the name 'Gaioz Vissarionov Nizheradze'. This Georgian name on his passport would seem more convincing to a border guard or a policeman looking at a man of Koba's appearance and with a Georgian accent than would the Russian name 'Ivan Ivanovich Vissarionovich' on his other passport, which had been fabricated at the Avlabar press.

Toward the end of November 1907 'the case of Mukhtarov and Dzhugashvili' was turned over to the St Petersburg Department of Police and then submitted for 'Administrative Decision of the Special Council of the Interior Ministry'.[18] This was the usual procedure for dealing with Okhrana officers and agents who were suspected of involvement in provocations. Soon after Koba's departure to Europe an Okhrana officer, Alexander Bagratuni, arrived in Tiflis for his Christmas vacation. He visited his friends in the Tiflis Okhrana headquarters, where he had served before the purge that had begun after the Tiflis bank robbery. He inquired of his fellow officers how the Dzhugashvili–Mukhtarov case had ended. 'Dzhugashvili shows improvement', one of the officers told Bagratuni, 'We'll watch what happens next. If Dzhugashvili misleads us again, we'll have to seal him in an envelope.' ('Sealing in an envelope' was an Okhrana expression for sending people into exile.[19])

At the time of Koba's departure for Europe, Lenin, who was in Finland, told his followers to cash the stolen 500-ruble banknotes – no minor feat, since there were 500 of these banknotes to be cashed. Having learned about Kamo's arrest, Lenin was worried that he, too, could be arrested as a common criminal and accomplice in the robbery. He and his wife, Nadezhda Krupskaya, fled from Finland by walking over the frozen surface of a lake to the nearest shore. They arrived in Berlin on 22 December 1907.[20] Lenin was met there by several of his followers, among them Koba. He stayed in Berlin for three days. Then he and his wife left for Switzerland. But the shadow of the Tiflis bank robbery pursued them even there. Krupskaya was to recall that 'the good Swiss burghers were frightened to death by this incident. The only thing we heard talked about was the Russian expropriators. They were discussed with horror around the dining table in the boarding house where Ilyich and I usually dined.'[21] Lenin kept silent about his role in the robbery.

Having found safety in neutral Switzerland, Lenin waited for his emissaries to cash the 500-ruble banknotes. The cashing was to be done simultaneously in various European cities in January 1908. Lenin put Maxim Litvinov in charge of this operation. Garting was well informed by his agent Zhitomirsky about the people involved in the cashing of the banknotes. He asked the police chiefs in various countries to arrest anyone trying to cash the stolen banknotes. After their meeting with Lenin, Koba and Litvinov left Berlin for Paris in late December 1907. Garting's agents reported that they saw Litvinov 'in the company of two Armenians whose identity they did not know'. Garting reported to Director Trusevich that according to the description of his agents, 'one of the Armenians was below medium height, with brown hair and a wedge-shaped beard; he looked like a Frenchman and was mean'. Garting continued: 'Here the two Armenians lived in the Hotel de Luxembourg, but because of a personal quarrel with the hostess they left and their whereabouts proved impossible to establish, but it is known that they had to take part in the cashing.' Garting reported that the name of the 'mean Armenian' was 'something like Sharshadze'.[22]

To Garting's French agents, Armenians and Georgians must have been indistinguishable. The Georgian name 'Nizheradze', used by Koba, sounded 'something like Sharshadze' to them. The second 'Armenian' was probably Koba's brother-in-law, Alexander Svanidze, a member of Kamo's band. Garting suggested that according to the information he had received, the cashing planned by Vallakh (Litvinov) was to be done by a large number of Armenians who had taken part in the Tiflis expropriation.[23] In his next report to St Petersburg, Garting wrote that, according to additional information from his French agents, the man with the 'something-like-Sharshadze' name was about 28 and had a heavily pockmarked face – 'the whole face and nose heavily pitted'. This 'pockmarked man', wrote Garting,

had 48 banknotes of 500 rubles each, and he had been assigned by Litvinov to cash them, but, fearing that the police had seen him on the street together with Vallakh [Litvinov], he took the banknotes to a certain Melik Osepian, who was also involved in the operation. Then, following the advice of 'Victor' and 'Diadia Misha' [Mikha Tskhakaya] he took these banknotes to a person known to me, but so far it has been impossible to retrieve them.[24]

The 'person known to' Garting was Dr Zhitomirsky. Not knowing that Zhitomirsky was Garting's agent, Koba brought the 48 banknotes to him. Garting could not retrieve them without blowing his agent's cover. Garting concluded that 'because of intelligence considerations it will be necessary to delay the search of this person'. He meant Dr Zhitomersky. Garting did not recognize Koba in the description of the pockmarked Armenian supplied by Zhitomirsky and the French agents, but Koba sensed the danger of an impending police crackdown and feared that he might be caught in the dragnet. On 2 January 1908 he and his companion disappeared from Paris. Garting reported to Trusevich that the 'two Armenians' left Paris two days prior to the arrest of Litvinov.[25]

Litvinov was arrested on January 4 1908. The next day Garting reported to Trusevich that

Vallakh [Litvinov] was under surveillance for three days and nights and all railway stations in Paris were guarded, for which purpose fifteen additional French police agents were needed besides all the available agents of the Foreign Agency. Vallakh has here a mistress, a medical doctor named Fanny Yampolskaya who also disappeared from her apartment three days ago, but it was established that Vallakh and Yampolskaya lodged together in another part of the city in the Hotel Moderue.[26]

Garting also reported that Litvinov had intended to go to London to cash there the Tiflis banknotes 'with the assistance of the old revolutionary Simon Kogan, whose sons have there a colonial and money exchange shop'.

Litvinov and his mistress Yampolskaya were arrested by the Paris police as they were about to board a train at the Gare du Nord. 'The police', Garting stated, 'found twelve banknotes of 500 ruble denomination from the Tiflis expropriation . . . and this fact, in the privately expressed opinion of a court investigator, is absolutely sufficient for the extradition of Vallakh to the Russian government as a common criminal, accused of an armed robbery.'[27]

But despite the material evidence, the French minister of justice, Aristide Briand, ordered that Litvinov and Yampolskaya be released from prison and expelled from French territory rather than extradited to Russia. The Russian government was outraged and protested. Garting reported to Trusevich that Briand was influenced by the socialist leaders in the French Parliament and also by 'pressure on him from Vallakh's lawyer, the influential socialist deputy Williams, and, finally, by the fact that Vallakh has good personal relations with Ely Rubanovich, who is known to the Department of Police'. Garting complained that the French government's official explanation for Litvinov's release from prison, namely, that the Russian ambassador's written request for the extradition of Vallakh was not received in time, was absolutely incredible, because no government could submit a request for extradition at the time of arrest. He concluded, 'In the opinion of all serious Frenchmen the act of the French Government in any case was incorrect.'[28] Garting nevertheless petitioned Trusevich to honor the director of the Sûreté Générale and other French officials with decorations and monetary compensation for their efforts in apprehending the criminals.[29]

As to other attempts to cash the 500-ruble banknotes from the Tiflis robbery, a number of Lenin's followers were arrested in the act on 4 January 1908, in Paris, Munich, Stockholm, Geneva, Copenhagen, Sofia and Rotterdam. However, only a small fraction of the total of 500 notes was recovered in these arrests.[30] While others were being caught in the dragnet, Koba was on his way to Tiflis. He stopped in Leipzig to change trains.[31]

According to Okhrana reports, Lenin also took part in the cashing of the banknotes and for this purpose traveled to Moscow, where he stayed until 11 February 1908. The chief of the St Petersburg Okhrana sent two coded telegrams, dated 25 January and 9 February 1908, to the chief of the Moscow Okhrana. The first telegram stated that 'an unknown woman has to give Lenin ten thousand rubles for the 500-ruble banknotes, having cashed them by private persons. On receiving this money Lenin will go to Geneva.'[32] The Moscow Okhrana received a photograph of Lenin with a detailed description of his appearance: 'not tall, stocky, short neck, round red face, beard and mustache shaved, sharp eyes, bold, high forehead, almost always carries in his hand a rainproof overall . . .'. On 1 March 1908 the chief of the St Petersburg Okhrana sent a second telegram to Moscow, stating that Lenin, having received the money, had left Moscow for Geneva on 11 February (1908).[33]

By this time Koba was back in Tiflis. He arrived there in the middle of January 1908 and learned that the chief of the Tiflis Okhrana, Colonel Zasypkin, the man who had sent him abroad to gather information about the banknotes and the identity of Kamo, had been replaced by Colonel Alexander Mikhailovich Eremin.

NOTES

1. See H. Barbusse, *Stalin*, New York and London, 1935, p. 40. Stalin told Barbusse that he conferred with Lenin in 1907 in Berlin on two occasions. See also Edward Ellis Smith, *The Young Stalin: the Early Years of an Elusive Revolutionary*, London, 1968, p. 448.
2. I. M. Dubinsky-Mukhadze, *Kamo*, Moscow, 1974, pp. 64–71.
3. Ibid., p. 68.
4. The events are described in Rafael Bagratuni's handwritten testimony, dated 8 May 1967, on file in I. D. Levine's archive. Copy in the author's archive. In his testimony, Bagratuni relates information he received from his relative, Alexander Bagratuni, a gendarme officer who served in the Tiflis Okhrana until the end of summer 1907.
5. Dubinsky-Mukhadze, *Kamo*, pp. 71–85.
6. Ibid., p. 84.
7. Rafael Bagratuni's testimony.
8. S. Alliluev, *Proidennyi put'*, Moscow, 1946, p. 182.
9. Rafael Bagratuni's testimony.
10. Svetlana Allilueva, *Dvadtsat' pisem k drugu*, New York, 1967, p. 70.
11. Dubinsky-Mukhadze, *Kamo*, p. 85.
12. Ibid., p. 86.
13. Ibid., p. 87.
14. Ibid., p. 86.
15. Ibid., p. 94.
16. Ibid., pp. 94–6.
17. I. V. Stalin, *Sochineniya*, vol. II, Moscow, 1946–51, pp. 408ff.
18. Rafael Bagratuni's testimony.
19. Ibid.
20. V. I. Lenin, *Polnoe sobranie sochinenii*, vol. XV, p. 571, and vol. XVI, Moscow, 1958–65, pp. 680–86.
21. N. K. Krupskaya, *Reminiscences of Lenin*, Moscow and London, 1959, p. 174.
22. Garting's report no. 11, dated 5/18 January 1908 (the two dates refer to Old Style and New Style). On file at the Hoover Institution. Copy in the author's archive.
23. Ibid.
24. Garting's report no. 13, dated 7/20 January 1908. On file at the Hoover Institution. Copy in the author's archive.
25. Ibid.
26. Garting's report no. 11, dated 5/18 January 1908. On file at the Hoover Institution. Copy in the author's archive.
27. Ibid.
28. Garting's report no. 29, dated 14/27 January 1908. On file at the Hoover Institution. Copy in the author's archive.
29. Garting's report no. 23, dated 10/23 January 1908, and his report no. 29, dated 14/27 January 1908. On file at the Hoover Institution. Copies in the author's archive.
30. A year later, a report to Garting describing money obtained by Lenin's cashier, Krasin, referred to the possibility that the 200,000 rubles mentioned in the report may have been obtained by cashing the money stolen in Tiflis in 1907. See report no. 127089, dated 5 April 1909, of the chief of the Okhrana Foreign Agency. On file at the Hoover Institution. Copy in author's archive. See Chapter 8 for a more detailed discussion of this report.
31. Lord Moran, *Winston Churchill: the Struggle for Survival*, London, 1966, p. 275. See also Stalin, *Sochineniya*, vol. XIII, p. 124.
32. *Bolsheviki*, Moscow, 1918, pp. 237f.
33. Ibid.

8

COLONEL EREMIN

Colonel Alexander Mikhailovich Eremin assumed the post of chief of the Tiflis Okhrana at the beginning of January 1908, at the age of 35. He was born in 1872 to a family of Ural Cossacks and, after receiving a traditional military education in cavalry and officer schools, was appointed in 1903 to the Corps of Gendarmes and served as a staff officer in Okhrana Sections in several cities.[1] In 1905 Eremin was appointed acting chief of the Kiev Okhrana, replacing Colonel Spiridovich, who had been seriously wounded in a terrorist attack. This turned out to be a fateful appointment, starting his rapid promotion within the Okhrana and leading to his eventual encounter with Koba. Eremin's involvement with the case of the Maximalist Solomon Ryss in 1906 gave him the opportunity to meet in person the director of the Department of Police, Trusevich, who transferred him to the Special Section of the Department of Police at St Petersburg. The Special Section was the Okhrana's virtual nerve center, a clearing house for its operations throughout the empire.

The Tiflis bank robbery took place during his tenure in the Special Section. Eremin was involved in the Tiflis bank robbery investigation, which made him the ideal man to participate in the effort to foil the 15 million ruble bank robbery planned by Kamo. The Special Section was called upon to locate the bank Kamo had in mind.[2] On 29 November 1907 Prime Minister Stolypin sent the Special Section a list of large banks in Russia with his handwritten instruction: 'To the Special Section. Determine through the chiefs of gendarmerie administrations the landscape surrounding these institutions.'[3] Among the 58 reports received by the Special Section there was one noting that a state bank in the city of Rostov-on-Don could be observed from a nearby mountaintop, and that a 'large group of Armenians and Georgians' had arrived in the city. Their arrival was connected with the planned bank robbery.[4]

Eremin was sent to Tiflis, possibly because the Tiflis bank robbery and the planned bank robbery in Rostov-on-Don were, in the minds of Eremin's superiors, linked to Kamo, and because Eremin had been involved in the investigation of the Tiflis bank robbery. (The planned robbery in Rostov-on-Don never took place. The would-be robbers realized that they were being watched and abandoned the scheme.) Shortly after

Eremin's arrival in Tiflis, Koba returned from his secret mission in Europe. Eremin summoned Koba to glean information on Kamo's identity and the whereabouts of the stolen banknotes. However, Koba did not reveal to Eremin all he knew; by holding back information and promising to deliver it later he wanted to convince Eremin not to exile him and keep him in the Okhrana. He could not reveal more than a fraction of what he knew to avert Eremin's suspicion that Koba had been an accomplice in the Tiflis robbery and had deliberately kept the Okhrana in the dark, as officer Mukhtarov had asserted. By January 1908 the administrative decision in the Dzhugashvili–Mukhtarov case had been received by the Tiflis Okhrana: Koba was to be exiled for two years in northern European Russia; Mukhtarov was to be exiled for three years in eastern Siberia.[5] Eremin had the option of arresting Koba or delaying his arrest and letting him continue to cooperate with the Okhrana. The information in Koba's file in the Tiflis Okhrana was contradictory, so Eremin must have had doubts about Koba's trustworthiness. Some of Koba's reports, such as the information he had furnished on the Avlabar press, had made an important contribution to Okhrana intelligence operations. But the provocation with the illegal leaflets, which had caused a scandal in the Tiflis Okhrana in 1901, and Koba's role in the Tiflis bank robbery must have made Eremin wonder. He decided to delay Koba's arrest but not to reinstate him as a Tiflis Okhrana agent. Koba was to live in Baku and relay information to Eremin through the chief of the Baku Okhrana, Captain P. I. Martynov.

Koba's personal life may also have played a role in Eremin's decision. Koba's wife Keke was in her last months of pregnancy. The decision to postpone Koba's exile until after the birth of their first child may have been Eremin's way of expressing recognition of Koba's service to the Okhrana. Keke gave birth to a son on 16 March 1908. Koba named his son Yakobi (Yakov in Russian), but called him Koba (the Georgian diminutive of Yakobi).[6] Koba therefore named his son after himself or, rather, gave the boy the name he had chosen for himself. Nine days later, on 25 March 1908, the administrative decision in the Dzhugashvili–Mukhtarov case caught up with Koba, and he was arrested, still carrying a passport in the name of 'Gaioz Vissarionov Nizheradze'. For the next six months, he remained in Baku's Bailov prison, waiting to be shipped to his next place of exile in north European Russia.[7] His wife and child left Baku and returned to her family in Didi-Lilo.

During his half year in the Bailov prison, Koba wrote several reports to Captain Martynov, who relayed them to Eremin.[8] Eremin was eager to determine Kamo's identity, so that the Russian government could file formal deposition papers for his extradition from Germany. The German police sent a photograph of Kamo to the Russian Foreign Ministry, which in turn passed it on to the Okhrana. On 22 April 1909, a month after Koba's arrest, Colonel Eremin wired a telegram to St Petersburg stating that 'the man in the photograph is Kamo Ter-Petrosian, a native of Gori'.[9] If Koba was the one to identify Kamo, it was not the first time he had betrayed his friend.

Kamo's extradition took time. Lenin's friend Karl Liebknecht, a leading German Social Democrat, retained a prominent lawyer, Oskar Kohn, a Social Democratic member of the Reichstag. Kohn declared Kamo mentally unfit to stand trial. A team of German psychiatrists was assigned to evaluate Kamo, who provided them with evidence of his insanity: he ate his own excrement, pulled his hair, tore his clothes, screamed, wept, and several times attempted suicide by hanging. Once, he was in convulsions when prison guards cut the rope and revived him. The court-appointed psychiatrists concluded that Kamo was afflicted with a neurotic disease of a 'hysterical type' and cited the possibility of a 'hereditary predisposition' and 'degeneration'. They argued that Kamo's 'characteristic behavior could not be simulated for a long period of time' and only a truly sick person in a state of mental retardation could behave in this way. The Russian government requested Kamo's extradition to Russia as a common criminal. The German Social Democratic press and left-wing members of the Reichstag loudly protested, accusing the German government of 'a betrayal of Russian revolutionaries to the tsarist hangmen'. Kamo was transferred to a psychiatric hospital. In his report to Director Trusevich, Garting stated that the reason for the transfer of Kamo was to make it possible for him to 'escape from there with the help of German Social Democrats who are supporting him'.[10]

At that time Koba was in the Bailov prison in Baku, where strange and bloody events were taking place. Koba spread the rumor that a prisoner, a young Georgian worker, was an Okhrana *agent provocateur*. Incited by Koba, the prisoners attacked the man, who had to be rescued by the guards, who carried him out, blood-covered and almost lifeless. Koba's cell mate, Semeon Vershchak, a Social Revolutionary, recalled years later that 'the prisoners began asking one another who had known that the man was an *agent*, a *provocateur*? Only much later did it become clear that Koba had started the rumor. Whether the Georgian was indeed a *provocateur* was never established.'[11] Koba's friend 'Mitka the Greek', a common criminal who at that time proclaimed himself a Bolshevik, stabbed to death a young Georgian. None of the prisoners knew the murdered man. It turned out that Mitka himself did not know his victim, and admitted that Koba had told him that the man was a police informer; Koba's allegation was never proven. (Both events were reminiscent of what had happened some six years earlier, in the Batum prison, when Koba had 'exposed' an alleged informer who, he claimed, was posing as a worker, thus provoking a murderous assault on the man.) Vereshchak pointed to Koba's strange trait: 'the ability to quietly provoke others but to remain himself on the sidelines'. Vereshchak stated that Koba had been involved in robberies and was friendly with counterfeiters and expropriators who were imprisoned together with him, but he was never tried for these crimes. Koba attacked in the most odious manner the Social Revolutionary Party (Esers) for their terrorist and expropriation activities.[12] He attributed his own crimes to 'false targets', Koba's fundamental trait.[13]

In his denunciations of the Mensheviks, Koba revealed an 'absolutely peculiar hatred'. He called them 'scoundrels' and declared that in the struggle against the Mensheviks 'any means are fair'.[14] Koba frequently stated that the Mensheviks were mostly Jews. He stated that:

Lenin is exasperated that God sent him such comrades as the Mensheviks. Really, what kind of people are these Martovs, Dans, Axelrods! Nothing but circumcised Kikes! And that old bitch, Vera Zasulich! All right! Go work with them! They won't fight and there is no rejoicing at their feasting, cowards and shopkeepers! Don't the workers of Georgia know that the Jewish people produce only cowards who are useless in the fight?![15]

A virulent anti-Semitism was at the heart of Koba's hatred of the Mensheviks. In a newspaper article that he wrote shortly after his return from the London Congress in 1907 Koba stated that 'somebody among the Bolsheviks remarked in jest that since the Mensheviks were the faction of the Jews and the Bolsheviks that of the native Russians, it would become us to have a pogrom in the party'.[16] Koba's anti-Semitic record in later years suggest that this 'somebody' was Koba himself and that he was not joking.

According to the administrative decision of the Special Council, Koba was to be exiled to the town of Sol'vychegodsk in the Vologda province in northern European Russia. On 29 September 1908 he left Baku in a group of convicts; by the end of October, he arrived in Sol'vychegodsk. He stayed there until the end of June 1909, when he 'escaped' with a passport from Eremin. Captain Martynov, the chief of the Baku Okhrana, sent Eremin a report on 30 September 1909 stating that Dzhugashvili had escaped from his place of exile, arrived in Baku, and 'now holds passport no. 982 in the name of Oganes Vartanov Totomyantz, resident of the city of Tiflis, issued by the Tiflis chief of police on 12 May of this year and valid for one year . . . '.[17] Martynov did not arrest Koba in September 1909, because he knew that Eremin had procured the passport for 'Oganes Vartanov Totomyantz' and sanctioned Koba's 'escape'. In May 1910, when this passport expired, Martynov supplied Koba with another one in the name of 'Zakhar Grigorian Melikantz'.[18]

An Armenian terrorist group, the Dashnaks, were assuming growing importance in Eremin's and Martynov's intelligence operations.[19] Having lived for a long time in Gori, Tiflis and Baku, all places with a large Armenian population, Koba spoke Armenian fluently and could pass for an Armenian. Eremin and Martynov hoped that Koba would be able to provide valuable information on the Dashnaks' criminal activities. Eremin also hoped to find out from Koba more information on the Armenian Kamo who had recruited some members for his band from among the Dashnaks.

The German authorities did finally extradite Kamo. On 19 October 1909, handcuffed and dragging his shackles and chains, Kamo arrived at the Tiflis prison.[20] Also on 19 October 1909 Captain Martynov sent Eremin a secret cable stating that Koba had 'departed for Tiflis to participate in the conference', after which he must 'return to Baku and be involved at once in technical matters'. Martynov asked Eremin to 'telegraph [Koba's] departure from Tiflis and the train number'.[21] Koba was summoned by Eremin to identify Kamo. Koba stayed in Tiflis for two days, living in a 'secret apartment', and he received there some Bolshevik friends which led to a strange encounter. Eremin was paying him a visit when one of Koba's friends appeared. When Eremin had left, Koba's friend asked, 'What do you have to do with the gendarmes? Why was that gendarme here?' Koba replied, 'He's helping us in the gendarmerie.'[22] In a way, Koba was right: Eremin was helping him avoid exile in Sol'vychegodsk, while Koba was helping Eremin tighten the noose around Kamo's neck.

But Kamo was not destined to be hanged. The European press demanded that the Russian government terminate his case, and Prime Minister Stolypin received numerous letters and telegrams from European human rights organizations. One of the wires read: 'The League of Defense for the Rights of Man and Citizen would consider it insulting even to suspect the Prime Minister of Russia capable of using for evil ends the unheard-of act of the Prussian police in regard to Ter-Petrosov.'[23] Stolypin wrote in the margin: 'What nonsense!' In a letter to the Governor of the Caucasus, he observed that the 'democratic press of Europe with special passion discusses the fate of Arshakov [a.k.a. Mirsky and Ter-Petrosian] . . . The press attacks would definitely increase if Arshakov-Mirsky were to be sentenced to death, and this would have a negative influence on Russian interests in the question of the extradition of anarchists.'[24] Indirectly, Stolypin was instructing the governor to prevent the execution of Kamo.

Eremin, having completed his investigation, submitted Kamo's case to the Tiflis military tribunal. Each of the six indictment articles called for the death penalty. But the tribunal, pressured by the governor, took into account the opinion of appointed psychiatrists that Kamo was 'no doubt mentally ill' and decided to set his case aside, ruling, on 26 April 1910, that 'Simon Ter-Petrosian has to be submitted to an examination and prolonged observation in a psychiatric hospital.'[25] On 20 September 1910 the chief psychiatrist of that hospital, D. I. Orbelli, stated in his diagnosis that 'Simon Ter-Petrosian at present suffers from hysterical psychosis evolving into senility', and that he was 'definitely mentally incompetent to stand trial.' The tribunal ordered Kamo moved to the psychiatric ward of the Tiflis prison.[26]

The Tiflis bank robbery had not been much help to Lenin, who had a falling out with his 'cashier' Leonid Krasin. This squabble became known to the Okhrana. On 5 April 1909, Garting received a report stating that Krasin had 'obtained close to 200,000 rubles . . . possibly, this is the result of the cashing of the money stolen in Tiflis . . . Lenin protested the violation of party rules and the snatching of party money by Krasin.'[27] But Lenin had other sources of money besides Koba and Kamo. In July 1907 he took 6,000 rubles from a group of expropriators under the command of Lbov, promising to deliver arms in return. He never fulfilled his promise. In 1909 a member of Lbov's band, 'Sasha', appeared in Paris, demanding that Lenin return the money. Lenin offered to pay 500 rubles in return for a 6,000 ruble receipt. Sasha complained to V. R. Menzhinsky (one of the future chiefs of the Soviet Secret Police), who at the time opposed Lenin. Menzhinsky formulated Sasha's complaint in an open letter to the Bolshevik Center, stating in part:

Comrades, stop this game . . . You took the money . . . And these years, when the members of the Lbov detachment had been caught one by one, when they were kept in prison, hungry and in rags, for months waiting for help, or for execution . . . you, comrades from the Bolshevik Center, used our money. Are you waiting for us all to be caught and hanged . . .? I appeal to you, comrades, workers. Sasha.

Sasha never received the money. Menzhinsky also attacked Lenin, accusing him of fraud.[28]

The fraud began in December 1905 when Nikolay Shmidt urged the workers at the furniture factory he had inherited to go on strike and burn the factory, which they did. Shmidt was then arrested and later died in prison. According to the testimony of M. I. Mikhailov, a lawyer and Bolshevik sympathizer, Shmidt bequeathed his estate to the Bolsheviks. The court, ignoring this assertion, ruled that the legal heir was Shmidt's younger brother, a minor. Lenin sent his emissaries to blackmail the boy into renouncing his claims to the inheritance in favor of his two sisters, Ekaterina and Elizaveta. Lenin ordered two of his followers to marry the Shmidt sisters and give him the money. The younger sister, Elizaveta, agreed to marry the Bolshevik V. F. Lozinsky, alias 'Viktor Taratuta', and gave all her money to Lenin. With the older sister, Ekaterina, Lenin encountered problems. He sent Nikolay Andrikanis, a paralegal, to marry her. Andrikanis, according to an Okhrana report, 'entered into an intimate relationship with Ekaterina Shmidt and lives with her in civil marriage, having made a declaration to the Central Committee that he is ready to give up one third of the inheritance. In view of this, the Central Committee decided to appoint a three-member court, because the Bolsheviks wanted to press the matter and to receive all the inheritance.'[29] Early in June 1908 the three-member court decided to divide Ekaterina's inheritance equally between Lenin and Ekaterina, who agreed to pay 125,000 rubles in cash. Another Okhrana report, dated 19 November 1908 stated that Lenin's representatives had 'received 45,000 rubles from the older sister, Ekaterina, and will receive from her 80,000 rubles; besides, the Bolsheviks will receive 500,000 francs from the younger sister'.[30]

Despite these riches falling into Lenin's hands, it probably never occurred to him to send Koba some financial help when he was in prison and exile. Koba also suffered a great personal tragedy. In the autumn of 1909, after his 'escape' from Sol'vychegodsk and return to Baku, Koba lost his wife, Keke, who left him a 1-and-a-half-year-old son. The cause of Keke's death has remained shrouded in almost total silence; she was 23 years old. Koba's childhood friend Iosif Iremashvili wrote that Keke, being a very religious woman, begged Koba before her death to arrange her funeral in accordance with the rites of the Georgian Orthodox Church. Iremashvili recalled Koba saying after her death, 'I promised Keke that she would be buried in accordance with Orthodox rites, and I shall keep my promise.' Iremashvili wrote that the Svanidze family, too, 'insisted on a church burial'.[31]

This repeated insistence on a burial according to Orthodox rites is puzzling. In Georgia, as well as in the whole of the Russian Empire, cemeteries were under the jurisdiction of various religious communities, which did not allow a burial without the appropriate rites. Keke would ordinarily have been buried in accordance with the rites of the Georgian Orthodox Church to which she belonged. Under only one circumstance would she have been denied these rites and therefore burial in a cemetery: if she had committed suicide. If Keke took her own life, that would explain the almost total silence that has surrounded her death: her family had to conceal the truth or she could not have been put to rest in a cemetery. This custom found its way into poetry devoted to the fate of a suicide: 'A doctor glanced at the corpse fleetingly and allowed it to be buried somewhere, without church eulogy, without incense, nothing that consecrates the grave.'[32]

Keke was buried near the village of Didi-Lilo. Koba walked behind the coffin in the funeral procession, carrying his little son. In his recollections, Iremashvili describes how Koba grasped his arm and whispered to him, 'Soso, this creature softened my heart; now she is dead, and with her passing goes my last drop of feeling for mankind.' His hand on his chest, Koba continued, 'Here, in here, everything is empty, unutterably empty.'[33]

Koba returned to Baku after the funeral. He was 30 now, a minor figure in the revolutionary movement. Toward the end of 1909 his relations with the Baku workers became strained. Members of the Baku Printers Union discovered that a leaflet distributed in the name of a mysterious 'Baku Social Democratic Committee' had been printed by Koba on a secret press run by the Okhrana. The president of the union accused Koba of being an *agent provocateur*.[34] The accusation was echoed by leading Baku Mensheviks. 'You are nothing but a *provocateur!*' one of them charged Koba.[35] The leader of the Baku Bolsheviks, Stepan Shaumian, who had known Koba since 1905 – and whom Koba had denounced to the Okhrana on several occasions – openly accused him of cooperating with the Okhrana.[36] Koba's difficulties came to a head when on 23 March 1910 the Social Democratic Party Committee in Baku called for a secret meeting to look into the accusation that Koba was an Okhrana agent. The chief accuser was Shaumian. Another charge involved a worker named Zharinov, who accused Koba of having instigated an almost lethal attack on him. He had been nursed back to health by peasants who had found his almost lifeless body.[37] Koba promised to come and face the charges, but the house where the meeting was to take place was surrounded by Okhrana officers, and all the members of the 'court' were arrested. Finding themselves in prison, they decided to carry the proceedings to an end, but, as one of them recalled dryly, 'the prison conditions were not exactly suitable for that. The trial was postponed.'[38]

Colonel Eremin, too, had found himself in a difficult position; as Okhrana General A. Spiridovich recalled some 40 years later: 'Eremin worked brilliantly in the Caucasus. He built an excellent agent network among the Social Democrats and broke up revolutionary parties active there, especially the party of Dashnaktsatyun (the Dashnaks). This turned the Viceroy's circles against Eremin.'[39] The Dashnaks, Armenian nationalists, were supported by wealthy and influential Armenian businessmen, many of whom had interests in the growing Baku oil industry. They needed the Dashnaks as protectors against local Muslims and as strikebreakers in their conflict with trade unions, which often instigated unrest among workers in Armenian-owned businesses. The Viceroy of the Caucasus, Count Vorontsov-Dashkov, had strong ties with wealthy Armenians. They pleaded with him to recall Eremin from the Caucasus. The recall was masked by a promotion: on 21 January 1910 Eremin was appointed Chief of the Special Section of the Department of Police, the third highest post in the Department.[40] General Spiridovich also recalled that when Eremin had been transferred from Kiev in 1907, he 'took with him to St Petersburg some of his secret collaborators whom . . . he was unable to pass on to his successor'.[41] But while working in the Special Section Eremin could not personally deal with agents and informers, because the Special Section did not have a budget to pay for their services. The Special Section served as the center for coordination of all Okhrana sections and did not have its own agents. Eremin could, however, transfer Koba to an officer in the St Petersburg Okhrana, or could have passed him on to Colonel I. I. Pastrulin, his successor. Eremin did neither, most likely because he suspected Koba of double dealing and did not want to impose him on someone who might think of Koba as a reliable agent.

Captain Martynov, chief of the Baku Okhrana, was transferred from the Caucasus for the same reason as Eremin – he, too, treated the Dashnaks harshly.[42] Martynov's transfer put an end to Koba's employment with the Baku Okhrana and to his Okhrana career in the Caucasus. Before leaving Tiflis, Eremin 'sanitized' Koba's file in the Tiflis Okhrana, removing from it all documents that could point to Koba's employment as an agent.[43] This was the usual procedure for an Okhrana handler, whose responsibility it was to protect the cover of his agents and informers. Only the handler who recruited them was supposed to know their identity. Captain F. I. Galimbatovsky, who had replaced Captain Martynov as chief of the Baku Okhrana, stated in his report to St Petersburg that because of Koba's 'two escapes from the locality of his exile, as a result of which he has not served a single administrative penalty imposed on him, I suggest that the strictest measure of punishment be applied to him – exile for five years to a remote district of Siberia'.[44] This report had to pass through the Special Section, and it was probably its new chief, Colonel Eremin, who softened the recommendation. In the end, Koba was exiled to Sol'vychegodsk to complete the remaining six months of his two-year prison term, arriving in Sol'vychegodsk on 29 December 1910.

Koba's clouded career in the Caucasus ended, and the memory of him began to fade among the revolutionaries of the region. Some of those who knew him were to recall that he had been suspected of being an Okhrana *agent provocateur* and of being the author of anonymous Ohkrana denunciations. Others remembered that 'Koba was considered a common coward in Georgia, a man capable only of provocations and of encouraging others to blackmail and expropriations, hiding his identity and keeping out of danger.'[45] Another revolutionary recalled that Koba left 'a strong sensation of something abnormal, something strange, in all his words, movements, manners . . . a dry, heartless and soulless robot in the shape of a man, who strives to destroy something, only to put something else in its place.'[46]

NOTES

1. *Padenie tsarskogo rezhima*, vol. VII, Moscow/Leningrad, 1925, p. 339.
2. I. M. Dubinsky-Mukhadze, *Kamo*, Moscow, 1974, p. 94.
3. Ibid., p. 95.
4. Ibid., p. 96.
5. Rafael Bagratuni's testimony, dated 8 May 1967, on file in I. D. Levine's archive. Copy in the author's archive.
6. Yakov's date of birth can be found in the newspaper *Völkischer Beobachter*, Berlin, 24 July 1941. The paper carried an article reporting the capture of Stalin's son by German troops at Liasno, near Vitebsk. He stated his date of birth as 16 March 1908. See also Edward Ellis Smith, *The Young Stalin: the Early Years of an Elusive Revolutionary*, London, 1968, p. 392, fn 262a, and Major A. N. Kolesnik, 'Voennoplennyi starshii leitenant Yakov Dzhugashvili', *Voenno-istricheskii zhurnal*, December 1988.
7. *Krasny arkhiv*, no. 2, 1934, p. 3.
8. See Martynov's letters to Eremin in Lavrenty Beria, *K Vosprosy ob istorii bolshevitskikh organizatsii v Zakavkazie*, Leningrad, 1936, p. 90, and M. D. Bagirov, *Iz istorii bolshevitskoi organizatsii Baku i Azerbaidzhana*, Moscow, 1946, pp. 101ff.
9. Dubinsky-Mukhadze, *Kamo*, pp. 64ff. See photocopy of Colonel Eremin's wire, dated 22 April 1908.
10. Ibid., pp. 112-22.
11. S. Vereshchak, 'Stalin v tur'me', *Dni*, 22 and 24 January 1928.
12. Ibid.
13. For a discussion of this kind of projection, see Walter C. Langer, *The Mind of Adolf Hitler*, New York, 1972, pp. 183-5.
14. Vereshchak, 'Stalin v turme'.
15. R. Arsenidze, 'Iz vospominanii o Staline', *Novyi zhurnal*, no. 72, June 1963, pp. 218-21.
16. I. V. Stalin, *Sochineniya*, vol. II, Moscow, 1946-51, p. 46ff.
17. Beria, *K voprosu ob...*, p. 90.
18. Ibid. See also Okhrana report no. 101145, dated 31 March 1911, and Smith, p. 230.
19. See General A. Spiridovich's letter, dated 13 January 1950, to Vadim Makarov. In I. D. Levine's archive. Copy in the author's archive.
20. Dubinsky-Mukhadze, *Kamo*, pp. 124ff.

21. Bagirov, *Iz istorii...*, pp. 101ff.
22. Roy Medvedev, *Let History Judge*, New York, 1971, p. 319 and fn 61.
23. Dubinsky-Mukhadze, *Kamo*, p. 134.
24. Ibid., pp. 134ff.
25. Ibid., pp. 134–9.
26. Ibid.
27. Report of the chief of the Okhrana Foreign Agency no. 127089, dated 5 April 1909. On file at the Hoover Institution. Copy in the author's archive.
28. Roman Gul', *Dzerzhinsky*, New York, 1974, pp. 150–3.
29. *Bolsheviki*, Moscow, 1918, pp. 101ff, fn.
30. Ibid.
31. J. Iremaschwili, *Stalin und die Tragödie Georgiens*, Berlin, 1932, p. 40.
32. N. A. Nekrasov, poem *Pokhorony* (Funeral), *Selected Works*, Gospolitizdat, Moscow, 1946, p. 85.
33. Ibid.
34. S. Vereshchak, 'Stalin v turme'.
35. Leontii Zhgenti, *Prichiny revolutsii na Kavkaze i rukovodstvo*, Paris, 1963, pp. 58-62.
36. Ibid. See also N. Vakar, 'Stalin po vospominaniyam N. N. Zhordania', *Poslednie novosti*, 16 December 1936.
37. Smith, *The Young Stalin*, pp. 208–10.
38. Zhgenti, *Prichiny revolutsii na Kavkaze i rukovodstvo*, pp. 58-62.
39. General Spiridovich's letter to Vadim Makarov, dated 13 January 1950 in I. D. Levine's and the author's archives.
40. *Padenie tsarskogo rezhima*, vol. VII, p. 339.
41. General Spiridovich's letter to Vadim Makarov, dated 13 January 1950, in I. D. Levine's and the author's archives.
42. See 'Spisok obschego sostava chinov otdelnogo korpusa zhandarmov, 1911', p. 613; quoted in Smith, *The Young Stalin*, p. 401, fn. 482.
43. See Chapter 9. Colonel Pastrulin, Eremin's successor in Tiflis, discovered in 1911 that Koba's file in the Tiflis Okhrana archive was almost empty.
44. Beria, *K voprosu*, p. 225.
45. H. Montgomery Hyde, *Stalin: the History of a Dictator*, New York, 1971, pp. 71ff. Hyde quotes Zhgenti and Zhordania, two leading Georgian revolutionaries.
46. Arsenidze, *Iz vospominanii*, p. 220.

9

KOBA AND MALINOVSKY

Shortly after Koba's arrival in Sol'vychegodsk, he sent a letter to one of Lenin's supporters in Paris, Issak Shwartz, addressing him as 'Comrade Semeon' and signing it 'K. S.' and in parentheses 'Ivanovich'. As Koba anticipated, his letter was read and copied by the Okhrana.[1] On 24 January 1911 Koba sent a letter to a Moscow Bolshevik, Vladimir Bobrovsky, stating, 'I end my exile in July of this year. Ilyich [Lenin] and Co. are enticing me to one of their centers, without waiting for the end of the term (a legal person has more leeway), but if there is a great need (I am waiting for their answer), then, of course, I'll take off.' Koba was intentionally candid in providing his full name and address: 'Sol'vychegodsk, Vologodskaya Gubernia, Political Exile Iosif Dzhugashvili.'[2] This was because he wanted the Okhrana to know that he was the author of this letter. He also lied: at this point 'Ilyich and Co.' knew nothing of Koba's intention to go to one of the 'centers'.

As Koba anticipated, his two letters attracted the attention of the Okhrana. The new director of the Department of Police, Stepan Petrovich Beletsky, had ordered the Okhrana to encourage divisiveness among the revolutionaries. Beletsky's policy was in complete agreement with Lenin's splinter tactics but for the Okhrana's own reasons: Beletsky strove to 'divide and conquer' the revolutionary movement. Lenin, on the other hand, wanted to usurp the party leadership. In the eyes of Beletsky, the Bolsheviks were an extremist fringe group that was easily infiltrated by Okhrana agents and could be controlled and used to weaken the much larger and more influential Mensheviks. As he himself stated, Beletsky wanted to split the Bolsheviks from the Mensheviks so that 'these two movements could not unite and form a formidable power, which would be difficult to defeat'.[3]

Copies of Koba's letters were sent to the chief of the Special Section of the Department of Police, Colonel Eremin, who sent one copy of each letter to the recently appointed chief of the Okhrana Foreign Agency in Paris, A. A. Krasilnikov. Arkady Garting had retired in November 1909. He could not have transferred Koba to Krasilnikov because he had lost contact with him in 1907, and Eremin's covering letter provided no information about Koba.[4] Krasilnikov did not communicate with agents personally, but left this to gendarmerie officers assigned to him.[5] The copies of Koba's two letters were placed in the archive of the Foreign Agency in Paris.

The centers which Koba promoted in his letters were to be established in St Petersburg and Moscow. A copy of Koba's 'Iosif' letter was sent to the chief of the Tiflis Okhrana, Colonel Ivan Iosifovich Pastrulin, who was ordered to provide information on Iosif Dzhugashvili. Pastrulin was the logical source for such information, since Koba mentioned Tiflis in his 'Iosif' letter, and his name, Dzhugashvili, suggested that he was Georgian. Pastrulin, who had succeeded Eremin in Tiflis, initiated an inquiry in the Tiflis Okhrana archives, but found Koba's file to be almost empty, containing only scant information about his arrests and exiles. Pastrulin then ordered his agents to gather information about Koba from Tiflis revolutionaries, but they provided contradictory data because memories of him had become blurred, since he had left Tiflis years earlier and his role in the underground had always been confusing. In his report, Pastrulin stated that, 'according to secret information' provided by his agents, in 1903 Koba had 'headed the Batum committee' and was known there under the alias *Chopur*, 'Pockmarked' in Georgian. This was indeed Koba's nickname; not among revolutionaries but among criminals.

Pastrulin also reported that Koba 'in 1906–1907 lived illegally in Batum, where he was arrested . . .'. In fact, Koba lived in Tiflis in 1906–07. He was arrested not once but twice in Baku, where he lived from the end of 1907 to the end of 1910. Pastrulin's agents knew nothing of Koba's involvement in the Tiflis bank robbery in 1907, but they reported to Pastrulin that Koba 'in 1905 was arrested in Tiflis and escaped from prison'. (In fact, Colonel Zasypkin had arrested and released him twice after Koba had signed a pledge to collaborate with the Okhrana.) The fact that information as important as an arrest and escape from prison was not mentioned in Koba's Okhrana file should have suggested to Pastrulin that Koba had been an Okhrana agent and that his file had been 'sanitized' to protect his cover. But if Pastrulin understood this, he could not mention it in his report: it was contrary to Okhrana rules to commit to paper anything that might expose an agent. On 14 March 1911 Pastrulin sent his report to the Special Section and to the chiefs of the Moscow and Vologda Okhrana.[6] On 18 May 1911 the chief of the Vologda Okhrana, Colonel Konissky, stated in his report: 'The mentioned Dzhugashvili lived in the house of Grigorov in Sol'vychegodsk from December 29 1910 to January 10 1911, but at present lives in the house of Kuzakova. It is true that only six months remain to complete his exile (from December 31 1910 to June 27 of this year).'[7]

Koba at that moment was in a delicate situation that threatened to become unpleasant. The widow Maria Kuzakova, in whose house he lived, finding herself pregnant, threatened to accuse Koba of having raped her. The scandal was heatedly discussed by the locals and exiles. The Okhrana, which supervised the conduct of the exiles, intervened and helped Koba settle the case.[8] Koba probably promised to marry Kuzakova and convinced her to withdraw her charges. Towards the end of 1911 she gave birth to a son and named him Konstantin Kuzakov, but by then Koba was no longer in Sol'vychegodsk. In the late 1920s, when Stalin was already the most powerful man in Russia, Mariya Kuzakova brought Konstantin, then still a teenager, to Moscow and asked Stalin to help her and the boy. Stalin indirectly, through subordinates, advanced the professional and party career of his illegitimate son, but avoided close personal encounters with him.[9] After Stalin's death, Kuzakov worked at the Moscow Television Station. His striking resemblance to Stalin often frightened people, who thought that they had encountered 'a strange double of Stalin, looking at them with the somewhat arrogant and impenetrable gaze of his yellow eyes . . .'.[10] Throughout his rule Stalin directed Kuzakov's appointments to well-paid positions and in 1947 protected him from arrest, saying, 'I do not see any reason for Kuzakov's arrest.' In 1995 Konstantin Kuzakov, by then an elderly man in his mid-80s, revealed his story for the first time and allowed publication of a 1935 photograph of himself, his mother, and his 3-year-old son.[11]

Koba's exile ended on 27 June 1911, but he stayed in Sol'vychegodsk until 19 July 1911, before moving to Vologda, to wait for Lenin's response to his idea of establishing 'Russian centers' at St Petersburg and Moscow. Lenin agreed to this idea in a letter sent via Sergo Ordzhonikidze, a 26-year-old former medical orderly who had long been involved with Koba and Kamo, and since 1902 had acquired a list of criminal credentials. He came from a family of impoverished Georgian gentry. An orphan from early childhood, he was unruly and a poor student. In 1902, when he was barely 16, Ordzhonikidze left his native village for Tiflis, where he met Koba, Kamo and Lado. He helped them print the leaflets, not suspecting that he was thereby participating in an Okhrana provocation. He was arrested in the course of the investigation of this case, but released shortly afterward as a minor. He took part in a number of Kamo's armed robberies, in the Tiflis bank robbery, and in the assassination of Prince Chavchavadze. After the murder of the prince, Ordzhonokidze went to Baku, where he was arrested and exiled to Siberia. He then escaped to Iran, but soon returned to his native village. Fearing arrest, he escaped abroad again and joined Lenin in Paris.

Ordzhonikidze's arrival in Paris coincided with Lenin's learning about

Koba's letters to Shwartz and Vladimir Bobrovsky. These letters convinced
Lenin to set up the 'Russian centers' that Koba had promoted in his
letters. Lenin decided to send Koba, Ordzhonikidze and Bobrovsky to
Moscow to set up a 'Russian Organizational Commission' there and select
delegates to a Bolshevik conference that Lenin planned to hold early in
1912 in Prague. According to Lenin's plan, Koba was to take part in
organizing this conference, and Ordzhonikidze was to convey this decision to Koba, who was still in Vologda.[12]

On his arrival in Moscow, Ordzhonikidze was introduced by Cecilia
Bobrovskaya, Vladimir Bobrovsky's sister, to a man by the name of Roman
Malinovsky. Cecilia thought of Malinovsky as a rising star in the workers'
movement, and admired him as 'a commanding person in all respects'.[13]
What she did not know was that Malinovsky was an Okhrana agent.
Ordzhonikidze revealed to Malinovsky Lenin's plan to hold a conference
in Prague and to make Koba a part of the Moscow center. Malinovsky
reported this information to the chief of the Moscow Okhrana, Colonel
P. P. Zavarzin, who decided to prevent Koba's arrival in Moscow in order
to promote Malinovsky to the position of the head of the planned 'Russian
center' there and to ensure that Malinovsky would head the Moscow
delegation to Lenin's conference in Prague. Zavarzin arrested Bobrovsky
and several other Bolsheviks, among them Aleksey Rykov (a future head
of the Soviet government), who in 1911 advocated unification with the
Mensheviks. In arresting Rykov, Zavarzin followed the 'divide and
conquer' strategy of the director of the Department of Police, Beletsky. He
also played into the hands of Lenin, who proclaimed that the Prague
conference would 'wipe out forever the vestiges of formal unity with the
Mensheviks and would *regenerate* our revolutionary Bolshevik Party. I un-
derscore *regenerate* because Bolshevism has existed as a trend of political
thought and as a political party since 1903!'[14] On 17 August 1911 Zavarzin
sent a letter, marked 'Absolutely Secret: Personal' to the chief of the
Vologda Okhrana, Colonel Konissky, notifying him that 'the money for
Koba's traveling expenses will be sent to Peter Alekseevich Chizhikov,
Ishmetov Store, Vologda'.[15]

Zavarzin requested the St Petersburg Okhrana to arrest Koba on his way
to Moscow. Zavarzin could not have known about Koba's Okhrana ties.
Nor did Koba have any inkling that Malinovsky was about to emerge as his
rival, not only in the party, but also in the Okhrana. Malinovsky in many
respects resembled Koba: some of the parallels appear almost uncanny.
Malinovsky was born in 1878 in the village of Gladova near the town of
Plotsk in the part of Poland that belonged to the Russian Empire. He was

a Pole and spoke Russian with a heavy accent; as a child he contracted small-pox, which left his face heavily pockmarked; he committed robberies, for which he received prison sentences in 1894, 1896 and 1899; he was also charged with a rape, sentenced and imprisoned for it. His parents, whom he lost in early childhood, were poor peasants. Malinovsky lived with distant relatives and wandered from one shelter to another. After working for several years in Germany as a tinker, he returned to Poland to work as a tailor's apprentice. In 1902 he enlisted in the Russian elite Izmailovsky Guards Regiment by resorting to a fraud: he impersonated a cousin having the same name and used his identity card to conceal his own criminal past and true age. He began his career as an Okhrana informer in 1902, reporting on soldiers and officers of his regiment.[16] After the Russo-Japanese War he was discharged from the army. In 1906, he came to St Petersburg and found a job as a lathe operator. The trade union movement was just getting organized, and he rapidly advanced as an activist because of his talent for demagoguery.[17]

Malinovsky began his career in the Okhrana in 1906 initially under the codename 'Ernest' as a 'shtuchnik' (piecemeal informer) usually paid 25–50 rubles for each report. He was 'arrested' by the Okhrana several times during the period 1906–09 and released for 'lack of evidence'. These arrests enhanced his popularity among the workers. Toward the end of 1909, however, Malinovsky's position in the union became shaky, as workers accused him of intrigues against the union chairman and members. Malinovsky was also charged with several instances of embezzlement and with being too extravagant, vain and quick tempered, but his arrest by the Okhrana on 15 November 1909 saved him from being fired from his union posts. After keeping him in prison for two months, the Okhrana terminated his service and exiled him to Moscow. He was a victim of a general purge of the Okhrana agent network in the wake of the scandal surrounding the exposure of the infamous Okhrana agent provocateur Evno Azef, which shook the entire police establishment.[18]

The party organization in Moscow was in the hands of the Mensheviks, but there was also a small group of Lenin supporters. On 13 May 1910 Malinovsky was arrested. He offered his services as an informer to Moscow Okhrana interrogator V. G. Ivanov, who reported the offer to Colonel Zavarzin. The colonel personally recruited Malinovsky as a 'secret collaborator', or salaried agent. By the end of 1911, Malinovsky had submitted 57 reports in poor Russian, signed Portnoy (tailor). When Malinovsky reported the arrival of Ordzhonikidze in Moscow, Zavarzin saw an opportunity to advance Malinovsky to the top of Lenin's organization and ordered him to declare himself a Bolshevik.

Ordzhonikidze directed Filip Goloshchekin, a dentist turned revolutionary who had just escaped from exile, to deliver Lenin's message and money to Koba in Vologda. Goloshchekin arrived in Vologda and, together with Koba, left for St Petersburg. An exile, M. M. Lashevich, wrote on this occasion, 'Filia [Goloshchekin] has been here, took Koba with him and left.'[19] The chief of the Vologda Okhrana, Colonel Konissky, sent cables to the Moscow and St Petersburg Okhrana, stating that Koba had boarded a train on 6 September 1911 and that he was carrying a passport in the name of 'Peter Alekseevich Chizhikov'.[20] Koba decided to stay in St Petersburg for a while. Goloshchekin proceeded to Paris to join Lenin there.

Koba could not have chosen a more unfortunate moment for renewing his contact with the St Petersburg Okhrana. On 5 September 1911, the day before Koba's departure from Vologda, Dmitry Bogrov, a member of the Social Revolutionary Party shot and killed Prime Minister Stolypin in a Kiev theater. The Okhrana was in turmoil: not only had it failed to protect the prime minister, but Bogrov also was soon revealed as having been an Okhrana agent. This inflamed suspicions that the Okhrana was involved in the murder. Various 'hidden hand' theories were born. The most popular version insisted that Bogrov was a 'blind tool' in the hands of an influential clique at the imperial court and of the empress herself, who were purportedly dissatisfied with Stolypin's policies.[21] The other conspiracy theory, propagated by 'Jewish-hand' theorists, focused on the fact that Bogrov was a Jew, and claimed that his motive was to protest at Stolypin's reputed anti-Semitism.[22]

A more likely explanation is found in the state of mind of the murderer. He had joined the Social Revolutionary Party, had been arrested by the Okhrana and, fearing severe punishment, had agreed to become an informer. When his friends suspected him of ties to the Okhrana, he pleaded with them not to doubt his loyalty, all the while despising himself for his cowardice and betrayal. Entangled in the contradictory circumstances of his life, Bogrov was a very confused young man, who decided with one shot to put an end to the emotional conflict that was consuming him. In assassinating Stolypin, he desperately wanted to prove to himself and to his friends that he was a true revolutionary.[23] This explanation has not convinced the proponents of conspiracy theories.[24]

The assassination of Stolypin once again exposed the danger of uncontrollable Okhrana agents and probably influenced Eremin's decision to agree to Koba's arrest. He could not but notice the warning signs in Koba's personality and in his checkered Okhrana career. There was also another problem: at that time Eremin already knew about Kamo's escape on 15

August 1911 from the psychiatric ward of the Tiflis Metekh prison. Kamo's escape had been daring. The rope on which he lowered himself from his prison window snapped, and he landed on the rocks of the Kura riverbank, badly injuring himself and losing consciousness. He recovered and with the help of friends escaped abroad. His bones not yet fully mended, he knocked at the door of Lenin's apartment in Paris. Lenin listened with amazement to Kamo's saga and advised him to restore his health by resting for a while, and then, as soon as possible, to go to the Caucasus to organize a bank robbery. As always, Lenin needed money.[25]

Eremin was aware of the connection between Kamo and Koba, who arrived in St Petersburg three weeks after Kamo's escape. Eremin feared that Kamo's escape might activate the Tiflis bank robbery case and threaten his own career. But his immediate reason for agreeing to Koba's arrest was Colonel Zavarzin's request to prevent Koba's arrival in Moscow by detaining him in St Petersburg. Koba visited Sergey Alliluev, who had moved to St Petersburg after the Tiflis Okhrana purge in 1907. Alliluev noticed Okhrana agents near his home and told Koba about them. Koba remained unperturbed.[26] In the evening, he went to the Hotel Rossiya, where he was arrested. He was brought to the Preliminary Detention prison and remained there for three months. Then he was allowed to choose his next place of exile for three years under open police surveillance for his crime of 'going over to an illegal status'.[27] Koba chose Vologda and received 'free passage' along with 'voyage document no. 23602'. On 14 December 1911 he took a train to Vologda.[28]

In his report to Director Beletsky, Colonel Zavarzin stated triumphantly that 'the arrest of Rykov and his supporters in August 1911 had an impact that was outstanding in its significance . . . All the representatives of the Leninist faction remain free and in control of the situation.'[29] Bolsheviks selected 'Bina' (Valentina Lobova) to represent them in Prague.[30] Her husband, Aleksey Ivanovich Lobov, a Bolshevik, was an important Moscow Okhrana agent.[31] Zavarzin threatened him with the arrest of his wife and ordered him to feign serious illness to prevent her departure for Prague. When Bina, not suspecting anything, declined to go to Prague, Zavarzin ordered another Okhrana agent, Kukushkin, to call a meeting of Moscow Bolsheviks, who selected Malinovsky as the delegate to the Prague conference. Malinovsky cabled Lenin, requesting that the opening of the conference be delayed until his arrival.[32]

Lenin greeted Malinovsky warmly. He liked what he said were the qualities of this 'good boy, not an intellectual'.[33] He later recalled that 'Malinovsky had appeared at the conference with the reputation of an outstanding leader of the labor movement . . . a man who was much discussed in Menshevik circles, which regarded him as one of their own, even calling him the "Russian August Bebel".[34] (Bebel was one of the founders of the German Social Democratic Party and a member of the Reichstag.) One of the delegates recalled that 'Malinovsky was tall, strongly built, and dressed almost fashionably. Deep, numerous pockmarks gave his face a fierce expression, as if it had been through a fire . . . his yellow eyes slid and jumped quickly from one object to another. He seemed too loud and fussy. Talking to him made me feel tired immediately.'[35]

The Prague conference opened on 6 January 1912 with only 13 delegates present. Three of them were Okhrana agents: M. I. Briandinsky, A. S. Romanov, and Malinovsky.[36] 'We had no people at all', complained Lenin's wife Krupskaya.[37] Lenin insisted on holding an election to the Central Committee of what he called 'the new Bolshevik Party'. He moved among the delegates, whispering the names of people he wanted to get elected and pleading to 'give a little vote to Malinovsky . . . he has connections, and he is a working man'. Then Lenin collected what he called secret ballots. Most of the delegates declared themselves to be against Malinovsky, but Lenin soon leaked out the 'confidential' news that Malinovsky had been elected. 'Everyone was astonished', one of the delegates recalled.[38] Lenin announced the members of the Central Committee: himself, Zinoviev, Malinovsky, Shwartz, Goloshchekin, Ordzhonikidze and Elena Stasova. After the vote, he proposed Malinovsky as the Bolshevik candidate to represent the workers of the Moscow Gubernia, the second largest electoral district in population, size and political clout, in the approaching elections to the Fourth Duma. His proposal was accepted.[39]

Lenin's complete break with the Mensheviks became widely known and provoked an angry controversy. The Okhrana intercepted a letter, dated 29 February 1912, in which an outraged Menshevik wrote that Lenin's conference was illegal: 'In short, nine-tenths of the party were absent . . . All the members are united against this usurpation of the party banner . . . today a meeting was held with 150 people present; all, with the exception of eight, agreed that this conference was illegal and that it was necessary to protest it.'[40] The Mensheviks appealed to the Second Socialist International for arbitration, complaining about the illegality of the Prague conference and demanding investigation of charges that Lenin had been involved in armed expropriations and that he had pocketed the loot. Lenin vehemently denied these charges. The investigation was scheduled to start in August 1914, some two-and-a-half years after the Prague conference, but the outbreak of the First World War made this impossible.

After the conference, Lenin 'co-opted' Koba as an 'agent of the Central Committee' without revealing to anybody, except Sergo Ordzhonikidze, the hidden meaning of this appointment: he sent Sergo Orzhonikidze to Vologda to instruct Koba to go to the Caucasus to meet Kamo there and help him carry out an expropriation. Koba told Sergo Ordzhonikidze that he was pleased by his appointment. On 24 February 1912 Ordzhonikidze sent a letter to Lenin. 'I have seen Ivanovich and have a definite understanding with him. He is greatly pleased with the turn of events and greatly impressed.'[41] Koba left Vologda for the Caucasus, where he expected to meet Kamo. He appeared in Tiflis early in March 1912, but Kamo was not there. He was in a Turkish prison, having been arrested in Constantinople for illegal transport of arms to the Caucasus. The Turks soon released him into the custody of the local Georgian priests, from whom Kamo escaped to Bulgaria, where he was rearrested. A prominent Bulgarian revolutionary, Blagoev, a friend of Lenin, engineered Kamo's escape from prison. Kamo loaded a small steamer with weapons and explosives and was on his way to the Caucasian shores when the Turks again arrested him. This time Kamo bribed his way out of prison, and at the end of summer 1912 he finally appeared in Tiflis.[42] By that time, Koba was no longer there.

Not finding Kamo in Tiflis, Koba went to Baku, where he was investigated by the local revolutionaries, who suspected him of being an Okhrana agent. They called a secret meeting and invited Koba. An Okhrana agent, David Vissarionovich Bakhradze, also known as 'Nikolay Stepanovich Eriyuv', who signed his Okhrana reports with the codename 'Fikus', was present at this meeting and sent the following report: 'To Baku Okhrana Section. Yesterday the Baku Committee of the RSDWP was in session. Dzhugashvili, who arrived from the center, and the Committee member "Kuz'ma", [S. Shaumian] and others were present. The participants at the meeting accused Dzhugashvili of being a *provocateur*, an Okhrana agent. Dzhugashvili responded with the same accusations against them. Fikus.'[43]

Investigation of the charges against Koba was entrusted to Boris Nikolaevsky, a prominent Menshevik (and future émigré historian). Nikolaevsky and Koba met at the home of a Baku Bolshevik, Lev Sosnovsky.[44] Koba sat down far from the light so that his face could not be seen. He denied that he was an Okhrana agent, but Nikolaevsky found his answers evasive. They agreed to meet again but Koba did not show up, having left Baku by the end of March 1912. Nikolaevsky noticed Okhrana agents following him, and was soon arrested.[45] Early in April 1912 Koba arrived in Moscow, where Ordzhonikidze introduced him to Malinovsky. This was their first encounter and Koba could not but notice some obvious similarities between himself and Malinovsky: both their faces were heavily pockmarked; both had yellow eyes with a quick, penetrating, almost predatory look, which made a memorable impression on people; both spoke Russian with an accent. Soon Koba made another discovery: he realized that Malinovsky was an Okhrana agent and that both of them made treachery a way of life. Superficially, they immediately became close friends. Koba visited Malinovsky's apartment in Moscow several times and became friendly with his wife and two sons. Once Koba came when only one of the boys was at home. Koba talked to him for some time, but suddenly took the boy by the shoulder and hit him on the cheek, saying he should remember who was talking to him. Malinovsky was baffled when his son told him about Koba's outburst.[46] Malinovsky reported Koba's and Sergo's presence in Moscow to Zavarzin, who ordered surveillance of both of them and sent a special report to Director Beletsky with a copy of the Bolshevik platform for the forthcoming elections to the Fourth Duma, which Malinovsky had borrowed from Sergo and copied for Zavarzin. In his report Zavarzin asked Beletsky to order the arrest of Koba and Sergo, but stressed that the existence of the platform was known only to them and Zavarzin's informer, and that the arrests and investigation of Koba and Sergo had therefore to be conducted extremely carefully and not in Moscow because it might expose his 'secret central agent'.[47]

On 9 April 1912 Koba and Sergo boarded a train leaving for St Petersburg. Zavarzin sent a cable there:

Urgent. Petersburg. Personally for the chief of the Okhrana Section. Central Committee Social Democrats Sergo and co-opted Koba departed from Moscow to Petersburg from Nikolaev station, train no. 8. Accept surveillance data from agents Andreev, Astakhov, Pakhomov . . . Liquidation is desirable, but must be done exclusively by local ties without revealing Moscow sources. Colonel Zavarzin.[48]

To protect Malinovsky's cover, Zavarzin insisted that the arrests not be made in Moscow. While boarding the train to St Petersburg, Koba noticed three 'tails', and realized that Malinovsky had betrayed them. Without telling Ordzhonikidze, he slipped away from him and the Okhrana agents. A few days after his arrival in St Petersburg, Ordzhonikidze was arrested. (He was imprisoned for three years and then exiled to Siberia, to be released only after the February Revolution.) After his own arrival in St Petersburg, Koba moved into the home of Bolshevik Duma Deputy N. G. Poletaev, who enjoyed parliamentary immunity, and lived there for several days, helping Poletaev edit the first issue of the Bolshevik *Pravda*, which was financed and controlled by the Okhrana.[49] Director of Police Beletsky wanted to strengthen the Bolshevik faction by enabling *Pravda* to compete with the Menshevik *Luch*. The first issue of *Pravda* was published on 22 April 1912; that very day, Koba was arrested and brought to the St Petersburg Preliminary Detention Prison. A few days before his arrest, Koba had written a letter to Klara Zetkin, a Polish Social Democrat and Lenin's friend, who lived in Paris. Koba learned from Ordzhonikidze that Lenin had given Klara Zetkin some of the Tiflis 500-ruble banknotes. Koba wrote to her, requesting that she transfer the party money she had been given for safekeeping to the Central Committee, for financing the election campaign in the Fourth State Duma. He did not sign the letter.[50] Koba knew that Klara Zetkin would show the letter to Lenin; he meant to remind Lenin that it was he who had organized the Tiflis robbery and therefore should have a say in how the money was spent. The letter was intercepted by the Okhrana and brought to Eremin's attention. On 20 April 1912, two days before Koba's arrest, Eremin sent a copy of the letter to the Okhrana Foreign Agency in Paris with a covering note, stating that he could not identify the author of the unsigned letter.[51]

Finding himself in prison, Koba attempted to bargain his way out by betraying Kamo and accusing Shaumian of planning an expropriation. On the basis of Koba's denunciation, the Okhrana sent the chief of the Tiflis Okhrana, Colonel Pastrulin, a cable stating: 'Please, report immediately about the measures taken in connection with Shaumian's expected attempt to escape from exile and the arrival with stated purpose of Kamo (Ter-Petrosian).'[52] Pastrulin's agents searched in vain for Kamo in Tiflis. Then Pastrulin himself rushed to Baku with a large retinue of officers and detectives, but Kamo was not to be found there either. On 6 June 1912 Pastrulin cabled to Beletsky: 'Simon Ter-Petrosian [Kamo] has not been found in Baku.'[53]

The reopening of the Tiflis bank robbery case threatened to expose Koba's role in the robbery as well as Eremin's coverup of Koba's criminal involvement in it. Eremin knew that the author of the letter to Klara Zetkin was Koba. In his covering note to the chief of the Okhrana Foreign Agency in Paris, he had lied when stating that he did not know who the letter's author was. In order to cover himself against the possible charge of concealing information, he sent an 'afterthought' letter to the chief of the Foreign Agency on 11 June 1912 in which he stated:

In addition to the report of April 20 1912, no. 100007, the Department of Police notifies Your High Excellency that the author of the document without signature from St Petersburg might be Iosif Vissarionov DZHUGASHVILI, a peasant of Tiflis *Gubernia* and province, village of Didi-Lilo, who was exposed as being engaged in revolutionary activity in the ranks of the Russian Social Democratic Workers' Party, and who had been exiled from St Petersburg to the town of Vologda under open police surveillance for three years, whence he escaped on February 29 of this year, but on April 22 of this year Dzhugashvili was arrested in St Petersburg.

The report was signed by Eremin and co-signed by Vice-Director S. Vissarionov.[54]

Eremin's uncertainty in stating that Koba 'might be' the author of the letter to Klara Zetkin appears furtive, in light of Koba's imprisonment in St Petersburg. Koba had been in detention for almost two months by the time Eremin sent this updated response, although it would have been easy for Eremin to determine whether Koba was indeed the author of the letter to Klara Zetkin. Besides, Eremin had a seven-page report to the Okhrana, handwritten by Koba in prison a week before Eremin had sent his updated covering letter, with information on the status of the revolutionary parties and their leaders. In his report, Koba twice mentioned money that Lenin had, but he called it money from the Shmidt inheritance. He did not mention the Tiflis banknotes. Eremin ordered his secretary to type two copies of Koba's report, leaving out only Koba's complaint that Malinovsky was an untrustworthy Okhrana agent. Eremin sent one copy to the St Petersburg Okhrana Section, where Ordzhonikidze was undergoing interrogation: the arrests of Koba and Ordzhonikidze were related, since both had been prompted by Zavarzin's request. Moreover, Koba mentioned 'Sergo' in his report as one of the leading Bolsheviks. Eremin sent the other copy of Koba's report to the chief of the Foreign Agency, Krasilnikov, together with his 11 June 1912 covering letter stating that Koba 'might be' the author of the letter to Klara Zetkin. This covering letter was attached to a copy of Koba's unsigned report without mentioning his complaint againt Malinovsky. In his covering letter, Eremin did not mention either this attached unsigned report or that Koba was the author of it. Eremin was determined not to reveal that the attached unsigned document was actually a copy of a report written by his former agent, Iosif Dzhugashvili.

Koba's report to the Okhrana is a strange document. The way it is written makes it difficult to recognize it as a report by an Okhrana agent. Were it not for a listing of Bolshevik leaders, their addresses, assignments and responsibilities, the document could pass for a partisan commentary on various Social Democratic factions by a devoted member of Lenin's organization. Entitled 'Personnel composition', the list reads:

CENTRAL COMMITTEE consists of seven members, among whom are known 'Sergo' and 'Semeon'.

CENTRAL ORGANS: 'Social Democrat' and 'Workers' Gazette' – Lenin, Grigory Radomyslsky [ZINOVIEV] and Kamenev.

BUREAU OF FOREIGN ORGANIZATIONS. 'Inesa' Armand, Dr. Britman, Aleksey, Semashko and Vladimirsky.

TRANSPORT – in Leipzig, in the hands of Tarshis (Piatnitsa).

BUREAU OF PARIS SECTION OF FOREIGN ORGANIZATIONS OF R.S.D. W. P. Aleksey (lives in the apartment of Shatsky, 1 rue Lenereux), Valentin (Sorokin), lives in Fonteray aux Roses, Chernov (Grechnev), lives at rue de Lolbiac, apartment number not known.

CORRESPONDENCE with Russian groups is in the hands of Lenin's wife. (4, rue Marie-Rose.) The most important Leninists live in Paris: Lenin, Grigory Radomyslsky, Yury Kamenev, Mikhail Morozov, Semashko, Vladimirsky, Grechnev, Shapovalov, Zhitomirsky, Aleksey, Yury Begzadian, Bogdan Zezulinsky, Isaak, 'Nikolay Vasilievich' and others.[55]

Koba's report must have made Eremin wonder what kind of person his former agent was. On the one hand, Koba provided valuable and detailed information about various party factions, including the Bolsheviks. Out of seven members of the Bolshevik Central Committee, he knew Lenin, Sergo Ordzhonikidze and Semeon Shwartz, and mentioned only them. But as if he had forgotten that he was writing a report for the Okhrana, Koba many times stressed with unmistakable admiration that Lenin's faction was 'the most active and the strongest', that 'the Leninist party', 'the Party of Lenin' was 'the only party that has strengthened its position in Russia and abroad', and so on. Other revolutionary groups, especially the Menshevik-liquidators, Koba treated with obvious disdain, stressing repeatedly that they were 'in a pitiful condition'. Koba in his report expressed contempt for Trotsky, who 'represents only literary power'. Eremin must have realized that Koba's allegiance was at this point not with the Okhrana, but with Lenin. It was an allegiance that had its logic. In Prague, Lenin had co-opted Koba to the position of an agent of the Central Committee, while the Okhrana had arrested Koba twice in the course of less than a year and seemed unwilling to promote him to a meaningful position. A year later, Eremin was to state in a report to Director Beletsky: 'After the election of Dzhugashvili to the Central Committee of the party in the city of Prague he, having returned to Petersburg, went over into open opposition to the Government and broke completely his connection to the Okhrana.'[56]

Eremin must also have realized that in his report Koba had purposely avoided mentioning the stolen Tiflis banknotes by making a crafty substitution: he referred twice to the Shmidt inheritance, as if it, rather than the Tiflis banknotes, had been the money he had in mind when writing to

Klara Zetkin. In fact, Lenin had spent the Shmidt inheritance years earlier.[57]

Although the typist who copied Koba's report corrected it here and there, some of his non-Russian-sounding phrases remained intact. Following Eremin's instruction, the typist did not copy a part in which Koba complained about Malinovsky's misleading the Okhrana. Clearly, Eremin did not want the fact that Malinovsky was an Okhrana agent mentioned anywhere, following the Okhrana's strict rule to protect its agents' identity. But he kept Koba's handwritten report, including his complaint against Malinovsky, intact and placed it in Koba's file in the archive of the Special Section.[58] One of the officers in the Special Section, Lieutenant-Colonel Ivan Petrovich Vasiliev, learned about Koba's complaint regarding Malinovsky, and this was to have far-reaching consequences.

NOTES

1. Koba's letter was intercepted by the Okhrana and a copy of it was sent to the Paris Okhrana head-quarters with covering letter no. 97373, dated 10 January 1911. On file at the Hoover Institution. Copy in the author's archive.
2. Koba's 'Iosif' letter was intercepted by the Okhrana and a copy of it sent to the Paris Okhrana head-quarters with a covering letter #98570, dated 7 February 1911. On file at the Hoover Institution. Copy in the author's archive.
3. See *Padenie tsarskogo rezhima*, vol. III, Moscow/Leningrad, 1925, p. 286. See also Alexander Kerensky, *The Crucifixion of Liberty*, New York, 1934, p. 246.
4. Covering letter no. 98570, dated 7 February 1911, sent with Koba's 'Iosif' letter. On file at the Hoover Institution. Copy in the author's archive.
5. See *Padenie tsarskogo rezhima*, vol. VII, p. 359. The names of the officers assigned to Krasilnikov were Dolgov, Ergardt, Liustikh and Likhovsky.
6. Okhrana Report no. 101145, dated 14 March 1911. On file at the Hoover Institution. Copy in the author's archive.
7. Okhrana report no. 217 from the chief of the Vologda Province Gendarme Administration, dated 18 May 1911. On file at the Hoover Institution. Copy in the author's archive.
8. V. Rudich's taped testimony citing Olga Shatunovskaya's statement that a commission of Old Bolsheviks during the Khrushchev era investigated the rape case against Stalin at the time of his exile in Sol'vychegodsk. See also S. Vereshchak's articles, recounting Stalin's conversation with S. Surin, one of the exiles there and an Okhrana agent, about his stormy relations with Kuzakova.
9. Alexander Kolesnik, *Mify i pravda o Staline*, Kharkov, 1991, p. 10.
10. Ludmila Kafanova, 'O velikom druge i vozhde', *Novoe russkoe slovo*, 24 March 1977, p. 29, fn 10. See also Svetlana Alliluyeva, *Only One Year*, New York, 1969, pp. 381ff.
11. Evgeny Zhirnov, 'K. Kuzakov – syn I. V. Stalina', *Argumenty i fakty*, No. 39, 1995.
12. I. M. Dubinsky-Mukhadze, *Ordzhonikidze*, Moscow, 1963, pp. 74ff.
13. T. S. Bobrovskaya, *Provocateurs I Have Known*, London, 1931, pp. 26ff.
14. Dubinsky-Mukhadze, *Ordzhonikidze*, p. 74.
15. Roy Medvedev, *Let History Judge*, New York, 1971, p. 321, quoting Zavarzin's 'Absolutely Secret; Personal' letter, dated 17 August 1911, to Colonel Konissky.
16. See N. V. Krylenko, *Za piat' let, 1918–1922 g.*, Moscow, 1923, p. 331; Ralph Carter Elwood, *Roman Malinovsky: a Life without a Cause*, Newtonville, MA, 1977, p. 24; see also *Vechernie izvestiya Moskovskogo soveta*, no. 91, 5 November 1918.
17. A. E. Badaev, *Bolsheviki v gosudarstvennoi dume*, Moscow, 1954, p. 156.
18. On Malinovsky's career see *Delo provokatora Malinovskogo*, Respublika, Moscow, 1992. Also Paul Sacardy, 'Lenin's Deputy: the Story of a Double Agent', unpublished manuscript on file at the

Radio Liberty Committee; B. K. Erenfeld, 'Delo Malinovskogo', *Voprosy istorii*, no. 7, 1965; *Padenie tsarskogo rezhima*, vol. VII, p. 374 and listed references; 'Ot ministerstva yustitsii', *Vestnik vremennogo pravitelstva*, 16 June 1917; *Bolsheviki*, Moscow, 1918, p. X.

Evno Azef, an engineer by profession, was the head of the terrorist arm of the Social Revolutionary Party and a top-secret Okhrana agent. He masterminded many terrorist acts, among them several assassinations of high government officials. Driven by dark predatory impulses, Azef managed for many years to remain beyond the suspicion of both the Okhrana and the revolutionaries. General A. A. Lopukhin (to whom Koba and Kamo in 1905 had attributed their forged 'Lopukhin Report') was outraged by Azef's duplicity and confided to Vladimir Burtsev, a Social Revolutionary journalist and self-appointed exposer of Okhrana spies, that Azef was an Okhrana agent. Lopukhin was exiled for his exposure of Azef, who managed to escape and died in anonymity in Berlin. His handler, chief of the St Petersburg Okhrana, General Gerasimov, was forced to resign. The Azef scandal resulted in a long and thorough investigation of Okhrana practices and in the firing of many of its agents and informers. (It was in the course of this investigation that Okhrana Colonel Zasypkin submitted the report about the exposure and liquidation of the Avlabar press.) The Okhrana purge created a vacancy for Eremin's transfer to St Petersburg and Beletsky's appointment to the post of acting Vice-Director of the Department of Police. On Azef's career, see B. I. Gul', *Azef*; see also *Padenie tsarskogo rezhima*, vol. VII, p. 300 and listed references. On Lopukhin and Gerasimov see *Padenie tsarskogo rezhima*, vol. VII, pp. 369 and 323 and listed references.

19. Report of the chief of the Vologda Gendarmerie Department no. 622, dated 14 October 1911, quoting Lashevich's letter, attached to Okhrana covering letter no. 97527, dated 25 February 1912, with enclosed copy of Zavarzin's report no. 292791, dated 17 February 1912. On file at the Hoover Institution. Copy in the author's archive.
20. Medvedev, *Let History Judge*, p. 322.
21. Yulian Semenov, a prominent Soviet writer, suggested in a manuscript based on Okhrana documents that Bogrov was a tool of the Okhrana. He told the author about his findings on 3 February 1988, in New York, in the presence of Ilia Levkov.
22. This opinion was widely held at the time.
23. See *Padenie tsarskogo rezhima*, vol. VII, p. 310 and cited references.
24. 'Shkola filerov', *Byloe*, no. 3 (25), 1917.
25. Dubinsky-Mukhadze, *Kamo*, Moscow, 1974, pp. 142–54. See also his book *Ordzhonikidze*, Moscow, 1963, pp. 70–2.
26. Anna S. Allilueva, *Vospominaniya*, Moscow, 1946, pp. 107–10; Lev Trotsky, *Stalin*, New York, 1941, p. 135.
27. Okhrana Report no. 102383, dated 11 June 1912. On file at the Hoover Institution. Copy in the author's archive.
28. *Krasny arkhiv*, vol. 2 (105), 1941, p. 23.
29. 'Bolsheviki i departament politsii', *Russkoe slovo*, 19 May 1917.
30. *Bolsheviki*, pp. 210ff.
31. Ibid., p. 211 and cited references.
32. Bobrovskaya, *Provocateurs*, pp. 26ff. P. P. Zavarzin, *Zhandarmy i revolutsionery*, Paris, 1930, p. 195; 'Bolsheviki i departament politsii', p. 1.
33. V. I. Lenin, *Polnoe Sobranie sochinenii*, Moscow, 1958–65, p. 36, in letter to Maxim Gorky.
34. *Delo provokatora Malinovskogo*, Moscow, 1992, pp. 49–53. See also Lenin's testimony before the Extraordinary Investigative Commission of the Provisional Government, 'Ot ministerstva yustitsii', *Vestnik vremennogo pravitelstva* 16 June 1917.
35. A. K. Voronsky, *The Waters of Life and Death*, London, 1936; quoted in Elwood, *Roman Malinowsky*, p. 27.
36. 'Bolsheviki i departament politsii'. See also references under their names in *Bolsheviki*.
37. N. K. Krupskaya, *Reminiscences of Lenin*, Moscow and London, 1959, p. 216.
38. Voronsky, *The Waters*, p. 312; quoted in Elwood, *Malinovsky*, p. 27.
39. Ibid.
40. Okhrana Report no. 98536, dated 16 March 1912, with an intercepted letter from 'Grisha' in Paris to N. N. Silinskaya in Odessa, dated 29 February 1912. On file at the Hoover Institution. Copy in the author's archive.
41. *Krasny arkhiv*, no. 5 (78), 1936, p. 21.
42. I. Dubinsky-Mukhadze, *Kamo*, Moscow, 1974, pp. 156–62.
43. Dmitry Tabachnik, 'Obyknovennyi provokator', *Rabochaya gazeta*, Kiev, 27 March 1989. Also

'Seksot', *Kaleidoskop*, no. 323, 30 March 1989, pp. 6–9. The report had been discovered in the Baku archive by G. A. Arutunov.

44. Lev Sosnovsky was a relative of the present author. A prominent Soviet journalist, he perished in the Great Purges.

45. Edward Ellis Smith, *The Young Stalin: the Early Years of a Revolutionary*, London, 1968, pp. 252–6 and p. 403, fn. 535a.

46. Medvedev, *Let History*, p. 337 and fn. 88. Medvedev's 'famous Bolshevik in Moscow' in 1912 can refer only to Malinovsky.

47. Ibid. See also *Krasny arkhiv*, vol. 2 (105), 1941, p. 26.

48. Dubinsky-Mukhadze, *Ordzhonikidze*, p. 104.

49. 'Bolsheviki i departament politsii'. See also S. T. Possony, *Lenin: The Compulsive Revolutionary*, London, 1966, p. 162, fn.

50. Stalin, *Sochineniya*, vol. II, p. 417. See also Smith, p. 257; Dubinsky-Mukhadze, *Kamo*, pp. 156ff. The copy of Koba's letter to Zetkin was apparently removed from the Hoover Institution by an earlier researcher. When the author looked for it in 1974, both it and Eremin's accompanying covering letter no. 100007, dated 20 April 1912, were missing from the archive. The only thing remaining was a reference (to both the letter to Zetkin and to Eremin's covering letter no. 100007) in Okhrana report no. 102383, dated 11 June 1912 and signed by Vice-Director Vissarionov and the chief of the Special Section, Eremin. However, some of the earlier researchers in the archive, including Stanford professor S. T. Possony and his wife, had seen Koba's letter to Zetkin and remembered what it said about the Tiflis money.

51. Covering letter no. 100007 of 20 April 1912. See previous reference.

52. Dubinsky-Mukhadze, *Kamo*, p. 163.

53. Ibid.

54. Okhrana report no. 102383, dated 11 June 1912. On file at the Hoover Institution. Copy in the author's archive.

55. Covering letter no. 102383, dated 11 June 1912 and printed on the Special Section stationery, was signed by Vice-Director S. Vissarionov and the chief of the Special Section, Eremin. Attached are seven typewritten pages of Koba's report to the Okhrana (unsigned) with a penciled note '*Spravka bez no.* (reference without number), 5/18 June 1912'. On file at the Hoover Institution. Copy in the author's archive.

Also see Z. Serebriakova, 'Stalin i tsarskaya okhranka', in *Sovershenno secretno*, no. 7, Moscow, 1990, p. 21. Serebriakova writes about two documents she found in Soviet archives: (1) Stalin's original handwritten statement, which includes a complaint about Roman Malinovsky and which Eremin preserved in his office and placed in Stalin's file; (2) the shortened copy of the same report, which Eremin sent to the St Petersburg Okhrana, where Sergo Ordzhonikidze was being interrogated. Serebriakova found this shortened copy (without the complaint against Roman Malinovsky) in Ordzhonikidze's file. The other shortened copy Eremin sent to the Okhrana Foreign Agency in Paris under the heading '*Spravka bez no.*, 5/18 June 1912.'

The report begins with a brief summary of the 'general condition' of the Russian Social Democratic Workers' Party and praises the 'Bolshevik–Leninist faction, the most active and most united, remains the only one with some financial means, which are left over from the Shmidt inheritance'. The report continues to downgrade and ridicule all other factions of the Russian Social Democratic party'and praises the 'Party of Lenin.' The report ends with a list of leading Bolsheviks, entitled 'Personnel composition.'

56. See Eremin's report to Beletsky in Chapter 10, below.

57. On the Shmidt inheritance see Chapter 7 above, and *Bolsheviki*, pp. 101 and 243.

58. Z. Serebriakova, who found the original in the Central State Archive, and a copy (from which Stalin's complaint against Malinovsky is missing) in Ordzhonikidze's Okhrana file, describes her discoveries in 'Stalin i tsarskaya okhranka'. Serebriakova writes that the original of Stalin's report (which appears in published form as 'Circular Letter No. 1 on the Final Composition of the Central Committee of the RSDWP' in Stalin's *Sochineniya*, vol. II, p. 417) 'miraculously survived and is now discovered, moreover, in two archival deposits'. (That was the handwritten version in the Central State Archive and the typed copy in Ordzhonikidze's Okhrana file.) 'This alone proves Stalin's ties to the Okhrana', Serebriakova writes.

Stalin's report to the Okhrana survived because Stalin redefined it when he found it in his St Petersburg Okhrana file. He began to refer to it as his first circular letter to the party. Stalin did not know that Colonel Eremin had shortened copies of this report made and sent to the Okhrana

Foreign Agency headquarters in Paris and to Ordzhonikidze's interrogator under the heading *Spravka bez no.*. The copy in Ordzhonikidze's file was discovered by Serebriakova in 1990. How Stalin's report to the Okhrana survived is told in subsequent chapters, as is the story of his Okhrana file.

10

THE 'GREAT STATE SCANDAL'

Lieutenant-Colonel Ivan Petrovich Vasiliev served in the Special Section of the Department of Police, where Colonel Eremin headed a staff of ten officers and 12 secretaries. Because of his rank and long career, Vasiliev was considered a senior assistant to Eremin and often signed covering letters for him. He was born in 1872. After graduating from a military school in 1891, Vasiliev served in reserve army units until 1900, when he was transferred to the Separate Corps of Gendarmes and assigned to the Moscow Okhrana. He served there under its chief, Zubatov. Vasiliev was known to his fellow officers as a notorious *Zubatovetz* (follower of Zubatov). He was involved in instigating Jewish pogroms and printing anti-Semitic pamphlets, among them the infamous *Protocols of the Elders of Zion*. He was also close to extreme chauvinist groups like the Black Hundreds.[1] Among his fellow officers Vasiliev was also known as a 'drunkard and intriguer'.[2] In May 1910, he was assigned to the Special Section of the Department of Police.

Koba, in his June 1912 report to the Okhrana, accused Malinovsky of being an untrustworthy agent who was misleading the Okhrana. This accusation attracted Vasiliev's attention. Koba probably repeated this accusation during interrogation by Okhrana officers, among them Vasiliev. It so happened that by summer 1912, when the campaign for the election to the State Duma was on its way, Malinovsky's name was gaining prominence as a likely candidate from the Moscow electoral district. Vasiliev took Koba's assertion of Malinovsky's ties to the Okhrana seriously. He also came to the conclusion that high Department of Police officials were manipulating the elections, intending to plant their agent in the State Duma. This insight had an obvious ramification: if Malinovsky were exposed, it would provoke a state scandal concerning the criminal meddling by high police officials in the Duma electoral process. Such a scandal would topple Vasiliev's superiors in the Okhrana, including Eremin, thus creating vacancies for his own promotion to the top of the police establishment. The man Vasiliev hoped to replace was his immediate superior, Colonel Eremin. Vasiliev knew that Koba, by trying to unmask Malinovsky, intended to take Malinovsky's place as Lenin's right-hand man and also to become at the same time the top Okhrana agent in the Bolshevik organization. Vasiliev had learned about Koba from reports that had been received by the Special

Section; he had even signed some of the covering letters referring to Koba.[3] Thus, the unmasking of Malinovsky would serve the mutual interests of Vasiliev and Koba.

The decision to promote the election of Roman Malinovsky to the Duma was made by the Okhrana soon after his return from Prague in January 1912. Malinovsky at that time reported to the chief of the Moscow Okhrana Section, Colonel Zavarzin, that Lenin wanted him to run for the Duma seat as a delegate from Moscow. Zavarzin immediately took a train to St Petersburg to personally report the news to director of the Department of Police S. P. Beletsky, who sent Vice-Director Vissarionov to Moscow to interview Malinovsky and to determine whether his candidacy might be derailed by any criminal record. According to electoral law, a candidate had to obtain a 'Certificate of Good Standing', stating that the candidate had no criminal record. Vissarionov learned that Malinovsky had been sentenced for rape and petty theft. Despite this revelation, Beletsky and Vissarionov were inclined to promote Malinovsky's election to the Duma, but the chief of the Special Section, Colonel Eremin, objected, pointing out that it was illegal to interfere in the Duma electoral process and, besides, it was too dangerous because Malinovsky's criminal background and ties to the Okhrana might be exposed and, if they were, there would be a 'great state scandal'.[4] Despite Eremin's objection, Beletsky decided to plant Malinovsky in the Duma. He reported his decision for approval to the assistant minister of the interior, I. M. Zolotarev, who personally informed the minister of the interior, A. A. Makarov. The minister gave his consent. For the sake of secrecy, it was decided that only Beletsky and Vissarionov would have contact with Malinovsky.[5]

Malinovsky went to his native Plotsk, where he bribed a town clerk into giving him the needed Certificate of Good Standing.[6] According to electoral law, he also needed proof of six months of uninterrupted employment. Malinovsky obtained a job at a textile factory near Moscow, but he quarreled with his foreman, who threatened to fire him. Malinovsky reported this to Colonel Zavarzin, who asked Director Beletsky's advice. Beletsky's response was confusing. He stated that Malinovsky 'should not be deprived of his full rights, which are very important to him at the moment'.[7] Zavarzin interpreted this statement to mean that the foreman should be temporarily arrested, and on 25 April 1912 he was.[8] (Several months later, after Malinovsky's election, the man was released.)

On 2 July 1912, when the Duma election campaign was in progress, Koba was exiled to the town of Narym in western Siberia. Soon after his arrival in Narym, Koba infuriated his fellow exiles by befriending an Okhrana officer named Kibirov. The exiles summoned Koba to a comradely court, demanding an explanation. Koba said that Kibirov was not an enemy at the moment, but that he would not hesitate to kill him in the future revolutionary struggle. Some time later, he was summoned again to a 'comradely court', where one of the exiles, a petty thief named Bulanov, was accused of stealing from the peasants of a nearby village. Koba defended him, saying: 'Bulanov is a fighter for the cause of the exploited classes.' Bulanov confessed the crime, cried, and promised not to steal again. The exiles were insulted by Koba's demagoguery and one of them, a Georgian Jew, made a passionate speech in protest. Koba angrily snapped back in Georgian: '*Uria mamatskhali*' ('stinking Jew'). A Georgian Menshevik shook his head and commented, 'Bolsheviks are Bolsheviks . . . now they suddenly turn into anti-Semites as well.'[9]

In Narym, Koba met Semeon Surin, an Eser-Maximalist whom he had first met in 1906 in St Petersburg while visiting Kamo. At that time Surin was a member of the Maximalist-Bolshevik group with which Kamo cooperated. Later, Koba and Surin had served terms of exile in Sol'vychegodsk. Having known each other for years, they met as old friends who had no secrets from each other. Surin asked Koba how his affair with Maria Kuzakova, who had accused Koba of raping her, had ended.[10] Surin also confided to Koba that a scheme to assassinate the Tsar was in progress and that the attempt would be made during the forthcoming celebration of the 300th Anniversary of the House of Romanov. Koba decided to use this information to reinstate his relations with the Okhrana. He sent two letters to Lieutenant-Colonel I. P. Vasiliev, asking him to arrange a meeting with a high official responsible for the security of the Tsar so that he could help thwart a planned assassination attempt.[11] Vasiliev passed Koba's message on to I. M. Zolotarev, the assistant minister of the interior, who was responsible for the security of the Tsar and the royal family. Zolotarev agreed to meet Koba. For Koba to meet a man as important as Zolotarev would have been a fantastic feat had Zolotarev not been anxious to obtain vital information about a planned attempt on the Tsar's life. Koba's offer was given credibility by corroborating reports from other sources, among them an Okhrana agent living in Paris. (The assassination scheme was abandoned because the conspirators were warned that their plan was known to this informer[12].)

On 1 September 1912 Koba, carrying a passport in the name of 'Ivanov', left Narym almost openly. A short while later, Semeon Surin also 'escaped' – together with an Okhrana officer posing as a journalist.[13] Surin became an Okhrana agent in September 1912, when he was brought to St

Petersburg and threatened with the death penalty for his role in the assassination conspiracy against the Tsar but he was offered clemency in exchange for helping to thwart the plot. (In April 1917, when many Okhrana agents were exposed, Surin was listed among them as 'a member of the Petrograd organization of the Social Revolutionary Party, who turned into a *provocateur* before the February Revolution'.[14])

Koba and Zolotarev met in a private room of a fashionable restaurant.[15] Koba offered to help the Okhrana foil the plot to assassinate the Tsar, saying: 'I can provide you with information – a terrorist act is being hatched, but I haven't yet fully uncovered it, I need some time, and for this I need money.' Zolotarev agreed to Koba's request.[16] He could not provide Koba with money out of his ministerial budget, which did not have a provision for payment to Okhrana agents and informers, but he could arrange for Koba to be employed by the St Petersburg Okhrana and authorize his compensation through the Okhrana payroll. On Zolotarev's recommendation, Koba was employed as an agent of the St Petersburg Okhrana section in September 1912.[17] In late September he went to Moscow, where he took part in a party meeting at which Malinovsky's Duma candidacy was approved.[18]

By this time, Colonel Zavarzin was no longer Malinovsky's handler. On 10 July 1912 Zavarzin had been succeeded by Colonel A. P. Martynov (not to be confused with the former chief of the Baku Okhrana) as the new chief of the Moscow Okhrana. On 30 September 1912 Malinovsky reported to Martynov that he had been chosen as one of the electors from Moscow.[19] Martynov requested Beletsky's opinion on whether the scheme of Malinovsky's election to the Duma should be allowed to proceed. Beletsky again consulted with Zolotarev and Interior Minister Makarov, and they gave their consent. Lenin contributed 300 rubles to Malinovsky's election effort. Two Moscow Bolsheviks and Okhrana agents informed the Okhrana about Lenin's contribution.[20]

On 11 October 1912 Vice-Director Vissarionov sent a letter to his superior Beletsky stating that electoral law prohibited people with a criminal record from running for a Duma seat and advised him to ask Interior Minister Makarov 'whether the Moscow Governor should be informed of this prohibition, or this person should go unnoticed by him'. Vissarionov had in mind the Moscow governor, General V. F. Dzhunkovsky, who by law had to approve Malinovsky's candidacy. Beletsky wrote on the margin of this letter: 'The minister was informed. Let the elections take their natural course. S. B.' General Dzhunkovsky, not suspecting the existence of Malinovsky's criminal record and of the

Okhrana's scheme to plant its agent in the Duma, approved his candidacy.[21] On 17 October 1912 Beletsky cabled Martynov: 'The question of the person known to you participating in the election to be left to its natural course.' Martynov replied: 'The case is left to its natural course. Success guaranteed. Colonel Martynov.'[22] On 26 October 1912 Malinovsky was elected to the Duma. The same day Martynov cabled Beletsky: 'Carried out successfully.'[23]

Lenin was triumphant. '*For the first time* we have an *outstanding worker-leader* among our people in the *Duma*', he wrote with heavy underscoring.[24] Malinovsky, with his wife and two sons, moved from Moscow to St Petersburg, where they rented a spacious apartment. In addition to his lucrative Duma salary, Malinovsky's Okhrana salary was raised from 100 to 500 rubles, and then increased to 700 rubles per month. By comparison, the salary of General Dzhunkovsky, the governor of Moscow, was only 500 rubles per month. Malinovsky was also paid 25–50 rubles for every piece of information related to party activities in Moscow that he sent to Moscow Okhrana Chief Martynov. He was given the status of a 'special agent of the Department of Police' with the codename 'X'. He reported only to Beletsky or Vissarionov, communicating with them either by a special telephone installed in his apartment, in private rooms of fashionable restaurants, or in their homes. Beletsky, Vissarionov and Martynov considered Malinovsky the 'pride of the Okhrana'.[25]

Lenin moved from Paris to the city of Cracow, in the Austrian part of Poland near the Russian border, to make it easier for him to maintain contact with Malinovsky and other Bolshevik Duma deputies. Among the 442 elected deputies were 13 Social Democrats, 6 Bolsheviks and 7 Mensheviks. Lenin insisted on the Menshevik–Bolshevik split, and Beletsky was just as strongly in favor of it.[26] Lenin sent drafts of his speeches to Malinovsky, who took them to Beletsky or Vissarionov for review and minor corrections and then delivered them in the Duma.[27]

But dark clouds began to appear over this Okhrana–Bolshevik symbiosis. Lieutenant-Colonel I. P. Vasiliev started a secret campaign, attempting to expose Malinovsky's ties to the Okhrana. He sent a number of anonymous letters to the Menshevik newspaper *Luch*, stating that Malinovsky was an Okhrana agent. The paper's editors ignored what they considered to be slanders, but rumors began to spread. Vasiliev then wrote an anonymous letter to Lidia Dan, the wife of the Menshevik leader F. I. Dan, offering to meet her secretly and prove that he was a high Okhrana official and that he had evidence of Malinovsky's duplicity. He suggested that Dan signify her agreement to this meeting by a certain newspaper advertisement; she ignored the offer.[28]

Koba, meanwhile, was hoping to expose Malinovsky for his own reasons.[29] Early in November 1912 he went to Cracow to see Lenin, intending to inform him of Malinovsky's Okhrana ties. Upon his arrival Koba quickly recognized the futility of any attempt to convince Lenin of Malinovsky's treachery, as Lenin was far too fond of having Malinovsky as his mouthpiece in the Duma. Koba decided that exposing Malinovsky would have to wait for an opportune moment. At the end of November 1912 Koba returned to St Petersburg to work on the editorial board of *Pravda*. Before parting with Lenin, he informed him that he had chosen a new alias, 'Vasiliev', to take the place of 'Ivanovich'. This alias reflected his secret alliance with his new Okhrana 'godfather', Lieutenant-Colonel Ivan Petrovich Vasiliev. From this point on, Lenin and other initiated party members referred to Koba as 'Vasiliev', or its derivatives 'Vasily' and 'Vaska'.

At the end of November 1912 Koba returned to St Petersburg. He initiated an editorial policy in total contradiction to Lenin's instructions and to the policy of Beletsky: instead of advocating a Bolshevik–Menshevik split, Koba's articles called for 'unity in the proletarian class-struggle . . . unity at all costs'.[30] Koba also delayed publication of Lenin's articles. He even refused to pay Lenin for them. Lenin was extremely annoyed: 'Why has the money not been sent yet? We *need* money. It is very *important*', he complained.[31] Spite against Lenin and the Okhrana for promoting Malinovsky instead of him was at the heart of Koba's new stance.

In December 1912, in a letter to the *Pravda* editorial board, Lenin attacked Koba personally. 'Get rid of Vasiliev as soon as possible, otherwise he cannot be saved; he has already done the most important work, but he is still needed.'[32] Perhaps what Lenin had in mind was that Koba had done important work in expropriations and might still be needed to do such work, and that otherwise there was no point in retaining him. Director Beletsky reported to Assistant Minister of the Interior Zolotarev, 'The situation in the Social Democratic Duma faction is such now that it is possible for the six Bolsheviks to be induced to split the faction into Bolsheviks and Mensheviks. Lenin supports this. See his letter.'[33] Zolotarev agreed to Beletsky's proposal that Malinovsky be instructed to provoke the split. Lenin intended to give the same instruction to Malinovsky. At the end of December 1912 he asked the Bolshevik Duma deputies to come to Cracow for a conference. Lenin summoned Koba too, in order to remove him from the *Pravda* editorial board. At the conference, Lenin insisted on splitting the Duma faction and all agreed. After the conference, Malinovsky sent a long and detailed report to Beletsky, listing all those present, among them Koba, and described the agenda discussed.[34]

Also after the conference, Koba wrote to Zolotarev, reminding the assistant minister of the interior that he had had the honor of being introduced to him in a restaurant and stating that he had observed Malinovsky closely at Cracow and that Malinovsky was at heart with Lenin and worked more zealously for the Bolsheviks than for the Okhrana. Koba asked Zolotarev to remove Malinovsky from the Okhrana and offered himself as the chief agent in the Bolshevik organization.[35] Zolotarev was extremely annoyed and threatened by Koba's letter. He was afraid of being held personally responsible, as in fact by law he was, for all Okhrana operations, including the scheme to plant Malinovsky in the Duma.[36] He also resented Koba's communication with him over the head of his Okhrana handler. On the margin of Koba's letter Zolotarev wrote that it was not permissible for an agent to go 'over the heads of his superiors', adding, 'This agent should be deported to Siberia for good. He is asking for it.'[37] Zolotarev gave Koba's letter to Vissarionov, who was substituting for Beletsky. Vissarionov placed the letter in Koba's file at the Special Section. A short while later, on 25 January 1913, Zolotarev resigned and was transferred to another post; two years later, he became a senator. General V. F. Dzhunkovsky, the governor of Moscow at the time of Malinovsky's election, was appointed the new assistant minister of the interior in place of Zolotarev.[38]

Koba hoped that his letter to Zolotarev would lead to the dismissal of Malinovsky from the Duma and the Okhrana. While waiting for Malinovsky's downfall, he tried his hand at theoretical writing. Lenin needed a non-Russian to publicize his views on the nationalities problem. Under Lenin's guidance, Koba wrote a short article, which was published on 12 January 1913 in the Russian newspaper *Sotzial-Demokrat* in Paris. He signed the article 'K. Stalin'. This was the first time he used the name by which he was to become known to history.[39] Early in January 1913 Lenin sent Koba to Vienna with an introductory letter to Alexander Troyanovsky and his wife, Elena Rozmirovich, who at that time joined Lenin's supporters. In their apartment, Koba met Nikolay Bukharin, a young Marxist from Moscow, who had just escaped from exile. The circumstances of his arrest had convinced Bukharin that Malinovsky was an Okhrana agent. Bukharin attempted to prove this to Lenin. He was unsuccessful: Lenin accused him of 'malicious slander' and threatened to brand him a traitor if he did not stop slandering Malinovsky. Lenin insisted that the Mensheviks were behind the 'dark campaign of slander being waged against this wonderful Bolshevik'.[40]

While staying in Troyanovsky's apartment, Koba for the first time met Lev Trotsky, who barely heeded him. Years later, all Trotsky recalled about the meeting was a 'glint of animosity' in Koba's 'yellow eyes'.[41] Koba and Trotsky were to remain enemies for the rest of their lives. As for Bukharin, Koba must have found him an eager, if unwitting, ally in his scheme to expose Malinovsky. While waiting for an opportunity to destroy his rival, Koba, on Lenin's advice, worked on an essay entitled 'Marxism and the Nationalities Problem', an enlargement of his earlier article. Lenin asked Bukharin and Troyanovsky to help Koba locate and translate related works by Austrian authors, since Koba knew no German, and he edited Koba's essay. The most striking feature of this essay was the attention it devoted to the Jews and the Jewish Bund: in all, there were 174 comments concerning Jews, all hostile. Again, Koba signed the essay K. Stalin.[42]

In January 1913, Lenin asked Koba to help Kamo organize a large expropriation in the Caucasus. Koba at once saw an opportunity to expose Malinovsky, and the advice he offered Lenin was in effect a tangled provocation. On Koba's suggestion, Lenin sent Elena Rozmirovich to Tiflis with a message to Kamo after providing her with 500-ruble banknotes with undoctored serial numbers. Before her departure, Koba sent an anonymous message to the Okhrana, revealing the time and purpose of her trip there and her plan to visit her parents in Kiev on her way to Tiflis. When Rozmirovich crossed the border, she came under the observation of Okhrana agents, who, knowing her destination to be Tiflis, gave her the codename 'Tiflisskaya'.[43] After her arrival in St Petersburg, on 20 January 1913, Rozmirovich was arrested. The Okhrana found on her 'highly incriminating material evidence' – a message to Kamo and the stolen Tiflis banknotes. A long prison sentence seemed unavoidable. A few days earlier, the Tiflis Okhrana reported Kamo's arrest.[44] Kamo had arrived in Tiflis at the end of the summer of 1912, after escaping from his Turkish and Bulgarian captors. Not finding Koba there, he had gone to Baku, where the local revolutionaries had urged him to abandon expropriations and escape abroad. Kamo then went to Moscow to visit Leonid Krasin, who had parted company with Lenin and was working as an engineer. 'You are indeed crazy if you are thinking of an expropriation at this time', Krasin told him.[45] Kamo returned to Tiflis and managed to gather a small band of local criminals with whom, on 24 September 1912, he unsuccessfully attacked a money transport on the Khodzhar highway. Heavy rain helped the robbers avoid capture. Colonel Pastrulin reported Kamo's robbery attempt to Director Beletsky, who ordered the Okhrana to spare no effort in apprehending Kamo. Nevertheless, Kamo managed to evade capture for several months, before being arrested in Tiflis on 10 January 1913.[46]

Elena Rozmirovich's parents notified her husband Alexander Troyanovsky about her arrest. Koba and Bukharin, who were still in Vienna, convinced Troyanovsky that Malinovsky had caused Elena's arrest. Troyanovsky sent a letter to Elena's parents in Kiev, stating that their daughter's arrest took place 'under strange circumstances. If she is not set free in the next few days, it will provide me with indisputable proof that a certain important party leader masterminded a provocation and I shall get even with him.' He threatened to expose this leader as an Okhrana agent and thus cause a great state scandal.[47] Troyanovsky's letter was intercepted by the Okhrana and a copy brought to Beletsky, who showed it to Malinovsky. Malinovsky immediately understood that Troyanovsky was threatening to expose him and became hysterical. He swore that he had nothing to do with Rozmirovich's arrest and pleaded, tears in his eyes, with Beletsky to release her at once. Beletsky attempted to calm him down and to explain that her release would only prove that Troyanovsky's suspicion was correct. Malinovsky would not listen, and Beletsky reluctantly ordered Rozmirovich's release.[48] As Beletsky predicted, Troyanovsky interpreted his wife's release as proof of Malinovsky's treachery and told Lenin about his conclusion. Lenin, however, once again categorically dismissed the accusation; as a result, Troyanovsky broke off contact with him. Elena Rozmirovich was greatly surprised by her release from prison. She did not suspect Malinovsky of having betrayed her, since she had not told him of her planned arrival in St Petersburg or her mission in Tiflis, and she sided with Lenin in defending Malinovsky against her husband.

Malinovsky, meanwhile, had no idea who had instigated the arrest of Rozmirovich. Koba behaved like an old friend towards him. On 20 January 1913, the day of Elena Rozmirovich's arrest, Koba sent Malinovsky a letter, stating 'From Vasily. Greetings, *druzhishche* [old pal].' He mentioned 'Galina' – Elena Rozmirovich's alias. He signed it, 'Your Vas.'[49] The fact that Koba twice refers to 'Galina' in his letter suggests the letter was meant as a diversion, intended to avert any suspicion of his involvement in the provocation of her arrest. Both Malinovsky and Beletsky were at a loss as to who had engineered the 'Rozmirovich provocation'. At first, Beletsky suspected Yakov Sverdlov, who shortly thereafter had come from Cracow to work on the *Pravda* board. Sverdlov was arrested on 10 February 1913. The suspicion proved unfounded, but Sverdlov was not released. On 15

February 1913 Beletsky arrested the editor of *Pravda*, M. E. Chernomazov, an Okhrana agent.[50] During his interrogation, Chernomazov convinced Beletsky that he had no knowledge of Rozmirovich's visit to Russia and could not have provoked her arrest.

Koba arrived in St Petersburg on 16 February 1913.[51] He hoped that, by this time, Malinovsky had been exposed. Koba did not know that Beletsky was racking his brains trying to determine who had provoked Rozmirovich's arrest. Malinovsky reported Koba's arrival to Beletsky, who ordered that Koba's Okhrana file be brought to him. Beletsky found there Koba's letter to Zolotarev, in which Koba accused Malinovsky of being an untrustworthy Okhrana agent, and Zolotarev's instruction to exile Koba to Siberia 'for good'. Beletsky also discovered in Koba's file his report to the Okhrana, in which he leveled the same charge against Malinovsky. Beletsky realized that Koba's obvious motive in provoking Rozmirovich's arrest was his intense rivalry with Malinovsky.

Rozmirovich's plan to go to Tiflis and establish contact with Kamo focused Beletsky's attention on Koba's Tiflis roots and also brought up the nagging question of his involvement in Kamo's current expropriation schemes and earlier crimes, including the Tiflis bank robbery. Beletsky, who had closely followed Kamo's case, knew that Colonel Eremin had played an important role in the investigation of the Tiflis robbery. He asked Eremin about Koba. Eremin replied that Koba had been his agent in the past and had supplied him with information at the time of his service in Tiflis.

On 22 February 1913 Beletsky ordered the release from prison of *Pravda* editor Chernomazov. The same day, Chernomazov told Malinovsky that in the course of his interrogations he understood that an Okhrana agent was operating at the top of the party leadership and that the Okhrana had known in advance that 'Galina' was to travel to Tiflis and Kiev. At the time of her arrest only a very limited number of the most important leaders could have known about her arrival in St Petersburg. Malinovsky immediately reported this conversation to Beletsky, saying that besides him another Okhrana agent was operating among the top Bolsheviks, someone who threatened him personally, and that 'all these circumstances prove, that there is a person near the "six" who is connected to the intelligence organs of the Empire'.[52] ('The six' referred to the six Bolshevik deputies in the Duma.) Beletsky confided in Malinovsky that this *agent provocateur* was Koba and that he would be exiled for a long time and would not be able to escape. Beletsky instructed Malinovsky to invite Koba to a fund-raising party for *Pravda*, scheduled to take place on 23 February 1913, so that Koba could be arrested. Koba came and sat at a table next to Bolshevik Duma deputy Shagov.[53] Several gendarmes walked into the hall and moved toward Koba. 'Dzhugashvili', one of the officers said, 'we have finally got you!' Koba angrily replied, 'I am not Dzhugashvili, my name is Ivanov.' The officer laughed, saying, 'Tell these stories to your grandmother', and ordered Koba to follow him.[54] Malinovsky walked next to Koba, protesting his arrest and promising to take all necessary measures to free him.[55]

Two days later Malinovsky sent a brief letter to Troyanovsky at his Vienna address. He twice mentioned 'Galia' (Rozmirovich) but refrained from making any reference to Koba's arrest.[56] Chernomazov, the editor of *Pravda* and an Okhrana agent, wrote to Lenin the same day, reporting Koba's arrest, using Koba's alias 'Vasily'. In his long and emotional letter, Chernomazov stated that he had been greatly surprised to see 'Vasily' at the fund-raising party. He concluded his letter on a highly emotional note, stating: 'Someone is interfering. I am racking my brains trying to figure out who it is. The situation is terrible. The snatching of the Georgian [Koba] has cast me down. I have the feeling of careening down the pass of misery . . .'.[57]

That same day, 25 February 1913, Lenin, as yet unaware of Koba's arrest, wrote to Malinovsky, 'Why is there no news from Vasily? We are worried.'[58] In another letter, sent on the same day to Bolshevik Duma deputy N. N. Podvoysky, Lenin wrote, 'Vaska must be protected. Of course, he is unstable, he is too sick.'[59] Five days later, on 1 March 1913, Lenin, still unaware of Koba's arrest, wrote to a St Petersburg Bolshevik, A. E. Akselrod, complaining that he had received only 'one letter from Vasily, the other was lost'.[60]

Among many Okhrana cases of concern to Beletsky at the time was the 'Finkelshtein case', which, it turned out, involved Koba. A Berlin newspaper applied for permission for its correspondent Finkelshtein (one of the aliases of Maxim Litvinov) to come to Russia to cover the celebration of the 300th anniversary of the House of Romanov. According to secret inform-ation received by the Okhrana, Finkelshtein intended to come to Russia under journalistic cover to take part in an attempt on the Tsar's life.[61] Litvinov probably intended to come to Russia to help Koba and Kamo organize an expropriation, as in Tiflis in 1907. (It is possible that Koba invented the assassination plot in order to divert attention from the Tiflis robbery case.) In the course of investigating the Finkelshtein case it was discovered that some of the documents had been lost. Beletsky summoned his assistant (a distant relative), N. V. Veselago, to his office, and asked him to locate these documents, since Veselago was in charge of this particular case. Veselago recalled years later that Beletsky suddenly became silent and pensive. 'Nikolay Vladimirovich', he then said to Veselago, 'if one of these documents – which, by the way, are to be obtained as soon as possible – refers to "Koba", bring it directly to me.' Veselago had never heard the name Koba. 'Yes, sir, but may I inquire who Koba is?', he asked. 'Might he appear in a document under another name?' Beletsky thought for a moment. 'You have a point', he replied. 'Koba might indeed be recorded as "Dzhugashvili" – his real name. He is one of our agents. That's all. Many thanks.'[62]

This may have been the point at which Meer Valakh's aliases 'Finkelshtein' and 'Maxim Litvinov' triggered an association with Koba and Kamo in Beletsky's mind. Beletsky knew the ruling of the Tiflis regional court: 'According to the deposition of the prosecutor, the defendant Simon Arshakov Ter-Petrosian [Kamo] at present does not suffer from disintegration of mental faculties.'[63] This meant a new investigation of the Tiflis robbery case, in which Kamo might incriminate Koba as his accomplice and implicate the Okhrana. A few days later, when Veselago was about to take a train to Moscow to work in the Okhrana archive there, Beletsky summoned him again. 'When you arrive in Moscow, tell Colonel Martynov that he should not worry about Malinovsky', he told Veselago. 'Everything is in order with Malinovsky. The Colonel will understand.'[64] Beletsky thought that in having arrested Koba he had eliminated the threat of Malinovsky's exposure, and he wanted to assure Martynov on this point.

Beletsky requested information on Koba not only from the Special Section, but also from the local Okhrana in places where Koba might have committed provocations. Reports on Koba from other Okhrana sections were piling up on Beletsky's desk.[65] One such report stated that Koba was 'not married; father Vissarion, place of residence unknown. Mother Ekaterina lives in Gori . . .'. Seven years after Vissarion's murder, Koba was still hiding his father's death from the Okhrana. The report also provided Koba's physical description: 'chin sharp, voice quiet, ears of middle size, usual posture, birthmark on left ear . . . second and third toes fused'.[66] Beletsky's and Eremin's fears that Kamo would expose Koba's real role in the expropriations did not materialize: Kamo did not produce any evidence against him. Kamo's interrogator reported: 'The defendant Ter-Petrosian gives very verbose testimony. The investigation is not able to trace his party contacts, or expose or indict his co-conspirators.'

On 1 March 1913, Kamo's case was brought for an open hearing before the Tiflis Military Tribunal. His lawyer later stated: 'Kamo did not deny facts that related to him personally, but he did not give any real data, either to the judges or the interrogators, about other persons.'[67] On 1 March 1913 Kamo was sentenced to death by hanging on four counts: taking part in the armed uprising in 1905; the Tiflis bank robbery in 1907; his escape from prison in 1911; and the armed robbery on the Khodzhar highway in 1912. But his death sentence was commuted to 20 years' imprisonment in the general amnesty declared on the occasion of the 300th anniversary of the Romanov dynasty.[68] Koba's case, on the other hand, was decided in secret, as were all cases of provocations by Okhrana collaborators. When Beletsky completed his investigation, he obtained a 'Decision of the Highest Authority' to exile Koba for four years to a remote Siberian village. On 2 July 1913 Koba was transported by train to the Siberian town of Krasnoyarsk, from where he was shipped down the Yenisey River to the village of Turukhansk.

Before closing Koba's case, Beletsky ordered Colonel Eremin to submit a written report on what he knew about Koba's Okhrana career. Eremin provided Beletsky with a brief summary of what he knew about Koba, which was typed on Department of Police Special Section stationery. The report read:

Benevolent Sir Stepan Petrovich,
Iosif Vissarionov Dzhugashvili, who has been exiled by Administrative Decree to the Turukhansk region, provided the Chief of Tiflis G.G.A. [Gubernia Gendarmerie Administration] with valuable intelligence information when he was arrested in 1906.

In 1908 the chief of the Baku Okhrana Section received from Dzhugashvili a series of intelligence reports, and afterward, upon his arrival in St Petersburg, Dzhugashvili became an agent of the St Petersburg Okhrana Section.

Dzhugashvili's work was distinguished by accuracy, but was fragmentary. After the election of Dzhugashvili to the Central Committee of the party in the city of Prague he, having returned to St Petersburg, went over into open opposition to the Government and broke completely his connection to the Okhrana.

I am informing you, dear sir, of the above for your personal consideration in the conduct of operational work.

With assurance of my high esteem,

A. Eremin[69]

The report was factual and fair, which was in line with the opinion of N. V. Veselago about its author: 'Colonel Eremin was a strict, demanding person and a follower of formalities.'[70] While writing his report, Eremin already knew that he had been demoted from the position of the chief of the Special Section and appointed chief of the Gendarmerie Administration in Finland. Eremin's demotion, Beletsky's request to Eremin to write a report on Koba, and Koba's exile happened at the same time and were not coincidences. Beletsky suspected Eremin of protecting a dangerous *provocateur*, and he also suspected him of helping Koba in his attempt to expose Malinovsky. Beletsky based his suspicion on the fact that Eremin from the very beginning was against the Okhrana's meddling in Malinovsky's election to the Duma. Besides, Beletsky knew that some high-placed Okhrana officer had sent anonymous letters to the Menshevik paper *Luch* and had contacted Lidia Dan, in an effort to expose Malinovsky. Beletsky suspected the wrong man: the treacherous high Okhrana officer was not Eremin but Eremin's assistant, I. P. Vasiliev. (Vasiliev did finally become chief of the Special Section of the Department of Police, but his tenure was short-lived. Appointed to the post on 15 January 1917 he surrendered to the Provisional Government on 1 March 1917).[71]

The order for Eremin's transfer to Finland was issued on 11 June 1913.[72] Eremin signed his last Special Section document on 19 June 1913. On the same day, Director Beletsky sent the 'top secret' instruction to all Okhrana sections to address all correspondence 'until further notice' to deputy chief of the Special Section M. E. Broetsky.[73] But on Friday 12 July 1913 Eremin was still in the Special Section, winding up his duties there.[74] Beletsky placed Eremin's report on Koba in a 'TOP SECRET' file marked IOSIF VISSARIONOV DZHUGASHVILI. The rubber-stamped warning on it read, 'NOT TO BE OPENED WITHOUT THE PERMISSION OF THE HIGHEST AUTHORITY', that is, the authority of the Tsar. Beletsky collected in this file all Okhrana reports on Koba that he had been able to locate: intercepted letters from and to Koba; Koba's letter to Zolotarev; Koba's prison photographs; his reports to the Okhrana; his signed depositions, and his signed receipts for money he had been paid by the Okhrana. The file with all these documents was sealed and placed in a large iron safe located in a guarded secret room of the Special Section of the Department of Police together with all files of former Okhrana agents who were no longer active because they had retired, died, or been dismissed.[75]

Beletsky could not have foreseen that future events in Russia would turn Koba's file into a time bomb of immensely destructive power, that it would shake off the archival dust and emerge at the center of secret conspiracies and bloody purges that would convulse the entire country and hurl millions of people into an abyss of suffering.

NOTES

1. See E. Evseev, 'Istoriya sionizma v tsarskoi rossii', *Voprosy istorii*, 5 (May 1973), p. 72.
2. *Padenie tsarskogo rezhima*, Moscow/Leningrad, 1925, vol. III, p. 176, and vol. VII, p. 314.
3. See Vasiliev's signature 'for the Chief of the Special Section' on the copy of Colonel Pastrulin's Report No. 53-C, dated 14 March 1911. On file at the Hoover Institution. Copy in the author's archive.
4. *Padenie tsarskogo rezhima*, vol. III, p. 281, and vol. V, pp. 212–13. See also 'Ot ministerstva yustitsii', *Vestnik vremennogo pravitelstva*, 16 June 1917; 'Bolsheviki i departament politsii', *Russkoe slovo*, 19 May 1917, p. 1.
5. *Padenie tsarskogo rezhima*, vol. III, pp. 108 and 280.
6. *Padenie tsarskogo rezhima*, vol. III, p. 283. See also N. V. Krylenko, *Za piat' let, 1918–1922 g.*, Moscow, 1923, p. 343.
7. *Rabochaya gazeta*, 62, 21 May 1917, p. 3. See also Ralph Carter Elwood, *Roman Malinovsky: A Life without a Cause*, Newtonville, MA, 1977, p. 82, fn. 62, for other references.
8. Ralph Carter Elwood, *Roman Malinovsky: a Life without a Cause*, p. 35.
9. See N. Karganov, 'Iz proshlogo Stalina', *Vozrozhdenie*, 13 January 1929.
10. S. Vereshchak, 'Stalin v tur'me: vospominaniya politicheskogo', *Dni*, 24 January 1928.
11. See Chapter 29, below for I. A. Zelensky's 'confession' at the Bukharin Show Trial. Zelensky 'confessed' that he had sent from his place of exile in Narym two letters to an officer of the gendarmerie whom he knew as 'Vasily Konstantinovich'. From Zelensky's forced 'confession' – one of many instances in which Stalin forced his victims to confess slightly altered versions of events in his own life – Stalin's relations with Vasiliev can be inferred.
12. See *Padenie tsarskogo rezhima*, vol. I, pp. 293, 298, 318, 319. V. L. Burtsev suspected a certain S. A. Shtakelberg and he convinced the conspirators to refrain from carrying out the attempt on the Tsar's life. Shtakelberg was indeed a secret collaborator of the Okhrana. Ibid., vol. VII, p. 438.
13. Boris Souvarine, *Stalin: a Critical Survey of Bolshevism*, London, 1939, p. 128; Karganov; Vereshchak; Edward Ellis Smith, *The Young Stalin: The Early Years of an Elusive Revolutionary*, London, 1968, p. 260.
14. *Russkoe slovo*, 15 April 1917, p. 3. 'Provokatory'.
15. See Alexander Orlov, 'The Sensational Secret behind the Damnation of Stalin', *Life*, 23 April 1956.
16. *Padenie tsarskogo rezhima*, vol. V, p. 62. After the February Revolution, Zolotarev testified about his encounter with a person in a private room of a restaurant, who offered to foil an assassination attempt. Zolotarev said that had he not agreed to the offer, the agent 'would have simply walked out on me' and the assassination conspiracy would not have been exposed.
17. Evidence of Koba's employment by the St Petersburg Okhrana is found in a report written by Eremin summarizing Koba's activities in the Okhrana.
18. I. V. Stalin, *Sochineniya*, Moscow, 1946–51, vol. II, p. 420.
19. *Bolsheviki*, Moscow, 1918, pp. X and XI.
20. The agents' names were A. A. Poliakov and A. S. Romanov. See 'Bolsheviki i departament politsii; Ot ministerstva yustitsii'; N. V. Krylenko, *Za piat' let, 1918–1922 q.*, Moscow, 1923, p. 334.
21. *Padenie tsarskogo rezhima*, vol. V, pp. 85ff.
22. *Bolsheviki*, pp. XI–XII; also 'Bolsheviki i departament politsii'.
23. Ibid.
24. V. I. Lenin, *Polnoe sobranie sochinenii*, 1958–65, vol. XLVIII, p. 133. See also Elwood, *Young Stalin*, p. 28.
25. *Bolsheviki*, Introduction. *Padenie tsarskogo rezhima*, vol. III, p. 280; vol. V, p. 212.
26. *Padenie tsarskogo rezhima*, vol. III, p. 286.
27. 'Bolsheviki i departament politsii'.
28. See *Pisma P. B. Akselroda i Yu. O. Martova 1902–1916*, pp. 291–92. Bertram Wolfe, *Three Who Made a Revolution*, New York, 1964, vol. II, p. 269. Wolfe writes:

> Some official high in the Ministry of the Interior or the Police was privy to the arrangement and did not like it. From the outset, this still today [1964] unknown personage tried to communicate with the socialist 'underworld' without revealing his identity. When Malinovsky was elected, *Luch* received an anonymous warning on his Okhrana ties. A year later the wife of Fedor Dan received a letter telling her that a high police official wanted to see her in confidence,

and that she could signify acceptance of the appointment by a code advertisement in a stipulated newspaper. Both warnings were ignored.

Given clues unwittingly provided by Stalin at the Bukharin Show Trial (see Chapter 29) and in other instances, the probability is high that the 'high police official' was I. P. Vasiliev.

29. John J. Dziak, *Chekisty*, Lexington, MA, 1988, pp. 8–9.
30. I.V. Stalin, *Sochineniya*, vol. II, Moscow, 1946–51, p. 417.
31. Lev Trotsky, *Stalin*, New York, 1941, p. 146.
32. Okhrana Report, dated 13 December 1912 (O.S.), with the attached intercepted letter, dated 14 December 1912 (O.S.), from N. Krupskaya to A. E. Akselrod in St Petersburg. (Krupskaya wrote Lenin's letters.) On file at the Hoover Institution. Copy in the author's archive.
33. *Padenie tsarskogo rezhima*, vol. I, p. 316; vol. III, p. 485; vol. V, p. 220; see also 'Bolsheviki i departament politsii'.
34. Trotsky, *Stalin*, p. 149ff.
35. Orlov, 'Sensational Secret'.
36. See *Utro rossii*, 23 June 1917. Clipping can be found in the Nikolaevsky Collection at the Hoover Institution. After the February Revolution Zolotarev was indicted in the Malinovsky case.
37. Ibid.
38. *Padenie tsarskogo rezhima*, vol. VII, pp. 342f. and p. 334.
39. Stalin, *Sochineniya*, vol. II, p. 437.
40. Wolfe, *Three Who*, vol. II, p. 269; D. Shub, *Lenin*, Garden City, NY, 1948, pp. 119ff. G. Aronson, 'Malinovsky – Agent Lenina', *Rossiya nakanune revolutsii: istoricheskie etudy*, 1962, pp. 24–60.
41. L. Trotsky, *Stalin*, New York, 1941, p. 244.
42. Ronald Hingley, *Joseph Stalin: Man and Legend*, New York, 1974, p. 72; also Smith, *The Young Stalin*, p. 294.
43. *Bolsheviki*, p. 227. Also F. N. Samoilov, *Vospominaniya*, Moscow/Leningrad, 1923–27, vol. III, pp. 27ff.
44. I. Dubinsky-Mukhadze, *Kamo*, Moscow, 1974, p. 169.
45. Ibid., pp. 164–8.
46. S. Shumsky, 'Troyanovsky', *Poslednie novosti*, Paris, 1 January 1934, p. 3. Also see Shumsky's unpublished manuscript in the Nikolaevsky Collection at the Hoover Institution.
47. Shumsky, 'Troyanovsky', p. 3.
48. Okhrana Report no. 94182, dated 25 January 1913, with attached copy of Stalin's intercepted letter signed 'Your Vas.' On file at the Hoover Institution. Copy in the author's archive.
49. *Bolsheviki*, p. ix.
50. Smith, *The Young Stalin*, p. 297; K. Sharikov, 'Vazhneishie mesta prebyvaniya i revolutsionnoi deyatelnosti I. V. Stalina v Peterburge-Petrograde-Leningrade 1909–1934', *Propaganda i agitatsiya*, no. 32, 1939, p. 60.
51. *Bolsheviki*, p. 131.
52. *Krasny arkhiv*, no. 62, 1935, p. 239; see also the note on the bottom of the same page.
53. David Shub, *Politicheskie*, New York, 1969, p. 122.
54. A. Shotman, *Kak iz iskry razgoralos' plamia*, Leningrad, 1935, p. 175.
55. Okhrana Report no. 95677, dated 26 February 1913 with attached copy of Malinovsky's letter to Troyanovsky, dated 25 February 1913, and signed 'R. Mal.' On file at the Hoover Institution. Copy in the author's archive.
56. Okhrana Report no. 95691, dated 27 February 1913, with attached copy of Chernomazov's letter, dated 25 February 1913. On file at the Hoover Institution. Copy in the author's archive.
57. Okhrana 'top-secret' covering letter no. 95796, dated 28 February 1913, to the chief of the Okhrana Foreign Agency, with attached copy of N. Krupskaya's letter, dated 25 February 1913, to 'Number 3' (i.e., to Roman Malinovsky, who was third in importance behind Lenin and Zinoviev). On file at the Hoover Institution. Copy in the author's archive.
58. Okhrana Report no. 96088, dated 16 March 1913, with attached copy of Lenin's letter, dated 10 March 1913 (N.S.), to N. I. Podvoysky. On file at the Hoover Institution. Copy in the author's archive.
59. Okhrana Report no. 96395, dated 13 March 1913, with attached copy of Lenin's letter to A. E. Akselrod. On file at the Hoover Institution. Copy in the author's archive.
60. Information on the Finkelshtein case is in a taped interview with N. V. Veselago, conducted by Edward Ellis Smith. The original and the translated English version are on file at the Hoover

Institution under the number MS HV 82256 S 646, see pp. 24–8. Veselago's handwritten recollections in Russian with his covering letter to I. D. Levine, dated 25 June 1956, are in I. D. Levine's and in the author's archives. See also Burtsev's testimony in *Padenie tsarskogo rezhima*, vol. I, pp. 318–20.

61. N. V. Veselago, interview and handwritten recollections.
62. Dubinsky-Mukhadze, *Kamo*, p. 170.
63. N. V. Veselago, interview and handwritten recollections.
64. See Zelensky's testimony at the Bukharin Show Trial, pp. 276ff.
65. Okhrana Report no. 97084, dated 19 April 1913, with attached copy of Okhrana Report no. 245, dated 21 March 1913, from the chief of the Tver' Gendarmerie Administration.
66. Dubinsky-Mukhadze, *Kamo*, pp. 171ff.
67. Ibid., p. 173.
68. See Chapter below 28 for a reconstruction of the original text of Eremin's report. For the reproduction of Stalin's forgery of Eremin's report, see I. D. Levine, 'A Document on Stalin as Tsarist Spy', *Life*, vol. 40, no. 7, 23 April 1956. See also I. D. Levine, *Stalin's Great Secret*, New York, 1956.
69. N. V. Veselago's letter, dated 25 June 1956, to I. D. Levine, with five pages handwritten in Russian, p. 2. The letter is in I. D. Levine's archive and a copy is in the current author's archives. See also N. V. Veselago's typed manuscript in English on file in the Hoover Institution archive at Stanford University (MS), Hv 8225 S 646, copy in the author's archive.
70. See Chapter 12 below.
71. Report of the Headquarters of the Separate Corps of Gendarmes no. 8468, dated 21 June 1913, to the Governor General of Finland. At the Okhrana archive in Helsinki, Finland. Copy in the author's archive.
72. See B. I. Kaptelov and Z. I. Peregudova, 'Byl li Stalin agentom okhranki', *Voprosy istorii KPSS*, April 1989, p. 97.
73. N. V. Veselago's letter, dated 25 June 1956, to I. D. Levine, p. 4. In I. D. Levine's and copy in the author's archive.
74. *Padenie tsarskogo rezhima*, vol. I, p. 317; V. Maksakov, 'Arkhiv revolutsii i vneshnei politiki XIX–XX vekov', *Arkhivnoe delo*, no. XIII, 1927.

II

'IOSIF DZHU . . . ? WE'VE FORGOTTEN. VERY IMPORTANT!'

Koba and a fellow exile, Yakov Sverdlov (who had also been arrested in February 1913), arrived in Turukhansk by the end of September 1913. Lenin asked Malinovsky to arrange Koba's and Sverdlov's escape. Malinovsky reported Lenin's request to Director Beletsky, who ordered the chief of the Yeniseisk Okhrana, Captain V. F. Zhelezniakov, to transfer Koba and Sverdlov to Kureika, a small settlement near the Arctic Circle. An escape from Kureika was considered virtually impossible.[1] As all political exiles, Koba received a monthly stipend sufficient to live on modestly. Occasionally, he wrote to Sergey Alliluev, who sent him parcels through the Red Cross. The outbreak of the First World War in August 1914 did not affect his way of life.

Lenin and Beletsky continued in their effort to split the Bolshevik and Menshevik factions in the Duma. On 27 October 1913 Malinovsky provoked the formal split of the Social Democratic faction in the Duma by pressuring the seven Menshevik deputies to submit to Lenin's leadership. When they refused, Malinovsky and Lenin, in a familiar move, accused *them* of splitting the faction.[2] In November 1913 Lenin called for a conference in the village of Pronin near Cracow where a resolution, sponsored by Lenin and Malinovsky, condemned Okhrana provocations and stressed the need for secrecy and for vigilance in combating Okhrana spies. Lenin appointed Malinovsky to head a committee responsible for protecting the party from Okhrana infiltration. Armed with Lenin's introductory letter, Malinovsky went to Paris to visit Vladimir Burtsev, a member of the Social Revolutionary Party (Esers) and the dedicated exposer of Okhrana agents, to discuss ways to combat provocations by Okhrana agents. Burtsev confided to Malinovsky that an officer in the Moscow Okhrana, Syrkin, had told him about 'a provocateur, not yet exposed, a man who plays an active role, a man with blood on his hands, who was involved in the affair with the Tiflis banknotes and in the smuggling of arms . . .'.[3] Burtsev was unaware of Koba's existence and erroneously took Dr Yakov Zhitomirsky to be the man described by Syrkin. Zhitomirsky was indeed an Okhrana agent but not the one Syrkin had in mind. Burtsev told Malinovsky, 'Take a trip to Moscow, check on some of my connections in the Department of Police. If I were there, I'd make a quick job of it . . .'. Malinovsky reported this information to Beletsky and to the Moscow Okhrana Chief, Colonel Martynov. Syrkin was arrested and sentenced to hard labor in Siberia.[4] While in Paris, Malinovsky delivered a highly emotional speech on the split in the Social Democratic faction of the Duma. He burst into tears as he described the bitter necessity of parting company with a man as highly honorable as Comrade Chkheidze, the Menshevik chairman of the faction. The blame for this bitter necessity Malinovsky assigned to the Mensheviks.[5]

Upon his return to Russia, Malinovsky attacked the use of Okhrana *agents provocateurs* against Social Democratic members and sponsored a Duma protest to the Minister of the Interior. He delivered ardent speeches, his voice ringing with indignation, denouncing the Okhrana. In his October 1913 Duma speech, he protested the arrest of workers by the Okhrana.[6] These impassioned performances won him widespread admiration.[7] Lenin, in enthusiastic praise of this vociferous champion, wrote, 'How wonderfully has the Workers' Party in the Duma carried out its duties.'[8] Malinovsky was a star, but his Okhrana career was nearing its end, and so was his career in the Duma.

On 14 January 1914 Beletsky resigned from the Department of Police and was appointed senator.[9] Shortly before that Vice-Director Vissarionov had also resigned.[10] The new director, V. A. Briun-de-Sent-Ippolit, and the new vice-director, A. T. Vasiliev (not to be confused with Lieutenant-Colonel I. P. Vasiliev, Koba's ally) refused to maintain the Okhrana's relationship with Malinovsky. Beletsky attempted to intercede on Malinovsky's behalf with A. T. Vasiliev, but Vasiliev refused, because the order to terminate all relations with Malinovsky came from the assistant minister of the interior, General V. F. Dzhunkovsky, who learned about Malinovsky's Okhrana ties from Lieutenant-Colonel Ivan Petrovich Vasiliev. I. P. Vasiliev had never given up trying to expose Malinovsky, but while Beletsky, Vissarionov and Zolotarev remained in office, his attempts would fail. (Vasiliev had even gone so far as to tell Burtsev about Malinovsky, but Burtsev had refused to believe him.[11])

Vasiliev tried to elevate his position within the Okhrana by exposing Malinovsky. He told General Dzhunkovsky about Malinovsky's Okhrana employment and how his election had been manipulated by the Okhrana.[12] Dzhunkovsky was genuinely outraged by the Malinovsky affair. As he was to testify several years later, he found this Okhrana meddling in the Duma elections intolerable.[13] He was also incensed to learn that, when he had been governor of Moscow, the Okhrana had concealed Malinovsky's criminal record, resulting in his approval of Malinovsky's candidacy.[14] An additional discovery did not mollify his anger: Malinov-sky's salary was higher than his own as governor of Moscow or as assistant minister of the interior. On 22 April 1914 Duma Chairman M. V. Rodzianko received an anonymous telephone call warning him that on Malinovsky's initiative the left-wing Duma deputies were planning to demonstrate against Prime Minister I. L. Goremykin during his speech in the Duma. Rodzianko called Dzhunkovsky and reported this information. Dzhunkovsky was furious. He hesitated for a moment, then asked Rodzianko to give him his word of honor to keep silent, confided that Malinovsky was an Okhrana agent and promised to force Malinovsky out of the Duma and out of the country.[15]

The planned Duma demonstration led by A. F. Kerensky submitted a resolution to postpone all Duma proceedings until complete parliamentary immunity and freedom of speech were guaranteed. The resolution was defeated by a vote of 140 to 76. Goremykin made one of his rare visits to the Duma to introduce the new state budget. His appearance was met by shouts and desk-pounding by left-wing deputies. Rodzianko suspended Malinovsky and ten other left-wing deputies for 15 days. Malinovsky walked out without resisting, but Trudovik A. F. Kerensky, Bolshevik G. I. Petrovsky and Menshevik I. I. Chkhenkeli were removed by the police. Shouting resumed when Goremykin started to speak again. After ten more deputies were removed, he was finally able to finish his address. Immediately after this incident Malinovsky was contacted by the chief of the St Petersburg Okhrana, P. K. Popov, who gave him 6,000 rubles and related to him Dzhunkovsky's orders: he was to resign from the Duma and leave the country. Popov left it to Malinovsky to find a suitable pretext for resigning.[16] Malinovsky realized that he had no choice but to comply. He began talking with his Duma colleagues about his disillusionment with parliamentary struggle and suggested calling the masses to revolutionary action.[17] His colleagues refused to support his idea. On 7 May 1914 Malinovsky provoked a scandal by making a blistering attack on the government, demanding the declaration of absolute freedom of speech. Kerensky read this proposed declaration in his speech to the Duma. Rodzianko warned him nine times to 'stop insulting the Duma' and then deprived him of the right to speak. When Malinovsky delivered his speech, Rodzianko, after two warnings, ordered him to stop, but Malinovsky refused. The Duma police removed him from the hall by force. The next day, Malinovsky walked into Rodzianko's office and threw his resignation on the desk, saying, 'Excuse me, I am leaving the Duma. I have no time. Excuse me.'[18]

On 13 May 1914 the Menshevik *Nasha rabochaya gazeta* printed a front-page article about the 'curious' silence of *Pravda* concerning 'rumors of Bolshevik *azefshchina*' (provocations like those of the infamous agent provo-cateur Evno Azef).[19] The right-wing *Rabochii* followed with a blunt report on Malinovsky's involvement with the Okhrana.[20] In the Duma, the right-wing deputy N. E. Markov II kept interrupting Bolshevik speakers with the sarcastic query, 'But where is Malinovsky?!' On 12 May 1914, Lenin wrote to Inessa Armand that 'the Malinovsky affair is warming up' and that newspapers were publishing stories in which 'Malinovsky is accused of being a *provocateur*. You can imagine what it means!! Very improbable but . . . [Lenin's ellipsis] you can easily imagine how much I am worried.'[21] On 15 May 1914 Malinovsky came to see Lenin in Pronin. He explained that he had left the Duma because the Okhrana had blackmailed him over a rape he had committed as a young man. After he left, Lenin established a three-man committee consisting of himself, and his assistants, Zinoviev and Y. S. Ganetsky. On 25 May 1914 the committee announced that it was 'convinced without a doubt of Malinovsky's political honesty'. Neverthe-less, Malinovsky was removed from all official party positions for his 'scandalous breach of discipline'. Lenin wrote, 'We have judged and resolutely condemned the deserter. There is nothing more to be said. The case is closed.'[22] The Mensheviks disagreed, and they set up a commission of inquiry to investigate the Malinovsky affair. However, the outbreak of the First World War made it impossible to complete the investigation.

When the war started, Malinovsky was arrested in Germany and placed in a prisoner-of-war camp. On 16 September 1914 it was erroneously re-ported that he had been drafted and killed in action.[23] Lenin wrote an obituary which appeared in the Bolshevik émigré journal *Sotsial-Demokrat*, stating that 'Roman Malinovsky . . . was an honest man, and accusations of political dishonesty were filthy fabrications.'[24]

Lenin learned that Malinovsky was very much alive when he received a letter from him from the prisoner-of-war camp. Malinovsky pledged personal loyalty to Lenin and devotion to socialism.[25] Lenin decided to use him in defeatist propaganda against the Russian government. In early 1915 Lenin secretly met in Zurich with Dr Alexander Parvus, an agent of the German Foreign Ministry and the General Staff whose real name was Alexander Helfand.[26] Parvus had in his youth taken an active part in the revolutionary movement in Russia. After the suppression of the 1905 Revolution, he had escaped to Germany and become an agent of German intelligence. With the start of the war in August 1914 Parvus, in a proposal to the German General Staff, described the Bolsheviks as the most extreme opposition group and pointed out that Lenin would welcome Russian military defeat since he saw it as an opportunity for his own advancement to power. Parvus's advice was to use Lenin's organization for anti-Russian defeatist propaganda. This idea was accepted. When Parvus met Lenin in Zurich, they struck a secret agreement according to which Parvus would channel German money to Lenin through intermediaries whom Lenin would designate.[27] Lenin created the 'Commission to Help Russian War Prisoners' and appointed his wife, Krupskaya, and his friend G. L. Shklovsky to distribute defeatist literature among Russian prisoners of war in Germany and Austria. Malinovsky became one of the most ardent agents of this commission, distributing its newspaper *V plenu* (In Captivity) and advocating the defeat of the Russian Army. Lenin was receiving 'very enthusiastic reports' about Malinovsky and began to correspond with him regularly. Krupskaya sent him parcels of clothing and food.[28] Parvus set up a 'Research Institute' in Copenhagen, where Russian émigrés, followers of Lenin, worked on 'scientific projects' financed by the Germans to obtain information about Russia. Russian military intelligence reported that the 'Institute' was engaged in espionage. Malinovsky's propaganda among the prisoners of war also came to the attention of Russian military intelligence.[29]

Another individual in whom Russian military intelligence and the Okhrana became interested was Maxim Litvinov. On 29 July 1915 the chief of the Okhrana Foreign Agency, Krasilnikov, sent an 'absolutely secret report' to the director of the Department of Police, V. A. Bruin-de-Sent-Ippolit, informing him that Maxim Litvinov had been engaged in spying on military installations in various parts of England. The report stated that 'Litvinov transmits the information to the Germans. Litvinov has lots of money in some bank, the origin of which is not known.' Krasilnikov further reported that 'Litvinov, in a group of his close friends, once said that he maintains ties with the German Social Democrats and corresponds with them through Holland . . .'. He described in detail Litvinov's behavior and his trips to areas where British defense industry was located, adding that 'the moral qualities of Litvinov are very questionable'. Krasilnikov concluded that the information he had obtained from his agents provided grounds 'for identifying a German spy in the person of Litvinov-Harrison'.[30]

Meanwhile, Koba was still in the Siberian settlement of Kureika. His official biography states that from there he sent a letter to Lenin, criticizing the

Social Democratic parties for their support of the war. Actually, he sent a letter, dated 27 February 1915 to the Okhrana Foreign Agency's old Paris address at 79 rue de Grenelle, not knowing that Garting had retired in 1909 and that, on the request of Eremin, the Agency's address had been changed in May 1910.[31] Koba's unsigned letter was delivered to Lenin, who was confused about the identity of its author. A report from Paris, dated 25 May 1915 from the chief of the Okhrana Foreign Agency Krasilnikov to his superior in the Department of Police in St Petersburg stated that:

according to agents' information, a letter that fell into Lenin's hands had been supposedly written in Zurich and addressed to the Russian Consulate in Paris, 79 rue de Grenelle. The letter described some sort of a conference of various factions of the Social Democratic Workers Party, and, by the way, the details indicate that the author had erroneous information about opinions of certain members of the [Jewish] Bund, and, according to Lenin's opinion, the author is a Bolshevik. . . .

Krasilnikov pointed out that Lenin was trying to determine who the author of the letter was. 'For some reason Lenin is not attempting to identify the handwriting. Very possibly, he knows only the contents of the letter.'[32]

Koba was suddenly on Lenin's mind. In a letter to Zinoviev in July 1915 he asked: 'Do you remember Koba's last name?' And in a letter to a Bolshevik, V. A. Karpinsky, Lenin wrote: 'Do me a big favor: find out from Stepko [Spandarian], or Mikha [Tskhakaya], or someone the last name of Koba. (Iosif Dzhu . . . ? We've forgotten. Very important.)'[33] Lenin's suspicion focused on the letter's distorted information about the Jewish Bund, because Lenin knew Koba's hostility toward the Jews. Another reason for Lenin's suspicion may have been hints by Malinovsky, with whom Lenin had renewed contact by the summer of 1915, pointing to Koba's ties to the Okhrana.[34]

In October 1916 all political exiles in Russia were ordered to appear before the mobilization boards to be drafted into the armed forces, which by this time had suffered five million casualties, almost two million dead and three million seriously wounded or taken prisoner. At the end of December 1916 Koba in a group of exiles arrived in Krasnoyarsk. The local military board rejected him for service in the army because of his short left arm.[35] But some exiles suspected him of having avoided the draft with the help of the local Okhrana, because they learned of a trip he had taken to the local Okhrana office in Eniseisk, near Krasnoyarsk.[36] Koba was allowed to spend the remaining several months of his four-year term in Archinsk, where, in the words of a fellow exile, 'the only brick buildings were a couple of churches and half a dozen houses belonging to well-to-do merchants. Nothing ever happened in this peaceful Siberian backwater, and life generally was dreary, drab, and cheap.'[37] In Archinsk, Koba often visited Lev Kamenev, also in exile, and his wife Olga, Trotsky's sister. In their home, Koba met many exiles, some of whom he accused of having ties with the Okhrana.[38] One of the exiles, Anatoly Baikalov, was struck by Koba's coarse manners and rudeness, and provocative and cynical attitude. Koba spoke haltingly, with a strong Georgian accent, like a poorly educated man whose main stock of ideas 'was borrowed from popular two-kopek Socialist pamphlets'.[39]

Meanwhile, momentous events were taking place in the Russian capital (renamed Petrograd because of anti-German sentiment). In February 1916, Prime Minister Goremykin had been replaced by Boris Vladimirovich Shturmer, a descendant of Russified German aristocracy, which outraged nationalist circles. The Kadet (Constitutional Democrats) party leader in the Duma, Pavel Miliukov, gave a sensational speech in which he mentioned the Tsarina, born a German princess, and Shturmer: he punctuated each reference to the Tsarina and Shturmer with the question, 'Is this stupidity or treason?'[40] A nationalist Duma deputy, Vladimir Purishkevich, accused the 'holy man' Rasputin of being the evil power behind the throne and of having a magic influence over the Tsarina. In December 1916 Purishkevich, Prince Yusupov and several of their friends lured Rasputin to a dinner, poisoned him with cyanide and shot him several times, then threw his body into the Neva. No one was charged with the murder.

Also in December 1916, the name of Roman Malinovsky suddenly reappeared in the Russian press under strange circumstances. Ivan Petrovich Vasiliev, who had risen to the rank of colonel, again told Burtsev that Malinovsky was an Okhrana agent and that his election to the Duma had been manipulated by the Okhrana. This time, Burtsev believed Vasiliev and published the information. He did not mention his source because, as acting chief of the Special Section of the Department of Police, Colonel Vasiliev would have been subject to severe punishment for any revelation of police secrets.[41] Vasiliev's aim was probably to establish his own reputation as that of a 'progressive' Okhrana officer, who had always opposed Okhrana provocations. In January 1917 Vasiliev was finally appointed chief of the Special Section.

On 8 March 1917 (23 February old style) crowds surged into the Petrograd streets, rioting against the bread shortage. Three days later, as rioting continued, the Tsar, who was at the Supreme Headquarters in Mogilev, ordered suspension of the Duma. His order was ignored. Duma deputies elected a Provisional Committee, composed mainly of members of the 'Progressive Bloc': Constitutional Democrats (Kadets) and Progressive Nationalists. The Committee included two members of the left-wing parties: the Trudovik (Labor) Party was represented by Alexander Kerensky; the Mensheviks were represented by N. S. Chkheidze, a Georgian. On the same day, 12 March 1917 (27 February 1917 old style) a group of workers entered Tavrida Palace, where the Duma sessions were being held, and proclaimed themselves the 'Petrograd Soviet of Workers' Deputies'. The February 1917 Revolution was under way.

The Tsar tried to reach Petrograd the next day, but his train was diverted to auxiliary rails in the town of Pskov. There, in his railroad car, the Tsar received his chief of staff, General M. V. Alekseev, several other top generals, and two Duma deputies, the Progressive Nationalist V. V. Shulgin and the Octobrist, A. I. Guchkov, all of whom pleaded with him to abdicate. The Tsar decided to abdicate in favor of his 12-year-old son, Tsarevich Alexey, but Alexey's personal physician stated that the Tsarevich suffered from hereditary hemophilia and that his life was always in danger. Because of the Tsarevich's disease, Tsar Nicholas resolved to abdicate in favor of his brother, Grand Duke Mikhail. But this decision came too late: at that very moment, the Provisional Committee of the Duma proclaimed itself the Provisional Government of Russia, without waiting for the Grand Duke's ascension to the throne, which, given this turn of events, Mikhail decided not to pursue. The 300-year-old dynasty of the Romanovs had come to an end.

The Duma deputies who participated in the negotiations with the Tsar could not have foreseen what kind of vacuum of power and legitimacy was to result from the Tsar's abdication and chain of events. Russia was thrown into the hands of power-hungry *besy*, the bestial creatures, 'those un-crowned lackeys', as Merezhkovsky called those Dostoyevskyan 'possessed' types, who had been waiting for this moment to emerge from the bottom of the Russian criminal underworld and put the country under the yoke of their merciless brutality.

At this time, Lenin was enjoying the hospitality of neutral Switzerland, while Koba in Archinsk was counting the days left of his almost completed term of exile.

NOTES

1. I. V. Stalin, *Solchineniya*, vol II, Moscow, 1946–51, p. 422.
2. Ralph Carter Elwood, *Roman Malinovsky: A Life without a Cause*, Newtonville, MA, 1977, p. 37.
3. *Padenie tsarskogo rezhima*, vol. 1, Moscow/Leningrad, 1925, pp. 313ff. Bertram D. Wolfe, *Three Who Made a Revolution*, vol. II, p. 537.
4. Bertram D. Wolfe, *Three Who Made a Revolution*, vol. II, New York, 1964, p. 537.
5. I. P. Koniavko, 'V podpolie i v emigratsii, 1911–1922', *Proletarskaya revolutsiya*, no. 16, 1926.
6. S. B. Chlenov, *Moskovskaya Okhranka i ee sekretnye sotrudniki*, Moscow, 1919, p. 69.
7. Paul Sacardy, 'Lenin's Deputy: the Story of a Double Agent', p. 11. Manuscript on file at Radio Liberty Committee Research Library. *Bolsheviki*, Introduction; 'Ot ministerstva iustitsii', *Vestnik vremennogo pravitelstva*, 16 June 1917. I. P. Koniavko, 'Parizhskaya sektsiya bolshevikov do nachala voiny', *Proletarskaya revolutsiya*, no. 4, 1923, pp. 166ff.
8. A. E. Badaev, *Bolsheviki v gosudarstvennoi dume*, Moscow, 1954, p. 198.
9. *Padenie tsarskogo rezhima*, vol. VII, p. 307.
10. Ibid., vol. VII, p. 317.
11. Ibid., vol. I, p. 315.
12. *Padenie tsarskogo rezhima*, Burtsev's testimony, vol. I, p. 315. I. M. Dubinsky-Mukhadze, *Ordzhonikidze*, Moscow, 1963, p. 78.
13. *Padenie tsarskogo rezhima*, vol. I, p. 315.
14. Ibid., vol. III, p. 498. See also M. V. Rodzianko, *Byloe*, no. 12, 1923, p. 249; V. l. Burtsev, 'Otvet na postavlennyi vopros', *Russkoe slovo*, 25 March 1917 (O.S.); 'Bolsheviki i departament politsii', *Russkoe slovo*, 19 May 1917.
15. *Padenie tsarskogo rezhima*, vol. III, p. 498; vol. V, pp. 81–8 and p. 222; vol. VII, pp. 167–8. Rodzianko's account in *Byloe*, no. 12, 1923, p. 249. A. T. Vasiliev, *The Okhrana*, London, 1930, p. 246.
16. *Padenie tsarskogo rezhima*, vol. V, p. 85.
17. Elwood, *Roman Malinovsky*, p. 45.
18. Rodzianko, *Byloe*, no. 12, 1923, p. 249.
19. Elwood, *Roman Malinovsky*, p. 48.
20. *Rabochii*, no. 5, 28 May 1914.
21. V. I. Lenin, *Polnoe sobranie sochinenii*, vol. XLVIII, Moscow, 1958–65, p. 293. (The last two sentences are in English in the original.)
22. Ibid., vol. XXV, p. 341.
23. The newspapers *Russkoe slovo*, 16 September 1914 and *Golos*, 13 October 1914, reprinted this report as front-page news. See Elwood, p. 58 and p. 94, fn. 110.
24. *Sotsial-Democrat*, no. 33, 19 October/1 November 1914, p. 2. See also Lenin's letter to V. A. Karpinsky in Lenin, vol. XLIX, p. 18, and Elwood, p. 58 and p. 94, fnn. 111 and 112.
25. V. I. Lenin, *Polnoe Sobranie Sochinenii*, letters to Zinoviev and Inessa Armand, vol. XLIX, pp. 261, 282–3. Lenin's correspondence with Malinovsky was submitted to the Investigatory Commission of the Provisional Government in May 1917 (see *Pisma P. B. Akselroda i Yu. O. Martova*, p. 292) but never published. See Elwood, *Roman Malinovsky*, p. 94, fn. 116.
26. David Shub, 'Politicheskie deyateli rossii', *Novy zhurnal*. See also Z. A. B. Zeman and W. B. Scharlau, *The Merchant of Revolution: the Life of Alexander Israel Helfand (Parvus) 1867–1924*, London 1966.
27. Shub, 'Politicheskie deyateli rossii', pp. 205ff.
28. Gerard Walter, *Lenine*, Paris, 1950, p. 251; quoted in Elwood, *Roman Malinovsky*, pp. 59, 94, fn. 119.
29. Elwood, *Roman Malinovsky*, p. 94, fn. 119.
30. Okhrana Report no. 933 from Paris, dated 29 July/11 August 1915. On file at the Hoover Institution. Copy in the author's archive.
31. Colonel Eremin's letter no. 125483, dated 13 May 1910, to the chief of Okhrana Foreign Agency A. A. Krasilnikov. On file at the Hoover Institution. Copy in the author's archive.
32. Okhrana Report no. 933 from Paris, dated 29 July/11 August 1915. On file at the Hoover Institution. Copy in the author's archive.
33. *Leninski sbornik*, edn 2, vol. XI, p. 193.
34. Elwood, *Roman Malinovsky*, p. 95.
35. Anna S. Allilueva, *Vospominaniya*, Moscow, 1946, pp. 81, 167. Also see 'Kakie bolezny

prepiatstvuyut postupleniyu na voennuyu sluzhbu', *Moskovskoye izd*; quoted in Edward Ellis Smith, *The Young Stalin: The Early Years of an Elusive Revolutionary*, London, 1968, p. 321.

36. Maya Ulanovskaya, taped interview, Israel, 1979. Her father was an anarchist exile in Krasnoyarsk and knew Stalin personally.
37. A. Baikalov, *I Knew Stalin*, London, 1940, p. 27.
38. Anton Antonov-Ovseenko, *Portret tirana*, New York, 1980, p. 178.
39. Baikalov, *I Knew Stalin*, p. 27.
40. Donald W. Treadgold, *Twentieth Century Russia*, Chicago, 1976, p. 119.
41. *Birzhevye vedomosty*, 5 December 1916. See also *Padenie tsarskogo rezhima*, vol. I, p. 315.

12

'VASILY ... SO FAR UNIDENTIFIED'

During the first days of the February Revolution street mobs stormed the Department of Police buildings in Petrograd. Bonfires burned day and night, consuming reference books, piles of loose documents and case files, which covered the floors and the courtyards. A mob also charged into the Moscow Okhrana headquarters located on Bolshoi Gnezdnikovsky Lane, causing similar devastation. All types of people were in the crowds: some were simply caught up in the excitement of the moment, others snatched documents, reference books and photographs as souvenirs.[1] Others were venting their hatred of the Okhrana for past persecution. But there were in the crowds also agents and informers who attempted to destroy evidence of their service in the Okhrana, which explains why many personal files of secret collaborators, agents' reports and intelligence notes disappeared from the Okhrana archives during the looting of the Okhrana and police headquarters.[2]

Despite this destruction, only a small part of the Okhrana archives perished. The Special Section of the Department of Police suffered almost no loss of documents. The safe with the politically most important files remained intact.[3] This safe contained the 'top-secret' files with the warning 'Do Not Open without the Permission of the Highest Authority', among them the 'dead' files of the former Okhrana agents Roman Malinovsky and Iosif Dzhugashvili.

On 3 March 1917 the Provisional Government ordered the police archive transferred for safekeeping, partly to the Petrograd Academy of Sciences and partly to the Petrograd Pushkin Museum. The files were transported without being indexed and were placed in rooms not suitable for storage. Another part of the archive was left in the Department of Police building. Thus, the original archive became fragmented.[4] The Extraordinary Investigative Commission of the Provisional Government, headed by the prominent attorney N. E. Muraviev, was set up to investigate officials of the tsarist regime who had been involved in Okhrana provocations. The Commission became known as the 'Muraviev Commission'. A research group, headed by P. E Shchegolev, was set up to inspect the Department of Police archive.[5] Shchegolev's group gathered a large amount of material to aid the Muraviev Commission in its investigation and it compiled a number of lists of the Okhrana's secret collaborators, which were published in 1917 by the Ministry of Justice of the Provisional Government.[6] The members of the Muraviev Commission were mostly interested in investigating criminal meddling in Roman Malinovsky's election to the Duma by top government and Department of Police officials.

One of the suspects was Eremin, the former chief of the Special Section. News of the February Revolution reached him in Finland, where, having been promoted to the rank of major-general, he was the head of the Finnish Okhrana Section. Hurriedly, he destroyed documents that could expose his secret agents. Examination of the Okhrana archives in Finland nevertheless revealed that Eremin had used a number of *agents provocateurs*.[7] Eremin fled abroad; for many years he and his family lived anonymously in Chile.[8]

Colonel I. P. Vasiliev on 15 January 1917 was appointed chief of the Special Section. His last day in office was 27 February 1917. Following the order of the chairman of the Duma for all Okhrana officers to surrender to the Provisional Government, Vasiliev went to the Duma on 1 March 1917 and was placed under arrest. On 6 March 1917 he submitted a special report to the Provisional Government, accusing top police officials of sponsoring numerous Okhrana provocations; he described these in great detail and provided the names of *agents provocateurs* and their Okhrana handlers.[9] He emphasized the case of the Okhrana's meddling in Malinovsky's election to the Duma, which he considered his trump card and the most criminal of all Okhrana provocations, pointing out that he had made a number of attempts to expose Malinovsky. Vasiliev's report was patently self-serving. He stressed that he, 'on his own initiative', had given written testimony to V. L. Burtsev describing the Malinovsky affair. Vasiliev described himself as an honest and 'progressive' Okhrana officer, who was on the side of the Revolution, and offered to serve the Provisional Government. He provided his home address: 'Petrograd, Zhukovsky Street, House No. 8, Apartment No. 5'.[10] Vasiliev was released from detention.

The news of the February Revolution and of the burning of the Okhrana archives reached Archinsk early in March 1917. On 8 March 1917 a group of exiles, among them Koba, boarded a train and headed for Petrograd. At each stop M. K. Muranov, one of the exiled Bolshevik Duma deputies, spoke before enthusiastic rallies. From the town of Perm (Molotov during Stalin's rule), the three returning Bolshevik exiles sent a telegram to Lenin in Switzerland: 'Fraternal greetings. Starting today for Petrograd. Kamenev, Muranov, Stalin.'[11] At this point, the pen name 'Stalin' replaced all other aliases, codenames and nicknames that Iosif Dzhugashvili had used in the past. He had used the name Stalin only twice before, once in signing his article on the nationalities question at the end of 1912, and once in signing his pamphlet on the same subject early in 1913. He signed the telegram to Lenin with the name Stalin because he could be reasonably sure that Lenin would remember that name from the article and pamphlet, both of which Stalin had written under Lenin's guidance. Lenin was more likely to remember this pen name than the alias 'Vasily', or the even earlier one, 'Ivanovich'. As for 'Dzhugashvili', Stalin may have doubted that Lenin would remember a name so strange to the Russian ear. 'Stalin' was to remain Iosif Dzhugashvili's name for the rest of his life.

Stalin arrived in Petrograd on 12 March 1917. On that day the Bolshevik newspaper *Pravda*, as well as other newspapers, published the first list of exposed Okhrana *agents provocateurs*. The newly formed Commission for the Research of Archives had decided to forward the discovered files of exposed Okhrana agents and informers to the Inter-Party Court of Conscience, which adopted the practice of punishing the exposed agents by jailing them and ruling that, after the Constituent Assembly had been formed, following elections, their fate would be decided there. A special bureau was created to provide newspapers with lists of exposed Okhrana agents.[12] Stalin scrutinized these published lists, afraid of spotting the name Iosif Dzhugashvili on one of them. That his name did not appear on any of the lists must have made him hope that his Okhrana file had been destroyed during the turmoil of the first days of the Revolution.

V. L. Burtsev, who had for many years specialized in exposing Okhrana agents, also scrutinized these lists, expecting to see the name of Roman Malinovsky; but it did not appear. Burtsev was interested in Malinovsky, because, early in December 1916, he had published information about Malinovsky's Okhrana ties without mentioning the name of his source, Colonel I. P. Vasiliev.[13] In March 1917 Burtsev, not finding Malinovsky's name among those of the exposed Okhrana agents, approached the former vice-director of the Department of Police, S. E. Vissarionov, and the former chief of the St Petersburg Okhrana, P. K. Popov, asking them to confirm or deny his information that Malinovsky had been an Okhrana agent. They confirmed it and provided Burtsev with details of Malinovsky's Okhrana career. In March 1917 Burtsev published the information they provided in the journals *Russkoe slovo* and *Rabochaya gazeta*. In his articles, he stated that Malinovsky 'for many years had been an agent of the Okhrana and the Department of Police'.[14] On the same day the Bolshevik *Pravda*, too, reported that Malinovsky had been exposed as an Okhrana agent. In publishing this report, the editors of *Pravda* – Muranov, Kamenev and Stalin – disregarded an article by Lenin arguing against the publication of such embarrassing revelations. Lenin refused to admit in his article that the former chief editor of *Pravda*, M. E. Chernomazov, had been an Okhrana agent, although Chernomazov's name had appeared on a published list of exposed Okhrana agents.[15] Lenin complained that the enemies of the Bolsheviks were using the issue of Okhrana *agents provocateurs* 'in an attempt to drown our party in slander and filth'.[16] Lenin's defense of Malinovsky was creating a scandal. Alexander Troyanovsky, in a letter to the newspaper *Edinstvo* (Unity), wrote: 'As early as summer 1913 many comrades insisted on an investigation of Malinovsky's behavior. Lenin and Zinoviev rejected this demand, thus assuming full responsibility. The details are scandalous. An investigation is imperative.'[17]

Lenin was against such an investigation, not only because it would expose Bolshevik ties to the Okhrana, but, more importantly, because it might reveal Lenin's and Malinovsky's cooperation with German intelligence in spreading defeatist anti-Russian propaganda. This was known to Russian military intelligence, which had collected information on Lenin and his contacts, among them Malinovsky, during the war. The Provisional Government received intelligence reports, identifying Lenin, Malinovsky, and others as German agents and their activities as treason. After the February Revolution, Alexander Parvus in a memorandum to the German government, advised increased financial support for the Bolsheviks, whom he described as 'an extreme left revolutionary movement' whose goals were compatible with German interests. He argued that the Bolsheviks would incite civil war and would promise to give land to the peasants, thus inducing them to desert from the army and return to their villages to take part in the land redistribution. Parvus promised that the Bolsheviks would agree to sign a separate peace with Germany. In two or three months, prophesied Parvus, the most dreadful anarchy would reign in Russia, and he advised that when that moment arrived, the German Army should launch an offensive and occupy large parts of Russian territory.[18]

The German government found Parvus's advice attractive and decided to expedite Lenin's departure to Russia. Parvus offered Lenin and Zinoviev safe conduct through German territory from Switzerland to Russia. But Lenin feared that if only he and Zinoviev were given safe conduct, they might be accused of being German agents. He sent a telegram to his and Parvus's intermediary, Y. S. Ganetsky, stating: 'Diadia [uncle] wants to know details. Official passage for only a few is unacceptable.' Ganetsky reported Lenin's objection to Parvus, who consulted with the German officials. They agreed to arrange passage through Germany for Lenin and 40 followers, among whom were Stalin's old friend Mikha Tskhakaya and several other participants in the Tiflis expropriations. Parvus's friend Karl Radek joined Lenin's group and told Lenin that Parvus was waiting for them in Stockholm. Lenin, unwilling to be compromised by a personal meeting with Parvus, used Ganetsky and Radek as intermediaries. On 31 March 1917 Parvus assured them that Germany would continue its substantial financial support for Lenin.[19]

Lenin crossed the Russian border on 3 April 1917 at Belo Ostrov. Kamenev and a small group of Lenin's supporters climbed aboard to greet him. Stalin was not among them. Lenin's first words were an angry rebuke to Kamenev: 'What's this you're writing in *Pravda*? We've seen several issues and have really cursed you!'[20] The 'we' was Lenin. His anger was not only directed at *Pravda*'s publication of reports about Malinovsky's ties to the Okhrana but also of the paper's editorial board advocating support of the Provisional Government in its policy to continue the war. On his arrival in Petrograd, Lenin made a declaration that became known to history as his 'April Theses'. He stated that the 'imperialist' war should be transformed into a 'civil' war between the 'bourgeois dictatorship', represented by the Provisional Government, and the 'revolutionary democratic dictatorship of proletariat and peasantry', represented by the Bolshevik Party, advancing the slogan 'All Power to the Soviets'. At the same time he stated: 'This transition is characterized, on one hand, by a maximum of legality (Russia is now the freest of all the belligerent countries of the world); on the other, by the absence of oppression of the masses.'[21] He hoped to exploit with impunity the 'maximum legality' that all of the parties in Russia enjoyed at the moment and he called for the overthrow of the Provisional Government. He appealed for an end to the 'imperialist war' by 'fraternization' between the soldiers of the opposing armies. The April Theses in their entirety repeated the main points of Parvus's memorandum to the German government.

Parvus's German aid to Lenin was cloaked in the guise of a business. He established an import–export firm in Stockholm with Ganetsky as manager. Germany sent to Ganetsky various goods for which there was great demand in Russia. The proceeds from sales were deposited to Parvus's account in the Nea Bank in Stockholm, and from there the money was transferred back to Russia, to a special account in the Siberian Bank in Petrograd. This account belonged to Mrs Sumenson, the Petrograd representative of the firm Nestlé. Lenin had full access to this account.[22] Two weeks after his arrival in Petrograd, Lenin began the publication of newspapers aimed at the soldiers at the front: *Okopnaya pravda* (Trench Truth), *Soldatskaya pravda* (Soldiers' Truth), and other Bolshevik newspapers, advocating an immediate separate peace and overthrow of the Provisional Government. Russian military intelligence reported to the Provisional Government that Bolshevik propaganda was financed by the well-known German agent Alexander Parvus.[23]

The Seventh Party Congress opened on 24 April 1917 without the Mensheviks. Lenin made a speech, declaring that 'international revolution' was approaching. He introduced Stalin and recommended his election to the Central Committee, stating: 'Comrade Koba has been known to us for a great many years . . . A good worker in all responsible jobs'.[24] Stalin was elected a full member of the Central Committee; he delivered a report on the nationalities question.[25] Lists of exposed Okhrana agents were still being published by the press. After his arrival in Petrograd, Stalin remained in the shadow of the *Pravda* editorial board. He stayed with the family of Sergey Alliluev. The children welcomed Stalin as one of the true heroes of the victorious revolution and an old friend of their father.

In May 1917 information about Malinovsky uncovered by the Muraviev Commission was leaked to the press. On 19 May 1917 the Petrograd newspaper *Russkoe slovo* (Russian Word) published a sensational article entitled 'Bolsheviks and the Okhrana' which questioned the legitimacy of the Bolshevik Party.[26] Starting on 21 May 1917, and for the next few days, Boris Nikolaevsky, a leading Menshevik, published a five-part article entitled 'The Malinovsky Affair' in the Menshevik paper *Rabochaya gazeta*, quoting extensively from testimony at the Muraviev Commission's hearings. He called Malinovsky the 'Bolshevik Azef'.[27] Nikolaevsky did not know that the true Bolshevik Azef was the new full member of the Bolshevik Central Committee, Iosif Stalin.

On 28 May 1917, Lenin and Zinoviev were subpoenaed to testify before the Muraviev Commission on what they knew about Malinovsky. The Commission ordered Lenin to submit all documents and correspondence relevant to the Malinovsky affair, but Lenin submitted only part of the correspondence.[28] He withheld anything that might have revealed his and Malinovsky's involvement in anti-Russian defeatist propaganda and could have been used as evidence of his treasonous ties with Germany. For Lenin, there were two sides to the Malinovsky scandal. The fact that Malinovsky had been an Okhrana agent was deeply embarrassing but was not a criminal matter. The Muraviev Commission was conducting an investigation of those high government and police officials who had been responsible for the manipulation of Malinovsky's election to the Duma, but Malinovsky himself and Lenin were not accused. On the other hand, Lenin's and Malinovsky's involvement in anti-Russian defeatist propaganda, financed by the Germans at a time of war, constituted the serious crime of treason.[29] The possibility of being accused of treason worried Lenin and dictated extreme caution in his handling of the Malinovsky affair. A related concern was the German money he had received, and was still receiving. To address both of these issues, in May 1917, Lenin created a secret group, which he called the 'Politburo'. It consisted of Lenin, Zinoviev, Kamenev and Stalin.[30] Lenin had previously (in March 1917) given the name 'Politburo' to the Stockholm group of Ganetsky, Kozlovsky, Radek, Vorovsky and Kollontay, who had served as intermediaries between him and Parvus.[31] He placed Zinoviev and Kamenev in the Petrograd Politburo because he considered them his most trusted confidants. In including Stalin as well, Lenin was probably motivated by another consideration: he knew that Stalin and Malinovsky had been rivals in the past and that Stalin had taken a lively interest in the Malinovsky affair and was the best informed man to deal with this particular case. It is also possible that Lenin remembered that Malinovsky had told him about Stalin's involvement with the Okhrana. Perhaps Lenin retained a small suspicion that Stalin had been the author of a letter to the former Okhrana headquarters in Paris that had come to his attention at the time when he was urgently inquiring about the full name of Iosif Dzhu.[32] At any rate, Lenin clearly thought of Stalin as someone potentially useful to him in dealing with this problem.

The Muraviev Commission held 88 hearings and questioned 59 witnesses. The story of the 'Rozmirovich provocation' and of the role that an Okhrana agent 'Vasily' had played in this provocation appeared in the testimony of the director of the Department of Police, Beletsky. The part of Beletsky's testimony before the Muraviev Commission mentioning 'Vasily' was omitted from the records of the Commission published in 1924–26 and entitled *Padenie tsarskogo rezhima* (The Demise of the Tsarist Regime), but it was remembered by some of those present at the hearings.[33] The Commission did not intend to prosecute 'Vasily', and it is doubtful that five years after his brief encounter with 'Vasily,' Beletsky would have remembered his actual name, Iosif Dzhugashvili. After all, even Lenin, who had already known Stalin for more than ten years, did not remember that name in 1915. More than likely, Beletsky did not even try to recall Vasily's name, since it was of no interest to him or the members of the Muraviev Commission. The Commission's focus was not Okhrana agents but the crimes of top police and government officials in connection with Malinovsky's election to the Duma. Okhrana agents themselves were not criminals in the eyes of the Provisional Government, but only in the eyes of the revolutionaries.

Colonel I. P. Vasiliev must have been invited to testify before the Muraviev Commission because he had attempted to expose Malinovsky in the past and had written about him in his special report, but whether he did in fact testify is not known. His name is not among those of the 59 witnesses whose testimonies were cited in the Soviet published record of the hearings. It is possible that he was murdered before he had a chance to testify. After the February Revolution, many Okhrana officers were murdered by their secret collaborators, who feared exposure. It is also possible that Vasiliev testified before the Muraviev Commission and was murdered after his testimony, which was years later expunged from the published record in the same way that his special report had been. At any rate, Vasiliev disappeared without trace in the summer of 1917. His name is neither among those of the officers killed during the civil war, nor among the names of those who fled abroad. Most probably, he was murdered on Stalin's order, possibly by Kamo, who had in the past murdered people on Stalin's instigation. Kamo was in Petrograd from May to July 1917, and he and members of his band often gathered in the Alliluev's apartment where Stalin lived at the time. During those days of upheaval, murders often went unrecorded.

What is certain is that there is no mention of Vasiliev's testimony in the censored seven-volume version of the Muraviev Commission's records, published during Stalin's rule as *Padenie tsarskogo rezhima*. By that time, Stalin's position would have made it easy for him to purge these records of references to the Okhrana agent 'Vasily'. Significantly, it was Stalin who ordered publication of the Muraviev Commission's records, which, in their Soviet published form, contained no reference to him. To remove Vasiliev's testimony could have been no more difficult than to withhold Vasiliev's special report, which also did not appear in the Soviet published record, even though it had existed in the complete original record of the Muraviev Commission. But in 1930, Stalin allowed publication of Vasiliev's special report, having purged it of all references to Malinovsky and 'Vasily'.[34] This omission is startling, since the exposure of Malinovsky had for years been Vasiliev's major preoccupation. In doctoring Vasiliev's report, Stalin in effect sought to 'prove' that Vasiliev had never written anything about Malinovsky and 'Vasily'.[35] By then, Stalin had removed all references to Malinovsky even from Lenin's collected works, which were published during Stalin's rule.

On 23 June 1917 the Muraviev Commission indicted six former tsarist government and police officials charged with fraud in Malinovsky's election to the Duma: I. A. Makarov, the minister of the interior; I. M.

Zolotarev, the assistant minister of the interior; S. P. Beletsky, the director of the Department of Police; S. E. Vissarionov, the vice-director of the Department of Police; A. P. Martynov, the Moscow Okhrana chief; and V. G. Ivanov, a Moscow Okhrana officer. The case was submitted to the Investigative Committee of the Supreme Tribunal.[36] Malinovsky was not indicted, but a special investigator was appointed to collect information about him. *Pravda* appealed to its readers to submit all available information about Malinovsky to the Commission.[37]

By that time, the country was more interested in the current political turmoil than in past Okhrana provocations, which were fading into history. On 3 May 1917 Prime Minister Prince Lvov had formed the first coalition government, in which Kerensky took over the post of defense minister. He went to the front to address soldiers declaring: 'I summon you forward, to the struggle for freedom, not to a feast, but to death. We revolutionaries have the right to death.'[38] By 1 July 1917, the Russian offensive against the Austrian forces in the direction of Lvov had been stopped. The Germans and Austrians counterattacked, and the Russian front collapsed. Soldiers fled in disorder, some deserting. Lenin urged the Petrograd Soviet to sponsor a demonstration against the Provisional Government. The Bolsheviks led a large crowd to Tavrida Palace, the site of the Provisional Government.[39] Minister of Justice P. N. Pereverzev delivered a speech before representatives of Petrograd military units, stating that Russian military intelligence had intercepted correspondence by Lenin that proved him to be a German agent and that this correspondence would be published. The newspaper *Zhivoe slovo* (Living Word) printed them under the headline 'Lenin, Ganetsky and Co. – German Spies.'[40] Military units loyal to the Provisional Government wrecked *Pravda*'s presses and editorial offices. Other Bolshevik newspapers were closed.[41] Newspapers published reports of the huge sums of money that Lenin had received from Germany.[42] Burtsev in the Menshevik *Lech* wrote: 'Parvus is not an *agent provocateur*. He is more than that. He is an agent of Wilhelm II.'[43] On 6 July 1917 the Provisional Government ordered Lenin, Zinoviev, Parvus, Ganetsky and other 'German spies' arrested. The Provisional Government accused Lenin of 'state treason' and of 'organizing an uprising against the existing government'.[44] 'Now they will shoot us all. This is the most suitable moment for them to do it,' Lenin told Trotsky. Years later, Trotsky commented: 'Our enemies were still lacking such consistency and such decisiveness.'[45]

Lenin together with Zinoviev went to the apartment of Duma deputy N. G. Poletaev, but someone started the rumor that Poletaev, according to documents of the Department of Police, was an Okhrana *agent provocateur*.[46]

This rumor gave Stalin an opportunity to prove his loyalty to Lenin. He convinced Lenin and Zinoviev to hide at a 'safer place', which turned out to be Alliluev's apartment. Lenin and Zinoviev stayed with the Alliluevs for five days, from 7 July to 11 July 1917. The apartment at that time was a hangout for members of Kamo's old band and other hard-core criminals who, like the political exiles, had been set free by the February Revolution. Kamo had walked out of the Kharkov prison on the morning of 6 March 1917 after the guards had left their posts following the collapse of the old regime. He had first gone to Tiflis, but in May 1917 he was already in Petrograd.[47] He frequented Alliluev's apartment, feeling at home with his comrades, among them Stalin and Ordzhonikidze, who had come to Petrograd from Siberian exile.

At that time, holdups, armed robberies, and murders became common-place occurrences in Petrograd.[48] The Provisional Government appointed an artillery colonel B. V. Nikitin, to organize a security unit to safeguard order, but his efforts in fighting the growing anarchy proved futile. Years later he was to reminisce that 'criminals formed the vanguard of countless hordes who came from the convict prisons and penal settlements of Siberia and other places of banishment. All over Russia the whole of the old criminal fraternity were liberated and swelled the ranks of the scum of the population which boiled over in the tragic upheaval . . .'.[49] Nikitin was powerless to deal with criminals like Kamo, let alone to arrest Lenin and other 'German agents'.

Most of Lenin's supporters thought that he should prove his innocence in court, and did not believe that the German government had spent huge sums, more than 50 million gold marks, to finance Bolshevik propaganda.[50] Only the very narrow circle of people around Parvus and Ganetsky and the Politburo members Zinoviev, Kamenev and Stalin knew about the German money, and they advised Lenin not to risk a trial. Lenin expressed the view that there would not be an open court. Stalin agreed, suggesting that the arresting officers would kill Lenin on the way to prison. That very moment Elena Stasova, Lenin's confidante, came in and said that a rumor had been spread that Lenin 'according to the documents of the police department, was a *provocateur*'. Everybody fell silent. Stasova's announce-ment 'produced an incredibly strong impression on Lenin. A nervous shudder ran over his face, and he declared with the utmost determination that he must go to jail.'[51] Lenin's determination was short-lived, however, and he decided to go into hiding. On 11 July 1917 he and Zinoviev wrote a letter to the Provisional Government in which they stated:

Everybody knows that Ganetsky had money deals with Parvus, but we had nothing to do with Ganetsky . . . . Not only have we never, either directly or indirectly, taken part in the business deals of Ganetsky and Kozlovsky, but in general we have not received even a kopek of money personally or for the party.[52]

Having sent this letter, Lenin put on a wig, which drastically changed his appearance, while Zinoviev shaved his head and glued on a mustache. Stalin led them to the small village of Razliv, near Petrograd, where a worker, N. A. Emelianov, and his three sons, had built a makeshift hut in a nearby forest for their summer outings. Lenin and Zinoviev stayed in this hut for a month and then escaped to Finland.[53] Trotsky had been in the United States during the war, and Lenin had not told him about the German money. Trotsky believed that Lenin's April Theses 'flowed unfailingly' from Trotsky's theory of 'permanent revolution'.[54] He did not know that Lenin's April Theses were also in full accord with the views of Parvus and the plans of the German government.

By August 1917, the Provisional Government was in a state of crisis. Kerensky became prime minister. With every passing day, his cabinet was weakened by military defeats at the front. The position of the Bolsheviks also deteriorated; Lenin and Zinoviev were in Finland, while Trotsky and Kamenev were in prison. Of the Politburo members, only Stalin was free, until he was joined by Kamenev who had been released from prison because he was able to prove that before the February Revolution he had been in exile and had had no contact with any German agent. Immediately after Kamenev's release, the rumor spread that he had been an Okhrana agent. Kamenev demanded an investigation to clear his name and to determine who had started this rumor. The Bolshevik Central Committee appointed Stalin to discuss with one of the leaders of the Social Revolutionary Party, Abram Gots, the creation of a 'commission in the case of Kamenev' to investigate this rumor.[55] Stalin himself had in the past spread such rumors about party comrades, including Yakov Sverdlov and Grigory Petrovsky, but apparently his comrades now entrusted him with the investigation of Kamenev. It is possible he maneuvered himself into this assignment to avert suspicion of any ties he may have had with the Okhrana and to remind all that he was a member of the Politburo, which had been created to deal with problems like the Malinovsky affair.

In an article published in August 1917, Stalin strongly defended Kamenev and attacked his 'counter-revolutionary' accusers with shrill denunciations that had a hidden meaning:

The reptilian hissing of the counter-revolution is again becoming louder. The disgusting serpent of reaction thrusts its poisonous fangs from around the corner. It will sting and slink back into its dark lair . . . The infamous baiting, the bacchanal of lies and calumnies, the shameless deception, the low-grade forgery and falsification assumed proportions hitherto unknown in history . . . At first they tried to smear tested revolutionary fighters as German spies, and that having failed, they want to make them out to be Tsarist spies. Thus they are trying to brand those who have devoted their entire conscious life to the revolutionary struggle against the Tsarist regime as Tsarist spies . . . The political meaning of all this is self-evident: the masters of the counter-revolution are intent at all cost on rendering Kamenev harmless and removing him as one of the recognized leaders of the revolutionary proletariat.[56]

Rhetorically, Stalin performed a convoluted trick here: he equated the accusation of the revolutionaries as being 'German spies' with that of their being 'tsarist spies'; then he dismissed both charges as calumnies. By this cunning equation, the Okhrana agent Stalin placed himself on an equal footing with Lenin and other accused 'German agents'. He also prepared a defense for himself in case he was accused of having been an Okhrana agent: he would call such claims 'infamous baiting, a bacchanal of lies and calumnies, shameless deception, low-grade forgery and falsification'.

The German offensive, which Parvus had advocated in his memoranda, began in August 1917. On 20 August Riga fell. German troops were moving toward Petrograd. Kerensky, fearing that Petrograd might fall into German hands, ordered the evacuation of the State Treasury and all archives. The preparations were haphazard, and the archive materials were broken up into disjointed parts, the files being placed in boxes and transported to various places: to the Kirillo-Belozersky Monastery in the north, to the Moscow State Archive, and to Kremlin basements. Boxes of files delivered to the monastery were piled up inside and in the rooms of its ecclesiastical school. Some parts of the archives remained in Petrograd, stored in boxes and ready for transportation.[57] During the March–August 1917 period, the Muraviev Commission had gathered some of the Department of Police files that it needed for investigation of the most important cases of Okhrana provocations. In September 1917 the Commission stopped its proceedings because of Kerensky's order to evacuate the archives, and its material together with the files of Okhrana agents were placed in boxes that were sealed and stored in expectation of evacuation, which, however, did not take place. The files remained in boxes for the next two years, and at the end of 1919 were transported to Moscow together with the archive of the Investigative Commission of the Supreme Tribunal.[58]

The file of Okhrana agent Iosif Dzhugashvili was not in this shipment. His name had not attracted the attention of the members of the Muraviev Commission, and they had not asked for his file.[59] In 1917 'Iosif Vissarionov Dzhugashvili', which was how Stalin's file was labeled, meant nothing to the people who searched the archives. Stalin's actual name might have been known only to a few people in the party and the Okhrana. Of those who once had known his name, not all remembered it. Even Lenin, who had personally known Stalin since 1905, was unable to recall his name in 1915. A Bolshevik Party history of the period before 1917, published in 1926, did not mention Stalin even once. Moreover, he was not included in its index of some 500 names of party members who were in any way prominent during this time. This index mentions only an 'Ivanovich' who was present at the Tammerfors conference. But the identity of the person hiding behind this alias remained a mystery to the party historians as late as 1926.[60] Stalin would have been interested in revealing who Ivanovich was except for the fear that this might have led to the realization that Ivanovich and the unidentified Okhrana agent 'Ivanov' were one and the same person. (Burtsev in his testimony before the Muraviev Commission referred to an unidentified Okhrana agent 'Ivanov' who in 1906 competed with the double agent Solomon Ryss in providing the Okhrana with information about the plans of the Bolshevik-Maximalist terrorists, among them Kamo. Burtsev knew nothing about Kamo's friend Dzhugashvili–Stalin.[61])

Many files of Okhrana agents were taken out of the archive and transferred to the Commission for the Investigation of Archives, which had offices in Petrograd and Moscow. The file with the name 'Iosif Vissarionov Dzhugashvili' was delivered to the Petrograd office of the Commission. It was there among the files that were in line to be inspected. But there was not enough time to do that. When the evacuation order was issued, all these files were placed in boxes for delivery to a Petrograd railway station. Whoever placed the file of Iosif Dzhugashvili into one of the boxes could have had no inkling that this file was a time bomb of enormous destructiveness. Some of the boxes were loaded into railway cars, while others were stored in warehouses for future transportation to Moscow, which was delayed until a more favorable time. Unpredictable events were rushing the country into an unknown future. (The stored boxes, neglected for years, were transported to Moscow in the summer of 1926, and it was then that the file of Iosif Dzhugashvili was discovered.)

The work of the Moscow Commission for the Investigation of Archives was not interrupted by evacuation. The Commission prepared lists of Okhrana agents in various parties, including the Bolshevik, basing its research on the documents of the Moscow Okhrana archive and information that emerged from the hearings of the Muraviev Commission. In April 1918, after the Bolsheviks came to power, the Commission published a book, titled *Bolsheviki*, which listed the 12 most important Okhrana agents in the Bolshevik Party: M. I. Briandinsky, I. A. Zhitomirsky, I. G. Krivov, A. I. Lobov, R. V. Malinovsky, A. K. Marakushev, A. A. Poliakov, A. S. Romanov, I. P. Sesitsky, M. E. Chernomazov, V. E. Shurkhanov, and one so far unidentified, who had the party alias 'Vasily'.[62]

Also in *Bolsheviki* is an index of names, aliases and codenames. This index has entries for the names 'Koba' and 'Dzhugashvili.' The entry under 'Koba' refers to 'Dzhugashvili'. The entry under 'Dzhugashvili' refers to two aliases, 'Koba' and 'Stalin', and to pages 100, 101 and 120. These pages do not mention 'Stalin'.[63] Stalin's aliases, 'Vasily' and 'Ivanovich', are also not mentioned. (It may seem strange that in 1918 no one remembered Stalin's party alias 'Vasily' that he had used six years earlier. Besides Lenin, Malinovsky and Chernomazov, no one among the Bolsheviks left any record of having known the alias 'Vasily', which implies that Stalin did not use it widely. Indicative of how ephemeral names were during that period is that in 1926, when the first history of the party was published, Stalin was not even mentioned and no one remembered Stalin's alias 'Ivanovich'. More than 500 prominent party workers were mentioned, but 'Ivanovich' was listed in the index only as an unidentified participant at a party conference.)

Researchers at the Moscow Commission for the Investigation of Archives did not have documentary evidence that Stalin had once had the alias 'Vasily'. The records of the Muraviev Commission, including the testimony of Director Beletsky and the special report of Colonel Vasiliev, were evacuated from Petrograd and were not available to the Moscow Commission. Of the few party members who knew who 'Vasily' was, Malinovsky was in a prisoner-of-war camp, Chernomazov was in hiding, and Lenin denied to the bitter end even the well-established fact of Malinovsky's ties to the Okhrana – hence he was unlikely, even if he remembered Stalin's alias 'Vasily', to admit that Stalin, a member of his government, might be a former Okhrana agent. (The fact that Stalin had ever had the party alias 'Vasily' was made public for the first time in 1940, after Stalin recovered his St Petersburg Okhrana file and allowed the publication of several reports taken from it.[64])

The researchers at the Moscow Commission for the Investigation of

Archives stated that the 12 mentioned Okhrana agents 'constitute only a small segment of all the *provocateurs* and ordinary "informers" who had worked in the Social Democratic Party. The publication of a complete list of these people is an undertaking for the, it is hoped, not-too-distant future.'[65]

NOTES

1. See V. Maksakov, 'Archiv revolutsii i vneshney politiki XIX i XX vekov', *Archivnoe delo*, no. XIII, 1927, pp. 29–35. Several partly burned documents were collected by an American journalist who witnessed the burning of the archives in Petrograd. These documents are on file at the Hoover Institution. Copies are in the author's archive.
2. Ibid.
3. Ibid., p. 35.
4. Ibid., pp. 35ff.
5. After the Bolsheviks came to power, Shchegolev became the chief of the Political Department of the Archival Fund, which was under the supervision of the Soviet Secret Police.
6. V. Maksakov, 'Archiv revolutsii i vneshei politiki XIX–XX vekov', *Arkhivnoe delo*, no XIII, 1927, p. 39.
7. *Russkoe slovo*, 14 April 1917, p. 3.
8. Letters from the Tolstoy Foundation, dated 9 October 1974, and 9 December 1974, report on the results of the search for Eremin's family in Chile. In the author's archive. In 1957, Eremin's two daughters came to New York with the intention of selling Eremin's papers; they found no buyer. After their return to Chile, they disappeared, most probably lured to Russia by a Soviet agent. The author obtained this information when interviewing I. D. Levine.
9. P. E. Shchegolev, *Okhranniki i avanturisty*, Moscow, 1930, pp. 138-49.
10. Ibid., p. 140.
11. *Leninsky sbornik*, vol. XIII, p. 271.
12. Maksakov, 'Archiv revolutsii', p. 30.
13. *Birzhevye vedomosty*, 5 December 1916. See also *Padenie tsarskogo rezhima*, vol. I, Moscow/Leningrad, 1925, p. 315.
14. V. L. Burtsev, 'Otvet na postavlennyi vopros', in *Russkoe slovo*, 25 March 1917 (O.S.). See also *Padenie tsarskogo rezhima*, vol. I, pp. 315ff, and Ralph Carter Elwood, *Roman Malinovsky: A Life without a Cause*, Newtonville, MA, 1977, p. 61.
15. V. I. Lenin, *Polnoe sobranie sochinenii*, vol. XXXI, Moscow, 1958–65, pp. 79–82 and 521f. See also Elwood, *Roman Malinovsky*, p. 96, fn. 8.
16. Lenin's letter, dated 17 March 1917 (O.S.), in Lenin, *Polnoe sobranie sochinenii*, vol. XLIX, p. 423.
17. *Bolsheviki*, Moscow, 1918, p. XIII, fn.* Quoting from *Edinstvo* and *Russkaya volia* (Russian Freedom), 24 April 1917.
18. David Shub, *Politicheskie deyateli rossii*, New York, 1969, pp. 213-27.
19. *Leninsky sbornik*, no. XIII. See also Shub, *Politicheskie*, pp. 213–17.
20. F. F. Raskolnikov, *Kronshtadt i piter v 1917*, Moscow/Leningrad, 1925, p. 54. See also Raskolnikov, *Na boevykh putiakh*, Moscow, 1964, pp. 63f.
21. Lenin, *Polnoe Sobranie*, vol. XX, pp. 109–45.
22. Shub, *Politicheskie*, pp. 217ff.
23. Ibid., pp. 217–21.
24. Robert M. Slusser, *Stalin in October – the Man Who Missed the Revolution*, Baltimore/London, 1987, p. 85.
25. Ibid., pp. 81–101.
26. 'Bolsheviki i departament politsii', *Russkoe slovo*, 19 May 1917.
27. 'Delo malinovskogo i dr.', *Rabochaya gazeta*, no. 62, 21 May 1917, pp. 2f. See also no. 63, 24 May 1917, p. 2; no. 67, 28 May 1917, pp. 2f.; no. 83, 17 June 1917, pp. 23; no. 85, 20 June 1917, p. 2; no. 87, 22 June 1917, p. 2.

28. *Pisma P. B. Akselroda i Yu. O. Martova 1902–1916*, p. 292.
29. *Padenie tsarskogo rezhima*, vol. II, p. 317.
30. I. Tovstukha, 'Joseph Stalin', in Georges Haupt and Jean-Jacques Marie, *Makers of the Russian Revolution*, Ithaca, 1974, pp. 67ff.; also quoted in Slusser, p. 96. See also Slusser, 'Lenin's Deal with Stalin, April 1917', lecture at Yale University, 26 January 1978; Slusser, 'On the Question of Stalin's Role in the Bolshevik Revolution', *Canadian Slavonic Papers*, vol. XIX, no. 4, December 1978. Also E. Yaroslavsky, *Landmarks in the Life of Stalin*, Moscow, 1940, p. 97.
31. Shub, *Politicheskie*, p. 218. D. Shub quotes from Z. A. B. Zeman and W. B. Scharlau, *The Merchant of Revolution: The Life of Alexander Israel Helfand (Parvus) 1867–1924*, London, 1926. Lenin had a history of inventing names for such emergency groups. The name 'Politburo' was no accident but had to do with his associating the word 'buro' with secret groups operating on foreign soil. The *Zagranichnoe Buro*, or 'Foreign Bureau', had been headed for years by Dr Yakov Zhitomirsky, Lenin's friend and an Okhrana agent. The Petrograd Politburo was a kind of extension of the Stockholm Politburo because both were addressing the same dangerous issue of the German money.
32. See Chapter 11 above.
33. The omitted portions of Beletsky's testimony were described by Shumsky in his article 'Troyanovsky', *Poslednie novosty*, 1 January 1934. See also the handwritten manuscript by Shumsky in the Nikolaevsky Collection at the Hoover Institution, file 132, box 4, no. 27. Shumsky describes the Rozmirovich provocation and Beletsky's conversation with Malinovsky as it was presented in Beletsky's testimony at the Extraordinary Commission's hearings and was also described in the article 'Bolsheviki i departament politsii'. Colonel I. P. Vasiliev's report on illegal Okhrana activities was not included in the seven volumes of the Extraordinary Commission material published in *Padenie tsarskogo rezhima*. Almost all references to Malinovsky and 'Vasily' had been removed from this censored version. Vasiliev's report in abbreviated form was published on Stalin's order in 1930 in a book by P. E. Shchegolev titled *Okhranniki i avanturisty*, Moscow, 1930, pp. 138–49. All references to Malinovsky and 'Vasily' are missing in this book.
34. Shchegolev, *Okhranniki i avanturisty*, pp. 138–49.
35. See Shumsky, 'Troyanovsky'. Also the author's interview with George Kennan in which Kennan described a book published in Czechoslovakia, depicting Stalin's Okhrana career. Kennan said that all the copies of the book had mysteriously disappeared. A distorted echo of this mystery could be found in a report, 'A Czarist Spy Named Stalin', *Newsweek*, 7 November 1966, which read:

> George Kennan, former US ambassador to Russia and an astute student of Russian affairs at Princeton's Institute for Advanced Studies, has long suspected that as a young Bolshevik Joseph Stalin was an agent of the Czar's secret police. Now Kennan has evidence. He recently learned that the passport Stalin used to attend a party congress at Stockholm in 1906 was issued by the secret police. Kennan's research also uncovered the fact that Stalin admitted during a party seminar in 1920 that he had been a Czarist agent. The statement was published in a Soviet theoretical magazine that disappeared a few months ago from all Russian libraries. Kennan traced the activities of each member of the seminar group, together with the Georgian and Armenian Communists who were closely associated with Stalin between 1906 and 1912 – and found that all had been liquidated in the twenties.

When a news reporter asked Ambassador Kennan about the accuracy of this account, Kennan declined to comment beyond stating that it was 'not entirely accurate'. See *New York Times*, 31 October 1966, and H. Montgomery Hyde, *Stalin: The History of a Dictator*, New York, 1971, p. 75, fn.
36. *Utro rossii*, 23 June 1917. (Newspaper clipping in the Nikolaevsky Collection at the Hoover Institution, file 132, box 4, no. 27.)
37. *Pravda*, no. 73, 17 June 1917, p. 3.
38. Donald W. Treadgold, *Twentieth Century Russia*, Chicago, 1976, p. 132.
39. Ibid., p. 133.
40. Slusser, *Stalin in October*, pp. 145ff, quoting Lenin, vol. XXI, pp. 9ff.
41. Ibid., p. 149; Slusser is quoting Rabinovich, *Prelude*, p. 201.
42. These reports were published in the Soviet journal *Proletarskaya revolutsiya*, no. 9, 1922.
43. *Luch*, 20 July 1917.
44. Shub, *Politicheskie*, pp. 219ff.

45. Lev Trotsky, *O Lenine*, Moscow, 1924, pp. 58f.
46. I. Dubinsky-Mukhadze, *Ordzhonikidze*, Moscow, 1963, p. 149.
47. I. Dubinsky-Mukhadze, *Kamo*, Moscow, 1974, pp. 180–2.
48. John Reed, *Ten Days That Shook the World*, New York, 1960; London, 1962, p. 49.
49. B. V. Nikitine, *The Fatal Years: Fresh Revelations on a Chapter of Underground History*, London, 1938, p. 24.
50. Eduard Bernstein, 'Ein dunkeles Kapitel', *Vorwärts*, Berlin, 14 January 1921. Also Shub, *Politicheskie*, p. 187.
51. Lev Trotsky, *Stalin*, New York, 1941, p. 211. See also Dubinsky-Mukhadze, *Ordzhonikidze*, p. 150.
52. Shub, *Politicheskie*, p. 186.
53. Roy Medvedev, *Let History Judge*, New York, 1971, pp. 200ff.
54. Lev Trotsky, *Stalin's School of Falsification*, New York, 1962, p. 5.
55. Trotsky, *Stalin*, p. 221.
56. Ibid., pp. 221ff.
57. V . Maksakov, 'Arkhiv revolutsii i vneshnei politiki XIX–XX vekov', p. 33.
58. Ibid., pp. 32f.
59. All materials and Okhrana files of the Extraordinary Commission were delivered to Moscow at the end of 1919. On Stalin's file, see Chapter 17 below.
60. Trotsky, *Stalin*, pp. 222ff.
61. *Padenie tsarskogo rezhima*, vol. I, p. 312.
62. *Bolsheviki*, Introduction, p. ix.
63. Ibid, p. 202.
64. See Chapter 30 below.
65. *Bolsheviki*, Introduction, p. xxix.

13

'THE GRAY BLUR'

On the eve of the October Revolution, Stalin was leading a secretive life, intently watching the rapidly unfolding events and fearing that he might get caught on the losing side. Lenin, from his hideout in Finland, demanded that the Bolsheviks stage an armed uprising against the Provisional Government. The commander in chief of the Russian army General Kornilov accused the Provisional Government of acting under the pressure of the Bolshevik majority of the Soviets who were in full agreement with the German General Staff.[1] Suspecting that Kornilov wanted to replace him as prime minister, Kerensky ordered his dismissal and appointed himself commander in chief; Kornilov, however, refused to relinquish his position.

By that time, Lenin had large sums of German money available and was financing a propaganda campaign aimed at weakening the Russian army and achieving a Bolshevik majority in the Soviets. He renewed his slogan 'All Power to the Soviets!' and called for resistance to 'Kornilov's counter-revolutionary mutiny' and 'conspiracy against the people', which, he insisted, aimed to reinstate the tsarist regime.[2] Kerensky, in his role as commander in chief, appointed General N. N. Dukhonin as chief of staff. By the end of September, Kerensky formed the Third Coalition Government, which consisted of ten socialists and six liberals. Under pressure from the radical left, he proclaimed Russia a federated republic and arrested several public figures who were critical of his policies. He also released from prison Trotsky and some other Bolsheviks accused in July of being German agents.

Kerensky's attempt to restore discipline in the army failed. The Bolshevik slogan 'Land and Liberty!' had a strong appeal to the soldiers, whom Lenin called 'peasants in uniform'. They deserted to take part in land redistribution, ignoring the appeals of the Provisional Government to stop and wait for the Constituent Assembly, which was expected to proclaim land reform.[3] By October, the price of food in Petrograd climbed as supplies dwindled. Plants and factories were closing down because of a shortage of raw materials and workers' unrest. In letters from Finland, Lenin declared that the moment was right to seize power: 'The victory is ours, because people are already close to desperation and *bestiality*.'[4] Lenin threatened to resign from the Central Committee if his demand for an uprising was not heeded. 'We shall ruin the revolution', he warned 'history will not forgive us if we do not assume power now.'[5]

The Provisional Government announced that elections to the Constituent Assembly would be held in November 1917. On 7 October 1917, 550 members of the Provisional Council of the Republic met to establish electoral procedures. The Bolsheviks walked out of the first session, preparing for an insurrection in late October. Kerensky declared, 'I have more strength than I need. The Bolsheviks will finally be smashed.'[6]

On 10 October the Bolshevik Central Committee met in the Petrograd apartment of a prominent Menshevik, N. N. Sukhanov, whose wife was an ardent follower of Lenin. Lenin insisted that the insurrection start at once and claimed that the Provisional Government was ready to surrender Petrograd to the Germans, and that the 'imperialist powers' were prepared to sign a separate peace treaty in order to strangle the Russian revolution and organize a 'second Kornilov mutiny'.

In reality, it was Lenin who was helping the Germans in their plan to capture Petrograd by subverting the Russian Army through German-financed propaganda, and it was Lenin who intended to sign a separate peace treaty with the Germans. And Lenin, not Kornilov, called for armed insurgency against the Provisional Government. Felix Dzerzhinsky, a recent recruit into Lenin's inner circle, did not know of the existence of the secret Politburo, which Lenin had formed in May 1917. He proposed to set up a 'Bureau for the Political Guidance of the Insurrection'. Lenin, Zinoviev, Kamenev and Stalin, the members of the original Politburo, were elected to this new Politburo, together with Trotsky, Sokolnikov and Bubnov. At the next meeting of the Central Committee, on 16 October 1917, Lenin again insisted on an immediate insurrection, stating: 'One cannot be guided by the mood of the masses for it is changeable and impossible to calculate; we must be guided by an objective analysis and assessment of the revolution.'[7] Lenin's resolution was approved, with only Zinoviev and Kamenev voting against.

On 18 October Kamenev published a letter in *Novaya zhizn'*, stating his and Zinoviev's objections to insurrection. Lenin, hiding in Finland, was furious. He wrote a letter to *Pravda*, in which he called Zinoviev and Kamenev 'strike-breakers' and demanded their expulsion from the party.[8] Stalin, in an unsigned editorial, defended Zinoviev and Kamenev, stating, 'The sharp tone of Comrade Lenin's article [against Zinoviev and Kamenev] does not change the fact that, fundamentally, we remain of one mind.'[9] The Second Congress of the Soviets was originally scheduled to open on 20 October 1917 but, because of organizational problems, was postponed to 25 October 1917, giving the Bolsheviks five more days to prepare for insurrection. On 24 October 1917 Fedor Dan, a leading Menshevik, and Abram Gots, a prominent Social Revolutionary, attempted to convince Kerensky to sign a peace treaty immediately and proclaim land reform. Kerensky interpreted this as an ultimatum and threatened to resign. The threat was an empty gesture; by then military units directed by Trotsky were already moving to take control of the nerve centers of Petrograd.

In Lenin's own words, the October coup was 'easier than lifting a feather'.[10] There was no resistance to the Bolshevik takeover, except for a short-lived skirmish in the Winter Palace, where the Provisional Government was defended by young cadets and a women's battalion. Bolshevik soldiers and sailors under the command of V. A. Antonov-Ovseenko overran the palace in the early morning of 26 October. The takeover claimed only six casualties. Kerensky fled in a car flying an American flag. The ministers of the Provisional Government were locked up in the cells of the old tsarist prison – the Peter and Paul Fortress. The victors helped themselves to the liquor and food stocked in the basement of the Winter Palace.

Stalin did not take part in the coup. He neither attended a Central Committee meeting held on 24 October in preparation for the coup, nor appeared at Smolny Palace the next day to take part in the assignment of duties. Instead, he spent the evening of 24 October and the day of 25 October with the Alliluev family.[11] The historian N. N. Sukhanov aptly notes that Stalin gave 'the impression of a gray blur, looming up now and then dimly, not leaving any trace'.[12]

The Second Congress of the Soviets opened during the Bolshevik uprising on 25 October, which became the official day of the 'October Revolution' (7 November, N.S.). Of the 650 delegates, 390 declared themselves to be Bolsheviks. Mensheviks and moderate Social Revolutionaries walked out in protest against what they called the 'Bolshevik adventure'. The Left Social Revolutionaries remained in the hall, indicating that they were the sole representatives of the peasantry.[13] They agreed to join the 'Soviet Government', which made it possible for Lenin to claim that his power was broadly based and represented the joint dictatorship of the proletariae and the poor peasantry. On 26 October 1917 Lenin announced the creation of the 'Council of People's Commissars', having rejected the traditional title of 'minister' as being too 'bourgeois', and named himself the 'Chairman of the Council'. He appointed Trotsky Commissar of Foreign Affairs. At the bottom of the list was the name of I. V. Dzhugashvili, the 'Commissar of Nationalities Affairs'.

Lenin saw in Stalin a 'non-Russian' spokesman on the nationalities problem, an important issue given the persistent conflict between various ethnic groups in the Russian empire. Lenin considered that his chief enemies were the Mensheviks, among whom were two prominent leaders, Tsereteli and Chkheidze, both Georgians. Lenin needed his own 'wonderful Georgian', a man who had the additional qualification of having written a theoretical pamphlet titled 'Marxism and the Nationalities Problems'. Lenin was also returning the favor for Stalin's past services: the expropriations and, more recently, Stalin's help in sheltering him in the Alliluevs' apartment and leading him to a hiding place in Rosliv when an order for his arrest had been out.

The first session of the Bolshevik government took place in Smolny Palace, in Lenin's office. Stalin attempted to strike up a conversation with Trotsky, who cut him short. Trotsky felt that Stalin's advances were out of place and found him unendurably vulgar. Stalin's face changed, and in his yellow eyes appeared the same glint of animosity that Trotsky had noticed during their brief encounter in Vienna in 1913.[14] On his first day on the job in Smolny Palace, Stalin furnished his corner of a room with a desk and two chairs, pinning above them a sheet of paper on which he had written, 'People's Commissariat of Nationalities Affairs'.[15] He moved from the Alliluevs' apartment to Smolny Palace and settled there in two small rooms on the ground floor.[16] This made it possible for him to be near Lenin at all times. At 2 am on 9 November 1917 Stalin was at Lenin's side when Lenin called the chief of staff of the Russian Army, General Dukhonin, and demanded immediate peace negotiations with the Germans. Dukhonin refused, so Lenin issued an order for the removal of Dukhonin and the appointment of N. V. Krylenko in his place. (At the outbreak of the First World War, Krylenko had deserted and fled abroad. In October 1915 Krylenko and his wife, Elena Rozmirovich, had secretly returned to Russia on an espionage mission of Parvus's 'Research Institute', settling in Moscow under the fictitious names 'Tsorn' and 'Sidorov', but on 4 November 1915 they had been arrested by the Okhrana and exiled. The February Revolution had set them free.[17]) Krylenko left for the Russian Army headquarters in Mogilev, where he instigated the execution of General Dukhonin by Red Guards. Krylenko ordered all front-line units to arrange their own cease-fire agreements with opposing enemy forces, and on 22 November 1917 concluded the preliminary armistice agreement with the Germans at Brest-Litovsk. Russian soldiers abandoned their trenches and headed home in entire units.

The German government concluded that the millions it had spent to support the Bolsheviks had been well invested. In his report of 3 December 1917 German Foreign Minister von Kuhlmann wrote:

Only when the Bolsheviks began to receive from us a constant flow of funds through various channels and under various names did it become possible for them to place their main organ *Pravda* on a sound footing, launch energetic propaganda, and to widen considerably the initially narrow base of their party. Now the Bolsheviks have come to power . . . They need peace to strengthen their own position . . . Signing a separate peace would mean the achievement of the desired military goal, namely, a breakup between Russia and her allies.[18]

On 17 November 1917 Parvus arrived in Stockholm and met Radek, who was elated – he considered Parvus one of the most influential people of the time and admired his financial success.[19] Parvus told him that he intended to ask Lenin's permission to return to Russia and was ready to defend himself against accusations of being a German agent. He asked Radek to relate his request to Lenin. Radek immediately left for Petrograd, accompanied by Ganetsky. On 18 November 1917 they crossed the Finnish border and sent Lenin a telegram, 'We travel by express train to Petrograd. We have a very important assignment. Asking for immediate conference.'[20] Lenin turned down Parvus's request, replying, 'The cause of the Revolution should not be marred by dirty hands.'[21] Lenin's reluctance to deal with Parvus was understandable; now that he had established direct contact with the Germans through their official representatives, he no longer had any use for Parvus, and any further association with the notorious German agent could only be a liability.

The news of the Bolshevik putsch reached Roman Malinovsky in his prisoner-of-war camp in Germany. He wrote a petition to the German Ministry of War, asking to be released and to be allowed promptly to return to Russia 'because the party to which I belong has taken power in Russia, my presence in Russia at this time could bring great benefits'.[22] The Germans, however, decided not to release Malinovsky until the general prisoner-of-war exchange took place as part of the peace settlement.

After the October insurrection the Bolshevik newspaper *Pravda* had declared, 'Comrades, by shedding your blood you have assured the convocation of the Constituent Assembly.'[23] Lenin accused Kerensky of sabotaging the elections to the Constituent Assembly on 12 November 1917 when, despite the well-financed Bolshevik propaganda, the results of the elections were not in their favor. Altogether 703 deputies were elected: 380 Right Social Revolutionaries, 39 Left Social Revolutionaries, 168 Bolsheviks, 18 Mensheviks, 17 Kadets and their allies, 4 Popular Socialists, and 77 representatives of minority groups.[24] Lenin ordered the arrest of several deputies in order to intimidate the others. He outlawed the Kadet Party. Two Kadet leaders, A. I. Shingarev and F. F. Kokoshkin, were arrested. A few weeks later they were murdered in a prison hospital. Lenin in his statements insisted that the Constituent Assembly would be allowed to convene on 18 January 1918, if it voted approval of the Soviet government. On 6 December 1917, there was an assassination attempt on Lenin's life, which gave him an excuse to unleash the 'Red Terror'.

Next day Lenin created the Soviet Secret Police, which became known as the Cheka (Extraordinary Commission to Combat Counterrevolution and Sabotage), of which Felix Dzerzhinsky was appointed chairman. Among the eight Cheka collegium members was Stalin's old friend Sergo Ordzhonikidze. The official duties of the Cheka were limited to preliminary investigation of criminal activities, but in fact it became Lenin's instrument of terror.

The Constituent Assembly held its opening session in Petrograd's Tavrida Palace on 18 January 1918. The leader of the Right Social Revolutionaries, Viktor Chernov, was elected chairman. Three resolutions were adopted: one on land reform, one on the appeal for a 'general democratic peace', and one proclaiming Russia a democratic federal republic. The session continued all night. At 5 am on 19 January 1918 a Red Guard sailor by the name of Zhelezniak interrupted the proceedings, declaring that the Assembly had to leave because 'the guards are tired'. At noon, the deputies returned but were prevented by Cheka detachments from entering Tavrida Palace. The Constituent Assembly was dispersed.

Peace negotiations with the Germans had begun at Brest-Litovsk on 22 December 1917. The Soviet strategy was based on the assumption that world revolution would start in the near future and it was necessary to stall the negotiations until the German communists came to power. 'Our final negotiations will be with Karl Liebknecht' (leader of the German Communists), declared Trotsky.[25]

German Foreign Minister von Kuhlmann and General von Hoffmann approached the peace issue from different perspectives. They considered the Bolsheviks to be German agents, deeply indebted to Germany for a sum in excess of 50 million gold marks that Lenin had received.[26] Von Kuhlmann had no intention of allowing the Bolshevik delegation to forget that they were on the payroll of the German government. On 5 January 1918 General von Hoffmann brought in a map and, pointing to a line on it, said that this was the future boundary of Russia. The line he indicated was the armistice front line, which cut deeply into the territory of former

Imperial Russia. On 8 February 1918 the Soviet government adopted the New Style (Gregorian) calendar, bringing Russia into line with the West. (Hereafter, all dates are given in New Style.) In early February, the Bolshevik Central Committee debated the German terms. Lenin proposed that they be accepted, but Trotsky advanced a strange 'no peace, no war' formula, while Bukharin was for a 'revolutionary war' against the Germans. Stalin voted with Lenin, but Trotsky's 'no war, no peace' formula was approved. Germany and Austria concluded a peace treaty with the Ukrainian *Rada* (parliament), which had proclaimed Ukrainian independence. To the astonishment of von Kuhlmann and General von Hoffmann, Trotsky declared that the Brest-Litovsk Peace Conference was closed and added, 'We are out of the war, but we refuse to sign the peace treaty.'[27] With these words, he left the conference and set out for Petrograd.

On 15 February 1918 the Germans announced the termination of the Brest-Litovsk armistice agreement and the German Army began its advance inside Russia. On 21 February 1918 Lenin's government proclaimed 'Holy Revolutionary War against the bourgeoisie and imperialists of Germany.'[28] Trotsky proposed to ask Britain and France, the allies of Imperial Russia, to provide the Bolsheviks with aid. Lenin sent a note to him, stating his agreement: 'I ask to add my vote in favor of taking potatoes and arms from the bandits of Anglo-French imperialism.'[29] On 23 February 1918 Berlin delivered new and much harsher German peace terms. Lenin demanded that the Central Committee immediately accept them. Stalin voted with Lenin. On 3 March 1918 the Bolshevik delegation, headed by Grigory Sokolnikov, signed the Treaty of Brest-Litovsk. The old Russian empire lost Poland, the Baltic states, the Ukraine, Finland, Bessarabia and a strip of Kars–Trebizond territory on the Russian–Turkish border. The total loss in population was close to 62 million people. A secret financial agreement was also added to the Brest-Litovsk Treaty, signed in Berlin and dated 27 August 1918. This reveals that Lenin shipped 90 tons of gold to Germany, which was probably the amount that the German government had spent to finance the Bolshevik takeover.[30]

In March 1918 the Seventh Party Congress approved the Brest-Litovsk Treaty and gave a new name to the party: 'Communist Party (b) – (Bolsheviks)'. The widespread popular disapproval of the Brest-Litovsk Treaty, the dispersal of the Constituent Assembly, and growing poverty and unemployment threatened Lenin's government. On 18 March 1918 Petrograd workers issued an appeal, stating that workers' committees in factories had been turned into the 'submissive tools of the Soviet government' and trade unions had become 'strictly government bodies and no longer express the opinions of the masses of workers'.[31] The anti-Bolshevik mood of Petrograd workers forced Lenin to order the evacuation of the Soviet government from Petrograd to Moscow on 12 March 1918. The evacuation was carried out secretly, as if it were a military operation.[32] Lenin's decision to seek security behind the ancient walls of Moscow's Kremlin was a symbolic reflection of the very essence of the Bolshevik putsch. The Bolsheviks claimed to represent the 'progressive' wave of the future communist utopia, but in fact they returned Russia to the medieval barbarity of the old Muscovy with its deranged Tsar Ivan the Terrible hiding behind the Kremlin walls. Stalin was one of the Soviet officials secretly moved from Petrograd to Moscow.

On 18 March 1918 the Petrograd newspaper *Vpered* (Forward) published an article by Menshevik leader Yuly Martov, stating that Stalin had been 'expelled from the party organization for having had something to do with expropriations'.[33] Stalin was enraged and demanded that Martov be tried for 'criminal libel of a Soviet official and slander of the Soviet government'. He stated with fervent indignation: 'Never in my life was I placed on trial before my party and expelled. This is a vicious libel . . . One has no right to come out with accusations like Martov's except with documents in one's hands. It is dishonest to throw mud on the basis of mere rumors . . . '.[34] Martov asked the court to collect affidavits from prominent Georgian revolutionaries who had expelled Stalin from the party and knew about the charge by a worker named Zharinov that Stalin had instigated an almost fatal attack on him.[35] The court assigned the prominent Menshevik and historian Boris Nikolaevsky to collect the testimony. When he returned to Moscow with the affidavits of the Georgian party members, he discovered that all the records of the court proceedings had disappeared. On 17 April 1918 the Petrograd newspaper *Zaria rossii* (Dawn of Russia) stated that the court refused to rule on Stalin's complaint because the complaint did not fall within its jurisdiction.[36]

In March 1918 a book titled *Bolsheviki* was published in Moscow with the stated purpose of relating the history of the Bolshevik party from 1903 to 1917. The introduction read:

The jubilant arrival of the Bolshevik leader Lenin on 4 February 1917 in Petrograd through Germany in a 'sealed' rail car created great turmoil in the minds of Russian citizens, inspiring endless gossip at all kinds of public gatherings and in the press. The Bolsheviks, until then known to very few, became a subject of discussion for the millions.[37]

Bolsheviki was intended to dispel the widely held notion of the Bolsheviks as German spies and Okhrana agents. But the book's authors could not erase from public memory the reports, published in 1917, about Bolsheviks like Roman Malinovsky who had been exposed as Okhrana agents, or the published Bolshevik list of 11 other such agents, among them one 'so far unidentified, who had the party alias Vasily'.[38]

The head of the Cheka, Dzerzhinsky, controlled the Okhrana archives in order to enlist into service former Okhrana officers and agents, as well as common criminals, prostitutes, and others vulnerable to blackmail. He issued a top-secret guide on how to recruit such people.[39] Dzerzhinsky had no specific interest in finding out who the unidentified Okhrana agent 'Vasily' was. Stalin, on the other hand, used his position as a member of Lenin's government to obscure the fact that he and 'Vasily' were the same person. It was at this point that Stalin made sure that the index of names, aliases and codenames in *Bolsheviki* would not identify him as either 'Vasily', or 'Ivanovich', or 'Ivanov'.

The new German Ambassador to Moscow, Count Wilhelm von Mirbach, arrived early in April 1918. After surveying the scene, he wrote to the German chancellor, Betmann–Gelveg:

The Bolshevik power in Moscow is mainly supported by Latvian battalions, and also by a large number of iron-plated cars, requisitioned by the government, which are continuously rushing around the city and can immediately deliver soldiers to vulnerable places when needed.[40]

On 17 May 1918 Mirbach sent a telegram to Foreign Minister von Kuhlmann stating,

I continue to do my best to counteract the efforts of the Allies and support the Bolsheviks. I, however, would be grateful to receive your instructions in regard to whether the general situation would justify spending large sums of money in our interests.

The next day, 18 May 1918, Mirbach received von Kuhlmann's reply:

Please spend large sums, because it is very much in our interests that the Bolsheviks remain in power. Ritzler's funds are at your disposal. If you need more money, please wire how much.[41]

The German money helped Lenin's government to survive, but it was the ruthless Red Terror of the Cheka that ensured the submission of the populace. Early in June 1918, popular anti-Bolshevik sentiment noticeably increased. Mirbach ascribed this to the manipulations of Russia's former allies, Britain and France. On 3 June 1918 Mirbach wired to the German foreign ministry: 'Because of the strong rivalry of the allies, three million marks a month are needed.' Mirbach's adviser, Trautmann, sent a memorandum to von Kuhlmann stating:

The fund which until now we had at our disposal for distribution in Russia has been exhausted. Because of this it is necessary for the Secretary of the Imperial Treasury to provide a new fund for our disposal. Taking into account the above-mentioned circumstances, this fund has to be, at least, no less than 40 million marks.[42]

By early June 1918 Russia was on the brink of famine and civil war, Lenin decided to organize 'Committees of Poor Peasants' which were intended to 'carry the class struggle to the village'. This was a policy of 'divide and conquer' by inciting the 'poor' peasants into attacking the 'rich' peasants, with the purpose of requisitioning their grain to feed the starving cities and the expanding party cadres. Rich peasants were labeled *kulaks* ('fist', an epithet for a peasant who keeps his crops in his tight fist) and were accused of keeping food from the starving population. In reality, there were no sharp class divisions among Russian peasants, almost all of whom owned some land and livestock. The 'Committees of Poor Peasants' attracted opportunists and lazy peasants who wanted to avenge private grievances. They formed an army of informers, who helped the Red Guards 'requisition' the crops of kulaks and often to execute them. The period of 'War Communism' had begun. The peasants were initially confused as to who was behind the state-organized requisition of the fruits of their labor: 'I am for the Bolsheviks but against the communists', was a typical claim. They remembered that the Bolshevik propaganda had promised them 'land, bread and peace'.

The Left Esers (SRs) assumed their traditional role of defenders of the peasantry, criticizing the 'Committees of Poor Peasants' as 'cliques of village loafers', and demanding termination of forced requisitioning of crops and annulment of the Brest-Litovsk Treaty. These demands fueled the conflict between the Bolsheviks and the Left Esers, who decided to carry out an anti-Bolshevik coup. The assassination of the German Ambassador von Mirbach was to serve as the signal for it. On 6 July 1918 two Left Esers, Yakov Blumkin and Nikolay Andreev, entered the German embassy at Number 5, Denezhny Lane in Moscow and asked to see Ambassador von Mirbach. Blumkin was a ranking member of the Cheka, while Andreev was a member of the Revolutionary Tribunal. They presented a Cheka document authorizing them to meet von Mirbach:

The All-Russian Extraordinary Commission delegates its member Yakov

Blumkin and the representative of the Revolutionary Tribunal Nikolay Andreev to enter into negotiations with the Ambassador to the Russian Republic in connection with a case that has direct relation to the Ambassador. Chairman Dzerzhinsky, Secretary Ksenafontov.[43]

Blumkin and Andreev were seated at a large marble table in a reception hall. Von Mirbach, his adviser Dr Ritzler, and a translator sat opposite them. Blumkin told a story about an arrest by the Cheka of a 'Count Robert von Mirbach', supposedly a relative of the Ambassador. When Von Mirbach said that he knew of no such relative, Andreev intervened, saying, 'Perhaps the Ambassador wants to know what measures will be taken by the Tribunal in the case of Count Robert von Mirbach?' This was an agreed signal. Blumkin opened his briefcase saying, 'Yes, yes, now I'll show the Ambassador . . .'. With these words, Blumkin drew a revolver and fired three shots, all of which missed. Von Mirbach rushed towards the door, but Andreev shot him in the back and threw a bomb, which exploded, killing Von Mirbach. Blumkin and Andreev jumped out of the window and were spirited away in a waiting car. German embassy officials called Lenin, who ordered Dzerzhinsky to go immediately to the German embassy. 'What do you say now, Mr Dzerzhinsky?' Ritzler reproached Dzerzhinsky, referring to the fact that the German embassy had repeatedly passed on to Dzerzhinsky information about plots to kill the German Ambassador. Ritzler showed Dzerzhinsky the Cheka authorization to meet the Ambassador, bearing Dzerzhinsky's own signature. Dzerzhinsky rushed to the Left Eser headquarters, where he learned that the uprising had already begun. A Left Eser leader by the name of Proshian said, 'Comrade Dzerzhinsky, do not bother looking for Blumkin. Count Mirbach was killed according to the decision of the party of Left Esers and the responsibility for the assassination we, the members of the Central Committee, take upon ourselves.'[44] Dzerzhinsky was disarmed and locked in a room. His assistant, M. I. Latsis, was captured in the Cheka Lubianka headquarters. 'No point in taking him anywhere, put this scum against the wall!' shouted a sailor, but one of the leaders, Alexandrovich, intervened, saying, 'There is no need to kill, comrades; arrest him, but do not kill.'[45] Dzerzhinsky's assistant Yakov Peters was urgently summoned by Trotsky, who ordered him to crush the uprising by attacking the Left Eser headquarters. Alexandrovich was caught at a railway station, and Latsis, whom he had saved from execution, personally shot him. Mass executions in Cheka prisons followed. Dzerzhinsky submitted his resignation to placate the Germans, who blamed him for not preventing the murder of Mirbach, but a month later was reinstated: 'Comrade Dzerzhinsky, whose resignation was accepted more than a month ago on his own request, is again appointed chairman of the VCheka [Cheka].'[46] Lenin needed Dzerzhinsky.

Stalin had left Moscow by train for the Volga port of Tsaritsyn on 3 June 1918, a month before the Left Eser uprising, on a mission to requisition grain from peasants in the Volga region. He was accompanied by Sergey Alliluev and Alliluev's youngest daughter Nadezhda, who had turned 17 and had asked to be Stalin's secretary. One night, Sergey Alliluev heard screams coming from Nadezhda's compartment. He rushed in with a pistol in his hand. Nadezhda, sobbing, told him that she had been raped by Stalin. Stalin pleaded with Alliluev not to turn the episode into a scandal and offered to marry Nadezhda. Because she was too young, their marriage was registered a year and a half later, on 24 November 1919.[47] Their son, who was born at that time, was named Vasily. The name Vasily continued to have special significance for Stalin.

NOTES

1. Donald W. Treadgold, *Twentieth Century Russia*, Chicago, 1976, pp. 135ff.
2. Ibid.
3. W. H. Chamberlain, *The Russian Revolution, 1917–1921*, vol. 1, New York, 1935, pp. 254ff.
4. David Shub, *Politicheskie deyateli rossii*, New York, 1969, p. 98.
5. V. I. Lenin, *Polnoe sobranie sochinenii*, 5th edn, vol. VI, Moscow, 1958–65, p. 217.
6. Treadgold, *Twentieth Century Russia*, p. 144.
7. Robert M. Slusser, *Stalin in October: the Man Who Missed the Revolution*, Baltimore/London, 1987, p. 230, quoting from *Protokoly tsentral'nogo komiteta RSDRP(b)*, August 1917 to February 1918, pp. 93ff.
8. Ibid., p. 109.
9. Ibid., p. 115.
10. Lev Trotsky, *Stalin*, New York, 1941, p. 239.
11. Anna S. Allilueva, *Vospominaniya*, Moscow, 1946, p. 61; quoted by Edward Ellis Smith, *The Young Stalin: the Early Years of an Elusive Revolutionary*, London, 1968, p. 374.
12. N. N. Sukhanov, *The Russian Revolution, 1917; Eyewitness Account*, vol. II, New York and London, 1955, pp. 229ff. Also quoted in Trotsky, *Stalin*, p. 194, and Smith, p. 345.
13. Ibid., vol. II, p. 624.
14. Lev Trotsky, *Stalin*, pp. 243ff.
15. Ibid., p. 245. Trotsky is quoting from Pestkovsky's memoirs.
16. Ibid., p. 243. Trotsky is quoting from Sergey Alliluev, 'Moi vospominaniya'.
17. *Bolsheviki*, Moscow, 1918, pp. 227ff.
18. Shub, *Politicheskie*, p. 232, quoting Z. A. Zeman, *Germany and the Revolution in Russia 1915–1917*, London, 1958, p. 95.
19. Shub, *Politicheskie*, p. 236, quoting A. Litvak, *Collected Works*, pp. 245, 252, 256.
20. Shub, *Politicheskie*, p. 234.
21. Ibid.
22. S. Passony, *Der Monat*, Heft 71, August 1954, p. 495.
23. *Pravda*, 26 October 1917.
24. Oliver Henry Radkey, *The Election to the Russian Constituent Assembly of 1917*, Cambridge, 1950, pp. 16ff.
25. Treadgold, *Twentieth Century Russia*, p. 152.

26. Shub, *Politicheskie*, pp. 187ff., quoting Eduard Bernstein, 'Ein Dunkeles Kapitel', *Vorwärts*, Berlin, 14 January 1921.
27. Trotsky, *Stalin*, p. 459.
28. Ibid., p. 460.
29. Treadgold, *Twentieth Century Russia*, p. 154.
30. *Lenin Sent Gold to Germany by the Ton*, see *Novoe Russkoe Slove*, 27 November 1997, p. 5. See also Dr Vladlen Sirotkin, 'Russian Gold and Real Estate Abroad', *International Life*, Moscow, 1997.
31. *Kontinent*, no. 2, 1975; reproduction on back cover.
32. I. Dubinsky-Mukhadze, *Kamo*, Moscow, 1974, pp. 81ff.
33. Y. Martov, 'Artilleriyskaya podgotovka', *Vpered*, 18 March 1918.
34. Bertram D. Wolfe, *Three Who Made a Revolution*, New York, 1964, p. 395.
35. See Chapter 8 above. See also Smith, *The Young Stalin*, pp. 208–10.
36. *Zaria rossii*, 17 April 1918. Also see Grigory Aronson, 'Stalinskii protest protiv Martova', *Sotsialisticheskii vestnik*, no. 7–8, 1939, pp. 84–9.
37. *Bolsheviki*, Introduction, p. i.
38. Ibid., p. ix.
39. A leading dissident, Petr Yakir, discovered this brochure in 1967 in the library of the widow of a high-placed Cheka official, and at that time showed it to many dissidents, among them Vitaly Svechinsky, Pavel Litvinov and Viktor Krasin. The brochure was taken from Yakir during a KGB search of his apartment in Moscow.
40. Shub, *Politicheskie*, p. 232, quoting Z. A. Zeman, *Germany and the Revolution in Russia 1915–1917*, London, 1958, p. 121.
41. Ibid.
42. Ibid., p. 233.
43. 'Roman Gul', *Dzherzhinsky*, New York, 1974, p. 114.
44. Ibid., pp. 113–22.
45. Ibid., p. 120.
46. *Iz istorii vserossiiskoi chrezvychainioi komissii, 1917–1921 gg.*, *Sbornik dokumentov*, pp. 150ff. Also P. I. Pimenov, 'Kak ya iskal shpiona Raili', *Materialy samizdata*, no. 14/72, 6 April 1972, p. 14.
47. Taped interview with I. P. Itskov.

14

RED TERROR

Before leaving for Tsaritsyn on 3 June 1918 , Stalin had expressed to Lenin and Sverdlov his strong opinion that the Tsar should under no circumstances be surrendered to the White Guards.[1] Stalin was preaching to the converted: Lenin had made up his mind long before the Revolution to destroy the Tsar and his entire family. He often quoted his idol Sergey Nechaev, who in one of his revolutionary appeals posed the question of who in the House of Romanov should be killed and answered it with the words: 'The full *ektenia*' (a prayer asking God to bless those mentioned in it, usually the entire royal family). '"Who of them, after all, should be killed?" a simple-minded reader would ask himself. "The entire House of Romanov!" was the answer he should have given himself. Look, this is so simple that it has the touch of genius.'[2] Lenin declared that it was 'necessary to cut off the heads of at least a hundred Romanovs'.[3] He considered Nechaev a 'titan of the revolution' and blamed Dostoyevsky for discrediting him in the eyes of Russian intelligentsia by depicting Nechaev as the *provocateur* Peter Verkhovensky in *The Possessed*. Nechaev in his *Revolutionary Catechism* had sermonized: 'A revolutionary knows only one science – the science of destruction and extermination. He lives in the world with this sole aim: to leave not one stone unturned; as many ruins as possible, the extinction of most of the revolutionaries – that is the perspective. Poison, the knife, the noose – the revolution consecrates everything.'[4] Lenin shared Nechaev's belief that the Revolution consecrated every crime – provided that it was Bolshevik driven.

After his abdication in February 1917 the Tsar and his family lived briefly in Tsarskoe Selo (Royal Village) near Petrograd, before being transferred by the Provisional Government to Tobolsk in Eastern Siberia. After the Bolsheviks came to power, the Tsar and his family were sent to Ekaterinburg at the end of May 1918 and placed under guard in a large brick house belonging to the local merchant Ipatiev. The Grand Duke Mikhail Romanov was sent to the town of Perm, where, on the night of 12 June 1918, he was the first to be murdered.[5] Lenin ordered the Ural Cheka Chief, Filip Goloshchekin, and the Ekaterinburg Cheka chief A. Beloborodov, to organize the murder of the Tsar and the royal family. They ordered Yakov Yurovsky, the commander of the detachment guarding Ipatiev's house, to shoot all members of the Tsar's family, as well as their servants, and secretly bury them.[6] On the night of 17 July 1918 Tsar Nikolay, Tsarina Alexandra, their son, Tsarevich Alexey, their four daughters, their maid Demidova, physician Doctor Botkin, the chef, and an attendant were led into a room in the basement of the Ipatiev house. Yurovsky, three assistants, and seven Latvian guards walked into the room. When Yurovsky started to read the death sentence, the Tsar asked, 'What?' and his daughters crossed themselves. Yurovsky drew his handgun and shot the Tsar. Then the other executioners started shooting. The bodies were loaded on a truck, which was driven to a long-abandoned mine deep in the woods, where they were buried under a pile of debris.[7]

On 18 July Sverdlov announced that 'The Presidium of the Ural Regional Soviet had adopted the decision to shoot Nikolay Romanov which was carried out on 16 July. The wife and son of Nikolay were sent to a secure place. Documents of the exposed conspiracy were sent to Moscow by special courier.'[8] Lenin listened to Sverdlov's announcement without lifting his head or taking his eyes from the papers in front of him, as if the murder had nothing to do with him. In response to repeated inquiries from the German Embassy about the fate of the Tsar's family, Radek and Foreign Commissar Chicherin insisted that only the Tsar had been shot, and that the members of his family were safe and well.

On 18 July a telegram signed by Beloborodov was sent to Sverdlov from the Urals stating that the former Grand Princes had been abducted in Alapaevsk 'by an unknown band'.[9] The corpses of the murdered princes were found in an abandoned mine after the White Army captured Alapaevsk. Autopsies revealed that Grand Prince Sergey Mikhailovich had been shot in the head. The other victims had been thrown into the mine alive, and their deaths had been caused by the fall.[10] The rest of the Tsar's relatives, who had been held as hostages in Petrograd's Peter and Paul Fortress, were executed there.

Ten years before the Revolution, Viacheslav Menzhinsky, a future head of the Soviet Secret Police, wrote that Lenin considered himself 'a natural heir to the Russian throne' and that if he ever became the ruler of Russia, 'this illegitimate child of Russian autocracy [would] really mess things up'.[11]

Lenin knew that the murder of the Tsar would cause turmoil and would throw the country into a maelstrom of violence and bloody civil war. This was in line with his agenda. 'Our slogan is civil war', he proclaimed. 'Let us raise the flag of civil war!'[12] He also knew that the murder of the Tsar would create an immense emotional void in the people and he intended to fill that void with his own persona. He wanted to establish a new legitimacy for his 'dictatorship of the proletariat', which in reality meant his own autocratic rule. The 'illegitimate child of Russian autocracy' did not mask his goal but stated brazenly that:

The speeches about equality, freedom and democracy in the present situation are gibberish . . . Already in 1918 I pointed out the necessity of one-person rule, the necessity of accepting the dictatorial power of one person from the point of view of implementing the Soviet idea. All phrases about equality are nonsense.[13]

Stalin, too, was an illegitimate child of Russian autocracy, who was to 'mess things up' no less than Lenin – but he was to do so while exercising great care in masking his actions with demagoguery.[14] Scholars have argued that in *The Brothers Karamazov* Dostoyevsky depicted Russian psychological types on the eve of the Revolution and that in the murder of Fedor Karamazov by the bastard Smerdiakov he foretold the murder of the Tsar. 'Where do they come from, these crowned lackeys, these Smerdiakovs, this triumphant rabble?' wondered D. Merezhkovsky, a prominent literary figure, as he watched the dregs of Russian society at the turn of the century rising from the pit of depravity to inundate the country: Okhrana *provocateurs*, expropriators, assassins, wild-eyed demagogues, political con artists and pretenders.[15] Hordes of criminals set free by the February Revolution joined in an orgy of violence. Marxist postulates served them as a convenient cover and justification for redressing real or imaginary grievances and for satisfying sadistic impulses.

Both Lenin and Stalin knew that the murder of the Tsar inflicted deep emotional injury on the Russian people, but Stalin sensed the severity of this injury more acutely than Lenin, for he had experienced a very similar trauma in his personal life: the murder of his father Vissarion was in psychological terms akin to the murder of *Tsar batiushka* (Father Tsar). Stalin instinctively understood the Russian people's collective trauma. For him, the Tsar assumed the enormously magnified image of Vissarion. Just as he kept silent about Vissarion's murder, Stalin during his rule also maintained absolute silence about the murder of the Tsar.

Having assumed power, Lenin continued to use criminal types to incite violence. Accounts of his encouragement of murders appeared in the press, which in early 1918 still dared to publish such information. In April 1918 the Petrograd newspaper *Novyi den'* (New Day) published an article titled 'The Case of the Shooting of Six Students', describing how a detachment of Red Sailors during a search of an apartment house on 2 March 1918 had arrested six students who were having a party with their girlfriends. The students were taken to Smolny Palace, where Commissar Panushkin, the head of the detachment, reported their arrest to Lenin. 'And what did you do with the arrested persons? Did you shoot them?' asked Lenin. 'No, we did not', answered Panushkin. 'Deliver them to Dzerzhinsky's Commission', said Lenin. 'But if something should happen to them on the way there, I would have nothing against it.' Panushkin interpreted Lenin's suggestion as the order to execute the students. Several Chekists volunteered to do the shooting. The students were driven to the outskirts of Petrograd and told to line up, facing a wall. When they refused, they were pushed against the wall by force and shot. Investigation of the case, initiated by parents anxious to find out what had happened to their sons, led to Lenin. Lenin claimed that he knew nothing about the shooting. The inquiry was soon terminated.[16]

Soon after the murder of the Tsar, attempts to assassinate Bolshevik leaders began. Lenin was alarmed. On 26 June 1918 he wrote a letter to Zinoviev castigating him for not ordering mass executions after Sergeev, a Petrograd worker, had shot the Bolshevik Volodarsky. On 9 August 1918 Lenin sent a telegram to the local Soviet in Nizhny Novgorod (later named Gorky) stating that 'You must immediately launch mass terror, shoot and exile hundreds of prostitutes who tempt soldiers to drink, former officers and so on. Not a minute to temporize. You must act with full might; mass searches. Shoot for keeping arms. Mass deportations of Mensheviks and unreliable people.'[17]

During one government meeting, he asked Dzerzhinsky how many people were in the Lubianka prison. Dzerzhinsky wrote down a figure and passed the note back to Lenin. Lenin put a cross next to the figure and returned it to Dzerzhinsky. Having glanced at the cross, Dzerzhinsky left the room to order the execution of all Lubianka prisoners. (The shootings generally took place in the prison's basement; the doomed prisoners were shot in the head with revolvers or rifles.) Krupskaya later on insisted that, in putting a cross next to the number of prisoners, Lenin had simply acknowledged the information, but Dzerzhinsky, knowing Lenin well, had no trouble decoding the real meaning.

Regarding the role of the courts in the unleashed terror, Lenin stated that 'The courts must not curb the [Bolshevik] terror, for to promise this would be a self-deception and deception, they must rather in principle guarantee and legalize the terror clearly, without falsehood and without embellishments.'[18] In a telegram Lenin sent in August 1918 he called for the establishment of a 'concentration camp' stating: 'It is necessary to launch merciless mass terror against kulaks, priests and White Guards; those about whom there are doubts should be placed in a concentration camp outside a city . . .'.[19] (A few years later Stalin and Hitler made concentration camps the mainstay of their regimes.)

On 30 August 1918 a Petrograd poet Leonid Kenigisser, who had just turned 20, assassinated the chairman of the Petrograd Cheka, M. S. Uritsky. Kenigisser was executed along with scores of other suspects.[20] On the same day, Lenin was severely wounded in an attempt on his life after addressing a meeting of workers at a factory in Moscow. He was about to get into his Rolls Royce (which had been the Tsar's personal car), when three shots were fired and he fell.[21] Two bullets struck him, one of them becoming lodged dangerously near his heart. Lenin's chauffeur raced to the Kremlin, where several prominent Moscow physicians, urgently summoned, saved his life. Cheka agents arrested Fannia Kaplan, a Right Eser who in 1906 had been sentenced to life imprisonment for a terrorist act, and released during the February Revolution. Kaplan confessed that she shot Lenin, but refused to name her accomplices.[22] She was executed in a Kremlin courtyard by the chief of the Kremlin guards.[23] (The execution was reported in the press, but for some reason the myth persisted for decades that Lenin spared her life and that she was sentenced to life imprisonment. As late as 1950, inmates in Butyrki prison in Moscow would point at a window in one of the towers, claiming that Kaplan was still incarcerated there.[24])

On the day after the attempt on Lenin's life, the Soviet government proclaimed the launching of 'Red Terror' and the Cheka declared the 'system of hostages' and 'mass executions of individually innocent class enemies.'[25] Soviet archives contain more than 7,000 unpublished documents with Lenin's signed orders, in which he instigates mass terror such as: 'Secretly prepare terror: necessary and quick'; 'Punish Latvia and Estonia by military means; for example, breach the border somewhere by at least one mile and hang 100–1000 of their bureaucrats and wealthy.' In these documents, Lenin calls for incitement to ethnic conflict, especially in the Caucasus, the 'sovietization' of Lithuania, Hungary, Czechoslovakia and Rumania, and the suppression of independence movements by means of mass executions. Lenin also gave orders to create concentration camps for foreign citizens and to wage campaigns to discredit foreign diplomats. (In December 1990, Soviet party officials discussed the publication of some 3,000 of these documents; the decision not to publish them being due to their embarrassing nature.[26])

On 30 August 1918, the day Lenin was wounded, the Soviet government published the statement: 'We do not doubt that here will be found the footprints of the hirelings of the English and the French.'[27] Cheka detachments broke into the British Embassy in Petrograd and murdered one of the diplomats, Captain Cromie. Dzerzhinsky declared that 'the main headquarters of counterrevolution are located in the foreign embassies and missions' and that it was necessary 'to gather unquestionable proofs of diplomats' criminal activities'.[28] (The Soviet government was at that time being financed through the German Embassy.)

On the night of 31 August the chief of the Kremlin guards, Malkov, broke into the Moscow apartment of Bruce Lockhart, who was representing British interests in Russia, and arrested him and his mistress Maria (Mura) Benkendorf, a Cheka agent. Lockhart was accused of plotting to overthrow the Soviet regime. The myth of the 'Lockhart Plot', the first Soviet international provocation, was born. It was to grow for decades into a highly profitable theme in the Soviet Union as well as in the West.

This provocation had a history. Before the signing of the Brest-Litovsk peace treaty, Lenin had asked the British to send troops to defend military supplies against German and Finnish attempts to capture them in the area of Archangel. After the signing of the treaty, the Germans demanded withdrawal of the British forces from the area. Lenin, Stalin and Dzerzhinsky decided to use Lockhart to infiltrate the headquarters of the commander of the British detachment in Archangel and to lure the British troops to a place where they could be easily surrounded and defeated.[29]

On Dzerzhinsky's order, a Cheka agent introduced himself to Lockhart as British intelligence officer Lieutenant Sidney G. Reilly. Actually his name was Rellinsky. He traded arms during the war and after the Bolsheviks came to power was arrested by the Cheka and recruited as an agent. His identity card with the name 'Sidney Grigorievich Rellinsky' was signed by a Cheka officer, former Okhrana agent V. Orlovsky.[30] He was sent to spy on the Whites during the Civil War, and later was assigned to work in the anti-Soviet organization 'Trest', created by the Cheka. (He was recalled to Moscow in 1927 and shot on Stalin's order as a British spy.[31])

Back in 1918 'Reilly' succeeded in befriending Lockhart, who was arrested with his lover Mura Benkendorf the day after the attempt on Lenin's life. Lockhart was accused of taking part in a 'plot to overthrow the Soviet government'. He was soon exchanged for the Soviet representative in London Maxim Litvinov, who had been arrested for spying for the Germans. Lockhart's lover Mura Benkendorf had been earlier recruited as a Cheka agent by Yakov Peters, Dzerzhinsky's assistant, who later wrote that she had been a 'German spy'.[32] Mura was released and sent abroad to carry out other Cheka assignments, among them to report on the activities of the writer Maxim Gorky. In 1920, she became the lover of H. G. Wells, who boasted that he had 'slept with Gorky's secretary'.[33]

In the summer of 1918 Stalin was in Tsaritsyn where, in one of his directives he demanded that villages in areas of resistance to Soviet rule should be burnt down to the ground.[34] The power entrusted to him by the Politburo in the area under his control made it possible for the first time in his life to arrange a mass murder. He ordered the arrest of military specialists – former Russian Army officers who had been drafted into the Red Army. The arrested officers were placed on a barge on the Volga. The floating prison was sunk, and the officers perished.[35] In this particular mass murder, Stalin went against Lenin and Trotsky, who considered military specialists indispensable for making the Red Army a credible fighting force in the civil war that had begun after the disbandment of the Constituent Assembly. Efrem Voroshilov and Semeon Budenny, on Stalin's urging, disobeyed orders of the Commander of the Southern Front former tsarist general N. N. Sytin. Trotsky complained to Lenin that Stalin had disrupted military operations. On 18 October Lenin recalled Stalin to Moscow and sent Trotsky to Tsaritsyn. At a small station, where their trains met and stopped briefly, Stalin asked Trotsky to be lenient with Voroshilov and Budenny.

On 22 October 1918 Stalin arrived in Moscow. The day after his arrival, he learned that his old rival Roman Malinovsky had just been arrested in Petrograd. Malinovsky had been released from a German prisoner-of-war camp in accordance with the Brest-Litovsk Treaty. He could have stayed in Germany, where he had once lived and worked, or he could have settled in his native Poland and begun a new life there. But he decided to return to Russia and attempt to gain readmission to the Bolshevik Party's top leadership. What mental gyrations led him to this decision is an intriguing question. He knew that he had been exposed as an Okhrana agent, yet for some reason he must have believed that, as in the past, Lenin would protect him and accept him into his inner circle. Bizarre though this belief may seem, it might have been based on more than wishful thinking. Malinovsky knew about Stalin's service in the Okhrana, having learned about it in 1913 from the director of the Department of Police, Beletsky. Having learned that Stalin had become a member of Lenin's government, Malinovsky may have surmised that his own Okhrana past would not be held against him and that he, too, might get a similar appointment. If this were his reasoning, he must not have known that Stalin had still not been identified as an Okhrana agent.

Zinoviev remembered Malinovsky and ordered his arrest when he appeared at Smolny Palace. Two days later Malinovsky was transferred to Moscow and was cross-examined by People's Commissar of Justice M. I. Kozlovsky (who a year earlier had been one of the intermediaries between Lenin and Parvus and accused by the Provisional Government of being a German agent). During his interrogation, Malinovsky insisted that he had returned to Russia because he wanted to 'redeem the sins of his life'. Kozlovsky complained that Malinovsky utilized 'all his remarkable talents in order to defend himself'.[36] The trial of Malinovsky took place on 5 November 1918 in the Kremlin in a secret session of the Highest Revolutionary Tribunal. The prosecutor was N. V. Krylenko, who, together with his wife Elena Rozmirovich, had been arrested by the Okhrana in 1915 as a German spy. Krylenko read the indictment, after which the Tribunal heard the testimonies of several witnesses, among them the former assistant minister of the interior, Dzhunkovsky, the former director of the Department of Police, Beletsky, and the former vice-director, Vissarionov, who were summoned from their prison cells to testify. Former Bolshevik Duma deputies Badaev and Petrovsky and Malinovsky's wife Stefania also testified. Malinovsky delivered a six-hour-long speech in his own defense. Lenin was present at the hearings, but did not testify. He listened to Malinovsky's speech without looking at him, at some points reacting with an occasional nod. While answering the accusation that he had received German money for his anti-Russian propaganda during the war, Malinovsky admitted the charge and said, 'It will ill become you to sit in judgment upon that.'[37]

No transcripts of the proceedings have ever been published, but several years later Krylenko stated in his memoirs that in his speech Malinovsky expressed remorse and declared that he deserved the death sentence for his crimes.[38] If Malinovsky had indeed said so, the reason may have been that he assumed his breast-beating would be seen as the obligatory rhetoric of contrition, to be rewarded with a mild sentence. But the Tribunal, unmoved, sentenced him to death. A few hours later, in the early hours of 6 November 1918 he was led into a Kremlin courtyard and shot. The tsarist officials Beletsky, Vissarionov, Dzhunkovsky and others were shot a few days later.

No information about whether or not Stalin was present in the courtroom has come to light. If any documents or recollections about his role in the court proceedings existed, he probably destroyed them during his rule. He also executed all those who had anything to do with Malinovsky's trial, including Krylenko, Rozmirovich and Kozlovsky. He destroyed everything that in his mind was in any way connected with Malinovsky, even to the point of obliterating every mention of Malinovsky's name in Lenin's writings published during Stalin's rule. The records of Malinovsky's interrogations, of his speech at the trial, the testimonies of witnesses, and other court documents are missing from the Soviet archives. Malinovsky's Okhrana file was not mentioned at the trial. Some pertinent documents, among them Lenin's testimony before the Muraviev Commission on 26 May 1917 and Zinoviev's testimony there on the same day, were found among Stalin's personal papers after his death. These were published for the first time in 1992.[39]

Malinovsky might have tried to expose Stalin as a fellow ex-Okhrana agent. If he had, Stalin could counter the accusation by calling it slander. He could – as he had done eight months earlier, when Martov had accused him of having been expelled from the party – defend himself by indignantly protesting that no one had the right to accuse a member of the Soviet government without documentary evidence. The existence of such evidence was not known at the time. Still, Stalin must have been apprehensive throughout the trial and very much relieved when it was over and Malinovsky had been silenced.

During Malinovsky's trial, Vladimir Burtsev, the famous exposer of Okhrana agents, was in prison and shared his cell with the former director of the Department of Police, Beletsky. Later Beletsky was executed, but Burtsev was released. He escaped abroad, settling for the rest of his days in Paris, where he wrote his memoirs, in which he recalled his conversations with Beletsky in prison. Burtsev's reminiscences make no mention of Beletsky's having remembered the Okhrana agent Iosif Dzhugashvili. Beletsky may have been aware that this ex-agent was now a member of Lenin's government, or may have feared the wrath of Stalin. Five years had passed since Beletsky had sealed the file of this agent and exiled him to Siberia. By 1918 Beletsky may well have forgotten the name 'Dzhugashvili'. For the director of the Department of Police, Iosif Dzhugashvili was one of innumerable Okhrana agents of no particular importance whom he encountered during his many years of service. Beletsky may well have been unaware that 'Dzhugashvili' and Stalin were one and the same person. The thought that any Okhrana agent would become one of the most important figures of the twentieth century was inconceivable in 1918.

NOTES

1. Lev Trotsky, *Stalin*, New York, 1941, p. 414. Trotsky is quoting Bessedovsky, who recalled Stalin saying: 'Under no circumstances must the Tsar be surrendered to the White Guards.'

2. V. D. Bonch-Bruevich, *Lenin o khudozhestevennoy literature*, Moscow, 1934, p. 18. See also David Shub, *Politicheskie deyateli rossii*, New York, 1969, pp. 92f.

3. V. I. Lenin, Polnoe sobranie sochinenii, Moscow, 1958–65, vol. XV, p. 285. See also Shub, p. 96.

4. S. Nechaev, *Revolutionary Catechism*, quoted in Roy Medvedev, *Let History Judge*, New York, 1971, p. 334. Medvedev states that Yuri Karyakin in his article on Dostoyevsky (in *Problemy mira i sotsialisma*, no. 5, 1963, and English translation in *World Marxist Review*, no. 5, 1963) drew an analogy between Stalin and Nechaev that had some validity. Karyakin also revealed to Medvedev that Nechaev's archive, thought to be lost, was returned to its place after 1953, from Stalin's office (p. 335).

5. N. Sokolov, *Ubiystvo tsarskoy semi*, Buenos Aires, 1969, pp. 265f.

6. Ibid., pp. 134ff. and p. 245.

7. Ibid., pp. 235ff.

8. Ibid., p. 246.

9. Ibid., p. 260.

10. Ibid., p. 264.

11. Roman Gul', *Dzerzhinsky*, New York, 1974, p. 154.

12. V. I. Lenin, *Polnoe sobranie sochinenii*, vol. XXXV, 4th edn, p. 129. Also quoted in Shub, *Politicheskie*, pp. 275–8.

13. V. I. Lenin, *Polnoe sobranie sochinenii*, vol. XXX, 4th edn, pp. 472–5. Also Shub, *Politicheskie*, p. 277.

14. How determined and methodical Stalin was in suppressing incriminating evidence has become apparent over the years. When V. Korotich, editor of the Soviet journal *Ogonek*, stated in 1988 that Stalin was responsible for mass terror, he was accused of slander by the Soviet State Prosecutor who argued that Stalin's responsibility could not be proved since Stalin's signature could not be found on any order of mass execution. Interview with V. Korotich by phone on 29 May 1992.

15. D. S. Merezhkovsky, *Griadushchii kham*, 1906, p. 21.

16. 'Delo rasstrela shesti studentov', *Novyi den*, no. 20, 17/4 April 1918.

17. V. I. Lenin, *Polnoe sobranie sochinenii*, XXXV. 4th edn, p. 286.

18. V. I. Lenin, *Polnoe sobranie sochinenii*, vol. XXVII, 2nd edn, p. 296.

19. V. I. Lenin, *Polnoe sobranie sochinenii*, vol. XXIX, 2nd edn, p. 489.

20. Gul', *Dzerzhinsky*, pp. 121ff.

21. I .P. Itskov, in a typed interview with the author, stated that at the time of the transfer of the Tsar from Tsarskoe Selo to Tobolsk, his staff had secretly dug a large hole in the ground and buried in it the Rolls Royce and the Tsarina's personal car, a Delane Belville, in the hope that the cars would be saved when the Royal Family returned to Petrograd. One of the Tsar's attendants was a sailor, Maxim Nikandrov. After the October insurrection, Nikandrov joined the Bolsheviks. He led Red Guards to the buried cars, and they were dug out. The Tsar's Rolls Royce was taken over by Lenin; the Tsarina's limousine was given to Trotsky. Nikandrov was rewarded by being appointed chief of the Kremlin garage.

22. Historian Boris Orlov of Jerusalem University claims in a research paper that Fannia Kaplan did not shoot Lenin and that she was only on a lookout for other Eser assassins, who escaped. See Boris Orlov, 'Mif o Fannia Kaplan', *Vremia i my*, nos 2 and 3, December 1975 and January 1976.

23. I. P. Itskov, taped interview.

24. The present author heard this story many times during his incarceration in Butyrki and Lubianka in 1950–55.

25. Trotsky, *Stalin*, p. 462.

26. Serge Schmemann, 'Soviet Archives', *The New York Times*, 8 February 1993, p. A-8.

27. P. I. Pimenov, 'Kak ya iskal shpiona Raili', *Materialy Samizdat*, p. 20.

28. Ibid., pp. 39–42.

29. Ibid., p. 17.

30. Ibid., p. 19. Rellinsky, born in Odessa in 1874, was the illegitimate child of a certain Rosenblum and learned English from sailors. Rellinsky had several wives, one of whom was the daughter of a British merchant marine captain by the name of Reilly. Rellinsky adopted and russified her name.

31. Pimenov, 'Kak ya iskal shpiona Raili', pp. 7–12.

32. Y. Piters, 'Rabota v cheka v pervye gody revoliutsii', *Proletarskaya revolutsiya*, no. 10, 1924, p. 29.

33. See the story of M. I. Zakrevskaya-Benkendorf-Budberg (Mura) in N. Berberova, *Zheleznaya zhenshchina*, New York, 1982.

34. *Pravda*, 20 September 1963; quoted in Medvedev, *Let History*, p. 15.

35. Medvedev, *Let History*, p. 13.

36. *Pravda*, no. 237, 1 November 1918, p. 4.

37. Vladimir L. Burtsev, 'Lenin i Malinovsky', *Russkoe slovo*, vol. I, no. 9/10, 17 May 1919, p. 139.

38. N. Krylenko, *Za piat' let, 1918–1922 g.*, Moscow, 1923, p. 348.

39. 'Delo provokatora Malinovskogo', *Respublika*, 1992, pp. 49–57.

15

'THE OLD MAN WANTS POISON'

On 11 November 1918 the First World War ended with the signing of the armistice agreement. The Hohenzollern and Hapsburg Empires were toppled not by socialist revolution, as Lenin, Trotsky and other Bolsheviks had prophesied, but by military defeat. The Soviet government annulled the Brest-Litovsk Treaty and ordered the Red Army to recapture the ceded territories. Winston Churchill called on the former allies of Russia to help the Whites in the Civil War to fight the Red Bolsheviks, but the Western democracies, exhausted by four years of bloody conflict, had no desire to enter another war. French Prime Minister Georges Clemenceau called merely for a *cordon sanitaire* around the Soviet state, perceiving Bolshevism as a kind of plague threatening mankind.

Early in 1919 Stalin and Dzerzhinsky were sent to the Ural front, where they immediately started summary executions. Then Stalin was sent to the southern front, where he interfered with the orders of career Russian army officers drafted in the Red Army, before being recalled to Moscow by Trotsky. At the Eighth Party Congress in March 1919 Voroshilov and Stalin's other 'Tsaritsyn boys' came out in opposition to the policy of drafting former tsarist officers as military specialists. Stalin claimed that this opposition was not aimed against Lenin, but against Trotsky. The Congress passed a resolution, stating that there was 'no military policy of Trotsky's . . . only the military policy of the Central Committee, which Trotsky was carrying out'. Stalin countered with a semantic diversion by proposing that opposition to the military policy not be considered as opposition.[1]

On 4 March 1919 Stalin and Nadezhda Allilueva were married. Nadezhda retained her maiden name, thus symbolically affirming the emancipation of women, which at that time was fashionable among party members. Soon after, their son Vasily was born. The family moved into a small apartment in the Poteshny (Amusement) Palace in the Kremlin, where all members of Lenin's government lived. On 16 March Yakov Sverdlov, whom Stalin had once accused of being an Okhrana agent, died suddenly. Rumor immediately spread that Sverdlov had been poisoned. At the time, no one suspected Stalin of poisoning a rival, but, given Stalin's later history, if this was a case of premeditated poisoning Stalin could be considered a likely suspect. Stalin was not averse to the idea of using poison, as is clear from a remark he made after hearing of the poisoning of an opposition leader in Turkey: 'This is how a political conflict should be ended . . .'.[2]

In October 1919 the White forces of General Yudenich were moving toward Petrograd and Zinoviev ordered evacuation of the city. Trotsky took personal command, reprimanding Zinoviev for losing his head; Zinoviev was deeply offended.[3] Toward the end of the year, the Whites retreated from Petrograd. In early December 1918 the White forces of Admiral Kolchak were defeated in Siberia and he was executed.[4] In April 1920 elements of the White Army regrouped in the Crimea under General P. N. Wrangel's command, but within a few months the Red Army defeated the Whites.

On 7 May 1920 the Polish Army of General Pilsudsky, the leader of Poland, occupied Kiev. Red Army units under the command of Mikhail Tukhachevsky (the future Soviet marshal) were sent to the Polish front. On 1 August 1920 those units broke through the northern sector of the Polish front and captured Brest-Litovsk. Ten days later Tukhachevsky was nearing the suburbs of Warsaw. In the rear of Tukhachevsky's army rode Felix Dzerzhinsky, a Pole, whom Lenin intended to appoint dictator of Poland. Dzerzhinsky savored the expected capture of Pilsudsky: 'I myself will put him against the wall and shoot him.'[5]

Stalin was sent to the southwestern front, where A. I. Yegorov was in command. On Stalin's insistence, Yegorov disregarded Trotsky's order to attack the Polish Army near Warsaw and led his cavalry in the direction of Lvov. On 15 August 1920 Stalin, urged on by Lenin and Trotsky, agreed to move Yegorov's cavalry to Warsaw, but it was too late. Tukhachevsky's army was defeated and retreated from Polish territory. The armistice treaty with Poland was signed on 12 October 1920. Tukhachevsky blamed Stalin for the defeat of his forces at Warsaw.[6]

In May 1920, Lenin signed a peace treaty with the Georgian Republic, where the Mensheviks were in power. But Lenin had no intention of relinquishing what he considered his inheritance from the tsars. Less than a year later, on 11 February 1921, the Red Army invaded Georgia. The decision to invade was made secretly by Lenin, Stalin and Ordzhonikidze; at the time Trotsky was in the Ural area. On 21 February 1920 Trotsky requested an explanation for the invasion of Georgia, asking, 'When did these operations begin, by whose order . . . ?'[7] The question was moot. By that time, Georgian Mensheviks, nationalists and other opponents of Soviet rule were being arrested by Cheka troops.

The Tenth Party Congress, which opened on 8 March 1921, adopted

Lenin's proposal to declare any kind of opposition to Politburo policy illegal. The Congress also approved Lenin's New Economic Policy (known as the NEP). The policy was Lenin's attempt to reach a compromise with the peasantry, which resisted forced requisition of food by refusing to produce it, thereby causing famine in many areas. In the Volga and Ukraine region cases of cannibalism were reported. Legions of abandoned children, whose families had been torn apart by the Civil War and famine, roamed the impoverished land in search of food and shelter. Lenin decided to strike a deal with the peasantry by replacing the forced requisition of food with a policy of taxation in kind. Lenin was also frightened by peasant uprisings in many areas, the largest of which flared up in the Tombov region. Red Army units were ordered to crush the peasant rebels who were called 'bandits'. An order of 1 September 1920 demanded the application of 'merciless Red Terror to the families of the rebels. Arrest all members of such families starting from the age of eighteen without regard to gender, and if the bandits want to continue the rebellion, shoot them.'[8] A special order was issued, listing the categories of peasants to be shot.[9] On 18 March 1921 Trotsky led Red Army units to crush the rebellion of sailors in the fortress of Kronstadt, near Petrograd, at the mouth of the Neva river. Four years earlier, the Kronstadt sailors had been the backbone of the Bolshevik putsch.

In July 1921, Stalin visited Tiflis for the first time in ten years. His son Yakov, who was 13 years old, and members of the family of his first wife, Keke Svanidze, came to see him. Yakov had been a year and a half old when his mother had died in 1909, and had grown up in the Svanidze family. It so happened that Yakov's school teacher was Iosif Iremashvili, Stalin's childhood friend, a Menshevik, who was in prison awaiting execution when Stalin arrived in Georgia. His sister pleaded with Stalin to save his old friend. Yakov may also have pleaded for his teacher. Stalin ordered the release of Iremashvili and allowed him to go abroad.

At the end of 1921 Yakov came to Moscow to join his father. Stalin was not in favor of having his son living with him, but Stalin's wife, Nadezhda Allilueva, accepted Yakov. She was only six years older than Yakov, but she was determined to be a good stepmother to the boy, who spoke almost no Russian. Because of the addition to his family, Stalin asked Lenin to assign him a larger Kremlin apartment. Stalin was by then an important member of the government, Commissar of Nationalities Affairs. In 1919 Lenin had appointed Stalin to the post of Chairman of the 'Workers and Peasants Inspection'. Stalin's responsibility was to fight corruption and criminal neglect in all branches of the Soviet government and industry. The position gave him the power to prosecute people, as well as to appoint his cronies in important positions. In a country suffering from hunger and shortages of every commodity, Stalin's appointments meant precious access to means of survival. Even Lenin felt his dependence on Stalin. In a letter dated 4 June 1921 he complained that he could not help his old friends find jobs. Stalin was placing his own men in key bureaucratic positions, paying no attention to even Lenin's recommendations, while accusing Lenin of favoritism.[10]

At the Eleventh Party Congress, which opened on 27 March 1922, Lenin proposed the creation of the post of general secretary to improve the effectiveness of party bureaucracy. Zinoviev suggested Stalin for the post. There were no other candidacies or objections, and the proposal was accepted.[11] 'It was one of many such events to which no one paid any attention', Lenin's friend Drabkina was to write years later.[12] The future was to reveal how mistaken this perception was. Stalin transformed a seemingly insignificant appointment into an office of great importance. He had a photographic memory for names, events and figures which he used to consolidate his power.[13] Stalin's memory and keen sense of spite made him a formidable enemy. Trotsky took note of Stalin's uncanny ability to remember: 'All of his hurts, resentments, bitterness, envy, and attachments he transferred from the small scale of the province to the grand scale of the entire country. He did not forget anything. His memory is above all spiteful. He creates his own five-year plan and even ten-year plan of revenge.'[14]

One of these plans of revenge Stalin realized on 14 July 1922. That day Kamo was run over by a truck as he rode his bicycle on his way home from his office. Stalin did not come to the funeral of his old friend, but shortly after, a special envoy from Moscow visited Kamo's wife and sisters and took all of his papers for 'transfer to the archives'. Suspicions arose that Kamo's murder had been orderd by Stalin and Ordzhonikidze, and the Georgian Bolsheviks made an attempt to bring both to trial for the crime.[15] During the preceding years Kamo had maintained contact with Lenin, who helped him get various government appointments. Early in 1922 he had been appointed chief of the Customs Administration of the Caucasian Region, with an office in Tiflis. In May 1922 Lenin contemplated 'taking Kamo along' on his trip to the Caucasus.[16]

Lenin continued to maintain friendly relations with Stalin until September 1922, when he learned that on Stalin's instruction the journal

Proletarskaya revolutsiya (Proletarian Revolution) had published two telegrams confirming the accusation that Lenin had been receiving German
money.[17] Lenin had always denied this.[18] The publication of the telegrams
exposed him as a liar and confirmed the Provisional Government's charges
that he had been an agent of Germany. Lenin learned that I. P. Tovstukha,
Stalin's protégé, who had earlier been the head of Stalin's Secretariat at the
Commissariat of Nationalities, had, on Stalin's behest, been appointed
editor of *Proletarskaya revoliutsiya*. It so happened that at the Ninth Party
Congress Kamenev had been asked to prepare for publication Lenin's
collected works, and he needed an assistant. Tovstukha was known for his
phenomenal memory, and Stalin recommended him, stating that Tovstukha
'knew Lenin's writings even better than Lenin'. Tovstukha searched the
Provisional Government archives, finding there Lenin's correspondence
with Parvus's agents, intercepted by Russian military intelligence. Lenin
interpreted the publication of the telegrams as a brazen attempt by Stalin to
blackmail him. Stalin, fearing that his full role in the intrigue might be
exposed, quickly sacrificed Tovstukha, whom he fired from all his posts.[19]
The post Tovstukha had held in the Central Committee went to his assistant A. N. Poskrebyshev.[20] (After Lenin's death Stalin reinstated Tovstukha
as the head of his Secretariat, and in 1927 Tovstukha published the first
biography of Stalin.[21] A year later, he developed tuberculosis and was fired
by Stalin who was afraid of becoming infected. Tovstukha soon died, and
Poskrebyshev was moved into his position.[22])

Lenin, not mollified by the firing of Tovstukha, decided to remove
Stalin from his position of power as general secretary. 'That cook will
prepare nothing but peppery dishes', he said to Trotsky, informing him of
his decision.[23] Lenin might have feared that other compromising archival
documents had wound up in Stalin's hands, as by this time he had developed a deep distrust of Stalin. In October 1922 Krupskaya, pointing at
Stalin's Kremlin apartment, told Trotsky in a hushed voice that Lenin
considered Stalin 'devoid of the most elementary honesty, the simplest
human honesty'.[24] Removing Stalin from his posts was no longer an easy
task, however. Lenin chose a political issue as a smoke screen behind which
he hid his real motives in attacking Stalin. He focused on an event that took
place in October 1922. In an angry clash with Georgian Bolsheviks in Tiflis,
Ordzhonikidze, as was his habit, struck one of them in the face. He routinely
used to beat his secretary Semushkin and to throw full ink pots at him.[25]
The Georgian Bolsheviks complained to Lenin about Ordzhonikidze's
brutality, and on 21 October 1922 Lenin sent Stalin a note, stating that
'conflict, conducted in a more seemly and loyal tone, should be settled

by the Secretariat'.[26] Shortly thereafter, Lenin received a letter from M. Okudzhava, a member of the Georgian Central Committee, who added more information to the previous complaint against Ordzhonikidze. Lenin decided to devote serious attention to the 'Georgian affair' and to accuse Stalin of encouraging violence.[27]

On 24 November 1922 Stalin suggested that a 'commission of inquiry' into the 'Georgian affair' be formed, with Dzerzhinsky as its chairman. Dzerzhinsky was still the chief of the Soviet secret police, recently renamed GPU (*Gosudarstvennoe politicheskoe upravlenie* or State Political Administration). Lenin's intention was to create the impression that the Cheka, notorious for its mass repressions, had been replaced by a more humane organ. In fact, the GPU was given much wider power than the Cheka had ever had. Unlike the Cheka it was, for instance, authorized to arrest party members; even they now began to fear Dzerzhinsky. Lenin, suspecting Dzerzhinsky of collusion with Stalin, objected and asked Aleksey Rykov, formerly one of his chief lieutenants and now Commissar for Internal Affairs, to go and personally investigate the Georgian complaint. On 9 December 1922 Rykov gave Lenin his version of the scandal, and three days later Dzerzhinsky submitted his report, which confirmed Lenin's suspicion that Stalin and Dzerzhinsky had been conniving to suppress the inquiry and to cover up Ordzhonikidze's violence, while protecting themselves from charges of complicity. Lenin's secretary Maria Fotieva recorded in Lenin's diary that Dzerzhinsky's report 'upset him deeply'.[28] On 13 December 1922, the day after reading Dzerzhinsky's report, Lenin sent a letter to Trotsky inviting him to join hands against Stalin. 'I think we have arrived at full agreement, and I am asking you to announce our solidarity at the plenary session', wrote Lenin.[29] Hours later, he suffered two heart attacks. On 16 December 1922, Lenin had another, very serious attack.

Two days later, at a meeting of the Central Committee, Stalin was appointed chairman of a medical *concilium*, consisting, besides himself, of Politburo members Kamenev and Bukharin, as well as several Kremlin doctors. The purpose of the *concilium*, the resolution stated, was to monitor Lenin's health, and to inform the party and the country of any changes in his condition. Stalin's duty was to keep informed about everything that happened at Lenin's bedside.[30] Citing his concern for Lenin's health, Stalin insisted on Lenin being isolated from all sources of information on current affairs that might upset him.[31] Krupskaya was allowed by Lenin's physician, Dr Forster, a member of the *concilium*, to take brief dictation from Lenin. Stalin learned about this and called her on the telephone, cursed her in obscene language, and accused her of 'disobeying doctor's orders'. She was deeply hurt, but decided not to tell Lenin about Stalin's outburst, fearing she would upset him. But she did complain to Kamenev, who promptly reported the conversation to Stalin.[32]

Several days later, on 23 December 1922, Lenin felt a little better. He summoned Maria Volodicheva, a secretary, and told her to take dictation, which he entitled 'Letter to the Congress'. He stated: 'Comrade Stalin on becoming general secretary concentrated enormous power in his hands and I am not sure he always knows how to use this power carefully enough.'[33] Knowing that Stalin had to be informed about everything that happened at Lenin's bedside, Volodicheva sent a copy of the dictation to him. The next day Lenin continued his dictation, belatedly telling Volodicheva, 'What was dictated yesterday and today is *absolutely* secret.' Volodicheva decided not to send Stalin a copy of the second dictation, but told Nadezhda Allilueva, Stalin's wife, who worked in Lenin's Secretariat, that Lenin had dictated some messages criticizing Stalin. Nadezhda passed this on to Stalin, who summoned Volodicheva, telling her to bring Lenin's dictation. In Stalin's office she found Zinoviev, Kamenev and Dzerzhinsky, all examining Lenin's dictations. 'Burn all of them', Stalin instructed her; Volodicheva refused. By this time she had begun to realize that Lenin's dictations were of great importance and ought to have been kept secret.[34] But the damage had been done; Stalin had learned that Lenin was plotting his downfall.

On 27 December 1922 Lenin dictated a letter to Politburo members in which he supported Trotsky in a conflict with Bukharin on the question of the State Planning Agency.[35] Bukharin did not realize that Lenin and Stalin were using political issues as props to hide their real motives and he wound up being an unwitting ally of Stalin against Lenin and Trotsky. Zinoviev and Kamenev also sided with Stalin, for personal reasons. They considered Trotsky the most likely successor to Lenin and feared that, if he came to power, he would threaten their positions in the party leadership. Zinoviev was afraid that Trotsky would remove him from his position, as he had done in October 1919. Besides, Trotsky had deeply offended Zinoviev and Kamenev by recalling in his published memoirs that they had opposed the October Revolution and that Lenin had branded them 'strike-breakers' and demanded their expulsion from the party. The fact that Stalin had defended them from Lenin's criticism inspired their gratitude. The personal resentment against Trotsky greatly contributed to the formation of the 'triumvirate' of Zinoviev, Kamenev and Stalin.

The triumvirate had existed in an embryonic state since 11 September 1922, when Lenin proposed to appoint Trotsky deputy chairman of the Soviet of People's Commissars – that is, in effect, his deputy – but Trotsky refused. Stalin, Zinoviev and Kamenev were relieved, but Stalin immediately decided to utilize Trotsky's refusal. On 14 September 1922 he submitted a motion to censure Trotsky for 'dereliction of duty' in refusing to accept Lenin's and the party's appointment.[36] By the end of December Lenin and Trotsky took a joint stand against the positions of the triumvirate on the questions of state monopoly. The members of the Central Committee supported Lenin and Trotsky. 'We have captured the position without firing a shot', Lenin said in a note to Trotsky. 'I propose that we do not stop, but press on with the attack . . .'.[37] On 4 January 1923 he did a brief dictation, advising the Central Committee to remove Stalin from the post of general secretary, stating that 'Stalin is too rude, and this defect . . . becomes intolerable in a general secretary. This is why I suggest that the comrades think about a way to remove Stalin from that post . . .'.[38]

On 24 January 1923 Lenin asked his secretary, Maria Fotieva, to bring him documents on the Georgian affair, but Stalin refused to release the documents, pointing to the Politburo's decision to allow Lenin, because of his health, only ten minutes a day for dictation and to forbid him access to any information that might be a 'cause for reflection and anxiety'. Fotieva repeated Lenin's request at the next Politburo meeting. 'Since Vladimir Ilyich insists, I think it would be even worse to refuse', said Kamenev, turning to Stalin, who replied with undisguised annoyance, 'I don't know. Let him do as he likes.'[39] Then, addressing all the Politburo members, Stalin declared that he wanted to be released from the responsibility of supervising Lenin's recovery. As he had expected, his request was denied.

Stalin's political survival depended on Lenin's total isolation. Fotieva attempted to obtain the documents on the Georgian affair from Aron Solts, a member of the Central Control Commission, whom many party members considered the conscience of the party. Solts said that the documents had disappeared. 'What do you mean disappeared?' she asked. 'Just disappeared', Solts answered.[40] Fotieva reported this conversation to Lenin, who at once set up a 'clandestine commission of inquiry' consisting of his personal secretaries Fotieva, Gorbunov and Maria Gliasser, and told them to locate the lost documents. On 14 February 1923 he dictated a note to Fotieva: 'Did Stalin know [of the Ordzhonikidze incident]? Why didn't he do something about it?' He added: 'The label "deviationist" for chauvinistic deviation and Menshevism indicates the same deviation among the Great Russian chauvinists.'[41] Lenin accused Stalin and Ordzhonikidze of brutal treatment of their own ethnic minority which was typical of Great Russian chauvinists. Lenin also identified Stalin's method of pinning labels on opponents and charging them with exactly the same crimes of which he himself was guilty. Identifying this method was easy for Lenin, since he himself had been a practitioner of it.

In the preceding years, some changes in Lenin's personality had taken place, suggesting that his attitude towards others was softening. In 1920, for instance, he helped his old enemy, the Menshevik leader Yuly Martov, to escape abroad, stating that 'some commissars are more Leninist than I'. He had Stalin in mind, knowing that Stalin sought revenge for the March 1918 article in which Martov had accused Stalin of having at one time been expelled from the party. When Lenin learned that Martov was dying in Berlin, he eulogized him by saying that Martov had been a wonderful comrade and what a pity it was that Martov was not at his side.[42]

Lenin was alarmed by Stalin's packing the Twelfth Party Congress with delegates loyal to him personally and invited Trotsky to join in attacking Stalin. 'I propose a bloc', said Lenin. 'It is a pleasure to form a bloc with a good man', answered Trotsky. Lenin dictated an article titled 'Better Fewer, But Better', in which he criticized Stalin's 'bureaucratic misrule and wantonness'. Stalin glibly observed, 'I suppose there is no need to print this, especially as we do not have Lenin's authorization.'[43] Trotsky demanded publication of the article, and Stalin's crony Valerian Kuibyshev suggested a 'compromise': to publish the articles in a bogus issue of *Pravda* and to show it to Lenin. Trotsky objected, and the idea was abandoned.[44]

During the month of February, Stalin appeared at Politburo meetings, in Trotsky's words, 'morose, his pipe firmly clenched between his teeth, a sinister gleam in his jaundiced eyes, snarling back instead of answering'. Trotsky's interpretation was that Stalin knew his fate was at stake and that he was resolved to overcome all obstacles.[45] Stalin had learned of the Lenin–Trotsky 'bloc' by listening in on telephone conversations between Lenin, Trotsky and other Politburo members on the secret Kremlin telephone system, called *vertushka* (cranker), which had been installed by a Czech engineer on Lenin's request when he had fallen ill. Stalin ordered a central listening device installed in his desk. When the system was ready, Stalin told Dzerzhinsky's assistant Genrikh Yagoda that the Czech engineer was a spy. He was then arrested and shot. Stalin secretly listened in on telephone conversations for hours.[46]

After a Politburo meeting at the end of February 1923 Trotsky, Zinoviev, Kamenev and Stalin remained alone; Stalin said that Lenin had asked to have poison brought to him. Trotsky knew that Dr Guetier had said a few days earlier, 'Vladimir Ilyich can get on his feet again. He has a powerful constitution.' Trotsky also thought of Lenin as the incarnation of the will to live. It did not occur to Trotsky to question the motive of Stalin's claim. (Only decades later Trotsky arrived at the conclusion that Stalin was doing the groundwork for a scheme in which Lenin's death by poison would be explained as suicide.) 'Naturally, we cannot even consider carrying out this request!' exclaimed Trotsky. 'Guetier has not lost hope. Lenin can still recover.' Trotsky was struck by how Stalin's face, a sickly smile transfixed on it, was extraordinarily enigmatic and out of tune with the circumstances of the request. 'I told him all that', Stalin replied with a touch of annoyance, 'but he wouldn't listen. The Old Man is suffering. He says he wants to have the poison at hand . . . he'll use it only when he is convinced that his condition is hopeless.' Trotsky, Zinoviev and Kamenev were familiar with the striking discrepancy between Stalin's facial expression and the substance of his words. This time Trotsky found this discrepancy utterly insufferable. The horror of it was magnified by Stalin's refusal to express any opinion about Lenin's request, as if he were expecting others to respond and wanted to catch their reaction without committing himself. Kamenev, who was sincere in his devotion to Lenin, stood pale and silent. Zinoviev appeared bewildered, as he always was in difficult moments. It was not clear to Trotsky whether Stalin's two allies had known about Lenin's request beforehand or whether Stalin's announcement was as great a surprise to them as to him. 'Anyway, it is out of the question', insisted Trotsky. 'He might succumb to a passing mood and take an irrevocable step.' Zinoviev seemed to agree. 'The Old Man is suffering', repeated Stalin, staring vaguely past his three colleagues and, as before, not committing himself one way or the other. This was an informal conference and no vote was taken, so Trotsky assumed that the agreement was not to send poison to Lenin, but he was left with the sensation that Stalin's behavior was baffling and that thoughts not in harmony with his words were running through his mind.[47]

Lenin learned about Stalin's rude treatment of Krupskaya. On 5 March 1923 he dictated a 'highly secret, personal' letter to Stalin, with 'copies to Comrades Kamenev and Zinoviev'. The letter read, 'You had the effrontery to call my wife on the phone and to swear at her . . . I do not intend to forget it so easily. What is done against my wife I consider done against myself.' Lenin asked Stalin to apologize or 'break all relations between us'.[48] Next day, Lenin called Volodicheva and dictated an urgent letter to Trotsky to be communicated immediately over the phone. The letter read, 'To Trotsky: I earnestly ask you to undertake the defense of the Georgian affair in the Central Committee of the party. That affair is now under 'prosecution' by Stalin and Dzerzhinsky, and I cannot rely on their impartiality. Indeed, quite the contrary!' Trotsky agreed. Fotieva wrote that Lenin 'is getting worse and is in a hurry to do what he can'. She added that Lenin was preparing a 'bombshell' for Stalin, which he intended to explode at the Twelfth Party Congress.[49] Kamenev learned about the 'bombshell' from Krupskaya, who told him that Lenin was planning to 'crush Stalin politically'. Kamenev then rushed to consult with Stalin and Zinoviev, who delegated to Kamenev the task of initiating negotiations with Trotsky, hoping that, as a member of Trotsky's family (he was married to Trotsky's sister), Kamenev would be able to reach an agreement with him. On 7 March 1923 Kamenev appeared in Trotsky's office. He seemed contrite and anxious to mollify Trotsky, and he told Trotsky that the triumvirate was ready to satisfy Lenin's and his terms. Trotsky forgot Lenin's warning about the 'rotten compromise' that Stalin would offer. 'I am against removing Stalin', he said, 'and I am against expelling Ordzhonikidze and disciplining Dzerzhinsky . . . but I agree with Lenin in substance.' Trotsky's terms were easy to satisfy: he asked Stalin to condemn 'Great Russian Chauvinism', apologize to Krupskaya, stop bullying the Georgians, and be more polite to his party colleagues. Stalin readily agreed to all these demands; he would have agreed to many more for the sake of his political survival.[50]

On that day, 7 March 1923, Lenin suffered a severe stroke. The right side of his body was paralyzed, and he lost the ability to speak. Trotsky had lost his powerful ally. He still had Lenin's notes on the Georgian affair and could have used them to remove Stalin, but his promise not to read them to the Twelfth Party Congress, which opened on 17 April 1923, overrode his earlier promise to Lenin to take up the defense of the Georgian affair and to crush Stalin politically. Instead, he submitted Lenin's notes to the Politburo, not to the Congress.[51] Stalin, trying to appease Trotsky, asked him to address the Congress in the name of the Central Committee. Trotsky, in a fit of fatal magnanimity, suggested that Stalin deliver the address as general secretary, to which Stalin modestly replied, 'No, the party would not understand it . . . the report must be made by the most popular member of the Central Committee.'[52] It was decided that Zinoviev would deliver the main address. Trotsky gave a report on economic matters. The Georgian Bolsheviks felt betrayed, and so did Lenin.

On 10 March 1923 newspapers had begun publishing daily bulletins on the state of Lenin's health, and on 15 May 1923 Lenin was moved from the Kremlin to a *dacha* in Gorki, in the rolling hills near Moscow. By July his health had dramatically improved. He took walks, made local visits, and

1. House of the Dzhugashvili family, where Stalin was born. [*Source*: David King Collection]

2. Stalin's mother, Ekaterina Georgievna Dzhugashvili (née Geladze). [*Source*: F. D. Volkov, *The Rise and Fall of Stalin*, Moscow, Spektor, 1992]

3. Kamo being delivered
from Germany in shackles
to the Tiflis prison in 1909.
[*Source*: I. M. Dubinsky-
Mukhadze, *Kamo*, Moscow,
Molodaya Gvardia, 1974]

4. Prison photographs of Stalin at the time of his last arrest in 1913, taken from Stalin's St Petersburg Okhrana file. [*Source*: David King Collection]

5. The 'Eremin Letter', published in *Life* magazine, 23 April 1956, in L. D. Levine's article 'A Document on Stalin as Czarist Spy'. Eremin's engraved signature on the silver decanter was displayed by Levine to prove that the signature on the 'Eremin Letter' was geniuine. The letter was actually fabricated by Stalin in June 1937. He forged Eremin's signature, adding to it a long slanted flourish to prove that the letter was a forgery, as well as some other detectable 'mistakes'. [*Source*: *Life* magazine]

МИНИСТЕРСТВО

ВНУТРЕННИХЪ ДѢЛЪ.

ДЕПАРТАМЕНТЪ

ПОЛИЦІИ.

По Особому Отдѣлу.

31 Марта 1911

№ 101145

По 3 Отдѣленію.

Секретно.

Завѣдующему Заграничной Агентурой.

Въ дополненіе къ предложенію отъ 7 минувшаго Февраля за № 98570, Департаментъ Полиціи препровождаетъ при семъ Вашему Высокоблагородію копію записки Начальника Тифлисскаго Губернскаго Жандармскаго Управленія отъ 14 сего Марта за № 53-с.

Исп.об.Вице-Директора

Завѣдующій Особымъ Отдѣломъ, Полковникъ

6. A copy of the original Okhrana document, dated 31 March 1911, with quite legible authentic signature of Colonel Eremin ending with Russian letter 'n' and a period. Eremin usually signed official Okhrana communications as 'Colonel Eremin' when addressing them as a military officer to a person with a military rank. This document is in the Okhrana archive at the Hoover Institution, Stanford University. [*Source*: courtesy of the Hoover Institution, Stanford University]

7. Ekaterina Svanidze, first wife of Stalin. [*Source*: F. D. Volkov, *The Rise and Fall of Stalin*, Moscow, Spektor, 1992]

8. Fabricated photograph of Lenin sitting next to Stalin. This propaganda fake of the two leaders was originally two separate photos of different sizes and the men were sitting on obviously different chairs. These two photos were pasted together in a crude fabrication intended to demonstrate their friendship on the eve of Lenin's death. This fabrication was published in numerous books. [*Source*: David King Collection]

9. Roman Malinovsky.
[*Source*: Edward Ellis Smith, *The Young Stalin*, London, Cassell]

10. Nadezhda Allilueva, Stalin's second wife, shortly before her suicide in 1932.
[*Source*: David King Collection]

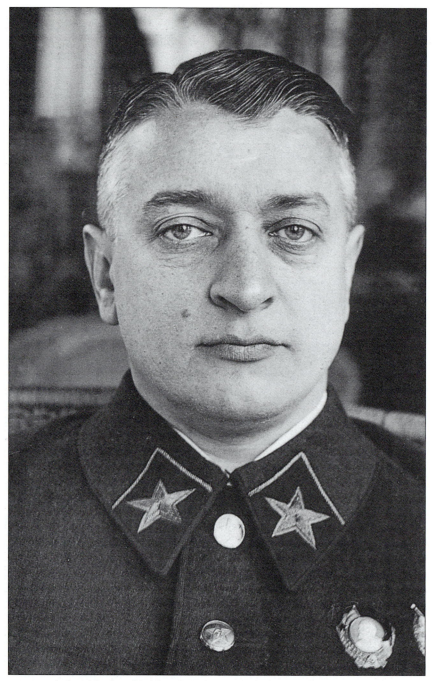

11. Marshal Mikhail Tukhachevsky. [*Source*: David King Collection]

12. Prison camp inmates building the White Sea–Baltic Canal. [*Source*: David King Collection]

13. Stalin with Yezhov (right) and Molotov and Voroshilov (left), at the opening of the White Sea–Baltic Canal. [*Source*: David King Collection]

14. People's demonstration in Red Square in 1938. [*Source*: David King Collection]

15. Chief prosecutor Andrey Vyshinsky at the Moscow show trial. [*Source*: David King Collection]

16. Stalin's son Yakov Dzhugashvili, captured by the Nazis. [*Source*: David King Collection]

17. Stalin and Ribbentrop watching as Molotov signs the Nazi–Soviet Pact in August 1939. [*Source*: David King Collection]

18. Lev Trotsky and his wife Natalia Sedova arrive in Mexico in 1937. [*Source*: David King Collection]

19. A Mexican policeman holds up the axe that killed Trotsky. [*Source*: David King Collection]

20. Funeral procession in March 1953 with the coffin of Stalin. In the first row are Beria, Voroshilov, Khrushchev and Mikoyan. [*Source:* David King Collection]

started to write with his left hand. In August he convinced his doctors to allow him to read newspapers. On 18 October 1923 he went to the Kremlin, took a walk in the streets of Moscow, visited an agricultural exhibition, and returned to his Kremlin office, where he sat for a while silently. Then, he returned to the Gorki *dacha*. A number of officials and friends visited him there between 24 November and 16 December 1923. Stalin was not among them.

On 16 December 1923 Stalin, despite optimistic prognoses of Lenin's physicians, ordered all visits to Lenin stopped. He was well aware that the improvement in Lenin's health boded ill for his own political survival. Isolating 'the old man' would at least hinder Lenin's struggle to demote him. The possibility of Lenin's recovery forced Stalin to look for ways to save himself. Zinoviev, Kamenev and Dzerzhinsky visited Stalin in his *dacha* in Zubalovo, near Moscow. They were drinking wine when Stalin said that his greatest pleasure in life was, 'To choose the victim, to prepare the blow with care, to slake an implacable vengeance, and then to go to bed . . . there is nothing sweeter in the world.'[53] Stalin knew that at the moment he had no greater and more powerful enemy than Lenin.

On 20 December 1923 Stalin invited Zinoviev, Kamenev and Bukharin to an informal Politburo meeting at which he stated that arrangements should be made for Lenin's funeral in case his health should take a turn for the worse. Stalin suggested that Lenin's body should be embalmed and placed in a mausoleum. He explained that Lenin was Russian, and that his funeral should be arranged in accordance with Russian customs and trad-itions. Bukharin, the only ethnic Russian in the group, was puzzled: he had never heard of such a custom in Russia. In the Russian Orthodox Church, the tradition of worshiping *moschi*, the skeleton remains of saints, existed, but Stalin proposed to preserve not Lenin's skeleton, but his mummy. This idea was more akin to the ancient Egyptian custom of embalming their Pharaohs than to the Russian tradition. Besides, the church was unlikely to canonize Lenin. Kamenev objected to the idea of embalming. Since the discussion was informal, no vote was taken. Lenin was alive, and the ques-tion seemed academic.[54] But it had been raised, and for Stalin it was not academic.[55]

On 18 December 1923 *Pravda* carried an article by Stalin in which he stated that party leadership without Trotsky was 'unthinkable'. Shortly afterwards Trotsky suddenly became ill. His physicians could not determine the nature of the infection. On 21 December 1923 five Kremlin doctors and the commissar of health, Semashko, signed the diagnosis of Trotsky's illness: influenza, catarrh in the upper respiratory organs, enlargement of bronchial glands, persistent fever, loss of weight and appetite, and reduced capacity for work. They advised that Trotsky be released from all his duties and sent to the Caucasus for a 'climatic cure for at least two months'. Ordinarily, a diagnosis of this nature was not made public, but this time it was published in *Pravda*, on 8 January 1924, without Trotsky's knowledge. Trotsky interpreted this as a 'polite way' of exiling him. On 18 January 1923 he left Moscow for the Caucasus.[56] On 19 January, as Trotsky's train was traveling hundreds of kilometers south of Moscow, Lenin watched a hunting party in a forest near his Gorki *dacha*. His health was improving.

On 21 January 1924 Lenin's health suddenly deteriorated. He called Gavril Volkov, his cook, and scribbled a note, 'Gavrilushka, I have been poisoned . . . Go fetch Nadia [Krupskaya] at once . . . Tell Trotsky . . . Tell everyone you can.'[57] Volkov called Maria Ulianova, Lenin's sister, who found him silently and helplessly crying. Lenin died the same day at 6:50 pm.

Stalin made all the arrangements for the funeral, and sent a coded wire announcing Lenin's death to Trotsky, whose train was approaching Tiflis. For Trotsky, Lenin's death was an unexpected and devastating blow. Before he left Moscow, Lenin's doctors had assured Trotsky that Lenin was on the road to recovery. Trotsky sent a message to Stalin, 'Lenin is no more. These words fall upon our mind as heavily as a gigantic rock falls into the sea. I deem it necessary to return to Moscow. When is the funeral?' Stalin replied, 'The funeral will take place on Saturday. You will not be able to return in time. The Politburo thinks that because of the state of your health, you must proceed to Sukhum. Stalin.' Trotsky followed Stalin's instructions.[58]

Stalin had lied. The funeral in fact took place six days later, on 27 January 1924, owing to difficulties in arranging the embalming. No embalming specialists could be found in Russia. GPU agents brought to Moscow from Kharkov a prominent pathologist-anatomist by the name of Vorobiev and his assistants, who joined Professor B. I. Zbarsky. Their experience was limited to embalming organs and animals for scientific purposes, but they could not disobey the mighty Politburo. The mummified body of Lenin, enclosed in a glass catafalque, was placed on display in the House of Columns. A long line of mourners inched along, day and night, in the freezing cold. People stopped briefly at burning piles of wood to warm themselves and then moved on to see Lenin's body. Stalin's farewell speech, which he read from a sheet of paper, was an odd litany in which overtones of Byzantine invocation were mixed with Marxist idioms, 'In leaving us Comrade Lenin ordained us to keep and strengthen the dictatorship of the proletariat. We vow to thee, Comrade Lenin, that we shall not spare our lives to fulfill your commandment.'[59] Stalin punctuated his speech with a plethora of vows of this kind.

Stalin's half-mythical oath before the corpse of his fallen enemy may appear to be sheer hypocrisy, but it should not be perceived as such. It was but a reflection of the workings of his peculiar mind, for at that moment Stalin may indeed have been overwhelmed by a deep need for identification with Lenin. Almost two decades earlier he had felt a strong emotional need to identify with his dead father, Vissarion, whose murder he had instigated. In his mind, Lenin had replaced Vissarion – the embodiment of his image of the stern and punishing father. Stalin also had an intuitive understanding of the emotional need of the Russian masses to identify with their dead leader. The great majority of the Russian people were deeply religious, illiterate peasants. The liturgical style of the invocation delivered by Stalin, a seminary dropout, evoked in them the memory of centuries-old religious traditions and found a ready response in the consciousness of all those in whom the murder of *Tsar batiushka* (Tsar the Father) had created a spiritual vacuum. Stalin sensed the longing for this vacuum to be filled, and at once set out to create a Lenin cult, in which he would assume the role of Lenin's heir. Zinoviev was the most active in fostering this cult, and on 30 January 1924, he wrote in an article in *Pravda* stating, 'How good that they thought of this in time! To bury Ilyich's body in the ground – that would be unendurable.'[60] By 'they' Zinoviev meant that he, Stalin, Kamenev and Bukharin had agreed on the embalming.

The official communiqué attributed Lenin's death to arterial sclerosis. When Trotsky returned to Moscow, he asked Kremlin doctors about the cause of Lenin's death. They disagreed with the official communiqué, but were at a loss to explain the death. Lenin's friends, who had been assured that Lenin was recovering, were equally stunned by his death.[61] An autopsy was not performed because the embalming made it impossible. Besides, Trotsky would not have demanded an autopsy, since at the time the thought that Stalin might have poisoned Lenin did not cross his mind. He also did not ask Krupskaya's opinion, because he did not want to cause her more pain. Some two years later, Trotsky asked Kamenev and Zinoviev about the circumstances under which Lenin had died. They answered in mono-syllables, avoided his eyes, and were unwilling to discuss the matter. Trotsky wondered whether they knew something or were merely suspicious; he began to suspect that they did know something but did not want to tell him.[62] Fifteen years later, Trotsky came to the conclusion that Stalin had resorted to embalming because, he may have feared that I would connect Lenin's death with last year's conversation about poison, would ask the doctors whether poisoning was involved, and demand a special autopsy. It was, therefore, safer in all respects to keep me away until after the body had been embalmed, the viscera cremated and a postmortem examination inspired by such suspicions no longer feasible.[63]

Genrikh Yagoda, Dzerzhinsky's assistant, had been a pharmacist before the Revolution. He took part in revolutionary activities and was arrested by the Okhrana and released after agreeing to become an Okhrana agent. His Okhrana file was found in the archives and wound up in the hands of one of Dzerzhinsky's assistants, M. A. Trilisser, who gave the file to Stalin.[64] Stalin kept such documents in his personal archive for use in blackmailing people into committing crimes on his instigation. Yagoda was one of the first victims of this kind of blackmail. His expertise in drugs allowed him to set up a secret laboratory to produce poisons.[65] Stalin asked Yagoda to make poison for Lenin and passed on to him Lenin's gratitude for sending him a 'means of deliverance'. Stalin explained to Yagoda that Lenin had 'written a few words to thank you . . . He is terribly distressed by the thought of a fresh attack . . .'.[66] Yagoda, fully aware that Stalin had at his hands the means of his destruction, was only too eager to believe the same invented story about Lenin's request for poison that Stalin had earlier told Trotsky, Zinoviev and Kamenev.

It is unknown which of Stalin's agents at the Gorki *dacha* put poison in Lenin's food. The nature of the poison remains also unknown. Bazhanov, Stalin's secretary, who fled abroad in 1926, wrote in his memoirs that Stalin had 'made a certain amount of progress since the days of Caesar Borgia' in using poison. Bazhanov suggested that Stalin used 'a culture of Koch bacilli mixed into food and systematically administered' which 'gradually led to galloping consumption and sudden death . . .'.[67] It is far more likely that Stalin used a conventional poison. (In later years cyanide became his poison of choice against his enemies.[68])

After Lenin's death, rumors that Stalin poisoned him began to circulate. These rumors originated mostly among Georgian Bolsheviks, who knew about the conflict over the Georgian affair and were familiar with Stalin's character.[69] Some old Bolsheviks did not believe the official explanation of Lenin's death. They thought that he had died of inherited or acquired syphilis. In the privacy of their homes, they would point at Lenin's portrait, which traditionally hung on a wall, and refer to Lenin as 'that *sifilitik*' (syphilitic), sometimes in the presence of their little children or grandchildren, who would point to Lenin's portrait, saying 'this is uncle Titi-Liti'.[70]

To direct suspicion away from himself, Stalin fabricated letters supposedly sent to the Politburo by ordinary people in the provinces, demanding the embalming of Lenin's body. He gave these to Professor Zbarsky, who wrote a book, stating 'The idea to preserve the body of V. I. Lenin originated in the very thick of the population. The most insistent demands came from the faraway provinces.' He then quoted at length some of these 'demands'. A group of Kiev railroad workers allegedly wrote: 'Immediately assign needed specialists to work on the problem of preserving the body of our dear Vladimir Ilyich for thousands of years . . .'. A group of 'Rostov-on-Don students' allegedly demanded that 'The body of Ilyich should not be buried in the ground but embalmed and placed in a central museum; by doing this the workers of the future centuries will have the opportunity to see the leader of the proletariat.'[71]

Half a century later Stalin's fabrications were still accepted as genuine letters. A Russian author, L. Lanina, stated that if the demands to embalm Lenin's body came from among the people, it means that 'having broken through all the restraining dikes, archaic instincts gushed from the depth of the unconscious to the very surface of life', and that only there could have originated 'the monstrous idea of embalming the *vozhd* [the leader] and to place him in a central museum'.[72] Actually, archaic instincts, with a considerable admixture of very pragmatic calculations by a hardened criminal, gushed to the surface not from the unconscious mind of the Russian people, but from the dark recesses of Stalin's own mind. Which is not to say that they did not find a response in the masses. In 1927 a marble mausoleum for Lenin's embalmed body was built in Red Square on Stalin's order. For the next quarter of a century, Stalin was to greet military parades and civilian demonstrations from the top of this mausoleum. Under his feet, Lenin's corpse lay enclosed in a glass sarcophagus.

Many years after Lenin's death, Stalin let slip unguarded references to the poisoning of Lenin. In the early 1930s, Stalin and Bukharin attended a dinner at Maxim Gorky's home in Moscow. The guests, as usual, were drinking a great deal. Stalin suddenly started to recount how the ailing Lenin had pleaded for poison so that he might put an end to his suffering. Stalin added a new detail to this invented story, stating that he had given Lenin his 'word of honor' to bring the poison. 'Lenin had complete trust in me', said Stalin, 'but I decided not to give poison to Lenin, but to ask the Politburo members to relieve me from the burden of my word of honor, and the Politburo members relieved me from my word of honor.' Stalin looked at Bukharin, who had listened silently. Stalin suddenly grabbed him by the beard. Turning to the guests, he shouted, 'Do you believe me, or do you believe Bukharin?' A chorus of frightened guests shouted, 'You! You!' One guest was slow to respond. 'Ah, you are afraid?' shouted Stalin, and the frightened man joined the chorus of believers.[73]

When drunk, Stalin sometimes let the truth out. Once in the mid-1930s, he invited a group of Soviet writers to a dinner in his *dacha*. He drank copiously, and at one point he suddenly began to brag that only he knew how and from what Lenin had died. I. M. Gronsky, at that time an *Izvestia* editor and Stalin's liaison with the literary circles, stayed sober, since it was his duty to maintain order and keep his eye on the guests. Gronsky realized that Stalin was bragging about his role in Lenin's death. He led Stalin to his room, where he fell asleep. 'What a sober man keeps in his mind, a drunk keeps on the edge of his tongue', Gronsky thought. He ordered the drunken writers to be driven home by bodyguards. When Stalin awoke, he began to recall what had happened at the dinner. He suddenly shouted, 'Ivan! Tell me the truth! What was I saying yesterday about Lenin's death?' Gronsky pretended to have heard nothing and claimed that everybody had been too drunk to remember anything. 'Ivan! But you were not drunk!' shouted Stalin. 'What did you hear?' Gronsky, realizing that all the maniacal suspiciousness of Stalin would be directed against him, claimed that he had heard nothing about Lenin. Soon afterward he was arrested as an 'enemy of the people', and spent more than 16 years in the Kolyma camp. Released and 'rehabilitated' after Stalin's death, he told this story. He was certain that Stalin had poisoned Lenin.[74]

In the mid-1980s, KGB researchers established that Stalin poisoned Lenin, but this discovery was not reported, although it circulated in KGB circles as 'confidential information'. Yulian Semenov, the author of many stories about daring exploits of Soviet intelligence, enjoyed the trust of KGB officers and the head of KGB Yury Andropov. Semenov stated that the KGB did not reveal Stalin's role in the poisoning of Lenin because this was a 'very sensitive subject'.[75]

NOTES

1. Roy Medvedev, *Let History Judge*, New York, 1971, pp. 12–15.
2. Anton Antonov-Ovseenko, *Portret tirana*, New York, 1980, p. 178.
3. Medvedev, *Let History Judge*, p. 41.
4. Lev Trotsky, *Stalin*, New York, 1941, p. 466.
5. Roman Gul', *Dzerzhinsky*, New York, 1974, p. 133.
6. Trotsky, *Stalin*, p. 467.
7. Ibid., p. 468.
8. S. Melgunov, *Kak bolsheviki zakhvatili vlast'*; quoted in Vladimir Maximov, *Novoe russkoe slovo*, 20 May 1988, p. 3.
9. Ibid.

10. Medvedev, *Let History Judge*, p. 19.
11. Ibid., p. 17.
12. E. Drabkina, 'Zimnii pereval', in Roy Medvedev's *Almanakh XX Vek*, no. 2, p. 17.
13. Andrey Gromyko, who knew Stalin well, claimed that Stalin had the memory of a computer.
14. Trotsky, *Stalin*, p. 415.
15. A. Avtorkhanov, *Zagadka smerty Stalina*, Frankfurt, 1976, p. 50.
16. I. Dubinsky-Mukhadze, *Kamo*, Moscow, 1974, pp. 216f., quoting V. I. Lenin, *Polnoe sobranie sochinenii*, Moscow, 1958–65, vol. LIV, p. 230.
17. *Proletarskaya revolutsiya*, no. 9, 1922, and David Shub, *Politicheskie deyateli rossii*, New York, 1969, p. 218.
18. Shub, *Politicheskie deyateli rossii*, p. 186, quoting *Rabochy soldat*, 26 July 1917.
19. Avtorkhanov, *Zagadka smerty Stalina*, pp. 19–24.
20. Alexander Poskrebyshev, who was to become Stalin's alter ego for the next three decades, was born in 1891 to a peasant family in a village near Ekaterinburg. His criminal career began on 16 July 1918, when, as a member of the Ekaterinburg Gubernia Soviet of Deputies, he signed the death sentence of the Tsar and the royal family. Later on, he distinguished himself in mass executions. In 1921, Stalin transferred Poskrebyshev to Moscow, where for a while he operated in Tovstukha's shadow.
21. I. P. Tovstukha, *Iosif Vissarionovich Stalin*, Moscow, 1927.
22. Interview with I. P. Itskov, in New York, 1989.
23. Trotsky, *Stalin*, p. 372.
24. Ibid., p. 375.
25. Interview with I. P. Itskov.
26. Lenin, *Polnoe sobranie sochinenii*, vol. XIV, p. 608.
27. R. Pipes, *The Formation of the Soviet Union, Communism and Nationalism, 1917–1923*, Cambridge, MA, 1964, p. 281.
28. Lenin, *Polnoe sobranie sochinenii*, vol. XIV, p. 596. See also L. A. Fotieva, *Iz vospominanii o V. I. Lenine, dekabr 1922 g.–mart 1923 g.*, Moscow, 1964, p. 54.
29. Medvedev, *Let History Judge*, p. 20.
30. Moshe Lewin, *Lenin's Last Struggle*, New York, 1968, pp. 70f.
31. Medvedev, *Let History Judge*, p. 22.
32. Lewin, *Lenin's Last Struggle*, p. 71.
33. Lenin, *Polnoe sobranie sochinenii*, vol. XLV, p. 345.
34. Medvedev, *Let History Judge*, p. 25.
35. Lenin, *Polnoe sobranie sochinenii*, vol. XXXVI, pp. 548f.
36. Isaac Deutscher, *The Prophet Unarmed*, New York, London, 1954, pp. 65f. Deutscher is quoting from Lev Trotsky's archive.
37. Ibid., p. 67. See also Lev Trotsky, *Stalin's School of Falsification*, New York, 1962, pp. 58–63.
38. Lenin, *Polnoe sobranie sochinenii*, vol. XLV, p. 346.
39. L. A. Fotieva, *Iz vospominanii o V. I. Lenine, dekabr 1922 g.–mart 1923 g.*, Moscow, 1964, pp. 64f.
40. Ibid., p. 75.
41. Lenin, *Polnoe sobranie sochinenii*, vol., XLV, p. 107. See also Lewin, *Lenin's Last Struggle*, pp. 96f.
42. Interview with I. P. Itskov, 1989.
43. Deutscher, *The Prophet Unarmed*, p. 68, fn. 2.
44. Ibid., p. 89.
45. Trotsky, *Stalin*, p. 374.
46. B. Bazhanov, 'Stalin', *Kontinent*, no. 8, 1978, pp. 296–300.
47. Trotsky, *Stalin*, pp. 376f.
48. Lenin, *Polnoe sobranie sochinenii*, vol. XIV, pp. 329f.
49. Ibid., p. 75.
50. Deutscher, *The Prophet Unarmed*, p. 90.
51. Trotsky, *Stalin's School of Falsification*, p. 73.
52. Trotsky, *Stalin*, p. 366.
53. Trotsky, *Stalin*, p. 378; also E. Lyons, *Stalin, the Czar of All the Russias*, Philadelphia/New York and London, 1940, p. 37.
54. Robert C. Tucker, *Stalin as Revolutionary*, New York, 1973, pp. 282f., citing N. Valentinov, 'Novaya ekonomicheskaya politika', *Vospominaniia* (Stanford, 1971), pp. 90–2.
55. Trotsky, *Stalin*, p. 382.

56. Ibid., p. 387.
57. See Elizabeth Lermolo, *Face of a Victim*, New York, 1956, pp. 136f.
58. Trotsky, *Stalin*, pp. 381f.
59. I. V. Stalin, *Sochineniya*, vol. VI, Moscow, 1946–51, p. 48.
60. *Pravda*, 30 January 1924.
61. See Lidia Shatunovskaya, 'Zagadka odnogo aresta', *Vremia i my*, no. 5, 1979, pp. 206–16.
62. Trotsky, *Stalin*, p. 382.
63. Ibid.
64. Alexander Orlov, *Tainaya istoria Stalinskikh prestupleniy*, New York, Jerusalem, Paris, 1983, pp. 248f. See also Robert Conquest, *The Great Terror*, New York, 1973, p. 75.
65. Trotsky, *Stalin*, p. 419. See Chapter 18 below for the poisoning of another enemy of Stalin's.
66. See Yves Delbars, *The Real Stalin*, London, 1953, pp. 129f. 'Yves Delbars' was a pen name of Nikolay Kossiakov. Kossiakov states that he learned about Lenin's poisoning from a man in Stalin's secretariat.
67. Trotsky, *Stalin*, p. 419.
68. Orlov, *Tainaya*, pp. 228f.
69. Avtorkhanov, *Zagadka smerty Stalina*, p. 50.
70. Interview with Pavel Litvinov (grandson of Maxim Litvinov) in Chappaqua, New York, 1975.
71. L. Lanina, 'Madam Tusso i tovarishch Krupskaya', Moscow independent journal *Referendum*; from the reprinted article in the Russian language journal *Panorama*, Israel, 3 July 1988, pp. 6f.
72. Ibid.
73. Taped interview with Boris Shragin in Chappaqua, New York, 1979.
74. Taped interview with Lidia Shatunovskaya-Tumerman. Also see Lidia Shatunovskaya, 'Zagadka odnogo aresta', pp. 206–16.
75. Yulian Semenov, in a conversation with the author in the presence of the publisher I. Levkov, 3 April 1988, in New York City.

16

'JEWISH ORIGIN'

Shortly after Lenin's funeral, the question of who would succeed him as chairman of the Council of the People's Commissars was raised at a Politburo meeting. Trotsky was still in the Caucasus and could not take part in the discussion. During Lenin's illness Kamenev had been the acting chairman – in effect, Lenin's deputy – since Trotsky had earlier refused the post. Kamenev's appointment as Lenin's successor appeared certain, but Stalin objected, claiming that Kamenev's 'Jewish origin' ruled him out as a Russian leader. 'We must consider the peasant character of Russia', said Stalin, adding that the Russian peasants, the great majority of the country, would resent having a Jew head their government.[1]

Stalin exaggerated Kamenev's 'Jewish origin'. His father was indeed a Jew (Rosenfeld by name), which in the eyes of many made Kamenev Jewish, although his mother was a member of the Russian nobility. Kamenev did not think of himself as Jewish. Zinoviev was unsuitable as Lenin's successor for the same reason – he was Jewish (his family name was Rodo-myslsky). It was also widely known that Trotsky, born Lev Davidovich Bronstein, was Jewish. The Politburo members silently accepted Stalin's argument. Anti-Semitism ran deep in Russia, even among those who did not express it openly. Stalin was able to make a point by stating that the Jewish origins of Trotsky, Zinoviev and Kamenev would prevent them from leading the country despite the fact that the party's major doctrine was 'internationalism'. The true irony was that Lenin himself was one-quarter Jewish. He had hidden the fact that his maternal grandfather, Alexander Blank, had been a baptized Jew. Responding to a census questionnaire in 1922, Lenin filled in the blank pertaining to his maternal grandfather with the statement: 'I do not know.'[2]

Even before Lenin's death, Stalin had tried to use the Jewish origin of Zinoviev and Kamenev to his advantage. He provoked the first show trial in Soviet history of a prominent party leader, Mirza Sultan-Galiev, whom he accused of Tartar nationalism and of plotting to cede Crimea to Turkey. Neither Zinoviev nor Kamenev knew that Stalin's secret goal in the Sultan-Galiev case was to bribe them with the promise of creating in the Tartar-populated Crimea a 'Jewish national home'. Stalin felt this idea would be attractive to Zinoviev and Kamenev as Jews, and as a result would turn them into his allies against Lenin and Trotsky. Stalin assigned to Mikhail Kalinin, the future president of the USSR, and to the journalist Mikhail Koltsov, a Jew, the task of propagating the idea of a 'Jewish Autonomous Region' in the Crimea. The Soviet press began the campaign with the slogan, 'Give the Crimea to the Jews.'[3] Stalin's would-be bribe was wasted: Zinoviev and Kamenev had no interest in this idea (and neither, for that matter, did Trotsky). They thought of themselves as 'internationalists' and considered the idea of a Jewish national home in Crimea, Palestine, or anywhere else totally foreign to them.

On 10 July 1923 at a session of the Party Central Committee Stalin attacked Sultan-Galiev and mentioned 'treasonable documents', which were supposedly found on Sultan-Galiev during a search. Stalin declared that these documents were 'genuine' and that Sultan-Galiev 'fully confessed his guilt and repented'.[4] Sultan-Galiev was sentenced to a prison term and soon perished. Zinoviev and Kamenev supported Stalin in this trumped-up charge, but were to express regret at having done so a few years later.[5]

The Thirteenth Party Congress, held in May 1924, was the first to take place without Lenin. Krupskaya wanted Lenin's letters, which she called 'Lenin's Testament', read to the delegates. Lenin had dictated these documents attacking Stalin, starting in December 1922. She gave copies of the 'Testament' to all Politburo members. After reading his copy, Stalin exploded with obscene swearing at Lenin in the presence of Kamenev and Zinoviev, an action ill-suited to the quasi-religious cult he had been creating around the dead leader.[6] In his 'Testament', Lenin criticized Stalin, calling him a 'social-nationalist' and 'crude Great Russian *Derzhimorda*' ('Ugly Mug', a repulsive character in Gogol's *Inspector General*, an uncouth, primitive, xenophobic character). Lenin stated that 'Stalin and Dzerzhinsky must be held politically responsible for this entire Great Russian Nationalist campaign.'[7] He complained about the concentration of 'enormous power' in Stalin's hands, his rudeness, lack of tolerance, disloyalty and capriciousness, and insisted on his removal from the post of general secretary. But Lenin also criticized Trotsky for 'excessive self-assurance' and 'excessive preoccupation with the purely administrative side of the work'. He warned the party of the danger of a conflict between Stalin and Trotsky, stating, 'These two qualities of the two outstanding chiefs of the present Central Committee may result in a split, and if our party does not take measures to prevent this, then the split could come about quite unexpectedly.' He added by stating that, 'the mutual relations of Trotsky and Stalin, this is no trifle, or rather, it is a trifle which may acquire decisive importance'.[8]

Trotsky chafed at Lenin's criticism of him and at being put on the same level with Stalin as one of 'the two outstanding chiefs of the present Central Committee'. Zinoviev and Kamenev, too, were upset: Lenin not only demoted them to secondary figures below Trotsky and Stalin, but had recalled the most shameful moment in their lives, the 'October episode' of 1917 when they opposed the Bolshevik insurrection. Like Stalin, they were against having Lenin's views made known to the delegates at the Congress, but feared that Trotsky would insist on revealing the 'Testament'. Trotsky, as Lenin had foreseen, agreed to a 'rotten compromise' with them: he agreed to have Lenin's Testament read by Kamenev at only the special closed session of the Central Committee on 22 May 1924. Boris Bazhanov, Stalin's secretary, described the scene: 'Terrible embarrassment paralyzed all those present. Stalin, sitting on the steps of the presidium, felt small and miserable. I studied him closely: notwithstanding his self-possession and show of calm, it was clear that his fate was at stake . . .'.[9]

It hardly seemed possible for the Central Committee members to ignore Lenin's wish, having loudly pledged to 'hold Lenin's word sacred'. But Zinoviev and Kamenev did the impossible. Stalin's fate was in their hands; they could have used Lenin's words to remove Stalin from power, but instead rushed to his rescue, imploring the Central Committee not to deny him the post of general secretary. 'Lenin's word is sacred', Zinoviev exclaimed. 'But Lenin himself, if he could have witnessed, as you all have, Stalin's sincere efforts to mend his ways, would not have urged the party to remove him.' Displaying a considerable flair for theatrical performance, Kamenev and Zinoviev persuaded delegates that Stalin was a reformed man.[10] The majority voted in Stalin's favor. Trotsky watched the scene, remaining aloof and silent. Stalin pretended to offer his resignation, but Zinoviev and Kamenev 'persuaded' him to stay. The decision was not to read Lenin's Testament to the delegates of the congress and not to enter it into the congressional record. Trotsky did not utter a word in protest against the suppression of Lenin's final words, although he had no illusion about the meaning of what was taking place. Karl Radek leaned toward him during the proceedings and said, 'Now they won't dare to go against you.' Trotsky disagreed. 'On the contrary', he said, 'they will have to go to the limit, and moreover as quickly as possible.'[11]

Why Trotsky did not use Lenin's 'Testament' as a weapon to fight Stalin remains an unanswered question. Perhaps he felt bound by his promise to Kamenev not to raise the matter of the 'Georgian affair', but more probably was held back by something else, an issue that paralyzed him then and years later. Two years later, he was to hint at this issue at a Politburo meeting, when he asked in indignation, 'Is it true, is it possible that in *our Party*, in *Moscow*, in *Workers' Cells*, anti-Semitic agitation should be carried out with impunity?!' The Politburo members pretended to know nothing of this anti-Semitic agitation and preferred to ignore the issue. Only Bukharin blushed with shame and embarrassment.[12]

Trotsky realized that Lenin saw in Stalin and himself not just two different personalities but symbols of two historical and ideological tendencies: internationalism and Great Russian chauvinism. Trotsky was paralyzed by a feeling of helplessness in the face of the emerging chauvinist mood in the party and the country, encouraged by Stalin. Zinoviev and Kamenev were blinded by their hostility toward Trotsky and did not realize the threat posed to them by Stalin. Trotsky did not help matters: he enraged Zinoviev and Kamenev in October 1924, by publishing his pamphlet *The Lessons of October*, in which he recalled their role in the 1917 'October episode' and mentioned that Lenin at that time called them 'strikebreakers of the revolution'. They were eventually bound to part company with Stalin because of their internationalist outlook. The major theme of Trotsky's pamphlet was his theory of 'permanent revolution', according to which the October Revolution was only the first in a series of forthcoming revolutionary upheavals elsewhere in the world. The theory was not new: Lenin and most Bolsheviks were convinced that socialism could not win in Russia without victorious revolutions in other countries, and were disappointed that the revolutions in Germany and Hungary had suffered defeat. In a pamphlet titled *Foundations of Leninism*, published in early 1924, Stalin stated that socialism could not be built in one country before the victory of revolutions in other countries. But his opinion underwent a sudden change a few months later when he published another pamphlet, entitled *Problems of Leninism*, in which he introduced his new theory of 'building socialism in one country, taken separately'. The essence of Stalin's new theory was that even if other countries did not follow the Russian example, the Russian people alone could go on building socialism. A moment would come, argued Stalin, when the other countries would join the world revolution. Trotsky interpreted Stalin's theory as a 'conservative nationalist deviation from Bolshevism'.[13]

Zinoviev and Kamenev initially paid little attention to Stalin's 'socialism in one country' idea and continued to support Stalin in his intrigues against Trotsky. In January 1925 the Central Committee removed Trotsky from his powerful position of war commissar. The fear was that he might use the Red Army to seize power. Trotsky did not fight back, stating, 'I know one must not be right against the party.' Stalin's slogan of 'socialism in one country' was approved by the majority of the delegates to the Fourteenth Party Conference in March 1926. By then, the triumvirate of Stalin, Zinoviev and Kamenev had broken up, and Stalin joined Bukharin, Rykov and Tomsky, the head of the Soviet trade union organization, in alliance against Zinoviev and Kamenev, who continued calling for international revolution. Kamenev was demoted to the status of 'candidate member' of the Politburo. After the congress, Stalin added to the Politburo his three supporters: Voroshilov, Kalinin and Molotov, whom he controlled by threatening to expose their past misdeeds.[14] Usually, he blackmailed such people with documents found in Okhrana archives.

By the summer of 1926, Stalin had considerably improved his position within the party apparatus by appointing the 'right' people to key posts. He was very close to his goal of achieving absolute power. His name, however, was still hardly known outside narrow party circles. The imminent defeat of Trotsky, Zinoviev and Kamenev, on whom Stalin was pinning the label 'Jewish intellectuals', appeared almost inevitable. It seemed that only a miracle could save them from annihilation at the forthcoming plenum (plenary session) of the Central Committee, which was to open on 14 July 1926. This miracle almost happened during the plenum.

NOTES

1. Roy Medvedev, *Let History Judge*, New York, 1971, p. 44.
2. See L. Horwitz, 'Lenin and the Search for Jewish Roots', *The New York Times*, 5 August 1992, p. A-22. The author reports that archival documents about Lenin's grandfather were on display in Lenin's Museum in Moscow in June 1992 (the museum was closed in October 1993). Soviet archivist V. V. Tsapeen reported in the Spring 1992 edition of the journal *Arkhivy rodiny* (Native Land Archives) that he found documents about Lenin's Jewish ancestry in Russian and Ukrainian archives. Lenin's grandfather, Israel Blank, was born in 1804 to Moshke and Miriam Blank and in 1820 applied for conversion to the Russian Orthodox Church to gain admission to the Medical-Surgical Academy, having changed his name to Alexander Dmitrievich Blank. He graduated in 1824. This information, suppressed by Stalin (who had found out about it earlier), was nevertheless known to Lenin's biographer Margorita Shaginian (Radio Liberty Committee, NY Program no. 103/72) and is referred to by Louis Fischer in *The Life of Lenin*, New York, 1964, p. 34.
3. Dr I. Frankel, ed., *Jerusalem University Collection of Documents on Soviet Jews*. See there M. I. Kalinin, *Yevrei-zemledel'tsy v soyuze narodov SSSR*, pp. 35f., and A. Bragin and M. Koltsov, *Sudba evreiskikh mass v sovetskom soyuze*, pp. 21–6.
4. I. V. Stalin, *Sochineniya*, Moscow, 1946–51, vol. V, p. 308.
5. Lev Trotsky, *Stalin*, New York, 1941, p. 417.
6. Trotsky, *Stalin*, pp. 375f.
7. V. I. Lenin, *Polnoe sobranie sochinenii*, vol. XLV, Moscow, 1958–65, pp. 356–60.
8. Ibid., pp. 345f.
9. Trotsky, *Stalin*, p. 376. Trotsky is quoting B. Bazhanov.
10. Isaac Deutscher, *The Prophet Unarmed*, New York, 1965, p. 137.
11. Trotsky, *Stalin*, p. 376.
12. Deutscher, *The Prophet Unarmed*, p. 258.
13. Trotsky, *Stalin*, p. 396.
14. Ibid., p. 388.

17

STALIN'S OKHRANA FILE
FOUND IN 1926

From the early days of Soviet rule, Stalin maintained a very close relationship with Felix Dzerzhinsky, the head of the Secret Police. Dzerzhinsky supplied him with documents, found mostly in the Okhrana archives, that revealed compromising information about Soviet officials and party members. Stalin gathered these documents in his own personal archive and used them to blackmail people into slavish obedience to him by threatening to expose their past. Those who refused to submit to him were crushed or committed suicide. A special group of Stalin's agents, headed by Matvey Shkiriatov and Yemelian Yaroslavsky, worked within the Central Control Commission, sorting out such documents. Stalin, for instance, kept in his archive a document exposing Kalinin, the figurehead 'President of the USSR', as an Okhrana collaborator.[1] Trotsky stated that Kalinin surrendered to Stalin 'gradually, groaning and resisting'.[2] Kalinin told friends that Stalin was a 'horse that would some day drag our wagon into a ditch.' Stalin placed a caricature of Kalinin in a Soviet magazine with the caption 'Last warning'.[3]

One of the first victims of blackmail was Trotsky's secretary Glazman, whose Okhrana file fell into Stalin's hands. Stalin warned Glazman by threatening to make public a document that confirmed an instance of his cooperation with the Okhrana. Glazman committed suicide, refusing to live in fear of exposure and slavish dependence on Stalin. His suicide shocked many party members.[4]

The search for files of Okhrana agents in the old police archives was proceeding slowly. In 1918, soon after the flight of Lenin's government from Petrograd to Moscow, Lenin ordered all old archives to be transferred there. Dzerzhinsky was interested in the records of former Okhrana officers, agents and informers, some of whom he hoped to recruit into the Cheka. His recruiting technique was highly effective: threat of exposure and execution unless they joined. In some cases, former Okhrana agents were tried in court and executed. Ex-agent Ivan Okladsky was one such example. Another Okhrana agent tried in open court was Anna Serebriakova. The files of both were found in 1924 in one of the Department of Police archives that had been transferred to Moscow that year. By that time, both these former agents were aged invalids of no use to the Cheka.

Okladsky's file revealed that as a young man in 1881 he had been a member of the terrorist group the People's Will, which had conspired to assassinate Tsar Alexander II. All members of this group were arrested and, according to the official report, sentenced to death and hanged. Okladsky was the only one to avoid the gallows by agreeing to turn informer. He was secretly released from prison and sent to Tiflis under a new name to work as an Okhrana agent. Several years later, he was summoned to St Petersburg by the director of the Department of Police, V. K. von Plehve, and offered a job as an Okhrana agent in St Petersburg, replacing the agent 'Landezen' (Landezen was Arkady Garting's codename – he eventually became the Chief of the Okhrana Foreign Agency in Paris), who had escaped abroad to avoid being exposed. Okladsky retired before the Revolution, and his file was placed in the 'top-secret' safe in the Special Section of the Department of Police. His file was found in 1924. Okladsky was arrested and shot.[5]

Anna Serebriakova's story was less convoluted. She was recruited in 1884; her handler was Zubatov, the Chief of the Moscow Okhrana. Although she never joined either the Mensheviks or the Bolsheviks, members of both parties used her apartment in Moscow as a 'safe house' and entrusted many party secrets to her. Her Okhrana codenames at different times were *Subotina*, *Tuz* (the Ace) and *Mamasha* (Mommy). In 1909, Burtsev published an article accusing her of being an Okhrana agent. Serebriakova and her husband and son indignantly denied the charge. The scandal died down, and she soon retired with an Okhrana pension of 1,200 rubles a year. In addition, she received several large emergency grants for medical treatment for an eye disease. She was completely blind when her file was found in 1924 and GPU agents came to arrest her. Initially, Serebriakova stubbornly denied any ties with the Okhrana, but admitted to it when the documents from her file were read to her. These included numerous receipts of Okhrana payments signed by her, the last one dated January 1917, the eve of the February Revolution. Her trial began on 15 April 1926 and continued for 11 days. Nineteen witnesses, among them prominent Soviet officials who had known her for many years, testified. Serebriakova's son appeared as a witness for the prosecution. He declared that he had lost all feelings for her as his mother and 'despite her blindness, I refuse to help her financially. I reject her as a mother and her future fate is of no concern to me.'[6] The trial proceedings included testimony by four 'experts on the Okhrana', who were summoned to advise the court on technical details of Okhrana operations, codenames and terminology encountered in various documents. They stated that Serebriakova's Okhrana file had been found only recently, in 1924, and that, contrary to the widely held assumption that the Okhrana archives had been destroyed, 'most of the Department of Police archives have been preserved.'[7]

On 26 April 1926 Serebriakova was sentenced to seven years in prison, confiscation of her property, and annulment of all her civil rights for five years following the end of her prison term. The verdict stated that her crime called for 'the highest measure of punishment', that is, the death penalty, but that the court took into account her advanced age, her blindness, and the fact that 'at present she does not pose any threat to society'. She was 69 years old at the time. Article 67 of the Criminal Code, under which she was sentenced, read: 'Active efforts or active struggle against the workers' class and the revolutionary movement while serving in responsible or highly secret agent positions during the tsarist regime.'[8]

In April 1925, at the time of Anna Serebriakova's trial in Moscow, another trial took place in Baku. Newspapers described the defendants as Mensheviks, Esers, Azerbaijanian mussavatists, Armenian dashnaks and White Army officers, all of whom were accused of collaboration with 'British interventionists' and of complicity in the murder of 26 Baku commissars in 1918, among them Stepan Shaumian (who on several occasions had accused Stalin of betraying him to the Okhrana). Only one of the condemned commissars, Anastas Mikoyan, had been able to convince the executioners to spare him. That Mikoyan had managed to save his own life by collaborating with the executioners was known to Stalin, who used this to keep Mikoyan 'on the hook'. The difference between the fate of Anna Serebriakova and Anastas Mikoyan was one of relative utility to Stalin: Serebriakova, useless, was sentenced to imprisonment in April 1926; Anastas Mikoyan was useful to Stalin as one of his close assistants at the Central Committee plenum when it opened on 14 July 1926.

This plenum was of great importance to Stalin: he intended to use it to destroy the United Opposition, headed by Trotsky, Zinoviev and Kamenev. In the spring of 1926, Zinoviev and Kamenev, having parted company with Stalin, invited Trotsky to form with them a United Opposition. Stalin was not impressed. 'Ah, they have granted themselves mutual amnesty', he said scornfully.[9] Zinoviev had been removed from his post as the head of the party organization in Leningrad (Petrograd was named Leningrad after Lenin's death). Stalin had sent Sergey Kirov to Leningrad to replace Zinoviev. An even more important change was that the Red Army fell under Stalin's control after the death of Mikhail Frunze, an old Bolshevik who had replaced Trotsky as war commissar a few months earlier. The death of Frunze was most convenient for Stalin. He had resisted GPU intervention in military affairs and refused to support Stalin in his conflict with the opposition. There were rumors that he was even preparing a military coup to depose Stalin. Frunze suffered from a stomach ulcer. Stalin, in charge of supervising the medical care of Soviet officials, ordered a council of Kremlin doctors to perform surgery. Frunze's physician objected, stating that Frunze's heart would give out if he were subjected to chloroform. Stalin nevertheless ordered that Frunze undergo surgery; he then died during the operation. (His death was depicted as a barely veiled murder in the 1927 story *The Tale of the Unextinguished Moon*, by Boris Pilniak. Stalin forced Pilniak to admit his 'error' in a public statement and ordered all copies of the book confiscated and destroyed.[10]) After Frunze's death, Stalin appointed his old crony Klement Voroshilov to Frunze's post as war commissar. Voroshilov was Stalin's creature because of incriminating Okhrana documents found in the old police archives.[11] With this appointment, Stalin came close to becoming an absolute dictator.

Stalin's confidence in being able to defeat the United Opposition at the July 1926 plenum might have turned out to be a bit premature. While the plenum was in session, an event took place that had the potential to utterly ruin him: some time in July 1926 Stalin's St Petersburg Okhrana file was found in one of the last shipments of the Okhrana archives to Moscow. The transfer of old archives to Moscow had begun in June 1918 when the Soviet government had issued a decree creating *Glavarkhiv* (the Main Archive Administration), which was ordered to gather all archives in Moscow. Toward the end of 1919, *Glavarkhiv* transferred to Moscow the files of the Provisional Government's Investigative Commission of the Supreme Tribunal. These contained the materials of the Muraviev Commission, which had investigated Okhrana provocations.[12] The file of Okhrana agent Iosif Dzhugashvili was not in this shipment. Transfer of the archives took place under the direction of the chairmen of *Glavarkhiv*, first by M. H. Pokrovsky, later by D. B. Riazanov. The files were shipped in boxes, sometimes in bags, and piled up in a number of temporary locations, none suitable for study, indexing and cataloguing. Following the decision of the collegium of *Glavarkhiv*, early in 1925 Riazanov ordered all the old displaced archives, including the Department of Police archives, to be moved to a specially equipped building in Moscow. Various archives were moved there, including the 'Petrograd Historic-Revolutionary Archive', parts of which had been stored in the former Department of Police building, in the Pushkin Museum, and in railroad warehouses and freight cars in Leningrad. 'In the summer of 1926, all archival materials of the Petrograd Historic-Revolutionary Archive were transferred to Moscow.'[13]

It was then, during the inventory of one of the last shipments in July 1926, that the file of Iosif Dzhugashvili was found. The director of the Department of Police, S. P. Beletsky, had placed it in the 'Top-Secret' safe in the Special Section. An employee of the archive, perhaps the same one who found the file, secretly sent the information to David Shub, editor of the Menshevik journal *Sotsialistichesky vestnik* in Berlin, stating that Stalin's Okhrana file contained documents proving that Stalin had for many years been an Okhrana agent. Shub felt that such monumental and unbelievable information could not be made public without supporting documentation, which this informant did not supply.[14] To Shub the thought that the leader of the Soviet Union was a former Okhrana agent appeared fantastic. For all his hostility toward the Bolshevik usurpers of the Russian Revolution, and especially toward the rising dictator Stalin, Shub could not imagine that Stalin, for all his duplicity, could be a creature of the Okhrana. In any case, he could not publish the information without having in his hands un-impeachable documentary proof. But Shub confided this information to a trusted friend, I. D. Levine, a prominent American journalist and author.[15]

The discovery of Stalin's Okhrana file coincided in time with Dzerz-hinsky's demise under very strange circumstances. As usual, the discovered file was brought to Dzerzhinsky, probably on 18 July 1926. He decided to stay overnight at his Lubianka office and remained there the next day, returning home at 3 am on 20 July 1926. Later in the morning he left home early and went to his Lubianka office, but stayed there only briefly and then went to the Kremlin to take part in the party plenum, which had already been in session for four days, to deliver a speech on the state of heavy industry.[16] At that time, Dzerzhinsky served as both chairman of the GPU and commissar of heavy industry. He had the fervent ambition to prove that he was capable of more than executing enemies of Soviet power and could also direct important sectors of the Soviet economy. Stalin had satisfied this ambition by making him the commissar of heavy industry. Dzerzhinsky knew that the leaders of the United Opposition – Trotsky, Zinoviev and Kamenev – considered him a narrow-minded fanatic in-capable of constructive leadership. He hated them for this, and knew his career depended on Stalin's victory over the opposition. Given this weighty reason for supporting Stalin, he must have been in agony over the question of what to do with the file of Okhrana agent Iosif Dzhugashvili.

On his arrival at the plenum, Dzerzhinsky behaved in a frantic, bizarre, almost hysterical fashion. Stalin noticed his odd behavior at once. He may have learned from secret agents in social-democratic circles in Berlin that David Shub had received information about the discovery of his Okhrana file. He knew that such files were always brought to Dzerzhinsky. Alarmed, Stalin sent Anastas Mikoyan to find out what was the matter with Dzerzhinsky. When Mikoyan reported to Stalin what he had learned, Stalin's suspicion increased. He decided to prevent Dzerzhinsky from speaking to the plenum and instead to assign Grigory Piatakov, Dzerzhinsky's deputy, to deliver the report on the state of heavy industry. 'Strange, Piatakov is my deputy, but he didn't even inform me about his intention to speak!' exclaimed Dzerzhinsky, and indignantly demanded to be allowed to address the plenum. Stalin gave in and let him speak, to keep him from creating pandemonium with his protest.[17]

Dzerzhinsky's two-hour-long speech was exceedingly disjointed and punctuated by hysterical outbursts, diatribes against the leaders of the opposition, threats and complaints of dubious meaning, and he was repeatedly interrupted by protests. At one point he shouted: 'You know perfectly well what my power consists of! I do not spare myself . . . And because of this you all here love me, because you trust me . . . I have never twisted my soul! It is difficult for me alone to tackle this problem and, therefore, I beg your help . . . '.[18]

Dzerzhinsky was tormenting his soul: Stalin's Okhrana file posed a dreadful dilemma for him. He saw no solution to it and was begging for help without being able to tell anyone about it. For two days before his appearance at the plenum, he had read with horror the file of Okhrana agent Iosif Dzhugashvili. He had read Colonel Eremin's letter to Director Beletsky, describing Dzhugashvili's Okhrana career, Dzhugashvili's letter to Assistant Minister of the Interior Zolotarev, complaining about Malinovsky's devotion to Lenin and disloyalty to the Okhrana, Zolotarev's instruction to exile Dzhugashvili to Siberia 'for good' as a punishment for his threat to expose Malinovsky. The file had Dzhugashvili's reports to the Okhrana, including his report on the condition of the Social Democratic Party which he wrote in June 1912, his signed pledges to cooperate with the Okhrana, and his signed receipts for the money he was paid for this cooperation. As head of the GPU, Dzerzhinsky saw a great many such Okhrana files, and he had no doubt that these were genuine documents, proving that Stalin had for many years been an Okhrana agent. Dzerzhinsky was a fanatic who made all his actions subservient to the Revolution: he recruited former Okhrana agents into the service of the Soviet secret police as willingly as he executed them if they were of no use to him. But the astounding fact that as despicable a creature as an Okhrana agent had wormed his way to the pinnacle of Soviet power was beyond his comprehension. He found himself in an untenable position at a crucial moment in the party's power struggle. Dzerzhinsky realized that by removing Stalin he would destroy himself, because victory by the opposition would mean that he, too, would be removed from all his posts. He also feared that Stalin would destroy anyone who knew of the file's discovery. Agonizing over what to do with Stalin's file, Dzerzhinsky on his way to the plenum on the morning of 20 July 1926 stopped at his Lubianka office and hid the file among personal papers.[19] He would never touch it again.

During his speech Dzerzhinsky drank from a glass of water that was periodically brought to him. Before finishing his speech, he suddenly turned pale, lost consciousness, collapsed and fell off the rostrum. He was carried to the lobby, where he died before the eyes of delegates who gathered around him.[20] Some of the delegates at the plenum had no doubt that Dzerzhinsky had been poisoned. Rumors to that effect immediately started to spread among the delegates and later in party circles in Moscow.[21] There was no investigation and no autopsy. Dzerzhinsky's body was cremated, and ashes that may or may not have been his were immured in the Kremlin wall, the usual way in later years to enshrine the remains of Kremlin dignitaries. But Stalin left some evidence that incriminated him.

The falsification of historical truth and the cover-up of the poisoning started immediately. Stalin concocted an official version of Dzerzhinsky's death from a heart attack, which allegedly took place not at the plenum but in Dzerzhinsky's apartment, in his own bed. Thus, the death was moved from the actual scene and time of the crime. This distortion and shifting of the event in space and time automatically resulted in Stalin's having an alibi. That many delegates saw Dzerzhinsky die at the plenum made no difference to someone as dedicated to 'rewriting' history as Stalin. The new version of Dzerzhinsky's death was presented by Stalin in his speech at the funeral and enlivened with a dizzying and confounding mixture of fact and myth:

Today the Party was struck by a heavy blow. Comrade Dzerzhinsky, the terror of the bourgeoisie, devout knight of the proletariat, noble-blooded fighter for the Communist Revolution, militant builder of our industry, eternal worker and fearless soldier of great battle, died suddenly of a heart attack. Comrade Dzerzhinsky died instantly, on returning home after his speech – as always a passionate one – at the Central Committee plenum. His ailing, completely overburdened heart refused to work and death struck him down in a single moment. Glorious death at a front line post![22]

Stalin was up to his old habit of rephrasing the same lie several times in order to plant it as the truth in the minds of his listeners and in his own mind. According to Stalin's fraudulent version, Dzerzhinsky died of a heart attack, 'suddenly . . . instantly . . . in a single moment' – not at the plenum, but 'on returning home after his speech'. This version was later enriched by Soviet authors with other fantastic inventions, among which could be found some surviving particles of truth. In one such story, Dzerzhinsky took ill and fell near the rostrum, but after a while he 'felt a little better, got up and headed home. . . . he was very pale and moved slowly. . . . he firmly shook his wife's hand and silently went into his bedroom. . . . he fell unconscious between the two beds. Belenky and Redens lifted and placed him on his bed.'[23]

Abram Belenky was the head of the Kremlin bodyguards at the time (he was to perish during the purges in the 1930s).[24] Stanislav Redens was Dzerzhinsky's assistant and nephew (he was also shot during the purges). Redens was married to the sister of Stalin's wife Nadezhda Allilueva, which made Stalin and Redens in-laws and Stalin and Dzerzhinsky remote relatives. What in fact had happened was that Stalin ordered Belenky and Redens to carry Dzerzhinsky's corpse home. It was they, not Dzerzhinsky, who 'firmly' shook his wife's hand and placed his body on the bed. He had dropped dead before the very eyes of bewildered plenum delegates. This was why Belenky and Redens had not taken him to the Kremlin Hospital. Furthermore, the reason they did not take his body to a morgue was that Stalin wanted to avoid an autopsy.

Dzerzhinsky was the first casualty of Stalin's Okhrana file after its emergence from the dusty archives. Stalin may have tried to talk himself into believing that Dzerzhinsky had destroyed the file, but the fear that it was preserved and might fall into the hands of his enemies must have continued to unnerve him.

NOTES

1. Taped Interview with Mikhail Agursky in Israel, in 1971. Agursky stated that documents establishing Kalinin's ties with the Okhrana were found among Stalin's personal papers after the dictator's death.
2. Lev Trotsky, *Stalin*, New York, 1941, pp. 388f.
3. Ibid., p. 388.
4. Ibid., p. 390.
5. See Lev Sheinin, *Zapiski sledovatelia*, Moscow, 1968, pp. 385–412. Okladsky's story was also told in a book by Larisa Raizner, the wife of the high Soviet official Fedor Raskolnikov. She obtained Okladsky's Okhrana file from the GPU with which she maintained close relations. She died suddenly in 1926, shortly after publishing her book. Ten years later, Raskolnikov, then the Soviet Ambassador to Bulgaria, defected and was thrown out of a Paris hotel window by Stalin's agents.
6. *Pravda*, 24 April 1926.
7. Ibid. See also *Arkhivnoe delo*, vol. XIII, 1927, p. 35.
8. *Pravda*, 27 April 1926.
9. Isaac Deutscher, *Stalin, a Political Biography*, New York and London, 1968, p. 307.
10. Trotsky, *Stalin*, p. 418.
11. On Voroshilov's connections with the Okhrana, see Lev Trotsky, *Stalin*, p. 388ff.
12. V. Maksakov, 'Arkhiv revoliutsii i vneshnei politiki XIX–XX vekov', *Arkhivnoe delo*, no. XIII, 1927, p. 32.
13. Ibid., p. 41.

14. David Shub's notification of the discovery of Stalin's Okhrana file and his reaction to it are described in a letter by I. D. Levine to the author, dated 7 August 1976. On file in the author's archive.
15. Interview with I. D. Levine. Levine's letter in the author's archive.
16. A. Tishkov, *Dzerzhinsky*, Moscow, 1974, p. 374.
17. Ibid., pp. 374f.
18. Ibid.
19. See Chapter 19 below for the discovery of Stalin's Okhrana file among Dzerzhinsky's personal papers.
20. Isaac Deutscher, *The Prophet Unarmed*, New York, 1980, p. 279.
21. Ibid. See also Anton Antonov-Ovseenko, *Portret tirana*, New York, 1980, p. 334.
22. Tishkov, *Dzerzhinsky*, pp. 377f.
23. Ibid., pp. 376f.
24. Abram Belenky's sister, Emilia Solomonovna Belenkaya-Ravich, an architect, was the author's neighbor in a Moscow apartment on Lobkovsky Street. She mentioned her brother and spoke of Dzerzhinsky's death.

18

'CASTRATED FORCES'

Beginning in July 1926, when his Okhrana file was found in the old archives, Stalin's behavior markedly worsened. He had always been irritable and quicktempered, but now members of his own family suffered from his increasing intolerance and angry outbursts. In August 1926, his relations with his wife Nadezhda Allilueva deteriorated to such an extent that Nadezhda left Stalin, taking along their 6-month-old daughter Svetlana and their 7-year-old son Vasily to live with her parents in Leningrad. Yakov, Stalin's 18-year-old son from his first marriage, stayed with his father but grew so unhappy that he attempted suicide by shooting himself in the chest in the kitchen of their now deserted Kremlin apartment. The wound was not fatal, and doctors at the Kremlin hospital saved Yakov's life. 'He can't even shoot straight', was Stalin's heartless comment.[1]

Stalin telephoned Nadezhda several times and pleaded with her to return. He finally succeeded in persuading her, but a few weeks after her return, she wrote to her sister Anna in Kharkov that she wanted to move in with her. Anna's husband Stanislav Redens had been transferred to the Kharkov GPU after the death of his uncle Dzerzhinsky. Anna advised Nadezhda to stay with Stalin and for the sake of the children not to break up the family. Nadezhda followed her advice. Her decision probably also had to do with her knowledge that by this time no one in Russia could hide from Stalin.

Nadezhda was deeply disappointed in Stalin. The revolutionary hero she had worshiped had turned out to have little to do with the reality of her marriage. The discovery of Stalin's Okhrana file and his fear of imminent exposure must have been on Stalin's mind day and night. He began to suffer from insomnia, and his shortened arm bothered him periodically. Stalin's condition worsened to the point where he sought the help of V. M. Bekhterev, the eminent Russian psychiatrist, neuropathologist and physiologist. Stalin also considered Bekhterev a political ally in the conflict with Trotsky over the question, much discussed in the mid-1920s among high Soviet officials, of whether to allow publication of Sigmund Freud's work. Trotsky was for publication, while Stalin insisted that Freud was a charlatan and consequently opposed it. Bekhterev was a supporter of Pavlov's theory of reflexes and considered Freud's psychoanalysis unscientific.

Stalin needed Bekhterev's reputation to dismiss Freud's theories and, at the same time, to deliver a blow to Trotsky which was ever a high priority on Stalin's agenda.

On 22 December 1927 Bekhterev left Leningrad for Moscow to take part in a congress of psychiatrists and neuropathologists. Just before his departure he received a telegram inviting him to visit Stalin in the Kremlin. He spent more time with Stalin than he had anticipated and arrived at the congress later in the day, after its opening. To his colleagues, who wondered why he was so late, he explained, 'I examined one short-armed paranoiac.'[2] (According to another version, Bekhterev said, 'Diagnosis is clear. Typical case of heavy paranoia.'[3]) Later in the day, Bekhterev mentioned that Stalin suffered from a severe case of split personality, paranoia and schizophrenia.[4] Bekhterev was elected honorary chairman of the congress, and many participants gathered around and were in a position to overhear his comments. Bekhterev was a sociable, candid and fearless man. Before the Revolution, he had expressed his ideas openly to the Tsar, who, upon being told of Bekhterev's arrival, used to tell court officials to give Bekhterev's institute everything he asked for, 'otherwise I would give him even more'. Bekhterev was politically on the side of liberal and socialist groups, and at times organized secret meetings of revolutionaries in his office. During the infamous Beilis trial, he delivered an impassioned speech against anti-Semitism.[5] Bolshevik rule did not change him and he voiced his thoughts as openly as ever. He had many years' experience in the treatment of paranoia. When he made the discovery that the general secretary was a paranoiac, he felt no compunction to keep his diagnosis from his colleagues.

Bekhterev's opinion was reported to Stalin. In the evening, Bekhterev and his colleagues went to the Bolshoi Theater. According to an account of what happened there, several men came up to Bekhterev during an intermission. They were not delegates and no one knew them. They led him to a buffet, where he had drinks and ate sandwiches. They then disappeared and were not seen again. That night Bekhterev died. The rumor spread that he had been poisoned on Stalin's order.[6] Bekhterev's son P. V. Bekhterev, a chief engineer in a weapons factory, wanted to bury his father in the family plot in the Leningrad cemetery, but he was told that, according to Bekhterev's wishes, his body would be cremated without autopsy. The urn supposedly containing Bekhterev's ashes was sent to Leningrad with permission for his son to bury it where he liked.[7]

The newspaper *Izvestiya* initially blurted out that Bekhterev had died on the evening of 23 December 1927, immediately after returning from the Bolshoi Theater, but subsequent reports moved the time of death to the next day. As usual, Stalin shifted the death further in time from when the murder had occurred. According to the official report, Bekhterev died of 'heart paralysis'.[8] But Bekhterev's son insisted that his father had been poisoned, although he suspected his stepmother rather than Stalin. Nevertheless, Bekhterev's son was arrested and sentenced to 'ten years in prison without the right to correspondence'. In fact, he was executed by shooting. His wife died in a prison camp, and their three children were sent to orphanages.

Bekhterev's diagnosis of Stalin was paranoia, a mental disorder characterized by highly systematized delusions of persecution or grandeur. Any fact that contradicts the delusion is dismissed by paranoiacs with contempt. People who do not share their convictions are considered enemies. Paranoiacs pursue their ideas stubbornly and with great inventiveness, and they are liable to accuse imagined 'enemies' of what they are guilty of themselves. Freud considered this trait as 'projection', the most characteristic symptom of paranoia. He wrote: 'The most striking characteristic of symptom formation in paranoia is the process which deserves the name of *projection*. An internal perception is suppressed, and, indeed, its content, after undergoing a certain degree of distortion, enters consciousness in the form of an external perception.'[9]

Stalin staged the infamous show trials, in which he paraded innocent people and forced them to 'confess' to crimes that he himself had committed, thus projecting on to his victims his own guilt. He suppressed his internal perception of the truth and, after it had undergone some distortion, it reappeared as an external perception, which he accepted as reality and believed his invented accusations against his 'enemies' were true. Early in 1928 Stalin instigated the prosecution of coal-mining engineers of the town of Shakhty in the Northern Caucasus. The engineers were charged with 'wrecking' the coal-mining industry. In a speech before a party plenum on 13 April 1928 Stalin declared: 'The facts show that the Shakhty affair was an economic counterrevolution, plotted by a section of bourgeois experts, former coal mine owners . . . We have internal enemies. We have external enemies. This, comrades, must not be forgotten for a single moment . . .'.[10]

The interrogations of the engineers, 50 of them Soviet citizens, three of them foreigners, were conducted by Stalin's friend Efim Evdokimov, the head of the GPU of the Shakhty region. He was a former common criminal who had been set free by the February Revolution. During the Civil War, he joined the Red Army in Tsaritsyn, where he met Stalin, who turned him into a drinking companion and in later years often invited him on vacation trips to the Caucasus. Staging the Shakhty case was decided on one such trip. Evdokimov gave the depositions of the 'wreckers' to the head of the GPU, Menzhinsky, who dismissed their 'confessions' as fabrications and declared that prosecution of such a case would be tantamount to sabotage of Soviet industry. Evdokimov complained to Stalin, who told him: 'Nonsense. Go back to the North Caucasus and immediately adopt whatever measures you consider necessary. From now on send all your information to me only, and I will take care of Comrade Menzhinsky myself.'[11]

The Shakhty trial was held in the Moscow Hall of Columns. A few of its highlights suffice to convey its grimness. One defendant did not appear because, as one of the judges explained, he had gone mad in his cell. When one of the accused engineers, Nikolay Skorutto, started to read his 'confession', his wife shouted, 'Kolia, darling, don't lie! Don't! You know you are innocent!' Thereupon Skorutto denied his guilt; the next morning he again confessed his guilt, saying that his wife's outcry had confused him.[12] Another of the defendants, a man of 80, denied his guilt and challenged one of the men who had confessed, 'Why do you lie, eh? Who told you to lie?' Yet another defendant, a Jew, shouted: 'One day another Zola will arise and will write another *J'Accuse* to restore our name to honor.'[13]

At one point during the proceedings a 12-year-old boy rose from his seat in the audience and proclaimed that his father, one of the defendants, the engineer Kolodub, was 'a traitor and enemy of the working class'. The boy demanded that his father be shot. 'I reject him and the name he bears', he shouted. 'From now on I shall no longer call myself Kolodub, but Shakhtin.'[14] Similar scenes of sons denouncing their fathers and demanding their execution were to take place during subsequent show trials. Stalin kept staging his personal trauma – his own court testimony against his father Vissarion in 1890 in Tiflis. The Shakhty trial ended with the defendants being sentenced to various prison terms. But Stalin re-enacted the events of his past not only on the stage of his show trials but in 'real life' as well, projecting them on to other people as if these events had taken place not in his own life but in theirs. In 1927 he ordered Menzhinsky to assign a GPU agent by the name of Stroilov to set up an 'underground Trotskyite printing press' and to plant illegal leaflets there in order to incriminate opposition leaders. Stroilov's press was liquidated by the GPU, and he was declared to be a White Guard officer, while opposition leaders were accused of counter-revolutionary activities. 'Stalin was a master of such little sensations', wrote Alexander Orlov, a top GPU officer at the time, not knowing that a similar provocation had been set up by the Okhrana informer Iosif Dzhugashvili in Tiflis as early as 1900.[15] Trotsky, Zinoviev and Kamenev complained to Menzhinsky that his GPU had staged a provocation. Menzhinsky did not deny the accusation and confirmed that the leaflets were forgeries. 'Do you think that Stalin alone would be able to cope with the task [of building socialism]?' Kamenev asked him. Menzhinsky skirted the question and asked instead, 'Why then did you let him grow into such a formidable force? Now it is too late.'[16]

Throughout 1927 Stalin turned the debates in the Politburo and Central Committee into spectacles aimed at destroying the 'United Opposition'. Trotsky, Zinoviev and Kamenev were expelled from the Politburo, Zinoviev was dismissed as the head of the Comintern (Communist International), which became virtually a GPU front. Stalin himself contemptuously referred to it as *'eta lavochka'* ('this criminal hangout').[17] The Central Committee became an appendix to Stalin's Secretariat. In Trotsky's words: 'The line of attack against the Opposition was prearranged . . . The tone of the baiting became more unbridled . . . The stage director of all this was Stalin. He walked up and down at the back of the presidium . . . and made no attempt to hide his approval when the swearing addressed to some Oppositionist assumed an utterly shameful character.'[18]

Stalin's resolve to eliminate the opposition was vehement. When one of his old Georgian friends, Budu Mdivani, once tried to persuade him to reach an agreement with Trotsky, Zinoviev and Kamenev, Stalin at first listened in silence, pacing back and forth. Then he suddenly walked up to Mdivani. The expression on his face was menacing. Rising up on his toes and raising one arm, Stalin screamed, 'They must be crushed!'[19] On 7 November 1927, the tenth anniversary of the October Revolution, two columns of demonstrators moved down Tverskaya Street toward Red Square. The right column was carrying placards with slogans approved by the Politburo, while the left column displayed those of the opposition, among them the slogan 'Let us carry out Lenin's Testament', a reminder of Lenin's advice to remove Stalin from his high party posts. Trotsky, Kamenev and a few other members of the opposition stood on the balcony of the Paris Hotel and greeted the demonstration. Suddenly, they were attacked by GPU agents hurling rotten eggs and shouting, 'Down with the traitor Trotsky!' The agents tore up the placards of the opposition and forced its column to join the 'correct' one.[20] Trotsky made several public speeches before Moscow workers. At the Paveletsky railway station his speech was interrupted by Molotov, who demanded in the name of the Central Committee that the 'illegal gathering' be disbanded. Trotsky, losing self-control, accused 'Stalin and his camarilla' of being the 'grave-diggers of the Revolution'. The next day a *Pravda* article accused Trotsky of 'creating an illegal party'.[21]

Stalin labeled the opposition 'Trotskyite deviation', and he referred to the opposition's members as 'Jewish intellectuals'. At the Fifteenth Party Congress in December 1927, Trotsky, Kamenev and Zinoviev were expelled from the party. Trotsky refused to accept expulsion and was exiled to Alma-Ata in Kazakhstan. Zinoviev and Kamenev renounced their opposition views, and Stalin benevolently allowed them to be readmitted to the party. Trotsky's supporters, on the other hand, he exiled to different parts of the country to make it difficult for them to communicate with each other. The 'castrated forces' of the opposition, as he called them, were scattered and no longer posed any danger to him. After the Fifteenth Party Congress, two Stalinists, Yan Rudzutak and Valerian Kuibyshev, were added to the Politburo.

In 1927 Stalin promoted a war psychology in Russia by kindling fear of foreign intervention. Soviet relations with the West deteriorated. Britain broke off diplomatic relations with Moscow, and France declared a *de facto* break. The Soviet ambassador to Poland, Peter Voikov, was assassinated in revenge for his role in the murder of the Tsar's family, of which he liked to brag. Stalin's policy toward China suffered a setback, which provided Trotsky with an opportunity to accuse him of serious mistakes. Trotsky continued advocating a policy of support for the Chinese communists, while Stalin formed an alliance with Chiang Kai-shek and his Kuomintang government. In April 1927 Chiang Kai-shek's troops massacred communists in Shanghai. Stalin recalled Soviet military advisers and called on the Chinese communists to rise in revolt against the Kuomintang. In December 1927 Chiang Kai-shek brutally suppressed the 'Canton commune'. Stalin reacted by ordering Karl Pauker, the chief of the GPU Operations Department and the head of Stalin's bodyguards, to arrest all the Chinese in Moscow. Pauker carried out the order, rounding them all up, from those running laundries to members of the Chinese section of the Comintern and university professors. Stalin then received a telephone call from the Comintern official Osip Piatnitsky, who complained that the entire staff of the Chinese section had been arrested. Stalin summoned Pauker and asked him, 'Did you arrest *all* the Chinese?' Pauker proudly answered 'yes', whereupon Stalin struck him in the face and ordered, 'Release them all!' Pauker scurried to carry out the order. All the Chinese were released as suddenly as they had been arrested. Pauker, carrying an understandable grudge, stayed away from Stalin's office for several days, and did not go on his usual trip with Stalin to his *dacha*. Stalin finally summoned him and awarded him the Order of the Red Banner and an edict explaining that the citation was in recognition of the 'exemplary carrying out of an important assignment'. The staff of Stalin's Secretariat joked that Pauker should wear the medal not on his chest, but on his cheek.[22]

Stalin's fear of the Chinese threat engendered a preposterous idea, which was made public some three months after Chiang Kai-shek's suppression of the Canton commune: the settling of Jews in the Birobidzhan area (named after its two rivers, Bira and Bidzhan), the eastern Siberia region along the Soviet–Chinese border. The plan under consideration called for the establishment in Birobidzhan of a 'Jewish Autonomous Region'. Stalin's earlier reason for suggesting the creation of a Jewish autonomous republic (in the Crimea) had been an attempted bribe to secure Zinoviev's and Kamenev's allegiance. He no longer needed that allegiance, and this newly proposed relocation of the Jews was meant to serve quite a different purpose.

On 28 March 1928 the Soviet government announced a plan to 'assign the Birobidzhan region for the settlement of the toiling Jewish masses'.[23] Mikhail Kalinin, by then the chairman of the Supreme Soviet, and Stalin's earlier mouthpiece on the proposal for Jewish resettlement in the Crimea, this time proclaimed:

The Jews as a nation [are] one of the most vital and politically influential nations. That is why the creation of the Jewish republic would have enormous significance. This is a weighty thing . . . I am a sinner, I proposed Biro-Bidzhan a long time ago, despite the fact that it is located near China . . . There were some cries: 'Only not under China!' Two hundred years ago China was beyond reach. But now people say, 'So what, it takes a week to reach China' . . . The Jewry, which in the USSR consists of about three million, should have at least a little republic. And then everybody would know, that this nationality has its own 'state title' on our territory, if I may say so.[24]

In fact, Kalinin was not the initiator of this 'crazy idea', and his statement that he had been in favor of sending Jews to Birobidzhan even earlier was a lie. He had earlier promoted Stalin's idea of giving the Crimea to the Jews. As was often the case in these scripted performances, Stalin's hidden motives inadvertently leaked out in Kalinin's statements: Stalin intended to make Birobidzhan a buffer area in case of military conflict with China and to use the Jews as hostages in this conflict. As a 'politically influential nation', they would mobilize world support for the Soviet Union in the event of a war with China.

A territory less suitable for colonization than Birobidzhan was difficult, if not impossible, to find in all of the Soviet Union. An investigation of conditions in the area undertaken by the Tsarist colonial administration established that it was 'unsuitable for agricultural colonization', because it had 'permanently frozen subsoil, marsh-ridden terrain, made uninhabitable by *gnus* [blood-sucking insects: gnats, horseflies, midges], floods, prolonged below 40° frosts, cultural isolation, more than a thousand *verst* [about 700 miles] distance from the sea, unbearable intensity of labor, short growing period under unfavorable seasonal distribution of precipitation . . .'.[25]

For Stalin to contemplate sending a large number of Jewish settlers into such an inhospitable region leaves no doubt that he was motivated by more than military considerations alone: his pathological anti-Semitism, too, was at work. While Stalin was hatching his monstrous plan, one prominent party official, Yan Sten, who knew Stalin quite well, noted in a small circle of personal friends that, 'Koba will do things that will make the trials of Dreyfus and Beilis pale in comparison.'[26] Trotsky, who knew Stalin less well and wanted to believe in communism as an international movement transcending the parochial ideas of nations and races, denied for a long time that Stalin was an anti-Semite. But he finally accepted the fact that 'Stalin and his henchmen even stooped to fish in the muddied waters of anti-Semitism.' He was outraged by the anti-Semitic cartoons in the party press, which were received with sly snickers. In response to Trotsky's protests, Stalin made the glib statement: 'We are fighting Trotsky, Zinoviev and Kamenev not because they are Jews, but because they are oppositionists.' Trotsky finally recognized the true intention of Stalin's statement: it was a reminder to all not to forget that the leaders of the opposition were Jews.[27]

On Stalin's order, the country's annual solemnization of Lenin's cult did not take place on Lenin's birthday, but on the anniversary of his death on 21 January. On that day in 1929, five years after Lenin's death, Politburo members approved Stalin's decision to exile Trotsky from the Soviet Union. Bukharin abstained from voting. The only country that agreed to accept Trotsky was Turkey, where he enjoyed the status of an 'Honorary Citizen', which the Turkish leader Kemal Atatürk bestowed on him for cooperation with the Turks during the Civil War in Russia. On 12 February 1929 Trotsky, his wife Natalia Sedova, his older son Lev Sedov, Sedov's wife Anna Riabukhina and their baby son were brought to the heavily guarded port of Odessa, where the freighter *Ilyich* – named in honor of Vladimir Ilyich Lenin – was waiting for them. Stalin liked such symbolic 'coincidences' and marked important events in his life with them.

Trotsky's younger son Sergey refused to go abroad, saying that he had nothing to do with the political activities of his father. Trotsky and his wife went aboard the *Ilyich* first, followed by Lev Sedov, but Sedov's wife Anna and their baby son were prevented from boarding and were led away. Trotsky, his wife, and Lev Sedov shouted their protests, but the guards ignored them. The *Ilyich* left Odessa and headed for Istanbul.

NOTES

1. I. D. Levine, *Stalin*, New York, 1931, p. 325; Svetlana Allilueva, *Twenty Letters to a Friend*, New York, 1967, p. 101.
2. Oleg Moroz, 'Poslednii diagnoz', *Literaturnaya gazeta*, 28 September 1988.
3. Lidia Shatunovskaya, *Life in the Kremlin*, New York, 1982, p. 75.
4. Taped interview with Vasily Rudich, 1976.
5. Oleg Moroz, 'Poslednii diagnoz'.
6. Ibid. Oleg Moroz quotes psychiatrist M. I. Buyanov: ' everyone invariably insisted that Stalin had murdered Bekhterev – of course not with his own hand, but with the help of his henchmen'.
7. Ibid.
8. Ibid. Oleg Moroz quotes from the journal *Vestnik znaniya*, no. 24, 1927.
9. Sigmund Freud, 'Psychoanalytic Notes upon an Autobiographical Account of a Case of Paranoia (Dementia Paranoides)', *Collected Papers*, vol. 1, ch. 3.
10. *Pravda* no. 90 18 April 1928. See also I. V. Stalin, *Sochineniya*, vol. XI, Moscow, 1946–51, pp. 53f.; H. Montgomery Hyde, *Stalin: The History of a Dictator*, New York, 1971, p. 277.
11. Hyde, *Stalin*, p. 277.
12. Robert Conquest, *The Great Terror*, New York, 1973, p. 732.
13. Hyde, *Stalin*, p. 279.
14. Ibid.
15. Alexander Orlov, *Tainaya istoria Stalinskikh prestuplenii*, New York, Jerusalem, Paris, 1983; Lev Trotsky, *Stalin*, New York, 1941, p. 392.
16. Trotsky, *Stalin*, p. 392.
17. Interview with Iosif Berger in Israel, 1969.
18. Trotsky, *Stalin*, pp. 413f.
19. Ibid., p. 414.
20. I. P. Itskov, 'Dvadtsatye gody', *Novoe russkoe slovo*, 22 September 1987, p. 14.
21. Isaac Deutscher, *The Prophet Unarmed*, New York, 1965, pp. 373–5.
22. Alexander Orlov, *Tainaya*, pp. 329–31.
23. I. Frankel, ed., *Jerusalem University Collection of Documents on Soviet Jews*, pp. 98–136, citing *Tribuna*, no. 6, 1928, p. 1.
24. Ibid., quoting M. I. Kalinin, *Evrei v SSSR*, pp. 12–15.
25. Y. Larin, *Evrei i antisemitism v SSSR*, pp. 183ff., quoted in *Collection of Documents on Soviet Jews*, pp. 102f.
26. Roy Medvedev, *Let History Judge*, New York, 1971, pp. 224f.
27. Trotsky, *Stalin*, pp. 399f.

19

BLUMKIN'S FAILED MISSION

In early 1929 Stalin ordered the head of the GPU, Menzhinsky, to appoint Yakov Blumkin in place of the GPU resident in Turkey, G. A. Agabekov, who had defected to the West. In October Blumkin was instructed to return to Moscow and on his way there to visit Trotsky, who had rented a house on the island of Prinkipo in the Sea of Marmora, near Istanbul. Stalin counted on Blumkin's ability to, in the words of an old Bolshevik, do the 'job of winning Trotsky's confidence and killing him'.[1] Stalin believed that Blumkin was capable of committing a murder, because in July 1918, as a young member of the Left Esser party and Cheka officer, he had made history by taking part in the assassination of the German ambassador Count von Mirbach. Blumkin was tried by a military tribunal and sentenced to death, but, thanks to the interference of Trotsky, was pardoned in order to 'expiate his guilt in the battles in defense of the Revolution'.[2] He served on Trotsky's staff during the Civil War and joined the Bolshevik Party during that time.[3] After the Civil War, he resumed his service in the Cheka, and during the 1920s he was often sent by Soviet intelligence on secret missions abroad.

Blumkin was a bachelor, and, when in Moscow, frequently invited guests to parties in his large, well-furnished apartment. He was popular with women, liked to brag about his conquests and to show off, at times in dramatic ways: once he drew a gun in a restaurant and threatened to shoot the poet Osip Mandelstam, a fragile and gentle man who, Blumkin felt, had insulted him. Mandelstam's wife, Nadezhda, related in her memoirs that 'Blumkin was always brandishing his gun'. She added that later, when it became known that Blumkin had joined the Cheka and went on secret missions abroad, she failed to understand 'how such ostentation could be reconciled with the secrecy demanded by his work'.[4]

The pretext for Blumkin's visit to Prinkipo was Trotsky's request to the GPU to have bodyguards assigned to him, since he feared an assassination attempt by White Guards who had escaped to Turkey and sought revenge for their defeat in the Civil War. Trotsky's request for protection probably gave Stalin the idea to use Blumkin in arranging the assassination of his hated enemy. Blumkin's first task, however, was to arrange an attempt on the life of another enemy of Stalin, his former secretary Boris Bazhanov, who had escaped abroad in January 1928 and been granted asylum in France. Blumkin, en route to Turkey, took a detour to Paris. There, he enlisted his cousin, Arkady Maximov, a GPU informer, to arrange the assassination of Bazhanov. The car accident Maximov staged was unsuccessful. (In the summer of 1935, Maximov fell, was pushed, or jumped to his death from the first level of the Eiffel Tower.[5]) Blumkin, on arrival at Trotsky's, explained that he wanted to determine how the GPU might provide for Trotsky's security.

Trotsky worried more about White Guard assassins than Stalin's agents, despite a warning given to him by Kamenev in 1925: 'You imagine that Stalin is preoccupied with how to reply to your arguments. Nothing of the kind. He is figuring out how to liquidate you without being punished.' Zinoviev had added at the time that Stalin 'could have put an end to you as far back as 1924' but 'postponed killing you until certain that he could do this with impunity.'[6] Having disregarded these warnings and having no inkling of Stalin's scheme, Trotsky treated Blumkin as an old revolutionary and friend. He even asked Blumkin to deliver a personal letter to a close friend of his in Moscow, David Riazanov, the director of the Marx–Lenin Institute. In the letter, he thanked Riazanov for contracting him to do translations of Marxist literature during his earlier exile in Alma-Ata. Without this income, Trotsky would have been in dire financial straits.[7]

Upon his arrival in Moscow, Blumkin reported to his superiors in the GPU about his visit to Trotsky and received permission to pass his letter on to Riazanov. Menzhinsky and the chief of the GPU Foreign Department, Meir Trilisser, valued Blumkin's work highly and planned to send him on a new assignment in Europe in December 1929.[8] While Blumkin was waiting for his new assignment, one of his friends, Rabinovich, the assistant chief of the Secret Political Department of the GPU, made a stunning discovery: he found Stalin's Okhrana file while inspecting the personal papers of Felix Dzerzhinsky. Rabinovich's position in the Secret Political Department gave him access to documents in the personal archives of Cheka–GPU chiefs. He was sorting through Dzerzhinsky's papers to prepare them for deposition in the GPU's general archive.[9]

The documents in Stalin's file stunned Rabinovich. For a communist of his generation, the thought that the leader of the Communist Party and Soviet Union could be an ex-Okhrana agent was outrageous. What to do with this damning discovery was an agonizing problem. By the end of 1929 any attempt to expose the ex-Okhrana agent Stalin within the borders of the Soviet Union would have been tantamount to suicide: the GPU with numerous agents and informers, Stalin's bodyguards, the army and party apparatus – all were in Stalin's hands. Rabinovich recognized that if Stalin learned of the discovery of his Okhrana file and in whose hands it was, he would easily retrieve it and destroy anyone who knew of its existence. He decided to ask Blumkin to undertake the dangerous mission of delivering Stalin's Okhrana file into Trotsky's hands.

Blumkin was no less stunned than Rabinovich by the documents in the file of Okhrana agent Iosif Dzhugashvili. He felt it was his revolutionary duty to save the country by exposing the entrenched Okhrana agent. Ironically, in December 1929, when these documents fell into Blumkin's hands, Stalin was mobilizing his entire propaganda apparatus for the cele-bration of his 50th birthday. The official slogan was 'Stalin is the Lenin of today.' At the same time Lenin's close comrades Trotsky and other heroes of the October Revolution and the Civil War were languishing in exile. This must have struck Blumkin as a monstrous perversion of everything he held sacred. He knew that fate had put into his hands the opportunity to destroy the dictatorship of the Okhrana impostor who had usurped the Russian Revolution.

Blumkin made one crucial mistake: rather than keeping his mission secret, he hinted at it in talking to Karl Radek, one of Trotsky's friends and allies in the past. Having spent most of 1929 abroad, Blumkin did not know that Radek had switched his allegiance to Stalin, who had allowed him to return to Moscow from exile and given him a party sinecure. What exactly Blumkin told Radek about the discovery of the file or his mission to smuggle it to Trotsky is not known, but whatever Radek learned, he promptly reported to Stalin, who realized that his Okhrana file was in Blumkin's hands.

Stalin at once resolved to lure Blumkin into a trap in order to recover the file. He ordered Menzhinsky and Yagoda, as well as the chief of the Foreign Department of the GPU, Trilisser, to arrest Blumkin at the railway station the moment he prepared to leave Moscow for his assignment abroad. Stalin also ordered that anyone with whom Blumkin established contact before his departure be placed under surveillance. Yagoda called into his office a GPU agent, Liza Gurskaya, a beautiful young woman, telling her to drop 'bourgeois prejudices' and enter into an intimate relation-ship with Blumkin in order to determine his plans 'in the interest of the Party'. She did her best to make Blumkin reveal his secrets, but Blumkin remained circumspect and the 'love affair' did not yield the hoped-for information.[10]

Blumkin's departure abroad was scheduled for 21 December 1929, the day of Stalin's 50th birthday. Blumkin went through the usual procedures for a GPU officer going on a secret mission abroad, receiving fabricated passports and a suitcase with foreign currency for expenses and payments to agents and informers. He placed Stalin's Okhrana file in his suitcase on top of the foreign currency. Blumkin was on his way to the railway station when he noticed GPU surveillance agents following him and realized that he was about to walk into a trap. The idea occurred to him somehow to get a passport with the photograph of a man resembling him in order to sneak out of the Soviet Union undetected. He thought of a prominent artist, Raphael Falk, who had just returned from Paris, where he had taken part in an international exhibition of artists promoting their paintings. Falk physically resembled Blumkin, and Falk's wife Raisa had been Blumkin's high-school sweetheart. The Falk couple's apartment was in the Vkhutekhmas (the All-Union Artistic and Technical Studios) building opposite the Post Office on Miasnitskaya Street. Luckily, Raisa was home, and she invited Blumkin to come in. Blumkin sat down on a sofa in the living room and placed the suitcase next to him. 'Raisa, I need your husband's passport', he said. His request frightened her, and she told him that she couldn't give it to him. 'My husband and I would go to prison for that. This would be a serious crime', she protested. Blumkin pointed to his suitcase and said, 'Look, in here is Stalin's Okhrana file, the documents proving that he was an Okhrana agent. I must smuggle this file abroad. Stalin's regime will collapse in 24 hours after I cross the border.' While Blumkin was explaining his reason for needing Falk's passport, friends of Raisa's came in. Seeing that she had company, they apologized and left. Their sudden appearance unnerved Blumkin. He clutched his head and said, 'I'm like a trapped mouse, I want to live. No matter how, no matter what, I want to live.' He again asked for the passport, but Raisa still refused to give it to him. He finally gave up, saying, 'Please, hide this suitcase and don't tell anybody about it.' With these words he rushed out of the apartment. From a window, Raisa saw several GPU agents seize him as he emerged from the building and push him into a waiting car. The car sped to the GPU's Lubianka headquarters a short distance away. Five agents of the GPU's Operational Department knocked on the door of the Falks' apartment. 'Was Blumkin here?' the one in charge asked. Raisa, knowing it would be futile and possibly lethal to lie, said yes. 'What did he tell you?' the agent asked, entering the apartment with the rest of his group. 'Blumkin was very upset. He was saying something I couldn't understand. He was obviously sick . . .', Raisa lied. 'We'll cure him', said the agent, and he asked her whether Blumkin had left anything with her. Raisa hesitated, but afraid to say nothing to the GPU, she pointed at the suitcase standing next to the sofa where Blumkin had been sitting a few minutes earlier. The agent in charge placed the suitcase on a table, took from his pocket an *otmychka* (a lock-breaking tool used by criminals), and prised the suitcase open. His attention was at once attracted by the neatly stacked bundles of foreign currency bills stuffed in the suitcase. On top of the bills was a file, which the agent lifted, but his eyes were fixed on the foreign bills. 'Valiuta!' he exclaimed. 'This is what Blumkin busied himself with!' The agents of the Operational Department did not know that when going on a mission abroad intelligence officers like Blumkin usually carried large sums of foreign currency. At that time, the Operational Department was heavily engaged in the 'mobilization of internal resources' campaign, the mass confiscation of all kinds of valuables from Soviet citizens: foreign currency, gold coins, paintings, and jewelry. Hiding or trading of those valuables was punishable by death. Satisfied that Blumkin was involved in currency smuggling and speculation, the agent placed the file back into the suitcase without looking at it. He took the suitcase, saying to his group, 'Let's go!'[11]

Blumkin and his suitcase were delivered to Menzhinsky, who looked through the documents in the file and at once understood why Stalin had been eager to trap Blumkin. Menzhinsky also realized that Stalin would destroy anyone who knew about the file and that he was inviting certain death if he dared give it to Stalin. He hid the file among his personal papers and did not tell Stalin about it.[12] But Menzhinsky feared that Blumkin, Rabinovich and another man, named Silov, who was also involved in the attempt to smuggle the file abroad, would reveal under interrogation that the file was in the suitcase that Blumkin had left with Raisa Falk. But Stalin might also reasonably assume that Blumkin had destroyed the file before being captured. If Blumkin was kept from talking, figured Menzhinsky, Stalin might never learn what had happened to his file. To guarantee Blumkin's silence, Menzhinsky immediately carried out Stalin's order to execute Blumkin. Also executed were Rabinovich and Silov, who were arrested on the same day as Blumkin's accomplices. Menzhinsky thus denied Stalin the opportunity to find out what had happened to the file.[13]

Menzhinsky worried that Raisa Falk might know something about the file. The day after Blumkin's arrest and execution Raisa Falk was summoned to the GPU Lubianka headquarters, where she was led into a half-dark room and invited to sit on a chair in a corner. A man sitting at a desk in the opposite corner, his face hidden in the dark, did not introduce himself. He apologized for summoning her to discuss 'Blumkin's case', mentioning in passing that Blumkin had been executed for 'counter-revolutionary activities'. Then he asked her what she knew about Blumkin. Raisa said that she had known Blumkin since their high-school years and had seen him afterwards on rare occasions; he had visited her the previous day, looking very upset, and had soon left. The official did not ask about Blumkin's suitcase. He thanked her graciously and parted with her with exquisite gallantry. She was surprised to have found so pleasant a man in the dreaded Lubianka prison and relieved to have gotten away so easily. Raisa was not summoned to the Lubianka again. She kept to herself for many years Blumkin's visit and her strange Lubianka interrogation.[14] What Raisa Falk did not know was that she had been interrogated by Menzhinsky himself. Other women interrogated by him were also impressed by his courteousness and 'insinuating manners, gestures and smiles.' Menzhinsky was 'charming in manner', one of them wrote. He behaved with the same gallantry toward women whom he sent to execution cellars as toward those whom he set free.[15]

Menzhinsky was a cruel and unscrupulous but very clever man. Stalin, after having poisoned Dzerzhinsky, appointed Menzhinsky to head the GPU, no doubt convinced that Menzhinsky would pass on to him any embarrassing documents that might have fallen into GPU hands should he come across any such document. Stalin's assessment was based on Menzhinsky's lack of scruples, on dark spots in his past, and on the fact that he was decidedly not a Bolshevik fanatic of the 'Iron Felix' Dzerzhinsky type. His father was a russified Pole and became a tsarist official with good connections at the court; his brother was a wealthy banker who escaped abroad. Menzhinsky had published a number of biting articles in the Russian émigré press in which he criticized the Bolsheviks and Lenin in particular, calling Lenin an 'illegitimate child of Russian autocracy', a 'political manipulator', and a 'political Jesuit'. Menzhinsky also drew a parallel between Lenin and Chichikov, the con man in Gogol's *Dead Souls*.[16] Lenin, in turn, called Menzhinsky 'my decadent neurotic.' Stalin trusted Menzhinsky because he blackmailed him with all these anti-Lenin statements. He referred to Menzhinsky as 'my amiable but watchful Polish bear'.[17]

The executions of Blumkin, Rabinovich and Silov were never officially announced, but the rumor that they had been secretly shot spread widely. With the exception of his execution, nothing has ever been revealed about the identity of Silov. Many foreign communists enquired in Moscow about Blumkin's fate. On Stalin's orders, Blumkin's execution was categorically denied. The communist Viennese newspaper *Die Rote Fahne* stated that the 'mythical Blumkin' had never existed and, therefore, could not have been executed.[18] On 25 December 1929 one of Trotsky's followers in Moscow

sent him a letter, signed 'Your N', in which he described rumors started by
Stalin:

You know, of course, about the execution of Blumkin and that it was done on
Stalin's personal insistence. This vile act of revenge already now worries quite
wide party circles. But they worry silently. They feed on rumors. One of the
sources of these rumors is Radek. His nervous verbosity is well known. Now
he is totally demoralized . . . Regarding Radek, the following is being spread:
Blumkin at first found Radek, with whom he used to meet more often than
with others during the last years and in whom he got used to seeing one of the
leaders of the opposition . . . He, of course, did not realize that the opposition
already has a bitter enemy in the person of Radek, who, having lost the last
remnants of moral equilibrium, would not stop at any infamy. Here one has
to take into account Blumkin's tendency to idealize people and his close
relationship with Radek in the past. Blumkin related to Radek the thoughts
and plans of L. D. [Trotsky] . . . Radek in response demanded that Blumkin
immediately go to the GPU and report everything. Some comrades say that Radek
threatened Blumkin that he would report him if he did not do it himself. This
is very likely in view of the present mood of this depraved hysteric. We have
no doubt that this was how it happened. Blumkin delivered Trotsky's letter to
one of the oppositionists and, because of this breach of discipline, demanded
to be shot (literally!). Stalin decided to 'satisfy' Blumkin's request and ordered
Menzhinsky and Yagoda to shoot Blumkin . . . How should one understand
this official version? Its fraudulence hits one in the eye. No exact information
is available, because Blumkin, according to what we know by now, did not
have time to send any information out of prison.[19]

'N' had no idea that Blumkin was executed for attempting to smuggle
Stalin's Okhrana file out of the country. Trotsky, too, knew nothing of the
file, but Boris Bazhanov, one of Stalin's secretaries who had fled abroad in
1926, learned that Blumkin had been shot for his attempt to smuggle
abroad 'highly sensitive documents'.[20]

   Several years after Stalin's death, when the fear of the 'security organs'
had considerably lessened, Raisa Falk finally dared to tell her son and a few
close friends about Blumkin's visit to her more than a quarter of a century
earlier and what he had then told her about Stalin's Okhrana file. The sofa
on which Blumkin sat that day was still in the same spot in her living room.
'Blumkin was sitting right there', said Raisa, pointing at the sofa as if asking
it to bear witness to the story that only she knew.[21]

NOTES

1. Roy Medvedev, *Let History Judge*, New York, 1971, p. 140, quoting a Latvian Old Bolshevik, I. I. Sandler, imprisoned in Varkuta.
2. Dmitry Volkogonov, 'Demon revolutsii', *Pravda*, 9 September 1988.
3. Lev Trotsky, *Stalin*, New York, 1941, p. 337.
4. Nadezhda Mandelstam, *Hope Against Hope: A Memoir*, London, 1989, pp. 101f. Mandelstam did not suspect that this irreconcilable contradiction may have been the fatal flaw that led to Blumkin's downfall. In her book's index of names, she writes that Blumkin was executed in 1929 for delivering to David Riazanov a letter written by Trotsky, a lie spread by Stalin.
5. Boris Bazhanov, *Kontinent*, no. 10, 1976, pp. 244f.
6. Trotsky, *Stalin*, p. 417.
7. *Biulleten oppozitsii*, ed. L. Trotsky, vol. I (1929–30), no. 9, 1930, pp. 9f.
8. Alexander Orlov, *The Secret History of Stalin's Crimes*, New York, 1953, pp. 192f.
9. Interview with I. P. Itskov, who knew Rabinovich, the assistant chief of the GPU Secret Political Department in the late 1920s. See also Chapter 26, describing how I. L. Shtein, the assistant chief of the NKVD Secret Political Department, discovered Stalin's Okhrana file in Menzhinsky's office in 1936. See also *Biulleten oppozitsii*, No. 10, April 1930, p. 1 on Rabinovich and Silov.
10. Alexander Orlov, *Tainaia istoriya stalinskikh prestuplenii*, New York, Jerusalem, Paris, 1983, pp. 191–3.
11. Taped interview with Vasily Rudich.
12. Alexander Orlov, 'The Sensational Secret behind Damnation of Stalin', *Life*, 23 April 1956. Orlov relates the discovery in Menzhinsky's office of Stalin's Okhrana file in 1936 by the assistant chief of the Secret Political Department, I. L. Shtein.
13. *Biulleten oppozitsii*, vol. I, no. 10, 1930, p. 1.
14. Taped interview with Vasily Rudich.
15. Roman Gul', *Dzerzhinsky*, New York, 1974, pp. 159f. Gul quotes P. Melgunova-Stepanova.
16. Ibid., pp. 153–5.
17. Ibid., p. 150.
18. *Biulleten oppozitsii*, vol. I, no. 10, 1930, p. 8, quoting *Die Rote Fahne*.
19. Ibid., vol. I, (1929–30), no. 9, 1930, pp. 9f.
20. Boris Bazhanov, 'Polet v nochi', *Kontinent*, no. 10, 1976, p. 245.
21. Taped interview with Vasily Rudich.

20

THE 'KUTEPOV DOCUMENTS'

When no hint of his Okhrana file appeared after the execution of Blumkin, Rabinovich and Silov, Stalin must have hoped that Blumkin had destroyed the file before his arrest. But the fear of its having fallen into unknown hands continued to haunt him. He decided to discredit the documents in the file in advance if it were to reappear, by 'proving' that the documents Blumkin had tried to smuggle abroad were forgeries. Stalin had resorted to a similar strategy in August 1917, when he published an article in which he had stated that the enemies of the Bolsheviks used 'low-grade forgery and falsification' to malign 'revolutionary fighters' as 'German and tsarist spies'.[1] A month earlier, Lenin and Trotsky had branded as calumnies the Provisional Government's accusations that Lenin was an agent of the German general staff.[2]

In 1926, soon after his Okhrana file was discovered, Stalin assigned V. Maksakov, a GPU 'expert' on Okhrana documents, to reconstruct the history of the Okhrana archives from the time of the February Revolution. With Stalin's heavy-handed 'advice', Maksakov published an article in which he declared that the 'enemies of the party of the proletariat' fabricated fraudulent Okhrana 'documents' (he bracketed the word documents with sarcastic quotation marks). Maksakov added: 'The old Okhrana officers widely used the tsarist archives, "serving" the Provisional Government in its struggle with the Bolshevik party . . . These "documents" were intended to serve as a weapon in the struggle with the hated Bolshevik party.'[3]

Again, Stalin's old habit of repeating a lie several times was at work, with the usual intention of giving the lie the appearance of unimpeachable truth in the minds of others, as well as perhaps in his own mind. In order to buttress this 'truth' even more strongly, Stalin decided to stage a show trial in which a tsarist general would be forced to confess that he had directed the fabrication of documents aimed at discrediting the Soviet leader. Stalin decided to parade the former tsarist army general A. P. Kutepov as the chief culprit at the trial. Kutepov lived in Paris, where he served as the chairman of the ROVS (All-Russian Union of Army Veterans), an émigré organization of White Guard officers. To carry out his scheme, Stalin ordered the

GPU to kidnap Kutepov in Paris and bring him to the Lubianka prison in Moscow.

On Sunday, 26 January 1930 at 10:30 am, General Kutepov left his apartment at 26 rue Roussel and headed for the Russian Orthodox Church at 81 rue de Mademoiselle. He did not appear at the church and did not return home. The Paris police were notified and started an investigation, but it was not until 30 January that they received information clarifying how the general was kidnapped. A witness reported that looking out of his window, he saw a man of medium height with a black beard walking down the rue Roussel. The man was passing a parked car when two tall and burly men dressed in yellow overcoats suddenly grabbed him and pushed him inside the car. A policeman who had been standing at the corner quickly walked to the car and got in next to the driver. The car sped away. The Russian émigré dailies in Paris, *Vozrozhdenie* (Rebirth) and *Poslednie novosty* (The Latest News), as well as the French press, protested the kidnapping of General Kutepov and demanded that the French Government break diplomatic relations with Moscow. A crowd of Russian émigrés threatened to storm the Soviet Embassy on rue Grenelle, but the police prevented the attack.

The French government initiated an official inquiry, while GPU agents spread an assortment of fanciful lies about Kutepov's disappearance. The most blatant of them, reported by the Soviet newspaper *Izvestiya* on 3 February 1930, was that Kutepov had stolen a large sum of money from the ROVS and escaped to South America. The French police learned that the day of his disappearance Kutepov wrote 'Sk' in his diary. At that time, the police did not decipher the meaning of the abbreviation. The name it stood for was not revealed until seven years later, during the investigation of a similar kidnapping in Paris, that of General E. K. Miller, Kutepov's successor. Only then was it established that Kutepov's assistant General N. V. Skoblin and his wife Nadezhda Plevitskaya were Soviet agents and had played an important part in the kidnapping of both tsarist generals. But in 1930 Skoblin and Plevitskaya pretended to be solicitous friends: they often visited Kutepov's wife to express their support, and they assured her that Kutepov would soon return.[4] Skoblin and Plevitskaya had been recruited by Dr Max Eitingon, a GPU resident stationed in Vienna. (Eitingon, interestingly, was a prominent psychoanalyst, one of Sigmund Freud's famous 'six disciples'. In 1922 Freud told Eitingon, 'I suggest we continue our relationship, which has developed from friendship to sonship, until the end of my days.'[5]) Max Eitingon's brother, Leonid Eitingon, codename 'Naumov', a tall, powerfully built top GPU operative, was one of the most trusted of

Stalin's agents.[6] (In 1940, Leonid Eitingon, on Stalin's orders, organized the murder of Trotsky.) He was one of the two men in yellow overcoats who abducted Kutepov. The other GPU agent was S. V. Puzitsky, also a man of imposing physique.[7] Thirty-five years later, on 22 September 1965, the Soviet Army newspaper *Krasnaya zvezda* (Red Star) published an article, stating that 'Commissar Second Rank of State Security Sergey Vasilievich Puzitsky took part not only in the capture of the bandit Savinkov and in the destruction of the counter-revoluntionary monarchist organization "Trust", but also brilliantly carried out the operation to arrest Kutepov.'[8]

Puzitsky was executed in 1937. The GPU agent dressed in a police uniform was Lev Rudminsky.[9] A number of Soviet diplomats, most of whom were GPU agents, were also involved in Kutepov's kidnapping and hastened to leave Paris for Moscow.[10] (Fifteen years later, the Soviet Army occupied Prague and Soviet Secret Police arrested Kutepov's wife and his son Pavel, who had moved there from Paris. They were incarcerated in the infamous 'Political Isolator', called Vladimir Central, where they spent more than ten years. After Stalin's death, both were released but not allowed to leave Russia, despite having French citizenship. They died soon after, still not knowing why Stalin had ordered the kidnapping of General Kutepov.[11])

Kutepov was brought to Moscow's Lubianka prison in early February 1930. He was accused of directing the fabrication of Okhrana documents that were planted in Russian archives to discredit Stalin. After Kutepov had been executed, Stalin assigned Alexander Svanidze, the brother of Stalin's first wife, to carry out the destruction of what he called the 'Kutepov documents'.[12] Trotsky received a report stating that 'some 150–200 people had been arrested in Moscow'.[13] GPU agents spread rumors that 'Trotskyites had sabotaged railway transports, derailing trains during the transfer of troops for the struggle with Chiang Kai-shek . . .'.[14] Trotsky wrote that Stalin spread this 'idiotic version in order to invent some kind of justification for his Thermidorian crimes against the Bolshevik-Leninists Blumkin, Rabinovich and Silov, who had nothing to do with "sabotage". The fact that Stalin till now has not admitted the execution of Blumkin indicates that he has nothing to say to justify his loathsome crime.'[15] Stalin must have been relieved to find that Trotsky did not know the true reason for Blumkin's execution.

Material evidence was needed to prove the charges against Kutepov: a forgery that could be proved to be Kutepov's fabrication. By the end of the 1920s Stalin had established a highly professional operation for the mass production of all kinds of fakes. Alexander Svanidze was in charge of a printing operation which, starting in 1927, was producing tens of millions of counterfeit dollars, inundating the markets of the United States, Europe and China. The FBI for some time had difficulty in identifying the counterfeit bills. Soviet agents used Chicago gangsters to launder them. On 4 January 1933 FBI arrested Dr Valentine Gregory Burtan, an American communist and heart specialist; he was sentenced to 15 years in jail for masterminding this operation.[16]

There was, however, a substantial risk with Kutepov's appearance at his show trial which would confirm his kidnaping on French soil. This had the potential to ignite an international scandal, possibly leading to a break in French–Soviet diplomatic relations. Besides, Stalin did not have a document from his Okhrana file which he could have doctored in a way that would prove it was fraudulent. These considerations forced Stalin to abandon the idea of a show trial, although toward the spring of 1930 the necessary testimonies were prepared and the trial was almost completely rehearsed.[17] The accused 'confessed' that they were members of a counter-revoluntionary organization TKP (Toiling Peasants Party), which supposedly consisted of some 200,000 kulaks, Social Revolutionaries and White Guards. This imaginary conspiracy was code-named *Vesna* (Spring), because the Kutepov show trial was scheduled for spring 1930. But Stalin changed his mind and ordered that all of the defendants be 'liquidated administratively', that is, secretly shot without formalities.[18]

Besides the charge of fabricating Okhrana documents, General Kutepov was also accused of forming a large monarchist organization in the Red Army. Some 800 military commanders, among them the head of the Military Academy, A. E. Snesarev, were accused of being members of this mythical organization and arrested. (In 1918, Snesarev, a former tsarist officer, had been appointed by Trotsky as commander of the Tsaritsyn front. Stalin had accused Snesarev of treason and had arrested him, but Snesarev had been reinstated on Lenin's and Trotsky's orders. Stalin had not forgotten this insult.) When Snesarev was arrested in early 1930 no one could save him.[19] During this period, Stalin's inflamed imagination conjured up several conspiracies. After the executions of General Kutepov and his 'accomplices', Stalin ordered preparations for another show trial of 'saboteurs and spies', which was scheduled to take place in autumn 1930. But Stalin suddenly canceled it and ordered that all 46 defendants be secretly shot.[20]

The 'Industrial Party' show trial opened in the Moscow's Hall of Columns on 25 November 1930. The chief defendant was Professor Leonid Ramzin, an old Bolshevik and a leading specialist on thermodynamics. He 'confessed' that he had been a 'wrecker' of the Soviet economy and the head of the 2,000-member 'Industrial Party'. The other seven accused men, officials of the *Gosplan* (State Planning Agency) also confessed. Ramzin testified that he had met Lawrence of Arabia in London; as it turned out, Lawrence was not in England at the time Ramzin supposedly visited him. He also confessed to having received 'wrecking instructions' from two wealthy Russian émigrés, Riabushinsky and Vishnegradsky. The Western press reported that both men had died long before their alleged meeting with Ramzin. Finally, Ramzin admitted to having met with President Raymond Poincaré of France and discussed plans for an invasion of Russia, an admission so absurd that Poincaré must have felt ridiculous when he denied it.[21] Stalin's mind, gripped by paranoia, was producing fantasies which the GPU investigators did not dare to question, knowing that any inquiries along rational lines might cost them their jobs, if not their lives. Nikolay Krylenko, the public prosecutor, expressed in an oddly garbled way his concern about the lack of documentary evidence supporting the charges. He was especially puzzled by the fact that the defendants in their signed depositions prominently mentioned various 'documents, circular letters, reports, and records' that were not produced in court. Krylenko pointed to this fact in his summation of the case: 'What evidence can there be? Are there, let us say, any documents? I inquired about that. It seems that where the documents existed, they were destroyed . . . But, I asked, perhaps one of them has accidentally survived? It would be futile to hope for that.'[22] When Krylenko asked Stalin about these missing documents, his reply reflected Stalin's wishful thinking and produced the glib answer, 'Where these documents existed, they were destroyed . . .' and 'it would be futile to hope' that even one of them survived. Stalin fervently hoped none had survived and possibly was able to convince himself of that. At the closing session of the show trial a familiar scene took place. A boy, the son of one of the defendants, Xenophon Sitnin, rose from his seat in the spectators' gallery and demanded that his father be shot. 'To me my father is a class enemy, nothing more!' declared the boy. The press glorified him as a model for Soviet youth.[23]

Stalin's Okhrana file appeared in a disguised form at the next show trial, that of the mythical 'Union Bureau of the Central Committee of the Menshevik Party'. This show trial took place in March 1931. The only Menshevik among the defendants was Nikolay Sukhanov, a prominent historian whom Lenin had praised highly for his *Memoirs of the Revolution*, but whom Stalin hated for having described him as a 'gray blur' hardly noticeable during the revolutionary period. Sukhanov was forced to 'recall' that in 1928 he had had a meeting with the Menshevik leader Rafael Abramovich, an émigré who allegedly had come secretly to Russia to organize an anti-Soviet plot. Abramovich issued a statement, declaring that he had not visited Russia and had been attending the International Socialist Congress in Brussels at the time.[24]

The Union Bureau 'members' were accused of attempting to wreck the Soviet economy. One peripheral accusation contained a particle of truth, distorted almost beyond recognition. A 45-year-old economist, I. I. Rubin, who was arrested on 23 December 1930, half a year after the arrests of other defendants, was accused of giving a 'sealed file of documents for safekeeping' to David Riazanov, the Director of the Marx–Engels–Lenin Institute, the same Riazanov whom Trotsky, in a letter delivered by Blumkin, had thanked for providing him with paid translation work in Alma-Ata exile.[25] Riazanov, an Old Bolshevik, was until 1926 the Chairman of *Glavarkhiv* (Main Archive Administration), which in Stalin's eyes may have made him a likely suspect in the discovery of his Okhrana file that year. But the fact that Blumkin had brought Trotsky's letter to Riazanov just before attempting to smuggle the file abroad may also have triggered Stalin's suspicion that his file was in Riazanov's hands. Any suspicion he might have had would have been fed by Stalin's long-standing hatred of Riazanov: back in 1921, at a party meeting, Riazanov sharply criticized Stalin, who shouted back, 'Shut up, you clown!' Riazanov's reply was equally rude.[26]

The Blumkin–Riazanov 'connection' in Stalin's mind assumed ominous significance. The purpose of Rubin's arrest was to 'prove' that Riazanov was hiding Stalin's Okhrana file. Rubin had no idea why the interrogators insisted on his implicating Riazanov, a man whom he highly respected and was indebted to for advancing his career. He came to realize that the only reason for his arrest was for him to accuse Riazanov of taking the 'sealed file of documents for safekeeping'. Rubin categorically denied that he ever gave any sealed file to Riazanov. He was transferred to a special prison converted from a centuries-old monastery in the ancient Russian town of Suzdal. In the distant past this monastery had been used for the incarceration of heretics in small cells, actually damp stone caves.[27] Rubin was locked in one of these caves. It was so small he could barely move, and he soon came down with influenza and an old ulcer flared up, which caused him excruciating pain. He was summoned to interrogations day and night, and was not allowed to sleep. The interrogators took turns questioning him in the 'conveyor' system. Sometimes they beat him, but mostly applied psychological pressure. His chief interrogator, M. I. Gay, played the part of the man concerned for Rubin's well-being: 'Isaac Ilyich, confess. It's necessary for the Party', he kept admonishing him. Gay expressed no interest in the nature of the documents in the 'sealed file' that Rubin had supposedly given to Riazanov.

On the night of 29 January 1931 Rubin was led from his cell to the prison basement. Several GPU officers were holding a prisoner whose name, they told Rubin, was Vasilevsky. Turning to Vasilevsky, one of the officers said, 'We are going to shoot you now, if Rubin does not confess.' Vasilevsky dropped to his knees and begged, 'Isaac Ilyich, what does it cost you to confess?!' Rubin kept silent, and Vasilevsky was shot before his eyes. On the next night, Rubin was again taken to the basement. A young man, whom the officers called Dorodnov, stood there surrounded by GPU officers. 'You will be shot, because Rubin does not want to confess', one of them said, Dorodnov tore open his shirt, baring his chest, and said quietly, 'Fascists, gendarmes, shoot!' He was shot before Rubin's eyes. Something shattered inside Rubin. He agreed to sign the confession stating that he had given the 'sealed file' to Riazanov. Sick and emotionally devastated, he was taken back to Moscow's Lubianka prison, where his old cellmates hardly recognized him.[28]

Riazanov was fired from his job and expelled from the party for 'aiding the Menshevik traitors'.[29] During a face-to-face confrontation with Riazanov in an interrogator's office, Rubin, pale and tormented by guilt and shame, turned to Riazanov and said, 'David Borisovich, you remember I handed you a file.' The confrontation was interrupted, and Rubin was taken back to his cell. When the door behind him closed, he beat his head against the wall in a futile attempt to take his own life.[30] On 1 March 1931 the 14 defendants, among them Rubin, went on trial. In his coat pocket Rubin carried his typed confession with Gay's corrections in red pencil. He testified how he had given Riazanov the 'sealed file'. 'Didn't you establish any organizational [Menshevik] connection?' Prosecutor Krylenko asked. According to the script of his signed deposition, Rubin was supposed to answer that he had indeed established such a connection, but for some reason, he rebelled. 'No, there was no organizational connection', he replied. 'There was only his great personal trust in me.' Krylenko announced a court recess. The defendants were taken to an adjacent room, where Krylenko came up to Rubin and said angrily, 'You did not say what you should have said. After the recess I will call you back to the stand, and you will correct your reply.' Rubin refused. In his closing speech Krylenko singled out Rubin for the most spiteful abuse. Instead of the agreed-upon sentence of three years' imprisonment, Rubin was sentenced to five years' solitary confinement. He was released in 1935 and decided not to return to

Moscow, ashamed to see his former acquaintances. In the fall of 1937, he was again arrested and this time he perished in prison. Riazanov was arrested after the Union Bureau show trial and was shot a few years later.[31]

Shortly after the Menshevik Show trial Stalin wrote and published a book entitled *Provokator Anna Serebriakova*, using the pseudonym 'I. V. Alekseev'. (The initials of Alekseev's first and middle name point to Stalin's usual manner of hinting at the truth.) This is the fascinating product of a mind observing itself while purportedly analyzing someone else. Its true authorship was never revealed, but there is a wealth of evidence pointing to Stalin as its author.[32] The book consists mostly of reports, circular letters, receipts and other documents reproduced from the file of the exposed Okhrana agent Anna Serebriakova, who had been imprisoned in 1925 and died in a Moscow prison. The book's concluding chapter gives a strikingly perceptive psychological profile of an Okhrana agent, actually Stalin's own psychological self-portrait. In the preface, Stalin stated that the show trials' defendants had been connected with their 'ancestral father . . . the *provocateur* of the tsarist Okhrana'. He wrote:

The village kulak who uses a stick and a sawn-off shotgun, the professor Ramzin and the writer Sukhanov, who had been preparing an intervention, are people of the same kind . . . The same class threads that bind together the kulaks, the professors, and the literati also stretch deep into history, thus uniting the past with the present. And there, in history, we find the ancestral father of the present day wrecker – the *provocateur* of the tsarist Okhrana.[33]

In his typical style of repeated similar questions Stalin continued:

does one have to write about *provocateurs* and spies? After all, this page was turned forever; the wheel of history does not spin backwards. Does one have to harass these archival bones, does one have to introduce the contemporary reader to the sphere of the gloomy and base deeds of tsarism?

Stalin provided the answer:

It seems to us that we should harass archival bones. The *provocateur*, – we say, – [the strange punctuation in the Russian original is left unchanged here] is a close relative of the kulak and the wrecker. Ramzin used the trust of the proletariat, just as Azef used the trust of his party. Azef – served the Okhrana, Ramzin – served the international bourgeoisie.

Stalin did not want his 'archival bones' to be harassed.

Anna Serebriakova was not involved in murders and armed robberies.

These crimes were committed by Azef, as well as by Stalin. But in this remarkable passage Stalin describes not Serebriakova but himself, as well as Azef. The preface concludes with a 'stern warning to all those who, out of cowardice, greed or by vocation, trade in people, as in merchandise'.[34] This was the warning to all those who would dare to harass his archival bones. This warning has a familiar ring to it. V. Maksakov, Stalin's 'expert' on Okhrana operations, wrote in his 1927 article that after the February Revolution the archival workers were selling lists of exposed Okhrana agents to newspapers for a 'certain honorarium'. Maksakov oddly gloated, 'This attempt, as one should have expected, did not benefit the initiators of it . . .'.[35] A similarly odd triumphant note creeps into Stalin's writing: 'The life story of the *provocateur* Serebriakova is, undoubtedly, instructive. Her story represents the history of the revolutionary movement reflected in the cross section of the life of one extraordinary person . . .'.[36]

Only one man in Soviet Russia could have made this startling statement. No one but Stalin would have dared to characterize an Okhrana agent as an 'extraordinary person' whose life story represented the 'the history of the revolutionary movement' – the turn of praise that described Stalin as he saw himself.

The book concludes with a sketch of an Okhrana agent's psychological profile. Stalin states that it is 'difficult to determine, imagine and describe' this profile, but he, nevertheless, points to '*psikhologicheskuyu razdvoennost*' (psychological duality) as the agent's 'two natures', his 'split personality', and his ability to 'separate his thoughts from his words', which demand 'gigantic will power' and 'stainless steel stamina to control his words'. Stalin admires such an Okhrana agent, stating,

This split personality did not crush Serebriakova. On the contrary, this duality became the foundation of her character, the pivot of all her life . . . The duality stopped being a torture that was forced on her from the outside and of which she had to remind herself in order to live under its control: the duality itself became the way of life, the meaning of life.[37]

The 'gigantic will power' and 'stainless steel stamina' of such an agent created a sense of pride in 'uniqueness' and 'importance' in being the 'keeper of a secret', which lifted the agent above all other people. Such an agent also experienced a 'feeling of superiority' over his Okhrana handler, saying to himself: 'On me and on people like me rests the security of the regime that you are called on to defend.' Stalin quite appropriately cited the habit of such an agent to accuse others of what he himself was guilty of, a habit that Stalin quite appropriately called the 'false target' method.[38]

The perceptiveness of this psychological profile raises the question to what extent was Stalin aware that he was practicing this selfsame method by attacking the 'false targets'. On the one hand, the psychological mechanism of freeing himself from guilt by transferring it to others would have been ineffective if Stalin had recognized himself in his projections.[39] On the other hand, the unmistakable praise that Stalin bestows on the Okhrana agent argues that on some level Stalin was perfectly aware of his own 'two natures', or 'two personalities'. He masterfully describes the psychological profile of the *agent provocateur*, noting coyly: 'We repeat, but we will not take upon ourselves the mission to unwrap the mystery of this person. If it is true that 'man's soul is darkness, then the "soul" of any provocateur is indeed a gloomy night and Serebriakova's soul is three times gloomier.'[40]

Stalin's fear that his Okhrana past might be discovered prompted him to systematically destroy and falsify archival documents in order to 'prove' by its omission that the information had never existed. Thus in 1924–27 the doctored and abridged version of the records of the 'Muraviev Commission' was published under the editorial direction of P. E. Shchegolev.[41] Shchegolev omitted all references to Stalin's rivalry with Malinovsky and all references to Elena Rozmirovich's arrest. In addition, the depositions of Lenin and Zinoviev in the case of Malinovsky, which they submitted to the Muraviev Commission in May 1917, are missing from the published record. Also missing is the testimony of Colonel I. P. Vasiliev of 21 March 1917 in which he described the Malinovsky case in detail, presenting it as the most outrageous Okhrana provocation. But Colonel Vasiliev's testimony suddenly surfaced in 1930 in the book *Okhranniki i avanturisty* (Okhrana Officers and Adventurers) written by the same P. E. Shchegolev. In this book, Shchegolev writes that Vasiliev 'presented himself as the exposer of the provocation schemes of his colleagues in the intelligence service, and, if anything, he could not be denied the honor of being the most informed man'. Given this glowing assessment of Vasiliev, the book suffers from a curious omission: the Malinovsky case had been Vasiliev's trump card. From 1912 on, he had been persistent in his attempts to expose Malinovsky, presenting himself as a 'progressive' Okhrana officer eager to expose Okhrana provocations. But Malinovsky appears nowhere in *Okhranniki i avanturisty*. Shchegolev claimed, 'I quote Vasiliev's report in its entirety.' In fact, he quotes the report very selectively, and among his major omissions is that of all mentions of the Okhrana agent 'Vasily'.[42]

NOTES

1. Lev Trotsky, *Stalin*, New York, 1941, p. 222.
2. Ibid., p. 210.
3. V. Maksakov, 'Arkhiv revolutsii i vneshnei politiki XIX–XX vekov', *Archivnoe delo*, no. 12, 1927, pp. 27–31.
4. B. Prianishnikov, 'Pokhishchenie generala Kutepova', *Novoe russkoe slovo*, 9 December 1979.
5. Stephen Schwartz, 'Intellectuals and Assassins – Annals of Stalin's Killerati', *The New York Times Book Review*, 24 January 1988, pp. 3 and 31. See also John J. Dziak, *Chekisty: A History of the KGB*, Lexington, MA, 1988, pp. 100–2.
6. Felix Svetlov, interview in New York City, 1990. Also see Vitaly Rapoport and Yury Alekseev, *Izmena rodine*, London, 1988, pp. 502f.; Stephen Schwartz, 'Intellectuals and Assassins', pp. 3 and 31; Dziak, *Chekisty*, pp. 100–2.
7. Interview with Felix Svetlov, New York City, 1993.
8. B. Prianishnikov, 'Pokhishchenie generala Kutepova', *Novoe russkoe slovo*, 9 December 1979.
9. The author served his prison term in the Norilsk prison camp while Lev Rudminsky was a prisoner there. A native of the Crimean town of Theodisia, Rudminsky had known the author's parents since childhood. Rudminsky was arrested in 1937 and worked as a labor manager in the construction of housing in Norilsk. He was supplied with opium by camp medical personnel. When he was high on opium, he sometimes bragged about his past heroic exploits, including the kidnapping of General Kutepov. Rudminsky never mentioned Blumkin or Stalin's Okhrana file – apparently he had no idea that the kidnapping of Kutepov had been connected with this file.
10. One of them was Lev Gelfand, who later defected to the West and lived to an advanced age as 'Mr Moore', an American businessman. See Priandishnikov, 'Pokhishchenie generala Kutepova'.
11. I. P. Itskov was an inmate with Kutepov's son in the Vladimir Central prison and got to know him.
12. Rafael Bagratuni. Letter to I. D. Levine, dated 8 May 1967. In Levine's archive. Copy in the author's archive.
13. *Biulleten oppozitsii*, no. 10, April 1930, p. 19.
14. Ibid., p. 8.
15. Ibid., p. 1.
16. Walter G. Krivitsky, *In Stalin's Secret Service*, New York, 1939, p. 133.
17. Roy Medvedev, *Let History Judge*, New York, 1971, p. 114.
18. H. Montgomery Hyde, *Stalin: the History of a Dictator*, New York, 1971, p. 282.
19. Medvedev, *Let History Judge*, p. 137.
20. Ibid., p. 114.
21. Hyde, *Stalin*, pp. 281–3.
22. Medvedev, *Let History Judge*, p. 119, quoting *Proletarskii prigovor nad vrediteliami-interventami* (record of court proceedings), Moscow, 1930, p. 32.
23. E. Lyons, *Stalin, the Czar of All the Russias*, Philadelphia/New York and London, 1940, p. 370. Also quoted in Hyde, *Stalin*, p. 280.
24. Hyde, *Stalin*, p. 283.
25. Medvedev, *Let History Judge*, pp. 132–7.
26. Ibid., p. 34.
27. Ibid., pp. 132f.
28. Ibid., pp. 132–4.
29. Ibid., p. 132.
30. Ibid., pp. 134–6.
31. Ibid., p. 132.
32. Even on the grammatical level there is evidence of Stalin's authorship: the book contains the same type of mistakes found in Stalin's other writings, which are common to people who are not native speakers. There are incorrect usages (*starchestvo* instead of the correct *starost* to describe Sebriakova's advanced age) and non-Russian sounding phrases: (*proshedshee s nastoyashchim* instead of the correct *proshloe s nastoyashchim*; *liudi odnogo poriadka* instead of *liudi odogno poshiba*; *krepkie sviazi* instead of *prochnye sviazi*).
33. I. V. Alekseev, *Provokator Anna Serebriakova*, Moscow, 1932, pp. 3f.
34. Ibid.
35. V. Maksakov, 'Arkhiv revolutsii . . . ,' *Arkhivnoe delo*, no. XIII, 1927, p. 30.

36. Alekseev, *Provokator Anna Serebriakova*, p. 4.
37. Ibid., pp. 160–80.
38. Ibid., pp. 175f.
39. See Sigmund Freud, 'Psychoanalytic Notes upon an Autobiographical Account of a Case of Paranoia (Dementia Paranoides)', *Collected Papers*, London, 1958–86, vol. 1, ch. 3. See also Walter C. Langer, *The Mind of Adolf Hitler*, New York, 1972, pp. 183–5.
40. I. V. Alekseev, *Provokator Anna Serebriakova*, p. 180.
41. *Padenie tsarskogo rezhima*, 7 vols, Moscow/Leningrad, 1925.
42. Shchegolev, *Okhranniki i avanturisty*, pp. 138–49.

21

'I KNOW WHAT KIND OF REVOLUTIONARY YOU ARE!'

In 1930, Stalin's wife Nadezhda Allilueva enrolled in the Industrial Academy to study textile manufacturing. The director of the academy was the only one there who knew that she was Stalin's wife. The GPU placed two agents in Nadezhda's class; other agents drove her to school and let her out a block away from the academy.[1] Stalin at that time ordered a campaign of forced collectivization of the peasantry. From her classmates Nadezhda learned about the horrors of executions and mass deportations of peasants, the systematic extermination of the kulaks, famine in the Ukraine, Northern Caucasus and other areas of the country. She learned about hordes of orphaned children searching for food and shelter, women who sold themselves for crumbs from the tables of privileged party bureaucrats. She told Stalin about what she had heard, but he dismissed the accounts as 'Trotskyite rumors'. When, on another occasion, Nadezhda told him about cases of cannibalism in the Ukraine, Stalin became enraged and accused her of spreading 'anti-Soviet propaganda of the enemies of the people'. He ordered Karl Pauker, the chief of the GPU Operations Department, to arrest the students from whom she had heard of these conditions. He also forbade Nadezhda to attend classes, but she resumed her studies when Avel Enukidze, Stalin's close friend and the family's 'good uncle', intervened and changed Stalin's mind.[2]

In May 1930 Stalin ordered that all institutions of higher education be purged of members of the 'right' opposition, headed by Bukharin, Rykov and Tomsky, which had emerged at the Fifteenth Party Congress in 1927, when he had proclaimed the policy of mass collectivization of the peasantry. Bukharin ventured that Stalin had in his hands something with which he could blackmail Politburo members Voroshilov and Kalinin and that gave him control over them.[3] A free peasantry was incompatible with Stalin's thirst for unlimited power. A peasant who could provide for his family and himself without being dependent on the dispensations of the Party apparatus was in Stalin's eyes a class enemy. Collectivization did not move Russia any closer to the socialism the Left Opposition leaders envisioned. It was throwing the country back into medieval serfdom.

Stalin personally supervised the purge of the opposition members in the

Industrial Academy. On the evening of 29 May 1930 one of the first-year students, Nikita Khrushchev, was called to a telephone in the dormitory. An unfamiliar voice said, 'This is Mekhlis, the editor of *Pravda*. Can you come over to my office right away? I'll send my car for you. I have an urgent matter to discuss with you.' Khrushchev was brought to Lev Mekhlis, Stalin's assistant, who read to him a letter about 'political machinations and illegal procedures which had been used to select a rightist delegation'. Mekhlis said that the letter had come from the Industrial Academy. 'Are you in agreement with the contents of this letter?' he asked. 'Yes, absolutely', replied Khrushchev. 'Would you be willing to put your signature on it?' asked Mekhlis. Khrushchev, unaware that the letter had been fabricated by Stalin, said, 'I don't even know who the author is.' Mekhlis replied, 'This is not important. Your name and the author's name won't figure in this business at all. I'm asking you to sign it because I trust you . . .', Khrushchev said, 'Very well, I'll sign it.'[4] This was the beginning of Khrushchev's Kremlin career. Years later, Khrushchev stated that this unsigned letter had been 'like a clap of thunder out of a clear blue sky. The academy was immediately thrown into a turmoil. Classes were suspended and . . . a meeting was called at which all the academy delegates to the Bauman District Conference were recalled . . . I was made chairman of the meeting and was put on the new delegation.'

The whole country was undergoing purges similar to the one at the Industrial Academy: the 'old Bolsheviks', Party members since before the Revolution, were bullied by the power-hungry and unscrupulous 'new' Khrushchev-type recruits. Khrushchev recalled that at the time he had enrolled in the academy in 1929, it was 'teeming with rightists, and they'd gotten control of the Party cell'. The chairman of the cell in the academy was Khakharev, a party member since 1906, whom Khrushchev described as belonging to 'what we called the Old Guard . . . [who were] against Stalin and the General Line of the Party. The Old Guard at the Academy consisted of Old Bolsheviks . . .'. Khrushchev states that Stalin disliked the Old Bolsheviks saying, 'The Central Committee doesn't have confidence in them so it removes them from their Party posts . . .' .

Stalin catered to the ambition of relatively new arrivals in the party such as Khrushchev. He was born in 1894 in a village on the Russian–Ukrainian border. When his father got a job at a coal mine in the Ukrainian town of Yuzovka, the family moved there. During the First World War, Khrushchev worked in the mine as a metal fitter, thus avoiding the draft, since mine workers were exempt. He was mobilized into the Red Army during the Civil War, when he joined the Bolshevik Party. In 1922, he returned to

Yuzovka and learned that his wife had died of starvation during the famine of the preceding year. He married a second time and for two years worked as a Party organizer in the mine. He also started to attend *Rabfak* (Workers' School), established to provide elementary education for workers. In 1925, Khrushchev was sent to the Ukrainian Ninth Party Congress, which was chaired by Stalin's protégé Lazar Kaganovich, who began promoting Khrushchev to various positions in the Ukrainian Party organization.

In 1927 Khrushchev was sent to Moscow to attend the Fifteenth Party Congress. There, he saw Stalin for the first time, witnessed the defeat of the opposition, and voted for Stalin's 'General Line'. In 1929, he was sent to study metallurgy at the Industrial Academy in Moscow, but at first was not admitted because of insufficient education. Kaganovich applied 'pressure from above', and Khrushchev was admitted as a first-year student. In May 1930, Kaganovich, in a conversation with Stalin, mentioned Khrushchev as his protégé. Stalin needed a student to sign the fabricated letter. Khrushchev attended as a 'non-delegate' the Sixteenth Party Congress in June–July of 1930 at which Stalin proclaimed his 'Five-Year Plan in Four Years' and called for 'the liquidation of the kulaks as a class'. After the congress, Khrushchev was appointed secretary of the party organization in the Industrial Academy. Stalin's speech to the graduating class made a great impression on him. In his memoirs, he recalls thinking, 'Here is the man who knows how to direct our minds and our energies toward the priority goals.'[5] Stalin noticed that Khrushchev looked at him with adoration. Years later, other people, too, noticed that Khrushchev was a 'receptacle' who tended to submit to strong personalities.[6]

In January 1931 the secretary of the party committee in the Bauman District of Moscow A. P. Shirin was arrested and executed. Khrushchev was appointed in his place. Six months later, in July 1931, the secretary of the Party committee of the Krasnaya Presnia district of Moscow, M. N. Riutin was arrested. Stalin appointed Khrushchev in his place. Riutin was the author of two anti-Stalin pamphlets known as the 'Riutin Platform' and his fate suggests that he knew of Stalin's Okhrana file. Martimian Nikitich Riutin was born in 1890 in the remote Siberian village of Verkhnee Riutino, on the shores of the Angara River. During the Civil War, Riutin served as a commissar in one of the Red Army units. He was appointed secretary of the party organization in Irkutsk and in 1924 was transferred to Moscow, where Stalin appointed him secretary of the party committee of the Krasnaya Presnia district. For the next six years, Riutin supported Stalin in his conflict with the opposition. At the Sixteenth Party Conference in April 1929, he was elected candidate member of the Party Central Committee.[7]

However, a little more than a year later, at the Sixteenth Party Congress in June–July 1930, Riutin angrily accused Stalin of being a 'great *agent-provocateur*' and the 'grave-digger of the Revolution'.[8] Stalin demanded that the GPU arrest and execute Riutin, but Menzhinsky (who by then had Stalin's Okhrana file in his hands) referred Riutin's case to the party's Central Control Commission, which decided to expel Riutin from the party and to arrest him for 'defamation of the party's leadership' and '*dvurush-nichestvo*' (double-dealing), a term invented by Stalin, meaning the double-dealing of Okhrana *agents provocateurs*. However, on 17 January 1931 the collegium of the GPU acquitted Riutin, citing the 'unproven accusations' against him. Riutin even received back his party card and his post of secretary of the Krasnaya Presnia district. Half a year later he was fired and on 23 September 1931 he was arrested again on the charge of having written two anti-Stalin pamphlets. One was some 50 typewritten pages and entitled 'Stalin and the Crisis of Proletarian Dictatorship'. The second was 200 pages long and entitled 'Appeal to All Party Members'. Riutin declared that Stalin was 'the evil genius of the Russian Revolution, who, motivated by a personal desire for power and revenge, brought the Revolution to the verge of ruin'.[9] Riutin wrote: 'Even the most daring, genius-like *provocateur* could not have invented anything better than what Stalin and his clique did to bring about the destruction of the proletarian dictatorship . . . we must put an end to Stalin's rule as soon as possible . . .'. Riutin and his friends had made copies of these pamphlets and distributed them among party members with an attached short note that read, 'Having read it, pass it on to another person. Multiply and distribute.' On 21 August 1932 a small group of people gathered for the discussion of the 'Riutin Platform' in the apartment of a minor Soviet official Peter Silchenko. Someone reported this discussion – not to the GPU but to Stalin personally.[10]

On 20 September Silchenko's apartment was searched. Three days later, all the participants in the discussion were arrested. Among those arrested was Peter Petrovsky, the son of Grigory Petrovsky, the former Duma deputy whom Stalin often invited to visit him and whom he had 'kept on the hook', blackmailing him with Okhrana documents found in the archives. 'We know everything about you', Stalin told Grigory Petrovsky. 'In 1905 you caroused with the chief of police in Pavlograd . . . Look out, it might prove unpleasant!'[11] On another occasion Stalin produced Petrovsky's Okhrana file and shouted at him, 'We shoot people like you, but I will have mercy on you.'[12] Grigory Petrovsky outlived Stalin, but his son Peter was charged with the crime of not reporting to the authorities about the 'secret meeting of the plotters' for the discussion of the 'Riutin

Platform' and was sentenced to ten years' imprisonment (after completing his prison term he was executed in 1941).

The intensity of Stalin's rage at the 'Riutin Platform' surprised many GPU officers. He demanded the immediate execution of Riutin. Menzhinsky refused and referred the case to Yan Rutzutak, the chairman of the Central Control Commission. The commission met in an extraordinary session at the beginning of November 1932 to decide the case of 'Riutin and others'. It ruled to expel them from the Party as 'degenerates' and 'traitors'. Among the 20 'plotters' were Zinoviev and Kamenev: both were accused of not reporting to the GPU what they knew about the Riutin Platform. The GPU was ordered to accuse both of them 'in accordance with the full severity of revolutionary justice'.[13] Stalin demanded the death penalty for all the accused, but Menzhinsky refused to execute them and referred the case to the Politburo, where Stalin met unexpected resistance from Kirov, Kuibyshev and Ordzhonikidze. He had to agree to 'soft' sentences of prison terms. Riutin was sentenced to ten years, but this was soon changed to 15 years.[14] He was incarcerated in the infamous 'Susdal Isolator'. His wife and his two sons, Vissarion and Vasily, as well as his younger daughter Luba were thrown out of their home. (A few years later, all of them except Luba had been executed.)

Stalin had good reason to suspect Riutin of knowing about his Okhrana file: in 1930 Riutin suddenly changed from an ardent supporter into an implacable enemy who accused him of being a 'great *agent provocateur*' and 'genius-like *provocateur*'. Although no direct information has yet surfaced to prove this, Riutin might have learned of Blumkin's attempt to smuggle Stalin's Okhrana file abroad. Riutin had supported Stalin for years, as late as at the Sixteenth Party Conference in April 1929, but he angrily attacked him as a 'great *agent provocateur*' at the Sixteenth Party Congress little more than a year later, which argues that a drastic change in Riutin's attitude toward Stalin occurred in the period between the conference and the congress. Two dramatic events stand out in that period: the discovery by Rabinovich of Stalin's Okhrana file among Dzerzhinsky's papers and Blumkin's attempt to smuggle the file abroad in December 1929. Stalin insisted on the death sentence for Riutin, which at the time was a departure from the norm. The execution of Blumkin at the end of 1929 was the first time a Party member had been secretly executed by the GPU, and such executions did not become routine for several years.

At the time of Blumkin's execution, and for a few years thereafter, rumors of Stalin's Okhrana file circulated in Moscow and reached foreign journalists abroad. In 1938, Isaac Don Levine, an American journalist and the author of one of the first Western biographies of Stalin, wrote that he had 'long been familiar with reports that some of the old Bolsheviks had in their possession a secret file from the archives of the Okhrana proving that Stalin was a super spy for the Czar . . .'.[15] The timing and the secrecy surrounding A. P. Shirin's execution in 1930 suggest that Stalin suspected him, too, of knowing about the file. Menzhinsky's refusal to execute Riutin alarmed Stalin. He suspected that Menzhinsky was plotting against him. Stalin ordered confiscation of all copies of the Riutin Platform and ordered the Soviet military intelligence chief Yan Berzin and his officers to conduct searches.[16] Having this document in one's home became a crime. Stalin was not mistaken: Menzhinsky indeed was plotting to depose Stalin.[17] He resisted not only Riutin's arrest and execution but also Stalin's drive to transform the GPU into Stalin's 'private power base'.[18] Menzhinsky probably hoped to use Stalin's Okhrana file, which he kept hidden in his office, to depose Stalin. But any such scheme was growing increasingly unrealistic. Stalin was surrounding himself with his cronies and an army of bodyguards. Menzhinsky was physically deteriorating: he suffered from progressive *tabes dorsalis* and became an invalid who spent most of his time lying on a sofa in his office. The GPU was effectively under the control of his assistant Yagoda.

One of the reports that reached Stalin's desk attracted his attention: a peasant boy, Pavlik Morozov, in the tiny Ural village of Gerasimovka denounced to the GPU his father Trofim Morozov, the chairman of the village soviet, accusing him of hiding grain and resisting the drive for collectivization. Pavlik testified in court against his father, something that must have reminded Stalin of how he, as a 10-year-old boy, had testified in a Tiflis court in 1890 against his father Vissarion. Stalin's overt reaction was one of disgust: 'What a little swine, denouncing his own father!' he said. But he quickly decided to glorify the boy and use him for propaganda in the collectivization campaign,[19] turning him into a hero and a martyr.

The tragedy of the Morozov family began when Pavlik's father Trofim left his wife and four children and moved in with another woman in the same village. His wife told their oldest 13-year-old son Pavlik to complain to the local GPU, hoping to scare Trofim and force him to return to his family. Her calculations turned out to be disastrously wrong. The GPU officers coached Pavlik on giving 'politically correct' testimony against his father in court. Trofim was sentenced to ten years in a labor camp. At this point, Stalin intervened in the affairs of the Morozov family and events moved quickly according to his script. Trofim Morozov perished in the camp under unknown circumstances, and on 6 September 1932 a relative of Morozov, a GPU informer by the name of Ivan Potupchik, led Gerasimovka peasants to the corpses of Pavlik and his younger brother Fedia, buried in a shallow grave in a nearby forest. He claimed that the boys had been killed by kulaks. What had in fact happened was that on 4 September 1932, two days before Potupchik 'discovered' the corpses of Pavlik and Fedia, the assistant chief of the provincial GPU, Kartashev, ordered his agent Potupchik to murder Pavlik and thus started the case of Pavlik Morozov's 'political murder'. Fedia accidentally witnessed the murder of his brother, and Potupchik was forced to silence him. The case was 'investigated' under the close scrutiny of Stalin. Stalin gave instructions through the head of the special sector of his personal secretariat, Poskrebyshev, a native of the area, who passed them on to Kartashev. A number of villagers and Pavlik's relatives on his father's side, including his 80-year-old grandfather, were arrested, accused of murdering Pavlik, and executed immediately after the trial. Kartashev was to boast sickeningly of how he executed kulaks: 'I counted that 37 persons were shot by me personally. I sent a large number of people to the camps. I can kill in such a way that the shot is not heard. The secret is this: I force them to open their mouths and shoot there. I am splattered by warm blood, like by a cologne, but nothing is heard. I am good at killing.'

Soviet newspapers declared that Pavel Morozov was not alone – there were legions of boys like him, who, if necessary, would place their fathers on the defendant's bench. During the following half century, a plethora of streets, squares, Pioneer houses, factories, and so on were named after Pavlik Morozov, and many books and articles were written about him. Stalin ordered a memorial statue of Pavlik to be placed at the entrance to Red Square and commissioned songs and poems, even a cantata for chorus and symphony orchestra after a poem titled 'Pavlik Morozov'. There was even the opera *Pavlik Morozov*, in which the father sang ruefully about his son, 'Why did I let him join the Pioneers?' – this despite the fact that at the time of Pavlik's murder that youth group did not exist in his village. As late as 1982 a Soviet writer stated that Pavlik's story 'still awaits its Shakespeare'.[20]

Two months after the murder of Pavlik Morozov and the arrest of Riutin's group, Stalin's wife Nadezhda Allilueva committed suicide. Her and Stalin's relationship had worsened in the course of the past several years, and they quarreled over personal as well as political matters. 'You are a tormentor, that's what you are!' shouted Nadezhda in one angry exchange. 'You torment your own son . . . You torment your wife . . . you torment the whole Russian people!'[21] Stalin as usual responded with curses and vulgarities. During one quarrel, Nadezhda shouted at Stalin, 'I know what kind of revolutionary you are!'[22] This was a barely veiled reference to Stalin's shameful Okhrana past, which she and her brother Pavel Alliluev knew.[23] Nadezhda had suffered for many years from the blatant contradiction between the deified image of Stalin presented by the Soviet press and the man she knew intimately. But what finally became unbearable was Stalin's despotism in family matters. By the autumn of 1932, Nadezhda, then 30, looked far older than her years. She was last photographed walking along a narrow Kremlin street, her head bowed, her back bent, her eyes hidden, a trapped and forlorn woman.

The 7 November 1932 was the fifteenth anniversary of the October Revolution. As usual, there was a military parade and civilian demonstrations with columns moving through Red Square past the Lenin mausoleum, on top of which stood Stalin and Politburo members. In the evening, Stalin and Nadezhda went to a dinner in Voroshilov's apartment. The guests, as usual, drank much vodka, toasting Stalin. Nadezhda did not drink, which angered Stalin. 'Hey, you, have a drink!' he shouted at her from across the table. 'Don't you dare "hey" me!' Nadezhda shouted back. One of their typical quarrels followed. Nadezhda rushed out of the room, and Molotov's wife Polina Zhemchuzhina followed to comfort her. The two women walked for some time around the Kremlin grounds and then wished each other good night. In her room, Nadezhda wrote a long letter to Stalin. Then, with a small pistol that her brother Pavel had given her as a present, she shot herself. When toward morning Stalin came home, Nadezhda was dead. Not knowing this, he went to sleep in his room. In the morning a housemaid found Nadezhda's body lying on the floor. One of the bodyguards was later to describe the scene: 'When we rushed in, she was lying on the floor, in a black dress, her hair done in curls. The pistol was on the floor.'[24] Stalin was awakened. Molotov, Enukidze and other family friends came to console him. They found Nadezhda's letter and gave it to him. He read it in silence, and then read it over and over again.[25] Years later, Stalin's daughter Svetlana was to reveal what she had learned about this letter from those who saw it. She wrote: 'It was a terrible letter, full of reproaches and accusations. It wasn't purely personal; it was partly political as well. Svetlana added that 'at times Stalin was gripped by anger, rage. This was because my mother left this letter for him.'[26]

The Soviet population learned for the first time that Stalin had had a wife from a brief official announcement: 'Party member and Stalin's comrade-in-arms Nadezhda Allilueva died suddenly and prematurely.'[27] Nadezhda's remains were placed in the Hall of Columns. Svetlana, then 6 years old, was led to the coffin. Seized by fear, the little girl drew back and started crying. Enukidze led her away and tried to calm her down. Stalin approached the coffin. Suddenly he pushed it away, turned on his heels and left.[28] He did not walk in the funeral procession to the Novodevichy Convent.[29]

NOTES

1. Alexander Orlov, *The Secret History of Stalin's Crimes*, New York, 1953, pp. 301f.
2. Ibid.
3. Donald W. Treadgold, *Twentieth Century Russia*, Chicago, 1976, p. 226.
4. N. S. Krushchev, *Khrushchev Remembers*, Boston, Toronto, 1970, pp. 40f. Khrushchev does not reveal whether he found out at a later time that the letter had been written by Stalin.
5. Ibid., pp. 37–42.
6. Soviet film director Efim Sevela stated in an interview with me in Chappaqua, New York, in 1971 that a well-known movie director of Stalin's era, Georgy Chukhrai, had described Khrushchev as a 'receptacle' of psychic influence.
7. Arkady Vaksberg, 'Kak zhivoi s zhivymi', *Literaturnaya gazeta*, 29 June 1988. Also Lev Razgon, 'Nakonets', *Moskovskie novosti*, no. 26, 26 June 1988.
8. Walter G. Krivitsky, *I Was Stalin's Agent*, London, 1939, p. 182.
9. Robert Conquest, *The Great Terror*, New York, 1973, p. 52, quoting Boris Nikolaevsky, *Power and the Soviet Elite*, New York, 1965, p. 29. Also Lev Razgon, 'Nakonets.'
10. Vaksberg, 'Kak zhivoi s zhivymi'.
11. I. D. Levine, *Stalin*, New York, 1931, p. 337. Roy Medvedev, *Let History Judge*, New York, 1971, p. 295. Medvedev quotes from papers in the archive of the Petrovsky family.
12. Medvedev, *Let History Judge*, p. 295. Medvedev quotes from papers in the archive of the Petrovsky family.
13. Vaksberg, 'Kak zhivoi s zhivymi'.
14. Razgon, 'Nakonets'.
15. I. D. Levine, 'Stalin Suspected of Forcing Trials to Cover His Past', *Journal American*, 3 March 1938.
16. Krivitsky, *I Was Stalin's Agent*, p. 182.
17. *Komsomolskaya pravda*, 13 November 1964.
18. *Izvestia*, 31 August 1964.
19. Robert Conquest, *Stalin: Breaker of Nations*, New York, 1991, p. 11.
20. Yury Druzhnikov, 'Saga o Pavlike Morozove', *Strana i mir*, no. 2(44), March–April 1988, pp. 114–17.
21. Alexander Orlov, *Tainaya istoria stalinskikh prestuplenii*, New York, Jerusalem, Paris, p. 303.
22. Elizabeth Lermolo, *Face of a Victim*, New York, 1956, p. 167.
23. Orlov, *Tainaya istoriya stalinskikh prestuplenii*, pp. 309–11.
24. Ibid., pp. 300f.
25. *Poslednie novosti*, Paris, 8 August 1934.
26. Svetlana Allilueva, *Dvadtsat pisem k drugu*, New York, 1967, pp. 107f.
27. *Izvestia*, 12 November 1932.
28. Svetlana Allilueva, *Twenty Letters to a Friend*, New York, 1967, p. 108.
29. Orlov, *Tainaya istoria stalinskikh prestuplenii*, pp. 306f.

22

'WHY DID YOU KILL SUCH A NICE MAN?'

At the Seventeenth Party Congress in January 1934 Stalin proclaimed that the Soviet Union was free from 'backwardness and medievalism'. The Soviet press reported that Stalin's speech was greeted by 'stormy and prolonged applause'. Khrushchev in his statement to the Congress called Stalin 'the greatest leader of all times and all peoples' and 'our Leader-Genius'. Kirov's speech produced a long standing ovation and shouts of 'Long live our Mironych [Kirov's patronymic]!' After the secret voting in the election of the Central Committee, V. P. Zatonsky, the chairman of the elections commission, counted the ballots. He discovered that 1,108 ballots out of the total of 1,966 had Stalin's name crossed out, while Kirov's name had been crossed out on only three. Zatonsky reported the results to Lazar Kaganovich and to Stalin. They decided to conceal the voting results and declared that Stalin's name had been crossed out by only three delegates, as had Kirov's.[1] During a Politburo meeting Stalin expressed his desire to resign. Predictably, all expressed confidence in him. Molotov stated, 'No one could replace you.' Stalin readily agreed: 'Only enemies can say that you can remove Stalin and nothing will happen!' Kirov, too, urged Stalin to remain in post, but advised him to be more sensitive in how he treated people. 'When I was walking out of Stalin's office', Kirov later told his friend Chudov, 'I had the feeling that my head was placed on the block. Stalin's stare was such . . . that I knew I had signed my own death sentence.'[2]

Actually, Kirov had signed his death sentence more than a year earlier when he had objected to the execution of Riutin – and he was not alone: Ordzhonikidze, Kuibyshev and Menzhinsky had also expressed opposition to the execution and were therefore on Stalin's list of 'enemies' to be disposed of as soon as possible or convenient. Menzhinsky tried to protect Riutin, which had given Stalin cause to fear that he was plotting against him. As a countermove, Stalin used the Seventeenth Party Congress to remove Menzhinsky from the Central Committee. Stalin had his secret schedule for the murders of Kirov, Ordzhonikidze, Kuibyshev, and Menzhinsky.

Menzhinsky was first on his list; Stalin decided to poison him. Menzhinsky's deputy Yagoda, a former pharmacist, had founded a secret poison laboratory in the GPU, which was at Stalin's disposal. Stalin kept in his personal archive Yagoda's Okhrana file, containing documents that exposed Yagoda as an informer. Meer Trilisser, the head of the GPU Foreign Department, had found this file in the old archives and had given it to Stalin with the purpose of exposing Yagoda; instead, Stalin had promoted Yagoda and fired Trilisser from the GPU, sending him to work in the Comintern and later ordering his arrest and execution.[3] Yagoda was 'on the hook', and Stalin assigned to him important murders. The poisoning of Menzhinsky was slow and elaborate. Yagoda's assistants Bulanov and Savolainen for several weeks sprayed a mixture of mercury and two ampules of a special poison dissolved in acid on curtains and carpets in Menzhinsky's office.[4] Menzhinsky died on 10 May 1934. His office was closed and remained sealed for more than two years. No one was allowed to enter it, ostensibly because of its poisoned air and furniture. (Stalin's Okhrana file remained hidden among Menzhinsky's personal papers, to be found two years later.[5]) Menzhinsky was cremated, and the urn with his ashes was placed with great fanfare in the Kremlin wall in the last slot to the right of the passage between the wall and Lenin's mausoleum. A spot on the wall immediately to the left of the passage was where Ordzhonikidze's urn would be placed three years later. The place immediately to the left of this spot Stalin reserved for Kirov's urn, and it was to be filled after Kirov's murder.[6]

Stalin's intention was to implicate the opposition leaders in Kirov's assassination, and he chose a more dramatic method to eliminate him. In the first attempt, Stalin's agents approached two imprisoned common criminals, the Vasiliev brothers, offering to set them free if they agreed to murder Kirov. The brothers agreed and were released from prison, but when they attempted to break into Kirov's apartment they heard the voices of several men inside and fled. When this was reported to Stalin, he immediately ordered their execution.[7] Another plan formed in Stalin's mind when he received a letter from a certain Leonid Nikolaev, a disgruntled low-level official who complained about the abuse he had suffered from Kirov and the Leningrad party apparatus. 'Dear Iosif Vissarionovich!' wrote Nikolaev. 'I have been driven to desperation by undeserved persecution. Now I am ready to do anything.' The words 'ready to do anything' attracted Stalin's attention. He ordered that Nikolaev be investigated. The report that he received stated that Nikolaev was a 30-year-old invalid who had been born a cripple and who until the age of 14 had been unable to walk. During the Civil War, Nikolaev had joined the Bolsheviks and taken part in requisitioning bread from peasants. He became a minor party functionary but was expelled when he refused to leave Leningrad to take part in the collectivization drive. At this point, he wrote his letter to Stalin.[8]

By that time, Stalin had rearranged the state security apparatus. On 19 July 1934 the GPU was absorbed by the NKVD (People's Commissariat of Internal Affairs, or secret police), and Genrikh Yagoda was appointed commissar of internal affairs. Stalin wanted to appoint Efim Evdokimov (a common criminal who on Stalin's order directed the 'investigation' of the Shakhty case in 1928) to the post of the deputy chief of the Leningrad NKVD, but the chief there, Filip Medved, strongly objected to this appointment. Stalin then arranged the appointment of another of his cronies, Ivan Zaporozhets, whom he had promoted in the security apparatus. During the Civil War Zaporozhets had been a prominent figure in the anti-Soviet anarchist peasant army of Nester Makhno in the Ukraine, and Stalin used this fact to blackmail him. Zaporozhets planted an agent in the circle of Nikolaev's friends. This agent gave Nikolaev a revolver, took him to target practice, and provided him with a pass to the Smolny Palace, where Kirov had his office. Nikolaev was twice arrested in the streets by Kirov's bodyguards when his behavior aroused their suspicion, but both times Zaporozhets ordered his release and the return to him of the revolver and a diary in which Nikolaev wrote about his intention to kill Kirov. On 1 December 1934 Nikolaev went to the Smolny Palace, where the guards, having checked his pass, let him in without inspecting his briefcase. Hiding behind the partly opened door to a men's room on the third floor, Nikolaev waited for Kirov, who appeared without his bodyguard Borisov, detained by NKVD agents on the instruction of Zaporozhets. Nikolaev shot Kirov in the head, killing him instantly. He then attempted to kill himself with a shot to his own head but succeeded only in stunning himself. He collapsed next to Kirov's body.[9]

Stalin was ready for the news of Kirov's assassination. He had prepared a special decree, ordering a speedy investigation, ruling out pardons, and making mandatory the immediate carrying out of death sentences. He summoned his old friend Avel Enukidze, the chairman of the presidium of the USSR's Central Executive Committee, and had him sign this decree, dating it 1 December 1934, the day of Kirov's murder.[10] The next day, Stalin's train with special NKVD troops arrived in Leningrad. Nikolaev, his head bandaged, was brought into Stalin's office. 'Why did you kill such a nice man?' asked Stalin in a voice touched with tenderness. Nikolaev said that he had 'fired at the Party'. Then Stalin asked, 'And where did you get the revolver?' Nikolaev gave a startling reply, having recognized Ivan Zaporozhets who was standing next to Stalin, as a man to whom he had been introduced by the friend who had given him the revolver. Nikolaev understood now that his 'friend' was a NKVD *provocateur*. 'Ask him!', said Nikolaev, pointing at Zaporozhets. 'He coached me for four months, saying that the Party needed it.' Stalin was enraged. He understood that Nikolaev could expose the murder as an NKVD provocation. 'Take him away!', he shouted. Snapping 'Bungler!', he threw Nikolaev's file in Yagoda's face. Zaporozhets, his head lowered, walked out of the room.[11] Stalin immediately started the coverup. Kirov's bodyguard Borisov was murdered with a blow by a heavy metal rod as he was being driven from prison to an interrogation.[12] Nikolaev's 'friend', the NKVD agent, was quietly executed.[13] Stalin delayed the execution of Nikolaev, intending to force him to implicate the opposition in the murder of Kirov. Since it might have taken some time to wrench from Nikolaev such an accusation, Stalin returned to Moscow, taking Kirov's body with him. The open coffin was placed in Moscow's Hall of Columns, where Politburo members took turns as honor guards. Stalin, apparently overcome with emotion, embraced the body and kissed it on the cheek. He said, 'Goodbye, my dear friend. We will avenge you.'[14]

Stalin's display of tenderness toward the enemy he had had murdered may appear an act of stark hypocrisy. But as in the case of the murders of many of his other enemies, the truth was more complicated. Stalin's capacity for reshaping reality to suit his political and emotional needs made it possible, now that Kirov was dead, for him to imagine that not he, but the opposition leaders, headed by Trotsky, had guided Nikolaev's hands and that Kirov had to be avenged. When parting with his dead victims, Stalin was prone to identify with them and to be sentimentally moved by their deaths, as if blameless.

Stalin invented a detailed scheme of how to implicate the opposition leaders in the murder of Kirov. He divided a sheet of paper into two sections by drawing a vertical line. One side he labeled 'Moscow Center', and he entered on it the name Kamenev; the other side he labeled 'Leningrad Center', and he entered on it the name Zinoviev and also the name Nikolaev. In the course of several days, Stalin added a total of 13 more names to the list, sometimes shifting the names from one side to the other.[15] Then he ordered the arrest of these people, who were accused of plotting to assassinate Stalin, Molotov and Kaganovich. The alleged assassins refused to admit their guilt. Nikolaev's diary did not contain the name of a single member of the opposition, and Stalin ordered the court to declare it a forgery.[16] Failing to obtain confessions, Stalin on 29 December 1934 ordered that Nikolaev and 13 co-defendants be executed.

The Soviet press and the resolutions adopted at the mass meetings around the country called for 'revenge' and 'vigilance,' vaguely referring to the plots of 'enemies of the people' and 'White Guards'. Since Nikolaev had refused to implicate the opposition leaders, Stalin initially placed the blame for the murder on former White Guards, who had plotted the assassination in alliance with some foreign power. But he did not abandon his original scheme to use the murder of Kirov as a convenient pretext for the annihilation of the opposition. In a secret letter to the party organizations titled 'The Lessons of the Evil Murder of Comrade Kirov', Stalin called for the arrest and expulsion from the Party of former oppositionists. He also ordered secret executions of jailed members of the opposition. Mass arrests took place in Moscow and Leningrad.[17] On 16 December 1934 Zinoviev and Kamenev were brought to the Lubianka from their places of imprisonment, where they had been serving terms for 'not reporting' on the Riutin Platform. They were now accused of instigating the murder of Kirov. They vehemently denied involvement, pointing out that during the two preceding years they had been in prison. Stalin reduced the charge to the milder one of 'responsibility for political and moral support' for the murder. On 15 January 1935 Kamenev, Zinoviev, and several opposition members admitted their 'mistakes' and were sentenced to various prison terms. Zinoviev was sentenced to ten years and Kamenev to five years in prison.[18] Yet Stalin was unhappy with these terms, and on 27 July 1935 Kamenev was secretly sentenced to ten years' imprisonment for plotting to poison Stalin. The verdict asserted that Kamenev's sister-in-law on Kamenev's instruction gave harmful medication to Stalin in the Kremlin Hospital where she worked. Kamenev's brother even testified against his own wife.[19]

But thousands of people faced a more terrible fate. Stalin was 'avenging' the murder of Kirov by mass executions. In a country in which people had grown accustomed to standing in line for everything from bread to shelter, a new type of line was added: prisoners in the Lubianka, Butyrki, Lefortovo and other jails waiting in line to be taken down to the cellar or courtyard for execution. 'No pushing! No crowding! Wait your turn!' the guards would shout amidst the din of shots and cries of the victims. At intervals, the line would stop moving while the executioners took time out to fortify themselves at a buffet of food and vodka. The corpses were disposed of in secret burial grounds.[20]

Ivan Zaporozhets and Filip Medved were charged with 'lack of vigilance' and sentenced to three years in a *kontslager* (concentration camp).[21] A specially furnished train delivered them to a camp, where they were given comfortable quarters and management positions in the camp administration and special privileges. Their wives were allowed to visit and spend time with them. Still, Zaporozhets felt that Stalin had treated him too harshly.[22] Not knowing Stalin well, he hoped to be set free soon. A few years later, he was executed. NKVD officers talked among themselves about the suspicious circumstances behind the murder of Kirov and pointed to Stalin as its instigator. Stalin, receiving reports concerning these rumors, was greatly dissatisfied with the way the affair had been handled.[23]

For Stalin's next murder, that of Valerian Kuibyshev, he reverted to poisoning. Kuibyshev had committed a number of sins in Stalin's book. As the chairman of *Gosplan* (the State Planning Committee) he had objected to the arrests of his subordinates, the defendants at the 'Menshevik' and 'Prompartia' show trials. He had also objected to the execution of Riutin and, in January 1935, protested the trial of Zinoviev and Kamenev. On 26 January 1935 ten days after that trial, it was announced that Valerian Kuibyshev had died of heart disease. (Three years later, his secretary Maximov-Dikovsky was accused of poisoning him.[24]) The Soviet news-papers praised Kuibyshev for his 'uncompromising struggle against all deviations from the general Party line . . .'.[25] His native town Samara was renamed after him, and his body was cremated and the ashes placed in the Kremlin wall to the left of Kirov's urn.

NOTES

1. Roy Medvedev, *Let History Judge*, New York, 1971, p. 156.
2. Ibid. See also A. Antonov-Ovseenko, *Portret tirana*, New York, 1980, p. 120.
3. Alexander Orlov, *The Secret History of Stalin's Crimes*, New York, 1953, pp. 259ff.
4. Bulanov described this type of poisoning in his 'confession' at the Bukharin show trial. See *Bukharin Trial*, New York, 1865, pp. 480–5.
5. See Chapter 26 for the discovery of Stalin's Okhrana file.
6. Taped interview with I. P. Itskov in New York City in 1989.
7. Medvedev, *Let History Judge*, p. 158.
8. Elizabeth Lermolo, *Face of a Victim*, New York, 1956, p. 73. See also Antonov-Ovseenko, *Portret*, pp. 121–3.
9. H. Montgomery Hyde, *Stalin: the History of a Dictator*, New York, 1971, pp. 302–5.
10. Medvedev, *Let History*, p. 161. See also N. S. Khrushchev, 'Special Report to the Twentieth Party Congress' *The New York Times*, 5 June 1956, also referred to as Khrushchev's secret speech.
11. Hyde, *Stalin*, pp. 306f.
12. Olga Shatunovskaya's testimony in interview with Vasily Rudich. See also Khrushchev's secret speech, and H. Montgomery Hyde, *Stalin*, p. 307.
13. H. Montgomery Hyde, *Stalin*, p. 308.
14. A. T. Rybin, 'Riadom s I. V. Stalinym', *Sotsiologicheskie issledovaniya*, no. 3, 1988.
15. Khrushchev's secret speech.
16. Medvedev, *Let History Judge*, p. 163.
17. Robert Conquest, *The Great Terror*, New York, 1973, pp. 86–8.
18. Ibid., pp. 89–92.

19. Vitaly Rapoport and Yury Alekseev, *Izmena rodine*, London, 1988, p. 277. Also Conquest, *The Great Terror*, p. 133, and Anton Ciliga, *The Russian Enigma*, London, 1940, p. 283.
20. Hyde, *Stalin*, p. 310.
21. Conquest, *The Great Terror*, p. 93.
22. Alexander Orlov, *Tainaya istoria stalinskikh prestuplenii*, New York, Jerusalem, Paris, 1983, pp. 17–55.
23. Ibid.
24. *Bukharin Trial*, Maximov-Dikovsky's testimony, New York, 1965, p. 679.
25. *Krasny arkhiv*, no. 68, 1935, p. 6.

23

THE STALIN INSTITUTE

In 1935 the journal *Krasny arkhiv* (Red Archive) published a lead article titled 'Revolutionary Vigilance'. The article quoted Stalin who had casti-gated 'archival rats' who 'dig out accidentally selected documents'. Stalin stated that 'The archival institutions must exercise special vigilance . . . in utilizing the historical documents. . . We know that wicked double dealers and contrabandists do not shrink from committing fraud and falsifica-tion . . . '. Stalin's subordinates echoed his concern in their statements. Politburo member P. P. Postyshev declared:

Archival work, after all, is the sector of the sharpest class struggle. A Trotskyite or a Nationalist, no doubt, will try to use and to interpret this or that archival material not in the interests of, but to harm the cause of socialism.[1]

Postyshev did not suspect that in mentioning 'double dealers and contra-bandists' Stalin had in mind Blumkin, who had been executed for the attempt to smuggle abroad Stalin's Okhrana file. Postyshev also did not know that it was Stalin who did not shrink from committing 'fraud and falsification' and that he created the 'Stalin Institute' specially for the fabri-cation of his 'true biography' and the glorification of his 'revolutionary past.' At the head of this factory of lies he placed Lavrenty Beria, whom he trusted with many of his secrets.

Beria was born in 1899 in a remote village in Megrelia, a western province of Georgia. His parents were divorced, and he left home early and went to Baku, where at the age of 16 he became an informer for the Okhrana officer M. Bagirov. After the Revolution, he continued to work for Bagirov, who became an officer of the secret police of the Musawat government in Azerbaijan. In 1919, Beria was an informer for the British Embassy during the occupation of Baku by the British Expeditionary Force.[2] In 1920, he moved to Georgia and became an agent of the Security Division of the Menshevik government there. After the Red Army occu-pied Georgia, Beria returned to Baku, where he became an assistant to his old 'handler' Bagirov, who by that time had established himself as the chairman of the Cheka in Azerbaijan. (On Dzerzhinsky's order, many former Okhrana officers were recruited into the Cheka.) In 1921,

Dzerzhinsky sent his assistant, Kedrov, to Baku to inspect Bagirov's staff, and Kedrov recommended firing Beria, finding him an untrustworthy agent of several intelligence services. Nothing came of this recommendation;[3] Dzerzhinsky trusted Bagirov, who in turn trusted Beria.

In 1928, Beria was transferred to the Georgian GPU. He met Stalin for the first time in the summer of 1931 while serving as security chief during Stalin's vacation at a *dacha* in the Georgian resort town of Tskhaltubo. Stalin must have known Beria's background: he did not entrust his security to anyone with whose past he was not familiar, and his photographic memory allowed him to retain information on a large number of people. Beria was recommended to Stalin by Bagirov, whom Stalin trusted and to whom he assigned the task of writing his falsified biography. Stalin decided that he could use Beria, and he frequently expressed his approval of him in calling him *karge bicho* ('good boy' in Georgian).[4] Soon after Stalin's return to Moscow in the fall of 1931, he summoned the Party leaders from the Caucasus and, as if in passing, mentioned Beria's appointment to the post of second secretary of the Transcaucasian Party Committee. He met with objection. 'I am not going to work with that charlatan!' protested the Georgian first secretary, Lavrenty Kartvelishvili. Stalin's proposal was not approved. Such insubordination was still possible in 1931, but Stalin was not about to give in. 'Well, so what, we'll settle this question in the routine way', he said. After the meeting, the Caucasian leaders went to Ordzhonikidze, who explained that he had refused to attend the meeting because he did not want to be present at the 'coronation of Beria'. Ordzhonikidze was familiar with Beria's background. 'I've been telling Stalin for a long time that Beria is a crook, but Stalin won't listen to me, and no one can make him change his mind', he said. Three months later, Stalin appointed Beria to the post of first secretary of the Georgian Communist Party; later, he made him first secretary of the entire Transcaucasian Federation.[5]

In July 1935, Beria delivered a speech to the Tbilisi (formerly Tiflis) Party committee, criticizing some Party leaders, including Stalin's friend Avel Enukidze, who had 'distorted certain historical facts and events'. Beria declared that 'we already gathered materials and documents from the history of our Party organizations' and that he was assigned to 'provide an explanation to *certain questions* (facts and events) from the history of the Bolshevik organizations of Transcaucasia and Georgia'. Beria criticized historians for not giving due tribute to the leading revolutionary role of the 'great Comrade Stalin', and declared that 'nothing that so far has been written reflects the real and true role of Comrade Stalin, who actually led the struggle of the Bolsheviks in the Caucasus for a good many years'. The congress decided to 'sharpen even more the vigilance of all party organiza- tions in Georgia against attempts at distortion of the history of Bolshevism' and to create the Stalin Institute to study Stalin's life.[6] Beria also recalled Stalin's 1931 article in which Stalin had written that it was necessary 'to sharpen vigilance against the Trotskyites and all the other falsifiers of the history of our party by systematically ripping off their masks'.[7]

Stalin ordered Beria to 'select' material and documents for his new biography and at the same time to 'purge' old archives of documents exposing Stalin's ties to the Okhrana. Such documents, referred to by Stalin as 'Kutepov documents', had, he claimed, been forged by former Okhrana officers to defame him.[8] Beria, although pretending to believe Stalin's claim, knew very well that there were no 'Kutepov documents' and that Stalin was worried about genuine archival documents that pointed to his collaboration with the Okhrana. Stalin ordered Beria and his subordinates to deliver to him personally all Okhrana documents in which the name 'Iosif Dzhugashvili' was mentioned.[9]

Dzerzhinsky, who had directed the recruitment of former Okhrana agents into the Cheka, had given Stalin documents from their files, which made them vulnerable to blackmail. Stalin trusted Beria and Bagirov because he knew of their Okhrana past. When Stalin's Okhrana files were discovered, Beria and Bagirov delivered them to Stalin, pretending that they believed them to be the 'Kutepov documents'. Stalin's Tiflis Okhrana file was discovered in 1925, but it did not contain incriminating evidence against Stalin, since it had been sanitized by Colonel Eremin in 1910. Stalin's Baku Okhrana file was discovered sometime in the early thirties. Bagirov, chairman of the GPU in Azerbaijan, delivered this file to Stalin. Stalin's Batum Okhrana file was discovered in the early 1930s by the historian Sepp, author of *The October Revolution in Documents*, on which he was doing research in the Batum Okhrana archives. Sepp delivered the file on informer Iosif Dzhugashvili to Beria, who immediately went to Moscow and gave it to Stalin. Stalin said that the file contained the 'Kutepov documents', and he thanked Beria for bringing them. Then he ordered Beria to execute Sepp. Following Beria's return to Tbilisi, Sepp was arrested and shot. When in the mid-1930s another researcher found a file with Iosif Dzhugashvili's secret reports in the Kutais Okhrana archive, he brought this file to Bakhcho Kabulov, a criminal turned head of the Kutais NKVD, who gave it to Beria. Beria then delivered this file to Stalin.[10] The name of the man who found the file remained unrecorded.

Starting in July 1935, *Pravda* began publishing Beria's articles about

Stalin's 'leading role in the Revolution.' By this time, Stalin's files from the Tiflis, Baku, Batum and Kutais Okhrana archives had been delivered to him. He knew that Blumkin had attempted to smuggle abroad his St Petersburg Okhrana file. He hoped, and may well have convinced himself, that this file had been destroyed.

One thing is certain: Stalin's past as an Okhrana agent was being systematically replaced by a new version of his past, in which he assumed the role of a great revolutionary and Lenin's closest comrade-in-arms. Beria and Bagirov wrote books, and the journal *Krasny arkhiv* published articles in which 'Okhrana documents' were reproduced that Stalin had had doctored to prove his invented history. Stalin had these documents doctored and perverted, inserting in them flattering statements and erasing embarrassing information. He did it in a peculiar way: these deceitful fakes were technically almost flawless, but contained crude absurdities. Stalin ordered the dates of many of the doctored Okhrana documents changed from Old to New Style, but kept part of the text intact. The doctoring of the documents was done in a secret Kremlin press headed by Alexander Svanidze, the brother of Stalin's first wife.[11] For example, the report of the chief of the Tiflis Okhrana, Captain Lavrov, which preceded the arrests of the members of Kurnatovsky's circle in Tiflis in 1901, had a clearly fictitious insertion and a wrong date. The forged report, dated 28 March 1901 states, 'According to agent information the following persons are included in the Tiflis Social Democratic circle: 'An employee in the Tiflis Physical Observatory, Iosif Dzhugashvili – an intellectual . . . ; an engineer-chemist Victor Kurnatovsky – an intellectual . . .'. A list of names follows.[12] Stalin had not been a member of the Kurnatovsky circle, and his name had not appeared at all on that list, let alone at the top of it. Kurnatovsky was the head of the circle and his name was on top of that list. The genuine report of Captain Lavrov was not dated 28 March 1901, but 15 March 1901 (the difference between the Old and New Style dates in the twentieth century being 13 days).[13] Another Okhrana document doctored by Stalin states, 'In autumn of 1901 the Tiflis Committee of the RSDWP [The Russian Social Democratic Workers' Party] sent Iosif Vissarionovich Dzhugashvili to the city of Batum as a delegate . . .'.[14] In fact, the Tiflis Committee at that time expelled Stalin from the Party for slander and intrigues against its leaders.[15] Yet another doctored Okhrana document, dated 21 March 1910 had an underlined statement, asserting that Stalin had '*always occupied a very important position*' in the revolutionary movement.[16] Again, the truth was a different story: in March 1910 Stalin was called to appear before a party court assembled in Baku to answer charges of having betrayed revolutionaries to the Okhrana. The members of the court were arrested before Stalin appeared to face the charges.[17]

Stalin placed many such forged documents in Soviet archives, labeling them with index numbers. Their lies were endlessly quoted in articles, books and dissertations, in which Stalin was exalted as the 'greatest revolutionary' and the 'leader of the world proletariat'. Trotsky was amazed by the fabrications of the Stalin Institute. He wrote, 'Never before under the vault of heaven had there been such large-scale invention of falsehood. I do not think that in all of human history anything could be found even remotely resembling the gigantic factory of lies which was organized by the Kremlin under the leadership of Stalin. And one of the principal purposes of this factory is to manufacture a new biography of Stalin.'[18]

Many authors were forced to disclaim their earlier published historical research and memoirs, which were in conflict with Stalin's new version. Stalin ordered destroyed anything containing contradictions to his invented biography. Stalin's close friend Avel Enukidze published an article, expressing his regrets about 'mistakes' he had made in his earlier writings about the revolutionary underground in the Caucasus. This repentant article appeared in *Pravda* on 16 January 1935. But Stalin was still not satisfied. 'What more does he want?', Enukidze complained to his friends, 'I am doing everything he asked me to do, but it is not enough for him. He wants me to admit that he is a genius.'[19] Stalin demanded from Enukidze not only effusive praise but unqualified support in the drive to destroy the opposition. Enukidze failed to satisfy Stalin's demands. Shortly before the trial of Zinoviev and Kamenev in January 1935, Enukidze admonished Stalin saying, 'Soso, there can be no argument that they have hurt you, but they have suffered enough for it: you have expelled them from the party, you have kept them in prison, their children have nothing to eat. Soso, they are Old Bolsheviks, as you and I. You will not spill the blood of the Old Bolsheviks! Think what the entire world will say about us!' Enukidze later recalled that Stalin looked at him 'as if I had killed his father, and said: "Remember, Avel, who is not with me, is against me!"'[20]

In February 1935 Enukidze was expelled from his apartment in the Kremlin and transferred to Tiflis; but Stalin was not satisfied with these half-measures. His suspicions of Enukidze were growing, as Enukidze knew the contents of Nadezhda Allilueva's last letter to Stalin, in which she had stated that she knew 'what kind of revolutionary' Stalin was. Once Stalin's suspicion of someone was aroused, the decision to eliminate this 'enemy' was not far behind, although there was sometimes a delay between the decision and its execution. At the beginning of July 1935 Nikolay Yezhov, Stalin's new crony, attacked Enukidze in *Pravda* for 'political and moral disintegration'.[21] Nikita Khrushchev, by then secretary of the Moscow party organization, and Andrey Zhdanov, who had replaced Kirov in the Leningrad party organization, made similar accusations in speeches against Enukidze.[22] Enukidze was arrested and charged with 'betrayal of the motherland and espionage', but was not executed until two years later.[23]

Enukidze deeply offended Stalin when he equated him with Old Bolsheviks like Kamenev and Zinoviev. Stalin considered himself vastly superior to any of the Old Bolsheviks, and he hated all of them, knowing full well that if they discovered his Okhrana past they would attempt to destroy him. On 25 May 1935 he ordered the liquidation of the Society of Old Bolsheviks as well as of their publishing house. Soon thereafter the Society of Former Political Exiles was also closed. Members of these societies were arrested one after the other. Grigory Petrovsky, the former Duma deputy, explained that Stalin did 'not like Old Bolsheviks'.[24] Stalin was comfortable only with people whose record, like Petrovsky's, was sullied by ties to the Okhrana.

In the paper blizzard of adoration for him, Stalin especially liked a short booklet by Karl Radek titled *The Architect of Socialist Society*, in which Radek described the ideal future of the USSR at the end of the twentieth century in the form of a lecture to be delivered by a history professor and devoted to the 'Great Stalin – the Genius of All Humanity'. Stalin ordered millions of copies of Radek's book to be printed.[25]

NOTES

1. *Krasny arkhiv*, no. 68, 1935, p. 12.
2. A. Sarkisov, 'Sudba Marshala', *Kommunist*, no. 147 (16426), 22 June, 1988.
3. I. Viktorov, *Podpolshchik, voin, chekist*, Moscow, 1968, pp. 71–7. Also quoted in Roy Medvedev, *Let History Judge*, New York, 1971, pp. 241–3.
4. Interview with Nugzar Sharia.
5. Medvedev, *Let History Judge*, pp. 242f.
6. Lavrenty Beria, *K Voprosy ob istorii bolshevitskikh organizatsii v zakavkazie*, 21–2 July 1935.
7. *Proletarian Revolution*, no. 6, 1931, quoting Stalin's article 'On Some Questions about the History of Bolshevism'.
8. See Chapter 20 above for General Kutepov's kidnapping and prosecution.
9. A. Sarkisov, 'Sudba Marshala'.
10. Medvedev, *Let History Judge*, p. 319.
11. Writen testimony of Raphael Bagratuni in I. D. Levine's and in the author's archives. Bagratuni stated: 'Svanidze gathered over many years materials in Soviet archives to compose a biography of Stalin; but this was a ruse. Svanidze, heading a group of loyal Georgians, destroyed documents in Soviet archives compromising Stalin under the pretext that they had been fabricated by Trotskyites. While he was destroying documents, Svanidze, backtracking in time (using the old orthography), reissued certain historical documents.

12. Beria, *K voprosu ob istorii bolshevitskikh organizatsi v Zakavkazie*, pp. 19f.; also Edward Ellis Smith, *The Young Stalin: The Early Years of an Elusive Revolutionary*, London, 1968, p. 78.
13. See Chapter 2 above.
14. Beria, *K voprosu*, pp. 96f.
15. See Chapter 2 above.
16. Beria, *K voprosu*, pp. 96f.
17. See Chapter 8 above.
18. Lev Trotsky, *Stalin*, New York, 1941, p. xiv.
19. Ibid., p. 389.
20. Alexander Orlov, *Tainaya istoria stalinskikh prestuplenii*, New York/Jerusalem/Paris, 1983, pp. 298f.
21. *Pravda*, 8 June 1935.
22. *Pravda*, 16 June and 19 June 1935.
23. See below Chapters 26–9.
24. Robert Conquest, *The Great Terror*, New York, 1973, p. 131.
25. Orlov, *Tainaya istoria . . .*, pp. 194f.

'OLD BEAR WITH A RING IN HIS NOSE'

Stalin knew that Maxim Gorky, whom he had proclaimed the 'great proletarian writer', was a longtime friend of Kamenev whom he planned to parade, together with Zinoviev, as 'enemies of the people' in a staged show trial in the summer of 1936. Stalin also knew that Gorky would voice objections to the trial. Many years of living in Italy had helped Gorky lose touch with the reality of the Soviet Union. After his return to the Soviet Union in May 1933, Gorky for some time supported Stalin. For instance, in an article 'If the enemy does not surrender, he should be destroyed', Gorky had justified the Prompartia show trial. Stalin ordered three million copies of this article to be printed. Gorky also praised the 'Menshevik Union Bureau' show trial held in 1931.[1]

Stalin hoped to use Gorky's pen for self-aggrandizement. Yagoda organized Gorky's visits to specially selected prisons and camps that would impress him favorably with the Soviet penal system. Initially, Gorky was misled. He visited the Solovky prison camp in the north of Russia and wrote a favorable article, describing the 'good' conditions there for reforming criminals.[2] After visiting the prison camps engaged in the construction of the Belomor–Baltic Canal, Gorky also approved the use of forced labor in the growing Soviet prison camp system, the Gulag. Gorky's apologetic writings have led some historians to accuse him of contributing to Stalin's 'spiritual enslavement of the country'.[3]

Stalin's cronies tried to induce Gorky to write a biography of 'The Great Stalin'. Yagoda, who bribed Gorky with privileges, ordered an NKVD officer by the name of Pogrebinsky to convince Gorky to write the biography. 'I approached Gorky from this side and from that side, but he stubbornly avoided conversation about the book', complained Pogrebinsky.[4] Stalin also ordered Yagoda to ask Gorky to write an article titled 'Lenin and Stalin' for *Pravda* on the occasion of the seventeenth anniversary of the October Revolution, but Gorky refused. He also refused to write articles against Kamenev and Zinoviev, whom Stalin accused of instigating the murder of Kirov, and of other crimes.[5]

On Gorky's insistence, Stalin freed Kamenev from prison in 1933 and allowed him to return to Moscow, where he was appointed assistant chairman of the publishing house Academia, chaired by Gorky, who hoped to publish works of great Russian writers, among them Dostoyevsky's *The Possessed* and *The Brothers Karamazov*.[6] Stalin considered Dostoyevsky's books to be dangerous propaganda, and in a sense they were, since characters like the 'possessed' Peter Verkhovensky and the revolting 'bastard' Smerdiakov bore a striking psychological resemblance to members of Stalin's entourage and indeed to Stalin himself. Stalin sensed that Dostoyevsky's books might help Soviet readers to recognize in these types the men who had control over them.

Stalin's relations with Gorky drastically deteriorated on 15 January 1935 when Kamenev and Zinoviev were imprisoned again. Gorky demanded that he be issued a passport allowing him to travel to Italy. His demand was not heeded. At the end of January 1935 David Zaslavsky, Stalin's mouthpiece, published two articles in *Pravda*, criticizing Gorky for promoting 'literary decay'.[7] Zaslavsky, whom Lenin described as 'a notorious slanderer,' had been before the Revolution an anti-Bolshevik journalist and a member of the Jewish Bund. He became Stalin's leading mouthpiece, while Lenin's closest comrades were sent to jail.[8] Gorky felt helpless and isolated from his friends. 'I am very tired', Gorky complained to I. Shkapa, who was soon to be arrested. 'It is as if I am surrounded by a fence – I cannot step over it! . . . Surrounded . . . trapped . . . not backward, not forward! I am not accustomed to this!'[9] In a letter to the French Communist writer Romaine Rolland, Gorky complained that he was trapped and felt like an 'old bear with a ring in my nose'.[10]

On 27 July 1935 Kamenev was secretly sentenced to ten years in prison for an 'attempt on Stalin's life'.[11] This new imprisonment of Kamenev troubled Gorky deeply. In July 1935 he was invited to attend the International Congress of Writers in Defence of Peace in Paris, but on orders from Moscow an NKVD agent Maria Kudasheva, the wife of Romaine Rolland, convinced her husband to visit Gorky in Moscow precisely at this time. Gorky's trip abroad was thus prevented. Stalin had good reason to fear that Gorky would not return to the Soviet Union. Gorky kept writing to Stalin, protesting the persecution of Kamenev and other Old Bolsheviks; Stalin did not respond. Letters that Gorky sent abroad were intercepted and handed over to Stalin.[12] Gorky asked Mikhail Koltsov, at that time the *Pravda* correspondent in Paris, to notify the French writers André Gide and Aragon of his urgent plea for them to visit him as soon as possible. Louis Aragon was to recall: 'The tone of Gorky's appeals, which we received through Koltsov, changed. In them one felt the fear of death.'[13]

Gorky feared that his 'archive', a suitcase containing letters to him from a large group of people, might fall into Stalin's hands and pose a danger to people who had corresponded with him. Before returning to the Soviet Union in 1933 he had given this 'archive' for safe keeping to Baroness Maria (Mura) Budberg (*a.k.a.* Maria Zakrevskaya-Benkendorf), who for many years belonged to the circle of Gorky's friends and occasionally did secretarial work for him. (Mura had become a Cheka agent at the beginning of 1918 and had taken part in the 'Lockhart Plot', having become a lover of Lockhart, a British diplomat. She was then sent abroad on Cheka assignment to infiltrate Gorky's circle of friends and gather information on Western intellectuals.[14]) After Gorky returned to the Soviet Union, Mura Budberg settled in London, having become a lover of the writer H. G. Wells, whom she first met in 1920, when he visited Gorky in the Soviet Union. Wells later ungallantly bragged that he had 'slept with Gorky's secretary'.[15] (In 1934, after an interview with Stalin, Wells gave a remarkable assessment of him, stating that he was a 'kindly man' who 'owes his position to the fact that no one is afraid of him and everyone trusts him'.[16])

In the summer of 1935 Gorky attempted to retrieve from Mura Budberg the suitcase containing his correspondence. His wife Ekaterina Peshkova approached Mura in London, but she refused to hand over the suitcase knowing that Stalin wanted to get hold of Gorky's entire archive.[17] After his Okhrana files were discovered in the old archives, these archival bones became even more of an *idée fixe* for Stalin, and the call for 'vigilance on the archival front' became his obsession. In the spring of 1936, an attempt was made by NKVD to steal Trotsky's papers from his home in Norway, and in the same year Stalin's agents stole Trotsky's archive at the International Institute of Social History in Paris, where Trotsky's son Lev Sedov headed a Trotskyite organization.[18] Also in 1936, Stalin ordered the NKVD to confiscate all of Gorky's letters in O. Piatnitsky's archive. In the same vein, a top-ranking NKVD officer conveyed to Mura Budberg Stalin's order to deliver the suitcase with Gorky's correspondence to Moscow, telling her that an officer would accompany her and provide a special railway car that would take her from the border crossing at Negoreloe to Moscow and then back to the border. Early in 1936 Mura Budberg secretly delivered Gorky's correspondence to Stalin and returned to London.[19]

With the letters in Stalin's hands, Gorky and his correspondents were in danger. Knowing that Gorky tried to hasten the arrival in Moscow of his friends, André Gide and Louis Aragon, the NKVD ordered Elsa Triole (Elizaveta Kagan), Aragon's wife and an NKVD agent, to prevent Aragon's journey, but she failed to do so. She did manage, however, to arrange their travel by boat to Leningrad, where she wanted to visit her sister Lilia Brik, former lover of the poet Vladimir Mayakovsky. Lilia Brik and her new lover, the commander of the Leningrad Military District, Vitaly Primakov, lived in a large luxury apartment and were at the center of the city's social life. Primakov, a legendary leader of the Red Cossacks during the Civil War, had abandoned his Jewish wife Anna Yakovlevna Kirshenblat, a gynecologist, and their 6-year-old son Evgeny Primakov.[20] (Evgeny Primakov grew up to become an MGB and then a KGB operative specializing in Arab countries and anti-Israeli propaganda. He became a high-ranking member of the Soviet intelligence service. After the collapse of the Soviet Empire he became chief of the Russian Intelligence Service and was later appointed foreign minister and then, on 10 September 1998, was appointed prime minister.[21])

Elsa Triole talked Aragon into staying in Leningrad for several days. Aragon years later was to recall: 'We, probably, should have rushed to Moscow, where Gorky was waiting for us. But, of course, my sister-in-law did not want to let us go easily.'[22] (Elsa Triole was to write in her memoirs in 1969: 'My husband is a communist. Communist because of me. I am a tool of Soviet power. I love to wear jewelry, I am a society woman, and I am a dirty whore.'[23]) On 6 June 1936 *Pravda* reported that Gorky had contracted influenza.[24] This was not the first time Gorky had been ill, but never before had the state of his health been reported in the press. He strongly objected to his illness being publicized, and Stalin ordered one issue of *Pravda* and one of *Izvestiya* to be printed for Gorky but without a medical report. In the regular issues, the reports were to be continued.[25] On 16 June Gorky felt much better, and his doctors predicted a speedy recovery. Gorky eagerly awaited the arrival of Gide and Aragon. 'The shadow of Gide and his forthcoming visit protects you', said one of Gorky's friends, Soviet writer Isaac Babel.[26] The report of Gorky's illness had made Gide schedule his departure for Moscow on 12 June 1936. On 11 June Soviet writer Ilya Ehrenburg arrived in Paris and phoned Gide. He told him that Gorky's health was improving and urged him to delay his visit because Moscow preferred his arrival to be 'not earlier than 18 June'.[27] Ehrenburg successfully carried out Stalin's urgent assignment to delay Gide's visit.[28] Gide arrived in Moscow on 17 June 1936. At the airport, he was met by Mikhail Koltsov. They went to see Gorky the following morning, but it was too late. Gorky died on 18 June 1936, at 11:10 am. His house was surrounded by security troops and the gates were closed. Aragon had arrived in Moscow on 15 June, but Elsa Triole had talked him into delaying his visit to Gorky until 18 June.[29] The next day, *Pravda* reported that Gorky died of 'paralysis of the heart'.[30] *Pravda* also reported that on

8 June 1936 Stalin, Molotov and Voroshilov had visited Gorky, who had been so elated that his health noticeably improved and 'he literally had risen from a coffin'.[31] But the rumor that Gorky had been poisoned spread.

Stalin ordered Yagoda to search Gorky's house. Yagoda found Gorky's diary in the library. When he finished reading it, he angrily cursed Gorky and muttered, 'No matter how much you feed a wolf, he always dreams of a forest.'[32] Stalin had 'fed the wolf' in vain.

Two years later, three physicians, Levin, Kazakov and Pletnev were accused of shortening Gorky's life by poisoning him.[33] Half a century later, on 4 February 1988, the Supreme Court of the USSR annulled the verdict and terminated the case against them for 'lack of criminal substance'.[34] Alexander Novikov, a former NKVD officer taken prisoner by the Germans during the Second World War, told a French prisoner of war, a fellow inmate in the Buchenwald camp, that Stalin had poisoned Gorky. Asked why the postmortem examination had failed to detect poison in Gorky's body, Novikov said, 'You don't understand anything! *The record of the examination had been compiled before his death!*'[35] A German communist, Brigitte Gerland, after being released from the Gulag and allowed to return to Germany in 1954, wrote that in a Vorkuta camp she met Dr Pletnev and learned from him that Gorky's health had suddenly deteriorated as a result of eating poisoned candies that Stalin had sent to him as a present, and that two medical orderlies, who were on duty that day and whom Gorky treated to the candies, also suddenly died.[36] In the summer of 1963 American author Isaac Don Levine, who had met Gorky on many occasions in the 1920s and 30s, visited Moscow and talked to Gorky's widow. He asked her whether Gorky had died a natural death. She became agitated and exclaimed, 'It's not quite so, but don't ask me about it! I won't be able to sleep a wink for three days and nights if I tell you!'[37]

NOTES

1. L. Fleishman, *Boris Pasternak v tridtsatye gody*, Jerusalem, 1984, pp. 30–3.
2. M. Geller, *Kontsentratsionny mir i sovetskaya literatura*, London, 1974, pp. 84–95.
3. M. Geller and A. Nekrich, *Utopia u vlasti*, vol. 1, London, 1982, p. 290.
4. Alexander Orlov, *The Secret History of Stalin's Crimes*, New York, 1953, p. 264.
5. Ibid., pp. 266f.
6. M. Gorky, 'Ob izdanii romana besy', *Pravda*, 24 January 1935.
7. D. Zaslavsky, 'Zametki chitatelia', *Pravda*, 20 and 25 January 1935.
8. V. I. Lenin, *Polnoe sobranie sochinenii*, 5th edn, vol. 49, Moscow, 1958–65, p. 441.
9. I. S. Shkapa, *Sem' let s Gorkim*, Moscow, 1964, pp. 318 and 383f.
10. J. Perus, *Correspondance Romain Rolland et Maxime Gorki*, Paris, 1991, p. 320, quoting Romain Rolland's diary. See Michele Nike, *K voprosu o smerti M. Gorkogo*, Paris, 1988, pp. 343f, fn. 90 and 93. Also P. Moroz, 'Gorky v SSSR. Vstrechi s Gorkim', *Sotsialisticheskii vestnik*, 1954, no. 1, pp. 15–18.

11. *Zinoviev Trial* (Report of Court Proceedings), Moscow, 1936, p. 174. See also Anton Ciliga, *The Russian Enigma*, London, 1940, p. 283.
12. Fleishman, *Boris Pasternak v tridtsatye gody*, pp. 239–42. Also Nike, *K voprosu o smerti Gorkogo*, pp. 345f., finn. 99–101; also Georges Duhamel, *Le Livre de l'Amertume*, Paris, 1983, pp. 185 and 417.
13. Michele Nike, 'K voprosu o smerti M. Gorkogo', pp. 329f., quoting L. Aragon, *L'Oeuvre poétique*, vol. VII (1936–7), pp. 96, 100, 107.
14. See Chapter 14 above.
15. N. Berberova, *Zheleznaya zhenshchina*, New York, 1982, pp. 261f. Also Boris Bazhanov, Paris, 1980, *Vospominania byvshego sekretaria Stalina*, p. 95.
16. H. Montgomery Hyde, *Stalin: The History of a Dictator*, New York, 1971, p. 316.
17. Berberova, *Zheleznaya Zhenshchina*, p. 264.
18. Ibid., pp. 259–65. See also Joel Carmichael, *Trotsky*, London, 1975, pp. 428f.
19. Berberova, *Zheleznaya zhenshchina*, pp. 264f.
20. Rakhil Mdinazadze, Georgian émigrée, of Brooklyn, NY.
21. The author knew Evgeny Primakov well, since they were classmates in the Moscow Oriental Institute (Arabic Division) in 1948–50.
22. L. Aragon, *L'Oeuvre Poétique*, vol. VII, Paris, 1977, pp. 115f.
23. Berberova, *Zheleznaya zhenshchina*, p. 269.
24. *Pravda*, 6 June 1936, p. 2.
25. One of the special copies is preserved in the Moscow Gorky Museum.
26. P. Herbart, *La Ligne de Force*, Paris, 1980, p. 105.
27. Nike, 'K voprosu o smerti M. Gorkogo', p. 344, quoting *Les Cahiers de la Petite Dame (1929–1937)* – 'Cahiers André Gide', 1974, vol. 5, pp. 539 and 547. Also R. Maurer, *André Gide et l'URSS*, Bern, 1983, pp. 53 and 96.
28. Ehrenburg recalls in his memoirs certain documents with 'yellowing' pages that Khrushchev found in Stalin's archive after Stalin's death and sent to Ehrenburg. He does not explain their nature, but clearly the documents were incriminating and were used by Stalin to blackmail Ehrenburg. See I. Ehrenburg, *Liudi, gody, zhizn'*, Moscow, 1967.
29. *Izvestia*, 18 June 1936, p. 2. See also Michele Nike, *K voprosu* . . ., pp. 344–6.
30. *Pravda*, 19 June 1936.
31. *Pravda*, 20 June 1936. Also *Kolkhoznik*, no. 6, 1936; Michele Nike, *K voprosu* . . . , p. 335, finn. 31–3.
32. Alexander Orlov, *Tainaya istoria stalinskikh prestuplenii*, New York, Jerusalem, Paris, 1983, p. 267.
33. See Chapter 29 below.
34. A. Loginov, 'Tri versii smerti Gorkogo', *Argumenty i fakty*, no. 1, January 1989.
35. Nike, *K voprosu o smerti Gorkogo*, p. 337, fn. 43. The letter of M. Braun, dated 16 December 1986, is in Nike's archive.
36. B. Gerland, 'Kto otravil Gorkogo', *Sotsialistichesky vestnik*, no. 6, 1954, pp. 109f.
37. I. D. Levine, *I Rediscover Russia*, New York, 1964, p. 175.

25

'THEY'LL SWALLOW IT'

In 1935 Stalin decided to stage a show trial finally to destroy Kamenev and Zinoviev, whom he now branded *podlye dvurushniki* (vile double-dealers), suggesting that they had been Okhrana *agents-provocateur*.[1] He ordered Yagoda to prepare documentary 'proof' to support this charge.[2] In June 1935 Stalin appointed Andrey Vyshinsky to the post of State Prosecutor and assigned to him the leading role in the show trial. He first met Vyshinsky in 1907 in Baku. At that time Vyshinsky was a Menshevik, but this was the least blemish on his record. Stalin kept in Vyshinsky's dossier an order, signed by Vyshinsky in 1917, to arrest Lenin. Vyshinsky kept in his safe a red file, sent to him by Stalin with a letter signed by a ranking Comintern official and the Soviet diplomat D. Z. Manuilsky, which Manuilsky had supposedly written to Stalin, warning him not to trust Vyshinsky, 'a man without principles', who had 'worked for the tsarist Okhrana'. The letter contained the names of several 'Baku Bolsheviks' whom Vyshinsky had supposedly betrayed. Stalin forwarded this letter to Vyshinsky, having written across its upper left corner: 'To Comrade Vyshinsky. I. St.'[3] Manuilsky may indeed have written this letter to Stalin, but it is also possible that Stalin had it fabricated and had given it to Vyshinsky in order to make him 'toe the line', and, at the same time, to attribute to him the betrayal of Baku Bolsheviks whom Stalin himself may have betrayed. Whoever was the author of the letter, Stalin's blackmail worked: Vyshinsky was his obedient tool. The Old Bolsheviks despised Vyshinsky, whom they called 'a rat in human image', and he hated them for this.[4] Stalin first used Vyshinsky's animosity toward the Old Bolsheviks in 1928 when he appointed Vyshinsky to preside over the Shakhty show trial.[5] Vyshinsky performed to Stalin's satisfaction, and Stalin chose him to play the leading role of prosecutor in the show trial of Kamenev, Zinoviev and other defendants scheduled for the summer of 1936.

In preparation for this trial, Stalin assigned N. I. Yezhov, whom he had appointed earlier in 1935 chairman of the Party Control Committee to supervise the interrogation of defendants. The chief of the NKVD Secret Political Administration, G. A. Molchanov, was given the responsibility of supervising a group of some 40 interrogators assigned to take depositions from the defendants. Yezhov announced Stalin's order that each NKVD interrogator should have on his desk at all times the text of the 7 April 1935 law allowing the death sentence to be passed on children of 12 years and over.[6] Three hundred members of the opposition, many of them parents and grandparents, were brought to Moscow from prisons, camps and places of exile. This group was deemed by Stalin to be a large enough pool of people from which to draw a sizable number of defendants who could be coerced into signing self-incriminating depositions to save their children and grandchildren.

Molchanov informed the interrogators that the Politburo had uncovered a large conspiracy headed by Trotsky and that the plotters were guilty of murdering Kirov, that they planned to assassinate Stalin, Voroshilov, Molotov and Kaganovich, and that their ultimate goal was the restoration of capitalism in the Soviet Union. This Politburo information, Molchanov claimed, was 'absolutely reliable'.[7] The interrogators had to force the defendants to confess their roles in the plot, the details of which had been provided by Stalin who probably convinced himself that the plot indeed existed. But to buttress his conviction, he felt the need to force the defendants to confess their involvement in it. When some of his subordinates dared to suggest that many people at home and abroad would not believe these accusations against Old Bolsheviks, Stalin's contemptuous reply was: 'Never mind, they'll swallow it!'[8]

Stalin created the show trial scenario in which true events in his life appeared in the 'confessions' of the defendants in distorted but recognizable versions where the truth was turned upside down and projected on to innocent people. For instance, in 1930, soon after the execution of Blumkin, Stalin had ordered a GPU agent Valentine Olberg to infiltrate Trotsky's circle in order to win Trotsky's confidence and organize his assassination. Trotsky, however, distrusted Olberg and ousted him.[9] In preparation for the Zinoviev–Kamenev show trial, Stalin decided to use Olberg again, but in a different role. Olberg was ordered to write a report, accusing several students of plotting to assassinate Stalin during a parade on Red Square. Molchanov explained to Olberg that he was chosen to help the party in exposing Trotsky at the forthcoming show trial. Molchanov promised Olberg that he would be set free and appointed to an important position. Olberg signed a deposition, stating that Trotsky's son Lev Sedov had sent him to the Soviet Union to organize a terrorist act against Stalin, and that Sedov was an agent of the Gestapo and that Trotsky was aware of it.

But Stalin decided that the testimony of Olberg was not convincing enough, and ordered Molchanov to force two more NKVD agents, Fritz David and K. B. Berman-Yurin, to 'confess' that in December 1932 they

had met Trotsky in Copenhagen and had received from him the assignment to assassinate Stalin and other Politburo members. This invention,
too, had a particle of truth turned upside down: a GPU agent, Yakov
Sobol, *had* met Trotsky in Copenhagen in 1932 on Stalin's orders and had
attempted to gain his confidence in order to murder him; the attempt
failed.[10]

None of the defendants was directly accused of being an Okhrana agent,
but one episode from Stalin's Okhrana career appeared in a disguised form
in the confession of the defendant E. S. Holtzman, who was forced to
testify that in 1932 he had met Trotsky's son Lev Sedov in Berlin and
arranged to go with him to Copenhagen for a conference with Trotsky.
'I agreed', Holtzman testified, 'but told him that we could not go together
for reasons of secrecy. I arranged with Sedov to be in Copenhagen within
two or three days, to put up at the Hotel Bristol, and to meet him there. I
went to the hotel straight from the station, and met Sedov in the lounge.
At about 10 am we went to Trotsky.' Holtzman testified that Trotsky had
told him that 'it was necessary to remove Stalin' and 'to choose cadres of
responsible people fit for the task'.[11] In fact, Iosif Dzhugashvili had gone to
the Hotel Bristol in 1906 to meet an Okhrana officer, who introduced him
to the chief of the Okhrana Foreign Agency, Arkady Garting.[12]

When Holtzman's testimony was published in the Soviet press, Trotsky
immediately declared that it was entirely false. Danish newspapers also
declared Holtzman's testimony a fabrication, informing their readers that
the Hotel Bristol in Copenhagen had been demolished in 1917, that is, 15
years before Holtzman's alleged meeting with Trotsky's son Sedov. The
'Hotel Bristol scandal' attracted the attention of the John Dewey Commission of Inquiry, which had been organized in the US to investigate the
Moscow show trials. In its published report the Commission stated: 'The
fact that there was not a Hotel Bristol in Copenhagen in 1932 is now a
matter of common knowledge. It would, therefore, have been obviously
impossible for Holtzman to meet Sedov in the lobby of the Hotel Bristol.'[13]
Stalin did not blame himself for the mistake. 'What the devil did you need
a hotel for?' he shouted at the NKVD chiefs. 'You ought to have said they
met at the railway station. A railway station is always there!'[14]

According to Stalin's scenario, besides Zinoviev and Kamenev, one of the
most important defendants at the show trial was Ivan Nikitich Smirnov,
a Civil War hero and close friend of Trotsky. Stalin wanted Smirnov to
confess that he had received 'coded instructions' from Trotsky to organize
a terrorist attempt on Stalin's life. Smirnov denied the accusations, pointing

out that he could not have committed the crimes of which he was accused, if only because he had been in prison since 1 January 1933. Yagoda's assistant Y. D. Agranov, who was assigned to interrogate Smirnov, said to Stalin: 'I am afraid that we won't be able to accuse Smirnov. He, after all, was in prison for a number of years.' Stalin gave Agranov an angry look and replied: 'Don't be afraid. Don't be afraid, that's all!' Agranov arrested Sergey Mrachkovsky, also a Civil War hero and Smirnov's friend and used him to break Smirnov. Mrachkovsky suffered from a mental disorder – he believed himself to be the greatest military strategist of all time – and Stalin was always quick to capitalize on people with mental problems. In 1932 Stalin urged Mrachkovsky to attack the opposition and offered him the post of commander of a large military region, on the condition that Mrachkovsky end his friendship with Smirnov and his relationship with the opposition. 'Break up with them', Stalin urged Mrachkovsky. 'What is binding you, a famous worker, to this Jewish Sanhedrin?' When he was arrested, Mrachkovsky expressed regret that he had not followed Stalin's advice. During a face-to-face confrontation with Smirnov, he said: 'Zinoviev and Kamenev have already agreed to testify. If they agreed to do this, it means that there is no other way out.' Smirnov was stunned. 'I will remind you, Ivan Nikitich', said Mrachkovsky, 'that I gave myself to the disposal of the Party. It means that I will have to testify against you in court!' Smirnov replied: 'I always knew you were a coward.'

Several days later Agranov showed Smirnov a deposition signed by his former wife, Safonova, who stated that in 1932 Smirnov had received 'terrorist instructions' from Trotsky. During an arranged confrontation between Smirnov and Safonova, she, sobbing, pleaded with her former husband to save her and himself by agreeing to testify at the trial. 'Then the whole world would be looking at all of you', she explained, 'and they would not dare to shoot you.' Smirnov agreed to testify on the condition that Safonova would not be hurt.

When it was reported to Stalin that Zinoviev and Kamenev had 'held firm' and refused to sign incriminating depositions, he shouted: 'Tell them – this goes for Zinoviev and Kamenev – that no matter what they do, they will not stop the advance of history. The only thing they can do is die or save their hides. Work on them until they crawl on their bellies with their confessions in their teeth.' When the chief of the NKVD Economic Administration, L. G. Mironov, reported to Stalin that Kamenev refused to confess and that there was little hope he could be broken, Stalin asked: 'Do you think that Kamenev will not confess? Do you know how much our state weighs, with all the factories, machines, the army with all the armaments, and the navy?' Mironov did not know what to make of Stalin's question, but Stalin insisted on an answer. Feeling like a schoolboy failing an examination, Mironov said: 'Nobody knows that, Iosif Vissarionovich. It is in the realm of astronomical figures.' Stalin goaded him: 'Well, and can one man withstand the pressure of that astronomical weight?' Mironov's answer was no. 'So, don't tell me anymore that Kamenev, or any other defendant, can withstand this pressure', Stalin concluded the lesson. 'Don't come to report to me until you have in this briefcase of yours Kamenev's confession.'

Zinoviev, too, refused to sign a confession. Stalin told Yezhov to offer him a deal. Zinoviev was brought to the office of Agranov. Also present were Yezhov, Molchanov and Mironov. Yezhov conducted the interrogation, constantly glancing at the list of Stalin's instructions. He stated at the outset that Zinoviev must help the party to 'deliver a crushing blow to Trotsky and his gang'. Zinoviev, suffering from asthma and chronic liver disease, was very pale and his breathing was heavy. 'What is demanded of me?' he asked. Yezhov said the Politburo wanted Zinoviev and Kamenev to testify in court that they, in agreement with Trotsky, had plotted the murder of Stalin and other Politburo members. Zinoviev angrily refused. Yezhov then read Stalin's conditions: if Zinoviev voluntarily agreed to face an open court proceeding and confessed to everything, his life would be spared; if he refused, he would be judged by a military tribunal behind closed doors. In this case, he and other members of the opposition would be liquidated. 'Tell Stalin that I refuse . . .', Zinoviev said in a weak voice. Yezhov made a similar offer to Kamenev, but he, too, refused to sign anything. Then, Yezhov showed Kamenev a deposition of one of the defendants, stating that Kamenev's son intended to assassinate Stalin and Voroshilov. Kamenev jumped to his feet and shouted that Yezhov was a scoundrel and a grave-digger of the Revolution. Yezhov left the room, a grimace of hate on his face. He soon summoned Kamenev and told him that his submission to the 'will of the Politburo' could save his and his son's lives. Kamenev said nothing. Yezhov lifted the telephone receiver and ordered Molchanov to arrest Kamenev's son.

In July 1936 Zinoviev requested a talk with Kamenev. Yagoda, seeing in this a sign that the chief defendants were about to give in, wanted to deny Yezhov, and claim for himself, the credit. He summoned Zinoviev to his office and agreed to allow he and Kamenev talk privately, having ordered microphones be installed in the office. During the meeting Zinoviev told Kamenev that it might be necessary to testify at the show trial, provided Stalin personally promised that their lives would be spared and their families and opposition members would not suffer. Kamenev, after some wavering, agreed, on the condition that Stalin make this promise in the presence of all Politburo members. Yagoda, Molchanov and Mironov reported to Stalin, who, rubbing his hands, exclaimed: 'Bravo, friends! Well done!' A few days later, Molchanov and Mironov delivered Zinoviev and Kamenev to Stalin's office in the Kremlin. Yagoda was already there. Stalin and Voroshilov were the only Politburo members present. 'Well, what are you going to say?' asked Stalin. 'We were told that our case would be discussed at the Politburo meeting', Kamenev protested. 'Before you is the commission of the Politburo that is empowered to hear everything that you say', said Stalin. Zinoviev rose and said that they had received many promises during the past several years, none of which had been kept. In a halting voice and with tears in his eyes, Zinoviev pleaded with Stalin to abandon the scheme for this show trial, which would besmirch not only them, but the whole party 'as a snake pit of intrigues, treachery and murders.' Zinoviev fell back in his chair, sobbing. Stalin waited for him to calm down and then in a quiet voice delivered a long speech, ending it with the words: 'You have only yourselves to thank if your case ends most sadly, so gravely that it could not be worse.' Kamenev asked Stalin, 'Where are the guarantees that we will not be shot?' Stalin looked at him with an air of amazement and exclaimed: 'Guarantees? Precisely what guarantee could there be here? Maybe you want an official agreement certified by the League of Nations?' Voroshilov stated that the two of them 'should fall on their knees before Comrade Stalin to thank him for saving their lives. If they do not want to save their hides, let them perish. To hell with them!' Stalin rose and began walking up and down the office. He called Zinoviev and Kamenev 'comrades' and said, 'we, Bolsheviks, are the pupils and heirs of Lenin and that we do not want to spill the blood of the old Party members . . .'. Stalin's words rang with deep feeling and sincerity. Zinoviev and Kamenev exchanged glances. Kamenev rose from his chair and said that he and Zinoviev agreed to testify at the show trial provided they received the promise that none of the Old Bolsheviks would be executed, that their families would not be persecuted, and that there would be no death sentences for past participation in the opposition. 'This goes without saying', said Stalin. The bargain was struck.[15]

But Stalin was not satisfied. He was consumed by the desire to wrench from Kamenev and Zinoviev a last-minute 'confession' about their ties to the Okhrana and continued to insist that Yagoda find proof that they had been Okhrana agents. Yagoda realized that it would be impossible to force these two Old Bolsheviks to confess to such a degrading crime and that they might refuse to testify at all. He also understood that by 'proof' Stalin meant the fabrication of false documents. This was a relatively simple task. The NKVD secret printing press fabricated many forgeries, but Yagoda pointed out to Stalin that it was dangerous to present such things in court because Zinoviev and Kamenev, as well as Trotsky, would demand that they be submitted to independent experts for analysis. He said that the best way would be to select former Okhrana officers, who would testify that they had recruited Kamenev and Zinoviev to spy on the revolutionary underground. Stalin agreed, but he also realized that the Okhrana charge against Kamenev and Zinoviev would enormously complicate the preparations for the show trial, which he wanted to start as soon as possible, and might delay or even thwart the trial. He, therefore, abandoned the idea.[16]

The show trial of the 'Trotskyite–Zinovievite Center' opened on 19 August 1936 in the October Hall of the Trade Union House. The hall had only 350 seats; all of them were reserved for NKVD officers and clerks. Of the more than 300 original defendants, only 16 were to be sentenced. The rest, except for the prominent scientist Ioffe, were executed 'administratively'. Stalin crossed Ioffe's name from the list of defendants, saying: 'Release him. He may be useful to us.'[17] Prosecutor Vyshinsky read the list of charges, while the chairman of the court, Vasily Ulrikh periodically glanced at the defendants. A sadistic bully, Ulrikh was remembered by many NKVD officers for his brutality during his earlier service in the Cheka.

In the course of three days, the defendants described their crimes, among them their roles in a conspiracy, headed by Trotsky, to assassinate Kirov and Stalin, their plans to wreck Soviet industry and agriculture, and so on. When Mrachkovsky testified that Smirnov had been the 'leader of the underground center', Smirnov made the sarcastic remark: 'You need a leader? Very well, take me!' Laughter in the audience dispelled for a moment the gloomy atmosphere of the trial.[18] Vyshinsky's closing speech at the trial was a shrill tirade: 'These mad dogs of capitalism . . . They killed our Kirov, they wounded our hearts . . . I demand that these dogs gone mad should be shot – every one of them!' The defendants read their 'final word' approved by Stalin who had crossed out all references to their revolutionary past, closeness to Lenin, former posts in the party and government, and had inserted self-denigrating epithets such as 'dregs of society, traitors and murderers who do not deserve any mercy'.[19] When these self-flagellations had ended, Kamenev asked permission to say a few words, addressed to his sons. One was an air force pilot, the other an adolescent (both eventually perished). 'No matter what my sentence may be', Kamenev said, 'I, in advance, consider it just. Don't look back. Go forward. Together with the Soviet people, follow Stalin.' Kamenev sat down and covered his face with his hands. Everyone seemed shaken. Even the faces of the judges for a fleeting moment lost their stony expression. Zinoviev, in a voice barely audible, read his own final words, which had Stalin's jargon-rife insert: 'My defective Bolshevism became transformed into anti-Bolshevism. And through Trotskyism I arrived at Fascism. Trotskyism is a variety of Fascism and Zinovievism is a variety of Trotskyism.'

At 2:30 am on 24 August 1936 Ulrikh announced that the defendants, without exception, were sentenced to death by shooting. All the defendants, including the planted NKVD agents, were executed the same night. Stalin fooled everyone, including the NKVD interrogators, many of whom had believed that Stalin would keep his promise to spare the lives of the defendants in exchange for their confessions.[20]

Yezhov, Yagoda and the head of Stalin's bodyguards, Karl Pauker, watched as the doomed men were led to the cellar. Kamenev walked as if in a dream. He was shot from behind. He fell, moaning. 'Finish him off!' shouted an officer, kicking Kamenev. Zinoviev was lying on his cot with a high fever when he was told to get dressed. 'We have orders to transfer you to another place', the same officer told him. Zinoviev could not walk. The guards threw a pail of water on his face and tried to drag him to the cellar, but even held by them he could not stand on his feet and fell to the floor. The officer ordered the guards to push him into the nearest empty cell and, grabbing his bushy hair and jerking his head down, put a bullet in it. He received a citation for acting expeditiously under difficult conditions.[21]

According to a rumor in NKVD circles, the 16 executed defendants, among them Kamenev and Zinoviev, were thrown into a mass grave in Khodynka Field. But there were many 'secret burial grounds' in Moscow. Khodynka Field may have become the rumored site because it was associated in the minds of Muscovites with a mass burial there 40 years earlier: in 1896 hundreds of people had been trampled to death there by a crowd celebrating the coronation of Tsar Nicholas II.

After the execution of the show trial defendants, Stalin, Yagoda and Pauker went to Stalin's *dacha* in the Caucasus, near Sochi. Before his departure on 1 September 1936 Stalin ordered Yagoda to execute 5,000 imprisoned members of the opposition. This was the first mass execution of party members.[22] Stalin thus strengthened his dictatorship. But another reason for this mass execution was probably his fear, fed by rumors that were reaching him, that his Okhrana file was in the hands of Old Bolsheviks.[23] He needed to destroy them before they were in a position to destroy him. Stalin ordered the chief of the Secret Political Department, Molchanov, to tell NKVD interrogators that preparations for a new show trial were soon to begin. Molchanov called a meeting in his office and declared: 'This year you'll have to forget about vacations. The investigation is not finished: that was just the beginning of it!'[24]

NOTES

1. *Krasny arkhiv*, no. 68, 1935, pp. 7-12.
2. Alexander Orlov, 'The Sensational Secret Behind Damnation of Stalin', *Life*, 23 April 1956.
3. *Inkvisitor* no. 6, Moscow, 1992, pp. 80–2.
4. Robert Conquest, *The Great Terror*, New York, 1973, pp. 37f.
5. See Chapter 18 above.
6. Alexander Orlov, *Tainaya istoria stalinskikh prestuplenii*, New York, Jerusalem, Paris, 1983, p. 56.
7. Ibid., pp. 56 and 71f.
8. Roy Medvedev, *Let History Judge*, p. 666. Also B. I. Nikolaevsky, 'Letter of an Old Bolshevik', p. 64; Walter G. Krivitsky, *In Stalin's Secret Service*, New York, 1939, p. 207.
9. Orlov, *Tainaya istoria*, p. 73.
10. I. D. Levine, *The Mind of an Assassin*, New York, 1959, p. 26.
11. *Zinoviev Trial*, Holtzman's testimony, Moscow, 1936, pp. 155–78.
12. See Chapter 6 above.
13. Dewey Commission Report, *Not Guilty*, New York, 1937, p. 85.
14. Orlov, *Tainaya istoria*, pp. 66–9.
15. Ibid. p. 105.
16. Alexander Orlov, 'The Sensational Secret Behind the Damnation of Stalin', *Life*, 23 April 1956.
17. Orlov, *Tainaya istoria*, p. 88.
18. Ibid., pp. 159–65.
19. Conquest, *The Great Terror*, pp. 167f.
20. Orlov, *Tainaya istoria*, pp. 165–9.
21. Conquest, *The Great Terror*, p. 170.
22. Orlov, *Tainaya istoria*, p. 170.
23. See Chapter 26 below for the rediscovery of Stalin's Okhrana file.
24. Orlov, *Tainaya istoria*, p. 170.

26

THE FATAL FIND IN MENZHINSKY'S OFFICE

During the preparations for the Zinoviev–Kamenev show trial, Yagoda assigned to the assistant chief of the NKVD Secret Political Department, Isaac Lvovich Shtein, the task of locating in the NKVD archive documents of former Okhrana officers, whom Yagoda intended to use as witnesses. These officers, according to Stalin, were needed to 'confirm' that they had recruited the 'double dealers' Kamenev and Zinoviev as Okhrana collaborators.[1] In connection with this search, Yagoda ordered the examination of the personal papers of Viacheslav Menzhinsky in his old office, which had been closed and sealed after his death in May 1934.[2] Around this time, it was also decided to renovate Menzhinsky's spacious office for Yezhov, who was spending much of his time in the Lubianka, supervising preparations for the show trials.

Shtein, Molchanov's deputy, had access to the papers of the heads of the secret police, as had his predecessor, the assistant chief of the GPU Secret Political Department, Rabinovich, who had discovered Stalin's Okhrana file in 1929 among Dzerzhinsky's papers and who had then been executed together with Blumkin.[3] Shtein's assignment was to sort through the personal papers of Menzhinsky and to place them in the central NKVD archive. While sifting through Menzhinsky's papers, Shtein came across the Okhrana file of 'Iosif Vissarionov Dzhugashvili'. He opened it and saw a prison photograph of the young Stalin and many documents that, at first glance, seemed to confirm the widely publicized heroic revolutionary past of the 'Great Soviet Leader'.[4] Shtein was elated. His first impulse was to report immediately to Yagoda that he had found documents of extreme historical importance, proof of Stalin's glorious deeds. But an instinctive doubt held him back, and he began to read the contents of the file. As he did so, his elation turned into horror when he realized that a number of documents in the file identified Stalin as an important Okhrana agent. He was most astounded of all by the letter of the chief of the Okhrana Special Section, Colonel Eremin, to the director of the Department of Police, Beletsky, in which Eremin described major points of Stalin's Okhrana career, and by Stalin's letter to the assistant minister of the interior, Zolotarev, in which

Stalin complained about the 'treachery' of Roman Malinovsky and advised that Malinovsky be dismissed from the Okhrana, offering himself for the position of top Okhrana agent in the Bolshevik Party.[5]

Shtein agonized for several days over what to do with this dreadful find. For a man as devoted to the Soviet state as he was, this was a terrible blow. His perception of Stalin suffered an abrupt change: no longer was Stalin Lenin's greatest comrade-in-arms, but an Okhrana imposter, a despicable traitor who had been exterminating the true revolutionaries, the Old Bolsheviks, Lenin's comrades. The mass purges, executions, and confessions at the show trials were suddenly cast in a very different light. Shtein knew that he could entrust his find neither to Yagoda nor to his immediate superior Molchanov – both of whom were unprincipled lackeys of Stalin. Shtein's closest friends, with whom he had worked since the days of the Civil War and whom he trusted, were in Kiev: the NKVD chief in the Ukraine, V. A. Balitsky, and his deputy, Zinovy Katsnelson. Taking Stalin's Okhrana file with him, Shtein took a train to Kiev.

Balitsky and Katsnelson were at first incredulous, suspecting that the documents were forgeries. But they put them through the necessary tests and came to the conclusion that they were genuine. Their decision was to do all they could to save the country from the ex-Okhrana agent. As well-informed NKVD officers, they knew the extreme difficulty of their task. Stalin surrounded himself with an army of bodyguards, and he had the mighty NKVD apparatus with multitudes of informers and troops at his disposal. The only force in the country that stood any chance of deposing Stalin was the Red Army, where Balitsky had close friends: Marshal Mikhail Tukhachevsky, first deputy commissar of defense and a candidate member of the Central Committee, and Yan Gamarnik, also first deputy commissar of defense and head of the political administration of the Red Army. Gamarnik was also a full member of the Central Committee. Balitsky gave them Stalin's Okhrana file, and together they decided to topple Stalin.

A conspiracy, headed by Marshal Tukhachevsky, was born. As usually happens in such cases, each of the plotters had his own trusted friends who joined the conspiracy. Among the first to join were Iona Yakir, the commander of the Kiev military district and a member of the Central Committee, I. P. Uborevich, the commander of the Byelorussian military district, and Corps Commander Boris Feldman, the chief of the main administration of the Red Army. A number of photocopies were made of documents in the file for the participants in the conspiracy.[6] The document most suitable for this purpose was the report of Colonel Eremin with a concise description of Stalin's Okhrana career. Some of the officers insisted that Stalin be executed and his Okhrana file presented to the Central Committee. Others thought that he should be arrested and put on trial, with his Okhrana file used as material evidence. The decision was to lure Stalin to the military maneuvers in the Byelorussian military district and to arrest him there. Tukhachevsky and Gamarnik insisted that Stalin should be judged by a secret party court. They feared that if Stalin's ties to the Okhrana were made public, it would discredit not only him but all the important achievements of the Soviet Union and would undermine the very legitimacy of Soviet power.

Corps Commander Boris Feldman was of a different opinion: he insisted that Stalin must be killed immediately and only then should his file be submitted to the party court. Feldman was convinced that a delay would risk the exposure of the conspiracy. 'Don't you see where all this is leading to?', he asked. 'He will strangle all of us, one by one, like baby chicks. We must act.' Tukhachevsky objected to what he saw as advice to overthrow the government, and he refused to participate.[7] Procrastination was threatening to doom the conspiracy – the widening of the circle of plotters increased the risk that Stalin would learn about it. Indeed, Stalin was alarmed by a report that some documents potentially harmful to him had wound up in the hands of Nikoly Tomsky, the head of Soviet trade unions. This report came from the NKVD agent Mark Zborovsky, who had penetrated the Paris circle of Trotsky's supporters. Trotsky's son, Lev Sedov, had received information about the discovery of Stalin's Okhrana file from the NKVD resident in Switzerland, Ignace Reiss, who, having learned from one of the plotters about the file's discovery, decided secretly to inform Trotsky about it. Trotsky, however, had long considered any reports about Stalin's ties to the Okhrana as fantastic inventions, and he forbade his son to take such reports seriously. Sedov, nevertheless, mentioned this 'fantastic invention' in the presence of Zborovsky and mentioned Tomsky. American journalist and writer Isaac Don Levine, too, learned about this report from people in Sedov's circle.[8]

Stalin immediately reacted to this report. On 23 August 1936 Vyshinsky mentioned Tomsky at the last session of the Kamenev–Zinoviev show trial as a suspect in a pending case of 'anti-Soviet conspiracy' that was under investigation. On the same day, Stalin, bringing a bottle of wine, visited Tomsky at his *dacha* in Bolshevo near Moscow. Perhaps Stalin hoped Tomsky would loosen up under the influence of alcohol and tell him what he knew about the Okhrana file. For a while Stalin and Tomsky spoke alone in Tomsky's study. Suddenly, the door was flung open and Stalin stormed out, followed by Tomsky, who was cursing him loudly. The car with Stalin and his bodyguards sped away. A few minutes later, Tomsky's son Yury heard a shot; Tomsky had committed suicide.[9]

NOTES

1. Alexander Orlov, 'The Sensational Secret Behind [the] Damnation of Stalin', *Life*, 23 April 1956. Also, R. S. Osinina (V. Svechinsky's aunt Rosa) worked as a secretary with Balitsky, Katznelson and Shtein in the Kharkov GPU before 1934. She remembered I. L. Shtein well. Taped interview with R. S. Osinina in Haifa, Israel on 18 August 1975. See also F. D. Volkov, *Vzlet i padenie Stalina*, Moscow, 1992, p. 18.
2. See Chapter 22 above.
3. See Chapter 19 above.
4. This photograph was later published by Stalin as a prison photograph taken in 1913.
5. See Chapter 10 above.
6. Orlov, 'The Sensational Secret,' pp. 35f.
7. Vitaly Rapoport and Yury Alekseev, *Izmena rodine*, London, 1988, p. 359.
8. I. D. Levine, 'Stalin Suspected of Forcing Trials to Cover His Past', *Journal American*, 3 March 1938. Also Levine's interview with the author.
9. Robert C. Tucker (ed.), *Stalinism*, New York, 1977, p. 213.

27

THE 'TUKHACHEVSKY DOSSIER'

While Marshal Tukhachevsky and his group of officers were waiting for an opportune moment to depose Stalin, he, without knowing of their plot, was fabricating and accumulating 'evidence' for a new show trial with Tukhachevsky as the chief villain. Stalin nursed an old grudge against Tukhachevsky dating back to the 1920s when he had started to gather what became known to history as the 'Tukhachevsky Dossier'. During the First World War, Tukhachevsky, an officer in the Russian Army, had been taken prisoner by the Germans. After the war he had returned to Russia and joined the Bolshevik Party and the Red Army. Because of his Polish name, Lenin and Trotsky appointed him commander of the Warsaw front during the Soviet–Polish war of 1920. Tukhachevsky blamed Stalin for the Red Army's defeat at Warsaw: Stalin had delayed carrying out Trotsky's order to send in the First Cavalry to bolster the Red Army at Warsaw. Stalin, in turn, called Tukhachevsky 'the demon of the Civil War'.[1]

In 1926 Stalin fabricated an unsigned letter to Mikhail Frunze, the commissar of defense, complaining about Tukhachevsky. Frunze wrote on this letter: 'The Party has always trusted Comrade Tukhachevsky, trusts him now, and will always trust him in the future.' After the execution of Blumkin in December 1929 several hundred former tsarist officers were arrested in preparation for the planned show trial of the kidnapped General Kutepov. Two of the arrested officers signed depositions stating that they had taken part in a 'monarchist plot' headed by Tukhachevsky. Stalin sent these to Sergo Ordzhonikidze with the note: 'I am asking you to familiarize yourself with this. Since the possibility of it is not excluded, it is possible.' In 1935, the NKVD received a report about a plot in the Red Army, headed by 'General Turguev'. (Tukhachevsky visited Germany in 1931 on an official mission, using the pseudonym Turguev.) On receiving this report, Yagoda shrugged it off as 'not serious material' and ordered it deposited in the archive.[2] But Stalin considered this 'material' very serious.

On 31 March 1935 *Pravda* published an article by Tukhachevsky in which he analyzed Hitler's aggressive intentions and predicted that Hitler would start a war by attacking European countries and the Soviet Union. Tukhachevsky's article sparked off a storm of protest in Berlin, where government and press accused him of fomenting Soviet–German conflict.

Tukhachevsky did not know that Stalin had initiated a secret policy of forming an alliance with Hitler, while the commissar of foreign affairs, Maxim Litvinov, was pursuing a policy of uniting European countries against German fascism.[3] Stalin decided to reassure the Germans that Litvinov's diplomacy was coming to an end. In late spring 1935, soon after the publication of Tukhachevsky's article, a Soviet official at a reception in the German Consulate in Kiev attracted the attention of German diplomats by confidently predicting that history would soon overtake Litvinov and make Soviet–German friendship a reality because it was 'absurd of Soviet Russia to ally herself with a "degenerate" state like France!'[4] Neither Litvinov nor Tukhachevsky knew that Stalin through his personal agents, was secretly attempting to enter into an alliance with Hitler.

Stalin's courting of Hitler began after Hitler, on 30 June 1934, crushed the putsch led by Ernst Roehm, the chief of staff of the SA and leader of the Brown Shirts. To Stalin, the bloody purge Hitler carried out suggested a kindred spirit. NKVD and Soviet military intelligence agents expressed the opinion that the Roehm purge was an indication of a deepening crisis in Germany, signaling the impending downfall of Hitler. Stalin disagreed and stated that, to the contrary, Hitler had enhanced his power by liquidating Roehm.[5] Hitler may well have been the example that encouraged Stalin to purge the Old Bolsheviks and murder Kirov. Stalin assigned to his personal agent David Kandelaki, a member of the criminal gang in Batum to which Stalin had also belonged some 30 years earlier, the task of initiating friendly contact with Hitler's circle.[6] Litvinov and Tukhachevsky were sure to voice objections to this policy on ideological, political and strategic grounds.

Defendants at the Kamenev–Zinoviev trial testified about a 'terrorist military group' of Red Army officers, mentioning the names of Shmidt, Kuzmichev and others, which added 'evidence' to the 'Tukhachevsky Dossier'. It was reported that the case of military officers was under investigation.[7] D. Shmidt, a tank division commander in the Kiev military district, and B. Kuzmichev, the chief of staff of an Air Force unit, were arrested at the beginning of July 1936 and accused of taking part in a 'counter-revolutionary plot'.[8] Shmidt had supported the opposition in the 1920s. During a conference in the Kremlin in 1927 he had come up to Stalin and, grabbing the hilt of his saber, had threatened to lop off Stalin's ears. Stalin turned pale but said nothing.[9] The episode was taken as a joke then, but Stalin had no sense of humor when it came to slights against him, and he had a long memory.

Shmidt was interrogated by the chief of the Special Department, M. I.

Gai, and his deputy, Z. M. Ushakov. When the commander of the Kiev military district, Iona Yakir, received permission to see Shmidt, he barely recognized him. To Yakir, Shmidt looked like a 'dweller of the planet Mars'. Shmidt told Yakir that all his 'confessions' had been obtained under torture. Yakir reported this to Voroshilov, who later called Yakir and told him that Shmidt had again confirmed his earlier testimony. Voroshilov did not reveal that after Yakir's intervention Shmidt had been forced to confess that he had prepared a revolt in his tank division on Yakir's instruction.[10]

In August 1936 Vitaly Primakov, the deputy commander of the Leningrad military district, was arrested.[11] (Louis Aragon and his wife Elsa Triole had stayed in Primakov's home a few days before Maxim Gorky's death.[12]) Whether Primakov was aware of Stalin's intrigue against Gorky is not known, but the main reason for his arrest was Stalin's desire to liquidate 'Tukhachevsky's nest' by forcing his friends, among them Primakov, to sign testimonies implicating Tukhachevsky. At the beginning of September 1936 another friend of Tukhachevsky's, Vitovt Putna, the military attaché in London, was recalled to Moscow and arrested.[13] As the 'Tukhachevsky Dossier' grew thicker with additional 'confessions', the noose around the marshal's neck was tightening.

Toward the end of 1936 the country faced a bizarre situation in which two files were in mortal combat for survival. The Okhrana file with genuine documents, exposing Stalin as a tsarist *agent provocateur*, was competing with the fabricated 'Tukhachevsky Dossier', containing fraudulent 'proof' of Tukhachevsky's treason. These two files were at the center of two conspiracies that depended on whether Stalin or Tukhachevsky would strike first. Stalin did not suspect that his Okhrana file was in the hands of Tukhachevsky, while Tukhachevsky did not know that he had been singled out by Stalin as his next victim.

During the Kamenev–Zinoviev show trial, the defendants mentioned the names of the leading Party officials – Bukharin, Rykov, Piatakov, Radek, and Uglanov – all of whom Stalin intended to put on trial together with Tukhachevsky. But Stalin met with opposition from Ordzhonikidze and the Politburo and Central Committee members Kosior, Chubar and Postyshev. On 10 September 1936 *Pravda* published a brief note stating that the case against Bukharin and Rykov had been terminated due to lack of criminal evidence.[14] In the middle of September 1936, Stalin received Yagoda's report on the public's reaction to the Kamenev–Zinoviev trial. Yagoda mentioned public opinion abroad, where the obvious fraudulence of the 'Hotel Bristol' testimony reinforced the opinion that the trial was nothing but Stalin's revenge on his political enemies. Yagoda also brought to Stalin's attention the growing sympathy among the Soviet population for the executed defendants and the appearance on the walls of factories of such slogans as: 'Down with the Murderer of the Leaders of October!' and, 'What a Pity They Did Not Finish Off the Georgian Skunk!'[15] Stalin was enraged. He interpreted Yagoda's report as advice to refrain from further show trials and, in particular, to abandon the planned trial of Tukhachevsky. Having decided to stage the trial, Stalin was annoyed by Yagoda's apparent advice to stop the purge. He was already dissatisfied with Yagoda's services, mostly because the murder of Kirov had been poorly managed and because Yagoda had failed to fabricate 'proofs' of Kamenev's and Zinoviev's ties to the Okhrana. Dissatisfaction with somebody invariably resulted in Stalin's suspecting that person of disloyalty. On 25 September 1936 Stalin sent a telegram to the Politburo members, signed by him and his new comrade-in-arms, Andrey Zhdanov. The telegram read: 'We consider it absolutely necessary and urgent that Comrade Yezhov be appointed to head the People's Commissariat of Internal Affairs. Yagoda has obviously proved unequal to the task of exposing the Trotskyite–Zinovievite bloc. *The GPU was four years late in this matter.* All party officials and most of the NKVD agents in the region are talking about this.'[16] Stalin suggested that the state security organs should have 'exposed' the members of the opposition four years earlier, in 1932. This was the year when the Riutin Platform was circulating among party members. As a result of Stalin's telegram, Yagoda was moved to the post of commissar of communications and Yezhov became the head of the NKVD.

At the end of 1936 Riutin was still alive. He had been incarcerated in the Suzdal Special Purpose Prison since the end of 1932, which made it difficult to accuse him of any new crime, but Stalin decided to include Riutin in the cast of defendants at the show trial of the 'Anti-Soviet Trotskyite Center', planned for January 1937. On Stalin's order Genrikh Liushkov, the deputy chief of the NKVD Special Department, sent an 'absolutely secret' order to deliver to the Lubianka 'political prisoner Riutin . . . in a separate train compartment under increased security and a special convoy'. On his arrival at the Lubianka, Riutin refused to sign any deposition and demanded paper to write a letter to Stalin. Liushkov gave him three uneven sheets of brown wrapping paper. Riutin wrote on them that he did not consider himself guilty of anything, was not going to incriminate himself and others falsely, and was not afraid of death; he dated this statement 4 November 1936. Stalin read Riutin's statement and ordered it to be placed in his personal archive, where it stayed for half a century until being published during the era of *glasnost*.[17] Toward the end of 1936 the telephone rang in the apartment of Riutin's sons. Liushkov called from his Lubianka office, and he handed the receiver to Riutin. This was the last time Riutin's family heard from him. This telephone conversation did not produce results: Riutin refused to sign any testimony. He thus cheated Stalin out of the pleasure of seeing the self-abasement of his hated enemy. Riutin's resistance made him unsuitable for the show trial and Stalin, enraged, ordered his execution. On 10 January 1937 Riutin was brought before the chairman of the Military Collegium of the Supreme Court, Vasily Ulrikh, who asked the usual questions and then recorded that Riutin refused to sign any testimony and to make his 'final statement'.[18] Immediately after the passing of the death sentence, Riutin was taken to the Lubianka basement and shot in the back of his head. His two sons were also shot, and his wife imprisoned and tortured to death in 1947. Only his daughter, Luba, survived.[19]

According to Stalin's plan, the defendants at the forthcoming show trial of the 'Anti-Soviet Trotskyite Center' had to confess that they had 'intended to seize power'. When one of the defendants, Karl Radek, was arrested, he complained to his interrogator Molchanov: 'After all I have done for Stalin – such ingratitude.' He had in mind his betrayal of Blumkin in December 1929, the book he had written glorifying Stalin, and the numerous articles in which he had maligned Trotsky and the opposition. Radek naively expected gratitude when he should have feared Stalin above all others: anyone who knew the true reason for Blumkin's execution – his possession of Stalin's Okhrana file – was bound to be on Stalin's list of enemies. Radek pleaded with Molchanov to arrange a meeting between him and Stalin. Initially, Molchanov refused. Radek was worked over by interrogators, who put him through a 'conveyor' – continuous questioning for days and nights without sleep. He was amazingly resilient. When Molchanov was conducting the interrogation, Radek said: 'All right, I agree to confess that I wanted to murder all of the members of the Politburo and place Hitler on the Kremlin throne. But to my confessions I want to add one small detail that, besides those co-conspirators that you have attached to me, I had one more conspirator, with the name of Molchanov.'[20] Frightened, Molchanov reported Radek's request to see Stalin to Yezhov, stating that Radek refused to sign any testimony until he spoke to Stalin. Yezhov told Radek to write a letter to Stalin, asking for a meeting with him. The meeting was arranged. Radek was led into Yezhov's office, where Stalin was waiting for him. Stalin promised to spare his life if he agreed to testify in court to having been Trotsky's agent and if he mentioned Tukhachevsky in his testimony. Radek agreed and on returning to his cell asked for a pen and ink. He composed his testimony, eloquently describing Stalin's fantastic charge of a Trotsky–Hitler conspiracy and assigning to himself and other defendants suitable roles. Stalin was delighted with Radek's creation and ordered the testimonies of all the other defendants rewritten to conform to Radek's new version.[21]

Radek's version sped up preparations for the planned show trial. Stalin was in a good mood. On 20 December 1936 he invited top NKVD chiefs to his *dacha* to celebrate his 57th birthday and the eighteenth anniversary of the founding of the Cheka, the original Soviet secret police. Newspapers published the usual congratulations from 'toiling people' all over the country and from abroad, where Stalin had many admirers in 'progressive circles'. As usual, the guests soon got drunk and asked Karl Pauker to perform the scene of Zinoviev's execution, which they knew Stalin relished. Stalin always enjoyed it when Pauker, a barber and the valet in the Budapest Operetta before the First World War, performed 'comical' scenes and told Jewish anecdotes with a Yiddish accent, which Stalin liked the most.[22]

Another reason for Stalin's good mood was that he was confident that he would soon be able to add more 'criminal evidence' to the 'Tukhachevsky Dossier'. He ordered A. Slutsky, the chief of the NKVD Foreign Department, to plant abroad fraudulent 'proof' of Tukhachevsky's links with Hitler and Trotsky. On arriving in Paris, Slutsky summoned Walter Krivitsky, the head of Soviet military intelligence in Europe, and told him that his mission was 'not a routine affair'. He said that the job 'involves a case of such colossal importance that I have had to drop all my other work and come here to put it through . . . . We have got to have two men who can play the part of thoroughbred German officers. And we have to have them at once. This job is so important that nothing else matters.'[23] Krivitsky said that his two best agents would report to Slutsky shortly. Slutsky ordered the two agents to impersonate officers of the German general staff and to give a film roll with a plan of a German attack on Czechoslovakia to a Soviet official, who would meet them in a certain café in Prague. Slutsky ordered the NKVD resident in the Soviet embassy in Berlin, Israilovich, to meet 'important officers of the German general staff', who would give him 'espionage information'. At the same time Slutsky notified the Czechoslovak police of the meeting with 'German spies'. Israilovich was arrested by the Czechoslovak surveillance agents and during interrogation 'revealed' that the German officers were his agents and that the film he had received from them contained photographs of secret documents from the German general staff. The police released him. President

Edvard Beneš of Czechoslovakia took the 'secret documents' seriously and was alarmed by their 'proof' of German conspiracy with Tukhachevsky. He instructed the Czech ambassador in Moscow to report the intercepted information 'if possible, to Stalin personally'. Stalin thanked Beneš warmly for the 'friendly act' and intimated that Israilovich had in fact maintained contact with German military intelligence as a go-between for Tukhachevsky.[24] Beneš sent this information to the British and French, who also took it very seriously.[25] Stalin put this incriminating 'evidence' into the 'Tukhachevsky Dossier'.

But Stalin was not yet satisfied. He developed a scheme to plant with Czech intelligence a briefcase full of 'espionage documents' implicating Tukhachevsky. At the end of December 1936, Slutsky had arrived in Prague with a briefcase containing a photocopy of a German 'military plan for the seizure of the Sudetenland' and several forged passports, a doctored photograph of Trotsky posing with a group of German officers, several documents with Tukhachevsky's signature, and a formula for making invisible ink. Slutsky assigned an NKVD informer to plant this briefcase in the apartment of a local Trotskyite by the name of Grilevich and then informed the Czech police that Grilevich was a German spy. Suspecting a provocation, the Czech police did not act on this information. Slutsky attempted to have Grilevich arrested, employing various machinations, including bribing Czech police officials – without success. An alarming telegram from Yezhov arrived: 'Ivan Vasilievich wants to know results of operation.' 'Ivan Vasilievich' was Stalin's NKVD codename. (The name had special meaning for Stalin: it included his pre-Revolutionary codenames 'Ivanov', 'Ivanovich' and 'Vasiliev'.) Slutsky knew that when 'Ivan Vasilievich' wanted to 'know the results', this meant that these results had better be delivered immediately. He paced his office in the Soviet embassy in Prague, cursing the 'shirkers and loafers' of the Czech police. 'Drunkards!' he fumed. 'If they had been told that Grilevich had hidden unlicensed vodka, they would have come running at once, but when they are given a serious political case, they sit like sleepy flies.'[26]

Slutsky returned to Moscow. During a discussion Stalin suddenly turned to him and told him that it was imperative for Piatakov to testify that he had received the instruction to assassinate Stalin from Trotsky personally during a trip to Oslo in December 1935. Piatakov had gone to Berlin in 1935 on an official mission to purchase heavy machinery. Stalin stated that Piatakov had used this opportunity to travel to Oslo. At the next conference Slutsky reported to Stalin that Piatakov's trip to Oslo from Berlin was quite improbable in view of the facts that the round trip there would have taken at least two days and that, while in Berlin, Piatakov had had daily appointments with German business leaders, who must have kept records of their meetings with him, and their records might prove that on the day of Piatakov's alleged trip to Oslo he was actually in Berlin. Stalin was not swayed. 'What you said about the train schedule might be true', he said, 'but why couldn't Piatakov fly to Oslo in an airplane? Such a flight there and back could most likely be made in one night.' Slutsky replied that planes carried only a few passengers and their names were registered by the airlines; it would be easy to verify that Piatakov had not flown to Oslo. Stalin was getting angry. 'It must be said that Piatakov flew in a special plane', he said with an air of finality. 'For such a job the German authorities would gladly provide an airplane.' Remembering the Hotel Bristol débâcle, Stalin ordered Slutsky to avoid mentioning any hotel in Piatakov's confession.[27] The conversation dismayed Slutsky. He understood that Stalin wanted to avoid repeating the Hotel Bristol mistake, but he was at a loss how to explain why Stalin was stubbornly insisting on this patently fictitious meeting of Piatakov with Trotsky in Oslo, just as he had earlier insisted on the fictitious meeting of Holtsman with Lev Sedov at the Hotel Bristol in Copenhagen. Slutsky had no idea about the meetings of Iosif Dzhugashvili with the chief of the Okhrana Foreign Agency, Arkady Garting, in 1906 in Copenhagen and in 1907 in Oslo, and he did not have any conception of Stalin's irresistible urge to attribute events of his life to his victims and to re-enact these events many times over by attributing them to innocent people. Searching for explanations to Stalin's inventions, Slutsky at times mentioned his doubts to his friends. Rumors about such conversations were bound to reach Stalin at some point.

The show trial of the 'Anti-Soviet Trotskyite Center', at which Piatakov was the chief defendant, opened on 23 January 1937 in the cold, dark October Hall of the House of Trade Unions. The judges – Ulrikh, Matulevich and Rychkov – sat facing the carefully selected audience. The prosecutor, Vyshinsky, sat behind his desk on their left. The defendants, one after another, 'confessed' their assigned roles in sabotage, espionage and plots to assassinate Soviet leaders on the orders of Trotsky and Hitler. Piatakov told about his flight to Oslo and meeting with Trotsky. Radek in his testimony mentioned as if in passing the name of Tukhachevsky, who, he said, did not take part in anti-Soviet activities.[28]

When Radek's testimony was published, General Walter Krivitsky, the chief of Soviet military intelligence in Europe, read it in a Hague newspaper. Turning to his wife, he said, 'Tukhachevsky is doomed.' She disagreed. 'But Radek again and again absolved Tukhachevsky from any connection with the conspiracy', she reasoned. 'Exactly', Krivitsky said. 'Does Tukhachevsky need absolution from Radek? Do you think for a moment that Radek would dare on his own accord to drag Tukhachevsky's name into the trial? . . . Don't you understand that Radek speaks for Vyshinsky, and Vyshinsky for Stalin! I tell you, Tukhachevsky is doomed.'[29] Krivitsky was not mistaken.

The chief defendant, although not present in court, was Trotsky, who was accused of meeting Adolf Hitler and Rudolf Hess for the purpose of coordinating the assassination of Stalin. In this accusation, as in other charges invented by Stalin, there was some perverse correlation with actual events. In reality, it was Stalin who at that moment was planning an attempt on Trotsky's life while Stalin's agents were engaged in secret negotiations with Hitler's aides. At the very time when the defendants were confessing their crimes, Stalin's personal agent David Kandelaki met on 29 January 1937 with Hitler's trusted intermediary Dr Hjalmar Schacht and offered to conclude a Soviet–German treaty. Two weeks later, on 11 February 1937, Hitler wrote to Schacht that 'if Russia were to develop further along the lines of absolute despotism supported by the army', then this proposal would certainly be considered.[30]

On 30 January 30 1937 the show trial came to an end. Thirteen defendants were sentenced to death and four, among them Radek, received prison terms. Radek's face lit up when he heard his 10-year prison sentence pronounced. He turned to his fellow defendants, shrugged, and flashed a guilty smile at the audience. The same night, the 13 condemned men were shot.[31]

Soon after the executions the Norwegian newspaper *Aftenposten* reported that 'Piatakov's conference with Trotsky in Oslo was quite improbable', because no airplanes had landed at the Oslo airport during December 1935 when Piatakov supposedly traveled there. Another newspaper *Arbeiderbladet*, the organ of the Norwegian Social Democratic Party, reported that not a single plane had landed at the Oslo airport during the whole period between September 1935 and May 1936. To counter these charges, Vyshinsky produced a document from the Soviet foreign trade mission stating that according to official information planes *could* land at the Oslo airport year round, which was true. But the fact remained that no airplane *had* landed there during the period in question. Trotsky cited this fact, as well as the 'Hotel Bristol' mix-up to prove that the 'confessions' were 'false from beginning to end'.[32]

The execution of Piatakov was a great blow to his superior, Ordzhonikidze. For years, Piatakov had been deputy commissar of heavy industry. Ordzhonikidze, a poorly educated man, was totally dependent on him and pleaded with Stalin not to persecute him. When he did not prevail, he arranged a personal meeting with Piatakov in prison. He told Piatakov that Stalin had given his word of honor not to execute him if he signed the self-incriminating testimony. Piatakov agreed to sign. After his execution, Ordzhonikidze realized that he had been cast in the role of a dupe shamelessly used by Stalin. He angrily accused Stalin of breaking his word. To scare him, Stalin ordered his Kremlin apartment searched. When Ordzhonikidze called Stalin and complained, Stalin said, 'That's nothing extraordinary. The NKVD is the sort of organization that's capable of searching my place too.' Then Stalin read to Ordzhonikidze some complaints against him. 'See what people say about you!' he admonished him. Ordzhonikidze cursed Stalin and hung up.[33]

On 18 February 1937 Stalin ordered Poskrebyshev, the chief of his personal secretariat, to go to Ordzhonikidze's apartment and shoot him.[34] At 5:30 pm Ordzhonikidze's wife, Zinaida, heard a shot. When she looked out the window, she saw a man running across the Kremlin lawn. She went into her husband's study, found him dead, and called Stalin, whose apartment was nearby. 'Heavens, what a tricky illness!' Stalin said, feigning shock and sadness. 'The man lies down to have a rest, and the result is a seizure and a heart attack!' The official medical report stated that the death resulted from 'paralysis of the heart'. Commissar of Health G. Kaminsky and two Kremlin doctors, Levin and Khodorovsky, were forced to sign this report. (Kaminsky was soon afterwards secretly shot, Levin and Khodorovsky were to appear as defendants at a show trial a year later.[35])

Ordzhonikidze's body was cremated, and the urn with his ashes was placed in the Kremlin wall in the long-vacant spot to the left of the passage to the mausoleum. Stalin ordered a pompous funeral to honor 'our beloved Sergo'. Khrushchev delivered an emotional oration in which, choking with tears and anger, he referred to the 'enemies', stating: 'It was they who struck a blow at thy noble heart. Piatakov, the spy, the murderer, the enemy of the working people, is caught red-handed, caught and condemned, crushed like a reptile.'[36] At the February–March party plenum Molotov spoke darkly about 'the special danger of present-day saboteurs and spies making themselves out to be Communists, ardent supporters of the Soviet regime'.[37] A show trial of 'German spies' headed by Tukhachevsky was planned to start soon.

In February 1937 Slutsky was still trying to induce the Czech police to arrest the Trotskyite Grilevich. He sent Grilevich registered letters in coded language and invisible ink, hoping that they would be intercepted and would trigger Grilevich's arrest. During a stay in Paris, Slutsky visited Alexander Orlov, the Soviet intelligence adviser to the Spanish Republican government, who was recuperating from an illness in a Paris hospital. Slutsky told Orlov about the 'flight of Piatakov to Oslo,' the assignment of two 'German officers, the Grilevich provocation and other strange fabrications of "Ivan Vasilievich" '. Orlov could find no logical explanation for these strange stories.

Soon after Slutsky left, Orlov had another visitor – his cousin Zinovy Katsnelson, the deputy chief of the Ukrainian NKVD, who happened to arrive in Paris on official business and learned of Orlov's illness. Katsnelson confided to Orlov what he knew about the discovery by Shtein of Stalin's Okhrana file and about the documents in the file exposing Stalin as an ex-Okhrana agent. He also told Orlov about the conspiracy of military officers to depose Stalin. His story provided some explanation for Stalin's bizarre behavior and a clue to his personality. Orlov, like Katsnelson, hoped that the plot headed by Tukhachevsky to depose Stalin would succeed.[38]

In March 1937 Stalin ordered the execution of a large group of NKVD officers who had served under Yagoda. Yezhov ordered all the chiefs of the departments besides Slutsky and Pauker to go on 'inspection tours'. They never returned. At the first stop outside Moscow they were arrested and shot. Their deputies, too, were executed. Some 3,000 NKVD officers were arrested and shot during this period. Molchanov, the chief of the secret political department, who had managed the preparations for the two Moscow show trials, was arrested and shot. There were many suicides among the NKVD officers at that time. Molchanov's deputy, Shtein, who had discovered Stalin's Okhrana file, also committed suicide – whether at this time or somewhat later is not clear.[39]

On 18 March 1937 Yezhov delivered a speech before newly recruited NKVD officers, devoting it to the liquidation of 'Yagoda's nest' and stating that Yagoda had been exposed as an 'Okhrana *agent provocateur*' who had wormed his way into the Soviet secret police to mastermind a network of spies in the NKVD and had attempted to escape abroad 'with a suitcase full of *valiuta*'. Stalin attributed to Yagoda not only the Okhrana past, but also projected on to him Blumkin's attempt to flee abroad with a suitcase full of foreign currency. Despite this grave charge, Yagoda remained free for two more weeks; he was arrested on 3 April 1937. When brought to Slutsky's office, Yagoda said: 'You may put it down in your report that I have said that there must be a God after all.' Slutsky was stunned. Yagoda explained: 'Quite simple. From Stalin I deserve nothing but gratitude for my faithful service. From God I deserve the most severe punishment for having broken his commandments a thousand times. Now, look where I am, and judge for yourself whether there is a God or not!'[40] According to Stalin's scenario, Yagoda and Tukhachevsky were to appear as chief defendants at the next show trial, the one concerning 'German spies' and 'Okhrana agents'.

Stalin was delaying Tukhachevsky's arrest while waiting for the 'evidence' against him to be discovered in the briefcase planted in Grilevich's apartment in Prague, as well as additional criminal evidence' that he expected to receive from Hitler's secret police. Somewhat earlier, on 16 December 1936, the former tsarist general N. V. Skoblin, an NKVD agent in Paris (who had taken part in the kidnapping of General Kutepov in 1930), on Slutsky's order relayed to a representative of the SD (German military intelligence) the 'information' proving that Tukhachevsky was heading a plot to depose Stalin and was in contact with top German Army generals and military intelligence officers. Skoblin provided the same 'information' to a Russian émigré group in Berlin, the 'Guchkov Circle', which had been infiltrated by several NKVD agents, including Guchkov's own daughter.[41] Skoblin's 'information' reached Reinhardt Heydrich, the head of the SD, who reported it to Hitler in order to plant in Hitler's mind suspicion about the loyalty of German Army generals. Heydrich also wanted to warn Hitler about the possibility that the dangerous 'Red Bonaparte' Tukhachevsky, who was known as a capable military strategist and as a man who held strong anti–German views, might come to power. Heydrich suggested to Hitler that 'evidence' be fabricated of Tukhachevsky's conspiring with the German high command, thus provoking his arrest, which would suit German interests. Hitler agreed with this idea and ordered the fabrication of the necessary documents to be passed on to Stalin. Heydrich's assistant, Janke, was against the forgery scheme, arguing that Skoblin might be a Soviet agent and his information might be fraudulent and intended to misinform the German government. Heydrich had Janke placed under house arrest and ordered SD forger Franz Putzig to add Tukhachevsky's signature to documents that had been stolen from the German general staff. Heydrich told his assistant, H. Behrens: 'Even if Stalin wanted simply to mislead us with this Skoblin information, I will supply our little Kremlin uncle with enough proof that his lie is a pure truth.'[42] Putzig fabricated 15 documents implicating Tukhachevsky.[43] Heydrich ordered Behrens to go to Prague to offer these forgeries to Czech president Beneš who referred him to the Soviet embassy in Berlin, to contact there an official by the name of Israilovich (who earlier had received 'espionage information' from 'two German officers'). Behrens showed Israilovich two letters with

Tukhachevsky's forged signature and offered to deliver the rest of the 15 documents. Israilovich asked about the price, but Behrens only shrugged. Several days later, Israilovich introduced Behrens to Leonid Zakovsky, who said that he represented Yezhov. Zakovsky looked through the documents and asked how much they would cost. Heydrich, in order to impress Stalin with the documents' value, had instructed Behrens to ask for three million rubles, but to lower the price if he met with resistance. Zakovsky did not bargain and silently nodded. The forgeries were in Stalin's hands at the beginning of May 1937.[44] (The three million rubles proved to be of no use to the Germans – they were in large banknotes and the serial numbers were known to the NKVD. German agents who used them were arrested.[45])

Stalin also received information about Tukhachevsky's 'espionage activities' from Soviet diplomats who repeated the rumors spread by NKVD agents. In January 1937, the Czech ambassador to Germany, Mastny, sent a coded cable to President Beneš stating that a group in the Red Army was plotting to depose Stalin, which could bring about a change in the balance of power in Europe in Germany's favor. Beneš repeated this information to the Soviet ambassador to Czechoslovakia, C. Alexandrovsky, who flew to Moscow to report it to Stalin. At the same time, French premier Eduard Daladier asked the Soviet ambassador to France, Vladimir Potemkin, whether there was any truth to reports that Red Army generals were involved in a conspiracy with the Germans. Potemkin wired a coded message, describing his conversation with Daladier.[46]

In the beginning of May 1937 the 'Tukhachevsky Dossier' was almost complete, containing numerous forgeries. Stalin was close to ordering Tukhachevsky's arrest. The only delay had to do with the suitcase planted in the Prague apartment of the Trotskyite Grilevich, who still had not been arrested by the Czech police. Slutsky was receiving angry inquiries from 'Ivan Vasilievich'. Stalin attributed great importance to this briefcase, because in it was 'proof' not only of Tukhachevsky's ties to the Germans but also to Trotsky, who appeared in one of the forged photographs in the company of German officers. Despite Stalin's urging, it took Slutsky almost five months to get Grilevich arrested. In June 1937, a bribe to a Czech police official finally had the desired effect, but Grilevich was soon released. Ironically, by then Stalin no longer had the slightest interest in Grilevich's briefcase. An event that occurred on 19 May 1937 forced him to realize that weaving a web of lies around Tukhachevsky had been a waste of time.

NOTES

1. Vitaly Rapoport and Yury Alekseev, *Izmena rodine*, London, 1988, p. 468, fn. 1.
2. Boris Viktorov, 'Zagovor krasnoi armii', *Pravda*, 29 April 1988.
3. Gustav Hilger and Alfred G. Meyer, *The Incompatible Allies*, New York, 1971, p. 271.
4. Ibid., p. 269.
5. Walter G. Krivitsky, *I Was Stalin's Agent*, London, 1939, pp. vii–xv.
6. Hilger and Meyer, *The Incompatible Allies*, p. 269.
7. *Zinoviev Trial*, Moscow, 1936, p. 36.
8. Robert Conquest, *The Great Terror*, New York, 1973, pp. 287f.
9. Alexander Barmine, *One Who Survived*, New York, 1945, pp. 89f.
10. P. I. Yakir and Y. I. Geller, *Kommandarm Yakir*, Moscow, 1963, p. 207.
11. I. Dubinsky, *Primakov*, Moscow, 1968, pp. 164 and 173.
12. See Chapter 24 above.
13. Conquest, *The Great Terror*, p. 290.
14. *Pravda*, 10 September 1936.
15. Alexander Orlov, *Tainaya istoria stalinskikh prestuplenii*, New York, Jerusalem, Paris, 1983, pp. 172f.
16. Roy Medvedev, *Let History Judge*, New York, 1971, p. 174.
17. Arkady Vaksberg, 'Kak zhivoy s zhivymy,' *Literaturnaya gazeta*, 29 June 1988.
18. Ibid.
19. Lev Razgon, 'Nakonets,' *Moskovskie novosti*, 26 June 1988. Also Arkady Vaksberg, 'Kak zhivoy s zhivymy'.
20. Orlov, *Tainaya istoria*, pp. 195f.
21. Ibid., pp. 197–200.
22. Ibid., p. 335.
23. Walter G. Krivitsky, *In Stalin's Secret Service*, New York, 1939, pp. 216–18.
24. Alexander Orlov, 'The Sensational Secret Behind Damnation of Stalin', *Life*, 23 April 1956, p. 36.
25. Winston Churchill, *The Second World War*, vol. 1, London, 1948, p. 224. Also John Erickson, *The Soviet High Command: A Military-Political History, 1918–1941*, London, 1962, p. 433.
26. Alexander Orlov, *The Secret History of Stalin's Crimes*, New York, 1953, pp. 206–8.
27. Ibid. pp. 181–3.
28. *Piatakov Trial*, Moscow, 1936, p. 146.
29. Krivitsky, *In Stalin's Secret Service*, p. 216.
30. Conquest, *The Great Terror*, p. 299.
31. Orlov, *Tainaya istoria*, p. 204.
32. Ibid., pp. 182f.
33. Conquest, *The Great Terror*, pp. 259f.
34. Ibid., p. 260. Also I. P. Itskov, taped interview.
35. Ibid., pp. 260f.
36. Conquest, *The Great Terror*, p. 261, quoting *Great Soviet Encyclopedia*, 2nd edn, under 'Ordzhonikidze'.
37. Ibid., p. 346.
38. Orlov, 'The Sensational Secret'.
39. Ibid.
40. Orlov, *Tainaya istoria*, p. 253.
41. Walter Krivitsky, *I Was Stalin's Agent*, London, 1939, p. 237. Also *Dlya vas*, no. 48, 27 November 1938, p. 12.
42. *Panorama*, no. 56, 3 July 1988, quoting from Paul Karell, *Hitler's War on Russia*, London, 1966.
43. Lev Nikulin, *Marshal Tukhachevsky*, Moscow, 1961, pp. 189–94.
44. Conquest, *The Great Terror*, p. 302.
45. *Panorama*, no. 56, 3 July 1988, quoting from Paul Karell.
46. Conquest, *The Great Terror*, p. 302.

28

THE FORGERY THAT
TELLS THE TRUTH

On the night of 19 May 1937, during a routine search of the apartment of one of the arrested Red Army officers, NKVD operatives happened upon a photocopy of a document from Stalin's Okhrana file. It was a copy of Colonel Eremin's report in 1913 to the director of the Department of Police, S. P. Beletsky, with a brief description of Stalin's Okhrana career.[1] The copy was handed over to Karl Pauker, the chief of the NKVD Operations Department, a man of limited intelligence and poor knowledge of the Russian language. Pauker, a drinking companion of Stalin for many years, radiated a dog-like devotion to him and had no idea about the danger this document posed to him. He at once brought it to Stalin.[2]

Stalin immediately grasped the document's meaning: his St. Petersburg Okhrana file was in the hands of military plotters who intended to destroy him. He ordered Yezhov to declare a state of emergency and to cancel all passes into the Kremlin, to surround it with NKVD troops, and to place detachments of bodyguards at his office and living quarters. The reason he cited for ordering these extraordinary security measures was that he had uncovered a vast conspiracy to murder Yezhov.[3] (As usual, he pointed at a 'false target' in order to divert attention from himself.) Stalin ordered Yezhov to arrest and execute a large number of Red Army officers whom he suspected of involvement in the conspiracy.

Stalin's vision of the 'enemy' underwent a drastic change. Having schemed to fabricate evidence of Tukhachevsky's imagined conspiracy, he was suddenly confronted with an actual conspiracy on the part of unknown plotters who were in possession of his Okhrana file and who in his thinking at this point had no connection with Tukhachevsky. This real threat of his Okhrana file wiped the invented 'Tukhachevsky Dossier' from his mind. Curiously, he did not suspect initially that Tukhachevsky had anything to do with his Okhrana file. He repeated his usual mistake of striking rashly at suspected plotters and destroying important sources of information. He ordered Yezhov to execute Karl Pauker and his deputy Volovich, stating that they were 'Polish and German spies'.[4] By murdering Pauker, Stalin denied himself the opportunity to determine where exactly the photocopy of Eremin's report had been found and to trace the threads of the conspiracy from there. He had done the same in December 1929, when he had ordered the execution of Blumkin without first finding out from him what had happened to the file Blumkin had tried to smuggle out of the country.[5]

On 22 May 1937, the day he left Moscow for The Hague, Walter Krivitsky, the head of Soviet military intelligence in Europe, paid a visit to Mikhail Frinovsky, Yezhov's deputy. Krivitsky asked what was the reason for the sudden outbreak of 'such a succession of arrests and executions that it seemed as if the Russian roof were falling in, and the whole Soviet edifice tumbling.' Krivitsky asked, 'Tell me, what's going on? What's going on in the country?' Frinovsky told him that the worst was over and that the country had lived through an extremely dangerous situation brought on by a conspiracy. 'We've just uncovered a gigantic conspiracy in the Army, such a conspiracy as history has never known', Frinovsky explained. 'And we've just now learned of a plot to kill Nikolay Ivanovich [Yezhov] himself! But we have got them all. We have got everything under control.' Far from convinced that everything was under control, Krivitsky departed. He left Moscow amidst great alarm and confusion. Something near panic had seized the officers corps of the Red Army as hourly reports of fresh arrests reached them. Krivitsky felt like he was leaving a city in the midst of a series of earthquakes.[6]

Every new arrest threatened to expose the military conspiracy headed by Tukhachevsky. Among the arrested might be an officer who under torture would reveal the names of other conspirators. A month earlier, Tukhachevsky's friends, Corps Commanders A. I. Gekker and I. I. Garkavi, had been arrested. Because Garkavi was married to a sister of Yakir's wife, Yakir arranged an audience with Stalin, who pretended to be friendly, saying that there were serious charges against Garkavi, but if he was innocent, he would be released.[7]

May began with the usual 1 May parade in Red Square. Tukhachevsky appeared a few minutes before the start and went to his place in front of the mausoleum, on top of which stood Stalin and Politburo members. Then came Deputy Commissar of Defense Yan Gamarnik. He did not look at Tukhachevsky. Both of them knew that Stalin was watching them from the top of the mausoleum. After the military parade Tukhachevsky left Red Square, not waiting for the civilian demonstration. On 4 May 1937 he was scheduled to go to London on an official visit, but his trip was suddenly canceled.[8]

Brigade Commander A. R. Medvedev was arrested on 8 May 1937 and accused of being a Trotskyite. He was forced by the investigator Z. M. Ushakov to sign a deposition stating that he had known since 1931 about the existence of a Trotskyite group in the Red Army, of which Tukhachevsky's friend Corps Commander B. M. Feldman was a member. Yezhov ordered Feldman's arrest.[9] The chief of staff of the Far Eastern Army, Corps Commander Lapin, and the head of the Frunze Military Academy, Corps Commander Kork, were arrested on 11 May 1937. The same day, Voroshilov notified Tukhachevsky that he had been appointed commander of the Volga military district.

On 19 May 1937 Ushakov, a notorious sadist, accused Feldman of taking part, together with Tukhachevsky and Yakir, in a plot to subvert the Soviet state. Two decades later, Ushakov testified: 'I summoned Feldman to my office, locked him and myself up, and towards the evening of 19 May Feldman wrote his testimony about the conspiracy with Tukhachevsky, Yakir, Eideman, and others taking part in it.'[10] Ushakov insisted that it was he who had uncovered the Red Army conspiracy and congratulated himself on having made history by forcing Feldman to confess, thus unleashing a gigantic purge in the Red Army. In fact, on 19 May Stalin did not pay attention to the confessions elicited by torture from military officers whom he had had arrested only to wrench from them 'criminal evidence' to be added to the 'Tukhachevsky Dossier'. From the moment when Pauker brought him the photocopy of Colonel Eremin's report, Stalin lost interest in contrived evidence against Tukhachevsky and became preoccupied with the search for his Okhrana file, not suspecting that Tukhachevsky was plotting to use it against him.

On 25 May 1937, before leaving for Kuibyshev to assume his new post as commander of the Volga military district, Tukhachevsky went to say goodbye to Yan Gamarnik, Deputy Commissar of Defense and Chief Political Commissar of the Red Army. Although Gamarnik was suffering from a cold, he had come to his Department of Defense office see Tukhachevsky off. Stalin's Okhrana file was hidden in Gamarnik's office, but, knowing that walls have ears, the two did not say a word about it. Both men knew that mass arrests and executions were claiming many of their close friends and must have fervently hoped that the opportunity to depose Stalin would present itself soon. 'Happy journey, Mikhail Nikolaevich!' Gamarnik said. 'Get well, Yan Borisovich!' replied Tukhachevsky.[11]

The following day, Tukhachevsky was arrested during a meeting at the Kuibyshev party headquarters. An express train delivered him to Moscow.

He was taken to the Lubianka prison and interrogated by Ushakov, who had earlier tortured Feldman.[12] 'Tukhachevsky was given to me', Ushakov was to testify two decades later: 'I already had him confessing on May 26.'[13] Tukhachevsky, bandaged and carried on a stretcher, was brought to the Kremlin for personal interrogation by Stalin.[14] It remains unknown which of the arrested officers broke under torture and revealed that Tukhachevsky knew that Stalin's Okhrana file was in the hands of Gamarnik. On 28 May, a detachment of NKVD troops surrounded the Department of Defense and NKVD agents sealed all the offices there. On 29 May, Voroshilov called the army commander I. P. Uborevich in Minsk and ordered him to come to Moscow. Uborevich's wife and daughter, who had come to the station to see him off, witnessed his arrest. The next day, Voroshilov called Yakir in Kiev and ordered him to come to Moscow immediately. Yakir was arrested during the stop of the Kiev–Moscow train at Briansk station. A 'Black Raven' (prison wagon) traveling at high speed delivered him to the Lubianka prison. The same day, 30 May 1937 A. S. Bulin, the newly appointed chief of the Cadres Administration of the Red Army and his deputy, I. V. Smorodnikov, on Stalin's order went to Gamarnik's apartment and took from him the keys to the safe in his office in the Department of Defense. There they found Stalin's Okhrana file, and turned it over to Stalin.[15] On 31 May at 5 pm Bulin and Smorodnikov returned to Gamarnik's apartment. This time, they had Stalin's order to murder him. The two men asked his wife to take them to the bedroom. She showed them the bedroom door and went to the kitchen. Shortly afterward, she heard two shots and in the hall saw Bulin and Smorodnikov getting ready to leave. They pretended to be as surprised as she was by the shots and together with her went back into the bedroom. Gamarnik was dead.[16] The next day, 1 June 1937, *Pravda* published a report, stating that 'former member of the Central Committee Y. B. Gamarnik, having been entangled with anti-Soviet elements, and fearing that he would be unmasked, had committed suicide.'[17] Voroshilov told Smorodnikov, 'as far as the funeral is concerned, the crematory has already received orders'.[18] Rumors about the two gunshots were spreading. Some NKVD officers were convinced that Gamarnik had been murdered.[19] (Somewhat later Bulin and Smorodnikov were accused of being Japanese spies and shot.[20])

Finally, the file Stalin had worried about for many years was in his hands. Now, he had to exterminate everyone who might have known about its existence. Soon after Gamarnik's murder, Alexander Orlov, the top Soviet intelligence adviser to the Spanish Republican government, had a conversation with G. K. Zhukov (the future marshal and Soviet defense minister) who in 1937 came to Spain from Moscow. Zhukov told Orlov that Voroshilov had been 'unable till now to recover' after the exposure of the military conspiracy: 'Only the determination of Stalin and the swiftness of Yezhov saved the situation. Yezhov's boys shot them [the conspirators] without ceremony. Klim [Voroshilov] said that in this case not a single hour could be lost . . . He was especially shocked by the treachery of Gamarnik. That was incomprehensible indeed: we all regarded Gamarnik as a saint . . .'.[21]

From 1 June to 4 June 1937 the Military Council, presided over by Voroshilov, castigated the 'renegade counterrevolutionary military fascist organization'. Stalin, his hands behind his back, walked up and down the hall, watching the reaction of the participants. Those who expressed doubts about the validity of the charges were arrested during the recesses.[22] Stalin singled out Gamarnik's 'treachery' for exceptionally violent posthumous abuse. On 6 June 1937 the Red Army newspaper Krasnaya zvezda (Red Star) labeled him a 'Trotskyite, Fascist and spy'.[23] Stalin's Okhrana file was not mentioned at the Military Council, or at the interrogations of the arrested military men. The arrested generals knew that any mention of it would bring about immediate execution and no interrogator would have dared to record such testimony. The generals were tortured and forced to sign their testimony as blood was dripping from their wounds. (Two decades later, during the Khrushchev years, the brownish spots on their 'confessions' were proved to be dried blood.[24]) Stalin's version of the conspiracy changed somewhat: instead of the initial charge of plotting to kill Yezhov, the generals were now accused of plotting to remove Voroshilov. The defendants were promised in the name of rukovodstvo (the leadership) that their 'good behavior' in court would favorably affect their sentence, that is, that they had better confirm their testimonies if they hoped to stay alive.

On 11 June, 1937, Pravda reported: 'The case of Tukhachevsky M. N., Yakir I. E., Uborevich I. P., Kork A. I., Eideman R. P., Feldman B. M., Primakov V. M. and Putna B. K. arrested by the organs of the NKVD at different times, has been brought to investigative conclusion and trans- ferred to the court. . .'.[25] The trial began on 11 June, at 9 am, and ended at 11 am. Ulrikh again was the presiding judge. Each of the defendants had an armed guard standing behind him and an interrogator sitting at his side. One by one, they stood up and said, 'Plead guilty, have no complaints.' At any departure from their scripted testimony, Ulrikh yelled, 'Don't deliver lectures, just testify!' As usual, particles of distorted truth appeared here and there in the testimonies. Uborevich testified that the generals had 'in essence conspired with Gamarnik to attack Voroshilov, and that Gamarnik said that he would come out 'krepko (sturdily) against Voroshilov'. In fact, the generals had assigned to Gamarnik, a member of the Central Committee, the role of attacking Stalin at the Central Committee meeting, presenting Stalin's Okhrana file, and strongly arguing the case against him as an entrenched Okhrana imposter. The incorrect, non-idiomatic Russian expression 'krepko' had a familiar ring: Stalin often used it in his statements. Here, too, he was the author of the 'confessions'. The generals in their 'final word' asked to be forgiven and expressed devotion to 'Comrade Stalin'. With the exception of General Vitaly Primakov's, their final word was brief. Primakov, who had been arrested in August 1936, nearly a year earlier than the other defendants, delivered a long speech. Its style of questions and answers, peculiar logic, and abundant repetition of the same idea left no doubt that it had been penned by Stalin:

I must tell the final truth about our plot. Neither in the history of our revolution, nor in the history of other revolutions, has there been such a plot as ours, neither in the composition nor in the means which this plot choose for itself. Of whom did this plot consist? Whom did the fascist banner of Trotsky unite? It united all the counterrevolutionary elements, all that was counterrevolutionary in the Red Army it gathered in one place, under one banner, under the fascist banner of Trotsky. What means did this plot chose for itself? All means: treason, betrayal, defeat of their country, wrecking, espionage, terror. For what purpose? For the reinstatement of capitalism . . . What forces did the plot gather to achieve this plan? I named to the investigation more than 70 people – the conspirators, whom I had recruited myself . . . I have formed an opinion about the social face of the plot, that is, of what groups our plot consists, the leadership, the center of the plot. The composition of the plot consists of people who do not have deep roots in our Soviet country, because every one of them has his own second motherland. Every one of them personally has family ties abroad. Yakir has relatives in Bessarabia, Putna and Uborevich in Latvia; Feldman is tied to South America no less than to Odessa; Eideman is more connected with the Baltic countries than with our country.[26]

The idea that the plotters were not Russian patriots, but Poles, Jews, Lithuanians, Latvians – and that their treachery could hence be seen as the plotting of outsiders – suggests that Primakov's final statement was a surviving relic of a testimony which was prepared for the planned show trial that Stalin had aborted. Whether Primakov actually delivered this speech, or it was just deposited in the archive is not clear. All of the defendants, including Primakov, received sentences of the 'highest measure of punishment'. They were shot immediately after the trial.

On the same day, 11 June 1937, not far from Moscow in the ancient town of Dmitrov, thousands of inmates, mostly common criminals, celebrated their release from the Gulag on the occasion of the opening of the Moscow–Volga Canal on the construction of which they had worked. They were awarded citations as *udarniki* (shock-workers). The citations, dated 11 June 1937, were signed by Zinovy Katsnelson, who had been earlier appointed chief of the Gulag.[27] On that day, Stalin still did not know that the conspiracy to depose him had begun in the summer of 1936, when Shtein brought his Okhrana file to Katsnelson and Balitsky.

From 23 to 29 June 1937 Stalin presided over a special party plenum. He planned to undertake a gigantic purge and demanded the approval of 'extraordinary emergency powers' for Yezhov. Osip Piatnitsky, the chief of the Political-Administrative Department of the Central Committee, objected, saying that he had information about illegal methods of investigation practiced by the NKVD under Yezhov's leadership. The next day, Yezhov declared that the NKVD possessed 'undeniable data, proving that before the Revolution, Piatnitsky had been an informer of the Okhrana Section of the Department of Police'. Yezhov suggested that the plenum cast a vote of no confidence in Piatnitsky and delegate to the NKVD the investigation of Piatnitsky's past 'to sort out the truth from the lies'.[28] Ironically, Stalin became reacquainted with the truth when his file fell into his hands: he had found there his report, *Spravka bez no. 5/18 June 1912*, in which he listed the names and aliases of the most important Bolsheviks, among them Piatnitsky, of whom he wrote: 'TRANSPORT – in Leipzig in the hands of *Tarshis* (Piatnitsa).'[29] (Tarshis was Piatnitsky's actual family name.) Krupskaya, Lenin's widow, pointed to the many years of friendship between Lenin and Piatnitsky and tried to intervene on his behalf, but Stalin warned her that if she did not stop bothering him, the party would proclaim that not Krupskaya but the Old Bolshevik Elena Stasova was Lenin's widow. 'Yes, the Party can do anything', Stalin told her.[30] Piatnitsky was arrested on 7 July 1937 and shot some time later. His wife, having gone insane, perished in a prison camp. His daughter Yulia survived.[31]

Toward the beginning of July 1937 Stalin learned that the conspiracy to depose him started with Shtein delivering his Okhrana file to Katsnelson and Balitsky.[32] Knatselson was arrested early in July and executed. Shtein, realizing that his arrest was imminent, committed suicide when he saw Yezhov walking into his office.[33] Balitsky was arrested somewhat later, in mid-July, in the course of Stalin's exceptionally uncanny provocation which was centered on a remarkable fabricated document, known to history as the 'Eremin Letter'. This forgery has continued to inspire debate among historians and biographers of Stalin, some of whom still believe it to be a genuine document.

Stalin's main purpose in fabricating the 'Eremin letter' was to discredit Colonel Eremin's genuine report and to 'prove' that this report had been forged by Stalin's enemies with the aim of maligning the revolutionary past of the great leader. On a quite rational level Stalin assumed that despite mass arrests and executions, some photocopies of the genuine Eremin report might have survived the dragnet and ended up in Trotsky's hands. Stalin hoped that the fabricated 'Eremin Letter' could readily be proven to be a bona fide forgery and would discredit the copy of the original document. But beyond that calculated rational motive Stalin was also satisfying a strong emotional need to discredit, in his mind, Eremin's genuine report. The 'two natures' and 'split personality' of an *agent-provocateur* he so masterfully described in his book *Provocateur Anna Serebriakova* were actually not her but his own psychological traits. He produced the 'Eremin Letter' forgery to convince himself, firstly, that Colonel Eremin's report and other genuine documents in his Okhrana file had been fabricated by his enemies.

While Stalin was engrossed in the mopping up of military and NKVD personnel whom he suspected of disloyalty, he also invented an ingenious cover-up scheme which was a carbon copy of his earlier scheme in 1930 when he concocted the bogus 'Kutepov documents' conspiracy. He ordered identical kidnapping of a White Guard general in Paris and devised plans for a gigantic show trial with numerous defendants, whom he intended to force to confess that they had fabricated Okhrana documents in order to falsely accuse him of having been an Okhrana agent. The only new twist to this old scheme was that this time he knew what documents were in his Okhrana file and was able to distort them to furnish material evidence of forgery. This idea was not new to Stalin. As early as August 1917 he had accused the Provisional Government of fabricating Okhrana documents in order to besmirch 'true revolutionary fighters'. On Stalin's order this accusation was repeated in 1927 by his assistant Maksakov who described the history of the Okhrana archives. Stalin repeated the same accusation in articles he published in the journal *Krasny arkhiv* (Red Archive) in 1935.

Stalin's scheme had many offshoots, but it began in Moscow. In June 1937 Stalin ordered Alexander Svanidze, the brother of his first wife Keke, to forge the 'Eremin Letter' and three other Okhrana documents. Svanidze was in charge of a secret Kremlin printing shop that had earlier specialized in producing counterfeit foreign currency and forged foreign passports for Soviet intelligence operatives. In the 1930s, Svanidze, on Stalin's orders, also forged Okhrana documents to glorify Stalin's revolutionary past and doctored actual Okhrana documents that had been found in the old archives, inserting in them laudatory statements about Stalin's role in the underground and often changing dates to conform to the New Style. These changes of dates and the laudatory insertions made these doctored Okhrana documents easy to recognize as forgeries. They were inserted in the Soviet archives. In forging the 'Eremin letter' and the three other Okhrana 'documents', Svanidze on Stalin's order made several intentional and glaring mistakes in all of them. Stalin knew that these 'mistakes' would be noticed, thereby 'proving' that the documents were forgeries. Svanidze fabricated an almost exact copy of the genuine Colonel Eremin report. In appearance and content, the forged report differed only slightly from the genuine one, but the 'mistakes' were easily detectable. Typed on a doctored version of stationery of the Special Section of the Department of Police, with rubber stamps, incoming and outgoing numbers and notations, the forgery was addressed to the 'Chief of the Yeniseysk Okhrana Section, Captain Aleksey Fedorovich Zhelezniakov.' It read:

M.V.D   Absolutely secret
CHIEF OF THE   P e r s o n a l
SPECIAL SECTION OF THE
DEPARTMENT OF POLICE
    ★★★★★★★★★★★

   12 July 1913
   # 2893

                                        To Benevolent Sir
                                        Aleksey Fedorovich!

Iosif Dzhugashvili-Stalin, who had been exiled by administrative decree to the Turukhansk region, provided the chief of the Tiflis G.G.A. [Guberniya Gendarmerie Administration] with valuable intelligence information when he was arrested in 1906.

In 1908 the chief of the Baku Okhrana Section received from Stalin a series of intelligence reports, and afterward upon Stalin's arrival in Petersburg Stalin became an agent of the Petersburg Okhrana Section.

Stalin's work was distinguished by accuracy, but was fragmentary.

After Stalin's election to the Central Committee of the Party in Prague, Stalin, upon his return to Petersburg, went over into open opposition to the Government and completely broke off his connection with the Okhrana.

I am informing you, Benevolent Sir, of the above for your personal considerations in the conduct of operational work.

Please, accept my assurance of my highest esteem.

Eremin's forged signature on the letter resembled his genuine signature,
except for a long downward curving flourish at the end of it instead of the
legible letter 'n' in the real signature, which did not have this flourish.[34]

Eremin's genuine report was addressed to the director of the Department
of Police, Stepan Petrovich Beletsky, while the forgery was addressed to
Captain Aleksey Fedorovich Zhelezniakov. The captain's actual name was
not Aleksey, but Vladimir; this 'mistake' was easy to spot, since the names
of Okhrana officers were published annually and reference books indicated
where their names were to be found in many archives and libraries. There
was also a grammatical 'mistake' in the stationery letterhead, and the letter
had the outgoing number 2893, which was not even close to the numbers
used at this time. The actual report of Colonel Eremin had no number,
since he labeled it 'Absolutely secret: Personal' and addressed it to Director
Beletsky in connection with Beletsky's personal investigation of a provocation by the Okhrana agent Iosif Dzhugashvili. The names of Okhrana
agents, even their codenames, were never mentioned in internal Okhrana
correspondence, which passed through certain channels and was assigned
outgoing and incoming numbers. Stalin did not change the salutation
'Benevolent Sir' with which Colonel Eremin addressed Beletsky, a civilian
official and Eremin's immediate superior. If Eremin had indeed addressed
his report to Captain Zhelezniakov, he would have used the salutation
'Your Honor' and would have signed the report 'Colonel Eremin,' as he
did in correspondence with gendarmerie officers. (In correspondence with
civilian officials, he signed his name not 'Colonel Eremin', but simply 'A.
Eremin.'[35])

Stalin did not change the text of the genuine report of Colonel Eremin,
reproducing it in full for the fabricated 'Eremin Letter', except for his
pen name 'Stalin' that had been inserted in several places. In 1913 the
Okhrana did not know this pen name. It knew his aliases 'Vasily', 'Ivanov',
'Ivanovich', and his nickname 'Koba'. He had used the pen name 'Stalin'
only once in 1913. The 'Eremin letter' forgery contained these obvious
mistakes: the addressee's wrong first name, Eremin's crudely forged signature, the improbable use of the name Stalin and the outgoing and incoming
numbers. In addition to the 'Eremin letter', Stalin also fabricated a report
allegedly written by a former Yeniseysk Okhrana officer, V. N. Russianov,
who, after the Civil War, escaped to China and lived with his family in
Shanghai, working as a driver for a wealthy American family. Russianov's

forged 'report' was addressed to M. D. Golovachev, 'Chairman of the Council of Representatives of Organizations of Autonomous Siberia' and was written in longhand on stationery with the letterhead:

Former
CHIEF OF THE YENISEYSK OKHRANA
SECTION
March 13 1935
No. 51

The report purportedly informed Golovachev that Stalin had been an Okhrana agent, and ended with the words: 'I believe my material in your reliable hands could be used now in full measure. I am certain, that you will be able to make it a weapon in the struggle against the Third International.'[36] It was signed 'Major General Russian'. The final 'n' in this signature was followed by a long downward-curving flourish identical to the one in the signature on the forged 'Eremin Letter', which suggests that both forgeries were fabricated by the same hand at the 'Stalin Institute'. The 'Russianov Report' listed four attached 'Okhrana documents, including the 'Eremin Letter' and a fabricated letter from Russianov to A. T. Vasiliev (the director of the Department of Police), as well as two reports from an agent by the name of 'David', dated 10 October 1915 and 12 January 1916. These two 'reports' had supposedly been sent by 'Turukhansk Okhrana Section Officer Kibirov' to the 'Chief of the Yeniseysk Okhrana section'. The events described in these two 'agent reports' indeed took place, but not in Turukhansk and not on those dates. They took place in 1912 in Narym, where Stalin briefly served his term of exile and maintained friendly relations with an Okhrana officer by the name of Kibirov, for which he was reproved by the 'comradely court' of his fellow exiles. Kibirov could not have sent the 'agent reports' from Narym to the Yeniseysk Okhrana, since Narym had no administrative ties to Yeniseysk.[37] The 'Eremin Letter,' the 'Russianov Report', and the two 'Kibirov Reports' — all purposely infested with easily detectable 'mistakes' were fabricated on Stalin's order in order to be identified as forgeries. All showed the same pattern of crude fabrications: they told a story he could easily discredit by pointing to 'mistakes' in the obviously forged documents.[38]

In mid-July 1937 Stalin summoned Genrikh Liushkov, whom he had recently appointed deputy chief of the NKVD Secret Political Department, replacing Shtein at this post, and appointed him to the post of chief of the Far Eastern NKVD. Stalin gave Liushkov the four forged Okhrana documents, among them the 'Eremin Letter', and ordered him deliver these forgeries to M. D. Golovachev, a Soviet agent in China, and to arrange with him for their publication in the émigré newspaper.[39] Stalin selected Liushkov for this top-secret personal mission because Liushov enjoyed Stalin's trust. A former member of Odessa's criminal underworld, Liushov was known among NKVD officers for his extensive use of provocations. Stalin entrusted to him especially important missions. During the preparations for the Zinoviev–Kamenev trial, Liushkov headed a team of 'interrogators' who tortured the defendants. In late 1936 Stalin had assigned him the interrogation of his much-hated enemy Riutin, and in early 1937, had sent him to conduct a purge in Rostov. He was described by a fellow NKVD officer as an 'arrogant, arbitrary and sadistic bully'.[40]

Toward the end of July 1937 Liushkov arrived in Khabarovsk at the head of a detail of two officers and five soldiers and called NKVD headquarters from the railway station. He spoke to V. A. Balitsky, who in April 1937 had been appointed chief of the Far Eastern NKVD. Liushkov asked Balitsky to pick him up at the station. (Liushkov had known Balitsky for a long time; he had worked with him, Katsnelson and Shtein in the Kharkov GPU for many years.[41]) Balitsky drove to the station and was seized at gunpoint by Liushkov's detail; an express train then transported him to Moscow. Liushkov drove to the NKVD headquarters in Balitsky's car and announced that he was the new chief 'with personal orders from Stalin'. He had a list of army men whom Stalin had ordered arrested and shot, and he was under orders by Stalin to watch closely the commander of the Far Eastern military district, Marshal V. Bliukher, who had just returned from Moscow, where he had reluctantly put his signature on the verdict to execute Tukhachevsky and the other generals.[42]

In July 1937, Liushkov traveled to Shanghai under an assumed name and gave the Eremin Letter and other forgeries to M. D. Golovachev, a Russian émigré and NKVD informer. Golovachev agreed to publish the forgeries in a Russian-language émigré newspaper in China on receiving Liushkov's signal.[43] Golovachev was also instructed to insist that he had received these documents from the former Okhrana officer Russianov. He knew from the outset that the documents he received from Liushkov were forgeries. Golovachev was a devious, unscrupulous man, after whom the lawyer Komarovsky, Lara's seducer in Boris Pasternak's largely autobiographical novel *Doctor Zhivago*, was patterned. Before the Revolution Golovachev had been a lawyer; during the Civil War he was a Cheka informer in Petrograd. Lenin appointed him assistant foreign minister of the puppet 'Far Eastern Republic'. In Pasternak's novel, Komarovsky, also a Petrograd lawyer, is appointed by Lenin to that same post. Golovachev went to China after this 'republic' became defunct, as does Komarovsky in the novel. At this point, Komarovsky disappears from Pasternak's novel.

Among the Russian émigrés in China, Golovachev had the reputation of being a suspicious character, and was suspected of being a Soviet agent who was setting up various kinds of societies and 'institutes' as fronts for Soviet intelligence.[44] Fearing that Japanese intelligence might take an interest in his activities, Golovachev left Harbin for Shanghai when the Japanese occupied Manchuria in 1934. In Shanghai, he misrepresented himself as 'Professor Golovachev', to account for the various 'institutes' he had been setting up. He kept his contacts with North Chinese publications, that is, Russian-language newspapers in Japanese-occupied Manchuria. The cultural attaché of the French embassy in Shanghai provided him with the following letter of reference for obtaining an American entry visa: 'Mr Golovachev is a highly cultured man who has made good use of his intelligence and knowledge in Shanghai intellectual circles, always keeping above the mêlée of politics. Mr M. D. Golovachev has acquired the best of reputations in the Chinese and foreign circles of Shanghai.[45] The letter left the exact nature of Golovachev's 'good use' of his intelligence unspecified.

Liushkov instructed Golovachev to claim that he had obtained the Okhrana documents from the former Okhrana officer Colonel Viktor Nikolaevich Russianov, who had served at the Yeniseysk Okhrana post before the Revolution. The plan was for the Chinese police on the Soviet government's advice to search Russianov's home and come up with criminal evidence. To prove that Russianov had been involved in the fabrication of the 'Eremin Letter' and other forgeries, Stalin had Liushkov plant in Russianov's home a package containing Okhrana stationery, rubber stamps, and other paraphernalia, among them ten photographs, including some of Stalin, Trotsky and Malinovsky.[46]

Stalin deliberately chose Russianov as a victim of this provocation. He must have remembered him well from the time of his last exile: before the February Revolution, Russianov had had the rank of subaltern and been assistant to the chief of the Yeniseysk Okhrana, Captain Zhelezniakov. He was appointed chief shortly before the Revolution.[47] The day after the February Revolution, he was arrested by the Menshevik Boris Nikolaevsky, at the time a political exile in Yeniseysk, who was elected mayor of the town. Nikolaevsky found Russianov burning records in his Okhrana office and ordered that he be arrested and kept in prison.[48] A few months later Siberia fell into the hands of Admiral Kolchak, and Russianov was released from prison. He joined the White Army, rising to the rank of colonel. After the defeat of the Whites, Russianov escaped to China. By August 1937, when Russianov was working as a chauffeur in Shanghai, the Eremin Letter and other forgeries were in the hands of Golovachev, who was waiting for Liushkov's signal to publish them. The package with the Okhrana paraphernalia had already been planted in Russianov's home in Shanghai.

The other part of the provocation was the kidnapping of General Miller in Paris which had to be carried out before Stalin gave the signal to publish the Eremin Letter. In preparation for the kidnapping, the deputy chief of the NKVD Foreign Department, Mikhail Shpigelglas, had arrived in Paris in July 1937. He summoned the resident of Soviet military intelligence in Europe, General Walter Krivitsky, and told him he needed to borrow two agents from him who could impersonate 'German officers', explaining only that he was on an 'especially important mission', but did not reveal that he needed the agents for the kidnapping of General Miller.[49]

On 22 September 1937 General Miller told his assistant, General Kusonsky, that he had to attend a business meeting. Before he left, he gave Kusonsky a sealed envelope and said, 'Don't think that I've lost my mind, but if I don't come back from this meeting, then, please, open this envelope and read my note.' Around 1 pm, one of General Miller's friends saw him and General Skoblin near the Soviet villa on the Boulevard de Montmorency. Skoblin motioned Miller to go inside. Behind Miller appeared a tall, husky man. The next moment all three disappeared behind the gates of the villa.[50]

Miller's wife recalled the kidnapping of General Kutepov and called General Kusonsky, who sped to Miller's office and opened the envelope left by Miller. The note inside read: 'I have an appointment at 12:30 today with General Skoblin at the corner of rue Jasmine and rue Raffat. He is to take me to a rendezvous with a German officer, Colonel Strohmann, a military attaché in one of the Balkan countries, and someone named Verner, an official in the local German embassy. They both speak Russian well. This meeting has been arranged at the initiative of General Skoblin. It is possible that this is a trap – this is why I am leaving you this note.'[51] General Kusonsky recalled what Miller had said to him seven years earlier: 'If you go to an unknown or suspicious meeting it is always necessary to leave a note. And Kutepov should have done that.'[52]

Skoblin, summoned to Kusonsky's office, denied knowing anything about the disappearance even when confronted with Miller's note. He was told to go to police headquarters. He was the first to walk out of the office while Kusonsky and the others traded glances. 'His behavior is strange, isn't it?' Kusonsky whispered to the others as they were leaving. They returned to the office briefly to exchange ideas. When they walked out, Skoblin was nowhere to be found.

The French police soon established some important facts: the Soviet ambassador to France, Vladimir Potemkin, had bought a gray truck on 13 August 1937; on 22 September 1937, the day Miller disappeared, this truck pulled up to a pier in Le Havre where the Soviet merchant liner *Maria Ulianova* (named after Lenin's sister) was docked, and two men carried a large wooden box on board; a few minutes later, the *Maria Ulianova* was on her way to Leningrad. Prime Minister Eduard Daladier was informed of these facts and, to appease French public opinion, summoned Ambassador Potemkin and demanded the return of the *Maria Ulianova* to Le Havre, threatening to send a military ship to intercept her. But an hour later, he called Potemkin to apologize, saying that the *Maria Ulianova* could not have been involved in the abduction of General Miller. With the threat of war with Germany looming, Daladier wanted to avoid straining relations with Stalin. Despite Daladier's reluctance to antagonize Stalin, the investigation proceeded. In Skoblin's home the French police found secret codes, bogus passports, and other evidence proving that he and his wife Nadezhda Plevitskaya were Soviet agents. Plevitskaya was arrested and on 5 December 1938 was sentenced to 25 years in prison. She died in prison in 1944, during the German occupation.

When the German Army occupied Paris in 1940, Gestapo agents searched the offices of the Russian Army Veterans' organization. They found secret microphones, wires from which led to the apartment of the Russian émigré Tretiakov, who lived on the floor above. Arrested by the Gestapo, Tretiakov confessed that he had been a Soviet agent and had cooperated with General Skoblin. He said that on the day of General Miller's kidnapping, in which he did not take part, Skoblin, instead of going to police headquarters as he had been ordered to do, went upstairs and hid in Tretiakov's apartment. Tretiakov knew nothing of what happened to Skoblin after that. Skoblin fled to the Soviet Union, where his fate is unknown.

Ten days after Plevitskaya was sentenced, the French police arrested Lidia Grozovskaya, an NKVD agent working under cover at the Soviet embassy in Paris. These developments made it clear to Stalin that it was impossible to use General Miller as a defendant at a show trial: his appearance would confirm Soviet criminal kidnapping on French territory and might explode into an international scandal, and lead to a break in diplomatic relations with France. Stalin was forced drastically to curtail the show trial that he had planned from the time his Okhrana file had fallen into his hands in May 1937. On 15 December 1937 the lives of many of the prospective defendants were cut short by a mass execution. The names of some of them were later made public.[53] Others were executed secretly, Generals Miller and Skoblin probably among them.

The scandal over the kidnapping of General Miller forced Stalin to abandon his plan for a show trial and to use the 'Eremin Letter' and other forgeries as criminal evidence, but the story of these forgeries did not end there. Like a genie let out of a bottle, they acquired lives of their own.

NOTES

1. See Chapter 10 above.
2. This reconstruction of the events is supported directly and indirectly by several things:
   (a) Yury Kogan, the son of one of the executed top officers in Uborevich's circle of plotters stated in two taped interviews that, during the search of the apartment of an arrested officer in Minsk, a copy of a document incriminating Stalin and pointing to the existence of a plot was discovered. Yury Kogan learned of this from one of his father's friends, who survived the purge. The interviews took place in 1979 in Jerusalem with Michael Meerson-Aksenov, a Russian Orthodox priest, and in 1981 in Beer-Sheva (Israel) with Viktor Shwartzburg.
   (b) As was revealed by Alexander Orlov, a number of photocopies of documents from Stalin's Okhrana file had been made by the plotters. The photocopy most likely to have been found during the search of the arrested officer's apartment was that of Eremin's report. That report was a one-page document concisely describing Stalin's Okhrana career. It hence lent itself perfectly to photocopying and distribution among the plotters. The fact that Stalin fabricated an almost exact copy of Eremin's report in order to discredit it (as this chapter shows) indicates that his motive was to discredit other copies of Eremin's report in case one or more of them survived his dragnet.
   (c) The fact that Pauker was secretly executed shortly after the copy of Eremin's report was found in the arrested officer's apartment suggests that it was Pauker who brought the copy to Stalin. Besides, as the chief of the Operations Department, Pauker was in charge of all arrests and searches. If there was anything to report to Stalin in the domain of Pauker's responsibilities, it was he who would personally bring it to Stalin's attention.
3. Walter G. Krivitsky, *In Stalin's Secret Service*, New York, 1939, pp. 229–31.
4. *Bukharin Trial*, New York, 1965, p. 582.
5. See Chapter 19 above.
6. Krivitsky, *In Stalin's Secret Service*, pp. 229–31.
7. P. I. Yakir and Ya. I. Geller, *Komandarm Yakir*, Moscow, 1963, p. 212.
8. N. I. Koritsky, *Marshal Tukhachevsky*, Moscow, 1965, pp. 128–34. Also I. Rachkov, 'Iz vospominaniy o Y. B. Gamarnike', *Voenno-istorichesky zhurnal*, no. 5, 1965, pp. 67–70.
9. Boris Viktorov, 'Zagovor krasnoi armii', *Pravda*, 29 April 1988.
10. Ibid.
11. I. Rachkov, 'Iz vospominaniy o Y. B. Gamarnike', p. 69.
12. Lev Nikulin, *Marshal Tukhachevsky*, Moscow, 1961, pp. 189–94.
13. Viktorov, 'Zagovor krasnoi armii'.
14. P. Yakir heard of Tukhachevsky's being interrogated by Stalin in the camps. The author heard of it in the Norilsk camp from an inmate, the former NKVD officer A. Y. Tsynman.
15. Unpublished memoirs of Olga Shatunovskaya, an Old Bolshevik and a member of a Party committee that investigated Stalin's crimes during the Khrushchev era. Shatunovskaya's recollections were related by Vasily Rudich in a taped interview with me. In my archive. Also, Rachkov, 'Iz vospominaniy o Y. B. Gamarnike', pp. 69–72, and Vitaly Rapoport and Yury Alekseev, *Izmena rodine*, London, 1988, p. 300.
16. Rachkov, 'Iz vospominaniy o Y. B. Gamarnike', pp. 69f.

17. *Pravda*, 1 June 1937, p. 4.
18. Rachkov, 'Iz vospominanii o Y. B. Gamarnike', p. 70.
19. Krivitsky, *In Stalin's Secret Service*, p. 232.
20. L. Gaglov and I. Selishchev, *Komissary*, Moscow, 1961.
21. Alexander Orlov, *The Secret History of Stalin's Crimes*, New York, 1953, pp. 238f. In his 1953 book, Orlov refers to Zhukov as 'General N', but in his 23 April 1956, *Life* article, 'The Sensational Secret Behind Damnation of Stalin', Orlov on p. 44 refers to Zhukov's photo, taken in Spain at the time of Orlov's service there, and writes: 'I knew General Zhukov when he came to Spain as an observer during the civil war. I talked to him a number of times and I carried away the impression that Zhukov was no courtier and no stooge of Stalin. The 1937 blot on the honor of the Red Army must have bothered his military conscience ever since.'
22. Viktorov, 'Zagovor krasnoi armii'.
23. *Krasnaya zvezda*, 6 June 1937.
24. Viktorov, 'Zagovor krasnoi armii'.
25. Ibid.
26. Ibid.
27. The award citation, dated 11 June 1937 and signed by Zinovy Katsnelson, is among the papers of the author's father Ya. I. Brakhtman, a former prisoner in the Dmitrov camp, who received the award on this day.
28. Genady Zhavoronkov, 'I edinozhdy ne solgavshiy', *Moskovskie novosti*, 10 April 1988. Also Iosif Kosinsky, 'Za chto borolis?', *Novoe Russkoe slovo*, 22 April 1988.
29. See Chapter 10 above for Colonel Eremin's cover letter, dated 11 June 1912 with attached *Spravka bez no. 5/18*, p. 7.
30. Orlov, *Tainaya istoria*, p. 262.
31. Yulia Piatnitskaya, *Dnevnik zheny bolshevika*, New York, 1987, p. 172. Also Zhavoronkov, 'I edinozhdy ne solgavshiy', and Kosinsky, 'Za chto borolis?'
32. The discovery of Stalin's Okhrana file in Menzhinsky's old office was to appear in a somewhat distorted form in the 'confessions' at the Bukharin show trial in March 1938 (see Chapter 29 below). Indications are that Stalin learned where the file was found from the arrested officers and he must have learned it sometime before July 1937, since he ordered the arrest of Katsnelson and Balitsky that month.
33. V. Lulechnik, 'Zagovor protiv Stalina i delo Tukhachevskogo', *Panorama*, no. 735, 10–16 May 1995, p. 20. Lulechnik states that E. G. Plimak 'firmly established the fact of I. L. Shtein's suicide after meeting distant relatives of Shtein's'. See also Evgeny Plimak and Vadim Antonov, 'Stalin znal, chto delal', *Novoe Russkoe Slovo*, 22 March 1996, p. 50.
34. The 'Eremin Letter' forgery was first published by Isaac Don Levine in his article, 'A Document on Stalin as Czarist Spy', in *Life* magazine on 23 April 1956, p. 47. See also John J. Dziak, *Chekisty*, Lexington, 1988, pp. 9–10.
35. Eremin's signature 'A. Eremin' appears on his letters addressed to civilian officials of the Department of Police. See, for instance, his letter no. 125483, dated 13 May 1910, to the chief of the Okhrana Foreign Agency, A. A. Krasilnikov. Eremin starts his letter with the salutation '*Milostivy Gosudar*' ('Benevolent Sir'), the same way he started his letter to Beletsky, and he does not mention his military rank.
36. Columbia University, New York, Library of Rare Manuscripts, Bakhmetiev Archive, M. P. Golovachev's Collection. See also reprints of Stalin's 'Okhrana documents' in the newspaper *Evreisky mir*, New York, 30 October (no. 23), 6 November (no. 24) and 13 November (no. 25), 1992.
37. N. Karganov, 'Iz proshlogo Stalina', *Vozrozhdenie*, 13 January 1929. See also Chapter 10 above.
38. Columbia University, New York, Library of Rare Manuscripts, Bakhmetiev Archive, M. P. Golovachev's Collection. See also reprints of Stalin's 'Okhrana Documents' in the newspaper *Evreisky mir*, New York, 30 October (no. 23), 6 November (no. 24), and 13 November (no. 25), 1992.
39. Alvin D. Coox, 'L'Affaire Liushkov', *Soviet Studies*, January, 1968, p. 62.
40. Roy Medvedev, *Let History Judge*, New York, 1971, pp. 244f.
41. Taped interview with R. S. Osinina, widow of Liushkov's assistant Osinin.
42. Coox, 'L'Affair Liushkov', p. 408.
43. Golovachev never revealed that he received the forgeries from Liushkov. He maintained that he had obtained them from the former Okhrana officer Russianov. His claim was an obvious lie for

several reasons: Russianov would not have made mistakes that clumsy in fabricating the forgeries. He would obviously be expected to know the first name and patronymic of Captain Zhelezniakov, a man under whose command he had worked for several years in Yeniseysk. Also, Stalin would never have assigned the planting of the forgeries to anyone he did not know personally and trust. Liushkov, who specialized in provocations and had carried out personal assignments for Stalin in the past, was the ideal choice – just as Golovachev was the ideal choice for Liushkov as a Soviet agent who could get the forgeries published in China.

44. Taped interview with General T. V. Gerbov, a Russian émigré in Harbin who knew Golovachev personally, Nayak, NY, in 1975. The tape is in the author's archive.

45. The letter, signed by Grosbois and dated 8 June 1948 is in I. D. Levine's archive. Copy in the present author's archive.

46. Russianov's son, who had emigrated to Australia, sent this package of Okhrana material to I. D. Levine. It was examined by the author in Levine's archive at his Virginia farm.

47. N. M. Ulanovskaya spoke in a taped interview about her husband, Soviet intelligence officer A. Ulanovsky, who met Stalin during his exile in Yeniseysk. She recalled that Stalin was known among the exiles for visiting the Okhrana office there.

48. H. Montgomery Hyde, *Stalin: the History of a Dictator*, New York, 1971, p. 613.

49. Krivitsky, *In Stalin's Secret Service*, pp. 216–18.

50. Lev Rudminsky, who was imprisoned in the Norilsk Gulag, had taken part in General Kutepov's and General Miller's kidnapping. He recalled that the fabrication of documents to defame Soviet leaders was the reason the generals were kidnapped. The timing of both kidnappings supports this claim: Kutepov's took place shortly after Blumkin's attempt to smuggle Stalin's file abroad, Miller's shortly after Stalin recovered his Okhrana file.

51. S. Rozhdestvensky, 'Pokhishchenie generala Millera', *Novoe russkoe slovo*, 19 May 1979.

52. Ibid.

53. *Bukharin Trial*.

29

THE STAGED 'TRIFLE'

Stalin considerably reduced the scope of his next planned show trial because of the scandal over the kidnapping of General Miller. He decided that at the trial no mention of the general and of the fabrication of Okhrana documents should be made. The trial was scheduled for the beginning of March 1938. But before it opened several important events took place.

In July 1937 Ignaz Reiss, the NKVD resident in Switzerland, had written a letter to the Central Committee, declaring his opposition to 'Stalin's counter-revolution' and calling for a 'return to Lenin, his teachings and his cause'.[1] Stalin was convinced that Reiss had learned about the discovery of his Okhrana file and was the source of the information about it that had reached Trotsky's son Lev Sedov. Stalin ordered the murders of Reiss, Lev Sedov, and two of Trotsky's aides, Erwin Wolf and Rudolf Klement, who had also learned about the file from Reiss.[2] In the early morning of 4 September 1937 the Swiss police found the body of Ignaz Reiss, the NKVD resident in Switzerland. Reiss's body was riddled with bullets. The murder of Reiss was carried out by a mobile group of killers under the command of Mikhail Shpigelglas, the deputy chief of the NKVD Foreign Department. Mark Zborovsky, an NKVD agent who had gained Lev Sedov's trust, learned where in Switzerland Reiss and his wife and daughter were staying. Shpigelglas ordered NKVD agent Gertrude Shildbach, a close friend of the Reiss family, to invite Reiss into her car, where the killers would be waiting for him. After Reiss's body was found, the police also found the car, which turned out to have been rented by Renate Steiner, another NKVD agent. Steiner was arrested, and she named the assassins and told the authorities at which hotel they were staying. By the time the police got there, the killers had left. In their rooms, the police found luggage containing a box of poisoned chocolates, Stalin's 'present', which Gertrude Shildbach for some reason had failed to give to Reiss's wife and daughter. The investigation of Reiss's murder threatened to expose a large network of Soviet agents in Europe and lead the police to the center of this network in the Soviet embassy in Paris. (Like the Okhrana's Foreign Agency before it, the main branch of the NKVD's Foreign Department was located in Paris.)

Soon after the murder of Reiss, the resident of Soviet military intelligence in Europe, Walter Krivitsky, defected to the West, fearing that
the same fate awaited him. His fear was well founded: he had refused
Shpigelglas's request to track down and murder his close friend Ignaz Reiss.
This refusal put Krivitsky high on the list of people to be eliminated. On 6
October 1937 he petitioned the French government for political asylum
and asked for protection from NKVD assassins. Shpigelglas was ordered to
murder Krivitsky, but the French police assigned heavily armed bodyguards
to protect him. Shpigelglas failed to carry out the mission. (In 1941
Krivitsky was shot dead in his room in a Washington hotel.[3])

In October 1937 Shpigelglas arrived in Spain to carry out several assassinations ordered by Stalin.[4] He had a meeting with Alexander Orlov, the
Soviet adviser on intelligence matters to the Spanish Republican government. During a long car ride Shpigelglas shared with Orlov his apprehension
about the mass arrests and executions, mentioning incidents when prominent Soviet officials 'disappeared together with their cars and personal
drivers'.[5] He mentioned several cases of suicide among NKVD and government officials, for which he could find no explanation. Orlov had earlier
learned from his cousin Zinovy Katsnelson of the discovery of Stalin's
Okhrana file, but decided not to reveal this information to anyone.
Shpigelglas asked Orlov to help him secure a transfer to Spain as Orlov's
assistant. Orlov realized that Shpigelglas feared for his life and hoped to find
shelter in Spain until the wave of arrests and shootings was over. He
thought that Shpigelglas wanted to bring his wife and daughter to Spain
and become a defector like Krivitsky.[6]

Meanwhile, events continued to unfold. By October 1937 most of the
Soviet agents in Europe had been recalled to Moscow and executed.
Despite their apprehensions, most of them returned to save the lives of
their wives, children and relatives whom they had left in the Soviet Union.
According to a 8 June 1934 decree, all the relatives of military personnel
who escaped abroad or refused to return to Russia were to be exiled for
ten years to Siberia, even if they had no prior knowledge of such 'betrayal
of the motherland'. By a secret addition to this law, all relatives of NKVD
'traitors' were to be executed if the traitor revealed 'state secrets'. Few
agents could bring themselves to face such consequences. Krivitsky's defection was followed by that of his two agents, 'Paul' and 'Bruno', who had
impersonated German officers in the kidnapping of General Miller and in
the earlier provocation in Prague in forging 'Tukhachevsky's dossier'.[7] Dr
Max Eitingon, the NKVD resident in Vienna, also defected. He was the
'handler' of the NKVD agents General Skoblin and his wife Nadezhda

Plevitskaya. She testified in a French court that Eitingon was her 'angel-protector' and for years had given her money and also paid for expensive dresses and jewelry.[8] Plevitskaya also mentioned that Eitingon had visited her and Skoblin in Paris after the kidnapping of General Miller to say good-bye before going to Jerusalem to settle there and open a psychiatric clinic. (He died, and possibly was assassinated, in Jerusalem in 1944.[9])

Among the recalled Soviet agents who complied with the order to return to the USSR was Sergey Efron, a literary critic and husband of the great Russian poet Marina Tsvetaeva (who did not know of her husband's connections with to the NKVD). After leaving Paris, he for a while corresponded with Tsvetaeva; then letters from him stopped. Their daughter went to Moscow to find out what had happened to her father and was arrested. (In 1939, Tsvetaeva, too, went to Moscow to find out what had happened to her daughter and husband. She was exiled to the remote Siberian village of Elabug, where she hanged herself on 31 August 1941. Efron was shot in prison in October 1941. Their daughter spent the next 16 years in the Gulag, emerging after Stalin's death an emotional and physical cripple.[10])

After the murder of Reiss, three people whom he had told about the discovery of Stalin's Okhrana file, were also murdered. On 16 February 1937 Trotsky's son Lev Sedov was murdered: Mark Zborovsky, an NKVD agent, brought Sedov to the hospital for an appendectomy and tipped off NKVD killers who murdered Sedov in his hospital bed. Zborovsky also guided the killers to Trotsky's secretaries Erwin Wolf and Rudolf Klement. Wolf was murdered in Spain. The decapitated body of Klement was found floating in the Seine. (Zborovsky settled in the United States after the occupation of France by the Germans and was arrested as a Soviet agent. He helped the FBI expose a large Soviet espionage network and struck a deal with the prosecution, pleading guilty to a perjury charge in exchange for a short prison term. After serving his sentence, he worked in various hospitals and universities.[11])

On 16 February 1937, the same day that Lev Sedov was murdered in Paris, Abram Slutsky, the chief of the NKVD Foreign Department, was poisoned. Yezhov's deputy, Frinovsky, invited Slutsky to his Lubianka office for a 'business discussion' and treated him to tea and cookies. Slutsky died instantly. Half an hour later, Frinovsky phoned Slutsky's deputy, Shpigelglas, and asked him to come over. Shpigelglas saw Slutsky's body slumped in an armchair. Frinovsky told him that the doctor had just left and that 'medicine can't help in this case'. He added that Slutsky had died of a heart attack. Slutsky's body lay in state in the NKVD club with a guard of honor, and his colleagues paid their respects. NKVD officers knew the rudiments of forensic medicine and noticed characteristic spots pointing to poisoning by hydrocyanic acid. *Pravda* published an obituary signed by a 'group of friends'. Stalin was destroying all people who, like Slutsky, knew too much. Slutsky had been in the habit of bragging to his friends of his closeness to Stalin and had mentioned to them some 'strange' behavior of Stalin. For example, he told some NKVD officers how Stalin insisted on attributing to Piatakov an obviously fictitious trip to Oslo. At the time he was murdered, Slutsky was taking an active part in preparations for the show trial scheduled to begin early in March 1938. He was assigned to interrogate Yagoda, one of the chief defendants, and related to friends Stalin's odd claims that Yagoda and other defendants had been Okhrana agents. Slutsky's talk was reaching Stalin.

Mass arrests and murders made foreign diplomats in Moscow wonder and whisper about the 'sick man in the Kremlin', surmising that Stalin's purges could only be the work of someone in the throes of persecution mania. But, as Alexander Orlov wrote, 'this was not the case. The almighty dictator was not a lunatic. When all the facts connected with the case of Tukhachevsky become known, the world will understand: Stalin knew what he was doing.'[12]

The role of the chief villain at the forthcoming show trial Stalin assigned to Nikolay Bukharin; the trial became known in history as the 'Bukharin Trial'. During the Kamenev–Zinoviev show trial, Bukharin's name was mentioned by some defendants. Speakers at public meetings demanded that Bukharin be 'put in the dock'. Bukharin was invited to Kaganovich's office, where a confrontation with his arrested friend Grigory Sokolnikov was arranged. Sokolnikov said that he and Bukharin belonged to an 'anti-Soviet organization'.[13] (Sokolnikov had struck a deal with Stalin, agreeing to incriminate himself and implicate Bukharin and others in exchange for Stalin's promise to spare his life and not persecute his family.[14])

Bukharin was summoned to the Central Committee Plenum and Yezhov, in Stalin's presence, accused him of treason, terrorist activities and involvement in the murder of Kirov. Stalin very calmly said that there was no need to hurry with Bukharin's arrest. Bukharin spent the next three months in his Kremlin apartment, which had formerly belonged to Stalin. His study was in the room where Nadezhda Allilueva had committed suicide. Bukharin felt guilty for causing harm to his second wife Anna, some 25 years his junior. A few months earlier, she had given birth to their first son. Once Anna saw Bukharin with a revolver in his hand, but he assured her that he would not commit suicide. He wrote Stalin several letters, addressing him as 'Dear Koba!' There was no reply. Early in February 1937 he wrote to the Central Committee: 'In protest against unheard of accusations. I declare a hunger strike to the death . . . '. A day later, three NKVD officers arrived with the order to evict him from his Kremlin apartment. Upon their arrival, the telephone rang. 'How are you doing, Nikolay?' Stalin asked. 'Here, they've come to evict me from the Kremlin', said Bukharin. 'And you send them to the devil's mother', said Stalin, and ordered that the eviction be stopped. Bukharin's former wife wrote Stalin a letter stating that she did not want to be a party member at a time when Bukharin, a true revolutionary, was falsely accused of monstrous crimes. She was arrested and executed.[15]

On 27 February 1937 Bukharin was summoned before the party plenum and arrested. Until 19 May 1937, when the mass arrests and executions started, the interrogation of Bukharin proceeded in the usual way: he was pressured to 'confess' his role in the assassination of Kirov and other 'anti-Soviet activities'. But on 19 May 1937 Stalin's attention was diverted to the discovery of his Okhrana file, and the case of Bukharin was put on ice for seven months. Then, on 15 December 1937, Stalin, having changed his mind, had a large number of the defendants summarily executed. (Among those who were executed was Stalin's old friend Enukidze, who was initially charged with being the mastermind behind anti-Soviet conspiracy.) At this point Bukharin became the leading villain at the revised show trial.

The 'Bukharin Trial' opened on 2 March 1938 in the October Hall of the Moscow House of Unions. The defendants, as usual, admitted their guilt and described crimes they had never committed. Stalin's old friend Enukidze, who had been executed on 15 December 1937, was presented as the past mastermind of a gigantic conspiracy. On 3 March 1938, the day after the trial began, Isaac Don Levine, an American journalist and writer, published an article in *Journal American* under the headline, 'Stalin Suspected of Forcing Trials to Cover His Past'. Levine wrote:

Is Stalin a former agent of the Czar's Okhrana trying to wipe out in blood the preserved traces of his past career in the secret service of the Romanoffs?

As the author of the first biography of Stalin, the writer has long been familiar with reports that some of the old Bolsheviks had in their possession a secret file from the archives of the Okhrana proving that Stalin was a super spy for the Czar when he joined forces with Lenin . . .

So incredible did this charge appear, in spite of the fact that there are suspicious circumstances in Stalin's career, that one did not dare to make it public without further substantiation . . .

Levine found this charge analogous to Benedict Arnold testifying 'that Alexander Hamilton had plotted the assassination of George Washington'.[16]

Levine's article was widely dismissed as sensationalist, but he had known for many years about the rumours of Stalin's links with the Okhrana. As early as 1926 he had received information about the discovery of Stalin's Okhrana file in the old archives.[17] Although he kept receiving bits and pieces of similar information, he long refrained from making any of it public without further substantiation. He had received the latest information about the discovery of Stalin's Okhrana file from Lev Sedov's assistants Erwin Wolf and Rudolf Klement, who had received it from Reiss. The murder of all four finally convinced Levine that the reports of the file's discovery were true and that the murders were the result of Stalin's drive to seal the lips of everyone who knew anything about the file.[18] Levine did not know at the time he published his article that Stalin had acted on the tip of the NKVD agent Mark Sborovsky, codename 'Etienne', who had penetrated the Sedov–Trotskyite group in Paris.

It was inevitable that Stalin would bring up the accusations of ties with the Okhrana at least against some defendants, and several alleged 'Okhrana agents' were scripted to confess their crimes. In the final script, the Okhrana charge against Bukharin was dropped, but instead he was pressed to admit that, having suspected Lenin of being a German spy, he had intended to kill him in 1917. 'Stalin wants to put the dead Lenin in the dock as well!' Bukharin exclaimed when his interrogator made these charges.[19] Stalin equated charges of collaboration with the Okhrana with the old claim that Lenin had been a German agent. In August 1917 he put these two charges on an equal footing in an article castigating the Provisional Government: 'First they tried to smear tested revolutionary fighters as German spies, and, that having failed, they want to make them out to be Tsarist spies.'[20] Bukharin categorically refused to sign testimony having anything to do with his alleged suspicion of Lenin having been a German spy, even after Stalin promised to spare his life. Stalin then ordered that Karl Radek be brought from the camp to the Lubianka prison, in order to show that he kept his word when he promised to spare someone's life. But Radek failed to extract from Bukharin testimony about his intention to murder Lenin. Bukharin's only concession was his agreement to testify that he had intended to arrest Lenin for a single day.[21]

The mysterious 'Rykov secret file' suddenly made its appearance in the proceedings of the Bukharin Trial. Yagoda's assistant P. Bulanov was testifying: 'I shall proceed directly to the specific crimes in which I personally

took part. I know from what Yagoda told me that the decision to assassinate Nikolay Ivanovich Yezhov . . .'. Vyshinsky abruptly interrupted,
'Did you know where Rykov's secret file was kept?' Bulanov immediately
replied, 'Yagoda had it.' Vyshinsky persisted, 'The conspiratorial file?'
Bulanov readily replied, 'If it was not conspiratorial, Rykov would hardly
have sought such a reliable place for it. I now pass to the attempt on the
life of Nikolay Ivanovich Yezhov. According to Yagoda . . .'. This time
Vyshinsky did not interrupt Bulanov and allowed him to proceed with his
fantastic story about vast conspiracies, poisonings and murders, which
Bulanov said had been directed by 'Enukidze, who acted on behalf of
Trotsky'. But his fellow defendant Rykov did not let the issue of the file
pass unchallenged. He interjected, 'Bulanov spoke here about my archives,
which were found in Yagoda's possession. I should like him to tell us about
what was found, where those archives came from, what their contents are,
and how he knows about them.' Vyshinsky called on Bulanov, who gave
a strange answer:

If I knew exactly what they contained and the dimensions of the archives, I
would most certainly answer my fellow-accused. Unfortunately, I have no
such information at my disposal. I spoke about those archives on the basis of
the following: when Yagoda was moving to different premises during the
renovation of the building, I do not remember under what circumstances it
happened, but, at any rate, I found a file of documents among some of the
things which had been lying for a long time in the safe. I asked Yagoda about
it. He said: 'Don't unpack them, these are Rykov's archives.' It seemed to me
that was sufficient grounds for me to make that statement.

At this point, Ulrikh cut short the enquiry into 'Rykov's secret archives'
and announced, 'Adjournment for 30 minutes.'
    During the next session, Yagoda described the poisoning of Menzhinsky,
Kuibyshev, Gorky and Gorky's son Peshkov, as well as the murder of
Kirov. He said that he had committed these crimes following the orders of
Enukidze. Yagoda did not mention Rykov's secret file, but Rykov used
the first opportunity to say, 'I have a question to ask Yagoda regarding the
archives about which Bulanov spoke.' Yagoda replied: 'I had no archives
of Rykov's.' Vyshinsky pursued the issue, 'I have a question to Bulanov',
he said. 'What archives of Rykov's did you say were in Yagoda's keeping?'
Bulanov's interrogators had not prepared him for such insistent questioning. Not knowing what to say, he displayed confusion and annoyance:

I spoke of that in my testimony to the court. I will repeat. While participating
in a change of premises, I discovered a number of documents of a personal

character. I don't remember what they were. It was clear that they were personal documents of Alexey Ivanovich Rykov. I asked Yagoda, who confirmed my opinion, but as to what was there, and how much of it, I have said and say now that I do not know.

This time Yagoda became curious about Rykov's file. He turned to Bulanov and said, 'Allow me to raise a question. Perhaps you will recall one document, at least, and will say what it was?' Bulanov's curt answer was, 'Had I remembered, I would already have said it.' Yagoda persisted, thinking aloud: 'Rather strange. He establishes that this was Rykov's archive, but by what documents? Just by name, or what?' Turning angrily to Yagoda, Bulanov said:

In reply to that, I can only say one thing: that Yagoda at one time did not doubt for a single second my ability to find my bearings and apprise things very rapidly under any circumstances. I don't know why he now denies a thing that is unquestionably clear to me: I said what I knew and considered it necessary to say so.

Yagoda had the final word on 'Rykov's secret archives': 'In any case, had the archives really existed, in comparison with the other crimes, the Rykov archives are a trifle.'[22] He did not know that this 'trifle' was the essence of Stalin's show. In Stalin's original script, which Stalin had considerably altered, Rykov was accused of having been an Okhrana agent while Bulanov was to state that Rykov's Okhrana file had been found in Menzhinsky's office 'during a change of premises'. Fragments of this original version survived and appeared at the Bukharin Trial. 'Rykov's secret file' was but one such fragment.

Several alleged 'Okhrana agents' testified that they had been Okhrana agents before the Revolution. Familiar details of Stalin's Okhrana career emerged in their testimony. The first 'exposed Okhrana agent' to testify on 3 March 1938 was V. I. Ivanov, People's Commissar of the Timber Industry. He declared: 'My first downfall dates back to 1911, when I was a student at the Tula gymnasium in the eighth grade. The tsarist Okhrana managed to recruit me as one of its agents.' Ivanov also stated, 'I was expelled from the university; a large number of students were expelled at that time.' Ivanov did not know that he was describing the expulsion of Tiflis seminarians that Stalin had provoked some four decades earlier. Ivanov further stated, 'In Moscow, the Okhrana department again got hold of me.'[23] Vyshinsky was satisfied by Ivanov's testimony and asked him few questions.

During the session on 5 March 1938, I. A. Zelensky, another 'exposed

Okhrana agent', who before his arrest was director of cooperative organizations, described his Okhrana career, beginning his testimony with the statement: 'First of all I must dwell on my gravest crime – my work in the tsarist Okhrana.' At one point in his lengthy testimony Zelensky said, 'It goes without saying that I used to meet at a secret rendezvous an officer of the gendarmerie. I did not know his name; he was called Vasily Konstantinovich.' Zelensky further testified that after his arrest by the Okhrana, he wrote a petition, 'requesting to be summoned for examination because I wanted to know the reason for my arrest'. He was summoned by 'Vasily Konstantinovich', who explained to him that it was 'better for you that we arrested you'. Zelensky probably did not suspect that he was describing not his but Stalin's relations with Okhrana gendarmerie Lieutenant Colonel I. P. Vasiliev. 'I remained in prison for six months, after which I was exiled to the Narym territory', stated Zelensky. 'Before starting out, I was visited in prison by the same officer of the gendarmerie with whom I had meetings at the secret rendezvous, and he demanded that I reported from my place of exile.' Zelensky testified that from Narym he had sent two letters to this officer, but addressed to 'Averbukh's print shop'. He added, 'I was told by my investigator, that later, on the basis of this testimony, Averbukh, when examined, fully confirmed what I had said.' (L. Averbukh, the husband of Yagoda's sister, by that time was in no position to confirm anything. He had been executed on 15 December 1937, when Stalin had modified the original scenario of the trial and ordered the shooting of a large number of defendants. Averbukh was one of the 'exposed Okhrana agents' who in the original scenario had been appointed to mouth fragments of Stalin's Okhrana past.)

Zelensky described recognizable events in Stalin's career in 1912, when Stalin began his cooperation with Lieutenant-Colonel I.P. Vasiliev. Zelensky also mentioned a '*provocateur* Polonko', stating: 'I must say that aside from being in direct contact with the gendarmerie officer, the Okhrana put me in touch with another agent – the *provocateur* Polonko, who delivered part of the information which I supplied . . . he was the liaison man.' Hiding behind '*provocateur* Polonko' was Stalin's rival in the Okhrana, Roman Malinovsky, a Pole, who was spitefully demoted by Stalin to the role of liaison man in this reinterpretation of the past. Zelensky further stated that he had broken off his relations with the Okhrana in 1912. Colonel Eremin in his report to Director Beletsky wrote that Stalin broke off contact with the Okhrana after the Prague conference in 1912.

Stalin's aliases 'Vasily' and 'Vasiliev' came up in the testimony of yet another 'exposed Okhrana agent', P. T. Zubarev, an official in the

Agriculture Commissariat. 'Tell us under what circumstances you became an agent of the tsarist Okhrana', asked Vyshinsky. Zubarev corrected him, 'Not the Okhrana, but the tsarist police.' Vyshinsky then asked, 'Is there any difference?' Zubarev replied, 'There is a slight difference, but in substance they are the same.' Vyshinsky agreed, 'I think so too.' (Stalin's rivalry with Malinovsky made this difference important: after his election to the Duma Malinovsky's status changed from an agent of the Moscow Okhrana to the top secret agent of the Department of Police; he reported exclusively to its Director and Vice Director.)

Zubarev described how he had been recruited by a police officer 'Vasiliev', who told him, 'If you, Zubarev, want to escape punishment, the only way you can do so is to accept my proposal that you become an agent of the police.' Zubarev said that he had agreed to Vasiliev's proposal and provided him with information on the revolutionary underground and 'on the character of some of its most active leaders'. Zubarev said that when he moved to another town, he resumed his work as an agent under the code-name 'Paren'. Vyshinsky then asked, 'This was your second pseudonym?' Zubarev replied, 'Yes, Vasily was my first one.' Then Vyshinsky asked, 'Did you have another pseudonym?' Zubarev said that in the city of Ufa he had had the pseudonym 'Prokhor'. Vyshinsky asked when he had acquired this pseudonym. 'At the beginning of 1916', Zubarev answered.[24] Asked by Vyshinsky on another occasion whether he received any remuneration for this work, Zubarev replied: 'On two occasions Inspector Vasiliev gave me 30 rubles.' 'Thirty pieces of silver on each occasion?' Vyshinsky asked. 'Yes', replied Zubarev. 'Twice as much as Judas received!' Vyshinsky exclaimed; Zubarev agreed.

At this point, Ulrikh intervened and said to Zubarev, 'Tell us about your espionage activities.' Zubarev began to elaborate on his supposed spying 'for the benefit of fascist Germany'. But he was interrupted by Vyshinsky, who wanted to return to the more pressing matter of Zubarev's recruitment by officer 'Vasiliev' in 1908. 'I request that inspector Vasiliev, who enlisted Zubarev, be called as a witness in order to verify this circumstance', said Vyshinsky. An elderly man was led into the courtroom. He said that his name was Dmitry Nikolaevich Vasiliev, that he was born in 1870, and that he had served as police inspector from 1906 to 1917. His appearance was greeted with a stir of approving whispers and laughter from the audience that even extracted the semblance of a good-natured smile from Vyshinsky's otherwise stern face. This time, Ulrikh led the questioning. He asked Vasiliev: 'In particular, did you enlist Zubarev?' to which Vasiliev readily replied, 'Zubarev . . . yes.' Ulrikh then said, 'Tell us in a few words how you did this.' Vasiliev told how he had recruited Zubarev some 30 years earlier and got a signed pledge from him. 'What was the nature of the pledge?', asked Ulrikh. 'To the effect that he undertook to supply the police with information. In making the pledge, he said that his pseudonym would be "Vasily"', replied Vasiliev. 'Did he say that?', asked Ulrikh, and Vasiliev readily replied, 'Yes, he said it. I remember it very well.' Vyshinsky interjected, 'How is it that you remember him so well? Much time has elapsed since then, and yet you remember this Zubarev so well.' To which Vasiliev replied, 'I have not set eyes on him since 1909.' Turning to Ulrikh, Vyshinsky asked, 'May I question Zubarev?' Given permission, he asked Zubarev, 'Do you remember? Is this man the Vasiliev who was the inspector at that time?' Zubarev was uncertain what he was supposed to say. 'Thirty years have elapsed since then and it's hard for me to remember', he said, hesitating for a moment, 'but I think that is the man . . . I don't deny it.' Vyshinsky probed further. 'Does he resemble him?,' he asked. 'Yes', said Zubarev. 'He was younger then', Vyshinsky encouraged him. 'Of course', Zubarev agreed. Vyshinsky then asked, 'Did you yourself choose the pseudonym "Vasily"?' Zubarev replied, 'I don't remember whether I adopted it myself, or whether he proposed it; I don't remember, and I wouldn't deny that he gave it to me, or that I chose it myself, but the fact occurred.'[25] Despite the fact that Zubarev claimed to have used the aliases 'Paren' and 'Prokhor' during the later and more important part of his alleged service for the tsarist police, only the alias 'Vasily' inspired Vyshinsky's keen interest. The source of this 'interest' was Stalin himself, who had instructed Vyshinsky to call 'Inspector Vasily' as a witness in order to 'establish' the origin of this alias which was mentioned in the documents in his Okhrana file.

On 12 March 1938 the Bukharin show trial ended. In their final pleas the defendants demanded severe punishment for their heinous crimes. Stalin had allowed Bukharin to modify his testimony and deny that he had intended to murder Lenin and taken part in the murders of Kirov, Menzhinsky, Kuibyshev and Gorky. For this concession, Stalin demanded that Bukharin deliver his last plea, written by Stalin. In it, Bukharin mentioned in passing that 'some of the Western European and American intellectuals' do not understand that 'in our country the antagonist, the enemy, has at the same time a divided, a dual, mind'. The statement was intended to attribute to Stalin's enemies the divided and dual mind of Stalin himself. Stalin perceptively described such a mind in his psychological portrait of the *provocateur* Anna Serebriakova. Bukharin denied that the psychology of Dostoyevsky's characters still existed in Russia. Dostoyevsky's characters were, he claimed, a thing of the remote past in the Soviet Union. Bukharin continued, 'Such types do not exist in our country, or exist perhaps only on the outskirts of small provincial towns, if they do even there. On the contrary, such psychology is to be found in western Europe.'[26] Stalin pointed Bukharin's finger far away from himself.

At 4 am on 13 March 1938 Ulrikh read out death sentences on 18 defendants, including Bukharin, Yagoda, Rykov and all 'exposed Okhrana agents'. Three defendants received long sentences that none of them survived. The death sentences were carried out immediately. Walter Duranty, the *New York Times* correspondent in Moscow for many years, described Ulrikh as a 'hard judge but a just one' in a book he published in 1942.[27] A few months earlier, Duranty had written that the Gamarnik's suicide 'proved that he had been engaged in some deal with the Germans'.[28] The American ambassador to the Soviet Union, Joseph Davies, in his report to Washington on 7 March 1938 wrote that the trials offered proof 'beyond reasonable doubt to justify the verdict of guilty of treason'.[29] In his lectures Davies drew laughter when in his reply to questions about a fifth column in Russia, he cracked the joke, 'There aren't any, they shot them all.'[30]

NOTES

1. Alexander Orlov, *Tainaya istoria stalinskikh prestuplenyi*, New Yorkm Jerusalem, Paris, 1983, p. 223.
2. I. D. Levine received information about the file from Wolf and Klement. Their subsequent murders convinced him that their claims were authentic. Interview with Levine in Chappaqua, New York, 1976.
3. Orlov, *Tainaya istoria . . .* , p. 224.
4. John J. Dziak, *Chekisty: A History of the KGB*, Lexington, 1988, pp. 99f. Also Stephen Schwartz, 'Intellectuals and Assassins – Annals of Stalin's Killerati', *The New York Times Book Review*, 24 January 1988.
5. Orlov, *Tainaya istoria . . .* , p. 188.
6. Ibid. p. 188f.
7. Ibid. pp. 223–5.
8. S. Rozhdestvensky, 'Pokhishchenie generala Millera', *Novoe russkoe slovo*, 19 May 1979.
9. Schwartz, 'Intellectuals and Assassins', pp. 3 and 29-31. The first reports about Max Eitingon's connections with Skoblin and Plevitskaya appeared in the Russian-Language émigré newspaper *Vozrozhdenie*, Paris, 9 December 1938 and in an earlier unsigned Russian-language manuscript, dated December 1937. See Dziak, *Chekisty . . .* , p. 99, fn. 79.
10. Robert Conquest, *The Great Terror*, New York, 1973, p. 444. Also Pavel Antokolsky, *Novy mir*, no. 4, 1966. Also Marina Tsvetaeva, *Izbrannye sochineniya*, Introduction, Moscow/Leningrad, 1964, Efron is listed among prisoners executed in October 1941.
11. Dziak, *Chekisty*, pp. 99f. Also Schwartz, 'Intellectuals and Assassins'.
12. Orlov, *Tainaya istoria*, pp. 228–32.
13. Felix Medvedev, *Ogonek*, no. 26–30, Moscow, 1987. See also *Soviet Media Digest*, Radio Liberty, 8 August 1987, nos 725–05 to 725–13.

14. Orlov, *Tainaya istoria*, p. 271. (The author met Yury Sokolnikov in the Norylsk Special Regime camp No. 4 in 1952 and was very close to him during the Norylsk uprising in the summer of 1953. After his release from prison camp Yury did not have permission to live in Moscow, but was allowed to settle 100 kilometers from Moscow, according to the regulations.)

15. Felix Medvedev, *Ogonek*, no. 26–30, Moscow, 1987. See also *Soviet Media Digest*, Radio Liberty, 8 August 1987.

16. I. D. Levine, *Journal American*, 3 March 1938. The article's subtitle reads: 'Levine Probed Reports of Secret File Proving Red Leader Czarist Spy.'

17. See Chapter 17 above for I. D. Levine's letter to the author, mentioning this report. The report about the discovery of the file reached the magazine *Sotsialistichesky vestnik*, published in Berlin, in 1926. Davis Shub, the editor of this magazine, told Levine about this report.

18. I. D. Levine in a conversation with the author in 1976 in Chappaqua, New York.

19. Orlov, *Tainaya istoria . . .* , pp. 271f.

20. Lev Trotsky, *Stalin*, New York, 1941, pp. 221f.

21. Alexander Orlov, *Tainaya istoria . . .* , pp. 271f.

22. *Bukharin Trial*, New York, 1965, pp. 478–99

23. Ibid., pp. 110f.

24. Ibid., pp. 272–5.

25. Ibid., pp. 144–9.

26. Ibid., p. 666. Stalin's deep distrust of Dostoyevsky's insight into a certain type of mind is indicated by his banning of Dostoyevsky's works.

27. Walter Duranty, *The Kremlin and the People*, New York, 1941, p. 37.

28. Ibid., p. 55.

29. Joseph E. Davies, *Mission to Moscow*, vol. 1, New York, 1941, p. 39.

30. Conquest, *The Great Terror*, p. 673.

THE MYSTERIOUS 'WORKER VASILY'

During 1937 and 1938 alone, Yezhov submitted for Stalin's signature 383 lists of party members selected for liquidation. These lists were usually signed, 'Approved: J. Stalin, V. Molotov'.[1] Sometimes Stalin and Molotov sanctioned the execution of more than 3,000 people a day.[2] The surviving Old Bolsheviks, most in prison camps, were frightened and kept silent when Stalin began to rewrite his biography in 1937. He published *A Short Course of Party History*, a book that bore little resemblance to the party's actual past. In rewriting his past, Stalin as usual did not replace the facts with complete inventions, but a distorted version of the mutilated truth.

Until 1939 all official biographies of Stalin listed his five arrests and four escapes from places of exile. But in his new biography, published in 1939 to mark his 60th birthday, Stalin listed seven arrests and six escapes, two of which he allegedly made from prison. Documents in his Okhrana file brought back his memory of two 'arrests' and 'escapes' in Tiflis in February 1905 and in March 1906 when he had been arrested by the chief of the Tiflis Okhrana, Colonel Zasypkin. On the first occasion he betrayed Stepan Shaumian, whom Zasypkin arrested; upon his second arrest Stalin had provided Zasypkin with information about the Avlabar press, which had led to its liquidation.[3] In his new biography, Stalin began to claim that he had organized the Avlabar press in 1903 and had directed its work from his prison cell!

Stalin also added a new detail to his 'escape' from Novaya Uda at the end of 1903. He asserted that he had fabricated the identity card of an Okhrana agent in his own name, and with this forgery had traveled to Batum, on his way there fooling a gendarmerie officer.[4] Mikhail Bulgakov was commissioned to write a play titled *Batum* about the 'leading role of Comrade Stalin in the Batum demonstration'.[5] In 1934 Stalin ordered that all published copies of his childhood biography be destroyed, but in 1939 he permitted publication of a new childhood biography: *Detstvo i yunost' vozhdia: documenty, zapiski, rasskazy* (The Childhood and Youth of the Leader: Documents, Notes, Recollections). This biography consists of quotes from documents, articles and the recollections of individual people. Stalin expunged the names of people he did not want mentioned and whole phrases he did not like. V. Kaminsky and I. Vereshchagin, identified as the 'compilers' of this biography, did not claim authorship. Their work carries the imprint of the two opposing impulses that were forever at war inside Stalin: on the one hand, the urge to tell the truth; on the other, the need to distort and hide it. The described events were turned out of context, but they still contained fragments of truth that hint at what actually had happened. Thus, for instance, the mass expulsion of the pupils of the Tiflis Seminary provoked by the young Koba is mentioned sarcastically: 'In the fall of 1899, 40–50 people (pupils of the ecclesiastical seminary) were forced "of their own volition" to leave the seminary for good.'[6]

Stalin did not destroy all the documents in his St Petersburg Okhrana file. For instance, he placed his original report to the Okhrana, dated 5/18 June 1912, in the Soviet archives, describing it as his 'circular letter to the Party no. 1' and he mentioned it in his collected works.[7] In 1941 for the first time Stalin also made public his alias 'Vasily', which was mentioned in two circular reports he found in his Okhrana file and also placed in the Soviet archives.[8] One of them, dated 7 March 1913, describes Stalin as having assumed the party aliases of 'Koba' and 'Vasily'. The other, dated 19 April 1913, also mentions these aliases.

In rewriting the story of his life, Stalin devoted great attention to creating a script for a movie about his role in the October Revolution. In the summer of 1938 he invited Aleksei Kapler, a prominent Soviet screenwriter, to his *dacha* in Kuntsevo and commissioned him to write a screenplay for a film about Lenin. Mikhail Romm, a prominent Soviet director, was chosen to direct the film. Stalin frequently discussed the script with Kapler and Romm, offering his advice. 'Here Stalin enters the hall', Stalin would say. Kapler would enquire what Comrade Stalin was saying at this point. 'Something wise, wise' was Stalin's answer.[9] One repercussion of Kapler's frequent visits was that Stalin's daughter Svetlana, 13 at the time, fell in love with Kapler, a handsome man of 34. (Stalin at first did not notice Svetlana's infatuation. When he did, he had Kapler accused of being a British spy and imprisoned.[10])

Kapler's script turned out much too long for one movie, Stalin ordered him to turn it into a two-part movie and suggested the titles: *Lenin in October* and *Lenin in 1918*. The major role in both films was assigned not to Lenin, nor even to Stalin, but to a mysterious character 'Worker Vasily', who appeared larger than life and had no family name or patronymic. His role was played by a movie star Nikolay Okhlopkov. 'Worker Vasily' overshadowed Lenin, who appeared in the movie helpless and without the wise advice of this mysterious personage. Stalin was presented in the movie in a modest role compared with that of 'Worker Vasily'. Critics were certain that this towering figure represented the wisdom of the proletarian masses.

Stalin attributed to 'Worker Vasily' the leading role in the film which had a familiar ring: in July 1917 'Worker Vasily' leads Lenin to a hiding place, a makeshift hut in the suburbs of Petrograd, whence Lenin later escapes to Finland. Infact, it was Stalin who led Lenin and Zinoviev to a hut in a forest near the village of Razliv to hide them 'from the blood-hounds of the Provisional Government' in July 1917. In 1939, when the movie appeared on the screen, no one was in a position to challenge this version of events: Lenin was dead; Zinoviev had been shot in 1936. The owner of this makeshift hut, the worker Emelianov, his wife, and their three sons had been arrested in 1935 and perished.[11] Krupskaya, who knew Emilianov and the story about this makeshift hut, died just before 'Worker Vasily' appeared on the screen. Rumors spread that she had been poisoned.[12]

It is clear that 'Worker Vasily' was Stalin's idealized 'double' and that Stalin, not Lenin, was the chief hero in the movies. In both movies Stalin substituted his past as Okhrana agent 'Vasily' with the enormously magnified screen image of 'Worker Vasily'. In his perception of himself, reality and fiction blended in a bewildering tangle of truth and myth. Thus, an Okhrana agent, one of the 12 listed in the 1918 book *Bolsheviki*, described there as 'yet unidentified, who had the alias "Vasily"', was 'unmasked' by Stalin during the Bukharin trial when P. T. Zubarev was forced to 'confess' that his Okhrana alias was 'Vasily' and that he had been recruited by an Okhrana officer by the name of Vasiliev. Stalin had forced Zubarev to 'confess' to an event in Stalin's own life.[13]

NOTES

1. Z. T. Serdyuk, speech to the Twenty-second Party Congress, *Pravda*, 31 October, 1961.
2. D. Volkogonov, TV interview; broadcast in the U S on NBC on 27 March, 1991.
3. See Chapter 5 above.
4. *Batumskaya demonstratsiya 1902-go goda*, Moscow, 1937, p. 140.
5. M. A. Bulgakov, *Sobranie sochinenii*, vol. III, Moscow 1990, p. 698.
6. V. Kaminsky and I. Vereshchagin, *Detstvo i yunost vozhdia*, Moscow; 1939, p. 88.
7. See I. V. Stalin, *Sochineniya*, vol. II, Moscow, 1946–51, p. 417. See also Z. Serebriakova, 'Stalin i tsarskaya okhrana', in *Sovershenno secretno*, no. 7, 1990, Moscow. Serebriakova found the original of Stalin's report in the Central State Archive and its copy in Ordzhonikidze's Okhrana file (Stalin's complaint against Malinovsky is missing in this copy). Serebriakova writes that the original of Stalin's report 'miraculously survived and is now discovered, moreover, in two archival deposits'. (That is, the handwritten version in the Central State Archive and the typed copy in Ordzhonikidze's Okhrana file.) 'This alone proves Stalin's ties to the Okhrana', states Serebriakova. Stalin's report to the Okhrana survived because Stalin redefined it when he found it in his St Petersburg Okhrana file, calling it 'Circular Letter No. 1 on the Final Composition of the Central Committee of the RSDWP.' What Stalin did not know was that Colonel Eremin had copies of this report made, ordering the typist to delete Stalin's complaint about Malinovsky, and sent the copies to the Okhrana Foreign Agency headquarters in Paris and to Ordzhonikidze's interrogator

under the heading 'Spravka bez no.' (reference without number). The copy in Ordzhonikidze's file was discovered by Serebriakova.

8. *Krasny arkhiv*, vol. 2 (105), Ogiz, Chief Archive Administration of the NKVD of the USSR, 1941, pp. 30f.

9. Taped interview with Efim Sevela at Chappaqua, New York, 1976. In the present author's archive.

10. Jennifer Dunning, 'Aleksey Kapler', *The New York Times*, 15 September 1979, p. 12.

11. Roy Medvedev, *Let History Judge*, New York, 1971, pp. 200f.

12. The author heard these rumors from various people.

13. H. Montgomery Hyde, *Stalin: The History of a Dictator*, New York, 1971, pp. 376f.

31

INHALING 'POISON GAS'

In May 1938 Stalin sent his personal assistant Lev Mekhlis and Yezhov's deputy Frinovsky to the Far East to 'liquidate' the 'Balitsky nest' in the NKVD and the 'Gamarnik–Bulin gang' in the Red Army. (A year earlier Stalin had ordered Bulin to murder Gamarnik. In June 1938 Khrushchev delivered a speech in which he called Balitsky a 'Fascist agent'.[1]) Trucks with arrested NKVD and Red Army officers were delivering their human cargo to the Khabarovsk prisons. Frinovsky personally shot 16 top NKVD personnel.[2]

The chief of the Far Eastern NKVD, Genrikh Liushkov, was not among the executed officers. Stalin was delaying sending an order to Liushkov to signal his permission to publish the 'Eremin Letter' and other forged Okhrana documents in the Russian émigré press in China . Stalin was uncertain about what to do with these forgeries. On the one hand, he did not need them as 'criminal evidence' against General Miller, who had been executed. On the other, he wanted them available to discredit any embarrassing Okhrana documents that might have survived his dragnet. Most of all, he wanted to have these forgeries to reinforce his own wishful thinking that the accusations about his Okhrana past were inventions of his enemies.

Liushkov was watching with alarm the purge that was swallowing up his associates. A morally blind former hardcore common criminal, he was not blind to his chances for survival. He knew that Stalin was delaying his arrest only because of the assignment to publish the 'Eremin Letter' and other forged Okhrana documents. Being familiar with Stalin's provocations, Liushkov realized that these forgeries were meant to discredit genuine Okhrana documents and probably surmised that Stalin intended the purge to cover up his Okhrana past. He knew that sooner or later the purge would swallow him as well.

On 9 June 1938 Liushkov told his deputy Grigory Osinin-Vinnitsky that he had to go to the Soviet–Manchurian border to meet a 'very important agent'. He left Khabarovsk, having taken from a secret fund 4,000 Manchurian gobi to 'encourage' this agent. Upon his arrival at a border guard detachment, Liushkov donned a civilian disguise. He was accompanied by an intelligence officer, who hid some distance behind Liushkov, waiting for his return. But Liushkov did not return; he faded into the night and the fog that soon turned into heavy rain.[3]

In the early hours of 12 June 1938 a Manchukuo border patrol noticed a strange figure lurking in the morning mist. Liushkov was apprehended and detained. A major in Japanese military intelligence, a linguist, interrogated him and promptly reported to the Japanese Army headquarters in Seoul, Korea, that he had encountered the 'escape of the century'. Liushkov was sent to Seoul, where incredulous officers at first suspected him of being a Soviet plant. The Japanese general staff ordered Liushkov's transfer to Tokyo. A report about Liushkov's defection was released on 1 July 1938. By this time Soviet diplomats had been instructed to insist that the real Liushkov was still in Russia and that the one in Tokyo was an 'imposter'.[4]

Liushkov's defection was widely disbelieved in the West. A 4 June 1938 *New York Times* editorial entitled 'Diary for a Japanese Schoolboy' depicted it as an anti-Soviet invention. The Germans, however, took his defection seriously. Admiral Wilhelm Canaris, the chief of Nazi intelligence, sent an agent to interrogate Liushkov. Major Schol, the German assistant military attaché in Tokyo, received information about the interrogation of Liushkov and shared it with his friend Richard Sorge, the top Soviet agent in Tokyo, who was posing as a correspondent for a German newspaper. Sorge was ordered to relate all available information on Liushkov: 'Transmit immediately', Moscow demanded.[5]

Liushkov was very selective in what he told his Japanese interrogators. He gave them some limited information about the location of Soviet troops but did not expose Soviet agents in China or Japan.[6] He also kept quiet about his own role in the mass purges and preparations for the show trials, such as his interrogation of Kamenev, Zinoviev, Riutin and other prominent party members. Nor did he talk about the deportation of Koreans from the Soviet Far East, which he had directed in December 1937 and for which he was given an award (Korea being then under Japanese rule).[7] Finally, Liushkov did not mention the forged Okhrana documents he had been assigned to plant in China. He did not have these forgeries to prove such a fantastic charge. Liushkov stood to gain nothing from implicating himself in Stalin's provocations, in the mass purges and show trials, and he had no desire to discredit either Stalin personally or the Soviet system, which had elevated him to one of the top positions in the NKVD. Despite the meagerness of the information that the Japanese obtained from him, there was a report that the Soviet embassy in Tokyo directed the Japanese Communist Party to liquidate Liushkov.[8]

After Liushkov's escape, the number of arrests and executions in the Far East increased sharply. Marshal Vasily Bliukher, the commander of the Far Eastern forces, was arrested, taken to Lubianka, tortured and shot. Twenty-two NKVD officers were executed, among them Liushkov's deputy, Grigory Osinin-Vinnitsky, who was declared a Japanese spy.[9] M. M. Zapadny, who had been appointed chief of the Far Eastern NKVD after Liushkov's defection, was also executed. On 29 July 1938 it was reported that the purge in the Far East had been ordered personally by Stalin in order to stop Japanese penetration of Soviet defenses.[10] Special troops replaced the frontier guards in the area of Liushkov's defection and several times opened artillery fire on Japanese positions across the border. The Japanese responded by attacking in the area of Khal Kin Gol and Lake Khasan, to verify Liushkov's information on Soviet troops. Large battles occurred in these areas, with substantial losses on both sides. The Soviet press maintained total silence about Liushkov. Stalin removed from Soviet archives all documents related to these battles.[11] After Liushkov's defection, Stalin performed one of his 'false target' escapades, which allowed him to vent his rage. He ordered Yezhov's deputy, Frinovsky to go to a border crossing to capture 'a dangerous spy' who was supposed to come there. Frinovsky was then arrested and executed for trying to 'flee abroad'.[12] (The final chapter of Liushkov's story was written in 1945. He was at the headquarters of the Japanese Army in the Manchurian city of Dairen when the Soviet Army entered the city. A Japanese general shot him dead to keep him from being captured alive by the Soviets.[13])

After Liushkov's defection, Romm and Nagi, two NKVD residents in China, and other Soviet agents there were recalled to Moscow and executed. M. D. Golovachev, the NKVD informer to whom Liushkov had given the 'Eremin Letter' and other forged Okhrana documents, was not recalled to Moscow, because he was not a staff intelligence officer, but one of numerous *shtuchniks* (piecemeal informers) who worked for the NKVD in various countries. After Liushkov's defection, Golovachev remained in possession of the forgeries, not knowing what to do with them. He was left without guidance by his NKVD handlers who had been recalled to Moscow.[14] Golovachev understood that the documents were intended to play an important role in some major provocation. He must have worried that this provocation might end up hurting him. He made no attempt to find out from Soviet officials what to do with these forgeries. (Three years later Golovachev attempted to sell the 'Eremin Letter' to the Germans.[15])

Soon after Liushkov's defection, an event took place that attracted no attention in the world press: Colonel Russianov, the man Golovachev had been instructed to implicate as the forger of the 'Eremin Letter' and the other forgeries, suddenly died. He was 59 years old. Russianov's family suspected that he had either been poisoned, or had committed suicide. His son found a strange package in their home, containing Okhrana stationery, rubber stamps and photographs of Stalin, Trotsky and Malinovsky. The son could not explain the origin of the package and decided to preserve it. There was no investigation into the cause of Russianov's death, he was one of many Russian émigrés in Shanghai who were of no interest to the Chinese police. His family did not press for an investigation: they wanted to bury him in the Russian Orthodox cemetery and feared that they would be turned away if it were established that the cause of death was suicide by poisoning. (Russianov's family left Shanghai ten years later before the capture of the city by the Chinese Communists and moved to Australia. In 1956, Russianov's son sent the package with the Okhrana paraphernalia to Isaac Don Levine, the American journalist who at that time was investigating the origin of the 'Eremin Letter'.[16])

On 9 July 1938 Alexander Orlov, the chief Soviet intelligence adviser to the Spanish Republican government, received Yezhov's order to return to Moscow.[17] He knew that this would be the end of him. He recalled his last conversation with Pavel Alliluev, the brother of Stalin's late wife Nadezhda. Orlov, long acquainted with Pavel, had met him in Paris at the Soviet exhibition in September 1937. They went for a long walk and recalled old friends, many of whom were no longer alive. Alliluev complained that NKVD agents were following him everywhere. Orlov asked Alliluev what was behind the execution of Tukhachevsky and other generals. Alliluev fell silent and then said very slowly: 'Alexander, don't ever enquire about the Tukhachevsky affair. Knowing about it is like inhaling poison gas.' A few months later Orlov read a short obituary in a Soviet paper: Pavel Alliluev had 'died while carrying out his official duties'. Orlov recalled Alliluev's 'poison gas' remark and concluded grimly that Stalin had had him murdered.[18] (Ten years later Stalin was to accuse Evgenia Alliluev, Pavel Alliluev's wife, of poisoning her husband.[19])

From his conversation with Alliluev, Orlov surmised that Alliluev knew about Stalin's Okhrana file and its role in the Tukhachevsky conspiracy, and that by 'poison gas' Alliluev had meant that acquiring knowledge about Stalin's Okhrana file was tantamount to committing suicide. Orlov himself had caught a whiff of this poison when his cousin, Zinovy Katsnelson, had told him in February 1937 about I. L. Shtein's discovery of Stalin's Okhrana file. Orlov knew that Katsnelson had been executed and Shtein had committed suicide. To escape their fate, Orlov drove across the border to France and, together with his wife and daughter, boarded a ship to Canada. On 13 August 1938 the Orlovs arrived in Washington and applied for political asylum, which he obtained without much difficulty. Then, he and his family lived anonymously for 15 years although he believed that the US authorities would in the long run be unable to protect him from the NKVD. Eventually, he wrote a book entitled *The Secret History of Stalin's Crimes*, but did not publish it until 1953, the year of Stalin's death, stating that the case of Marshal Tukhachevsky and the other executed generals was 'destined to occupy a much more significant place in history than it deserves in its own right'. Orlov wrote:

I am making this assertion because I know from an absolutely unimpeachable and authoritative source that the case of Marshal Tukhachevsky was tied up with one of Stalin's most horrible secrets which, when disclosed, will throw light on many things that seemed so incomprehensible in Stalin's behavior.[20]

(In 1956 he published an article in *Life* magazine, recounting what he knew about the Tukhachevsky plot.[21])

In December 1938 Yezhov was removed from the post of NKVD chief and Beria appointed in his place. Stalin then ordered him to destroy 'Yezhov's nest'. Yezhov was still alive in March 1939 when he appeared as a delegate at the Eighteenth Party Congress. During one of the sessions, Stalin asked Yezhov to come close to the podium. 'Well, what do you think about yourself? Can you be a member of the Central Committee?' he asked him. Yezhov, his voice breaking, said that he had devoted his whole life to the party and Stalin and that he loved Stalin more than his own life. 'Is that so?' asked Stalin with an air of amazement and enquired: 'Then who was Frinovsky? Did you know Frinovsky?' Yezhov answered, 'Frinovsky was my deputy.' (Frinovsky, arrested for his alleged attempt to escape across the Manchurian border, was by then signing depositions accusing Yezhov.) Before Yezhov could go on, Stalin interrupted him to ask who Shapiro was, who Ryzhova was, who Fedorov was. All of these aides of Yezhov had been shot by then. 'Iosif Vissarionovich! But you know it was I – I myself! – who exposed their plot. I came to you and reported', Yezhov pleaded. Stalin interrupted him with an angry tirade:

Yes, yes, yes! When you thought you were going to get caught, then you came all in a hurry. But what happened before that? Did you organize a plot? Did you want to kill Stalin? Top people in the NKVD were hatching a plot and you supposedly had nothing to do with it! Do you think I don't see anything? Well, let me refresh your memory. Who was it that you sent to stand guard over Stalin one day? Who? Did they have revolvers? Why be near Stalin with revolvers? To kill Stalin? And what if I hadn't noticed? What then?[22]

Stalin was again rewriting history. He wanted to forget that on 19 May

1937, after Karl Pauker brought to him a photocopy of Colonel Eremin's report, he had declared a state of alert, and Yezhov and Frinovsky had placed armed guards to protect him from 'a gigantic conspiracy in the Army, such a conspiracy as history has never known'.[23] Yezhov knew it was useless to argue when Stalin turned these events upside down. 'Well? Get going! That's all', Stalin concluded. Addressing the audience, he mused, 'I don't know, comrades, can this man remain as a member of the Central Committee?' He paused as if pondering the question and added, 'I have my doubts. Of course, you think it over . . . It's up to you, as you wish . . . But I have my doubts!'[24] Soon thereafter, Yezhov was arrested and executed. Stalin explained to Alexander Yakovlev, a leading airplane designer: 'That scoundrel Yezhov! He finished off some of our finest people. He was utterly rotten. That's why we shot him.'[25]

The greatest devastation was suffered by the party apparatus, the cadres of the NKVD, and the army in the Ukraine, where, as Stalin found out, the Tukhachevsky conspiracy against him had taken root. The purge there was directed by Nikita Khrushchev, who was appointed first secretary of the Ukrainian Party in January 1938. Khrushchev executed all members of the Ukrainian Politburo. Out of the 102 members of the Central Committee of the Ukrainian Party only three remained alive, among them Grigory Petrovsky. All members of the Ukrainian government were arrested.[26] Stanislav Kossior, the head of the Ukrainian government, was brought to Stalin's office for interrogation. Stalin also summoned Grigory Petrovsky. 'Well, talk!' Stalin said to Kossior. 'What can I say? You know I'm a Polish spy', Kossior replied. Turning to Kossior, Petrovsky objected, 'Stasik, why do you tell lies about yourself and me?' Kossior replied meekly, 'I made depositions and I won't take them back.' Stalin exclaimed, 'There, you see, Petrovsky, you didn't believe that Kossior had become a spy. Now do you believe he is an enemy of the people?' Petrovsky did not respond at once, and Stalin ordered that his file be brought in. 'We shoot people like you', he shouted at Petrovsky, 'but I will have mercy on you.'[27] Petrovsky's file contained a document with information about his ties to the Okhrana, yet despite this, or maybe because of it, he was never arrested, although both of his sons were imprisoned.[28]

Many of the people arrested at that time were accused of having been Okhrana agents. One was the respected theater director Vsevolod Meyerhold, who was accused of working for the Okhrana under the alias 'Semenych',[29] and of being a Japanese spy. This latter accusation was probably a consequence of Liushkov's escape to Japan. It so happened that soon after Liushkov's escape, a Japanese couple, Yoshido Yoshima and his wife, came to Moscow to study Meyerhold's approach to theater. They were arrested and accused of being spies and were executed (after Stalin's death, they were declared innocent). Meyerhold was arrested on 20 June 1939. A few days later the body of his wife, Zinaida Raikh (formerly married to the poet Sergey Esenin), was found in their apartment. Her body had 17 knife wounds, and her eyes had been cut out, apparently from the superstitious fear that they retained the image of her murderers. The only things taken from the apartment were documents. Their NKVD file was opened under the joint name of 'Meyerhold–Raikh, V. E.' On 13 January 1940, three days before his trial, Meyerhold wrote an appeal to Vyshinsky, not knowing that Vyshinsky was no longer the chief prosecutor but had been promoted to the position of deputy commissar of foreign affairs. Meyerhold wrote: 'Interrogator Rodos broke my left hand and left my right one unbroken so that I could sign my depositions with it. My depositions are false: I could not withstand tortures and denigration. He forced me to drink urine, to crawl – me, an old man.'[30] Meyerhold was brought before Ulrikh, who hurriedly asked a few formal questions. Meyerhold denied the accusations, and was then taken to the Lubianka cellars and shot in the back of the head.

Usually, the bodies of executed men and women were disposed of in secret 'burial grounds'. One such mass grave was located on the outskirts of Moscow, near the Abelman *Zastava* (checkpoint), in a deep ravine next to the Kalitnikovskoe cemetery. An old road paved with wornout cobblestones led to a former slaughterhouse. Since long before the Revolution, this road had been known as *Skotogonnaya Doroga* (Cattle Drive Road). It had been used by peasants from villages near Moscow, who drove their livestock there to supply Moscow with meat. In the 1930s this road was often traveled by covered gray-blue trucks in which NKVD officers in yellow rubber aprons delivered the bodies of executed men and women, usually some 30 corpses per delivery. The officers swung the corpses by the hands and feet and threw them into the ravine and hurriedly threw shovels of earth over them. There were layers upon layers of corpses.[31]

NOTES

1. Robert Conquest, *The Great Terror*, New York, 1973, p. 348, fn. 74 (which cites *Bilsovik ukrainy*, 6 June 1938).
2. Conquest, *The Great Terror*, pp. 617f.
3. Vladimir Mikhailov and Viacheslav Bondarenko, *Kurier*, no. 58, 3–9 June 1993, pp. 1 and 24.
4. Alvin D. Coox, 'L'Affaire Liushkov', *Soviet Studies*, January 1968, p. 411.
5. Ibid.

6. Mikhailov and Bondarenko, *Kurier*, no. 58, 3–9 June 1993, pp. 1 and 24.
7. Coox, 'L'Affaire Liushkov', p. 400, citing *Pravda* report on Liushkov, dated 20 December 1937.
8. Ibid. p. 413, fn. 21.
9. R. S. Osinina, who was earlier divorced from Gregory Osinin-Vinnitsky, provided this information in a taped interview with the author in Haifa, Israel, in 1979. She was an aunt of Vitaly Svechinsky. In the author's archive.
10. Coox, 'L'Affaire Liushkov', p. 407.
11. V. A. Korotich, the former editor of *Ogonek*, provided this information in a telephone interview with the author on 9 September 1992, when he was in Massachusetts. Korotich stated that he had attempted to find these documents with the help of KGB chief Kruchkov.
12. Roy Medvedev, *Let History Judge*, New York, 1971, p. 323.
13. A. Antonov-Ovseenko, *Portret tirana*, New York, 1980, p. 209. See also Mikhailov and Bondarenko, *Kurier*, no. 58, 3–9 June 1993, pp. 1 and 24.
14. See Chapter 28 above.
15. See Chapter 34 below.
16. The author examined this package at I. D. Levine's farm in Waldorf, Virginia. It is in Levine's archive.
17. Alexander Orlov, *Tainaya storiia stalinskikh prestuplenii*, New York/Jerusalem/Paris, 1983, p. 13.
18. Ibid., pp. 309–11.
19. I. P. Itskov, taped interview. Itskov, a lawyer, represented Evgenia Allilueva in her 'rehabilitation case'. See also Svetlana Allilueva, *Twenty Letters to a Friend*, New York, 1967, pp. 182f.
20. Alexander Orlov, *The Secret History of Stalin's Crimes*, New York, 1953, p. 240.
21. Alexander Orlov, 'The Sensational Secret Behind Damnation of Stalin', *Life*, 23 April 1956, pp. 34–44.
22. Medvedev, 'Dvadtsatyi vek', *Obshestvenno-politicheskii i literaturnyi almanakh*, no. 2, pp. 41f.
23. See Chapter 22 above.
24. Medvedev, 'Dvadtsatyi vek', pp. 41f.
25. H. Montgomery Hyde, *Stalin: The History of a Dictator*, New York, 1971, p. 377.
26. Conquest, *The Great Terror*, pp. 348–50.
27. Medvedev, *Let History Judge*, pp. 295f.
28. Ibid., p. 295. Medvedev quotes from papers in the archive of the Petrovsky family.
29. Ibid., p. 316.
30. V. A. Chalikova, 'Arkhivnyi yunosha', *Neva*, October 1988, p. 152.
31. Alexander Milchakov, 'Ovrag na kalitnikovskom', *Semiya*, no. 40, Moscow, 1988.

32

THE MURDER OF TROTSKY

Soon after the murder of Ignaz Reiss, Stalin ordered the NKVD to assassinate Trotsky.[1] After Reiss informed Trotsky's son Lev Sedov about the discovery of Stalin's Okhrana file, Sedov in turn reported this information to his father. Stalin feared that Trotsky might publicize this information. The first attempt on Trotsky's life was made in January 1938, shortly before the murder of Sedov. Trotsky escaped unharmed. His suspicion that Stalin was behind this assassination attempt increased after his son's murder in February and the murders of Trotsky's aides Rudolf Klement and Erwin Wolf. Trotsky and his wife, Natalia Sedova, were greatly hurt by the death of their son, in whom they lost not only a beloved son but a devoted assistant as well. Ironically, if Sedov reported to Trotsky the discovery of Stalin's Okhrana file, the news fell on deaf ears: Trotsky always denied all accusations that Stalin had ever been an Okhrana agent. To Trotsky, such blasphemy seemed inconceivable.

Trotsky devoted the summer of 1938 to drafting the program for the Founding Congress of the Fourth International, which opened on 3 September 1938 in the house of Alfred and Marguerite Rosmer outside of Paris. Twenty-eight delegates, representing Trotsky's supporters in 11 countries, were present. Trotsky could not attend because he had no passport: his Soviet citizenship had been terminated and he did not want to apply for citizenship elsewhere. In Stalin's words, Trotsky was a 'passportless vagrant'. He was living in a villa in Coyoacan, a suburb of Mexico City.

At the congress, the fear of the Kremlin's long hand hung over the delegates. They decided to have only one session in order to prevent Stalin's agents from infiltrating the congress. But Mark Zborovsky, the NKVD agent who had organized the murder of Lev Sedov, was an active participant: he officially represented the 'Russian Section' of the Fourth International. Another NKVD agent, whose true name was Ramon Mercader, attempted to attend the congress but was not admitted. Sylvia Agelof, one of Trotsky's secretaries, introduced Mercader to Alfred and Marguerite Rosmer as Jacques Mornard. Agelof met Mercader for the first time – by accident, she thought – shortly before the opening of the congress, when she arrived in Paris from New York. In fact, her meeting with Mercader had been carefully orchestrated by NKVD agents in New

York and Paris. The encounter was part of Stalin's scheme to assassinate Trotsky.

Stalin entrusted the assassination of Trotsky to Beria and Leonid Eitingon, who had in the past carried out assignments of special importance, among them the kidnapping of generals Kutepov and Miller and the murder of Reiss and Sedov. During the Spanish Civil War, Eitingon had directed a group of assassins, for the most part South Americans, who on Stalin's orders murdered 'unreliable' representatives of various leftist parties. Caridad Mercader, Cuban by birth and a fanatical communist, became Eitingon's mistress. Her son, Ramon, was recruited by the NKVD and carried out various assignments, playing the role of a wealthy and charming young man. Because Sylvia Agelof was known as Trotsky's trusted assistant and had easy access to him, she was selected as the object of Mercader's courtship; he was to charm and 'marry' her, to gain access to Trotsky's household. Their 'accidental' meeting in Paris was the beginning of a love affair.[2]

Mercader showered Agelof with attention. Agelof was a young woman active in the Russian–Jewish emigrant leftist circles of New York. She was plain and unaccustomed to being courted by men, and fell for Mercader's charm. In February 1939 she returned to New York, and in September of that year Mercader arrived there carrying a bogus Canadian passport with the improbably spelled name 'Jacson', a mistake by the NKVD forger. He explained that he was using this passport to avoid being drafted into the Belgian Army. In October 1939 Mercader left for Mexico, telling Agelof that he was going there on business. She promised to visit him and at the same time to help Trotsky with his book on Stalin, which he was writing at the time.

Toward the end of 1939 Agelof went to Mexico. Mercader often drove her to Trotsky's villa and picked her up after work. The villa was like a small fortress surrounded by a high wall. One of Trotsky's followers was always on guard at the gate. The Mexican police had also built a brick hut nearby to keep Trotsky's villa under surveillance. Mercader's assignment at that time was merely to learn about the villa's defenses, while Eitingon, in preparation for an attack, gathered together the group of assassins, who by that time had returned from Spain to Mexico. Among them was one of the leaders of the Mexican Communist Party, the prominent painter David Siqueiros, who was also a leading official in the miners' union. Other members were Vittorio Codovilla, one of the founders of the Argentine Communist Party, and Vittorio Vidali, Eitingon's assistant in Spain.[3]

At 4 am on 23 May 1940 four cars dropped off at Trotsky's villa 20 of

Eitingon's assassins, dressed in the uniforms of Mexican police. The guard at the gate let them in and was then overwhelmed. The assassins swooped into the courtyard, forced the other guards to surrender, placed a machine gun in front of Trotsky's bedroom and opened fire. Trotsky and his wife crawled under their bed. After firing at the house for 20 minutes, the assailants left as suddenly as they had arrived, taking with them Trotsky's two cars and a guard. Trotsky got away with minor scratches from broken window glass. Colonel Salazar, the head of the Mexican secret police, asked Trotsky whether he suspected anyone. 'The author of the attack is Joseph Stalin', replied Trotsky.[4]

Four days later Sylvia Agelof introduced Mercader to Trotsky as her husband. Two weeks later, Mercader, claiming he had to go to New York on business and would soon be back, generously left his car for Trotsky to use. During Mercader's absence, the Mexican police established the names of the attackers. The corpse of the guard who had been kidnapped by the assassins was found buried in the courtyard of the farm they had rented. David Siqueiros was arrested, but released on bail. The Chilean poet Pablo Neruda, a prominent communist and a diplomat, helped Siqueiros escape to Chile. The rest of the assassins were tried in court for stealing Trotsky's cars. The charges of attacking Trotsky's villa and murdering the guard were dismissed. The question of Stalin's involvement in the assassination attempt was not raised.

Upon his arrival in New York, Mercader was given a new assignment by Eitingon and Gaik Ovakimian, the NKVD agent who was officially the Soviet General Consul in New York. They received instructions from 'Ivan Vasilievich' (Stalin's codename in secret communications), spelling out exactly how Mercader should murder Trotsky. Enraged by the failure of the 23 May assassination attempt, Stalin had decided to direct the assassination of Trotsky personally and to provide detailed instructions how the murder should be carried out. A number of years later, in January 1948, Stalin acted out his compulsion to re-enact the murder of his father Vissarion. He ordered his secret police to murder Solomon Mikhoels by striking him on the head with an 'axe wrapped in a wet quilted jacket'.[5] Stalin decided that the assassination of Trotsky was to be carried out by Mercader, who was to use an 'axe wrapped in a wet quilted jacket' as the murder weapon. Stalin's instruction must have made little sense to Eitingon, Ovakimian and Mercader, but they were in no position to argue with 'Ivan Vasilievich'. Nevertheless, to wear a quilted jacket would have been absurd in Mexico in the summer. Eitingon and Ovakimian therefore decided that Mercader would wrap the axe in an overcoat. They told Mercader that the fate of his mother would depend on the success of his mission, since she would be executed if he failed.

Mercader returned to Mexico in a highly nervous state. On 17 August 1940 he went to Trotsky's villa. The day was hot, but he wore a hat and was clutching a black overcoat. He said that he had written a draft of an article about the split among American Trotskyites and asked whether Trotsky would look at it and make corrections. Trotsky sat down behind his desk and started to read the draft. Mercader waited, his hat still on and his overcoat in his hands. His strange behavior made Trotsky feel uneasy, and ten minutes later he came out of his study visibly upset. He told his wife and his chief bodyguard, Joseph Hansen, that he was through with Mercader. He suspected that Mercader was engaged in some 'shady financial machinations' and had ties with the fascists.

But three days later, on 20 August 1940, Trotsky yielded to Sylvia Agelof's request and again agreed to take a look at Mercader's article. That day, too, Mercader wore a hat and kept hugging a black overcoat. Trotsky's wife asked him, 'Why are you wearing a hat and carrying a rain-coat in the sun?' He replied, 'It might rain.'[6] Trotsky, interrupting his work on Stalin's biography, invited him into the study and, sitting down behind the desk, began reading Mercader's article. Mercader, sitting on the edge of the desk, quietly took the axe out of his overcoat and brought it down hard on Trotsky's head. The plan had apparently been for him to kill Trotsky on the spot and to leave the villa unnoticed. Eitingon was waiting for him in a car parked not far from the villa, ready to speed him away before the murder was discovered. Instead, a wild scene ensued. Trotsky let out a terrible cry, leapt to his feet, and flung his recording machine and everything he could lay his hands on at Mercader. Then, he hurled himself at his assassin, bit Mercader's hand, and yanked the axe out of his grip. Stunned by the attack, Mercader had no opportunity to pull out the dagger hidden in his overcoat. Natalia and the guards rushed in and subdued him. Afraid his guards might kill Mercader, Trotsky murmured slowly, spacing the words: 'He must not be killed . . . he must talk.' Mercader, fearing Trotsky's guards would kill him nevertheless, shouted: 'They made me do it. They're holding my mother, they have put my mother in gaol!'[7] Trotsky died the next day, 21 August 1940.

That day Stalin, as usual, arrived in his Kremlin office at noon. His secretary, Poskrebyshev, quietly placed before him a telegram: 'Trotsky has been mortally wounded, possibly killed. Details later.'[8] Poskrebyshev knew how important this report was to Stalin. He had experienced Stalin's hatred of Trotsky in his own life. A few months earlier, on 30 April 1940, Stalin had ordered Beria to poison Poskrebyshev's wife Bronislava, one of whose sisters had been married to Trotsky's son Lev Sedov.[9] By that time, Trotsky's younger son Sergey had been executed in a prison camp in Kazakhstan, and most of the relatives of Trotsky and his first wife had been arrested and perished in the camps. The arrests of Trotsky's relatives began shortly after his exile abroad. One of his friends in Moscow wrote to Trotsky soon after the execution of Blumkin in December 1929 that Trotsky's eldest daughter (from his first marriage) had been arrested and that his younger daughter had died in prison. 'Platon Volkov, the husband of your [older] daughter, was sent into exile two months ago', wrote the friend. 'M. Nevelson, the husband of your deceased daughter, has been in prison for a long time. But this revenge is too common and therefore insufficient.' The friend added:

The thirst for revenge was stronger than Stalin. In Party circles the story is often mentioned how Stalin one evening in 1923 in Zubalovo said to Dzerzhinsky and Kamenev: 'To choose the victim, to prepare the blow with care, to slake an implacable vengeance, and then to go to bed . . . there is nothing sweeter in life.' Bukharin hinted at this conversation ('Stalin's philosophy of sweet vengeance') in his discussion last year about the struggle with the Stalinists.[10]

When Trotsky's death was confirmed, Stalin wrote an editorial for *Pravda*, headed 'The Death of An International Spy'. Stalin declared that Trotsky 'was finished off by the same terrorists whom he had taught to murder from behind a corner' and that he had 'worked for the intelligence services and general staffs of England, France, Germany, Japan . . .' and that having 'organized the villainous murders of Kirov, Kuibyshev, M. Gorky, he became the victim of his own intrigues, betrayals, treason, evil deeds . . .'.[11] The Soviet satirical journal *Krokodil* displayed a caricature of Trotsky on its cover, his skull split wide open with an axe and blood pouring into a large metal basin.[12]

Stalin was in a good mood when he received Caridad Mercader, the mother of the assassin, and presented her with decorations for her and her son.[13] Eitingon was also received by Stalin, who embraced and decorated him with the Order of Lenin, and promised him that he would not allow a 'hair to be touched' on Eitingon's head.[14] Ramon Mercader was sentenced by a Mexican court to 20 years in jail. He did not reveal that he had murdered Trotsky on orders from the NKVD. Stalin paid for his silence by arranging the most comfortable prison condition possible for Mercader: a sunny cell with an open patio. He was also allowed female companionship on a regular basis, his food was brought to him from the best restaurants, and he was supplied with books, newspapers and journals.[15] (In August 1960, Mercader walked out of prison and was greeted by representatives from the Czechoslovakian Embassy, who handed him a passport. Until the 'Prague Spring' and Soviet invasion of 1968, Mercader lived in Prague. He was spirited off to Moscow after the invasion and soon became known among well-connected Moscovites as the man who had murdered Trotsky and who always had Western cigarettes, liqueur and imported food.[16] When he died, his gravestone in a Moscow cemetery gave his name as 'Reimond Lopez'. His mother, a hopeless addict, died, a victim of the drugs with which the secret police supplied her. Ramon Mercader's brother, Louis, was for years a lecturer in the Communications Institute in Moscow. He left the Soviet Union with his family and settled in Madrid, where he wrote a book about his brother, the murderer of Trotsky.[17])

Stalin had many reasons for murdering Trotsky. Among the most compelling of these was that he learned of Trotsky's intention to accuse him of poisoning Lenin.[18] He probably also suspected that Trotsky would accuse him of having been an Okhrana agent. Trotsky was finally shedding his remaining illusions about Stalin, writing prophetically that Stalin 'seeks to strike, not at the ideas of his opponent, but at his skull'. Stalin knew that Trotsky was working on a biography *Stalin* and that he was to point out the true significance of the 'confessions' at the show trials. Shortly before his death Trotsky wrote:

With his monstrous trials Stalin proved much more than he wanted; rather, he failed to prove what he set out to prove. He merely disclosed his secret laboratory, he forced 150 people to confess to crimes they never committed. But the totality of these confessions turned into Stalin's own confession.[19]

Trotsky was an implacable enemy of fascism and was a fervent critic of Stalin's policy of *rapprochement* with Hitler and of the non-aggression pact with Germany that Stalin signed in 1939. In 1938 he wrote:

Fascism goes from victory to victory and finds the main help . . . in Stalinism. Terrible military threats knock at the door of the Soviet Union, but Stalin chooses this moment to undermine the Army . . . The time will come when not he, but history will put him on trial.[20]

NOTES

1. Roy Medvedev, *Let History Judge*, New York, 1971, p. 140, fn. 23. See also Volkogonov's chapter on Trotsky 'The Demon of the Revolution', published in *Pravda*, 9 September 1988, p. 4 (see note 8 below). Although the fact that Stalin ordered the murder of Trotsky is widely known, no official confirmation of it has ever been published during the Soviet and post-Soviet period. Party and government spokesman Colonel-General Dmitry Volkogonov in his biography of Stalin devoted a whole chapter, titled 'The Demon of the Revolution', to Trotsky. (Volkogonov considers Trotsky the 'Demon' and describes him with unrestrained hostility.) Volkogonov comes close to admitting that Trotsky was murdered on Stalin's order. He hints: 'After Trotsky's death, Beria received promotion. In the West it was held for a long time that Beria was the chief executioner and organizer of the decision regarding Trotsky. I think, however, that in the foreseeable future it will be impossible to obtain documentary evidence to support or deny these versions.' Despite numerous revelations of Stalin's crimes that have been published since his death, many of his crimes still remain unacknowledged by government and archive officials. The murder of Trotsky is one of these official secrets.
2. Robert Conquest, *The Great Terror*, New York, 1973, pp. 600f.
3. Ibid., p. 599.
4. Joel Carmichael, *Trotsky*, London, 1975, pp. 473f.
5. See Chapter 36 below for the murder of Mikhoels in 1948. For the murder of Vissarion, see Chapter 4 above.
6. Carmichael, *Trotsky*, pp. 477f.
7. Ibid., pp. 480f.
8. D. Volkogonov, 'Demon revolutsii', *Pravda*, 9 September 1988.
9. Bronislava had been earlier married to a prominent Party member, I. P. Itskov, whom she divorced to marry Poskrebyshev, hoping that this would protect her relatives from persecution. On the day of her murder, Beria phoned her and told her to come to his Lubianka office, saying that he had something important to show her. Bronislava's body was carried out of Beria's office in a bag and taken to the Lubianka's Internal Prison, where her death was recorded as heart failure. Then the body was delivered to the Moscow crematorium and her cremation registered the same day. Itskov reconstructed these events from official records two decades later. Taped interview with I. P. Itskov in New York in 1989. In the author's archive.
10. *Biulleten oppositsii*, no. 9, February–March 1930, pp. 9–11.
11. *Pravda*, 24 August 1940.
12. *Krokodil*, September 1940. The cartoon was one of the author's childhood recollections.
13. Conquest, *The Great Terror*, p. 603, quoting from E. Castro Delgado, *J'ai Perdu la Foi à Moscou*, Paris, 1950.
14. Vitaly Rapoport and Yury Alekseev, *Izmena rodine*, London, 1988, p. 504.
15. Conquest, *The Great Terror*, p. 603.
16. Boris Shragin, interview in Chappaqua, New York, in 1976.
17. Interview with Felix Svetlov in New York, 4 August 1991. Also, interview with Vladimir Gutkin in New York in 1993. Gutkin worked with Louis Mercader in Moscow. In the author's archive.
18. Lev Trotsky, *Stalin*, New York, 1941, p. 373. and fn. 2. In 1937, Trotsky for the first time wrote down his recollections of the days in 1923-24 when, as he came to believe, Stalin arranged the poisoning of Lenin. In October 1939 Trotsky wrote a magazine article describing these events. Stalin no doubt had received information about Trotsky's intention to publish his recollections in this article and in the book he was writing.
19. Trotsky, *Stalin*, p. 421.
20. *Biulleten oppositsii*, vol. 65, 1938. Quoted in Volkogonov, 'Demon revolutsii'.

33

'IVAN SUSANIN' AND THE
'EASTERN QUESTION'

After Stalin's Okhrana file fell into his hands in May 1937, he was able to conjecture through whose hands it had passed. By a strange coincidence, the major roles in the history of this file were played by persons of Polish descent, or, more precisely, by people whom Stalin considered to be Poles because of their Polish family names, although some of these 'Poles' had been Russified generations back. Of such remote Polish descent was the director of the Department of Police, S. P. Beletsky, who, after having investigated the Stalin–Malinovsky feud, had ordered Stalin's exile and placed his file in the archive. Elena Rozmirovich came from a prominent military family of Russified Polish gentry. Stalin's arch rival in the Okhrana, Roman Malinovsky, was a Pole also. In the summer of 1926, when Stalin's Okhrana file was discovered in the old archives, it fell into the hands of the chief of the secret police, Felix Dzerzhinsky, another Pole. Then, after Blumkin's arrest, the file was intercepted by Dzerzhinsky's successor, V. P. Menzhinsky, yet another Pole. Finally, the file wound up in the hands of Marshal Tukhachevsky, who came from a long-Russified Polish family.[1] V. A. Balitsky, S. V. Kossior and other Russified Poles played an important role in the Tukhachevsky conspiracy. Stalin ordered executions not only of the participants in the conspiracy but of the families and relatives of Dzerzhinsky, Menzhinsky, Tukhachevsky, all four Kossior brothers, Stanislav Redens – the NKVD chief in Moscow and Dzerzhinsky's nephew – and many other 'Polish spies'.[2]

Stalin had the psychological trait of transferring his hatred of individuals to the entire social or ethnic groups to which he believed they belonged. The purge swallowed thousands of foreign communists and many officials of the Comintern (Communist International), but usually Stalin spared the lives of a small group of leaders of 'fraternal communist parties'. The Polish Communist Party was completely liquidated. A single Polish leader, Wladislaw Gomulka, survived because he was in a Polish prison at the time of the massacre. Ten thousand Poles were shot in Moscow and 50,000 in the provinces.[3] The wives of the arrested Poles received the standard sentence of eight years, forced labor. Few survived, and the orphanages were filled with the children of imprisoned and executed Poles. These children were taught to chant: 'We thank Comrade Stalin for our happy childhood!'[4]

In 1937 Stalin acquired the strange habit of going to the Bolshoi Theater performances of Glinka's opera *Ivan Susanin* (which before the Revolution had been known as *A Life for the Tsar*). He never stayed to the end, always leaving abruptly in the middle of the second act after a scene depicting the death of Polish soldiers in a forest near Moscow. This scene re-created an episode that took place in 1613 at the time of the Polish invasion of Russia. According to popular tradition, Ivan Susanin, a peasant from a village near Moscow, volunteered to guide a detachment of Polish soldiers to Moscow the shortest way, but instead lured them into a dense virgin forest where they all perished. Susanin's heroic deed gave birth to many poems and songs, including a poem by K. F. Ryleev, which Glinka adopted as the libretto for his opera. Stalin avidly watched the scene of the dying Polish soldiers. In front of him in his secret box stood a large plate of hard-boiled eggs. From time to time he would take an egg and eat it, all the while keeping his eyes fixed on what was taking place on the stage.[5] (An interesting similarity is found between Stalin's behavior and that of an accused murderer examined by Bekhterev in 1898. Bekhterev was assigned by a court to examine a certain Russian country squire named Shebalin, who was accused of murder. Bekhterev's diagnosis was paranoia, persecution mania combined with megalomania, and he concluded that the lives of others had no value for Shebalin, who lived in constant fear of assassination. Shebalin's diet consisted mostly of hard-boiled eggs because he thought it was impossible to inject them with poison.[6])

Stalin's obsessive interest in the death of Polish soldiers in *Ivan Susanin* was indicative of his hatred for the entire Polish people. Having destroyed tens of thousands of Poles on Soviet territory, Stalin became obsessed with the idea of partitioning Poland between Germany and the Soviet Union and, at the same time, securing a Soviet–German alliance, using Poland as the bait. The Munich agreement to partition Czechoslovakia, signed by the Western democracies with Hitler on 30 September 1938, was interpreted by Stalin as the capitulation of Britain and France, which strengthened his respect for Hitler and his contempt for the 'decadent' European democracies. Vladimir Potemkin, whom Stalin had made assistant commissar for Foreign Affairs, began openly to promote the idea of the partition of Poland in order to attract Hitler's attention. 'My poor friend, what have you done?' Potemkin said to the French ambassador to Moscow, R. Coulondre, shortly after the end of the Munich conference. 'I don't see any other conclusion than a fourth partition of Poland.'[7] (The three partitions of Poland, in 1772, 1793 and 1795, by Russia, Austria and Prussia respectively, had been part of an intricate diplomatic arrangement between these three great European powers at the time, the purpose of which was to avoid military conflicts over the 'Eastern Question', that is, over their competing claims in dividing up the inheritance of the decaying Ottoman Empire. The Ottoman Turks were retreating from the European continent, from the Balkans, and from North Africa and the Near East; the European powers used Polish territory as an exchangeable commodity to compensate each other for concessions made when their interests were in conflict. As a result of the three partitions, the Russian Empire absorbed eastern Poland with its large Ukrainian, Byelorussian and Jewish populations.)

Stalin's scheme of the 'fourth partition' of Poland completely lacked the geopolitical considerations that had been at the heart of the three partitions of Poland at the end of the eighteenth century. His true aim was to provoke the Germans into attacking Poland in order to destroy it, using Hitler as his 'hit man'. The scheme was in line with his customary approach of murder by proxy – only the scale of the crimes changed: whereas before the Revolution Stalin had provoked the murders of individual victims, he now provoked mass executions and toward the end of the 1930s he prepared for the destruction of the entire Polish nation.

Until March 1939, Stalin's attempts to reach an agreement with Hitler failed despite the efforts of his personal emissary David Kandelaki.[8] In the words of the German ambassador to Moscow, Count F. W. Schulenburg, Kandelaki 'enjoyed the confidence of Stalin'.[9] On 10 March 1939 Stalin in his speech at the Eighteenth Party Congress warned of unidentified 'war-mongers who are accustomed to have others pull chestnuts out of the fire for them'. He expressed the Soviet Union's desire to improve Soviet–German relations and stated that the British, French and American press had been trying to 'incense the Soviet Union against Germany, to poison the atmosphere, and to provoke a conflict, when no sensible reasons for such a conflict exist'. The Soviet Union intended to stay out of the 'new imperialist war', which, Stalin stated, was 'already in its second year'. These declarations were received favorably in Berlin.[10] Hitler did not suspect that Stalin's aim was to destroy Poland and that *he* had been chosen to pull the Polish chestnut out of the fire for Stalin.

The United States embassy in Moscow reported to Washington that the message of Stalin's speech was that Germany 'may count on Soviet neutrality in the event of war against the Western powers'.[11] The German embassy in Moscow in its report to Berlin offered an interpretation of

Stalin's motives that was closer to the truth, pointing out that the Soviets wanted to 'bring about war between Germany, France and Britain, while they, to begin with, preserve their freedom of action and further their own interests'.[12] Hitler acted soon after Stalin's speech. On 15 March 1939 the German Army occupied Czechoslovakia. Hitler was faced with the problem of what to do with the 700,000 Ukrainians living in the part of Czecho-slovakia known as Ruthenia, or Carpatho-Ukraine. They proclaimed their independence and requested the protection of the Third Reich. On 3 December 1939 Schulenburg wrote to Berlin that Stalin was against grant-ing independence to Carpatho-Ukraine and thought it might become 'a crystallizing point for the Ukrainian independence movement'.[13] both the Soviet Union and Poland had large Ukrainian populations. Hitler initiated secret negotiations with Poland, offering Carpatho-Ukraine in exchange for the port city of Danzig (Gdansk) and a 'corridor' (a strip of land for rail and road through Polish territory, linking Germany with east Prussia). He promised to support future Polish gains at the expense of the Soviet Ukraine. When his offer was rejected, Hitler began to consider seriously Stalin's idea of partitioning Poland between Germany and the Soviet Union.[14] Hitler ceded Carpatho-Ukraine to Hungary, which had possessed this area before the defeat of the Austro-Hungarian Empire in the First World War, and ordered Schulenburg to improve Soviet–German relations.[15]

On 3 April 1939 Hitler ordered the Wehrmacht to prepare for an attack on Poland, and on 28 April 1939 he renounced the Polish–German peace treaty. Stalin was certain that his idea of the partition of Poland had been accepted by Hitler and that negotiations on this issue would soon start. On 17 April 1939 Soviet Ambassador to Berlin Aleksey Merekalov suggested to the German foreign ministry that a process of improvement be started in Soviet–German relations.[16] Throughout April 1939 emissaries of Stalin, operating under diplomatic cover, broached the theme of improving rela-tions in talks with German officials.[17]

One man obviously unsuited for negotiation with Hitler was the Commissar of Foreign Affairs Maxim Litvinov, since he was known in Berlin as a supporter of *rapprochement* with the Western democracies and was a Jew. On 1 May 1939 Litvinov was present at the usual military parade and civilian demonstration in Red Square, but later that day was dismissed from his post. The next evening Stalin called him and ordered him to give to Molotov a list of the most important foreign ministry officials. Stalin appointed Molotov People's Commissar of Foreign Affairs. V. M. Molotov, L. P. Beria, his assistant, V. G. Dekanozov, and Stalin's assistant, G. M. Malenkov, entered Litvinov's office. Molotov placed on Litvinov's desk the list of 30 diplomats that had been prepared by Litvinov. One after the other these diplomats were summoned to Litvinov's office, where Beria and Dekanozov questioned them, after which each one was arrested. (Only one, Evgeny Gnedin, the illegitimate son of Alexander Parvus, survived torture and prison to be released after Stalin's death.) From May to August 1939 Lubianka interrogators were preparing a show trial of 'Litvinov's case', and the arrested diplomats were forced to sign depositions accusing Litvinov of various crimes. In the end Stalin decided to abandon the idea and spare Litvinov's life.[18]

The Soviet chargé d'affaires in Berlin, Grigory Astakhov, was ordered to find out Hitler's reaction to the dismissal of Litvinov. Astakhov reported that Hitler was very pleased by the fact that his replacement, Molotov, was not Jewish. (Schulenburg, an ardent supporter of improvement in Soviet–German relations, knew about Hitler's 'distaste' for Jews and did not report to him that Molotov's wife Polina Zhemchuzhina was Jewish.) Hitler said that the dismissal of Litvinov was the 'decisive' factor in his decision to start negotiations with Stalin.[19] He ordered Schulenburg to approach Stalin with the suggestion of an agreement between the Soviet Union and Germany.[20] In a letter to Mussolini, Hitler pointed to the 'readiness on the part of the Kremlin to arrive at a reorientation of its relations with Germany, which became apparent after the departure of Litvinov.'[21]

On 20 May 1939 Schulenburg suggested to Molotov the starting of trade negotiations between Germany and the Soviet Union. Molotov replied that a 'necessary political base' had to be established first.[22] Stalin wanted to arrive at an agreement with Hitler on the partitioning of Poland before the trade questions were addressed. Hitler agreed to that. On 23 May 1939 Hitler told German generals that he intended to invade Poland even if Britain and France came to Poland's defense. The generals objected to starting a war over Poland against the Western powers, especially since Russia, too, might come to the defense of Poland. Hitler responded by stating that it was not out of question that Russia would show itself disinterested in the destruction of Poland.[23] He did not suspect that the destruction of Poland was the main motive behind Stalin's drive to improve relations with Germany. The German foreign minister, Joachim von Ribbentrop, predicted that if Hitler could secure a friendly agreement with Stalin to maintain at least neutrality in the German–Polish conflict, Britain and France would not declare war on Germany. A week later, on 30 May 1939, Ribbentrop's deputy Weizsacker sent to the German embassy in Moscow the following coded wire: 'Contrary to the policy previously planned, we now have decided to undertake definite negotiations with the Soviet Union.'[24]

On 27 July 1939 Julius Schnurre, the man in charge of commercial negotiations with Russia, invited the Soviet officials Astakhov and Baburin to a dinner in a Berlin restaurant and during the dinner conversation pointed out that such 'virile countries' as Russia and Germany were more similar to each other in world outlook than they were to the 'decadent' democracies. Astakhov agreed and asked what would be the fate of the Ukrainian and Byelorussian parts of Poland if Poland should cease to exist. Schnurre acknowledged Soviet interest in these parts of Poland. Astakhov then pointed out that the Soviet Union was interested in the Baltic states and the Bessarabian part of Rumania. Schnurre said that Germany sympathized with Soviet aspirations. Astakhov reported the conversation to Moscow.[25]

Hitler set the date for the invasion of Poland for the end of August 1939, before the autumn rains would render Polish roads difficult to use for the Wehrmacht's motorized divisions. On 18 August 1939 Hitler ordered Ribbentrop to sign the Soviet–German treaty. Stalin attempted to delay the signing, but Hitler sent him a personal letter, urging that Ribbentrop sign the treaty by 23 August 1939. Stalin wired his assent. When Stalin's reply was brought to Hitler, he pounded on the wall with his fists and shouted: 'I have the world in my pocket!'[26]

On 23 August 1939 Ribbentrop arrived in Moscow, and the same evening signed the non-aggression pact. The partition of Poland was spelled out in an additional secret protocol. Poland was to be divided between Germany and the Soviet Union by a line that ran through the middle of the country along the Vistula river. Stalin put his signature on the map on which the line was drawn. (More than half a century later, the secret protocol with this map was found in the Soviet Communist Party archive and was published.[27]) It also stated that Estonia, Latvia and Finland were in the sphere of interest of the Soviet Union, while Lithuania was relegated to the German sphere. (Somewhat later, Stalin exchanged the Polish-populated area of Lublin for Lithuania.) Stalin also expressed his interest in the Bessarabian part of Rumania, and the Germans took note of this.

The signing ceremony was followed by a reception and a banquet. 'I know how much the German nation loves its Führer', Stalin said in his toast. 'I should therefore like to drink to his health.' Ribbentrop toasted Stalin and Molotov.[28] When in the morning the German delegation was leaving the Kremlin, Stalin took Ribbentrop by the arm and said: 'The Soviet government takes the pact very seriously. I can guarantee on my word of honor that the Soviet Union will not betray its partner.'[29] The next day, Ribbentrop gave Stalin a draft for a joint communiqué. Stalin read it, smiled wistfully and said: 'Don't you think that we have to pay a little more attention to public opinion in our countries? For many years we have been pouring buckets of slop over each other's heads . . . Public opinion in our country, and probably in Germany too, will have to be prepared slowly for the change in our relations which this treaty is to bring about . . . '.[30]

Stalin's more moderately worded communiqué was accepted. On his return to Berlin, Ribbentrop said that in Stalin's entourage he felt as if he were among his old Nazi comrades. He was praised for his accomplishment by a jubilant Hitler, who called him the 'new Bismarck'. Hitler intended to order the German Army to march into Poland on 26 August 1939 but the British, having received a report about his plan from their intelligence service, surprised him by repeating on 25 August 1939 their earlier pledge to come to Poland's defense, if attacaked. Hitler was furious. 'What now!' he shouted at the 'new Bismarck', who had predicted that Great Britain would cave in if the Soviet–German pact was signed. Hitler rescinded the order for the invasion.[31] For Hitler and Stalin the next several days were filled with anxiety. Hitler's top-secret memorandum of 1936 had envisioned the German economy being able to support a major war by 1940, but now he risked such a war a year earlier. Stalin, eager to see Hitler crush Poland, was afraid that the threat of a wider war might force Hitler to abandon the attack on Poland. But toward the end of August 1939 Hitler made the fateful decision to order the German Army into battle. 'Let us not have another war of flowers', he said. 'Even the bravest army becomes demoralized by bloodless victories like those we had in the Rhineland, in Austria and in Czechoslovakia.'[32]

Hitler expected that at the time of the German attack, Stalin would move the Red Army into the territory assigned to the Soviet Union by the secret protocol and he was alarmed by intelligence reports about the Soviet Army's withdrawal from the Polish frontier. Molotov provided a dubious explanation to the effect that the USSR was a constitutional state and that the Soviet–German pact had to be ratified by the Supreme Soviet, which had not yet found time to do so. Hitler, however, would not stand for such nonsense. The Supreme Soviet ratified the pact on 31 August 1939. The next morning, German troops crossed the Polish frontier.

On 3 September 1939 Britain and France declared war on Germany. 'May God have mercy on us, if we lose', said Goering when he heard the news.[33] On 6 September 1939 a Polish request for help arrived in Moscow, but Molotov told the Poles that his government had no intention of helping them. By then the Polish Army was in disarray. Outnumbered and lacking in modern equipment, it was, for all its gallantry, no match for the mechanized German divisions. The Wehrmacht rolled across Poland, approaching the secretly agreed-upon Soviet–German border along the Vistula River. Schulenburg kept telling Molotov to move in Soviet troops to claim Russia's share of Poland. But Stalin was not yet ready to issue marching orders. He was aware that in the eyes of the civilized world his partnership with Hitler in the division of Poland would be seen as a criminal act and, as usual, was looking for ways to hide responsibility for it and to create the impression that he had nothing to do with the destruction of the Polish state. 'Of course, it's all a game to see who can fool whom', he said. 'I know what Hitler's up to. He thinks he's outsmarted me, but actually it's I who have tricked him.'[34]

On 17 September 1939 Stalin finally ordered the Red Army to cross the Polish border. The Soviet propaganda machine presented the move as an innocent act of extending a 'brotherly hand' to the Ukrainian and Byelorussian peoples, who were supposedly threatened by the advancing German Army. The Soviet Army met no resistance. Polish General Mecheslav Smoravinsky ordered his troops not to fight the advancing Soviet units, and the Polish government ordered all units of the Polish Army to surrender to Soviet troops. Soviet planes dropped leaflets with appeals to Polish soldiers to kill their officers and government officials. Many Polish officers were killed by Soviet troops at the time of their surrender, and some 15,000 officers were taken prisoner and transported to the Soviet interior, where they were interned in three separate camps. Most of the officers were reservists who had been called to active duty at the onset of the war. In December 1939 they were allowed to send Christmas cards to their families, which they assumed to be an indication of their speedy release.

Immediately after the partition of Poland, 180,000 Poles were deported to Siberia from the Soviet-occupied area. Another 1,200,000 were sent there in the course of the next two years. On 5 March 1940 Stalin called a Politburo meeting and got approval for his proposal to execute the 14,700 Polish officers held in the camps in Kozelsk, Starobelsk and Ostashkovo, as well as 11,000 arrested Polish officers, factory owners, landlords, government officials, and priests held in various prisons and camps in territories incorporated into the Soviet Union. Stalin put his signature on the record of this decision. (The record was found in October 1992 in the personal archive of Mikhail Gorbachev, and was published by the Yeltsin government.[35]) The chiefs of the NKVD in the annexed Polish territories directed the executions in these areas.

A special system was instituted for the execution of the Polish officers in the three camps. B. Z. 'Bakhcho' Kobulov, deputy of Lavrenty Beria, summoned the chiefs of the NKVD administrations in the Smolensk, Kalinin and Kharkov regions and read to them the 'highest authority' order to execute the Polish officers held in the camps in their areas. The officers from the Ostashkovo camp were driven to the NKVD prison in Kalinin on Sovetskaya Street, where the commandant, NKVD Lieutenant A. M. Rubanov, prepared a special sound-proof death chamber. The Polish officers were led into the adjacent 'Lenin room', and their hands were tied with ropes. Then, they were pushed into the death chamber, where Rubanov and a Moscow representative, Major B. M. Blokhin, waited behind the door and shot their victims in the back of the head. The massacre went on for many days. The same method was used in the Kharkov NKVD prison, where the Starobelsk camp officers were murdered.[36]

The execution of the Kozelsk camp officers was carried out differently. They were told that they would be transported to another camp. Before the departure, they were vaccinated – against typhus and cholera, they were told. Their personal belongings were not taken from them. Only after their arrival in the Katyn Forest near Smolensk did the officers begin to suspect that this was the end. One of them, Major Solsky, kept a journal in which he recorded his observations until moments before his death. He made his last entry on 9 April 1940: 'A few minutes before 5 am they woke us up and put us on trucks which had little cells, each one guarded. We arrived in a little wood which looked like a holiday place. They took away our rings and watches which showed the time was 6:30 am. What will happen to us?'[37]

The officers' hands were tied with ropes; they were herded in small groups and led to prepared graves, where they were shot, one by one, in the back of the head. The executioners were rushed to finish their assignment and did not search the corpses. Because of this, many personal items and documents, including Major Solsky's diary, were buried in the mass graves. Some Poles offered resistance; they were dragged to the grave with their long military tunics tied over their heads, pushed to the edge of the pit, and shot. Some had their heads crushed, others were finished off with bayonets. When it was over, the executioners covered the graves with earth and planted young pine trees to cover the traces of the massacre. The murdered Polish officers were educated men. Some of them may have even heard the opera *Ivan Susanin*, but they could not have imagined that their execution was a bizarre re-enactment of a scene in this opera, orchestrated by Stalin.

On 26 October 1940 Beria signed a secret order to present 144 NKVD officers in the Smolensk, Kalinin and Kharkov regions with various awards 'for successful execution of special assignments'. Forty-four officers were awarded an extra month's salary, the rest received 800 rubles each. At the top of the list of those given rewards was the name of Captain F. K. Ilyin, the deputy chief of the NKVD in the Smolensk region. He directed the Katyn Forest massacre. Not much is known about the others on that list. One of them, Sukharev, who bragged after the incident that 'today I have done a good job' and was awarded 800 rubles, shot himself years later. Rubanov and Blokhin became drunkards and also committed suicide. As for the others, in the words of Adam Ulam, 'Besides the Last Judgment, nothing threatens them.'[38]

After the partition of Poland, relations between Stalin and Hitler continued to be good for several months, but signs of trouble began to appear here and there. On 27 September 1939, Ribbentrop came to Moscow. Stalin told him that 'to partition the Polish population would create sources of unrest from which discord between Germany and the Soviet Union might arise . . .'. Stalin offered to give to Germany the Lublin region, populated by Poles, in exchange for Lithuania. Ribbentrop agreed, but requested that the oil-rich Drogobych area be given to Germany, because the Soviet Union already had a great deal of oil while Germany had none. Stalin said that 'the Ukrainian people had strongly pressed their claims to the area' and promised to sell oil to Germany.[39] The Soviet–German communiqué stated that since the disappearance of Poland from the political map of Europe was a fact of life, there was no need for the continuation of the war and declared that Britain and France were the aggressors, responsible for the hostilities. It also stated that the Soviet Union and Germany intended 'to engage in mutual consultations in regard to necessary measures' in case the war should continue.[40] The two countries also agreed to a mutual exchange of citizens. The NKVD handed over to the Gestapo a large number of German refugees, most of them German Jews who had sought safety on Soviet soil. The agreement had a provision for consultations to coordinate police measures in combating Polish nationalist agitation.

In October 1939 Stalin forced Latvia and Estonia to sign a 'mutual assistance' pact that allowed Soviet bases on their territories. He attempted to coerce Finland into a similar arrangement, but the Finns balked. On 29 November 1939 Stalin accused Finland of shelling the Leningrad area, and the Red Army invaded Finland. Otto Kuusinen, a Finnish communist whose son was imprisoned in Moscow, was made the head of a puppet government ready to be installed in Finland. The Finns, however, put up strong resistance, the Red Army suffering 250,000 casualties: 50,000 dead and 200,000 wounded – this number exceeded that of the entire Finnish Army. The heroic Finnish resistance inspired an outpouring of sympathy in the Western democracies as well as in Germany. Great Britain and France were urgently debating sending military help to the Finns. The Soviet Union was expelled from the League of Nations. In March 1940 Stalin sued for peace, settling for minor mutual land concessions. The Finnish campaign dramatically exposed the weakness of the Red Army after the mass arrests and executions of its officers following the failure of the Tukhachevsky plot. Stalin, as usual, did not blame himself. In March 1940 he ordered the NKVD to prepare a new show trial of 'not yet exposed participants of the Tukhachevsky conspiracy'. A new wave of arrests swept through the Red Army.

Stalin's show trials made a strong impression on Hitler. They convinced him that Stalin was an enemy of 'Jewish Bolshevism' and that Stalin's personal dictatorship was quite compatible with German fascism. Hitler expressed his admiration for Stalin. He called him 'the cunning Caucasian', and stated that Stalin commanded his 'unconditional respect' and was, 'in his own way, just one hell of a fellow! He knows his models Genghis Khan and the others very well.' In a paroxysm of praise Hitler described Stalin as 'one of the most extraordinary figures in world history'.[41] In a letter to Mussolini, he wrote: 'Stalin pretends to have been the herald of the Bolshevik Revolution. In actual fact, he identifies himself with the Russia of the Tsars, and he merely resurrected the tradition of Pan-Slavism. For him Bolshevism is only a means, a disguise designed to trick the German and Latin peoples.'[42] Hitler also considered Stalin a 'worthy rival'.[43] He felt that in Stalin he had found a 'kindred soul'.[44]

Stalin, too, considered Hitler a kindred soul, nowhere more so than in the question of their shared hatred of the Jews. On this issue Stalin could not help but envy the openness with which Hitler preached and practiced his anti-Semitism. Stalin had to pretend to be an avid internationalist and to pay lip service to the proclaimed Bolshevik doctrine. Stalin may well have been envious of Hitler's credentials: Hitler was not an imposter but a true ideologue and the founder as well as the leader of the German National Socialist Party. He had no need to fear being exposed as a traitor to his party by archival documents. But the inevitable break in relations between Hitler and Stalin had nothing to do with this difference in their pasts nor with hidden envy on the part of Stalin. Rather, its roots lay in an irreconcilable conflict of interest in the perennial 'Eastern Question'.

Events did not unfold in the way that the two dictators had planned. On 10 May 1940 Winston Churchill became the British prime minister. That same day Hitler ordered the German Army to attack France, the Netherlands, Luxembourg and Belgium. On 21 May the German Army advanced to the English Channel, forcing the British to flee from Dunkirk. The French Army was crushed. On 10 June 1940 Italy declared war on Britain and France. French Prime Minister Paul Reynaud, who had earlier replaced Daladier, resigned. The new French prime minister, Marshal Pétain, a First World War hero, promptly sued for peace. For the moment, the defiant Britain of Winston Churchill faced the Germans alone.

The fall of France led Stalin to believe that German victory was near. He promptly ordered the occupation of Estonia, Lithuania and Latvia, and in July 1940 these Baltic states were 'admitted' into the USSR as constituent republics. In late June 1940, Stalin annexed Bessarabia and northern Bukovina as well, proclaiming this formerly Rumanian territory part of the Moldavian Soviet Socialist Republic. But in annexing northern Bukovina, Stalin had gone beyond the agreed limits of the secret protocol. Hitler decided not to wait for Stalin to swallow what was left of Rumania. In August and September 1940 the German Army moved into Rumania, and Hitler assigned part of its Transylvanian province to Hungary and the province of Dobrudja to Bulgaria. The dark shadow of the 'Eastern Question' fell over German–Soviet relations. Territories that once were part of the Ottoman Empire turned into a bone of contention between Germany and Russia, as had happened in the late eighteenth century in relations among Prussia, Russia and Austria. But this time Poland was already partitioned, and sections of it could not be used as a bargaining chip in the territorial aspirations of Stalin and Hitler. Bukovina was only the beginning of the conflict between the two dictators over the 'Eastern Question'.

In September 1940 the Tripartite Pact of Germany, Italy and Japan was signed. Stalin intended to join this victorious coalition in order to participate in the distribution of the spoils. The purpose of Molotov's visit to Berlin in November 1940 was to reach an agreement with Hitler on the conditions under which the Soviet Union would join the Berlin–Rome–Tokyo 'Axis'. Hitler greeted Molotov warmly on his arrival in Berlin on 12 November 1940. After a few words of welcome, he went into a long presentation of his grandiose plans for the division of the world between Germany and its allies. Molotov listened with great attention and replied that he agreed in principle, though some terms would have to be clarified.[45] On the same day Ribbentrop told Molotov what he thought were Hitler's terms for the division of the world. Speaking about German and Italian *Lebensraum* ('living space') Ribbentrop said that the German aspirations were limited to the former German colonies of Central Africa, while the interests of Italy were focused on North and East Africa. Then, Ribbentrop suggested that Russia might also turn to the south, in the direction of the Persian Gulf and the Arabian Sea, for a natural outlet to the open sea. He asked whether at the same time certain aspirations of Russia in this part of Asia – in which Germany was completely uninterested – could not also be realized.[46] Molotov liked the offer. The problem was that Ribbentrop did not know about Hitler's latest plans for the area of the Persian Gulf and the Arabian Sea.

The next day Hitler took over negotiations with Molotov. Ribbentrop no longer mentioned the Persian Gulf and the Arabian Sea as the focal point of Soviet aspirations. Instead, he spoke of the future partition of the British Empire, suggesting that the Soviet Union should extend its sphere of influence in the direction of India and find there an outlet into the Indian Ocean. Gustav Hilger, the German foreign ministry's expert on Soviet affairs, wrote that 'the conflict of aims of the partners in the negotiations became so obvious that it was clear even then that there was little hope for the possibility of reaching an understanding'.[47] Hitler declared that, according to a Soviet–German oral agreement, the former Austrian territories were to fall within the German sphere of influence.[48] This meant that the Balkan states, which at one time had belonged to the Ottoman Empire and later were part of the Austro-Hungarian Empire, were within the German sphere. Hitler pointed out that the underlying rationale of the secret protocol of the 1939 Soviet-German Pact was the agreement to restore the territorial possessions of the two empires he and Stalin had inherited. Hitler viewed himself as the heir of the old German and Austrian empires, whereas Stalin wanted to restore the old Russian Empire. It was unavoidable that the two dictators would also inherit the old claims and bitter rivalries that had divided these empires.

After his conversation with Molotov on 12 November 1940 Hitler told Goering of his decision to crush the Soviet Union.[49] Hitler was not present at the final discussion, which was conducted in an air-raid shelter because of the British bombing of Berlin on the evening of 13 November 1940. Ribbentrop said that the decisive question was whether the Soviet Union was 'prepared and in a position to cooperate with us in the great liquidation of the British Empire'. He offered the German draft of a new secret protocol, expressing the hope that 'an agreement could be reached on possible Soviet aspirations in the direction of British India, if an understanding were reached between the Soviet Union and the Tripartite

Pact'.[50] Molotov insisted on Soviet interest in the 'Near East', in Turkey, Bulgaria, Rumania, Hungary, Yugoslavia and Greece. Ribbentrop asked Molotov to sign another secret protocol with the statement: 'The focal point of the territorial aspirations of the Soviet Union would presumably be centered south of the territory of the Soviet Union in the direction of the Indian Ocean.'[51] Molotov said that he could not take a 'definite stand' on this without Stalin's agreement.[52]

That the last conversation between Molotov and Ribbentrop took place in a bomb shelter made a deep impression on Stalin because it drove home a coded message he had received on 11 November 1940, the day before Molotov's arrival in Berlin: the Soviet ambassador to Great Britain, Ivan Maisky, had reported that in his opinion Germany had lost the air war over England. This message and the British air raid on Berlin led Stalin to believe that Hitler was in a weak position and that therefore the time was right to extract from him concessions in the area of the Near East. On 25 November 1940 Stalin sent Hitler a note stating that 'The Soviet Union is prepared to accept the draft of the Four Powers Pact' with a modification (the Four Powers being Germany, Italy, Japan, and the Soviet Union). The main modification was the point that 'the area south of Batum and Baku in the general direction of the Persian Gulf is recognized as the center of aspirations of the Soviet Union'. In his note, Stalin repeated this idea twice. He also demanded the establishment of a Soviet naval base on the Bosporus and the Dardanelles, and stated that, in the case of Turkish resistance, 'the Soviet Union agrees to work out and carry through the required military and diplomatic measures'.[53]

Before November 1940 Hitler had not expressed much interest in the Near East, but by the time of Molotov's visit to Berlin, his strategic thinking had undergone a drastic change: he decided to make the Near East a zone of German interest. This decision was dictated by the German defeat in the air war over Britain, which threatened to prolong the conflict. It meant a sharp rise in German dependency on oil supplies from abroad, as Germany had no oil resources of its own. An important factor in Hitler's decision to occupy Rumania in August 1940 was the need to secure for Germany the oil-producing Rumanian Ploesti fields. (Stalin had earlier refused Hitler's request to cede to Germany the oil-producing region of Drogobych.) Hitler was attracted by the vast oil resources of Iran and Iraq, where his agents were inflaming anti-British rebellions and where various organizations sympathetic to Germany were active. Stalin's claims to the 'territory south of the Batum–Baku line', meaning Iran and Iraq, were in direct conflict with Hitler's plans. Hitler was also driven by irrational motives, the most powerful of which was his pathological hatred of the Jews. The Jewish population of Palestine, which was under British mandate, appeared to Hitler as a major 'Jewish threat', and he intended to destroy it. In 1939 Arab fanatics in Palestine set up a shadow cabinet under the leadership of Hajji Amin al-Husseini, the Mufti of Jerusalem, who incited riots that led to the Arab rebellion of 1939. The result was a bloody Jewish pogrom. The Mufti al-Husseini openly sided with Hitler, and joined in hate propaganda against Britain and the Jews. He appealed to Hitler to destroy the Palestine Jews and free the Muslim world from 'the Jewish and British yoke'. (In May 1941, the pro-German organizations were crushed by the British, and al-Husseini fled to Germany.[54]) Hitler cultivated pro-German feelings among Arab nationalists, who agitated against Britain's policy of creating a 'national home' for the Jews in Palestine.[55] In 1939 German radio took over from the Italians the Arabic-language broadcasting of anti-Jewish and anti-British propaganda.[56] Hitler viewed all these activities as indications of Germany's favorable prospects in the Near East and decided that Stalin's claims to this area were incompatible with German interests. He did not answer the Soviet note of 25 November 1940. On 18 December 1940 he signed a secret order, code-named 'Operation Barbarossa', to the German high command, stating: 'The German Wehrmacht must be prepared to crush Soviet Russia in a quick campaign.'[57] The date for the invasion was set for 15 May 1941.

NOTES

1 J. Pilsudski, *Rok 1920 z povody pracy M. Tuchaczewskiego 'Pochod za Wisle'*, Warsaw, 1931, Tukhachevsky's Polish 'origin' was the reason he was appointed commander of the Soviet forces advancing on Warsaw in the 1920 Soviet–Polish war. Also V. Primakov in his 'last word', which was almost certainly penned by Stalin, referred to the non-Russian ethnic origin of his fellow defendants at the 11 June 1937 trial (see Chapter 28 above).

2. Robert Conquest, *The Great Terror*, New York, 1973, p. 582.

3. Ibid., pp. 583–5.

4. Recollections of Richard Vinaver, one of the Polish children who were placed in orphanages. Interview with Vinaver in Moscow in 1957.

5. Galina Vishnevskaya, Bolshoi Theater singer and the wife of cellist Mstislav Rostropovich, states in her recollections that in Stalin's box 'there was always a big bowl of hard boiled eggs on a table . . .'. See the excerpt from her autobiography *My Russia, My Love*, New York Post, 26 September 1984, p. 31.

6. Oleg Moroz, 'Poslednii diagnoz,' *Literaturnaya gazeta*, 28 September 1988.

7. R. Coulondre, *De Staline à Hitler*, Paris, 1950, p. 165.

8. Walter G. Krivitsky, *I Was Stalin's Agent*, London, 1939, pp. 38f.

9. Lionel Kochan, *The Struggle for Germany 1914–1945*, New York, 1967 p. 118, fn. 65, quoting Schulenburg's report to Berlin, GFM-2/1907/429293-4.

10. *Documents on German Foreign Policy 1919–1945*, series D, vol. VII, Washington and London, 1954–62, pp. 225–9.

11. Kochan, *The Struggle for Germany*, p. 73, quoting *Foreign Relations of the United States, Soviet Union 1933–1939*, pp. 748f.
12. *Documents on German Foreign Policy, 1918–45*, series D, vol. III, p. 139.
13. Ibid., series D, vol. V, pp. 138–40.
14. Donald W. Treadgold, *Twentieth Century Russia*, Chicago, 1976, p. 335.
15. Kochan, *The Struggle for Germany*, p. 120, fn. 89, quoting *Documents on German Foreign Policy, 1918–1945*, series D, vol. IV, pp. 441, 590.
16. Adam B. Ulam, *Stalin*, New York, 1973, p. 508, quoting R. J. Sontag and J. S. Beddie (eds), *Nazi–Soviet Relations 1939–1941: Documents from the Archives of the German Foreign Office*, p. 2.
17. Kochan, *The Struggle for Germany*, p. 74, and p. 120 fn. 90, quoting *Nazi–Soviet Relations, 1939–1941*, vol. I, pp. 1f.
18. Evgeny Gnedin, *Katastrofa i vtoroe rozhdenie*, Amsterdam, 1977, pp. 107–09.
19. *Documents on International Affairs, 1928–1963*, vol. I, 1939–1946, p. 446.
20. Gustav Hilger and Alfred G. Meyer, *The Incompatible Allies*, pp. 296f.
21. *Nazi–Soviet Relations 1939–1941*, Washington, 1948, p. 81.
22. Ibid., p. 6.
23. *International Military Tribunal*, vol. XXXVII, Nuremberg, 1947, p. 550.
24. Ulam, *Stalin*, p. 508.
25. Ibid.
26. Ibid., p. 510.
27. The secret protocol with the map and Stalin's signature was published by the Yeltsin government, *New York Times*, 19 August 1989, pp. A1–5.
28. *Documents on German Foreign Policy 1919–1945*, series D, vol. VII, Washington and London, 1954–62, pp. 225–29.
29. Alan Bullock, *A Study in Tyranny*, New York, 1964, p. 531.
30. Hilger and Meyer, *The Incompatible Allies*, p. 304.
31. Ulam, *Stalin*, p. 512.
32. Albert Speer, 'Nazi Invasion of Poland ? September 1 1939,' *The New York Times*, 31 August 1979, p. A–23.
33. Ulam, *Stalin*, p. 512.
34. N. S. Khrushchev, *Khrushchev Remembers*, Boston, Toronto, 1970, p. 128.
35. *The New York Times*, 15 October 1992, pp. 1 and 8.
36. *Novoe vremia*, no. 46, 1992, p. 48.
37. Report of the Polish Red Cross, *The New York Times*, 17 February 1989, p. A–9.
38. Ulam, *Stalin*, p. 513.
39. *Novoe vremia*, no. 46, 1992, p. 48.
40. *Documents on German Foreign Policy 1918–1945*, series D, vol. VIII, p. 160.
41. Solomon F. Bloom, *Commentary*, May 1957, p. 417.
42. Ibid.
43. Robert G. L. Waite, *The Psychopathic God: Adolf Hitler*, New York, 1977, p. 76.
44. Bloom, *Commentary*, p. 417.
45. Hilger and Meyer, *The Incompatible Allies*, p. 323.
46. *Nazi–Soviet Relations 1939–1941*, Washington, 1948, pp. 221f.
47. Hilger and Meyer, *The Incompatible Allies*, p. 323.
48. *Nazi–Soviet Relations 1939–1941*, pp. 234–37.
49. Alan Bullock, *A Study in Tyranny*, New York, 1964, p. 622.
50. *Nazi–Soviet Relations 1939–1941*, pp. 221f.
51. Ibid., pp. 247–54.
52. Ibid.
53. Ibid., pp. 258f.
54. George E. Kirk, *A Short History of the Middle East*, New York, 1964, pp. 194–99.
55. Ibid.
56. Ibid.
57. *Documents on German Foreign Policy 1918–1945*, series D, vol. XI, p. 899.

34

THE WAR AND THE OCTOBER 1941 MASSACRE

Events in Yugoslavia prevented Hitler from attacking the Soviet Union on 15 May 1941 as originally planned. On 20 March 1941 Yugoslavia joined the Axis, but the overthrow of the Belgrade government by Serbian officers opposed to an alliance with Germany forced Hitler to order German troops, which had been moving into Poland, to move into Yugoslavia and suppress the rebellion.[1] This development postponed the invasion of the Soviet Union by more than a month.

On 3 April 1941 Churchill sent a message to Stalin, informing him of Hitler's intention to invade the Soviet Union.[2] Stalin was receiving similar warnings from various sources, but shrugged them off as attempts by Britain to sow discord between him and Hitler. A former Czech agent in Berlin, code-named 'Shkvor', reported to Soviet intelligence the concentration of German troops along Soviet borders. Stalin read Shkvor's report and wrote on it in red pencil, 'English provocation'. He ordered the NKVD to assassinate Shkvor.[3] A number of warnings of the impending German attack came from Richard Sorge, the Soviet master spy in Japan. Stalin disregarded his information (Sorge was arrested by the Japanese and executed in 1943). Stalin's own intelligence organs did not help matters: Marshal F. I. Golikov, chief of Soviet military intelligence, presented warnings about an imminent German invasion as coming from 'doubtful sources'. Golikov was afraid he would be seen by Stalin as an 'English *provocateur*'.[4]

Stalin, meanwhile, was confronting his 'enemies' in the military, whom he suspected of plotting to kill him. A new wave of arrests of officers had started in spring of 1940. They were accused of taking part in a military conspiracy to assassinate Stalin and were forced to sign depositions accusing the deputy commissar of defense, General K. A. Meretskov, of heading this conspiracy. Some 40 such depositions had been signed by the end of spring 1941. Stalin planned to arrest Meretskov in June and to stage his show trial soon thereafter. Thereafter, several events conspired to change his mind.

On 5 April 1941 late at night, Stalin invited the Yugoslav ambassador, Milan Gabrilovic, as the representative of the anti-German rebel government to Moscow, to sign a non-aggression pact. Hitler interpreted this as a clear challenge to Germany.[5] Over the next few days, the Wehrmacht occupied Yugoslavia and Greece. On 13 April 1941 the 'Neutrality Pact' between the Soviet Union and Japan was signed. After a Kremlin dinner Japanese Foreign Minister Yosuke Matsuoka was driven to the Moscow railroad station to board a trans-Siberian train for his trip home. Suddenly, to the astonishment of the diplomats and reporters who had come to see Matsuoka off, Stalin appeared at the station. He embraced Matsuoka, saying to him, 'We are both Asiatic.' He told Matsuoka that he considered Britain and the United States to be enemies of the Soviet Union. Then, he went up to the German ambassador, Count Schulenberg, put his arm around his shoulders and said, 'We must remain friends, and you must do everything to that end!' He found in the crowd General Hans Krebs, the acting German military attaché, and told him, 'We will remain friends with you – whatever happens!'[6]

On 1 May 1941 Stalin appeared as usual on top of the Lenin mausoleum, reviewing the military parade and civilian demonstration. Next to him, always a position of honor, stood the newly appointed ambassador to Germany, Beria's assistant, V. G. Dekanozov. An Armenian native of Gori and a common criminal in his youth, Dekanozov enjoyed Stalin's trust. On 6 May 1941 Stalin assumed the post of chairman of the Council of People's Commissars, a position equivalent to prime minister. Schulenburg reported to Berlin that, in his opinion, Stalin wanted to correct the recent mistakes of Molotov's foreign policy, which had led to the cooling of Soviet–German relations.[7] In the opinion of Gustav Hilger, who was Schulenburg's adviser at the time, Stalin wanted to 'use all the authority of his person and his official position' to improve Soviet–German relations. Hitler, however, had other plans. On 30 April 1941, Schulenburg returned to Moscow after a brief visit to Berlin, where he had had an audience with Hitler. Schulenburg left for Moscow, convinced that Hitler had secretly decided to attack the Soviet Union. 'The die has been cast', he told embassy officials when his plane landed at the Moscow airport. 'War against Russia has been decided!'[8]

On 13 May 1941 the Soviet news agency TASS stated that 'rumors' of the German intention to launch an attack against the Soviet Union were without foundation.[9] Trying to appease Hitler, Stalin ordered the closing of the Yugoslav and Greek embassies. On 18 June 1941 the Soviet ambassador to Great Britain, Ivan Maisky, reported to Stalin the transfer of 147 German divisions to areas along the Soviet borders – information he had learned from British Foreign Secretary Anthony Eden. Despite this, Stalin left on the same day for his annual vacation in the Caucasus, having issued an order to avoid 'provocations' along the Soviet–German border. Stalin arrived in Sochi on 20 June and there received Commissar of the Navy Nikolay Kuznetsov's report that all German merchant ships had left Soviet waters. Stalin took this report more seriously than previous warnings and gave several orders to increase combat preparedness. He also ordered Molotov to start a diplomatic offensive through Schulenburg to repair ties with Hitler. At 9 pm on 21 June 1941 Molotov met with Schulenburg, who promised to do his best to improve relations between their countries.

Early next morning German troops attacked along the entire Soviet–German border from the Baltic to the Black Sea. Motorized divisions of the Wehrmacht moved rapidly inside Soviet territory, easily breaking the Red Army's resistance and taking entire units prisoner. Schulenburg returned to Molotov's office early in the morning and read the declaration of war. 'I know it is war', said Molotov. 'Your aircraft have just bombarded some ten open villages. Can it really be that we have deserved that?'[10] At noon Soviet radio transmitted Molotov's announcement that the war had begun with a sudden attack of the 'fascist brigands'. For the next ten days Stalin did not issue a single statement to the Soviet people, who expected him to rally them for the defense of the country. War with Germany did not fit into his plans, and he did not want to part with his wishful vision of his alliance with Hitler. Stalin's tendency to mistake wishful thinking for reality was in full force: to accept the fact that the alliance was a thing of the past took time. At a time when the motorized units of the Wehrmacht were moving deeply inside Soviet territory, Stalin clung to the notion that the attack was a 'provocation' by some undisciplined German units.[11] His attention was fixed on the imaginary plot of General K. A. Meretskov, whom he intended to 'expose' at the planned show trial.

The day after German troops moved into Soviet territory, General Meretskov received the order to come to Moscow immediately. He was arrested as soon as he arrived. Beria's deputies V. N. Merkulov and L. E. Vladzimersky accused the general of taking part in a 'military conspiracy' and in 'conspiring with Kork and Uborevich to give battle to Stalin'. The non-Russian sounding phrase 'to give battle to Stalin' indicates that the author of this accusation was Stalin. Meretskov was shown depositions of some forty military 'plotters' who had confirmed this charge. He denied ever having plotted with Kork and Uborevich, who had been executed in June 1937 together with Tukhachevsky. Merkulov and Vladzimersky applied to Meretskov 'measures of physical influence', a euphemism for beatings with rubber sticks, to obtain a confession.[12] Among Meretskov's 'co-conspirators' were People's Commissar of the Defense Industry B. L.

Vannikov, Lieutenant-General Y. V. Smushkevich, Colonel-General G. M. Shtern, and several other top military commanders. Two days after the war started, Major Maria Nesterenko, an Air Force ace and commander of a special purposes brigade, was arrested. She was married to Lieutenant-General P. B. Rygachov, one of the arrested officers. The accusation against her read: 'Having been the darling wife of Rygachov, she could not but know about the treacherous activities of her husband.'[13]

During the first week of the war, Stalin refused to see any Politburo members except Beria, with whom he discussed the depositions of Meretskov and other 'plotters' and the scenario of the planned show trial. But on 30 June 1941 a group of Politburo members saw Stalin and pleaded with him to take immediate steps to improve the situation at the front.[14] Stalin began to face the reality of the threat the war posed to his regime. He appointed himself supreme commander-in-chief and head of the *stavka* (military headquarters). His radio address was tape-recorded in Sochi and the tape was broadcast several times during 3 July 1941 while Stalin was on his way to Moscow. He spoke in a nervous, halting voice with the familiar Georgian accent. His train made frequent stops along the way while the track was checked for mines (Stalin chose to travel by train because he was afraid of flying).[15]

Upon his arrival in Moscow, Stalin ordered Beria to force several arrested men to sign depositions stating that Mikhail Kaganovich, the younger brother of Politburo member Lazar Kaganovich, was Hitler's agent and that Hitler intended to appoint him 'vice president of Russia' after German victory. Before the war Mikhail Kaganovich had been the people's commissar of the aviation industry, and because of this Stalin also accused him of ordering aircraft factories to be built near the border so that the Germans would capture them in case of war. Stalin informed the Politburo members of these charges; Lazar Kaganovich said, 'Well, so what? If it's necessary, arrest him!' Stalin praised Lazar Kaganovich for being a 'man of principles'. Mikhail Kaganovich was taken to Mikoyan's office for a face-to-face confrontation with a prisoner who had been ordered to repeat the accusations. As usual, the charges contained a generous measure of truth about Stalin himself, which he projected on to Mikhail Kaganovich. Hitler had expressed the opinion that it would be best, after victory over Russia, to entrust the administration of the country to Stalin – under German supervision – since he was the best man to handle the Russians.[16] And it was Stalin who had ordered the construction of airplane factories near the border with Germany because he considered Hitler an ally and did not foresee a war against him. According to Mikoyan's assertion, Mikhail Kaganovich asked permission to go to the toilet, from where a shot was heard moments later.[17] It is unlikely that Kaganovich shot himself – with the exception of Stalin's bodyguards, no one was allowed to enter the Kremlin with firearms. Most probably, Kaganovich was shot by Stalin's bodyguards. He was buried at the Novodevichy cemetery, near the grave of Stalin's late wife, Nadezhda Allilueva. Mikhail Kaganovich's wife was to be buried there a few years later.[18]

The rapid advance of the German Army inside the Soviet Union forced Stalin to seek help from the Western democracies. On 11 July 1941 the 'Agreement for Joint Action' between Britain and the Soviet Union was signed and took effect immediately.[19] Among those present was Maxim Litvinov, former commissar of foreign affairs, whom Stalin suddenly appointed ambassador to the United States. By the end of July, Harry Hopkins, President Roosevelt's special emissary, arrived in Moscow. He was impressed by Stalin's knowledge of Soviet military needs and by his ability to remember details and figures. Hopkins did not know that Stalin had a photographic memory, and he came away with the impression that talking to Stalin 'was like talking to a perfectly coordinated machine'. Litvinov interpreted the conversation. His sudden reappearance in the Kremlin reminded Hopkins of 'a morning coat which had been laid away in moth-balls when Russia retreated into isolation from the West, but which had now been brought out, dusted off, and aired as a symbol of changed conditions'. Stalin asked Hopkins to relate to Roosevelt that the Soviet government 'would welcome American troops on any part of the Russian front under the command of the Americans'.[20]

On 16 July 1941 the Germans captured near Vitebsk hundreds of thousands of Red Army soldiers and officers. Among them was 33-year-old First Lieutenant Yakov Dzhugashvili, Stalin's older son by his first wife. German planes dropped leaflets with a photo of Yakov with the appeal to Soviet soldiers to follow his example and surrender. When one of the leaflets was brought to Stalin, he ordered the arrest of Yakov's Jewish wife, Yulia Meltser, accusing her of being a German spy and of 'tricking Yakov into German hands.' The daughter of Yulia and Yakov, Gulia Dzhugashvili, was 4 years old.

Yakov refused to cooperate with the Germans. One of the German interrogators recorded: 'Good, clever face of a typical Georgian. Behaved properly. For the last time spoke to his father by phone before going to the front. Categorically rejected a compromise between capitalism and communism. Did not believe in German final victory.'[21] In the autumn of 1941 Hitler ordered that preferential treatment be extended to Yakov.[22] He was placed in the Hotel Adlon in Berlin, where an attempt was made to use him for propaganda purposes. Georgian immigrants in Germany were allowed to visit him, but Yakov refused to cooperate with them as well as with the Germans. In April 1942 he was transferred to a prisoner-of-war camp near Lübeck where his bunk neighbor in the barrack was René Blum, son of the former prime minister Léon Blum. Hitler offered to trade Yakov for captured Field Marshal von Paulus, but Stalin sent a reply through Count Bernadotte, the Swedish chairman of the Red Cross, stating: 'I do not trade marshals for soldiers.' Yakov often felt depressed and refused to eat. He was especially hurt by Stalin's slogan: 'There are no prisoners-of-war, only traitors', which was repeatedly transmitted by the camp radio. After several attempts at escape, Yakov was transferred to the Sachsenhausen death camp. His fate was marked by an irony: his close friends in the camp were Polish officers who had been captured by the Germans in 1939. They, like the British and French officers, were receiving parcels and money transfers from their relatives through the Red Cross and they also received aid from the Polish government in exile in London. Yakov and the other Soviet prisoners-of-war received nothing from relatives or the Soviet government. Polish officers allotted to Yakov a monthly portion from their parcels of food, and he became friendly with Poles who spoke Russian. Together with them he attempted to escape on several occasions.[23] On the night of 14 April 1943 a scuffle broke out between Yakov and some British officers who accused him of not cleaning up after himself, and one of them hit Yakov in the face. He ran out of the barrack and threw himself on the electrified barbed wire. A guard on duty fired. Yakov was killed, and his body was burned in the camp crematorium.[24] (Two years after Yulia's arrest, Stalin ordered her release from solitary confinement in Lefortovo prison when he learned that Yakov had been killed in the prisoner-of-war camp and that Yakov had refused to collaborate with the Germans. Yulia left the prison a cripple. She died some time later.[25] Gulia, their daughter, survived.[26])

In August 1941, Churchill and Roosevelt held a conference aboard a warship off the coast of Newfoundland and agreed to set up the Lend-Lease program to help the Soviet Union. William Bullitt, who had been the American ambassador to the Soviet Union, urged Roosevelt to insist that Stalin, in return for Lend-Lease, issue definite, written, public pledges of no territorial expansion in the Far East and the pledge that the postwar boundaries of the Soviet Union in Europe should be those of August 1939. He warned Roosevelt of Stalin's imperialistic claims, which would only be checked if Stalin renounced Soviet territorial acquisitions in Poland, the Baltic states and Rumania. Roosevelt disagreed. 'I just have a hunch that Stalin is not that kind of man', said Roosevelt. 'Harry [Hopkins] says he's not . . . and I think that if I give him everything I possibly can and ask nothing from him in return, *noblesse oblige*, he won't try to annex anything and will work with me for a world of democracy and peace.' Bullitt replied that when Roosevelt 'talked of *noblesse oblige* he was not speaking of the Duke of Norfolk, but of a Caucasian bandit whose only thought when he got something for nothing was that the other fellow was an ass'. Roosevelt was annoyed and ended the exchange by saying, 'It is my responsibility not yours, and I'm going to play my hunch.'[27]

On 28 September 1941 the British minister of aircraft production, Lord Beaverbrook, and Roosevelt's roving ambassador, Averell Harriman, arrived in Moscow. That day German tanks broke through Red Army defenses and were about to capture Orel, the last major city on their rapid advance to Moscow. Stalin had persistently asked Churchill to open a second front 'somewhere in the Balkans' or France, but in September 1941 he suddenly requested the landing of some 30 British divisions in the Soviet port of Archangel or their transfer to the Soviet Union through Iran. Churchill had great difficulty raising *two* divisions for defense of the Middle East from the advancing German army. 'It is almost incredible that the head of the Russian Government with all the advice of their military experts could have committed himself to such absurdities', commented Churchill. 'It seemed hopeless to argue with a man thinking in terms of utter un-reality.'[28] On the other hand, Harriman and Beaverbrook saw in Stalin a capable leader who understood the reality of the threat to his country. During a meeting on 30 September 1941 Beaverbrook noticed that Stalin was doodling numerous pictures of wolves and was filling in the background with red pencil.[29] Others on different occasions also noticed Stalin's habit of drawing wolves. Beaverbrook did not know that the wolf symbolized an 'enemy' for Stalin.[30] He also did not know that Stalin was occupied by the imaginary threat of the military 'plotters', whom he intended to execute with a stroke of his red pencil.

All the arrested military men, except for Colonel-General A. D. Loktionov, signed confessions extracted under torture. During a face-to-face confrontation with Meretskov, the purported head of the conspiracy, Loktionov, writhing in pain and stretching his bleeding hands toward Meretskov, pleaded, 'Kirill Afanasievich, you know that this did not happen, did not happen, did not happen!' He fell silent when his eyes met the tired stare of Meretskov, who had lived through the same torture.[31]

But, in what must have seemed a miracle to them, Stalin decided to release from prison some of the accused plotters. By the end of September 1941 he realized that they would be more useful to him alive than dead. People's Commissar of the Defense Industry B. L. Vannikov, having been tortured and forced to sign fantastic confessions, was expecting execution when he received Stalin's order 'to describe in writing your proposals in regard to the development of production of armaments under condition of commenced military actions'.[32] Vannikov was released and reinstated in his post. Stalin also ordered the release of General Meretskov, whom he invited to visit him in the Kremlin. When Meretskov entered his office, Stalin took several steps toward him. He greeted him, 'Good day, Comrade Meretskov! How do you feel?'[33] Meretskov, too, was returned to his post. But a different fate awaited the other arrested military men. On 15 October 1941 most were evacuated from Moscow with the instruction that the investigation of their 'case' be continued.

By mid-October 1941 German troops had advanced to the suburbs of Moscow. Panic and looting of stores erupted in several sections of the capital. Stalin ordered all government offices evacuated to the city of Kuibyshev (Samara). He told the relatives of his late wife, Nadezhda Allilueva, to leave Moscow. A special train was waiting for him at a secret junction ready to depart for Kuibyshev, where a deep underground shelter would protect him. Earlier, on 7 October 1941, Stalin had appointed G. K. Zhukov commander of the western front and had ordered him to defend Moscow.[34] Zhukov transferred some 400,000 troops from Siberia and the Far East and deployed them in the city's defense. Stalin had been assured by Richard Sorge, the Soviet master spy in Japan, that the Soviet eastern borders were safe because the Japanese were preparing to attack American bases in the South Pacific. (Sorge's intelligence was to prove correct two months later when the Japanese attacked Pearl Harbor on 7 December 1941.) Because of the transfer of the Siberian reinforcements and the unusually early onset of a bitterly cold winter, for which the German troops were woefully unprepared, the German offensive came to a halt.

Despite the panic in Moscow, Stalin paid attention to the case of the 'military plotters'. On 18 October 1941 he gave the order to terminate the investigation and to execute immediately 25 especially important defendants who were undergoing interrogation. On 28 October Maria Nesterenko was being questioned in the Kuibyshev NKVD when Beria's assistant Rodos suddenly entered the room and said to her, 'Let's go!' Shortly thereafter, five covered trucks left the prison, heading toward a special lot near the small village of Barbysh, where 20 accused officers were executed.[35] The remaining five defendants could not be found in the Kuibyshev prison because they had been transferred by mistake to Saratov. On 28 October 1941 they were executed there. Executed at the same time in the city of Orel were the wives and children of Gamarnik, Kork, Uborevich and other Red Army generals who had been shot in 1937 together with Marshal Tukhachevsky.[36] All these executions were, in Stalin's mind, connected with the conspiracy of Tukhachevsky and the history of his Okhrana file.

But Filip Goloshchekin was executed at that time because in Stalin's mind he was connected with Roman Malinovsky. Generals G. M. Shtern and Y. B. Smushkevich were also executed in Kuibyshev. They had directed the fighting with the Japanese in the Far East in 1938, which Stalin connected with the defection of Genrikh Liushkov and the planting of the 'Eremin Letter'. Also in October 1941, Stalin ordered Beria to promise Alexander Svanidze, the brother of his first wife, that his life would be spared if he confessed that he had fabricated Okhrana documents to discredit Stalin. 'What should I ask forgiveness for?' Svanidze replied, 'I have committed no crime.' He was executed. 'See how proud he is!' said Stalin. 'He died without asking forgiveness.'[37] As always, Stalin's accusations contained fragments of distorted truth. Svanidze had indeed forged Okhrana documents in the secret Kremlin printing press, but had done so on Stalin's orders to glorify Stalin's revolutionary past. Stalin placed these forgeries in Soviet archives. On Stalin's order, Svanidze had also fabricated the 'Eremin Letter' and similar fakes intended to discredit true documents linking Stalin with the Okhrana. The execution of Svanidze was connected in Stalin's mind with events in far away Shanghai that reminded him of the 'Eremin Letter' forgery. When German troops reached the suburbs of Moscow in October 1941 M. D. Golovachev decided to sell the 'Eremin Letter' – which he had received from Liushkov – to the German embassy in Shanghai, thinking that Stalin's regime was about to be destroyed. On 26 November 1941 a cable with Golovachev's offer was sent to the German foreign office in Berlin. Soon, a request for additional information about the origin of the 'Eremin Letter' and its history went from Berlin to Shanghai. On 5 January 1942 the German embassy in Shanghai sent a secret cable to Berlin, stating that Golovachev's document 'had been hidden at the time by tsarist police officers' and that it was 'smuggled out only in 1934'.[38] Gustav Hilger, a top specialist in Russian affairs at the German foreign office in Berlin, at that time took part in the discussion of what to do with Golovachev's offer. He recollected that it was decided not to follow up on this matter because German officials felt that during the war they would be unable to put the 'Eremin Letter' through the necessary external tests.[39] Stalin no doubt knew from Soviet intelligence reports of Golovachev's attempt to sell the forgery to the Germans.

In November 1941 Soviet troops under the command of Zhukov rolled the German units back from the suburbs of Moscow. The commander of the German panzer divisions, General H. Guderian, wrote in his diary early in December 1941: 'The offensive on Moscow has ended. All the sacrifices and efforts of our brilliant troops have failed. We have suffered a serious defeat.'[40] The decisive battle took place around Stalingrad (Tsaritsyn Volgograd), where one of the Soviet army corps was commanded by General Rodion Malinovsky. The general's name was mentioned during a meeting in Stalin's office. Stalin grew alarmed and asked Khrushchev several times, 'Who is this Malinovsky?' Khrushchev did not know what to say. 'When you return to the front, you'd better keep a close watch on him', Stalin urged. 'Check up on all his orders and decisions. Follow his every move.' Khrushchev replied, 'Very well, Comrade Stalin, I won't let Malinovsky out of my sight.' Not knowing that the name 'Malinovsky' reminded Stalin of his Okhrana rival Roman Malinovsky, Khrushchev was puzzled by Stalin's order. He wrote in his memoirs: 'When I got back to the front I had to spy on Malinovsky every hour of the day. I had to watch him even when he went to bed to see if he closed his eyes and really went to bed to sleep. I did not like having to do this one bit.' Khrushchev added that in General Malinovsky's case 'perhaps the practical demands of wartime reality compelled Stalin to hold his anger and suspiciousness in check'.[41]

NOTES

1. *Documents on German Foreign Policy 1918–1945*, series D, vol. XII, Washington and London, 1954–62, p. 126.
2. H. Montgomery Hyde, *Stalin: The History of a Dictator*, New York, 1971, p. 426.
3. John Erickson, *The Soviet High Command*, London, 1955, p. 577. Also Hyde, *Stalin*, p. 427.
4. Hyde, *Stalin*, p. 427, citing Soviet source G. A. Deborin, quoted in *Survey*, April 1967, p. 443.
5. Gustav Hilger and Alfred G. Meyer, *The Incompatible Allies*, New York, 1974, pp. 327f. The authors state, 'Nothing the Russians did between 1939 and 1941 made Hitler more angry than the treaty with Yugoslavia; nothing contributed more directly to the final break; and Stalin must have sensed it'. years later wrote Gustav Hilger, the adviser to Count Schulenburg, the German ambassador to the Soviet Union.
6. Winston Churchill, *The Second World War*, vol. II, London, 1948, p. 511. Hyde, *Stalin*, p. 429, quoting *Documents of German Foreign Policy 1918–1945*, series D, vol. XII, p. 537.
7. *Documents on German Foreign Policy 1918–1945*, series D., vol. XII, p. 870.
8. Hilger and Meyer, *The Incompatible Allies*, p. 329.
9. *Nazi–Soviet Relations 1939–1941, Documents from the Archives of the German Foreign Office,*

Washington, 1948, p. 345.

10. Hilger and Meyer, *The Incompatible Allies*, p. 336.

11. Hyde, *Stalin*, p. 435, quoting Khrushchev's 'Special Report to the Twentieth Party Congress' (his secret speech).

12. Arkady Vaksberg, 'Taina Oktiabria 1941-go', *Literaturnaya gazeta*, 1988; reprinted in *Mir*, no. 165, 5–11 May 1988.

13. Ibid.

14. Khrushchev's secret speech.

15. Hyde, *Stalin*, pp. 438f.

16. Albert Speer, *Inside the Third Reich*, New York, 1970, p. 306.

17. Roy Medvedev, *Let History Judge*, New York, 1971, p. 310.

18. I. P. Itskov in a taped interview with the present author.

19. Sir Ernest Llewellyn Woodward, *British Foreign Policy in the Second World War*, London, 1962, pp. 152f.

20. Robert E. Sherwood, *The White House Papers of Harry L. Hopkins*, vol. I, 1949, pp. 343–5.

21. A. N. Kolesnik, 'Voennoplennyi starshii leitenant Yakov Dzhugashvili', *Voenno-istoricheskii zhurnal*, Moscow, December 1988.

22. Speer, *Inside the Third Reich*, p. 306.

23. A. N. Kolesnik, 'Voennoplennyi starshii leitenant Yakov Dzhugashvili'.

24. *The New York Times*, 19 February 1968, p. 7.

25. Svetlana Allilueva, *Dvadtsat' pisem k drugu*, New York, 1967, pp. 151f. See also Ya. L. Sukhotin, 'Iosif Vissarionovich bolshoe gnezdo . . .', *Novoe Russkoe Slovo*, April 8–9 1996.

26. Recollections of Nadine Brackman, the present author's wife, who was a classmate of Gulia in the second through sixth grades. She remembers that Yulia and her daughter Gulia lived in the secret police building on Bolshoi Komsomolsky Lane not far from the Lubianka. Gulia attended school no. 644 in the nearby Armiansky Lane. In the morning, a maid would accompany her to school, carrying her books and notes. After classes, the maid escorted her home. The girl was a loner. She hardly talked to her classmates and usually stood alone near a corridor window during breaks between classes.

27. Beatrice Farnsworth, *William C. Bullitt and the Soviet Union*, 1967, pp. 3 and 173.

28. Churchill, *The Second World War*, vol. III, pp. 405 and 411.

29. Sherwood, *The White House Papers of Harry L. Hopkins*, vol. I, p. 392.

30. See Chapters 35 and 36 below.

31. Arkady Vaksberg, 'Taina Oktiabria 1941-go'. *Litteraturnaya gazeta*, reprinted in *Mir*, no. 165, 5–11 May 1988.

32. Ibid.

33. Ibid.

34. Hyde, *Stalin*, pp. 459f.

35. Vaksberg, 'Taina Oktiabria 41-go'.

36. V. A. Chalikova, 'Arkhivnyi yunosha', *Neva*, October 1988, p. 153.

37. Medvedev, *Let History Judge*, p. 311. Also Khrushchev's secret speech.

38. The 'J' letter is on file in I. D. Levine's archive, and a copy of it is in the present author's archive. This confidential letter from a high State Department official, who signed the letter 'J', to Isaac Don Levine, dated 17 July 1956. The Letter referred to two secret cables, dated 26 November 1941 and 5 January 1942, from the German mission in Shanghai to the German foreign office in Berlin. The cables were discovered in File AA/18 at the Alexandria Repository of captured German Second World War documents.

39. Ibid.

40. Avon, the Earl of, *The Reckoning*, London, 1960–65, p. 206.

41. N. S. Khrushchev, *Khrushchev Remembers*, Boston, Toronto, 1970, pp. 203–5.

35

GENERALISSIMO WITH A CRIPPLED ARM

Paradoxically, the war years were psychologically the most normal time during Stalin's rule: for once, the country was not fighting 'enemies of the people' who were figments of his imagination. The threat of defeat forced Stalin to seek help even from those he most hated, among them the Polish people: he agreed to allow the formation of a Polish Army on Soviet territory. At the end of July 1941 General Wladislaw Sikorsky, the head of the Polish government in exile, and Ivan Maisky, the Soviet ambassador to Britain, signed an agreement that all Polish citizens and prisoners-of-war would be released from Soviet camps and jails and allowed to join the Polish Army. The question of the Soviet–Polish frontier was left unsettled. It was stated only that all the Nazi–Soviet treaties of 1939 had 'lost their validity'. The existence of the secret protocols on the partition of Poland was not known at the time.

In October 1941, when German troops were threatening Moscow, Beria summoned to his office Polish General Zigmunt Berling, one of the few surviving Polish officers who had been released from prison following the Soviet–Polish agreement, to discuss a plan for organizing the Polish Army. General Berling said that, according to information he had received, there were many Polish officers in three camps in Kozelsk, Starobelsk and Ostashkovo; there would be enough to organize the Polish Army. Beria's assistant V. N. Merkulov dropped an alarming hint: 'No, not these. In regard to them we made a big mistake.'[1]

The Polish ambassador to the Soviet Union, Stanislav Kot, was received by Stalin on 14 November 1941 and during the meeting asked Stalin to 'ensure' that all Polish officers and citizens be released. 'Are there Poles not yet released?' asked Stalin, pretending to be surprised and ignorant about the fate of the 15,000 executed Polish officers. 'We have names and lists', said Kot. 'Do exact lists exist?' asked Stalin. Kot explained that the names of all officers were known to the Polish government in exile. Stalin pretended to be incredulous. He picked up the telephone. 'NKVD?' he said into the receiver. 'This is Stalin. Have all the Poles been released from prison?' Stalin waited for a few seconds, as if listening to a reply, and then said, 'Because I have the Polish Ambassador with me and he tells me they haven't all been released.' Again Stalin pretended to be listening for few moments. Then he put down the receiver and turned to Kot, muttering as if confused, 'They say they've been released.'² During a meeting with Stalin two weeks later, Ambassador Kot, General Sikorsky and General Wladislaw Anders, who had been appointed commander of the Polish forces on Soviet territory, asked again for the release of the 15,000 Polish officers who were not in German prisoner-of-war camps and had not returned to their homes in Poland. Stalin feigned extreme surprise. 'That's impossible', he said. 'They've fled.' General Anders asked, 'But where could they flee to?' Stalin had an idea: 'Well, for instance, to Manchuria,' he suggested, perhaps recalling Liushkov's defection there. 'It isn't possible that they have all fled', General Anders protested. 'They must have been released, only they haven't arrived yet', insisted Stalin. 'Please understand that the Soviet Government has no reason whatever for detaining a single Pole.'³

Stalin's comment about people he sent to their deaths was: 'There is no need to remember the victims, because they all are *odnim mirom mazany* ['tarred by the same brush'].'⁴ The silence of mass graves seemed to assure Stalin that his victims had been forgotten. But the case of the murdered Polish officers began to haunt him soon after the Germans found the secret burial grounds in occupied Soviet territory. Hitler did not attach much importance to these mass graves, but paid attention to the one discovered in the Katyn Forest near Smolensk when told that it contained the remains of executed Polish officers. The discovery was made by accident: in July 1941, when the Germans occupied Smolensk, one of two NKVD officers who had been assigned to detonate explosives in the NKVD archive, had instead shot his partner and defected to the Germans, handing them the archive intact. Among the documents were records of the execution of the Polish officers in the spring of 1940. An elderly peasant named Parfen Kiselev and a village smith named Ivan Krovozertsov led the Germans to the mass graves of the Polish officers. Exhumation began a year later, and the first report about the Katyn massacre of thousands of Polish officers by the NKVD was broadcast by Berlin radio on 13 April 1943. Two days later, Soviet radio accused the Germans of the massacre of Polish officers in the Katyn Forest in the summer of 1941 when the Germans occupied the Smolensk region.

Germany invited representatives from several countries and the Red Cross to investigate the case. The Red Cross commission established the identities of the executed officers by their personal belongings, like diaries and letters, as well as by their uniforms. It also established that the executed officers were from the Kozelsk camp and had been murdered in the spring of 1940 that is, more than a year before the German invasion. General Sikorsky forwarded the report of the Red Cross commission to Winston Churchill, but Churchill decided not to publish it, stating that if the officers were dead then nothing could bring them back to life.[5] Nevertheless, the Polish government in exile persisted in demanding that the Soviets account for the Katyn massacre and for the fate of the officers in the Starobelsk and Ostashkovo camps. Stalin decided to break off relations with Sikorsky's government and to set up a puppet Polish government on Soviet territory. Soon thereafter, Sikorsky died in a plane crash.

After the Soviet Army recaptured the Katyn area in January 1944 a column of covered trucks delivered wooden boxes with the bodies of 925 Polish officers from Katyn to the Moscow Institute of Judicial Medicine, where NKVD personnel manipulated the remains, equipping them with 'material proof' like newspaper articles and forged diaries, aimed at substantiating Stalin's assertion that the executions took place after the German occupation of the Smolensk area. The next night these trucks carrying the remains headed back to Katyn. On 24 January 1944 the Soviet government published a statement that a 'special commission' had determined that the execution of the Polish officers had taken place in the summer of 1941 when the area was under German occupation. (After the war Stalin attempted to include the Katyn massacre in the record of the Nuremberg Nazi War Crimes Tribunal, but after briefly considering the case early in July 1946 the tribunal decided not to list Katyn among the Nazi crimes. The British and American governments also decided not to submit to the Nuremberg Tribunal the Red Cross report charging the Soviet Union with the Katyn massacre and thus pointing to Stalin as a war criminal. On Stalin's order a small stone monument was erected at Katyn. The inscription read: 'Here were buried prisoners – officers of the Polish Army, who perished in horrible torment at the hands of German-Fascist occupiers in the fall of 1941.'[6])

Stalin hoped to implicate his Western Allies in a mass murder similar to the Katyn Forest massacre: during the Teheran Conference, which started on 27 November 1943 he at one point suddenly suggested to Roosevelt and Churchill that 50,000 German officers be executed at the end of the war. Churchill objected: 'The British Parliament and the public will never tolerate mass executions. The Soviets must be under no delusion on this point.' Stalin insisted, saying, 'Fifty thousand must be shot. The general staff must go.' Churchill was outraged. By that time he knew from the Red

Cross report that the Katyn massacre had been perpetrated by Stalin's secret police. 'I would rather be taken out into the garden here and now and shoot myself than sully my own and my country's honor by such infamy', he said. Roosevelt intervened, joking, 'I have a compromise to propose. Not 50 thousand, but only 49 thousand should be shot.' His son Elliott, who had been invited to the dinner, said that he wholeheartedly agreed with Marshal Stalin's plan and was sure that the United States Army would support it. Churchill, greatly annoyed, left the table, saying that he resented 'this intrusion'. Stalin followed him, claiming that all this had been a 'joke'.[7]

During the Teheran Conference Roosevelt was eager to establish a close personal relationship with Stalin. He tried to please Stalin by teasing Churchill and making disparaging remarks about him. Roosevelt later recalled Stalin's reaction: 'A vague smile passed over Stalin's eyes, and I decided I was on the right track . . . I began to tease Churchill about his Britishness, about John Bull, about his cigars, about his habits . . . I kept it up until Stalin was laughing with me . . . The ice was broken and we talked like men and brothers.'[8] Sir Alan Brooke, the British chief of the imperial general staff, wrote in his diary: 'This conference is over when it has only just begun. Stalin has got the President in his pocket.' Brooke realized that Stalin had by then definite ideas as to how he wanted the Balkans run after the war, and that he intended to bring Turkey and the whole Eastern Mediterranean into the sphere of Soviet influence.[9] What Brooke did not know was that Stalin had a few years earlier attempted to reach an agreement with Hitler about the inclusion of these very areas in the Soviet sphere of interest, and that his disagreement with Hitler in this matter had led to the war between Germany and the Soviet Union. The perennial 'Eastern Question', which had historically led to conflict, was now threatening relations between Stalin and his Western allies.

Churchill was annoyed by Roosevelt's attempts to please the Soviet dictator and saw in a possible Roosevelt–Stalin alliance a threat to British interests. He was alarmed when Stalin invited Roosevelt to move into the Soviet embassy compound during the Teheran Conference under the pretext that Soviet intelligence had uncovered a German plot to kidnap Roosevelt and to assassinate Churchill and Stalin. Roosevelt accepted Stalin's invitation. Stalin visited him and they spoke for an hour through their interpreters. Roosevelt said that he was in favor of self-determination for the peoples of the British Empire, and he mentioned with pride that the United States had given independence to the Philippines. He warned Stalin not to mention the question of India, as if he and Stalin had already agreed on Indian independence and Churchill was their adversary in this issue.

Stalin readily assumed the role of the earnest champion of independence of all the peoples of the world, saying that India was unquestionably a painful problem for Churchill. Roosevelt said that the change in India should start at the bottom; Stalin agreed, noting that 'reforms from the bottom mean revolution'.[10]

By the time of the Teheran Conference, Stalin felt confident of victory. The German Army had suffered defeat at Stalingrad and had been driven from the Caucasus, which opened the route for delivery of aid through Iran by his Western allies. On 6 March 1943 Stalin bestowed upon himself the rank of 'Marshal of the Soviet Union', and he was proclaimed 'the greatest strategist of all times and all peoples'. In June, Stalin received a report that British and American troops had landed on the shores of Normandy, opening the second front.

On 20 June 1944 a group of German officers attempted to assassinate Hitler, hoping that with him out of the way Germany would be able to end the obviously lost war. The plotters were executed. Goebbels's propaganda machine poured hate on them in a manner reminiscent of Vyshinsky's oratory at the Moscow show trials. In the newspaper *Angriff* he stated: 'Degenerates to their very bones, blue-blooded to the point of idiocy, nauseatingly corrupt, and cowardly like all nasty creatures − such is the aristocratic clique which the Jew has sicked on National Socialism . . . We must exterminate this filth, extirpate it root and branch.'[11] The attempt on Hitler's life reminded Hitler of Stalin's mass purge in the military in 1937–38. Hitler expressed regret that he had failed to follow Stalin's example and purged the German Army the same way. He said that he had always believed the charges in the Moscow show trials to have been trumped up, but after the attempt on his life his new-found insight was that he could no longer exclude the possibility of treasonous collaboration between the Russian and German general staff. Hitler stated that the assassination attempt on his life had made him, finally, realize that in trying Tukhachevsky, Stalin had taken the decisive step toward successful conduct of the war. This new interpretation of the Tukhachevsky case inspired Hitler's confidence that he had reached the great turning point in the war. 'The days of treason are over', he exclaimed. 'New and better generals will assume command.'[12]

By the end of July, the Soviet Army had reached the Vistula River. Warsaw was within Stalin's reach, but he ordered General K. K. Rokossovsky not to cross the river without his personal order. He knew from Soviet intelligence sources that the Polish underground army, under the command of General Tadeusz Bor-Komorovsky, was ready to stage an armed uprising against the Germans. The uprising began on 1 August 1944.

The German Army was ordered to crush the Poles and to destroy whole sections of Warsaw. Churchill, Roosevelt and the head of the Polish government in exile, Stanislav Mikolajczyk, pleaded with Stalin to help the Poles, but on 16 August 1944 Stalin cabled Churchill: 'Things being what they are, Soviet headquarters have decided that they must dissociate themselves from the Warsaw adventure since they cannot assume either direct or indirect responsibility for it.' On 20 August 1944 Churchill and Roosevelt sent Stalin an urgent message: 'We hope that you will drop immediately supplies and munitions to the patriot Poles in Warsaw, or you will agree to help our planes in doing it very quickly. We hope you will approve. The time element is of extreme importance.'[13]

Stalin was only too happy to have the Poles slaughtered by the Germans. The Polish uprising lasted for two agonizing months. When the Germans finally crushed it, some 15,000 Polish fighters had been killed and 250,000 inhabitants of Warsaw met their deaths under the ruins of their city. On 17 January 1945, three months after the surrender of General Bor-Komorovsky and his fighters, the Soviet Army entered Warsaw. Churchill bitterly complained that the Russians found there 'little but shattered streets and the unburied dead'.[14]

Churchill was well informed about Roosevelt's desire to promote movements for independence in the British colonial possessions in the Far East and the Mediterranean. Churchill was forced to seek Stalin's support in the hope of counterbalancing Roosevelt.[15] On 9 October 1944 Churchill arrived in Moscow. Roosevelt refused to travel there, because of the presidential election in which he, despite failing health, was running for his fourth term. 'Let us settle our affairs in the Balkans', Churchill said at his first session with Stalin. 'So far as Britain and Russia are concerned, how would it do for you to have 90 per cent predominance in Rumania, for us to have ninety per cent of the say in Greece, and go 50–50 per cent in Yugoslavia?' While Stalin was listening to the translation of this offer, Churchill took a piece of paper and wrote '50–50 per cent for Hungary, 75 per cent for Russia in Bulgaria'. Churchill pushed the paper across the table to Stalin, who, after a short pause, took a blue pencil and signed his consent. Then he pushed the paper back to Churchill and Eden. 'Might it not be thought rather cynical if it seemed we had disposed of these issues, so fateful to millions of people, in such an offhanded manner?' asked Churchill introspectively. 'Let us burn the paper.' Stalin, who had no intention of honoring any agreement, was not concerned with such trifles. 'No', he said without hesitation, 'you keep it.'[16]

In January 1945, Stalin's attention was drawn to reports of Soviet intelligence that a Swedish diplomat Raoul Wallenberg had helped save a large number of Hungarian Jews. Wallenberg was not Jewish, but had strong ties to the Jews of Palestine, where he had worked in the banking system. Wallenberg was asked by a group of American Jews to join the Swedish embassy in Budapest in order to save Jews from death in Nazi concentration camps. On his arrival in Budapest in July 1944, Wallenberg issued 20,000 Swedish passports to Hungarian Jews and placed 13,000 more of them in Swedish-owned houses. Stalin assumed that Wallenberg was an 'American and Zionist spy'. Stalin had earlier opposed the Allies' plans to bomb Nazi concentration camp crematoriums because he did not want to stop the killing of the Jews.[17] On 17 January 1945 Soviet troops entered Budapest and the 33-year-old Wallenberg was arrested by V. S. Abakumov, the head of *Smersh* ('Death to Spies'), the Soviet counterintelligence organization. The Swedish foreign ministry was informed that Wallenberg was under Soviet 'protection', but later inquiries of the Wallenberg family, the Swedish government, and various Jewish organizations met with the claim by Soviet authorities that they knew nothing of his fate. On 17 July 1947 the head of the Lubianka Prison Hospital Dr A. L. Smoltsov sent a report to the minister of state security V. S. Abakumov (who as chief of Soviet counterintelligence had arrested Wallenberg two and a half years earlier) stating: 'I report that the prisoner Wallenberg, of whom you know, suddenly died at night in his cell, apparently of myocardial infarction. In view of your instruction to personally observe Wallenberg's condition, I request your instruction as to whom to assign the autopsy.' Smoltsov, after delivering this report to Abakumov, returned to his office and recorded the following: 'I personally reported to the minister. His order was to cremate the body without autopsy.' On the same day, Abakumov sent a report to the minister of foreign affairs, V. M. Molotov, notifying him about the termination of the 'Wallenberg case' in view of his 'sudden' death.[18] The body was cremated, and the cremation recorded under a secret number by the registrar of the Moscow crematorium.[19] Molotov had been besieged by enquiries about Wallenberg's fate, which annoyed him and Stalin. Molotov passed on to Abakumov Stalin's decision to quietly liquidate this 'spy'. Abakumov, in turn, ordered Dr Smoltsov or another agent to poison Wallenberg and to cover up the poisoning by cremation of the body without autopsy.

The question of the future of Poland proved to be the most difficult. Churchill did not know about the existence of the Soviet–German secret protocol, detailing the partition of Poland, and agreed to an unspecified percentage of Soviet hegemony over Poland in exchange for Stalin's promise to back Britain's control over Hong Kong and not to threaten her possessions in the Middle East. (The record of Churchill's negotiations with Stalin in Moscow in October 1944 were made public 30 years later, in 1973, by the opening of British wartime archives. However, the part dealing with the 'political conversations' between Stalin and Churchill was found in complete disorder, with many documents missing. Officials at the archives claimed they were at loss to explain the papers' disappearance.[20])

The 'Eastern Question' and the fate of Poland were again discussed at the Yalta Conference, which started on 5 February 1945. Stalin declared that the Polish territories that had been taken over by the Soviet Union in September 1939 would not be returned, but that Poland would be compensated by German Silesia, which was rich in mineral resources. Churchill objected, saying that Poland would not be able to absorb the large German population of Silesia, but Stalin stated, 'When our troops come in, the Germans will run away.' Stalin demanded most of east Prussia with Königsberg as compensation for the Soviet Union. He promised to declare war on Japan within three months of victory over Germany in exchange for large Soviet territorial acquisitions at the expense of Japan: the Kuril Islands, the southern part of Sakhalin Island, access to the port of Dairen, the lease of Port Arthur as a Soviet naval base, and joint Sino-Soviet operation of the Manchurian railroads. Roosevelt took upon himself to secure Marshal Chiang Kai-shek's acceptance of these agreements, which were spelled out in secret protocols signed by Roosevelt and Stalin. Churchill, for the sake of unity, reluctantly added his signature. British Foreign Secretary Anthony Eden called these secret protocols 'a discreditable by-product of the Conference'.[21]

On 12 April 1945 Stalin learned of Roosevelt's death and sent the new American president Harry S. Truman a letter of condolence, describing the late president as 'a great statesman of world stature and champion of post-war peace and security'.[22] Soon thereafter, Stalin sent a letter to General Dwight D. Eisenhower, asking him to hold his armies back to allow Soviet troops to enter Berlin before the Western Allies, 'according to [the] agreement with Roosevelt and in view of the amount of blood our people had shed'. Eisenhower halted his offensive.[23] Stalin's aim was for Soviet forces to capture Hitler. He was also eager to capture the German foreign ministry archive to prevent the world from learning of the existence of the secret protocols detailing his and Hitler's agreement in 1939 on the partition of Poland and the absorption of the Baltic states by the Soviet Union.

On 21 April 1945 Soviet armies commanded by Generals Zhukov, Konev and Rokossovsky began their final drive on Berlin by massive bombardment followed by street fighting. Most of the city was in flames. On 30 April 1945 Hitler and his mistress Eva Braun committed suicide, and on 1 May the German General Hans Krebs reported the deaths of Hitler and Braun to the Soviet headquarters and presented the offer of the new German government to start capitulation talks. Zhukov called Stalin, who said, 'So the play was up, the scoundrel. It's a pity that we couldn't capture him alive. Where is Hitler's body?' Zhukov replied that according to General Krebs, Hitler's body had been burned.[24] On the morning of 2 May 1945 Soviet troops broke into the courtyard of Hitler's Chancellery, where they found two badly burned bodies wrapped in still smoldering rugs and buried in a shallow grave. The gasoline that had been splashed on the bodies had been partly absorbed by the freshly dug ground. The bodies were not burned completely. Hitler's dentist confirmed that the jaw and teeth matched those on Hitler's x-rays.[25] Hitler's body was flown to Moscow for an autopsy, which was performed on 8 May 1945.

On 8 May 1945, the day on which the autopsy of Hitler's body was recorded in Moscow, Soviet Deputy Foreign Minister Vyshinsky came to Berlin with Stalin's instruction to Zhukov to suppress information about Hitler's death. Zhukov at a press conference abruptly changed his story about Hitler's death and declared: 'The circumstances are very mysterious. We have not identified the body of Hitler. I can say nothing about his fate. He could have flown out of Berlin at the very last moment.'[26] (Two decades later, in 1965, long after Stalin's death, Zhukov was to state publicly for the first time that 'Hitler and Goebbels, seeing no other way out, ended their lives by suicide.'[27]) In his statements to the allies, Stalin insisted that Hitler was hiding 'somewhere'. He also said that Hitler had fled in a large submarine to Japan; on other occasions, he mentioned South America as the place from which Hitler continued to threaten the human race. As always, Stalin pointed at a 'false target' to deflect attention away from himself. The implications of these innuendoes were that the Western powers were Hitler's protectors and had inherited Hitler's mantle as the enemies of mankind, while the Soviet Union was mankind's greatest hope and a bastion of peace and democracy. On 9 May 1945 Stalin, standing on top of Lenin's mausoleum, reviewed the Victory Parade by Red Army units, during which captured German flags were thrown on the ground before his eyes. On this occasion Stalin bestowed upon himself the rank of 'Generalissimo', the 'Order of Victory', and the medal of 'Hero of the Soviet Union'.

The Potsdam Conference was scheduled to open on 15 July 1945. Truman, Churchill and Stalin intended to settle some problems left unresolved after the war. The conference was delayed by a report that Stalin had suffered a slight heart attack. As always, Stalin refused to fly because he was afraid to travel by air, and a special train of 11 cars delivered him and his entourage, and a large contingent of security troops. The train included four luxury cars that had belonged to the Tsar's family and had been taken from a museum. Stalin chose to travel through Lithuania and east Prussia in order to circumvent the normal route through Poland, which he considered dangerous. He apologized for the one-day delay when he paid a courtesy call on Truman, saying that his doctors would not let him fly due to a 'weakness in the lungs'. Truman invited Stalin to stay for lunch. Apparently fearing that he might be poisoned, Stalin said that he could not. 'You could, if you wanted to', replied Truman. Stalin, persuaded by Truman's bluntness, stayed. During lunch, Stalin baffled Truman by insisting that Hitler was alive and hiding somewhere in Spain or Argentina. The previous day, while waiting for Stalin's arrival, Truman and Churchill had gone on a tour of Berlin ruins and had been shown Hitler's bunker in the Reich Chancellery. Soviet soldiers had pointed to a spot where they had found the badly burned bodies of Hitler and Eva Braun. Truman could not believe his own ears when Stalin said that a careful search by Soviet investigators had found no trace of Hitler's remains or any other positive evidence of his death.[28]

The evening before Stalin's arrival, Truman received a report about the successful test of the first atom bomb at the Alamogordo Air Base in the New Mexico desert. He passed the news on to Churchill, noting that Soviet entry into the war with Japan would not matter much in view of America's mighty new weapon. Churchill remarked that here was a speedy end to the Second World War and perhaps to much else besides.[29] They decided to inform Stalin about the bomb. Stalin displayed no interest in it, saying, 'That's fine. I hope you make good use of it against the Japanese.'[30] In fact, Stalin was not surprised by the news, since Soviet intelligence was keeping him informed about progress on America's development of the atom bomb. But he knew that the successful test considerably strengthened the position of the Western powers in negotiations, and he wanted to downplay the bomb's importance in order to elicit concessions from the Allies. Stalin had a sizable list of demands, all of them related to the 'Eastern Question'. He wanted to absorb Iran, or at least its northern part with its Azerbaijanian population, into the Soviet Union. He demanded that Libya be brought into the Soviet sphere of interest and claimed the Soviet right to participate in the international administration of Tangier. His most insistent demands were for the establishment of a Soviet naval base in the Bosporus. All these demands were rejected by Truman and Churchill. In Truman, Stalin did not have as accommodating an ally as he had had in Roosevelt. Truman did not seek to please Stalin and did not harass Churchill, whom he respected and whose opinions he took seriously. Churchill, seeing that Stalin had established tight control over the Soviet-occupied eastern European countries, thus breaking his October 1944 agreement, came to the conclusion that Stalin did not keep his word. Pointing to the Soviet secret police's reign of terror in these countries, Churchill in Truman's presence said that 'an iron fence has come down' on eastern Europe. 'All fairy tales', retorted Stalin.[31]

During the Potsdam Conference the Labour Party's landslide victory in the British general election led to Clement Attlee taking over as prime minister. Churchill's defeat gave Stalin no advantage, since at this point Truman assumed the role of the guardian of the West's interests. On 1 August 1945, at the closing of the Potsdam Conference, a camera recorded this strange scene: Stalin, dressed in his generalissimo uniform, was briskly walking to a chair. A witness described the scene: 'his crooked left arm jerked and dangled helplessly from the shoulder, as though its mechanism had suddenly gone out of control. Then that swinging, dangling arm, which appeared to have no connection with him, like the arm of a marionette, gradually resumed its normal position.[32]

Less than a week after Stalin returned from Potsdam the first atom bomb was dropped on Hiroshima. On 6 August 1945, Svetlana came to the Kuntsevo *dacha* with her 3-month-old son, Iosif. All the Politburo members were there, but no one paid attention to her because they were absorbed in the news of the Hiroshima bombing. Stalin realized that Japan's surrender was imminent and that he had to enter the war at once if he was to claim his share of the spoils. On 8 August 1945 he declared war on Japan, and Soviet troops crossed the border into Manchuria. The second atom bomb was dropped on Nagasaki, and Japan's unconditional surrender followed, but Soviet troops continued their advance. Genrikh Liushkov, the former chief of the Far Eastern NKVD, who had defected to the Japanese in 1938, was in the Manchurian city of Port Arthur, having been sent there from Tokyo as a 'consultant on Russian affairs'. Fearing capture by the approaching Soviet troops, Liushkov escaped to the headquarters of the Japanese Kwantung Army in the Manchurian city of Dairen and demanded to be immediately evacuated to Tokyo. General Yanagito Gendzo, the chief of staff of the Kwantung Army, decided that if Liushkov refused to commit suicide, he should be shot. On 19 August 1945, at 9 pm, General Takeoka invited Liushkov to his office and for two hours tried to convince him to commit suicide. Liushkov kept refusing and insisting that his escape to Tokyo be arranged. Pretending that he would take Liushkov to the port at Dairen to find a boat suitable for his escape, General Takeoka led him downstairs into the courtyard, where, he shot him in the chest. Liushkov's body was cremated, and the urn with his ashes was placed in a Buddist Temple in Dairen under the name of a Japanese officer. General Takeoka recounted the story of Liushkov's death to Soviet interrogators and later told it to the inmates of a Kolyma prison camp. Liushkov's urn is still in the Buddhist Temple in Darien.[33] With Liushkov's death, Stalin was now the only person alive who knew the truth behind the 'Eremin Letter'.

The Soviet spy Klaus Fuchs employed in the top secret 'Manhattan Project' in Los Alamos, where American physicists were developing the bomb, passed information to the Soviets. In 1943 I. V. Kurchatov started to work on a similar atom bomb project. On 25 January 1945 Stalin discussed this project with Beria, Molotov and Kurchatov. By this time the Soviet spies, Fuchs, Julius and Ethel Rosenberg, as well as a not-yet-identified spy code-named 'Parseus', provided Beria with considerable information about the first American atom bomb. Stalin demanded that Kurchatov create and test an atom bomb as soon as possible. He inquired whether there was enough plutonium for two bombs, so that one could be held in reserve.[34]

Winston Churchill was the first to sound the alarm over Stalin's aggressive designs. In a speech at the American College in Fulton, Missouri on 5 March 1946 he said:

From Stettin, in the Baltic, to Trieste, in the Adriatic, an iron curtain has descended across the Continent. Behind that line lie all the capitals of the States of Central and Eastern Europe – Warsaw, Berlin, Prague, Vienna, Budapest, Belgrade, Bucharest and Sofia . . .[35]

Stalin's angry response appeared in an interview published in *Pravda* on 13 March 1946, in which he compared Churchill to Hitler, calling him 'the warmonger of the Third World War'.[36] He invited a delegation of the British Labour Party, which included Alice Bacon, the left-wing Member of Parliament. She declared that Stalin was 'very human, a man with a fine sense of humour and keen intellect'.[37] Other visitors came away with a different impression. Lord Montgomery recalled in his memoirs that during a conversation Stalin abruptly asked him, 'Have you seen Lenin?' Baffled by the question, Montgomery answered, 'I thought he was dead.' Stalin agreed, 'So he is. But all the same you ought to go and see him in the mausoleum in Red Square.' Recalling his tour of Lenin's mausoleum, Montgomery wrote that Lenin looked to him 'pretty waxen and yellow'. He also recalled that Stalin looked much older than two years earlier, when they had met at the Potsdam Conference.[38]

When the British Labour government announced its decision to withdraw its assistance to Greece, Stalin instigated a civil war there. Stalin's scheme included absorbing Greece into the Soviet sphere of interest and forcing Turkey to acquiesce in the establishment of a Soviet military base in the Bosporus. Stalin's ambitions were frustrated by President Truman, who on 12 March 1947 declared America's determination to take 'immediate and resolute action' in support of any nation resisting communist aggression. In what became known as the Truman Doctrine, he stated:

I believe that it *must* be the policy of the United States to support free peoples who are resisting attempted subjugation by armed minorities or outside pressures. I believe that we *must* assist free people to work out their own destinies in their own way.[39]

In July 1947 Stalin rejected the Marshall Plan, which aimed at fostering peaceful economic development of all the countries ravaged by the war. Thus began the Cold War. In the ensuing months, Stalin's health declined. He suffered from high blood pressure and periodically experienced heart trouble. In the summer of 1947, Stalin renovated his *dacha* at Kuntsevo. He improved security arrangements, adding a safety zone around the *dacha* with two rows of barbed wire between which there was a passage for guard dogs. In January 1948 Yugoslav Politburo member Milovan Djilas visited Stalin and was invited to Kuntsevo for dinner. Djilas noticed that Stalin had aged. He was surprised that Stalin laughed at stupid jokes cracked by Politburo members. At the end of the dinner Stalin proposed a toast: 'To the memory of Vladimir Ilyich [Lenin], our leader, our teacher – our all!' Djilas was unable to decide whether Stalin was serious or joking. During the dinner Stalin asked Djilas whether there were many Jews in the Yugoslav Politburo, noting that in his there were none. He suddenly shouted at Djilas, 'You are an anti-Semite, an anti-Semite!' Stalin turned on a record player and tried to dance a Caucasian *lizginka*, but soon stopped, saying, 'Age has crept up on me and I'm already an old man!' Politburo members began to chant, 'No, no, nonsense. You look fine. You're holding up marvelously.' As the guests were about to leave, Stalin played another record, a loud cacophony of yowling, barking and howling wolves or dogs. Stalin kept laughing until he noticed that Djilas was baffled.

'Well, still it's clever, devilishly clever', said Stalin.[40] Djilas did not know what to make of Stalin's odd excitement. He had no idea that Stalin symbolically saw wolves as Jews and that there was a connection between Stalin's earlier comments about Jews and the sounds on that record. At the time of Djilas's visit, Stalin was already planning the mass deportation of Jews, a scheme that, had he lived to see it carried out, would have resulted in millions of deaths.

NOTES

1. A. Antonov-Ovseenko, 'Katyn', *Novoe russkoe slovo*, 27 May 1988, p. 20.
2. Stanislaw Kot, *Conversations with the Kremlin and Dispatches from Russia*, London, 1963, p. 106.
3. Ibid., p. 140.
4. V. A. Chalikova, 'Arkhivnyi yunosha', *Neva*, October 1988, p. 153.
5. Nikolas Betell, 'Katyn 1940', *Kontinent*, no. 11, 1977.
6. Antonov-Ovseenko, 'Katyn'.
7. Lord Moran, *Winston Churchill: the Struggle for Survival 1940–1965*, London, 1966, pp. 141f.
8. Frances Perkins, *The Roosevelt I Knew*, London, 1974, pp. 70f.
9. Lord Moran, *Winston Churchill*, pp. 133–5.
10. H. Montgomery Hyde, *Stalin: the History of a Dictator*, New York, 1971, pp. 491–3. See also Robert E. Sherwood, *The White House Papers of Harry L. Hopkins*, vol. II, 1949, pp. 771f; the Soviet Government publication of the complete transcript in *International Affairs*, Moscow, July and August 1961, nos. 7 and 8; and Winston Churchill, *The Second World War*, vol. V, London, 1948, p. 303.
11. Albert Speer, *Inside the Third Reich*, New York, 1970, p. 390.
12. Ibid., pp. 390f.
13. Winston Churchill, *The Second World War*, London, 1948, vol. VI, pp. 118–20.
14. Ibid., p. 128.
15. The wartime papers of Sir Winston Churchill were made public in August 1973. They revealed that his fear of Roosevelt's hostility to British colonial interests was the reason why Churchill sought Stalin's support in a deal that sealed the fate of Poland. See 'Churchill, Stalin Made Polish Deal', *The New York Times*, 5 August 1973.
16. Churchill, *The Second World War*, vol. VI, p. 198.
17. Arthur D. Morse, *While Six Million Died*, New York, 1967, p. 290.
18. *The New York Times*, 28 Dec. 1991, p. 6.
19. I. P. Itskov, taped interview with the author in New York in 1989. Itskov investigated the murder of his former wife, Bronislava, and searched the Lubianka archives, as well as the records of the Moscow crematorium. He was also interested in the fate of Raoul Wallenberg, and in doing his research kept Wallenberg in mind. He came to the conclusion that Wallenberg was poisoned in 1947 and was cremated. The author remembers Dr A. L. Smoltsov, a man of medium height, about forty years old, with a very low forehead and cold, small black eyes, who made regular visits to the Lubianka prison cells.
20. 'Churchill, Stalin Made Polish Deal', *The New York Times*, 5 August 1974.
21. Avon, the Earl of, *The Reckoning*, London, 1960–65, p. 513.
22. I. V. Stalin, *Stalin's Correspondence with Churchill, Attlee, Roosevelt and Truman 1941–1945*, Moscow and London 1957–58, vol. II, p. 214.
23. Hyde, *Stalin*, p. 331.
24. G. K. Zhukov, *Vospominaniya i razmyshleniya*, Moscow, 1974, pp. 631f.
25. Erich Kuby, *The Russians and Berlin, 1945*, London, 1968, p. 175.
26. Churchill, *The Second World War*, vol. II, p. 903.
27. G. K. Zhukov, 'Bitva za Berlin', *Voenno-istoricheskii zhurnal*, June 1965.
28. James MacGregor Burns, *Roosevelt: The Soldier of Freedom 1940–1945*, London, 1971, p. 68.

29. Churchill, *The Second World War*, vol. VI, p. 552.
30. James F. Byrnes, *Speaking Frankly*, New York and London, 1947, p. 263.
31. Ibid., p. 76.
32. Robert Payne, *The Rise and Fall of Stalin*, New York, 1965, London, 1966, p. 624.
33. V. Mikhailiv and V. Bondarenko, 'Zhizn' i smert' komissara Liushkova', *Kurier*, 3 June 1993. See also Alvin D. Coox, 'L'Affaire Liushkov', *Soviet Studies*, January 1968, p. 418; Also A. Antonov-Ovseenko, *Portret tirana*, New York, 1980, pp. 208f.
34. Serge Schmemann, article in *The New York Times*, 14 January 1993, p. 14.
35. *The Times*, London, 6 March 1946.
36. *Pravda*, 13 March 1946.
37. *Daily Herald*, London, 16 August 1946.
38. Hyde, *Stalin*, p. 555, citing Field Marshal Montgomery, *Memoirs*, London, 1958, p. 445.
39. Harry Truman, *Years of Trial and Hope 1946–1953*, London, 1966, p. 111.
40. Milovan Djilas, *Conversations with Stalin*, New York and London, 1962, pp. 157–61.

36

'MURDERERS IN WHITE GOWNS'

At the end of November 1947 Solomon Mikhoels, the director of the Moscow Jewish Theater and chairman of the Jewish Anti-Fascist Committee, delivered a speech before a largely Jewish audience in the hall of the Polytechnic Museum in Moscow. Mikhoels began his speech by saying that A. A. Gromyko, the Soviet representative to the United Nations, had declared Soviet support for the creation of a Jewish State in Palestine and thus pointed out the road to the Land of Israel. The applause was deafening. When the event was reported to Stalin he at once ordered the arrest of people who directly or indirectly had connections to Mikhoels.[1]

The economist I. I. Goldshtein was arrested on 19 December 1947; the literary critic Z. G. Grinberg was arrested on 28 December. At the same time, several of Stalin's relatives were also arrested, among them Anna Redens, the sister of Stalin's late wife Nadezhda Allilueva (Anna's husband Stanislav Redens had been executed in 1938), and Olga Allilueva, the widow of Nadezhda's brother Pavel Alliluev, who had died suddenly in 1938. Olga had remarried, and her second husband, a Jew, was arrested together with her. Stalin explained to his daughter Svetlana that the reason why her aunts had been arrested was, 'They knew too much. They blabbed a lot. It played into the hands of our enemies.'[2] He did not tell Svetlana that Olga was also accused of poisoning her husband Pavel Alliluev. Stalin suspected that Stanislav Redens and Pavel Alliluev had known about his Okhrana past, the discovery of his Okhrana file, and the true reason behind the execution of Tukhachevsky and other generals. He probably also suspected that Redens and Alliluev had shared these secrets with their wives, who might 'blab' about them to their Jewish friends. Among those arrested were Olga's neighbors Lev Tumerman and Lidia Shatunovskaya, who also knew Mikhoels personally. Anna, Olga and their neighbors were initially accused of taking part in an anti-Soviet conspiracy headed by Mikhoels. But after 13 January 1948 their interrogation records were rewritten, and the name of Mikhoels was erased from them. A few months later the defendants were sentenced by the MGB Special Council to various terms of imprisonment in the Vladimir Tsentral Jail.[3]

On 10 January 1948 V. S. Abakumov, the minister of state security, gave Stalin the signed depositions of I. I. Goldshtein and Z. G. Grinberg, who 'confessed' that Mikhoels was an American and Zionist agent.[4] Stalin summoned the Politburo members and, choking with rage, called Mikhoels a traitor who must be killed at once. 'Mikhoels must be struck on the head with an axe wrapped up in a wet *telogreika* [quilted cotton jacket] and run over by a truck', Stalin shouted.[5] The Politburo members were puzzled by Stalin's rage and his bizarre instructions but afraid to question his orders. They could not know that two murders Stalin had instigated many years earlier had merged in his mind: the murder of his father Vissarion in 1906 by Kamo, who used an axe wrapped in a rain-soaked quilted jacket, and the murder of Kamo, who in 1922 on Stalin's order was run over by a truck. Immediately after this meeting, Stalin called Abakumov and ordered him to liquidate Mikhoels. Shortly after Stalin's death Lavrenty Beria submitted a report to the Presidium of the Communist Party's Central Committee, dated 2 April 1953, which said that in his deposition Abakumov (who had been arrested) had stated: 'As I recall, the head of the Soviet Government, I. V. Stalin, gave me an urgent order – to organize immediately the liquidation, by MGB USSR personnel, of Mikhoels, assigning it to special persons.'[6] Abakumov further revealed that Stalin ordered him to assign the MGB officers Ogoltsov and Shubnikov, as well as the minister of state security of Byelorussia, Lavrenty Tsanava, a nephew of Beria, to carry out the assassination, which could look like a road accident.[7]

While visiting Minsk, Mikhoels was invited by Tsanava's agent to a wedding on the evening of 13 January 1948. Mikhoels and his companion, the literary critic V. Golubov-Potapov, an MGB agent, were driven by a 'friend' to Tsanava's *dacha* outside Minsk. They arrived there around 10 pm and were taken out of the car and murdered. Their bodies were run over by a truck. At midnight their bodies were taken to one of the deserted snow-covered streets and dumped there. The next morning the severely mutilated bodies were found by passers-by.

Stalin's daughter Svetlana visited her father the evening of Mikhoels' murder. As she walked into the room, the telephone rang. Stalin listened to the caller and then quietly, as if he were making a suggestion, said, 'Well, it's an automobile accident.' He hung up and greeted her. A few minutes later he told her, 'Mikhoels was killed in an automobile accident.' Svetlana realized that what she had witnessed was the report of a murder ordered by her father. She concluded that Stalin had invented the car accident to cover up the crime. 'I knew all too well my father's obsession with "Zionist" plots around every corner', she was to recall.[8]

The newspapers reported that Mikhoels and Golubov-Potapov had died

in a car accident. The coffin with Mikhoels's body was placed on the stage
of the Moscow Jewish Theater. Deep wounds left by the axe blows were
clearly visible despite the heavy makeup. A large crowd gathered outside
the theater because there was not enough room inside. Although Mikhoels
was buried with full official honors, the rumor spread that he had been
murdered by MGB agents.[9] At the time of the murder of Mikhoels the
Jewish Anti-Fascist Committee (JAFC), of which he had been the chairman for a number of years, was already under investigation by the MGB.
Members of the JAFC were accused of 'Jewish bourgeois nationalism' and
of involvement in an 'anti-Soviet conspiracy', headed by Mikhoels.

The JAFC was created on Stalin's order in August 1941 when the German
Army was rapidly advancing deep into Soviet territory. Stalin hoped
through this organization to mobilize Jewish support in the West for the
Soviet war effort. He believed that the Jews had great political and financial
clout. On 24 August 1941 S. A. Lozovsky, the deputy foreign minister and
the head of the Soviet Information Bureau, was ordered by Stalin to set up
the JAFC.[10] Initially, Stalin planned to make the JAFC an international
organization. He ordered Beria to release from prison Henrik Erlich and
Victor Alter, two widely known Jewish Social Democratic leaders in Poland,
who were awaiting execution, having been arrested as 'spies' in September
1939 in the Soviet-occupied part of Poland. Their death sentences were
annulled and they were released from prison and on 24 September 1941
they appealed to Polish Jews to enlist in the Polish Army, which was being
formed on Soviet soil. Erlich and Alter often met with the Polish ambassador to the Soviet Union, Stanislav Kot, who at that time was trying to
determine what had happened to the 15,000 Polish officers held in three
prisoner-of-war camps. Among these officers were many Polish Jews. After
being evacuated from Moscow to Kuibyshev in October 1941, when the
German army came close to the suburbs of Moscow, Erlich and Alter were
placed in a hotel in Kuibyshev (Samara). In the privacy of their rooms, they
discussed the rumors about the disappearance of the Polish officers. Their
conversations were tapped and reported to Stalin. On 4 December 1941
Erlich and Alter were arrested and executed as 'German spies'. Stalin
appointed Solomon Mikhoels chairman of the JAFC, having dropped the
idea of making it an international organization. During the war, Mikhoels
directed the effort to mobilize Jewish support in various countries for the
Soviet Union.[11] His appeal found an enthusiastic responce in the Jewish
community in Palestine which sent money and medical supplies to the
Soviet Union. This good will led to consequences reaching far beyond the

immediate war needs. Stalin became interested in Palestine and sent a number of agents to explore the possibility of using the Jewish community to advance Soviet strategic interests in the Middle East. Soviet agents were impressed by the strong leftist pro-Soviet sentiment in the Jewish community in Palestine at the time and by the 'socialist nature' of its economy. As the war was coming to an end, Stalin decided to support the creation of a Jewish state, hoping to turn it into a Soviet anti-Western satellite with the help of the communist and other leftist parties. After the war Stalin watched closely the struggle of the Palestine Jews against the British, who prevented them from transporting Jews to Palestine from camps for displaced persons in Europe.[12] Early in 1946 Stalin ordered Soviet intelligence to use Jewish–British conflict to promote his scheme of bringing the new state of Israel into the Soviet sphere of interest.[13] The resident of Soviet intelligence in London, Viktor Kukin, told Mordekhai Oren, one of the leaders of the Jewish leftist party Mapam, that the left-of-center Jewish groups in Palestine, striving to create a socialist Jewish state, would have Soviet support if they followed a pro-Soviet policy in international relations. 'We are going to help you', said Kukin.[14]

Mikhoels did not travel to Palestine, which had not much to offer by way of donations. Early in 1943 he and poet I. S. Fefer (an MGB agent) traveled to America to raise funds for the Soviet war effort. In New York, Mikhoels met Chaim Weizman, the future president of Israel. When they were alone for a few moments, Weizman asked in Yiddish, 'How do the Jews fare in Russia?' Mikhoels cast a frightened look around, raised his hands to heaven, and, expressing his horror, whispered, 'Gewalt!' Weizman recorded this episode in his diary.[15]

Soon after Mikhoels's murder, Stalin ordered his agent to poison the Secretary of the JAFC, Shakhno Epshtein. This agent, posing as a representative of the Central Committee, spoke with Epshtein for a few minutes behind closed doors. Then the door opened and the visitor announced that Epshtein had died of a heart attack.[16] The members of the JAFC were arrested one by one and accused of plotting to turn the Crimean peninsula into an 'American-Zionist base for an attack on the Soviet Union.'[17] (This accusation was rooted in the idea that had originated in Stalin's own mind early in 1923, then he had ordered Mikhail Kalinin to promote the creation of a 'Jewish Autonomous Republic' in the Crimea. Three years later he had decided to send the Jews not to the Crimea but to the Birobidzhan area in the Siberian Far East.) In 1944, after ordering the mass deportation to Siberia and Central Asia of the Crimean Tartars, the native population of the Crimea, Stalin decided to implicate the Jews in this crime. He instructed

Solomon Lozovsky, the chairman of the Soviet Information Bureau who was also a member of the JAFC, to suggest the idea of 'Crimea for the Jews' to members of the JAFC and tell them to put it in a petition addressed to him. On 15 February 1944 Lozovsky told Solomon Mikhoels, Shakhno Epstein, and I. S. Fefer to send Stalin a letter, proposing the creation of a 'Jewish Crimean Autonomous Republic'. The rumor about the idea of 'giving Crimea to the Jews' was briefly circulated among the Jewish refugees and in the camps for displaced persons in Europe. Stalin soon dropped the idea and it faded away, but Stalin did not forget it. On 12 October 1946 the MGB, on Stalin's order, sent to the Council of Ministers a report titled, 'On Nationalistic Manifestations of Some Members of the Jewish Anti-Fascist Committee', accusing it of plotting to create a Crimean 'anti-Soviet base'. On 26 November 1946 M. A. Suslov, a Secretary of the Central Committee and an ideological watchdog, sent a similar report to Stalin, in whose mind the scenario for a 'Crimean case' had already taken shape.[18]

At the beginning of November 1948 Suslov summoned all the members of the JAFC to his office and said that 'the time to act has arrived'. In the opinion of the Central Committee, a Jewish Autonomous Republic must be created on the basis of the Jewish Autonomous Region in Birobidzhan . . . All the Jews living on the territory of the Soviet Union must be re-settled in this Autonomous Republic.'[19] Solomon Lozovsky responded by saying that he, an internationalist all his conscious life, did not see anything positive in resettling the Soviet Jews in Birobidzhan. The poet Peretz Markish, who became chairman of the JAFC after the murder of Mikhoels, also expressed his objection to the idea, stating in conclusion, 'I cannot stab my people in the back.'[20] Suslov fidgeted in his chair while listening and then ended the meeting. He reported to Stalin the JAFC members' response. On 20 November 1948 Stalin submitted to the Politburo Resolution Number 81 which read:

The Bureau of the Council of Ministers of the USSR orders the Ministry of State Security of the USSR to liquidate the Jewish Anti-Fascist Committee, because, as the facts proved, this committee has been the center of anti-Soviet propaganda and has regularly supplied the organs of foreign intelligence with anti-Soviet information. In connection with this decision, the newspapers of this committee must be closed and the files confiscated. For the time being not to arrest anybody.[21]

On 13 January 1949, the first anniversary of the murder of Mikhoels, Politburo member G. M. Malenkov summoned Lozovsky and demanded that he confessed his role in the conspiracy to separate the Crimea from the Soviet Union and turn it into an 'American and Zionist base'. (Stalin's old habit of marking certain dates that were meaningful to him by staging notable events had resurfaced.) Malenkov confronted Lozovsky with 'criminal evidence' of his guilt: the letter, dated 15 February 1944 signed by Mikhoels, Epshtein and Fefer, in which they supported Stalin's own idea of creating a 'Jewish Autonomous Republic' in the Crimea. On 18 January 1949 Lozovsky was expelled from the party. Eight days later he was arrested; by then, all the other members of the JAFC had also been arrested.[22]

Stalin had been anti-Semitic from his early youth, prone to making derogatory statements about Jews, although he learned to hide his anti-Semitism behind the mask of the official party line of internationalism. His hatred became more intense in the late 1930s when he learned that a large number of Jews had played important roles in the history of his Okhrana file: Rabinovich, who found the file among Dzerzhinsky's papers; Yakov Blumkin who tried to smuggle the file abroad; I. L. Shtein, who discovered the file in Menzhinsky's office; Zinovy Katsnelson who received the file from Shtein; Yan Gamarnik, who kept the file in the safe in his office and who, together with Tukhachevsky, headed the military plot against Stalin; Ignaz Reiss, who informed Trotsky's supporters about the file's discovery; the chief of the Far Eastern NKVD, Genrikh Liushkov, to whom Stalin assigned the task of planting the forged 'Eremin Letter' and who escaped to Japan; Walter Krivitsky and Alexander Orlov, both of whom defected to the West and who also were connected in Stalin's mind with knowledge of his secrets. His hatred for Jews grew even more intense than his loathing of the Polish people. Stalin's daughter Svetlana wrote that her father was an anti-Semite but 'did not yet express his hatred of the Jews openly – he started doing so only later, after the war'.[23] Khrushchev, too, wrote that Stalin during the last five 'crazy' years of his life 'couldn't keep his anti-Semitism hidden'.[24] Stalin's intense hatred of the Jews hurt Svetlana's personal life: he exiled the screenwriter Aleksei Kapler, her first love, and refused to meet her Jewish husband, Grigory Moroz.

One of the most bizarre aspects of Stalin's anti-Semitism was its explosion precisely at a time when he was pursuing a policy of support for the new-born State of Israel. He hoped to turn Israel into a Soviet satellite similar to the 'Popular Democracies' he was setting up in Eastern Europe. The murders of Mikhoels and Epshtein and the arrests of the members of the JAFC actually took place after Stalin had decided to turn the Jewish state into a Soviet satellite. At the end of the Teheran Conference Roosevelt told Stalin that he intended 'to review the entire Palestine question' with the king of Saudi Arabia. Stalin replied vaguely that the Jewish problem was 'extremely difficult' and that the Soviet Union had tried to establish a national home for the Jews, but they had stayed there only two or three years before returning to the cities. The Jews were 'natural traders', he informed Roosevelt, and he added that only 'small groups' of them were settled in agricultural areas. Stalin had in mind Birobidzhan and the project he intended to undertake: the relocation of all Soviet Jews, and perhaps Jews from other countries as well, to the 'Jewish Autonomous Area' of Birobidzhan in the Siberian Far East.[25]

When the creation of the State of Israel was proclaimed on 14 May 1948, Soviet and American recognition followed almost immediately. Stalin, hoping to bring Israel into the Soviet sphere of interest, ordered that Israel be supplied with weapons when the armies of seven Arab states attacked Israel. Since the Suez Canal was under British control, Stalin entertained the idea of building an alternate canal through the Negev desert to connect the Mediterranean and the Red Seas.[26]

Meanwhile, events in eastern Europe, especially the example of a 'Popular Democracy' in Poland that Stalin had installed, were a clear warning to many Israeli Jews. The communist coup in Czechoslovakia in February 1948, and the murder of Czech foreign minister Jan Masaryk was another warning. Masaryk's body was found lying in the courtyard of the foreign ministry. A bullet hole behind his ear indicated that he had been shot and then thrown out of the window.[27] The conflict between Stalin and the president of Yugoslavia, Marshal Joseph Tito, in the summer of 1948, as well as the Soviet blockade of Berlin in the same year, also alarmed many Jews in Israel. Israeli president Chaim Weizmann opposed the Jewish leftists who worshipped Stalin. Prime Minister David Ben-Gurion had no illusions about Stalin. In 1938 he had protested against the Moscow show trials, denouncing Stalin as a *kham ha-gruzini* (a coarse Georgian bully).[28]

Molotov's Jewish wife Polina Zhemchuzhina, like her husband, was a fanatical admirer of Stalin. At a Kremlin reception she dared to say a few friendly words in Yiddish to the first Israeli ambassador to Moscow, Golda Meir. Zhemchuzhina was promptly arrested and exiled. Beria periodically whispered in Molotov's ear: 'Polina is alive.'[29] Hardly anyone could have imagined at the time that Stalin and the Politburo members were discussing a plan to exile all the Soviet Jews to the Siberian wilderness of Birobidzhan and other remote areas. But precursors of this impending catastrophe were already appearing. On 30 December 1949 all Jews in the towns of Kuntsevo and Davydkovo, which were close to Stalin's *dacha*, were evicted. Their neighbors, encouraged by MGB agents, helped themselves to the belongings of the expelled Jews.[30] Stalin started a campaign against 'cosmopolitans, rootless parasites, people without kith and kin, and passportless wanderers' whose obviously Jewish names were supplied in parentheses. These code phrases were easily recognized as transparently anti-Jewish. (For Stalin, the collective image of the 'passportless wanderer' stood for Trotsky, to whom he had denied Soviet citizenship in 1930 and who died a 'passportless wanderer'.) The MGB began mass arrests of 'cosmopolitans, Jewish bourgeois nationalists, and Zionists'. No information about these arrests appeared in the Soviet press.

Stalin's 70th birthday occurred on 21 December 1949. Presents from all over the world were placed in a special museum. Among them was a fur coat made by some Jewish tailors in New York. (His greatest present Stalin had already received in August 1949, when the successful test of the first Soviet atom bomb was announced.) The Soviet propaganda machine was convulsed by paroxysms of flattery. The writer Leonid Leonov in a *Pravda* article predicted that Stalin's birthday would be celebrated by people all over the world and that the new calendar would begin not with the birth of Christ but with that of Stalin.

In May 1950 Israel sided with the United States in condemning the communist aggression in Korea. Stalin realized that his plan of making Israel a Soviet base in the Middle East had failed. He was infuriated by what he perceived to be Jewish ingratitude and betrayal. The Soviet press kept silent about the retreat of the North Korean troops. It devoted most of its pages to Stalin's articles titled, 'The Question of Linguistics'. The hidden theme was the 'Jewish Question', although the Jews were not mentioned at all. Stalin had become interested in 'linguistics' by accident: during the mass arrests of Jews in 1949 and confiscations of their privately held *Jewish Encyclopedia*, which became criminal evidence of 'Jewish bourgeois nationalism.' Stalin examined the 16 volumes of this Russian-language Jewish Encyclopedia which had been published in 1913. He spotted there a brief entry under the heading 'Georgian Language,' stating that at the turn of the century a young linguist by the name of Niko Marr postulated a theory that the Georgian language was of Semitic origin. In 1896 Marr wrote an article in the Georgian journal *Iveria* and in 1907 published a short pamphlet arguing his theory.[31] Toward the end of his life, Marr became a prominent Soviet academician. When he died in 1934, he left behind many disciples who were not even aware that in his youth he had 'sinned' before Stalin by postulating the Semitic origin of the Georgian language.

The long-deceased Marr (he died in 1934) could not be forced to recant his heretical theory. Nevertheless, in his articles Stalin furiously attacked Marr, castigating the dead linguist on the pages of *Pravda*.[32] Stalin invited the Georgian linguist and academician A. S. Chikobaba to a dinner at the Kremlin and brought up the subject of linguistics. Khrushchev, who was present at the dinner, did not know what to make of Stalin's sudden interest in linguistics.[33] Stalin ordered A. N. Poskrebyshev, the chief of his secretariat, to find pre-Revolutionary publications on linguistics. At one point, he interrupted a meeting with an admiral when Poskrebyshev brought in some of these old books. 'What doesn't Stalin study!' thought the admiral in awe and admiration.[34]

Stalin never revealed the true reason behind his attack on Marr whose offense was too hideous even for condemnation. In his articles, Stalin dismissed all of Marr's views and claimed that language was not a 'super-structure', but was simply language. Deep down Stalin feared that there was some truth to Marr's theory. In 1949, he ordered that the name of the Georgian magazine *Iveria* (the ancient and poetic name for Georgia in the Old Georgian language) be changed to *Sakartvelo* (Georgia in contemporary Georgian language). Marr had cited the word 'Iveria' as evidence of the Semitic origin of the Georgian language. Stalin ordered that the word *Iveria* be expunged from all publications, including his own childhood poems. Marr's disciples were fired from their jobs, their dissertations annulled, their careers ruined and many of them arrested. None of them suspected that Stalin was punishing them for Marr's almost forgotten theory of the Semitic origin of the Georgian language.

Stalin was also disturbed by another linguistic theory, that the Basques, Albanians and Georgians all belonged to the Iberian group of people who lived in the Mediterranean basin in ancient times. His 'insight' probably was that *Iveria, Iberian, Evrei* (Jew in Russian) and *Uria* (a derogatory word for Jew in the Georgian language) were all words of the same root, point-ing to the perception that the Jews, as well as Georgians, belonged to the 'Iberian group'. This would explain why he began to develop a strong dis-like for Georgians too. He told his daughter Svetlana that the Georgians 'open their mouths and yell like fools'.[35] He started denying his Georgian origin and began statements with the words: 'We Russians . . . '. His interest in questions of ethnic origin startled some of his visitors. During a meeting with Yugoslav Vice Premier Edvard Kardelj, Stalin suddenly asked him, 'What is the origin of the Albanians?' Kardelj said that the Albanians were descendants of the Illyrians. 'I remember Tito told me they were related to the Basques', said Stalin. 'Yes, that's right,' replied Kardelj. 'They seem to be rather primitive and backward people', Stalin said. 'But they are very brave and faithful', Kardelj replied. 'Yes, they can be as faithful as a dog; that's one of the traits of the primitive', retorted Stalin.[36] Stalin attempted to provoke the Yugoslavs to attack Albania and destroy it. To Yugoslav Politburo member Milovan Djilas he said, 'Yugoslavia is free to swallow Albania any time she wishes to do so.' To illustrate his point, he licked his lips, pointed his finger at his throat, and made his eyes big, imitating a boa constrictor devouring its prey. Djilas was disturbed to see the 'Greatest Leader' so cavalier about the forceful annexation of a country. 'Comrade Stalin, there is no question of swallowing Albania, only one of friendly and allied relations between the two countries', he protested. Whereupon Molotov attempted to reassure him with the statement, 'Well, this is one and the same thing.'[37]

The failure to turn Israel into a Soviet satellite added fuel to Stalin's anti-Semitism. The director of the Stalin Automobile Factory in Moscow, A. I. Likhachev, received a report that the Jewish engineers working there were involved in sabotage. Likhachev told one of his Jewish friends, Georgy Meerson, whom he had known for many years, 'Take my advice, Georgy, quit your job at once. Otherwise, I'll have to fire you in order to save you. Don't ask questions.'[38] Meerson quit his job, and was the only one to survive, all the other Jewish engineers at the factory being arrested and executed in a *spets. uchastok* (special lot) outside Moscow. The guards ordered them to run and unleashed their dogs. Chief Engineer Edinov died first. Weakened by torture, he was unable to run.[39]

Late in 1951, Stalin had a regular checkup by his personal physician, Professor V. N. Vinogradov. During the examination Stalin said that the Politburo members A. S. Shcherbakov (in 1946) and A. A. Zhdanov (in 1948) had been poisoned by Kremlin doctors. Stalin mentioned the names of the doctors, all of whom were Jewish. Vinogradov knew them well and said he had absolute trust in their honesty and professional competence. After the checkup, Vinogradov advised Stalin to rest more and work less. To Stalin this advice had a familiar ring: three decades earlier, plotting to hasten Lenin's death and pretending to worry about his health, he had insisted that Lenin be kept from his daily duties. Stalin at once suspected Vinogradov of conspiring against him and ordered his arrest. Vinogradov, who came from a family of prestigious Russian physicians, was accused together with a group of Jewish Kremlin doctors of poisoning Shcherbakov and Zhdanov. The fact that Stalin accused Kremlin physicians of poisoning these Soviet leaders points to his habit of accusing 'false targets' and suggests that these leaders were poisoned on his own orders, and, as in other cases, he felt the emotional need to attribute the crimes to someone else. Both deaths at the time they took place were attributed to heart disease. In August 1947 Stalin's daughter Svetlana, who by then had divorced her Jewish husband and married Zhdanov's son Yury, was present at a family dinner at which Stalin suddenly turned to Andrey Zhdanov and shouted, 'Look at him sitting there, like Christ, as if nothing was of concern to him! There – looking at me now as if he was Christ!' Zhdanov turned pale and drops of sweat appeared on his forehead. Everyone fell silent.[40] In 1947 Stalin's illegitimate son Konstantin Kuzakov was pressed by the MGB to accuse Zhdanov of 'loss of vigilance in atomic espionage'.[41] The 'Leningrad case' broke out in 1949–50, when the whole of 'Zhdanov's nest', as Stalin called it, was destroyed and thousands of Leningrad officials, headed by Politburo member and Deputy Chairman of the Council of Ministers N. A. Voznesensky, were dismissed and many executed. Molotov, Khrushchev and Malenkov dared to mention Voznesensky's name in Stalin's presence. 'Before you go on, you should know that Voznesensky was shot this morning', Stalin told them, 'Are you telling me that you, too, are enemies of the people?'[42]

In May 1951 Stalin, ordered M. D. Riumin, the chief of the MGB Special Investigative Department, who had earlier worked in Stalin's personal secretariat, to induce the Kremlin hospital x-ray technician Lidia Timashuk, an MGB 'unofficial collaborator', to write a report accusing Jewish doctors, her superiors, of poisoning Zhdanov and Shcherbakov.[43] Using her report, Riumin fabricated the 'case of the Kremlin doctors' and handed it for approval to the minister of state security, Abakumov, who in turn reported it to Beria. Both realized that the case was a monstrous anti-Semitic provocation that might explode into a great scandal, and that its upshot might well be that the MGB and they personally would be charged with a lack of vigilance in protecting the security of Soviet leaders. Abakumov called Riumin a 'stupid adventurer' and ordered him to throw out the charges of poisoning. Riumin complained to Stalin that Abakumov and Beria were obstructing the investigation.[44] Stalin for the moment took no action and went to Georgia for a vacation. He ordered his daughter not to visit Beria, telling her, 'I don't trust that man!'[45]

Stalin ordered the arrest of all of 'Beria's men' in order to create a vacuum around Beria. He issued a secret decree, accusing the Mingrelians, an ethnic subgroup of Georgia to which Beria belonged, of treason, and decided to exile all Mingrelians to Siberia.[46] Stalin summoned the chief of the

Georgian MGB, N. M. Rukhadze, to the Barzhomi *dacha*, ordering him to arrest all Mingrelian generals. On the way back to Tbilisi, Rukhadze smoked one cigarette after another. 'Is anything wrong?' his driver, Colonel Samson Parulava, a Mingrelian, asked him. 'Bad, very bad', Rukhadze replied.[47]

After his return from Barzhomi in August 1951, Stalin learned that Abakumov had arrested Riumin for his refusal to drop the poisoning charge against the Kremlin doctors. Abakumov was frisked and arrested by General Vlasik, the head of Stalin's bodyguards, as he entered an elevator to Stalin's second-floor Kremlin office. Vlasik took away Abakumov's belt, ripped off his shoulder bands and drove him to the Lubianka prison. Colonel Mironov, the chief of the MGB Lubianka Internal Prison, could not believe his eyes when he saw the new prisoner, the minister of state security, to whom he had submitted a routine report a few hours earlier. Pointing at Abakumov, Vlasik said, 'Take him!'[48] Abakumov wound up in the same cell from which a few minutes earlier Riumin had walked out with Stalin's order to press on with the investigation of the doctors' case.

On 20 October 1951 S. D. Ignatiev, the new minister of state security, signed the order for the arrest of Lev Sheinin, an investigator of 'specially important cases', who for years had carried out many of Stalin's personal assignments and had written books about the heroic exploits of the Soviet secret police. Sheinin was accused of being a foreign spy and the head of the 'murderers in white gowns', meaning the Jewish Kremlin doctors.[49] Stalin was punishing Sheinin for his attempt to investigate the murder of Solomon Mikhoels. Sheinin did not know that Mikhoels had been murdered on Stalin's order, and he refused to accept the 'automobile accident' cover-up version. Stalin sent an MGB general to 'explain' to Sheinin that 'Zionists killed Mikhoels, a staunch Soviet patriot, because he would not cooperate with them'. Sheinin did not accept this explanation and continued to search for the murderers. Annoyed by Sheinin's meddling in his affairs, Stalin ordered his arrest. As the interrogation of Sheinin progressed, Stalin changed the original accusation and removed him from the list of defendants in the case of the 'murderers in white gowns' and transferred him to another case, that of Jewish writers and poets who wrote in Russian. The accused included Vasily Grossman, Alexander Stein, and Konstantin Finn.[50] The screenwriter Aleksei Kapler, with whom Svetlana had fallen in love some years earlier, was brought to the Lubianka from the Vorkuta camp and included in the cast of the writers' case. (Earlier he had been accused of being an English spy.) Kapler was now charged with being a 'Jewish nationalist'.

In the summer of 1952, for the first time in many years, Stalin did not go to the Caucasus on vacation. He intended to stage a show trial of the Jewish Anti-Fascist Committee defendants. The military tribunal of the Soviet Supreme Court disposed of the 'Crimean Case' in secret proceedings that took place from 8 May to 18 July 1952. The arrested members of the JAFC, among them writers, poets and actors, were accused of conspiring to make the Crimea a 'Zionist and American base'. Thirteen defendants, among them Solomon Lozovsky, were sentenced to death by shooting. Lina Shtern, a leading expert on longevity, a topic of great interest to Stalin, was sentenced to a three-year prison term. One of the accused died during interrogation. Another group of 110 Jewish intellectuals arrested in connection with the 'Crimean Case' were secretly tried later. Ten were executed, five died during interrogation, the others were sentenced to various prison terms, ranging from five to 25 years.[51]

On 5 October 1952 Stalin opened the Nineteenth Party Congress, the first since 1939. Khrushchev, Malenkov and Poskrebyshev in their reports stressed the need for 'political vigilance' and warned against aggression by the 'American imperialists'. They portrayed the United States and the West as 'warmongers.' Stalin made a brief statement about the 'struggle for the preservation and maintenance of peace'. He was greeted with a roar of applause. In a photograph taken during the congress he appears in his generalissimo uniform in the midst of a large group of marshals, generals and admirals. Stalin's intention was to blackmail the West with the threat of nuclear war. He was encouraged by the successful test of the Soviet hydrogen bomb in 1952 and gave orders to speed up the production of long-range jets and rockets capable of delivering nuclear weapons on to American soil.[52] 'We will show this Jewish shopkeeper how to attack us!' Stalin was fond of saying (he had somehow become convinced that President Truman was Jewish). An air force colonel, a friend of Stalin's son Vasily, told Svetlana, 'Now is the time to fight and to conquer, while your father is alive. At present we can win!'[53]

During the Party Congress, the Politburo was renamed 'Presidium' and enlarged from nine to 25 members. (Years later Khrushchev wrote that by replacing the old Politburo with the Presidium Stalin intended to 'annihilate the old Politburo members and, in this way, to cover up all of [his] shameful acts'.[54] But Stalin's intentions were more complex. In erasing the very name of 'Politburo' he intended to obliterate yet another connection to the past and to his Okhrana career. He was the only surviving member of the original Politburo, which had been set up by Lenin in great secrecy in May 1917 to deal with the scandal connected with the exposure of Roman Malinovsky, Stalin's rival in the Okhrana and in Lenin's entourage.)

The 7 November 1952 was the 35th anniversary of the October Revolution. As usual, Stalin stood on top of the mausoleum, reviewing the military parade and civilian demonstration. In the evening, he attended a reception at the Bolshoi Theater. Whenever his name was mentioned, the audience rose and cheered. *Pravda* described him as 'the wise leader and teacher, the organizer and inspirer of the historic victories of the Soviet people, the genius of all progressive mankind'. The Indian ambassador Krishna P. S. Menon, who was present at the reception, wondered by what means Stalin, that short, ageing and graying man, 'wielded greater, and more concentrated power, than any mortal had ever had'.[55]

During November 1952 Stalin's attention was fixed on the show trial that was being staged in the People's Court in Prague. The defendants were Czechoslovak leaders, most of them Jews. The chief defendant was the secretary general of the Communist Party, Rudolf Slansky. They had been arrested in November 1951, when Anastas Mikoyan arrived in Prague with instructions from Stalin to the Czechoslovak president Klement Gotwald to arrest Slansky, who might otherwise 'escape abroad'. Slansky and the other defendants were accused of providing Israel with weapons during the Arab–Israeli war of 1948–49. In fact, the defendants considered themselves 'internationalists' and were ideologically opposed to Stalin's policy of supporting the Jewish State. True to form, Stalin blamed them for a failed policy that he himself had ordered. Mordekhai Oren, one of the leaders of the Israeli leftist party Mapam, was arrested in Czechoslovakia. (Five years earlier, in 1946, Oren had told a Soviet intelligence officer in London that the Jews in Palestine would create a pro-Soviet state.) Now, Oren was interrogated by M. T. Likhachev, the deputy chief of the MGB Investigations Department for Especially Important Cases, who had been assigned to Prague. 'Why did you fool us?' Likhachev asked Oren.[56] The question echoed Stalin's outrage that the leftist Jews in Israel had 'fooled' him by failing to carry out their pledge to turn Israel into a Soviet satellite. 'So they thought they could fool Stalin! Just look at them, it's Stalin they tried to fool!' was his angry response to the Jewish 'betrayal'.[57]

The Prague show trial ended with Slansky and ten other defendants being sentenced to death by hanging, a highly unusual form of execution in Czechoslovakia and in the Soviet Union. Stalin re-enacted the hanging of the two Georgian peasants in the Gori public square, which he, then a

12-year-old boy, had watched, imagining that one of the condemned was his hated father Vissarion. Memorable events of his distant youth were becoming vivid in Stalin's mind while his memory of contemporary events was becoming increasingly faulty. During the last years of his life Stalin often could not recall the names of even close associates with whom he was in daily contact. During a dinner at his *dacha* he turned to N. A. Bulganin, his defense minister, and started to say something but stopped. 'You there, what's your name?' he asked. When Bulganin replied, Stalin said, 'Of course, Bulganin. That's what I wanted to say.'[58] Childhood traumas, on the other hand, Stalin remembered well, and was driven to re-enact.

Early in 1953 he encouraged a rumor in Georgia that Jews murdered Christian children with the aim of using their blood in the making of matzo. On his prompting the secret police let a hysterical woman, Nataly Kavtaradze, run in the streets of Tbilisi, screaming that the Jews had been caught murdering Christian children and rolling them in wooden barrels studded with nails, in order to drain their blood for use in matzo.[59] Such an accusation had last been heard in Georgia in Stalin's early childhood, when several Georgian Jews had been accused by a Russian investigator of killing a Christian girl and using her blood, drained in a barrel studded with nails, for making matzo. Her body was found with numerous little wounds on it, which the police took to be nail punctures. This accusation instilled in many Georgians fear for their children. The mass hysteria continued for some time, even after several prominent Russian lawyers repudiated the police version and proved in court that the girl had drowned during heavy rain and that her wounds were the bites of small animals. The Jews were acquitted.[60]

Stalin also reenacted one of his early traumas on the stage of the Moscow Youth Theater. He commissioned the play *Pavlik Morozov* and 'suggested' the script, according to which Pavlik, in the key court scene, condemns his father Trofim. Pavlik's mother also accuses Trofim, 'He was a beast, and remained a beast!' A friend of Pavlik's father, exclaimed, 'Way back Trofim came to me, begging, "Be my boy's godfather . . .". I agreed. Ugh, if I had only known what kind of little serpent I was baptizing, I would have drowned him in the font . . . '.[61] Stalin ordered a statue of Pavlik Morozov to be placed at the entrance to Red Square. Fearing that Pavlik's remains might reveal the secret of his death, Stalin ordered the transfer of his grave to a new place beneath a two-yard-deep concrete foundation under his statue in the center of Pavlik's native village. This transfer of Pavlik's remains was done at night.[62]

Toward the end of his life, Stalin decided to destroy all evidence of his crimes. The task was formidable. He needed, for one thing, to obliterate the 'burial grounds' containing the remains of hundreds of thousands of his executed victims so that these mass graves could not be discovered, as had happened with the Katyn Forest graves of Polish officers. To destroy thousands of mass graves all over the Soviet Union was a titanic undertaking and needed time. A number of these graves, such as the one in Kuropaty near Minsk, were excavated and the skeletons destroyed.[63] Then there was evidence in print that needed to be destroyed. In January and February 1953 Komsomol (Communist Youth) and Party members were mobilized to peruse newspapers and magazines in Soviet libraries and archives and to remove articles containing negative references to Stalin or positive statements about 'enemies of the people', such as Trotsky and other members of the opposition.[64] Stalin also had Soviet agents destroy newspaper articles dating as far back as 1917 – on file in American and European libraries – that described Bolshevik–Okhrana ties.[65] Stalin also was urgently trying to ensure his immortality by having numerous statues of himself erected, some consuming hundreds of tons of bronze.[66]

Early in January 1953, the Ministry of Internal Affairs of the USSR printed a million copies of a booklet titled, *Why It Is Unavoidable to Exile Jews from the Industrial Centers of the Country*.[67] The booklet was written on Stalin's instruction by D. I. Chesnokov, a lecturer on Marxism-Leninism at Moscow University, who was a friend of Svetlana's husband Yury Zhdanov and was promoted to the post of editor – firstly of the journal *Problems of Philosophy* and then of the journal *Communist*. Chesnokov was at the right place at the right time when he was invited to Svetlana's birthday party. He was introduced by Yury Zhdanov to Stalin. During his conversation with Stalin, Chesnokov stated that he was interested in developing the theoretical basis for the deportation of Chechens, Volga Germans, Crimean Tartars and others, whom Stalin had exiled a few years earlier. Stalin told Chesnokov to concentrate on the deportation of the Jews and sent him to the Central Committee's *dacha* near Moscow to prepare publication of a thesis on Jewish deportation. By the beginning of February 1953 this theoretical analysis had been approved by Stalin and millions of copies were printed and ready for distribution.[68] (Earlier, on 5 October 1952, when Stalin chaired the Nineteenth Party Congress, he had promoted Chesnokov to membership of the newly formed Presidium.)

By that time Gulag prisoners were being used by the ministry of internal affairs in the hasty construction of numerous barrack complexes, actually concentration camps, in Birobidzhan, the island of Novaya Zemlia, and other areas of Siberia to which the deported Jews were to be brought.[69] Stalin created a special 'Deportation Commission' accountable only to him. He appointed M. A. Suslov chairman, and N. N. Poliakov secretary of this commission. Poliakov revealed years later, that, according to Stalin's initial plan, the deportation was to begin in the middle of February 1953, but the monumental task of compiling lists of Jews had not been completed by that time. There were two types of lists: the 'pure-blooded' Jews were to be deported first. Those Jews with one Jewish parent, the so-called *polukrovki* (half breeds) were to be deported later. The delay in compiling the lists forced Stalin to order a strict timetable: the trial of the Kremlin doctors was to be held over 5–7 March 1953. Their executions (on the *lobnoe mesto* – the center of Red Square, where executions had taken place centuries earlier) were to take place on 11 and 12 March.[70] According to Stalin's plan, the public hanging of the Kremlin doctors in Red Square before the eyes of the incensed populace was to serve as the signal for a Jewish pogrom. Stalin intended to use this pogrom as justification for the exile of the Jews. He planned to play the role of the 'savior' of the Jews, who would be sent to 'safe places' to protect them from the enraged Russian populace.[71]

On 13 January 1953, the fifth anniversary of the murder of Mikhoels, *Pravda* published the first report by the Soviet news agency TASS about the arrest of a group of Kremlin doctors, who were accused of being agents of the Jewish organization the Joint Distribution Committee and of American intelligence, and whose orders had supposedly been passed on to them by the 'well-known bourgeois nationalist Solomon Mikhoels'.[72] The doctors were also accused of shortening the lives of the Politburo members Zhdanov and Shcherbakov, as well as of harming the health of Soviet marshals, generals and admirals. Doctor Vinogradov was accused of being an agent of British intelligence. *Pravda* in a front-page editorial, titled 'Foul Spies and Murderers under the Mask of Doctors and Professors', also accused the 'gang of doctors-poisoners' and their American and British 'bosses' of 'feverishly preparing for a new world war' and blamed the 'organs of state security' for their 'lack of vigilance', reminding readers that the doctors Levin and Pletnev had earlier 'killed the great Russian writer A. M. Gorky and the outstanding Soviet statesmen V. V. Kuibyshev and V. R. Menzhinsky'.[73]

The charge of 'lack of vigilance' was directed against Beria and the arrested minister of state security, Abakumov. In the beginning of 1953 Stalin spread the rumor that Beria was a Jew. Arrested MGB generals, all of whom were Mingrelians, were accused of a plot to separate the west

Georgian province of Mingrelia from the Soviet Union. They were forced to sign confessions confirming their guilt and implicating Beria. In Stalin's mind, the Jews and the Mingrelian 'plotters' became connected.[74] The files with the signed depositions of the Mingrelian generals were brought to Stalin for review, and he gave instructions not to forget 'the chief Mingrelian' (that is, Beria). On the files, Stalin wrote in red pencil, 'Death to the Mingrelian bandits.'[75] The houses and apartments of Mingrelians in Tbilisi and other Georgian cities were placed on special lists in expectation of the order for their exile to Siberia, which was to take place at the same time as the exile of the Jewish population. Cossack troops with sabers and whips arrived in Mingrelian cities to carry out the order. Their appearance and pre-revolutionary uniforms startled the local population.[76]

The daily barrage of statements against the 'murderers in white gowns' created a pogrom atmosphere in the country. The deprived populace sensed blood in the air. The Gulag administration was ordered to incite the inmates to murder Jewish prisoners.[77] The relentless anti-Jewish campaign did not remain unnoticed in Israel. On 9 February 1953 Jewish terrorists exploded a bomb in the Soviet embassy in Tel-Aviv. Stalin used this incident to break diplomatic ties with Israel. He gave the general director of TASS, Ya. S. Khavinson, and the chief of the Party Propaganda Department, M. B. Mitin, both Jews, a list of prominent Soviet Jews who had to sign an appeal to Stalin, the text of which he himself wrote. The appeal condemned the 'murderers in white gowns' and called for their execution, while pleading with the 'great and wise *vozhd* [leader] Comrade Stalin' to save the Jewish population from the 'understandable indignation of the Russian people' by 'relocating' the Jews to 'safe areas' in Siberia and the Far East. Khavinson and Mitin, who enlisted the prominent journalist David Zaslavsky and the academician and historian I. I. Minz, signed this appeal and promised to ask the prominent Jews on Stalin's list to sign it too and help to convince the Jews to cooperate with the authorities during the 'relocation to the safe areas'. They went to all the prominent Jews mentioned on Stalin's list and asked them to sign. Most of them did, fearing Stalin's wrath. Only a few refused: General Yakov Kreizer, the singer Mark Reizen, the writer Veniamin Kaverin, and Professor Arkady Ierusalimsky, Svetlana's teacher. The writer Ilya Ehrenburg in a letter to Stalin asked his advice on whether he should or should not sign the appeal, pointing out that the deportation of Jews might do much harm to the Soviet image abroad and to the peace movement. Stalin did not reply.[78]

Years later, the rumor was spread that Lazar Kaganovich had refused to sign the appeal and had thrown his party card on Stalin's desk in protest. In fact, Kaganovich was appointed by Stalin to direct the deportation.[79] His name on this Jewish list was crossed out in red pencil by Stalin. Stalin's choice of Kaganovich, a Jew, for carrying out the deportation was a clever ruse: who could accuse a Jew of anti-Semitism? Stalin saw Kaganovich not as a Jew but as a fellow criminal who had sided with him even in the murder of his own brother Mikhail. He could count on Kaganovich – who was not merely a fellow criminal but also an anti-Semitic Jew and an utterly depraved and immoral creature – to help him in the extermination of the Jewish people. Khrushchev, unaware that anti-Semitism is rooted in psychological makeup, found it difficult to believe, exclaiming in his memoirs: 'A Jew himself, Kaganovich was against the Jews!'[80] If Kaganovich had refused to sign the appeal, he would not have survived this act of insubordination. But rumors often contain a particle of truth. Someone in Stalin's entourage *did* protest and refuse to sign the appeal. The signing of the appeal took place around 13 February 1953. On 14 February 1953 *Pravda* announced that 'one of the prominent leaders of the Communist Party and the Soviet Union, the member of the Central Committee' Lev Mekhlis had died of heart failure.[81]

Stalin assigned to Khrushchev an important role in inciting anti-Semitism in the Ukraine, the area of Khrushchev's responsibility at the time. 'The good workers at the factory should be given clubs so they can beat the hell out of those Jews,' he told Khrushchev. At the beginning of 1953, Stalin invited Khrushchev and two Ukrainian high officials, Melnikov and Korotchenko, to a dinner. As usual, they soon got drunk, and Stalin told the Ukrainian officials that they should organize pogroms in the Ukraine. At first they were surprised to hear the 'great internationalist' Stalin making such statements, but they knew that Stalin's instructions had to be carried out.[82] On their return to the Ukraine, they organized the pogroms.[83] Leonid Brezhnev, a protégé of Khrushchev, was elevated to candidate member of the Presidium in October 1952. Stalin sent him to Moldavia to supervise the deportation of the Jewish population from this area.

Some of Stalin's cronies had Jewish wives who became objects of Stalin's most intense suspicion, because in his mind they were connected with the Biblical story of Esther, a story he, the ex-seminarian, knew well. He knew that at the end of February and beginning of March 1953 the Jews would celebrate Purim, thanking God for giving them Esther, a Jewish wife of an ancient Persian king. She had saved the Persian Jews from the hands of their enemy Haman, who had plotted to destroy them. Stalin planned to start the pogrom during Purim to show the Jews that this time that they would be celebrating their deliverance prematurely. But Stalin feared that among the Jewish wives of his subordinates was a new Esther, who might prevent him from carrying out the deportation. He exiled Voroshilov's Jewish wife and called Voroshilov a British spy. He ordered the arrest of Andrey Andreyev's wife, Dora Khazan. Andreyev was expelled from the Politburo and lived in fear of arrest. Molotov's wife, Polina Zhemchuzhina, had earlier been exiled to Kustanai, Kazakhstan, where she remained under the codename 'Object Number 12' until January 1953 when she was trans-ferred to the Moscow Lubianka prison and included in the cast of the Kremlin doctors' case. (She was released by Beria a few days after Stalin's death and returned to Molotov.[84]) Stalin accused Molotov of being an American spy. General Khrulev's Jewish wife was arrested and imprisoned in the top-security prison Vladimir Tsentral. Many Jewish wives were kept there.[85] Marshal Zhukov was one of those he suspected of being Jewish.[86] Before exiling Zhukov to the Urals, Stalin showed him a report, signed by Beria, stating: 'We established that Marshal G. K. Zhukov for more than 15 years has been an agent of British Intelligence and continuously informed the hostile power about the defense secrets of the Soviet Union.'[87] Lieutenant-General N. Vlasik, the chief of Stalin's bodyguards for many years, was arrested on 15 December 1952 and accused of 'loss of vigilance', having maintained friendly relations with his Jewish neighbor, to whom he allegedly passed on secret information.[88] Early in January 1953, Stalin fired the chief of his personal secretariat, Alexander Poskrebyshev, his closest assistant for many years. Stalin remembered that Poskrebyshev's Jewish wife, who had been poisoned on his order in 1940, was a distant relative of Trotsky. Poskrebyshev expected to be arrested.[89]

Most of February 1953 Stalin spent in Kuntsevo with his bodyguards, mainly Russians and a few Georgians from his native town of Gori. He fired all the Mingrelians. He ordered the minister of state security, Ignatiev, to torture Vinogradov and the other Kremlin doctors, threatening, 'If you do not obtain confessions from the doctors, we will shorten you by a head.'[90] He viciously cursed Ignatiev. Khrushchev later recalled, 'Stalin was crazy with rage, yelling at Ignatiev and threatening him, demanding that he throw the doctors in chains, beat them to a pulp and grind them into powder.'[91] The 'liberation' of the Soviet Union from the 'Jewish yoke' was openly discussed in party and government circles.[92] The technical problems of transportation of Jews to Birobidzhan were addressed in the Council of Ministers. 'I thought I would go crazy when I learned about it', recalled the Old Bolshevik O. I. Goloborodko, who worked there at the time.[93]

When Stalin was told about the difficulty in transporting a large number of Jews to the remote area, he replied, 'Half of them will die on the way there.'[94] Some ten years earlier, hundreds of thousands of Crimean Tartars, Chechens, Kabardins and Volga Germans had been exiled in cattle trains from their native lands to Siberia and the Far East. Almost half of them had perished on the way to their destinations.

On 17 February 1953 Stalin invited Krishna P. S. Menon, the Indian ambassador to the Soviet Union, who was the last foreigner to see Stalin alive. As they talked, Stalin, as usual, kept doodling wolves in various aggressive postures, standing alone, in pairs and in packs. Noticing that Menon was looking at his drawings, Stalin suddenly said: 'The Russian peasant is a very simple man but a very wise one. When the wolf attacks him, he does not attempt to teach it morals, but tries to kill it. And the wolf knows this and behaves accordingly.'[95] The thought occurred to Menon that for Stalin the wolves symbolized his enemies. He was startled when Stalin suddenly asked about the impurity of the languages spoken by the peoples of India. Menon had no idea about Stalin's hatred of the Jews or his outrage at Niko Marr's theory of the Semitic origin of the Georgian language.

In the last days of February 1953, Stalin's daughter Svetlana felt an atmosphere of rising fear in which 'everything grew quiet, as before a storm'.[96] Stalin ordered his defense minister, Bulganin, to bring to Moscow and other large cities hundreds of cattle trains which were to be put on reserved lines nearby. Stalin planned to organize assaults by 'people's avengers' on the deported Jews.[97] By the estimation of one historian, 30–40 per cent of the deported Jews would not have reached their destination.[98]

At the end of February 1953 Stalin was ready to stage the trial of the Kremlin doctors. That year Purim was to start at sundown on Saturday, 28 February. According to the Jewish lunar calendar, it was the 14th day of the month Adar, 5713.

NOTES

1. Yakov Aizenshtat, *O podgotovke Stalinym genotsida evreev*, Jerusalem, 1994, p. 38.
2. S. Allilueva, *Only One Year*, New York, 1969, p. 154.
3. Interview with Lidia Shatunovskaya and Lev Tumerman in Rehavot, Israel, 1975. In the author's archive.
4. 'V komissii Politburo TK KPSS', *Izvestia TK KPSS*, January 1989. Protocol no. 7, dated 29 December 1988.
5. Taped interview with Vasily Rudich. In the author's archive. See also N. S. Khrushchev, *Khrushchev Remembers*, Boston, 1970, pp. 261f. Vasily Rudich related the testimony of Olga Shatunovskaya, a member of the Special Commission of the Presidium of the Central Committee. She together with N. M. Shvernik (the Special Commission's chairman), the general prosecutor of

the USSR, R. A. Rudenko, the chairman of the KGB, A. N. Shelepin, and the director of the Central Committee Section on Administrative Organs, N. R. Mironov, interrogated Politburo member G. M. Malenkov, who described Stalin's order to murder Mikhoels.

6. A. Borshchagovsky, *Obviniaetsia krov'*, Moscow, 1994, pp. 5–8, and Aizenshtat, *O podgotovke . . .* , pp. 39–41, quoting a report by Beria, dated 2 April 1953, to the Presidium of the Party Central Committee.
7. Ibid. Also Robert Conquest, *Stalin: Breaker of Nations*, New York, 1991, p. 306.
8. Allilueva, *Only One Year*, p. 154.
9. The present author with his classmate Mikhail Margulis were present at the funeral and heard the rumor. Two years later, Soviet movie director Mikhail Kalik was arrested and accused of stating that Mikhoels was murdered by MGB agents.
10. *Pravda*, 25 August 1941.
11. Y. A. Gilboa, *The Black Years of Soviet Jewry*, Boston, Toronto, 1971, pp. 42–56.
12. George E. Kirk, *A Short History of the Middle East*, New York, 1964, pp. 202–6.
13. Interview with Matetiahu Shmulevich in Yaffa, Israel, 1969 (in the author's archive); see also Y. A. Gilboa, *The Black Years of Soviet Jewry*, pp. 202–06 and 64ff.; See also interview with Samuil Tornopoler in Tel-Aviv, Israel, February 1969 (in the present author's archive). see also interview with David Ben-Gurion in Sde-Boker and Tel-Aviv in 1969 (in the author's archive); see also Ben-Gurion's letter to Gilboa, dated 31 January 1967 in Y. A. Gilboa, *The Black Years of Soviet Jewry*, p. 352, fn. 20.
14. Interview with Mordekhai Oren in Israel in 1969. In the author's archive.
15. Interview with Boris Guriel, director of Chaim Weizman's archive, in Tel-Aviv in 1969. In the author's archive.
16. Interview with Natalia and Alexander Rodovsky in Haifa, Israel, 1979. In the author's archive.
17. Interview with Lidia Shatunovskaya and Lev Tumerman, Rechavot, Israel, 1973.
18. 'V komissii Politburo TK KPSS', *Izvestia TK KPSS*, January 1989. Protocol no. 7, 29 December 1988, p. 37.
19. A. Vaisberg, 'Evreisky antifashistsky komitet u M. A. Suslov', *Zveniya-istorikeskii almanakh*, Moscow, 1991, pp. 535–54.
20. Ibid., p. 546.
21. 'V komissii Politburo TK KPSS', *Isvestia TK KPSS*, January 1989. Protocol no. 7, dated 29 December 1988. See also Arkady Vaksberg, *Stalin Against the Jews*, New York, 1994, pp. 198–202.
22. Ibid.
23. Allilueva, *Dvadtsat' pisem k drugu*, New York, 1967, p. 150.
24. Khrushchev, *Khrushchev Remembers*, Boston, Toronto, 1970, pp. 258–69. Also Khrushchev, *Khrushchev Remembers?The Last Testament*, Boston, 1970, pp. 78 and 150.
25. Edward R. Stettinius, Jr, *Roosevelt and the Russians: the Yalta Conference*, London, 1950, p. 278.
26. Interview with David Lifshitz in Tel-Aviv, Israel, 1969. In the author's archive; interview with Matetiahu Shmulevich in Yaffa, Israel, 1969. In the author's archive; G. S. Nikitina, *Gosudarstvo Izrail*, Moscow, 1968, pp. 58f, fn. 74.
27. Henry Kamm, 'Inquiry on Jan Masaryk's Death', in 1948 is demanded in Prague, *The New York Times*, April 3 1968. Also C. L. Sulzberger, 'Foreign Affairs: Murder Will Out,' *The New York Times*, April 17 1968. C. L. Sulzberger, 'Foreign Affairs: Murder Will Out', *The New York Times*, 17 April 1968.
28. Interview with David Ben-Gurion in Sde-Boker and Tel-Aviv in 1969.
29. Yury Idashkin, 'Lichny drug Stalina: Bogi zhazhdut,' *Literaturnaya Russia*, 22 July 1988.
30. Interview with Anna and Boris Glick, residents of Davydkovo and victims of the exile order, in New York, 1967. In the author's archive.
31. *Evreiskaya entsiklopedia*, vol. VI, St Petersburg, 1913, pp. 808f.
32. M. Gorbanevsky, 'Tovarishch Stalin vy bolshoi ucheny'. Interview in *Nedelia*, no. 45, 5–11 November 1990, p. 4.
33. Khrushchev, *Khrushchev Remembers*, pp. 270f.
34. Roy Medvedev, *Let History Judge*, New York, 1971, pp. 332f.
35. Allilueva, *Twenty Letters to a Friend*, New York, 1967, p. 187.
36. Vladimir Dedijer, *Tito Speaks: His Self Portrait and Struggle with Stalin*, London, 1953, pp. 300–12.
37. Milovan Djilas, *Conversations with Stalin*, New York and London, 1962, pp. 176–81.
38. Interview with Mikhail Meerson-Aksenov, son of Grigory Meerson, in New York in 1989. In the author's archive.

39. A. Antonov-Ovseenko, *Portret tirana*, New York, 1980, p. 325.
40. Allilueva, *Only One Year*, p. 384.
41. Evgeny Zhirnov, 'K. Kuzakov – syn I. V. Stalina', *Argumenty i fakty*, no. 39, 1995.
42. H. Montgomery Hyde, *Stalin: the History of a Dictator*, New York, 1971, p. 575, citing Khrushchev's secret speech (Special Report to the Twentieth Party Congress.)
43. Nikita Khrushchev's secret speech. Also Khrushchev, *Khrushchev Remembers*, pp. 282–6.
44. Boris Nikolayevsky, 'The Strange Death of Mikhail Ryumin', *The New Leader*, 4 October, 1954, pp. 15–18. See also John J. Dziak, *Chekisty: A History of the KGB*, Lexington, MA, 1988, p. 127.
45. Allilueva, *Only One Year*, p. 386.
46. Khrushchev, *Khrushchev Remembers*, p. 312.
47. Interview with Nugzar Sharia in Sag Harbor, New York, 1972.
48. Taped interview with I. P. Itskov in New York City in 1988.
49. Arkady Vaksberg, 'The Grand Inquisitor's Right-Hand Man', *Literary Gazette International*, vol. I, no. 5, April 1990, p. 7.
50. Ibid.
51. 'V komissii Politburo TK KPSS', *Izvestia TK KPSS*, January, 1989. Protocol no. 7, dated 29 December 1988.
52. Interview with Israeli diplomat Yakov Yanai in Tel-Aviv, Israel, 1971. In the author's archive. Yanai met a Soviet general in a prison camp who told him about Stalin's interest in the building of a long-range bomber that would make it possible to attack the US with nuclear weapons.
53. Allilueva, *Only One Year*, p. 155.
54. Nikita Khrushchev's secret speech.
55. K. P. S. Menon, *The Flying Troika*, London, 1963, p. 7.
56. Interview with Mordekhai Oren, Israel, 1969,
57. Allilueva, *Only One Year*, p. 392.
58. Khrushchev, *Khrushchev Remembers*, pp. 307f.
59. Interview with Nugzar Sharia, Sag Harbor, 1971.
60. *Evreiskaya Entsiklopedia*, vol. IX, pp. 938–40.
61. *Pravda*, 18 January 1953.
62. Yuri Druzhnikov, 'Saga o Pavlike Morozove', *Strana i mir*, no. (2)44, March–April 1988, p. 119.
63. Zenon Pozniak and Evgeny Shygalev, 'Kuropaty–doroga smerti', *Novoe russkoe slovo*, 24 June 1988, p. 6. Also Yury Turin, 'S odnoi storony, s drugoi storony', *Ogonek*, no. 39, Moscow, 1988.
64. Interview with Yakov and Diana Vinkovetsky (Pavel Litvinov's friends) in Chappaqua, New York, 1975. They took part in this censoring operation.
65. The author in 1974 discovered that collections of Russian newspapers in the libraries at Columbia, Stanford, Yale, and several other universities had articles on Bolshevik–Okhrana ties removed. A 19 May 1917 article was missing from the newspaper *Russkoe slovo*, and one of 16 June 1917 was missing from the newspaper *Den'*. The collections were otherwise intact.
66. Medvedev, *Let History Judge*, p. 508.
67. Antonov-Ovseenko, *Portret Tirana*, p. 326.
68. Aizenshtat, *O podgotovke Stalinym* . . . p. 79. Also, Z. Sheinis, *Grozila deportatsiya*, Moscow, 1991.
69. Antonov-Ovseenko, *Portret Tirana*, pp. 325f. Also Medvedev, *Let History Judge*, p. 496, and interview with Boris Zubok, who saw the Novaya Zemlia barracks. His interview with the author in Chappaqua, New York, 1975.
70. Z. Sheinis, *Provokatsiya veka*, Moscow, 1994, quoting the record of the testimony of the secretary of the Deportation Commission, N. N. Poliakov.
71. Aizenshtat, *O podgotovke Stalinym*, pp. 70–4.
72. *Pravda*, 13 January 1953.
73. Ibid.
74. Conquest, *Stalin: Breaker of Nations*, p. 306.
75. Interview with Nugzar Sharia, Sag Harbor, New York 1972. Sharia told the author about the recollections of his uncle Peter Sharia, one of the arrested 'Mingrelian bandits' to whom Beria had shown the files.
76. Ibid. Nugzar Sharia recalled the account of the Hero of the Soviet Union Meliton Kantaria, a Mingrelian. Also *The New York Times*, 31 December 31 1993, p. A-24.
77. The present author witnessed incidents of Jewish prisoners being attacked in the Norilsk prison camp by criminal inmates.

78. Aizenshtat, *O podgotovke Stalinym*, pp. 70–2. Also *Strana i mir*, Munich, 1984, no. 10, p. 4. Ehrenburg's letter is published in Vaksberg, *Stalin Against the Jews*, pp. 263f.
79. Antonov-Ovseenko, *Portret Tirana*, p. 325. Also Medvedev, *Let History Judge*, pp. 495–7.
80. Khrushchev, *Khrushchev Remembers*, p. 243.
81. *Pravda*, 14 February 1953, p. 1.
82. Khrushchev, *Khrushchev Remembers*, pp. 258–64.
83. Medvedev, *Let History Judge*, pp. 495f.
84. Vaksberg, *Stalin Against the Jews*, p. 272. See also Khrushchev, *Khrushchev Remembers*, p. 308.
85. Interview with Lidia Shatunovskaya, Rechavot, Israel, 1973. She was one of the prisoners in Vladimir Tsentral.
86. Djilas, *Conversations with Stalin*, pp. 160f.
87. Antonov-Ovseenko, *Portret Tirana*, p. 327.
88. A. N. Kolesnik, 'Glavny telokhranitel' vozhdia', *Voenno-istoricheski zhurnal*, no. 12, 1989, pp. 85–92.
89. Interview with I. P. Itskov, New York City, 1988.
90. Medvedev, *Let History Judge*, p. 494.
91. Khrushchev, *Khrushchev Remembers*. pp. 286f.
92. Allilueva, *Only One Year*, p. 155.
93. Antonov-Ovseenko, *Portret Tirana*, p. 326.
94. Interview with Alexander Radovsky in Haifa, Israel, 1990.
95. K. P. S. Menon, *The Flying Troika*, London, 1963, p. 29. Also H. Montgomery Hyde, *Stalin: The History of a Dictator*, New York, 1971, p. 591.
96. Allilueva, *Only One Year*, p. 155.
97. Aizenshtat, *O podgotovke Stalinym*, p. 70 and pp. 74f, quoting Bulganin's statement to Professor Yakov Etinger, in 'Khronika dela vrachey', pp. 4–7.
98. The historian was E. V. Tarle. He is quoted in Yakov Aizenshtat, *O podgotovke Stalinym*, p. 83.

37

THE MURDER OF 'DR MOREAU'

Stalin spent the last days of February 1953 mostly at his Kuntsevo *dacha*. He stayed there late on Saturday night 28 February and went to bed at 4 am. On Sunday morning, 1 March 1953, the bodyguard Gogi Zautashvili, a native of Gori, was manning a control board on which bulbs lit up indicating which of the doors in Stalin's three identical rooms were open. Gogi Zautashvili became alarmed when one of the bulbs lit up and did not go off. It meant that Stalin had opened a door to one of his three rooms and the door had not closed after him automatically, as it should have. Zautashvili waited for a few moments, then notified the chief bodyguard on duty that night, M. Starostin who at first was afraid to disturb Stalin, but an hour later he tried calling him on the internal telephone. There was no response. After several more attempts to reach Stalin by phone, Starostin ordered the guards to break through the steel-plated door of his apartment. They found Stalin lying on the floor in the doorway between the second and third rooms, his body curled in a fetal position, his head resting on his arm. He could not talk. The right side of his body was paralyzed. The bodyguards and Stalin's maid placed him on a couch.[1] Starostin reported Stalin's condition to S. D. Ignatiev, the minister of state security, who refused to take action and told Starostin to call Politburo members Beria and Malenkov. Beria did not answer his phone. Malenkov called back half an hour later and said, 'I couldn't find Beria. Try to find him yourself.' Then Beria called and ordered, 'Don't tell anybody about Stalin's illness, and don't call anybody!' Beria and Malenkov arrived at Kuntsevo at 3 am Monday morning, 2 March. Malenkov took off his squeaky shoes and tiptoed over to Stalin. Beria was already looking intensely at Stalin's face. He knew that Stalin intended to destroy him and saw in Stalin's condition the chance to save himself by murdering him. Turning to the bodyguard in the room, he snapped, 'Don't raise a fuss, don't bother us, and don't disturb Comrade Stalin.' Then he cursed Starostin in the Kremlin slang, unprintable except for the words: 'Who appointed you idiots to serve Comrade Stalin?' Beria and Malenkov left, saying that physicians would arrive soon. They arrived around 9 am, six hours later.[2]

Meanwhile, Beria was bringing his own order to the Lubianka. Ignatiev went immediately over to Beria's side and arrested the chief of the department for special cases, Riumin, and all his assistants. The arrested Mingrelian generals, disoriented and suffering from the effects of months of torture, were led from their cells to Beria's office, where he gave them belts for holding up their pants, the buttons of which had been cut off. He showed them their interrogation files, on which was written in red pencil, 'Death to the Mingrelian bandits' and the signature, 'I. Stalin'. Cursing Stalin, Beria told them that their tormentor had had a stroke. 'The *gotferan* [pederast, in Georgian] is almost dead', Beria said. 'We have no time to lose. Go back to your offices and resume your duties.' Communications with Kuntsevo and the Kremlin were taken over by Beria's men.[3]

The Kuntsevo *dacha* was isolated from the rest of the country. Only a very narrow circle of people knew what was happening, but none of those in the know who were close to Stalin could have imagined that Beria had decided to murder him. Their own fanatical worship of Stalin would have made the mere thought of such an act blasphemy. Beria, very far from worshiping Stalin, nevertheless played the game and pretended to do all he could to save him. He brought to the *dacha* several prominent physicians, including the heart specialist P. E. Lukomsky, without telling them who their patient was to be. When they saw Stalin, they were so frightened that they began to shake. Beria scared them even more with the grim question, 'Do you guarantee Comrade Stalin's life?'[4]

V. A. Negovsky, the founder of Soviet 'reanimation science,' and his assistant Galina Chesnokova were brought to Kuntsevo. They carried their equipment to an assigned room, were followed every step by armed bodyguards, and told, 'Sit down. The members of the government want to talk to you.' Beria, Malenkov, and other Politburo members entered the room. 'Now, you will tell us what you intend to do, and I will listen to you very attentively!' Beria said to them. Chesnokova recalled later, 'We immediately felt that here he [Beria] was the foremost boss.' They were led into a large living room where Stalin was lying on a sofa, his clenched fists on a white sheet. Next to him sat his daughter Svetlana.[5]

On Sunday, 1 March, Svetlana had tried to telephone Stalin but had not been able to get through because all communication with the Kuntsevo *dacha* had been cut off. Monday morning, 2 March, Svetlana was attending a lecture at the Institute of World Literature, when she was told that her father was ill and that she should go to Kuntsevo. On her arrival there, she met Khrushchev and Bulganin, who arrived at the same time. 'Let's go in. Beria and Malenkov will tell you everything', they said to her. They, like Svetlana, had been told that morning to come to Kuntsevo. When she walked in and saw her father, she felt that 'He was dying . . . everything around, the whole house, everything was dying in front of my eyes. They all felt that something portentous, something almost majestic, was going on in this room, and they conducted themselves accordingly.' Only Beria behaved differently: 'There was only one person who was behaving almost obscenely. That was Beria. He was extremely agitated . . . He was trying so hard, at this moment of crisis, to strike the right balance, to be cunning, yet not too cunning. It was written all over him . . .'. Stalin was dying a horrible death. His face darkened and changed, gradually his features became unrecognizable, his lips blackened. During the last two hours he was suffocating. Svetlana wrote that at the end something very strange happened:

The agony was awful. He literally choked to death. At what seemed like the very last moment, he suddenly opened his eyes and cast a glance over everybody in the room. It was a horrible glance, insane or perhaps angry and full of fear of death . . . then something incomprehensible happened . . . He suddenly lifted his left hand as though he was pointing to something above and bringing down a curse on us all . . . The next moment, after a final effort, the spirit wrenched itself free from the flesh.[6]

Stalin raised his crippled left arm as if he was cursing his enemies, the 'wolves' he had meant to destroy, and their prototype, his father Vissarion, who had caused him so much suffering. When Stalin breathed his last, Beria suddenly ordered, 'Take Svetlana away!' No one paid attention. A few minutes earlier, Stalin's son Vasily, drunk as usual, had been led out of the room when he shouted, 'Scoundrels, you murdered my father!' Seeing that Stalin was dead, Beria in a triumphant voice ordered the chief bodyguard, Khrustalev: 'Get my car!' Svetlana recalled that 'Beria could hardly restrain his joy. Not only I, but many people there understood that. But he was much feared, and they all knew that at the moment of my father's death no one in Russia had as much power as this horrible person.'

Other close associates of Stalin were crying. Khrushchev, in the old peasant tradition, dropped to his knees next to Stalin, loudly sobbing. The servants and bodyguards one after the other came close to the body of their *khoziain* (boss), whom they had venerated for many years, to pay their respects. Tears rolled down their faces. Soon all left except Svetlana, Bulganin and Mikoyan. On the morning of 5 March Stalin's body was removed in a white ambulance. It was embalmed.[7] In having Stalin embalmed, Beria destroyed any traces of poison in Stalin's body, and he did not destroy the 'personality cult' by treating Stalin's body with the same veneration that had been accorded to Lenin's remains. In the circle of the Mingrelian generals, whom he had set free, Beria bragged that he had poisoned Stalin and thus saved them from death and prevented the deportation of the Mingrelians and Jews to Siberia.[8]

Stalin's embalmed body was placed in the Hall of Columns, where he had staged the show trials and where thousands of defendants had confessed to crimes that they had never committed. Stalin's 'comrades-in-arms', the 'guard of honor' headed by Beria, stood next to his body. Past them moved grief-stricken mourners in a long line stretching for many streets. Thousands of mounted militiamen, security police and soldiers tried to maintain order, but they could not stop the human avalanche. Large crowds were pouring into Moscow's streets, stampeding and crushing under their feet thousands of crazed worshipers of Stalin, whom he was dragging along with himself into the grave even after his death. The death toll was especially high near Trubnaya Square.[9] A similar frenzy had seized the city more than half a century earlier, in 1896, when Moscovites had rushed to Khodynka Field to celebrate the coronation of Tsar Nicholas II. The crowd crushed under its feet hundreds of people. Moscovites proved to be unchanged in their emotional fervor, whether they celebrated a coronation or mourned the demise of their idols. One difference was that in 1896 they solemnized the ascendance of the legitimate heir to the Russian throne, the scion of a 300-year-old dynasty, while in March 1953 they lamented the death of the greatest criminal in history, whose appalling carnage they could not comprehend then and would be unable to admit to decades after his death.

Shortly before his death Stalin ordered the translation into Russian and publication of H. G. Wells's scientific fiction *The Island of Dr Moreau*. Stalin did not realize that the horror story of Dr Moreau could some day be seen as an allegory of his own true atrocities. In Wells's tale, the deranged Dr Moreau is driven by a craving to create ideal human beings by exploring the 'extreme limit of plasticity in a living shape'. He performs plastic surgery and organ transplanting on the oxen, wolves, apes, pigs and other animals who survive the torture of his experiments only to be forced to chant certain commandments, known as 'the Law' which become woven into their minds without any possibility of disobedience or argument. Finally, while Dr Moreau is performing an operation on a puma, the animal breaks its fetters and runs away. He pursues the terrified and bleeding puma and is killed in the ensuing struggle. The rumor that their tormentor is dead spreads among the deformed and terrified creatures. As time passes, dread of the mad doctor fades from their minds, and they slowly revert to their original animal state.[10] Wells first published this masterpiece of the macabre in 1896. He could not have foretold the emergence of the Soviet dictator. He did not recognize the mad doctor in Stalin when he interviewed him in 1934. Wells described Stalin as a very kind man who 'owes his position to the fact that no one is afraid of him and everyone trusts him'.

After Stalin's death millions of Gulag prisoners sensed that the end to their misery was in sight. A few victims of the Great Purge were still alive then and some sincerely cried, lamenting Stalin's demise.[11] But the great majority rejoiced. A prisoner, Roman Romanyuk, a Ukrainian, shouted joyfully, 'I just heard the mustached scum bag either got sick or dropped dead.'[12] Like Dr Moreau's tortured animals, the Soviet people, paralyzed by fear, needed time to shed it. Beria was the first among those close to Stalin to defy his legacy, but he was cautious not to move too quickly. He began the process of eroding the 'personality cult'. Beria immediately rescinded Stalin's order to deport the Jewish and Mingrelian populations to Siberia and terminated the 'case of the Kremlin doctors'. Those who had survived torture were in appalling physical condition. He ordered that they be given medical help and good food. On 3 April 1953, a month after Stalin's death, the doctors were released and driven to their homes. They could barely walk and were unable to climb even a few stairs without the help of the guards. The next day, an event unprecedented in the history of the Soviet Union took place: *Pravda* announced that the 'former USSR ministry of state security' had acted 'incorrectly and without any lawful basis' in arresting the Kremlin doctors and that all doctors 'accused in this case have been completely exonerated of the accusations against them . . . and released. The persons accused of incorrect conduct of the investigation have been arrested and criminal charges have been brought against them.'[13] Beria abolished Stalin's new Presidium and reinstated the old Politburo with its pre-October 1952 composition. He also abolished the ministry of state security and merged it with the ministry of internal affairs to concentrate two main organs of power in his own hands.

Soon after Stalin's death Beria invited Molotov to his office. When Molotov walked in, his wife Polina Zhemchuzhina rushed to him. They embraced and kissed and cried, while Beria stood behind his desk, smiling. He released all the other imprisoned Jewish wives, as well as Stalin's relatives Anna Redens and Olga Allilueva together with their neighbors and friends. Among the released prisoners was the screenwriter Aleksei Kapler.[14] The overcrowded cells of the Lubianka and other prisons were almost emptied. Beria proceeded with a mass 'unloading' of the Gulags. On

27 March 1953, three weeks after Stalin's death, an amnesty for millions of
prison camp inmates was issued, which also applied to 'political prisoners'
with sentences of up to five years.[15]

On 6 April 1953 *Pravda* published an editorial, titled 'Soviet Socialist
Legality Should Not Be Violated', which accused 'despicable adventurers
of the Riumin type' of inflaming national antagonism and slandering the
Soviet people. The article stated that 'careful investigation has established,
for example, that an honest public figure, the People's Artist of the USSR,
Mikhoels, was slandered in this way'.[16] Stalin's close associates knew that it
was he who had ordered not merely Mikhoels' slander but his murder, but
they kept silent. The process of dismantling the 'personality cult' was only
in its initial stage. The veneration of the dead dictator as 'the greatest genius
of mankind' was prevalent among the common people as well as among
the Politburo members, with Beria being the only exception.

The millions of released Gulag prisoners were the first to shed their fear
of the dead dictator. In May 1953 'special regime' camps in Norilsk,
Vorkuta, Karaganda, and other areas were swept by uprisings. During
Stalin's rule such a thing would have been unthinkable. Any such uprising
would immediately have been suppressed by force and ended in mass
executions. The uprising in the Norilsk camps was triggered by the shooting of a prisoner for his refusal to go to work on 3 May 1953. On 7 May a
special commission arrived from Moscow, telling the prisoners that 'Lavrenty
Pavlovich Beria himself sent us to discuss your demands'. A secret prisoners'
committee submitted a list of demands, which included review of all
sentences, removal of numbers from prisoners' garb, and permission to
correspond with relatives.[17] In June 1953 a workers' uprising in Soviet-
occupied East Berlin was suppressed by tanks under the command of
Marshal Zhukov.

Zhukov continued to admire Stalin and thought naively that he had
been exiled because of an espionage charge fabricated by Beria. He shared
with Bulganin a resentment against Beria. The two started a conspiracy to
arrest him. They were joined by Khrushchev, who at that time was on
friendly terms with Bulganin. All three plotters were united by the suspicion that Beria had shortened Stalin's life and by the fear that he intended
to change drastically Stalin's domestic and foreign policies. For Khrushchev
and Bulganin their hostility toward Beria was a natural extension of Stalin's
plan to destroy 'Mingrelian bandits'. As for domestic policy, they objected
to Beria's reversal of Stalin's idea of 'russifying' all Soviet republics and
ethnic groups. Beria revoked Stalin's order to appoint Russian officials to
all top positions in the non-Russian republics, especially to the posts of first

secretaries. Khrushchev and Bulganin saw manifestations of Beria's Georgian nationalism in these changes. They considered Stalin to be a Russian, but Beria remained in their minds as a Georgian, and they were incensed that the destiny of the Soviet Union was in the hands of a non-Russian. They were equally opposed to Beria's foreign policy. Beria wanted to ease international tension by withdrawing Soviet forces from Austria and East Germany.[18] To Khrushchev, Bulganin and Zhukov, all of these actions meant the betrayal of Stalin's legacy.

On the morning of 26 June 1953 Bulganin secretly summoned to his office Colonel-General K. Moskalenko, Lieutenant General P. Batitsky, Major General A. Baksov, Colonel I. Zub, and Lieutenant-Colonel V. Yuferov whom Zhukov recommended. Riding in two cars together with Zhukov and Bulganin, the group was admitted to the Kremlin under the pretext of attending a conference. They entered a small room next to Stalin's former office. Khrushchev and Bulganin walked in. 'Do you know why we invited you?', Khrushchev asked. They did not. 'You are assigned to arrest Beria', Khrushchev said and warned them that should the operation fail, they would be declared 'enemies of the people'. Zhukov and the five officers entered Stalin's former office, where Politburo members were gathered for a conference. They surrounded Beria. 'Comrades, don't worry!', Zhukov said to the Politburo members, most of whom did not know what was happening. Turning to Beria, he snapped, 'Get up! Follow me!' and he ordered the officers, 'Shoot him on the spot if he tries to escape.' Beria was placed in the underground shelter of the headquarters of the Moscow military district. Bulganin told the five officers, 'Forget all you know and all you've seen.' He promised to award them with Hero of the Soviet Union medals and kept his promise.[19]

On 10 July 1953, two weeks after Beria's arrest, *Pravda* announced that Beria was 'an enemy of the Communist Party and the Soviet people' and was detained to face trial. That day, Beria's 'personal representative', Colonel Kuznetsov, and his group of negotiators disappeared from Norilsk. At the beginning of August, all six special political camps of the Norilsk Gulag were surrounded by the troops of the ministry of internal affairs. The soldiers opened fire and the uprisings were suppressed, with many dead and wounded. The uprisings in Vorkuta and other areas of the Gulag were also brutally suppressed. Stalin was dead, but his methods turned out to be very much alive. The most active participants in the camp uprisings were sent to prisons and punishment camps. Among the inmates in one punishment camp, 101 kilometers from Norilsk was a certain Chabuk Amiragibi, a scion of a long line of Georgian grand dukes. He was one of the authors of the appeal connected with the uprising in Norilsk Camp Number 4. Shortly before Beria's arrest, he received a message from his sister Rodam, a wife of the poet Mikhail Svetliv and a close friend of Beria. She wrote that Chabuk would soon be released, that Beria would empty the Gulag camps, increase the production of goods, and improve relations with the West by withdrawing Soviet troops from Germany and Austria.[20]

Beria's arrest slowed down the de-Stalinization process. Khrushchev and Bulganin, supported by Zhukov and the Army, assumed power. In September 1953 the 'security organs' were re-created under the name of 'Committee of State Security' (KGB). In October 1953 it was announced that the Soviet hydrogen bomb had been successfully tested, which assured Khrushchev of the eventual victory of the 'Lenin–Stalin undertaking'. At that time, Stalin was still Khrushchev's idol. Beria was interrogated by the officers who had arrested him. They were forbidden to record any statement in which he accused Stalin of any crimes. During the interrogation they forbade him even to mention Stalin's name. They replaced all reference to Stalin with the word *instantsiya* (authority) in Beria's testimony. One of the officers, I. Zub, elevated to the rank of general for his role in Beria's arrest, wrote years later: 'Three and a half months after Stalin's death nobody had yet whispered a word about the cult [of personality]. For everybody in the country Stalin still remained Stalin – the great, the infallible, the indisputable. At that time the sorrow of his death had not yet settled in the hearts of the people.'[21] 'Beria's case' grew into 19 volumes. More than 200 women testified that he had raped them. He did not deny that charge, but, when accused of murder, he repeatedly stated that he had only carried out Stalin's orders – 'the orders of *instantsiya*', as the interrogators wrote. When he was accused of collaborating with the Mussavatist government of Azerbaijan and with British intelligence, he answered that Stalin had been an agent of the Okhrana. The interrogators ordered him to stop mentioning this. When he was accused of fabricating false charges against innocent people, including Marshal Zhukov, Beria replied that these charges were fabricated by Stalin, who forced him to sign them. When he was charged with shortening Stalin's life, he did not deny the charge, but stated that Stalin intended to destroy all Politburo members, including him, and that his death had prevented the deportation of the Jewish and Mingrelian populations.[22] Beria's testimony was read by Politburo members, and it may have been then that Khrushchev began to suspect that 'the greatest genius of mankind' had been an evil genius of mankind and to surmise that Beria, by shortening Stalin's life, had saved millions of people, including Khrushchev, from death. But at that time

Khrushchev was still very far from putting an end to Stalin's personality cult. He decided to place on Beria all responsibility for Stalin's crimes.

Beria's secret trial took place on 18–23 December in the headquarters of the Moscow military district. His six close assistants, Dekanozov, Vlodzimersky, Merkulov, Meshik, Goglidze and Kobulov were tried at the same time. The chairman of the court was Marshal Konev, the state prosecutor was Rudenko. All the defendants were sentenced to death by shooting. Beria was executed first. His hands were tied behind his back and he was taken to the bomb shelter, where he was tied to a large wooden board (to keep bullets from rebounding and striking the executioners). Marshal Konev and all the officers who had taken part in Beria's arrest, except for Marshal Zhukov, took part in the execution. Prosecutor Rudenko read the sentence. 'Allow me to say', Beria began, but Rudenko interrupted him: 'You have already said everything. Plug his mouth with a towel. Carry out the sentence.' General Batitsky volunteered to do the shooting and took out his pistol. Batitsky pulled the trigger and Beria's body slumped. It was wrapped in a bed sheet and delivered to the crematorium. Beria's assistants were executed the same day.[23]

NOTES

1. Taped interview with Nugzar Sharia in 1972, in Sag Harbor, NY. These events were described by Gogi Zautashvili to Nugzar Sharia. In the author's archive; see also A. Rybin, 'Riadom s I. V. Stalinym', *Sotsiologicheskie issledovaniya*, no. 3, 1988.
2. Ibid.
3. Interview with Nugzar Sharia, Sag Harbor, NY, 1972. Sharia recounted the recollections of his uncle Peter Sharia and other Mingrelian generals. Peter Sharia, one of the top Mingrelian officials in the Kremlin, was the only one to survive. His sentence was 10 years' imprisonment in Vladimir Tsentral.
4. Rybin, 'Riadom s I. V. Stalinym'.
5. V. Likholitov, 'Interview c meditsinskimi rabotnikami prisutstvovavshimi pri smerti', *Meditsinskaya gazeta*, 11 November 1988, p. 8.
6. Svetlana Allilueva, *Dvadtsat' pisem k drugu*, New York, 1967, pp. 5–10.
7. V. Likholitov, 'Kak balzamirovali Stalina', *Meditsinskaya gazeta*, 10 August 1988.
8. Interview with Nugzar Sharia, who recounted recollections of Stalin's Georgian bodyguards who had spoken openly about Beria's role in poisoning Stalin, recalling how he had bragged that he had saved the Mingrelian generals from execution and the Mingrelian population from deportation to Siberia by hastening Stalin's death.
9. Recollections of author's wife Nadine Brackman. Also interview with Nathan Finegold, New York City, 13 June 1974.
10. H. G. Wells, *Ostrov doktora Moro* (Russian [Island of Dr Moreau]) (Moscow, 1955).
11. Interview with Vitaly Svechinsky. In the author's archive.
12. The author heard Romanyuk's jubilant words.
13. *Pravda*, 4 April 1953.
14. *The New York Times*, 15 September 1979, p. 12.
15. *Pravda*, 28 March 1953.
16. *Pravda*, 6 April 1953.

17. Chabuk Amiragibi, presently a member of the Georgian parliament, and the author wrote this appeal. See also Semen Badash, *Kolyma ty moya, Kolyma*, New York, 1986, pp. 68–79.
18. Amy Knight, 'Beria, the Reformer', *The New York Times*, 3 November 1993.
19. S. Bystrov, 'Dozvoleno k pechati', *Krasnaya zvezda*, 18–20 March 1988.
20. Chabuk Amiragibi told the author about this message during the incarceration at the '101 Kilometer Camp' in August–September 1953.
21. Bystrov, 'Dozvoleno k pechati'.
22. Taped interview with Nugzar Sharia.
23. Bystrov, 'Dozvoleno k pechati'. Also A. Antonov-Ovseenko, 'Beria', *Yunost*, December 1988.

38

'YOU CAN'T WHITEWASH A BLACK DOG'

Soon after Beria's execution Khrushchev and the Party Politburo assigned a secretary of the Central Committee, P. N. Pospelov, to write a report on Beria's crimes.[1] An accidental discovery changed Khrushchev's mind. Construction workers converting Stalin's Kremlin apartment into a museum found a secret safe inserted in a wall. The safe was brought to Khrushchev. Years later, he mentioned only one of the documents he found in it: the letter in which Lenin had threatened to break off all relations with Stalin. 'I was astonished that this note had been preserved. Stalin had probably forgotten all about it', Khrushchev wrote in his memoirs.[2] Khrushchev did not reveal the nature of any of the other documents he had discovered in Stalin's safe. His colleagues in the Politburo strongly objected to revelations of any embarrassing information about Stalin's past.[3] The other documents in the safe were too scandalous for Khrushchev even to mention them. But slowly these documents continued to erode Khrushchev's veneration of Stalin and he decided to attack his 'personality cult'. Despite the objections of Politburo members, Khrushchev delivered a secret report on 24 February 1956 at the Twentieth Party Congress, condemning Stalin's 'personality cult'. His report became known as 'Khrushchev's secret speech'. Its transcript was secretly read to party members at various places of work all over the Soviet Union.[4] Leaders of Communist Parties in eastern Europe also received the text of Khrushchev's secret speech, which was leaked to the West and published there.[5]

Alexander Orlov, the NKVD general who had defected to the United States in 1938, read Khrushchev's secret speech. In April 1956 *Life* magazine published Orlov's article 'The Sensational Secret Behind Damnation of Stalin', in which Orlov revealed the information he had received in February 1938 from his cousin Zinovy Katsnelson about the discovery of Stalin's Okhrana file and about the Tukhachevsky conspiracy. Orlov wrote: 'However it happened, it seems to me certain that the documentary proof that Stalin had been a czarist police agent was placed before the current collective leadership.'[6]

In the same issue of *Life* magazine, Isaac Don Levine, the first Western biographer of Stalin, published an article titled 'A Document on Stalin as Czarist Spy', in which he stated that the 'Eremin Letter' brought to the United States by M. D. Golovachev in 1946 was a genuine document.[7] In his article Orlov did not mention the 'Eremin Letter', but he told Levine privately that, although it probably reflected the truth, the letter, in his opinion, was a forgery that had been fabricated by someone who knew the truth.[8] By the time Levine came across the 'Eremin Letter', it had gone through a tortuous history. Golovachev, after his failure in 1941 and 1942 to sell it to the German embassy in Shanghai, came to the United Stated in 1946 and attempted to sell it to the US government. George F. Kennan, the leading expert on Soviet affairs at the time, about to be appointed ambassador to the Soviet Union, remembered that 'for various reasons it did not seem to me suitable that our government should occupy itself with material of this nature, and therefore the document was not purchased'.[9] Golovachev sold the 'Eremin Letter' for $15,000 to three prominent Russian émigrés: the former Russian ambassador to the United States, Boris Bakhmetiev, a pioneer of Russian aviation, Boris Sergievsky, and a research engineer, Vadim Makarov, the son of a famous Russian admiral. They passed the letter on to Clare Boothe Luce, a conservative politician and diplomat married to the publisher of *Life* magazine. In 1946 Luce invited Levine to her Connecticut estate and asked him to investigate the letter to determine whether or not it was a genuine document.

Levine was greatly interested in the answer. Since 1926, he had been receiving reports from various sources about Stalin's ties to the Okhrana and the discovery of Stalin's Okhrana file in the old Okhrana archives. During the Bukharin show trial in March 1938, Levine published an article titled, 'Stalin Suspected of Forcing Trials to Cover His Past', in which he stated that he had long been familiar with reports about the discovery of Stalin's Okhrana file, exposing him as a tsarist agent.[10] Levin hoped that the Eremin Letter might finally be documentary evidence proving Stalin's service in the Okhrana.

For the next ten years Levine tried to establish whether the 'Eremin Letter' was genuine. He questioned former Okhrana officers and asked specialists on documents for their opinion. His research took him to the outskirts of Paris, to the home of the émigré Okhrana general Alexander Spiridovich, who had known Eremin well. Spiridovich showed Levine a silver decanter and told him it had been presented to him by his subordinates after his recovery from a 1905 assassination attempt. Among the several signatures engraved on the decanter was Eremin's. His signature looked very similar to that on the 'Eremin Letter'. Spiridovich gave the decanter to Levine as a present. 'I was deeply moved by his gift', Levine wrote. 'I now owned the final piece of evidence which proved to me that Stalin had been a czarist spy.'[11]

From the time in 1946 when Levine began his investigation of the Eremin Letter, Soviet agents in the United States and Europe must have reported to Stalin about his enquiries, but Stalin did nothing to prevent the publication of the forgery he himself had manufactured. He may have held on to his original idea of using its publication in the West as the opportunity to discredit not only the forgery itself, by pointing out its obvious mistakes, but, by a logical extension, to discredit the very notion that he had ever been an Okhrana agent. Stalin was devious but not subtle, and it probably did not occur to him that the 'mistakes' he had inserted in the forgery might be viewed as much too glaring, much too easy to detect to have been made unintentionally. It probably did not occur to him that the unavoidable conclusion would be that these mistakes had been done on purpose in order to discredit the truth and that the only person interested in doing that would be Stalin himself.

Levine's and Orlov's articles were published under the headline: 'What Khrushchev Isn't Telling: Stalin's Guiltiest Secret'. Orlov's article was met with almost total silence. Historians and Sovietologists avoided the question of Stalin's service in the Okhrana and the role Stalin's Okhrana file might have played in the history of the Soviet Union. They could not completely dismiss the information presented in Orlov's article, because his 1953 book, *The Secret History of Stalin's Crimes*, was accepted as a credible and important source that was widely quoted, and especially because Khrushchev's secret speech substantiated many of Orlov's claims. Nevertheless, Orlov's revelations about Stalin's Okhrana file and the Tukhachevsky conspiracy were ignored for decades by the historians of the West. One exception was Bertram D. Wolfe, who stated, 'If the Levine document [the Eremin Letter] requires further checking, the Orlov article carries complete conviction.'[12]

Levine's article citing the 'Eremin Letter' started a heated controversy. Stalin was dead, but KGB agents and Soviet sympathizers in the United States attempted to discredit Levine personally and thus to prove that the letter was a forgery. Martin K. Tytell, who presented himself as an 'expert on questionable documents', delivered a lecture, titled 'Exposing a Documentary Hoax', in which he attacked Levine's veracity.[13] (Tytell had earlier been a witness for the defense at the trial of Alger Hiss, accused of spying for the Soviet Union.) The US Senate Internal Security Subcommittee held several hearings on the question of the role of Soviet intelligence in the campaign to discredit the 'Eremin Letter'.[14] Grigory Aronson, a scholar of Soviet history, took a radically different tack, arguing that the question of whether Stalin was a tsarist spy was a 'trifle' and should not be used to divert attention from the issue of exposing the truly horrible facts about his reign of terror.[15] Levine replied that 'the Free World has had quite a dose of these facts, although there can be no limit to the quest for truth. . . If it were established that Stalin was a Czarist spy and a traitor to the Revolution, we could deliver a blow which at the moment would rock the Soviet dictatorship to its foundation.' He added that his forthcoming book would 'leave not a shadow of a doubt that Stalin was a Czarist agent' and would be 'but an opening chapter in the hunt for the solution to the great mystery in Stalin's life'.[16] In his book *Stalin's Great Secret*, Levine insisted that the 'Eremin Letter' was a genuine document.[17]

In June 1956, amidst heated debate over the 'Eremin Letter', M. G. Golovachev, who had brought the letter to the West in 1946, published an article in the Russian-language newspaper *Rossia* in New York, denying accusations that he had sold a forged document. 'I must state that this is an unquestionably genuine document which is a part of official archival material that relates to the role of Stalin in pre-Revolutionary Russia', wrote Golovachev. He promised to publish in the near future additional documents proving Stalin's ties to the Okhrana and to reveal how these documents had fallen into his hands.[18] Golovachev died before making any further revelations. For obvious reasons, he could not prove the genuine-ness of the 'Eremin Letter' or of the other forgeries in his possession, and he had no intention of telling the truth: that he had obtained all these docu-ments from Stalin's agent, the chief of the Far Eastern NKVD, Genrikh Liushkov. After Golovachev's death his widow donated his entire 'official archival material', including three additional forgeries, to the Bakhmetiev Archive at Columbia University in New York. They are still there.[19]

The fact that the 'Eremin Letter' was a forgery was established in 1957 when the Okhrana Foreign Agency archive was open for research at Stanford University's Hoover Institution. The 16 large wooden crates con-taining the Okhrana Foreign Agency's documents had been brought there from the Russian Imperial Embassy in Paris in 1924 by the ambassador of the Russian Provisional Government to France, Vasily Maklakov. He donated the documents to the Hoover Institution. In accordance with a signed agreement, these documents were not to be shown to the public until at least three months after Maklakov's death.[20] The Okhrana archive at the Hoover Institution contained many documents with Colonel Eremin's signature. It was established that his signature did not end with the long slanting curve as did the signature on the forged 'Eremin letter'.

The archive also had on file the register of the Okhrana officers on active duty in 1913, which listed the name of Captain Vladimir Fedorovich Zhelezniakov. The Eremin Letter was addressed to 'Alexey Fedorovich Zhelezniakov'. These 'mistakes' alone proved that the 'Eremin Letter' was a forgery, which led many scholars to the conclusion that it had been fabricated in order to discredit Stalin and, consequently, that Stalin had not been an Okhrana agent. This was precisely the reaction Stalin had counted on. Not all scholars were taken in, however. George F. Kennan declared that the 'Eremin Letter' was 'one of those curious bits of historical evidence of which it can be said that the marks of spuriousness are too strong for us to call it genuine, and the marks of genuineness are too strong for us to call it entirely spurious'.[21]

Soon after the 'Eremin Letter' was exposed as a forgery in 1957, Eremin's two daughters arrived in New York from Chile, hoping to find someone interested in buying their recollections about their father, Alexander Eremin, since his name had been mentioned prominently in Levine's article. They were too late. By then, interest in the 'Eremin Letter' and their father had subsided; besides, they had no documents that might have thrown light on Stalin's career in the Okhrana. Eremin himself had died – no one asked his daughters when or how. Finding no buyer for their story, they returned to Chile.[22] An attempt to locate them in 1974 was unsuccessful. A report from Chile stated that 'indeed the Eremin family lived at one time in Chile. Now it is impossible to find any trace of them.'[23]

Until 1989 the Soviet press did not mention the 'Eremin Letter', but it had been secretly discussed in the Kremlin since its publication in the West in 1956. Khrushchev, in the wake of his secret speech, assigned to a group of several surviving Old Bolsheviks the task of investigating Stalin's crimes, including the accusation of his service in the Okhrana. A special commission within the Party Control Committee was created for this purpose. The commission established that Stalin had doctored and fabricated Okhrana documents in order to glorify himself as a great revolutionary and had inundated Soviet archives with these doctored documents and forgeries. A Soviet historian, who took part in the inquiry, stated that 'In 1962 O. G. Shatunovskaya, a member of the Party Control Committee and of the commission dealing with the rehabilitation of the victims of the personality cult, raised before the Central Committee of the Communist Party the question of making public all the materials exposing Stalin as an Okhrana agent.' But Khrushchev at that time did not yet dare openly to disclose the commission's findings, claiming that to do so 'would reveal that for more than 30 years the country was ruled by an agent of the tsarist Okhrana . . .'.[24]

The Old Bolsheviks established that several of Stalin's Okhrana files had been found in the old archives and delivered to Stalin.[25] They submitted to Khrushchev the articles by Orlov and Levine, from which he learned about the discovery of Stalin's Okhrana file by I. L. Shtein, about the rivalry between Stalin and the top Okhrana agent Roman Malinovsky, and about the Tukhachevsky conspiracy.[26] Khrushchev must have recalled how, during the war, Stalin had become alarmed by mention of the name of general Rodion Malinovsky and had ordered Khrushchev to follow the general's every move. He must have realized that the rivalry with the Okhrana agent Roman Malinovsky was the cause of Stalin's sudden suspicion.

By 1962 Khrushchev began to think of exposing Stalin as an Okhrana agent. Probably on Khrushchev's order, the 'Eremin Letter' was stolen from the Bakhmetiev Collection at Columbia University and delivered to Moscow. (In 1956, the forgery had been placed in the safe of the Tolstoy Foundation in a New York bank.[27] Later it was deposited in the Bakhmetiev Archive at Columbia University. Access to this collection has been almost unrestricted.) In 1962 several party historians, assigned by Khrushchev to research Stalin's Okhrana past, were allowed to examine the 'Eremin Letter' when it was delivered to Moscow.[28] By 1962 a sinister picture of a tsarist spy haunted by the fear of exposure, a mass murderer bent on covering up his ignoble past, emerged in Khrushchev's mind.

The question of Stalin's service in the Okhrana was not the only cause of Khrushchev's growing hatred of his former idol. He was increasingly consumed by the emotional need to avenge the humiliations to which Stalin had subjected him personally. Stalin had been in the habit of cleaning his burning pipe by knocking it against Khrushchev's bald head, saying, '*Durachok ty, Nikitushka, durachok!*' ('You're a little fool, Nicky boy, a little fool!'), while Khrushchev had to ingratiate himself, smiling and cringing with pain.[29] Stalin also liked to place burning paper between the fingers of Politburo members and watch how they endured this torture.[30] Khrushchev recalled how Stalin used to force him, an overweight and ageing man, to drink glasses of vodka and dance the Ukrainian *gapak*, causing him excruciating pain, to the enjoyment of Stalin's guests. He was ashamed to recall how he, in boundless devotion to Stalin, cried, kneeling next to the body of the dead dictator and kissing his hand.[31] These and similar recollections filled Khrushchev with hatred of Stalin and shame of himself. He was driven by the urge to expose the tyrant, the despicable creature of the Okhrana, and to avenge his own humiliation. But Khrushchev met with stubborn resistance from most of the Politburo members, who had the backing of the party bureaucracy.

In 1957 Politburo members Molotov, Kaganovich and Malenkov attempted to depose Khrushchev, accusing him of undermining the Soviet system by exposing Stalin's crimes. Khrushchev was supported by Marshal Zhukov, whose command of the army assured his victory. Molotov, Kaganovich and Malenkov were sent to 'work' far away from Moscow. Bulganin and Voroshilov, too, were soon removed from the Politburo. Khrushchev, having used Zhukov, dismissed him, accusing the marshal of harboring 'bonapartist schemes'. The places of Stalin's old cronies in the Politburo were taken over by Khrushchev's protégés, among them the future general secretaries Brezhnev, Chernenko and Andropov. Although this new crop of Politburo members did not owe their rise to power to Stalin, they did not share Khrushchev's hatred of him, and felt that exposing Stalin as an Okhrana agent would discredit the Soviet system, cutting off the branch on which they were sitting.

Khrushchev's anti-Stalin drive created a rift in the communist camp. Mao Tse-tung and Albania's staunch Stalinist leader Enver Hoxha refused to attend the Twenty-second Party Congress, which opened in Moscow in October of 1961. In his speech, Khrushchev said that all he was trying to accomplish by criticizing Stalin was to prevent a similar 'personality cult' from emerging ever again. He accused the Albanian leader of using Stalin's methods of repression against his own people.[32] Because of the opposition of the majority of Politburo members, Khrushchev decided not to deliver his prepared speech in which he intended to accuse Stalin of organizing the murder of Kirov.[33] But Khrushchev delivered a blow to Stalin in another way: during the night of 31 October 1961 Stalin's embalmed body was secretly removed from the mausoleum and buried near the Kremlin wall. A black granite plate with inscription 'I. V. Stalin 1879–1953' was placed over the grave. Stalin's name, too, was removed from the mausoleum. Lenin was once again the sole occupant of this shrine. Stalin's burial was carried out by a detachment of soldiers under the headlights of military vehicles.[34]

In the summer of 1962 the remains of Ivan the Terrible, idolized during the Stalin era as one of Russia's greatest statesmen, were removed from his tomb in the Kremlin Cathedral of the Archangel Michael, where they had been since the Tsar's death in 1584. The remains were subjected to scientific analyses. One test revealed the presence of a considerable amount of arsenic, raising the possibility that the Tsar had been poisoned. A prominent Soviet anthropologist, Mikhail Gerasimov, who had earlier reconstructed the facial features of the prehistoric Java and Peking men, made a bust of Ivan the Terrible based on the skeletal remains. Gerasimov determined that

Tsar Ivan had been 6ft 3in tall, a giant by sixteenth-century standards.[35] Not content with disturbing the Tsar's tomb and demythologizing Ivan by the cold light of science, Khrushchev initiated a press campaign against Stalin's glorification of Tsar Ivan. Books praising Ivan were sharply criticized.[36]

With the passing of time, Khrushchev began to imagine that he could outdo Stalin, in whom he began to see a competitor for his own place in history. Once, during a reception in the Yugoslav embassy, Khrushchev got drunk and dropped down on all fours, declaring that he was the 'loco-motive of history'. When drunk, he began to tell his generals that under his leadership the Soviet Union would achieve greater victories in any war with capitalist countries than Stalin had achieved in the war with Hitler's Germany. In a fit of self-aggrandizement, he ordered that Soviet nuclear rockets be installed in Cuba. He visited the United States, declaring that he would show the West 'where the crayfish spends the winter', and he made the famous boast: 'We will bury you!' During a speech at the United Nations he took off his shoe and banged the podium with it. Americans were intrigued by this peculiar way of making a point. They tried to determine the meaning of the Russian saying to show someone 'where the crayfish spends the winter' – which is roughly equivalent to 'teaching someone a lesson'. The explanations of media commentators were quite varied, one indication of the width of the chasm between the West and the world from which Khrushchev came.

Khrushchev kept pursuing his aim to discredit Stalin. Early in March 1963 he delivered a speech about class struggle in which he mentioned Stalin several times. At one point he said that in the history of the Bolshevik Party there had been 'more than one case of betrayal and treason to the cause of the Revolution, for example, the activities of the double agent Malinovsky, a member of the Bolshevik faction of the State Duma'.[37] Khrushchev's hint of 'more than one case of betrayal' was not lost on those who suspected Stalin of ties to the Okhrana. In the summer of 1964, some KGB officers learned that Khrushchev decided to make public the history of Stalin's rivalry with Malinovsky by publication of an article exposing Stalin's ties to the Okhrana. The KGB officers knew that the Politburo opposed Khrushchev's decision.[38] On 19 July 1964 Khrushchev delivered a speech at a reception in Moscow in honor of a Hungarian Party delegation. At one point he shouted in a high-pitched and halting voice: 'In vain are the attempts of those who want to alter the leadership in our country and take under their protection all the evil deeds that Stalin committed . . . No one can whitewash him . . . You can't whitewash a black dog . . .'.[39] For the first time Khrushchev also publicly hinted that Stalin had been murdered: 'In human history there have been many cruel tyrants, but all of them met their death by an axe, the same axe with which they had maintained their power.'[40] This part of his speech was cut from the version published in the Soviet Union. The metaphor of the axe suggests that Khrushchev knew Stalin had been murdered by his own henchman, Beria. In view of Khrushchev's revelations of Stalin's crimes, this made Beria not the villain, as he was officially portrayed, but a hero, and his poisoning of Stalin a heroic deed. But Politburo members were against such a radical rewriting of Soviet history. They were also alarmed by a statement made by Enver Hoxha on 24 May 1964: 'The Soviet leaders are plotters who have the impudence to say openly, as Mikoyan has been doing, that they secretly hatched a conspiracy to murder Stalin.'[41] Hoxha had in mind Khrushchev as one of the 'plotters': by 1964 of all of Stalin's close 'comrades-in-arms', only Khrushchev and Mikoyan remained members of the Politburo.

Brezhnev and his Politburo allies decided that in revealing Kremlin secrets Khrushchev was behaving irrationally and that he should be removed from power. When Khrushchev was vacationing in the Black Sea resort of Pitsunda in October 1964, they accused him of 'voluntarism' and of harboring 'harebrained ideas'. Brezhnev, on assuming power, suppressed the story of the Stalin–Malinovsky rivalry that was about to be published. Only the part related to Malinovsky's Okhrana story was printed in 1965.[42] It did not mention Stalin at all.

Brezhnev attempted to restore Stalin's prestige as a 'Great Leader', but he failed: Khrushchev's secret speech at the Twentieth Party Congress had considerably tarnished Stalin's reputation. The speech itself was no longer secret after its publication in the Soviet Union in 1959.[43] Another force opposing Brezhnev's attempt to rehabilitate Stalin was the millions of prisoners who had been released from the Gulag system during Khrushchev's rule. The Gulag story entered Soviet literature with the Khrushchev-sponsored publication in 1962 of Alexander Solzhenitsyn's *One Day in the Life of Ivan Denisovich*. The prison-camp jargon, created by generations of Gulag inmates, poured into the Russian language. Dissident groups appeared, secretly writing and distributing anti-Soviet *samizdat*. In June 1968 Pavel Litvinov (a grandson of Maxim Litvinov) and a group of dissidents staged a protest in Red Square against the Soviet invasion of Czechoslovakia. They were arrested and exiled. But the repressions did not stop the dissident movement. The fear of Stalin's era was fading away from the 'island of Doctor Moreau'.

After Brezhnev's death, his successors renewed attempts to rehabilitate Stalin. Minister of Defence D. F. Ustinov declared at the 12 July 1984 Politburo meeting: 'In general there would not be that outrageous infamy that Khrushchev permitted in relation to Stalin. Stalin, whatever you might say, is our history. Not one foe brought us as much grief as Khrushchev with his policy in relation to the history of our Party and state, and in relation to Stalin.' The chairman of the Council of Ministers N. Tikhonov concurred, proclaiming that Khrushchev 'dirtied us and our policies and blackened them before the whole world'. The chairman of the KGB, V. M. Chebrikov, added: 'Apart from that, under Khrushchev a whole series of people were rehabilitated illegally. The fact of the matter is that they were punished entirely justly. Take, for example, Solzhenitsyn.'[44]

On becoming General Secretary Mikhail Gorbachev proclaimed the policy of *perestroika* (reconstruction) and *glasnost* (openness), promising to fill in all the 'blanks' in Soviet history. His actual intention was not to change the Soviet system but merely to make it more efficient. He wanted to retain party and police control over the political and economic life of the country. The 'blanks' were being filled in by the revived memories of a no-longer frightened people. The Soviet empire was collapsing, the satellite states of eastern Europe were breaking away, self-determination movements in the Soviet republics were asserting themselves. Gorbachev did not expect that by proclaiming *perestroika* and *glasnost* he would speed up the disintegration of the system he wanted to save. Filling in the blanks in Soviet history slipped out of Gorbachev's control. Information about Stalin's crimes, kept under the lid for generations, broke out in a torrent of revelations. Newspapers began reporting the discoveries of mass graves all over the Soviet Union.[45] A Memorial Society was created. Its members at a 1988 meeting in Moscow stated that the Soviet Union was a 'country built on skeletons'. A former inmate of the Vorkuta camps, Igor Dobroshan, added: 'There is no one who was not touched by Stalin's repressions. The terror during the French Revolution is incomparable to the Stalinist terror. We will be busy eradicating this infection for 200 years.'[46] L. Lanina, a journalist, wrote in a Moscow independent magazine:

In millions of nameless mass graves rest nameless victims with tags on their feet . . . in Kolyma and Solovky, in Vorkuta and Kazakhstan. These graves are the real sacred shrines that have been trampled down, and the salvation and expiation of the nation depends now on whether it will find the sacred path to them.[47]

Heated polemics erupted all over Russia in 1989 after a history professor at the Moscow Institute of International Relations, F. D. Volkov, stated that Stalin had been an Okhrana agent, citing the 'Eremin Letter' as proof. He declared, 'For 30 years we were ruled by a tsarist agent.'[48] In an article in *Moskovskaya pravda*, Volkov argued that the 'Eremin Letter' was a genuine document.[49] On 19 April the journal *Voprosy istorii KPSS* ('Problems of the History of the Communist Party of the Soviet Union') published a long official rebuttal in an article titled, 'Was Stalin an Okhrana Agent?' The article's authors pointed to a number of errors in the 'Eremin Letter' and stated that it was a forgery. They insisted that the Soviet archives had no documents pointing to Stalin's service in the Okhrana. Nevertheless, they were careful to note: 'In pursuing our review of documents and publications we by no means attempted to answer definitely the question of whether Stalin was a secret [Okhrana] collaborator.'[50]

On 2 July 1989 *Moskovskaya pravda* published 'Official Reference of the Central State Archive of the October Revolution', which described in detail the mistakes in the 'Eremin Letter', concluding that it had been fabricated with the purpose of discrediting Stalin. In support of this conclusion, the officials of the archive stated that even 'the most critically disposed biographers of Stalin, including his most bitter enemy Trotsky, having in mind the issue of Okhrana provocation, rejected this charge as monstrous and absolutely unprovable.'[51]

The conflicting views in the Soviet press about Stalin's Okhrana ties confused many readers. An author of one letter offered to resolve the controversy in what he thought a very simple way: 'Everything would be perfectly clear to the supporters and opponents of the Okhrana version if the personal file of the secret agent I. V. Dzhugashvili were to be unfolded before them.'[52]

Another question widely discussed was whether Stalin had been mentally ill. It was reported that Bekhterev had diagnosed Stalin as a paranoiac before his death. Some prominent Soviet psychiatrists agreed with this diagnosis, while others suggested a number of other definitions of Stalin's malady: 'paranoid schizophrenia, delirious condition, derived from paranoid psychopathy, heavy psychopathy', placing Stalin in the category of 'epileptic-psychopaths'. During a panel discussion, a psychiatrist stated that Stalin was 'cruel, devoid of any feeling of pity, completely amoral, easily excitable. I personally consider [his condition] a psychical monstrosity, a moral depravity. It is an anomaly but not a sickness.' Another psychiatrist reminded the audience of Hamlet's 'method in the madness', adding that Stalin was afflicted with 'megalomania of a limitless scale'. Another objected that too little was known about Stalin to allow a final judgement:

Psychopathy is a depravity of character, which is formed either genetically or emerges as a result of various traumas in childhood. It cannot exist without manifestations in the early stages of life, in the early years and the period of maturation. But what do we know about Stalin of this time of his life? Nothing special, except that he was cruel to animals.

But a colleague argued that what was known about Stalin made clear that 'for 30 years the country was ruled by a man with a sick soul'. A moderator of the discussion, a layman, concluded:

We simply have no other alternative, because if we accept Stalin as a sane man – the man who senselessly destroyed the flower of a great nation – this would mean that all of us were insane, and it would be enlightening to learn, how it happened that tens of millions of my fellow countrymen were murdered.[53]

Russel V. Lee, clinical professor emeritus at the Stanford University Medical School, wrote:

An inquiry in depth into the role of madness in human affairs would provide a fascinating field to be cultivated by a team of historians and psychiatrists. The harvest of bizarre events wrought by deranged leaders would be a rich one. The events of the terrible twentieth century provide the best example of the power of madmen to abolish rational behavior. In our time we have seen one of the most highly developed and intellectual peoples of all time completely subjected to the absolute power of a textbook paranoiac – Adolf Hitler. Such phenomena, alas for mankind, tend to be recurrent . . . In Russia there was Joseph Stalin, the man of steel and ruthless slayer of millions of his own people; completely devoid of scruples of any kind, he was a sociopath, a moral imbecile, and in complete control of Russia.[54]

NOTES

1. N. S. Khrushchev, *Khrushchev Remembers*, Boston, Toronto, 1970. p. 344, fn. 14; also p. 345, fn. 15.
2. Ibid., p. 44; also fn. 12.
3. Ibid., pp. 347–51.
4. The author was present at the reading of Khrushchev's secret speech at the Rossmetaloproekt firm in Moscow, in March 1956.
5. A member of the Polish Communist Party, Seweryn Bialer, defected to the West with a copy of Khrushchev's speech.
6. Alexander Orlov, 'The Sensational Secret Behind Damnation of Stalin', *Life*, 23 April 1956, p. 44.
7. Isaac Don Levine, the first Western biographer of Stalin, published an article titled 'A Document on Stalin as Czarist Spy', *Life*, 23 April 1956, p. 51.
8. Interview with I. D. Levine in Chappaqua, New York, 1976.
9. George F. Kennan, 'The Historiography of the Early Political Career of Stalin', a lecture read on

12 November 1970 and published in the *Proceedings of the American Philosophical Society*, Vol. 115, no. 3, June 1971, p. 167.

10. *Journal American*, 3 March 1938.
11. I. D. Levine, 'A Document on Stalin as Czarist Spy', *Life*, 23 April 1956, p. 51.
12. *Life* magazine, 11 May 1956.
13. *Senate Internal Security Subcommittee Report*, hearings held on 8 February 1957, p. 4184.
14. Ibid., hearings held on 1 October 1957, pp. 4126–56.
15. Grigory Aronson, 'Was Stalin a Tsarist Agent?', *The New Leader*, 20 August 1956.
16. I. D. Levine, 'Stalin Was a Tsarist Agent', typescript of an article for *The New Leader*, in I. D. Levine's archive. Copy in the author's archive.
17. I. D. Levine, *Stalin's Great Secret*, New York, 1956. The book reiterates the points made in Levine's article in *Life*.
18. The clipping of Golovachev's article in *Rossia* is in M. P. Golovachev's collection in the Bakhmetiev Archive in the Library of Rare Documents and Manuscripts at Columbia University. These documents were reprinted in the New York Russian-language newspaper *Evreisky mir*, 30 October (no. 23), 6 November (no. 24), and 13 November (no. 25), 1992.
19. These forgeries are in the M. P. Golovachev collection in the Bakhmetiev Archive in the Library of Rare Documents and Manuscripts at Columbia University. The forgeries were reprinted in the New York Russian-language newspaper *Evreisky mir*, 30 October (no. 23), 6 November (no. 24), and 13 November (no. 25), 1992.
20. Edward Ellis Smith, *The Young Stalin: The Early Years of an Elusive Revolutionary*, London, 1968, p. vii.
21. Kennan, 'The Historiography of the Early Political Career of Stalin', p. 167.
22. Interview with I. D. Levine, Chappaqua NY, 1976.
23. Letters from the Tolstoy Foundation, dated 9 October 1974 and 9 December 1974. In the author's archive.
24. F. D. Volkov, *Vzlet i padenie Stalina*, Moscow, 1992, p. 23.
25. Roy Medvedev, *Let History Judge*, New York, 1971, pp. 315–23. Also Medvedev, 'Dvadtsatyi vek', *Obshchestvenno-politicheskii i literaturnyi almanakh*, no. 2, London, 1977, pp. 10f.
26. A letter written by O. G. Shatunovskaya and C. B. Shaboldaev to the editors of *Moskovskaya pravda*, where it was published on 2 July 1989, p. 4. Also Alexander Orlov, 'The Sensational Secret Behind Damnation of Stalin', *Life*, 23 April 1956, p. 37.
27. I. D. Levine, 'A Document on Stalin as Czarist Spy'.
28. *Moskovskaya pravda*, 30 March 1989. Also F. D. Volkov, *Vzlet i padenie Stalina*, Moscow, 1992, p. 16.
29. Taped interview with Nugzar Sharia in Sag Harbor, Long Island, NY in 1972.
30. Medvedev, *Let History Judge*, p. 331.
31. B. Ravich, a chemistry professor and secretary of the Communist Party organization at the Moscow Institute of Nonferrous Metals (and my neighbor in Moscow communal apartment) related Khrushchev's behavior to me. It was well known at that time among Party officials. See also Svetlana Allilueva, *Dvadtsat' pisem k drugu*, p. 6. Svetlana recounts Khrushchev crying at the time of Stalin's death. Khrushchev in his memoirs attributes to Beria his own behavior, stating: 'Beria threw himself on his knees, seized Stalin's hand, and started kissing it.' *Khrushchev Remembers*, p. 318.
32. T. T. Rigby, *The Stalin Dictatorship: Khrushchev's Secret Speech and Other Documents*, Sydney, 1968, p. 95.
33. Taped interview with Vasily Rudich in Chappaqua, NY in 1975. Rudich related the testimony of O. G. Shatunovskaya, a member of the Party Control Committee, who recalled that A. N. Shelepin, the KGB chief at the time, kept Khrushchev from delivering the planned part of the speech relating to Kirov's murder. Shelepin, nicknamed 'Iron Shurik' was at the time 're-Stalinizing' the Soviet secret police. In November 1961 he was promoted to the Central Committee secretariat. See John J. Dziak, *Chekisty: A History of the KGB*, Lexington, MA, 1988, p. 152.
34. F. Konev, 'Kak perezakhoranivali Stalina,' *Voenno-istoricheskii zhurnal*, Moscow, 1989.
35. *The New York Times*, 28 April 1963; 29 July 1963. See also Robert Payne, 'A Man Like No Other', *The New York Times*, 8 September 1963.
36. S. M. Dubrovsky, 'Protiv idealizatsii deyatelnosti Ivana IV', *Voprosy istorii*, no. 8, August 1956, pp. 121–8.

36. *Pravda*, 10 March 1963.
38. Interview with Yury Krotkov, the author of the book *The Red Monarch* and a KGB agent who defected to the West, in New York in 1972. Krotkov related the inside story of Khrushchev's intention to make public the Stalin–Malinovsky rivalry in the Okhrana. The article he mentioned was published in censored form after Khrushchev had been removed: the part detailing the Stalin–Malinovsky Okhrana rivalry was suppressed. See B. K. Erenfeld, 'Delo Malinovskogo', *Voprosy istorii*, no. 7, 1965, pp. 106–16.
39. *Pravda*, 20 July 1964.
40. Radio Moscow I, 19 July 1964, *Radio Liberty Archive*, monitoring tape recording.
41. Robert Conquest, *The Great Terror*, New York, 1973, p. 172.
42. B. K. Erenfeld, 'Delo Malinovskogo', *Voprosy istorii*, no. 7, 1965.
43. Khrushchev, *Doklad na zakrytom zasedanii XX s'ezda KPSS*.
44. *The New York Times*, 8 February 1993, p. A-8.
45. *Ogonek*, no. 39, 1988; *Sputnik*, no. 109, 1988; Zenon Pozniak, 'Perezhitoe', *Moskovskie novosty*, 1988; Zenon Pozniak and Evgeny Shygalev, 'Kuropaty–doroga smerti', *Literatura i mastatstva*, Minsk, 3 June 1988; *Komsomolskaya pravda*, Moscow, 7 August 1989; *Novoe russkoe slovo*, 24 June 1988; *The New York Times*, 25 March 1989; *Novoe russkoe slovo*, 7 March 1989.
46. Shmidt-Choier, *Sputnik*, Israel, 17 November 1988, pp. 4f.
47. L. Lanina, 'Madam Tusso i tovarishch Krupskaya', *Panorama*, 3 July 1988. A reprint from the Moscow *samizdat* journal *Referendum*.
48. Shmidt-Choier, *Sputnik*, pp. 4f.
49. G. Arutunov and F. Volkov, 'K sydu istorii', *Moskovskaya pravda*, 30 March 1989.
50. B. I. Kaptelov and Z. I. Peregudova, 'Byl li Stalin agentom okhranki?', *Voprosy istorii KPSS*, Moscow, April 1989.
51. 'Versiya ne podtverzhdaetsa', *Moskovskaya pravda*, 2 July 1989, pp. 4f.
52. Ibid.
53. Oleg Moroz, 'Poslednii diagnoz', *Literaturnaya gazeta*, 28 September 1988. Also *Novoe russkoe slovo*, 18 August 1989, pp. 6f.
54. Russel V. Lee, 'When Insanity Holds the Specter', *The New York Times*, 12 April 1974.

AFTERWORD

Almost half a century after Stalin's death, Russia still lives in his shadow. Millions were executed or perished in the Gulag prison camps, with no family left untouched. Having exterminated ten million Russian peasants, Stalin enslaved the rest of them as serfs in his *kolkhoz* (collective farm) system. He left behind a dysfunctional economic system that defeats all attempts at economic and land reform. The great majority of Russians continue to suffer from the abject poverty, misery and deprivation while a few corrupt nouveau riche, the oligarchs, and mafiosi enjoy opulence and privileges in the post-Soviet Russia, as did the party elite during Stalin's reign. Stalin threw Russia back to the barbarity of the medieval reign of his favorite Tsar, the deranged Ivan Grozny (Ivan the Terrible).

Stalin's legacy permeates the daily lives of the country in the most striking and incessant way: all Soviet leaders since Stalin, except for Boris Yeltsin, have had a secret police career. Lavrenty Beria was the head of Soviet secret police for many years. Nikita Khrushchev began his Kremlin career in the 1930s as Stalin's *agent provocateur* and later served as Stalin's henchman during the purges. Leonid Brezhnev carried out the purges in Ukraine in the 1930s. Stalin sent him to Moldavia in the early 1950s to exile the Jewish population to Siberia. Yury Andropov had been the head of KGB for many years before becoming General Secretary in November 1982. Konstantin Chernenko started his career during the purges in the 1930s as a head of an execution detachment in the Far East, and then joined Brezhnev in Dnepropetrovsk, and later in Moldavia. Chernenko became General Secretary in February 1984. With his death on 10 March 1985 the line of Stalin's heirs, who had been involved in the bloodshed of the purges, ended. But the dominant role of the secret police at the pinnacle of power in Russia was far from over.

Mikhail Gorbachev became General Secretary of the Party in March 1985. Because of his age, he had not been involved in the Great Purges. But, in a somewhat different way, he was also a creature of the Soviet secret police, which had helped him get enrolled in the Moscow University's Law Department, where he was 'elected' secretary of the Komsomol (Union of Communist Youth) cell, a post in Stalin's time reserved for MGB (Ministry of State Security) collaborators. He rose up the party ranks with the support of the KGB (Committee of State Security, after 1953), and became a close friend of KGB Chief Andropov, who made him a member of the Politburo. It was in fact Andropov who introduced the word *perestroyka* ('reconstruction') and initiated the reconstruction of the Soviet system to save it from economic and political meltdown. When he become General Secretary Gorbachev promised to institute *perestroyka* and *glasnost* ('openness') and to fill in the 'blanks' in Soviet history. In fact, he intended to preserve the communist system and perpetuate himself as paramount Soviet leader. The result of his half-measures was the eventual disintegration of the Soviet Union.

Boris Yeltsin was elected President of Russia. Unlike his predecessors, he became a party member *after* Stalin's death, when the dominance of the secret police was greatly diminished. He was appointed secretary of the Sverdlovsk party organization because he was a successful industrial manager with an engineering education. Of course, no one in the party apparatus in Soviet times was totally isolated from the secret police, but in Yeltsin's case the ties to it were minimal. He was the timeliest figure among the Soviet party elite to break with the Stalinist past. As President, he was in the best position to re-establish the legitimacy of power in Russia, which had been brutally interrupted on 17 July 1918, when the Tsar and his family were murdered on Lenin's order. Eighty years later, on 17 July 1998, Yeltsin took part in a state funeral of the discovered remains of Tsar Nicholas II and his family. Yeltsin told the nation the horrible truth in his TV address: 'The truth has been concealed for 80 years. And we have to tell the truth tomorrow, and I should take part. This will be the right thing to do from the human point of view.'[1] But despite the many revelations during the Gorbachev and Yeltsin years, far from the whole truth was told to the Russian people. During the Yeltsin presidency in 1993 a law prohibiting release of information from Russian archives was approved. This is why many Russians still venerate Stalin and Lenin as sacrosanct idols. Crowds still visit Lenin's embalmed corpse in his mausoleum in the Red Square, and some 25 percent of Russians voted for the Communist Party in the 1999 Duma elections. Yeltsin resigned on the eve of new millennium, apologizing to the Russian people for not being able to fulfill all their hopes.

Yeltsin, for all his good intentions, succumbed under the weight of Stalin's legacy, which still burdens the life of the Russian people. Yeltsin twice unleashed brutal war against the Chechen people, all of whom Stalin had exiled to Siberia on 23 February 1944. Shortly before his resignation, during his visit to Peking, Yeltsin rattled the Russian nuclear saber, threatening the West with Russia's 'full nuclear arsenal'. This was reminiscent of

Khrushchev's banging his shoe on the podium in UN and threatening the West with 'We will bury you.'

Yeltsin compensated for a lack of KGB ties in his career by appointing three KGB career officers, Sergey Stepashin, Evgeny Primakov and Vladimir Putin, to the post of Russian prime minister. On the day of his resignation he appointed Putin Acting President of Russia, thus making it almost certain that he would be elected the next President of Russia. Putin served for years as KGB liaison officer with the notorious East German secret police, the STASI, spying on the West and the Germans on both sides of the Berlin wall. His KGB nickname was 'Stasy'. Putin's popularity soared when he promised to 'liberate' Chechnya, to destroy 'bandits and terrorists' and to restore 'Russian national pride'. He bragged of having 'liberated Grozny,' not mentioning the fact that the Russian Army had actually obliterated the city, with no building left standing to fly the Russian tricolor. Putin stopped any uncensored reporting from Chechnya from reaching the Russian people and the world, and ordered monitoring of e-mail and Internet use. He sharply increased the budget of the secret police. The Russian intelligence service is being merged with the interior ministry, creating a new KGB-style colossus.[2]

Grigory Yavlinsky, the leader of the liberal Yabloko Party, described the alliance of Putin supporters and the large communist Duma faction as an 'aggressive and obedient majority'. A century and a half earlier the great Russian poet Mikhail Lermontov had been sent into exile. On his departure he said: 'Goodbye unwashed Russia, the land of slaves and masters, and goodbye to you, blue uniforms, and to you, obedient to them people'. In Pushkin's time some 90 percent of the Russian population were enslaved serfs and the 'blue uniforms' were officers of the Separate Corps of Gendarmes, the secret police. 'Blue uniforms' reach deep into Russian history, pointing to a continuity that could be traced back to *oprichniki* (separate corps), actually palace guards, recruited mostly from criminals who terrorized the country during the reign of Ivan Grozny, murdering anyone whom his deranged mind perceived as enemies. The Separate Corps of Gendarmes was the backbone of the Okhrana, the Russian secret police at the turn of the twentieth century. This period became known in history as *Zubatovshchina*, after a practice of using Okhrana *agent provocateurs* to dominate the political life of the country, introduced by the Moscow Okhrana chief Zubatov, also known as 'Police Socialism'.

Stalin was a creature of the Okhrana. His secret police under its various names was an enormously magnified Okhrana. This has been Stalin's most enduring legacy and is the essence of this book, which tells a largely unknown story. People who do not know history are doomed to repeat it. It will take generations to overcome habits of thought formed during Stalin's long and brutal rule. By the law of nature, nations and individuals can find happiness only in freedom, and no nation can be free if it continues to suppress its own and other peoples. The struggle for a free Russia goes on.

NOTES

1. 'Yeltsin, in Reversal, Will Attend Rite for Czar and Family', *The New York Times*, 17 July 1998, p. A-3.
2. *New York Post*, 11 February 2000, p. 26.

Select Bibliography

NON-ENGLISH-LANGUAGE BOOKS

Agafonov, V. K. *Zagranichnaya okhranka*, Petrograd, 1918.

Aizenshtat, Yakov. *O podgotovke Stalinym genotsida evreev*, Jerusalem, 1994.

Alekseev, I. V. *Provokator Anna Serebriakova*, Moscow, 1932.

Alliluev, S. *Proidennyi put'*, Moscow, 1946.

Allilueva, Anna S. *Vospominaniya*, Moscow, 1946.

Allilueva, Svetlana. *Dvadtsat' pisem k drugu*, New York, 1967.

Antonov-Ovseenko, Anton. *Portret tirana*, New York, 1980.

Aragon, L. *L'Oeuvre poétique*, vol. VII (1936–37), Paris, 1977.

Arkhomed, S. T. *Rabochee dvizhenie i sotsial-democratiya na Kavkaze*, Geneva, 1910. Also published in Moscow/Petrograd, 1923.

Assmann, K. *Deutsche Schicksalsjahre*, Wiesbaden, 1950.

Avtorkhanov, A. *Zagadka smerty Stalina*, Frankfurt, 1976.

Badaev, A. E. *Bolsheviki v gosudarstvennoi dume*, Moscow, 1954.

Badash, Semen. *Kolyma ty moya, Kolyma*, New York, 1986.

Bagirov, M. D. *Iz istorii bolshevitskoi organizatsii Baku i Azerbaidzhana*, Moscow, 1946.

Bazhanov, Boris. *Vospominania byvshego sekretaria Stalina*, Paris, 1980.

Bega, F. F. and V. G. Aleksandrov. *Petrovsky*, Moscow, 1963.

Berberova, N. *Zheleznaya zhenshchina*, New York, 1982.

Berdiaev, Nikolay. *Russkaya ideya*, Paris, 1971.

—— *Dukhi russkoi revolutsii*, Paris, 1971.

Beria, Lavrenty. *Lado Ketskhoveli*, Moscow, 1938.

—— *K Voprosy ob istorii bolshevitskikh organizatsii v zakavkazie*, Leningrad, 1936.

Bonch-Bruevich, V. D. *Lenin o khudozhestvennoy literature*, Moscow, 1934.

Borshchagovsky, A. *Obviniaetsia krov'*, Moscow, 1994.

Bulgakov, M. A. *Sobranie sochinenii*, vol. III, Moscow, 1990.

Chlenov, S. B. *Moskovskaya okhranka i ee sekretnye sotrudniki*, Moscow, 1919.

Coulondre, R. *De Staline à Hitler*, Paris, 1950.

Darvichewy, Joseph, *Ah! Ce qu'on Rigolait Bien avec Mon Copain Staline*, Paris, 1979. Quoted in Daniel Rancour-Laferriere, *The Mind of Stalin*, Ann Arbor, 1988, pp. 36f.

Delgado, E. Castro, *J'ai perdu la foi à Moscou*, Paris, 1950.

Dmitrievsky, S. V. *Stalin*, Berlin, 1931.

Dmitrevsky, Vladimir, *Piatnitsky*, Moscow, 1971.

Dubinsky, I. *Primakov*, Moscow, 1968.

Dubinsky, I. V. *Naperekor vetram*, Moscow, 1964.

Dubinsky-Mukhadze, I. M. *Kamo*, Moscow, 1974.

—— *Ordzhonikidze*, Moscow, 1963.

Dubinsky-Mukhadze, I. M. *Shaumian*, Moscow, 1965.

Duhamel, Georges. *Le Livre de l'Ámertume*, Paris, 1983.

Ehrenburg, I. *Liudi, gody, zhizn'*, Moscow, 1967.

Enukidze, A. S. *Nashi podpolnye tipografii na Kavkaze*, Moscow, 1925.

Fleishman, L. *Boris Pasternak v tridtsatye gody*, Jerusalem, 1984.

Fotieva, L. A. *Iz vospominanii o V. I. Lenine, dekabr' 1922 g.-mart 1923 g.*, Moscow, 1964.

Gaglov, L. and I. Selishchev. *Komissary*, Moscow, 1961.

Gegeshidze, Z. T. *Lado Ketskhoveli*, 1959.

Geller, M. *Kontsentratsionny mir i sovetskaya literatura*, London, 1974.

Geller, M. and A. Nekrich, *Utopia u vlasti*, vol. 1, London, 1982.

Gnedin, Evgeny. *Iz istorii otnoshenii mezhdu SSSR i fashistskoy Germaniei*, New York, 1977.

—— *Katastrofa i vtoroe rozhdenie*, Amsterdam, 1977.

Gul', Roman. *Dzerzhinsky*, New York, 1974.

Gusarov, V. N. *Moi papa ubil Mikhelsa*, Frankfurt, 1978.

Herbart, P. *La ligne de force*, Paris, 1980.

Iremaschwili, J. *Stalin und die Tragödie georgiens*, Berlin, 1932. (English translation is in the author's archive.)

Kaminsky, V. and I. Vereshchagin. *Detstvo i yunost' vozhdia: documenty, zapiski, rasskazy*, Moscow, 1939.

Kazbegi, A. *Izbrannye sochineniya*, Tbilisi, 1957.

—— *Otseubiitsy, izbrannye sochineniya*, vol. I, Tbilisi, 1941.

Khrushchev, N. S. *Doklad na zakrytom zasedanii XX s'ezda KPSS o kulte lichnosti i ego posledstviyakh*, Moscow, 1959.

Kleist, P. *Zwischen Hitler und Stalin*, Bonn, 1950.

Kolesnik, Alexander. *Mify i pravda o Staline*, Kharkov, 1991.

Koritsky, N. I. *Marshal Tukhachevsky*, Moscow, 1965.

Kozmin, B. P. *Zubatov i ego korespondenty*, Moscow, 1928.

Krylenko, N. V. *Za piat' let, 1918–1922 g.*, Moscow, 1923.

Kurlov, P. G. *Gibel' imperatorskoi Rossii*, Berlin, 1923.

Larin, Yu. *Evreii i antisemitizm v SSSR*, see *Jerusalem University Collection*.

Lenin, V. I. *Polnoe sobranie sochinenii*, 5th edn, Moscow, 1958–65.

Leninsky sbornik, 2nd edn, vol. XI, Moscow–Leningrad, 1931, vols. XIII and XXV, Moscow, 1933.

Lomonosov, Yu. *Vospominaniya o martovskoi revolutsii 1917 g.*, Stockholm/Berlin, 1921.

Maisky, I. M. *Vospominaniya sovetskogo poslannika*, Moscow, 1964.

Makharadze, F. E. *Ocherki revolutsionnogo dvizheniya v Zakavkazie*, Tiflis, 1927.

Masanov, I. F. *Slovar' psevdonimov, russkikh pisatelei, uchenykh i obshchestvennykh deiatelei*, Moscow, 1956–60.

Medvedeva Ter-Petrosian, S. F. *Geroi revolutsii (Tovarishch Kamo)*, Moscow, 1925.

Melgunov, S. *Kak bolsheviki zakhvatili vlast'*, Paris, 1953.

Melgunov, S. P. *Na putiakh k dvortsovomu perevorotu*, Paris, 1931.

Merezhkovsky, D. S. *Griadushchii kham* (1906), *Polnoe sobranie sochinenii*, St Petersburg/Moscow, 1912.

—— *Griadushchii kham, Polnoe sobranie sochinenii*, vol. 15, Moscow, 1973.

Nadezhdin, P. *Kavkazskii krai, priroda i ludi*, Tipografia. V. N. Sokolova, Tula, 1901.

Nike, Michele. *K voprosu o smerti M. Gorkogo*, Paris, 1988, p. 344, fn. 29 (referring to Vsevolod, Ivanov. *Vstrechi s Gorkim*, Moscow, 1947, p. 315, and Bykoutseva, L. *Gorky v Moskve*, Moscow, 1968. p. 315).

Nikitina, G. S. *Gosudarstvo Izrail*, Moscow, 1968.

Nikulin, Lev. *Marshal Tukhachevsky*, Moscow, 1961.

Novitsky, V. D. *Iz vospominanii zhandarma*, Leningrad, 1929.

Orlov, Alexander. *Tainaya istoria stalinskikh prestuplenii*, New York/Jerusalem/Paris, 1983.

Perus, J. *Correspondance Romain Rolland et Maxime Gorki*, Paris, 1991.

Piaskovsky, A., *Pervaya (Tammerforskaya) konferentsiya RSDRP*, Moscow, 1951.

Piatnitsky, O. A., (ed.) *Prazhskaya konferentsiya RSDRP*, Moscow, 1937.

Piatnitskaya, Yulia. *Dnevnik zheny bolshevika*, New York, 1987.

Pilsudsky, J. *Rok 1920 Z povody pracy M. Tuchaczewskiego 'Pochod za Wisle'*, Warsaw, 1931.

Rapoport, Vitaly and Yury Alexeev. *Izmena rodine*, London, 1988.

Raskolnikov, F. *Na boevykh putiakh*, Moscow, 1964.

Raskolnikov, F. F. *Kronshtat i Peter v 1917*, Moscow/Leningrad, 1925.

Rozkanov, F. *Zapiski po istorii revolutsionnogo dvizheniya v Rossii (do 1913 goda)*, Izd. Dept. Politsii, St Petersburg, 1913.

Samoilov, F. N. *Vospominaniya*, vol. III, Moscow/Leningrad, 1923-27.

Shaginian, Marietta. *Semiya Ulianovykh*, Moscow, 1963.

Shchegolev, P. E. *Okhranniki i avanturisty*, Moscow, 1930.

Sheinin, Lev. *Zapiski sledovatelia*, Moscow, 1968.

Sheinis, Z. *Grozila deportatsiya*, Moscow, 1991.

—— *Provokatsia veka*, Moscow, 1994.

Shkapa, I. S. *Sem' let s Gorkim*, Moscow, 1964, 1989.

Shotman, A. *Kak iz iskry vozgorelos' plamia*, 2nd edn, Leningrad, 1935.

Shub, David. *Politicheskie deyateli rossii*, New York, 1969.

Shveitser, V. *Stalin v turukhanskoi ssylke*, Moscow, 1943.

Sokolov, N. *Ubiystvo tsarskoy semyi*, Buenos Aires, 1969.

Sokolova, A. I. *Moskovskaya suysknaya politsiya*, Petrograd, 1916.

Solomon, G. A. *Lenin i ego semiya*, Paris, 1931.

Solzhenitsyn, A. S. *Arkhipelag Gulag*, New York, 1974.

Spiridovich, A. I. *Istoriya bolshevizma v rossii ot vozniknoveniya do khvata vlasti, 1883–1903–1917*, Paris, 1922.

Stalin, I. V. *O Lenine*, Moscow, 1951.

—— *Marxizm i natsionalnyi vopros*, Moscow, 1953.

—— *Sochineniya*, vols I–XIII, Moscow, 1946–51.

Tishkov, A. *Dzerzhinsky*, Moscow, 1974.

Tovstukha, I. P. *Iosif Vissarionovich Stalin*, Moscow, 1927.

Trifonov, Yu. *Otbleski kostra*, Moscow, 1966.

Trotsky, L. *O Lenine*, Moscow, 1924.

—— *Moya zhizn'*, New York, 1930.

Tsereteli, I. P. *Vospominaniya o fevralskoi revoliutsii* (2 vols), Paris, 1963.

Tsvetaeva, Marina. *Izbrannye sochineniya*, Moscow–Leningrad, 1964, Introduction.
—— *Sochineniya v dvukh tomakh*, vol. 1, Moscow, 1968, Introduction.
Urutadze, G. I. *Obrazovanie i konsolidatsiya gruzinskoi demokraticheskoi respubliki*, Munich, 1956.
Viktorov, I. *Podpol'shchik, voin, chekist*, Moscow, 1968.
Volchek, G. and V. Voinov. *Viktor Kurnatovsky*, Moscow, 1961.
Volin, B. M. *12 Biografii*, Moscow, 1924.
Volkov, F. D. *Vzlet i padenie Stalina*, Moscow, 1992.
Walter, Gerard. *Lenine*, Paris, 1950.
Weingart, A. *Ugolovnaya taktika*, St Petersburg, 1912.
Yakir, P. I. and Ya. I. Geller. *Kommandarm Yakir*, Moscow, 1963.
Zavarzin, Pavel P. *Zhandarmy i revolutsionery. Vospominaniya*, Paris, 1930.
—— *Rabota tainoi politsii*, Paris, 1924.
Zhgenti, Leontii. *Prichiny revolutsii na Kavkaze i rukovodstvo*, Paris, 1963.
Zhilin, P. A. *Kak fashistkaya Germaniya gotovila napadenie na sovetskii soyuz*, Moscow, 1966.
Zhukov, G. K. *Vospominaniya i razmyshleniya*, Moscow, 1974.
Zubov, N. *F. E. Dzerzhinsky, biografiya*, Moscow, 1963.

ENGLISH–LANGUAGE BOOKS

Allilueva, Svetlana. *Only One Year*, New York, 1969.
—— *Twenty Letters to a Friend*, New York, 1967.
Amba, A. *I Was Stalin's Bodyguard*, London, 1952.
Avon, the Earl of. *The Eden Memoirs*: vol. I, *Full Circle*; vol. II, *Facing the Dictators*; vol. III, *The Reckoning*, London, 1960–65.
Avtorkhanov, A. *The Reign of Stalin*, London, 1953.
Backer, G. *The Deadly Parallel: Stalin and Ivan the Terrible*, New York, 1950.
Baikalov, A. *I Knew Stalin*, London, 1940.
Balabanova, A. *My Life as a Rebel*, New York and London, 1938.
Barbusse, H. *Stalin*, New York and London, 1935.
Barmine, Alexander. *One Who Survived*, New York, 1945.
Beer, Israel. *Israeli Security*, Tel Aviv, 1966.
Bessedovsky, Gregory. *Revelations of a Soviet Diplomat*, London, 1931.
Bezymenski, Leo. *The Death of Adolf Hitler: Unknown Documents from Soviet Archives*, New York, 1968.
Billington, J. H. *The Icon and the Axe: an Interpretive History of Russian Culture*, New York, 1970.
Bissonette, G. A. A. *Moscow Was My Parish*, New York, 1956.
Bobrovskaya, T. S. *Provocateurs I Have Known*, London, 1931.
Bronstein, J. *The Politics of Murder*, New York, 1950.
Bullock, Alan. *Hitler and Stalin: Parallel Lives*, New York, 1991.
—— *A Study in Tyranny*, New York, 1964.
Burns, James MacGregor. *Roosevelt: the Soldier of Freedom 1940–1945*, London, 1971.
Bychovsky, Gustav. 'Joseph Stalin: Paranoia and the Dictatorship of the Proletariat', in

Benjamin B. Wolman (ed.), *The Psychoanalytic Interpretation of History*, New York/ London, 1971.

Byrnes, James F. *Speaking Frankly*, New York and London, 1947.

Carmichael, Joel. *Trotsky*, London, 1975.

Chamberlin, W. H. *The Russian Revolution, 1917–1921*, vol. 1, New York, 1935.

Churchill, Winston. *The Second World War*, London, 1948.

Ciliga, Anton. *The Russian Enigma*, London, 1940.

Cleckley, Harvey, M. D. *The Mask of Sanity*, St Louis, 1955.

Cole, D. M. *Josef Stalin: Man of Steel*, London, 1942.

Conquest, Robert. *The Great Terror*, New York, 1973.

—— *The Soviet Deportation of Nationalities*, London, 1960.

—— *Stalin: Breaker of Nations*, New York, 1991.

Custine, Marquis Astolphe de. *Journey for Our Time – The Russian Journals of Marquis de Custine*, Chicago, 1951.

Davies, Joseph E. *Mission to Moscow*, 2 vols, New York, 1941; London, 1942.

Deacon, Richard. *A History of the Russian Secret Service*, New York, 1972.

Dedijer, Vladimir. *Tito Speaks: His Self Portrait and Struggle with Stalin*, London, 1953.

Delbars, Y. *The Real Stalin*, London, 1953.

Deutscher, Isaac. *The Prophet Armed: Trotsky, 1879–1921*, New York, London, 1954.

—— *The Prophet Unarmed*, New York, 1965.

—— *Stalin: A Political Biography*, New York and London, 1968.

Dewar, H. *Assassins at Large*, London, 1951, Boston, 1952.

Dewey Commission Report. *Not Guilty*, New York, 1937.

Djilas, Milovan. *Conversations with Stalin*, New York and London, 1962.

Donovan, R. J. *The Assassins*, New York, 1955; London, 1956.

Duranty, Walter. *The Kremlin and the People*, New York, 1941.

Dziak, John J. *Chekisty: A History of the KGB*, Lexington, MA, 1988.

Elwood, Ralph Carter. *Roman Malinovsky: A Life without a Cause*, Newtonville, MA, 1977.

Erickson, John. *The Soviet High Command: A Military-Political History, 1918–1941*, London, 1962.

Essad-Bey (pseudonym). *Stalin: The Career of a Fanatic*, New York and London, 1932.

Farnsworth, Beatrice. *William C. Bullitt and the Soviet Union*, 1967.

Fischer, Louis. *The Life and Death of Lenin*, New York, 1952; London, 1953.

—— *The Life of Lenin*, New York, 1964.

Fishman, J. and J. B. Hutton. *The Private Life of Joseph Stalin*, London, 1962.

Florinsky, Michael T. (ed.). *McGraw-Hill Encyclopedia of Russia*, New York, 1961.

Freud, Sigmund. 'Dostoyevsky and Parricide', *Standard Edition of the Complete Psychological Works of Sigmund Freud*, vol. XXI (1927–31), London, 1961, pp. 172–94.

—— *Freud: Dictionary of Psychoanalysis*, ed. Nandor Fodor and Frank Gayner. With a preface by Theodor Reik, New York, 1969.

—— *Moses and Monotheism*, New York, 1939.

—— 'Psycho-analytic Notes on an Autobiographical Account of a Case of Paranoia (Dementia Paranoides)', *Standard Edition of the Complete Psychological Works of Sigmund Freud*, vol. XII, London, 1958–86, pp. 3–82.

Gilboa, Y. A. *The Black Years of Soviet Jewry*, Boston, Toronto, 1971.

Harcave, Sidney. *First Blood: The Russian Revolution of 1905*, New York, 1964.

Harris, Thomas A. *I'm OK – You're OK*, New York, 1973.

Haupt, Georges and Jean-Jacques, Marie. *Makers of the Russian Revolution*, Ithaca, 1974.

Hilger, Gustav and Alfred G. Meyer. *The Incompatible Allies*, New York, 1971.

Hingley, Ronald. *Joseph Stalin: Man and Legend*, New York, 1974.

Hitler, Adolf. *Mein Kampf*, New York, 1939.

Hutton, J. *Stalin, the Miraculous Georgian*, London, 1961.

Hyde, H. Montgomery, *Stalin: The History of a Dictator*, New York, 1971.

Jones, Ernest, M. D. *Psycho-Myth, Psycho-History*, 2 vols, New York, 1974.

Karell, Paul. *Hitler's War on Russia*, London: Transworld Publishers, 1966.

Kerensky, Alexander. *The Crucifixion of Liberty*, New York, 1934.

Khrushchev, N. S. *Krushchev Remembers*, Boston, Toronto, 1970.

—— *Khrushchev Remembers – The Last Testament*, Boston, 1970.

Kirk, George E. *A Short History of the Middle East*, New York, 1964.

Klimov, G. *The Terror Machine*, New York and London, 1953.

Kochan, Lionel. *The Struggle for Germany 1914–1945*, New York, 1967.

Kot, Stanislaw. *Conversations with the Kremlin and Dispatches from Russia*, London, 1963.

Krivitsky, Walter G. *In Stalin's Secret Service*, New York, 1939.

—— *I Was Stalin's Agent*, London, 1939.

Krottov, Yury. *The Red Monarch: Scenes from the Life of Stalin*, New York, 1979.

Krupskaya, N. K. *Reminiscences of Lenin*, Moscow and London, 1959.

Kuby, Erich. *The Russians and Berlin 1945*, London, 1968.

Langer, Walter C. *The Mind of Adolf Hitler*, New York, 1972.

Lermolo, Elizabeth. *Face of a Victim*, New York, 1956.

Levine, I. D. *I Rediscover Russia*, New York, 1964.

—— *Stalin*, New York, 1931.

—— *Stalin's Great Secret*, New York, 1956.

—— *The Man Lenin*, New York, 1924.

—— *The Mind of an Assassin*, New York, 1959.

Lewin, Moshe. *Lenin's Last Struggle*, New York, 1968.

Lockart, B. H. *Memoirs of a British Agent*, London, 1932.

Ludwig, E. *Stalin*, New York, 1942.

Lyons, E. *Stalin, the Czar of All the Russias*, Philadelphia/New York and London, 1940.

Maclean, Fitzroy. *Eastern Approaches*, London, 1941.

Maisky, Ivan. *Journey into the Past*, London, 1962.

Mandelstam, Nadezhda. *Hope Against Hope: A Memoir*, London, 1989.

Medvedev, Roy. A. *Let History Judge*, New York, 1971.

—— 'New Pages from the Political Biography of Stalin', in *Stalinism*, ed. Robert C. Tucker, New York, 1977.

Menon, K. P. S. *The Flying Troika*, London, 1963.

Michaelis, Meir. *Mussolini and the Jews*, New York, 1979.

Montgomery of Alamein, Field Marshal Viscount. *Memoirs*, London, 1958.

Moran, Lord. *Winston Churchill: The Struggle for Survival 1940–1965*, London, 1966.

Morse, Arthur D. *While Six Million Died*, New York, 1967.

Nikitine, B. V. *The Fatal Years: Fresh Revelations on a Chapter of Underground History*, London, 1938.

Nikolaevsky, B. I. *Azef, the Spy, Russian Terrorist, and Police Stool*, Garden City, NY, 1934; *Azef, the Russian Judas*, London, 1934.

—— *Power and the Soviet Elite*, New York, 1965.

Orlov, Alexander. *The Secret History of Stalin's Crimes*, New York, 1953.

Orlov, V. *The Secret Dossier*, London, 1953.

Payne, Robert. *The Rise and Fall of Stalin*, New York, 1965; London, 1966.

Perkins, Frances. *The Roosevelt I Knew*, London, 1947.

Pipes, R. *The Formation of the Soviet Union, Communism and Nationalism, 1917–1923*, Cambridge, MA, 1964.

Possony, S. T. *Lenin: The Compulsive Revolutionary*, London, 1966.

Radkey, Oliver Henry. *The Election to the Russian Constituent Assembly of 1917*, Cambridge, 1950.

Radzinsky, Edvard. *Stalin*, New York, 1996

Rancour-Lafferriere, Daniel. *The Mind of Stalin*, Ann Arbor, MI, 1988.

Rapoport, Louis. *Stalin's War Against the Jews*, New York, 1990.

Reed, John. *Ten Days That Shook the World*, New York, 1960; London, 1962.

Rigby, T. T. *The Stalin Dictatorship: Khrushchev's Secret Speech and Other Documents*, Sydney, 1968.

Serge, V. *From Lenin to Stalin*, New York, 1937, London, 1937.

—— *Memoirs of a Revolutionary 1901–1944*, Oxford, London, 1967.

Shatunovskaya, Lidia. *Life in the Kremlin*, New York, 1982.

Sherwood, Robert E. *The White House Papers of Harry L. Hopkins*, vols. I and II, 1949.

Shub, D. *Lenin*, Garden City, NY, 1948.

Slusser, Robert M. *Stalin in October – The Man Who Missed the Revolution*, Baltimore/London, 1987.

Smith, Edward Ellis. *The Young Stalin: The Early Years of an Elusive Revolutionary*, London, 1968.

Souvarine, Boris. *Stalin: A Critical Survey of Bolshevism*, London, 1939.

Speer, Albert. *Inside the Third Reich*, New York, 1970.

Stalin, I. V. *Marxism vs. Liberalism*, interview by H. G. Wells, New York, 1935; *Stalin–Wells Talk*, London, 1934.

—— *Stalin's Correspondence with Churchill, Attlee, Roosevelt and Truman 1941–1945*, 2 vols, Moscow and London, 1957–58.

—— *Stalin's Kampf: Joseph Stalin's Credo, Written by Himself*, ed., M. R. Werner, New York and London, 1940.

Stettinius, Edward R. Jr. *Roosevelt and the Russians: The Yalta Conference*, London, 1950.

Sukhanov, N. N. *The Russian Revolution, 1917; Eyewitness Account*, 2 vols, New York and London, 1955.

Svanidze, Budu. *My Uncle Joe*, Introduction by Gregory Bessedovsky, London, 1952.

Tokaev, G. A. *Stalin Means War*, London, 1951.

Treadgold, Donald W. *Twentieth Century Russia*, Chicago, 1976.

Trotsky, Lev. *Stalin*, New York, 1941.

—— *Stalin's School of Falsification*, New York, 1962.

Truman, Harry. *Years of Trial and Hope 1946-1953*, London, 1966.

Tucker, Robert C. *Stalin as Revolutionary 1879-1929*, New York, 1973.

—— (ed.) *Stalinism*, New York, 1977.

Ulam, Adam B. *The Bolsheviks: The Intellectual, Personal and Political History of the Triumph of Communism in Russia*, New York, 1968.

—— *Stalin: the Man and His Era*, New York, 1973.

Vaksberg, Arkady. *Stalin Against the Jews*, New York, 1994.

Vasiliev, A. T. *The Okhrana*, London, 1930.

Vogeler, Robert A. *I Was Stalin's Prisoner*, New York, 1951.

Voronsky, A. K. *The Waters of Life and Death*, London, 1936.

Waite, Robert G. L. *The Psychopathic God: Adolf Hitler*, New York, 1977.

Weisberg, Alexander. *The Accused*, New York, 1951.

Winks, Robin W. *The Historian as Detective*, New York, 1970.

Wolfe, Bertram D. *Khrushchev and Stalin's Ghost*, New York and London, 1957.

—— *Three Who Made a Revolution*, 2 vols, New York, 1964.

Woodward, Sir Ernest Llewellyn. *British Foreign Policy in the Second World War*, London, 1962.

Yaresh, Leo. 'Ivan the Terrible and the Oprichnina', in Black, Cyril E. (ed.), *Rewriting Russian History*, New York, 1962.

Yaroslavsky, E. *Landmarks in the Life of Stalin*, Moscow, 1940, London, 1942.

Zeman, Z. A. *Germany and the Revolution in Russia, 1915–1917: Documents of the Archives of the German Foreign Ministry*, London, 1958.

Zeman, Z. A. B. and Scharlau, W. B. *The Merchant of Revolution: the Life of Alexander Israel Helfand (Parvus) 1867–1924*, London, 1966.

Zinger, Ladislaus. *Lenin and Women*, Stuttgart, 1970.

NON-ENGLISH-LANGUAGE PERIODICALS

Abramovich, R. 'Chingiz Khan 20-go veka', *Sotsialisticheskii vestnik*, no. 12, 30 December 1949.

Agursky, M. S. *Novoe russkoe slovo*, 2 April 1974.

Alliluev, S. 'Moi vospominaniya', *Krasnaya letopis'*, no. 5, 1923.

—— 'Vstrechi s tovarishchem Stalinym', *Proletarskaya revolutsiya*, no. 8, 1937.

Amlinsky, Vladimir. 'Mysli o Molotove', *Literaturnaya gazeta*, 7 September 1988.

Anisimov, N. 'I. V. Stalin v gody solvychegodskoi i vologodskoi ssylok', *Istorik-marksist*, no. 9, 1940.

Antonov-Ovseenko, Anton. 'Katyn', *Novoe Russkoe slovo*, 27 May 1988.

—— 'Beria', *Yunost'*, December 1988.

Aronson, G. 'Malinovsky – agent Lenina', *Rossiya nakanune revoliutsii: istoricheskie etiudy*, 1962, pp. R4–60.

—— 'Stalinskii protest protiv Martova', *Sotsialisticheskii vestnik*, no. 7–8, 1939.

Arsenidze, R. 'Iz vospominanii o Staline', *Novy zhurnal*, no. 72, 1972.

—— 'L. Beria: K Voprosu ob istorii bolshevitskikh organizatsii v Zakavkazie', *Caucasian Review*, no. 1, 1955.

Arutunov, G. and F. Volkov. 'K sydu istorii', *Moskovskaya pravda*, 30 March 1989.

Avtorkhanov, A. 'Koba i Kamo', *Novy zhurnal*, no. 110, 1973, pp. 266–87.

Badaev, A. E. 'Arest dumskoi piaterki v 1914 g.', *Krasny arkhiv*, no. 3 (64), 1934.

—— 'Russkie bolsheviki do revoliutsii', *Byloe*, no. 1, 1926.

—— 'O Staline', *Pravda*, 19 December 1939.

Bakai, M. E. 'Iz Vospominanii M. E. Bakaia o chernykh kabinetakh v Rossii', *Byloe*, no. 11, 1908.

Bazhanov, Boris. 'Polet v nochi', *Kontinent*, nos. 8–10, Paris, 1976.

—— 'Stalin', *Kontinent*, no. 8, 1978.

Bedia, E. 'Pervoe Maya 1901 goda v Tbilisi', *Izvestia*, 27 April 1937.

Bednyi, D. 'S podlinnym verno!', *Pravda*, 20 December 1929.

Beria, Lavrenty. 'Lado Ketskhoveli', *Pravda*, no. 189, 11 July 1937.

Bernstein, Edward. 'Ein Dunkeles Kapitel', *Vorwärts*, Berlin, 14 June 1921.

Betell, Nikolas. 'Katyn 1940', *Kontinent*, no. 11, 1977.

Bialik, B. 'Stalin i Gorky', *Krasnaya nov'*, no. 12, 1939.

Bokov, I. 'Sila Stalina', *Pravda*, 24 December 1939.

Burtsev, V. L. 'Lenin i Malinovsky', *Russkoe slovo*, vol. I, no. 9/10, 17 May 1919.

—— 'Otvet na postavlennyi vopros', *Russkoe slovo*, 25 March 1917 (O.S.).

Bystrov, S. 'Dozvoleno k pechati', *Krasnaya zvezda*, 18–20 March 1988.

Chalikova, V. A. 'Arkhivnyi yunosha', *Neva*, October 1988.

Chlenov, S. B. 'Moskovskaya okhranka i ee sekretnye sotrudniki', Moscow, 1919.

Drabkina, E. 'Zimnii pereval', *XX vek*, no. 2, London, 1977.

Drapkina, F. 'Tsarskoe pravitelstvo i pravda (documenty)', *Istoricheskii zhurnal*, nos 3–4, Moscow, 1937.

Druzhnikov, Yury. 'Saga o Pavlike Morozove', *Strana i mir*, no. 2(44), March–April 1988.

Dubrovsky, S. 'Protiv idealizatsii deyatelnosti Ivana IV', *Vosprosy istorii*, no. 8, August 1956.

Erenfeld, B. K. 'Delo Malinovskogo', *Voprosy istorii*, no. 7, 1965.

Evseev, E. 'Istoriya sionizma v tsarskoi Rossii', *Voprosy istorii*, 5, 1973.

Gerland, B. 'Kto otravil Gorkogo?', *Sotsialistichesky vestnik*, no. 6, 1954.

Golubovich, V. 'Molodoi Stalin', *Istorik-marksist*, no. 1, 1940.

Gorbanevsky, M. 'Tovarishch Stalin vy bolshoi ucheny', *Nedelia*, no. 45, 5–11 November 1990.

Gorky, M. 'Ob izdanii romana besy', *Pravda*, 24 January 1935.

Gudava, T. and E. Gudava. 'Ubiistvo Ili Chavchavadze v arkhivnykh dannykh', *Novoe Russkoe slovo*, 1 April 1988.

Idashkin, Yury. 'Lichny drug Stalina: Bogi zhazhdut', *Literaturnaya Rossia*, 22 July 1988, Moscow. Reprinted in *Novoe Russkoe Slovo*, New York.

Itskov, I. P. 'Dvadtsatye gody', *Novoe russkoe slovo*, 22 September 1987.

Ivanov, B. 'V novoi ude', *Pravda*, 25 December 1939.

Kafanova, Ludmila. 'O velikom druge i vozhde', *Novoe russkoe slovo*, 23 and 24 March 1977.

Kaptelov, B. I. and Z. I. Peregudova. 'Byl li Stalin agentom okhranki?', *Voprosy istorii KPSS*, April 1989.

Karganov, N. 'Iz proshlogo Stalina', *Vozrozhdenie*, Paris, 13 January 1929.

Kolesnik, A. N. 'Glavny telokhranitel vozhdia', *Voenno-istoricheskii zhurnal*, no. 12, Moscow, 1989.

—— 'Voennoplennyi starshii leitenant Yakov Dzhugashvili', *Voenno-istoricheskii zhurnal*, Moscow, December 1988.

Konev, F. 'Kak perezakhoranivali Stalina', *Voenno-istoricheskii zhurnal*, Moscow, 1989.

Koniavko, I. P. 'V podpolie i v emigratsii, 1911–1922', *Proletarskaya revoliutsiya*, no. 16, 1926.

—— 'Parizhskaya sektsiya bolshevikov do nachala voiny', *Proletarskaya revoliutsiya*, no. 4, 1923.

Kosinsky, Iosif. 'Za chto borolis?', *Novoe russkoe slovo*, 22 April 1988.

Lanina, L. 'Madam Tusso i tovarishch Krupskaya', *Panorama*, Israel, 3 July 1988, a reprint from the Moscow *samizdat* journal *Referendum*.

Likholitov, V. 'Interview s meditsinskimi rabotnikami prisutstvovavshimi pri smerti Stalina', *Meditsinskaya gazeta*, 11 November 1988.

—— 'Kak balzamirovali Stalina', *Meditsinskaya gazeta*, 10 August 1988.

Loginov, A. 'Tri versii smerti Gorkogo', *Argumenty i fakty*, no. 1, January 1989.

Lulechnik, V. 'Zagovor protiv Stalina i delo Tukhachevskogo', *Panorama*, 10–16 May 1995.

Maksakov, V. 'Arkhiv revolutsii i vneshnei politiki XIX–XX vekov', *Arkhivnoe delo*, no. XIII, 1927.

Margushin, P. 'Lenin i Innesa Armand', *Novoe russkoe slovo*, 17 November 1985.

Martov, L. 'Artilleriyskaya podgotovka', *Vpered*, Petrograd, 18 March 1918.

Matasova, F. 'Nabludenie za V. I. Leninym v dekabre 1905 g.– yanvare 1906 g.', *Krasnaya letopis'*, no. 1(12), 1925.

Medvedev, Roy. 'Dvadtsaty vek', *Obshchestvenno-politicheskii i literaturnyi almanakh*, no. 2, London, 1977.

Meglakelidze, S. and A. Iovidze. 'Revolutsiya 1905–1907 gg.', *Novoe vremia*, St Peterburg, 27 April 1906.

Mikhailiv, V. and V. Bondarenko. 'Zhizn' i smert' komissara Liushkova', *Kurier*, 3 June 1993.

Milchakov, Aleksander. 'Ovrag na kalitnikovskom', *Semya*, no. 40, Moscow, 1988.

Moroz, Oleg. 'Poslednii diagnoz', *Literaturnaya gazeta*, 28 September 1988.

Moroz, P. 'Gorky v SSSR. Vstrechi s Gorkim', *Sotsialisticheskii vestnik*, no. 1, 1954.

Nikolaevsky, B. I. 'K delu Malinovskogo', *Rabochaya gazeta*, 24 and 28 May, 17, 20, and 22 June 1917. In the Nikolaevsky Collection at the Hoover Institution, Stanford University.

Nikolashvili, N. 'Stikhi yunnogo Stalina', *Zaria Vostoka*, 21 December 1939.

Nord, L. A. 'Marshal Tukhachevsky', *Vozrozhdenie*, nos. 63–69, Paris, 1957.

Orlov, Boris. 'Mif o Fanni Kaplan', *Vremia i my*, no. 2, December 1975 and no. 3, January 1976.

Passony, S. 'Der Monat', *Heft 71*, August 1954.

Peskina, E. 'V Naryme', *Pravda*, 26 December 1939.

Pilsudsky, J. *Rok 1920 Z povody pracy M. Tuchaczewskiego 'Pochod za Wisle'*, Warsaw, 1931.

Pimenov, P. I. 'Kak ya iskal shpiona Raili', *Materialy samizdat*, Leningrad, 1968. See Samizdat Archive, Radio Liberty, New York, 6 April 1972.

Piters, Y. 'Rabota v cheka v pervye gody revoliutsii', *Proletarskaya revoliutsiya*, no. 10, 1924.

Pozniak, Zenon and Evgeny Shygalev. 'Kuropaty–doroga smerti', *Literatura i mastatstva*, Minsk, 3 June 1988; *Novoe russkoe slovo*, New York, 24 June 1988.

Prianishnikov, B. 'Pokhishchenie generala Kutepova', *Novoe russkoe slovo*, 9 December 1979.

Rachkov, I. 'Iz vospominaniy o Y. B. Gamarnike', *Voenno-istoricheskii zhurnal*, no. 5, 1965.

Raskolnikov, F. 'V iyulskie dni', *Proletarskaya revoliutsiya*, no. 5, 1923.

Razgon, Lev. 'Nakonets', *Moskovskie novosti*, no. 26, 26 June 1988.

Reiman, Mikhail. 'Agent v Politburo – k istorii sovetskoy politiki v 1932–1933 gg.', *Strana i mir*, no. 8, Munich, 1985.

Rozhdestvensky, S. 'Pokhishchenie generala Millera', *Novoe russkoe slovo*, 19 May 1979.

Rudnev, D. 'V Solvychegodske', *Pravda*, 16 December 1939.

Rybakov, Anatoly. 'Deti arbata', *Druzhba narodov*, no. 4–5, 1987.

Rybin, A. T. 'Riadom s I. V. Stalinym', *Sotsiologicheskie issledovaniya*, no. 3, 1988.

Serdyuk, Z. T. 'Rech' na XXII s'ezde partii', *Pravda*, 31 October 1961.

Serebriakova, Z. 'Stalin i tsarskaya okhranka', *Sovershenno secretno*, no. 7, Moscow, 1990.

Sharikov, K. 'Vazhneishie mesta prebyvaniya i revoliutsionnoy deyatelnosti I. V. Stalina v Peterburge–Petrograde–Leningrade 1909–1934', *Propaganda i agitatsiya*, no. 32, 1939.

Shatunovskaya, Lidia. 'Zagadka odnogo aresta', *Vremia i my*, no. 5, 1979.

Shengelaya, D. 'V Gori', *Pravda*, 14 December 1939.

Shub, David. 'Iz davnikh let', *Novy zhurnal*, no. 110, New York, 1973, pp. 288–95.

—— 'Noveishaya fabrikatsiya istorii KPSS', *Novoe russkoe slovo*, 23 December 1963.

Shumiatsky, Ya. 'Iosif Vissarionovich Stalin, biograficheskaya spravka', *Komsomolskaya pravda*, 21 December 1929.

Shumsky, S. 'Troyanovsky', *Poslednie novosti*, Paris, 1 January 1934.

Snegov, A. V. 'Neskolko stranits iz istorii partii', *Voprosy istorii KPSS*, no. 2, 1963.

Stalin, K. 'O voine', *Pravda*, no. 10, 16 March 1917.

—— 'Natsionalnyi vopros i sotsial-democratiya', *Prosveshchenie*, no. 3–5, March–May 1913.

Tabachnik, Dmitry. 'Seksot', *Kaleidoskop*, New York, no. 323, 30 March 1989, reprinted from 'Obyknovennyi provokator', *Rabochaya gazeta*, Kiev, March 1989.

Tsapeen, V. V. Report on data about Lenin's Jewish ancestry found in Russian and Ukrainian archives, *Arkhivy rodiny*, Spring 1992.

Tsiriulnik, Solomon. 'Ispoved' na popelishche', *Vremia i my*, no. 42, June 1979.

Turin, Yury. 'S odnoi storony, s drugoi storony', *Ogonek*, no. 39, Moscow, 1988.

Vaisberg, A. 'Evreisky antifashistsky komitet u M. A. Suslova', *Zveniya-istoricheskii almanakh*, Moscow, 1991, pp. 535–54.

Vakar, N. 'Stalin po vospominaniyam N. N. Zhordania', *Poslednie novosti*, Paris, 16 December 1936.

Vaksberg, Arkady. 'Kak zhivoi s zhivymi', *Literaturnaya gazeta*, June 29 1988.
—— 'Nazvat poimenno', *Novoe russkoe slovo*, 24 May 1988.
—— 'Taina oktiabria 1941-go', *Literaturnaya gazeta*, reprinted in *Mir*, no. 165, 5–11 May 1988.
Valentinov, N. 'O liudiakh revoliutsionnogo podpolia', *Novy zhurnal*, no. 73, September 1963.
Vereshchak, S. 'Stalin v tur'me: vospominaniya politicheskogo zakliuchennogo', *Dni*, 22 and 24 January 1928.
Viktorov, Boris. 'Zagovor krasnoi armii', *Pravda*, 29 April 1988.
Volkogonov, D. 'Demon revolutsii', *Pravda*, 9 September 1988.
Yaroslavsky, E. 'Vazhneishie vekhi zhizni i deyatelnosti tovarishcha Stalina', *V pomoshch' marksistsko-leninskomu obrazovaniu*, no. 10, Moscow 1939.
Yurasov, Dmitry. 'Vernite pravo na pamiat'', *Sobesednik*, no. 22, May 1988.
Zaslavsky, D. 'Zametki chitatelia', *Pravda*, 20 and 25 January 1935.
Zhavoronkov, Genady. 'I edinozhdy ne solgavshiy', *Moskovskie novosti*, 10 April 1988.
Zhilinsky, V. 'Organizatsiya i zhizn' okhrannogo otdeleniya vo vremia tsarskoi vlasti', *Golos minuvshego*, nos 9–10, 1917.
Zhirnov, Evgeny 'K. Kuzakov – syn I. V. Stalina', *Argumenty i fakty*, # 39, 1995.
Zhukov, G. K. 'Bitva za Berlin', *Voenno-istoricheskii zhurnal*, June 1965.
Zhukov, Y. 'Gori-Tbilisi', *Novy mir*, no. 12, 1939.

NON-ENGLISH-LANGUAGE PERIODICALS

'Bolsheviki i departament politsii', *Russkoe slovo*, 19 May 1917.
'Delo Malinovskogo i. dr.', *Rabochaya gazeta*, no. 62, 21 May 1917.
'Delo passrela shesti studentov', *Novy den'*, no. 20, 17/4 April 1918.
Dlia Vas, no. 48, Harbin, China, 27 November 1938.
'Epoka reaktsii (1908–1910)', *Krasny arkhiv*, no. 1 (16), 1934.
'Iz istorii prazhskoi konferentsii', *Krasny arkhiv*, no. 6 (97), 1938.
'Iz otcheta o perlustratsii departamenta politsii za 1908 g.', *Krasny arkhiv*, no. 2 (27), 1928.
'Iz proshlogo: stat'i i vospominaniya iz istorii bakinskoi organizatsii i rabochego dvizheniya v Baku', *Bakinskii proletarii*, 1923.
'Iz vospominanii russkogo uchitelia pravoslavnoi gruzinskoi dukhovnoi seminarii', *Russkaya pechatnia*, 1907.
'K delu Malinovskogo', *Vestnik vremennogo pravitelstva*, 22 June 1917.
'Kak departament politsii otpustil Lenina zagranitsu dlia bolshevitskoi propagandy', *Byloe*, vol. II, 1926.
'Kakie bolezni prepiatstvuyut postupleniyu na voennuyu sluzhbu', *Moskovskoe izd.*, Moscow, 1915.
'Neopublikovannye materialy iz biografii tovarishcha Stalina', *Antireligioznik*, no. 12, 1939.
'Novye dannye ob ubiistve Lado Ketskhoveli', *Krasnyi arkhiv*, no. 6, (91), 1938.

'Provokatory', *Russkoe slovo*, 15 April 1917.
'Shkola filerov', *Byloe*, no. 3 (25), 1917.
'V komissii Politburo TK KPSS', *Izvestia TK KPSS*, January 1989, Protocol no. 7, 29 December 1988.

ENGLISH–LANGUAGE PERIODICALS

Aronson, Grigory. 'Was Stalin a Tsarist Agent?', review of *'Stalin's Great Secret'* by I. D. Levine, *The New Leader*, 20 August 1956.
Bloom, Solomon F. *Commentary*, May 1957.
Coox, Alvin D. 'L'Affaire Liushkov', *Soviet Studies*, January 1968.
'Czarist Spy Named Stalin, A.' *Newsweek*, 7 November 1966.
Dunning, Jennifer. 'Alexsey Kapler', *The New York Times*, 15 September 1979.
Duranty, W. 'Stalin: Man, Mouthpiece, Machine', *The New York Times Magazine*, 18 January 1931.
Hansen, Joseph. 'With Trotsky to the End', Paris, October 1940.
Horwitz, L. 'Lenin and the Search for Jewish Roots', *The New York Times*, 5 August 1992.
Kamm, Henry. 'Inquiry on Jan Masaryk's Death', *The New York Times*, 3 April 1968.
Kennan, George F. Review of *The Young Stalin: the Early Years of an Elusive Revolutionary*, by Edward Ellis Smith, *American Historical Review*, October 1968.
—— 'The Historiography of the Early Political Career of Stalin'. *Proceedings of the American Philosophical Society*, vol. 115, no. 3, June 1971.
Kernberg, Otto. 'Structural Derivatives of Objective Relationships', *International Journal of Psycho-Analysis*, vol. 47, 1966.
Khrushchev, N. S. 'Special Report to the Twentieth Party Congress', *The New York Times*, 5 June 1956.
Knickerbocker, H. R. 'Stalin, Mystery Man Even to His Mother', *New York Evening Post*, 1 December 1930.
Knight, Amy. 'Beria, the Reformer', *The New York Times*, 3 November 1993.
Lee, Russel V. 'When Insanity Holds the Specter', *The New York Times*, 12 April 1974.
Levine, I. D. 'A Document on Stalin as Czarist Spy', *Life*, 23 April 1956.
—— 'Stalin Suspected of Forcing Trials to Cover His Past', *Journal American*, 3 March 1938.
Medvedev, Felix. *Soviet Media Digest*, 8 December 1987.
Nikolayevsky, Boris. 'The Strange Death of Mikhail Ryumin', *The New Leader*, 4 October 1954, pp. 15–18.
Orlov, Alexander. 'The Sensational Secret Behind Damnation of Stalin', *Life*, 23 April 1956.
Schmeman, Serge. 'Soviet Archives', *The New York Times*, 8 February 1993.
Schwartz, Stephen. 'Intellectuals and Assassins – Annals of Stalin's Killerati', *The New York Times Book Review*, 24 January 1988.
Slusser, Robert M. 'On the Question of Stalin's Role in the Bolshevik Revolution', *Canadian Slavonic Papers*, vol. XIX, no. 4, December 1978.

Speer, Albert. 'Nazi Invasion of Poland – September 1 1939', *The New York Times*, 31 August 1979.

Sulzberger, C. L. 'Foreign Affairs: Murder will Out', *The New York Times*, 17 April 1968.

Vaksberg, Arkady. 'The Grand Inquisitor's Right-Hand Man', *Literary Gazette International*, Moscow–Washington, vol. I, no. 5, April 1990.

PUBLISHED AND UNPUBLISHED REFERENCE MATERIALS

Agursky, M. 'My Father and the Great Terror'. A letter dated 15 June 1975.

Arkhivnye materialy o deyatelnosti I. V. Stalina, 1908–1913 gg. Krasny arkhiv, No. 2, 1934.

Avlabarskaya nelegalnaya tipografiya kavkazskogo soyuznogo komiteta RSDRP (1903–1906 gg.); Sbornik materialov i documentov. Tbilisi, 1954.

Bagratuni, Rafael, handwritten letter, dated 8 May 1967. In I. D. Levine's archive; copy in the author's archive.

Batumskaya demonstratsiya 1902-go goda. Moscow, 1937.

Biro-Bidzhanskii raion Dalne-Vostochnogo kraya, Komitet po zemelnomu ustroistvy trudiashchikhsia evreev, 2 vols. Moscow, 1928–30.

Biulleten oppositsii, ed. Lev Trotsky. New York.

Bolsheviki. Documenty po istorii bolshevizma s 1903 po 1916 gody byvshego moskovskogo okhrannogo otdeleniya, ed. M. A. Tsiavlovsky, Zadruga. Moscow, 1918.

Brakhtman, Ya. I. An award citation to labor camp prisoner Ya. I. Brakhtman (the author's father) on the occasion of the Moscow–Volga Canal completion, dated 11 June 1937 and signed by the chief of the Gulag, Zinovy Katznelson. In the author's archive.

Bukharin Trial: The Great Purge Trial, ed. Robert C. Tucker and Stephen F. Cohen. New York, 1965. Referred to as 'Bukharin Trial'.

'Chrezvychainoe sobranie upolnomochennykh fabrik i zavodov, Petrograd'. A leaflet published in *Kontinent*, no. 2, 1975, back cover.

'Chetvertyi (obyedinitelnyi) syezd RSDRP, April 1906 goda: protokoly'. Moscow, 1959.

Delo provokatora Malinovskogo. Moscow, 1992.

Dnevnik Imperatora Nikolaya II. Berlin, 1923.

Documents on German Foreign Policy 1918–1945, series D, vols VIII–XII. Washington and London, 1954–62.

Documents on International Affairs, 1928–1963, London, 1929–1973, Annual Record of Royal Institute of International Affairs, 1938, vol. I, 1939–1946.

Dvadtsat' piat' let bakinskoi organizatsii bolshevikov. Baku, 1924.

Eighteenth Congress of the Communist Party, The. Moscow, 1939.

Entsiklopedicheskii slovar'. St Petersburg, 1893–1906.

Evreiskaya entsiklopediya (Jewish Encyclopedia in Russian) 16 vols. St Petersburg, 1913.

Golovachev, M. P. Collection in the Bakhmetiev Archive at Columbia University's Library of Rare Manuscripts.

Gruzia v datakh, 'Khronika vazhneishikh politicheskikh, ekonomicheskikh i kulturnykh sobytii'. 1961.

History of the Communist Party of the Soviet Union (Bolsheviks) Short Course, New York, 1939.

International Military Tribunal, Trial of the Major War Criminals, vol. XXXVII, Nuremberg, 1947.

Iz istorii vserossiiskoi chrezvychainioi komissii 1917–1921 gg., *Sbornik Dokumentov*, Moscow, 1958.

'J.' A confidential letter to I. D. Levine, dated 17 July 1956, from an unidentified high State Department official who signed his letter 'J', describing two secret cables, dated 26 November 1941 and 5 January 1942, that had been sent from the German mission in Shanghai to the Foreign Ministry in Berlin concerning Golovachev's proposed sale of the 'Eremin Letter' (forgery). The cables were found in File AA/18 at the Alexandria Repository of captured German documents. 'J' letter contains a reference to Gustav Hilger's verbal statement that the German Foreign Ministry did not follow up on Golovachev's proposal because of the difficulty during the war of obtaining the documents and putting them through the customary external tests.

Jerusalem University Collection of Documents on Soviet Jews, ed. I. Frankel, Jerusalem, 1965.

Levine, I. D. Typewritten statement 'The Perjury Record of the Daily Worker's Distinguished Scientist – the Man who Built the Hiss Typewriter', 20 January 1958, Waldorf, MD.

—— Letter to author, dated 9 July 1974, referring to the visit to New York of Eremin's daughters.

—— Letter to author, dated 7 August 1976, with the reference to the 1926 report from Moscow to *Sotsialisticheskii vestnik* about a discovery of Stalin's Okhrana file. In the author archive. The 1926 Moscow report about the discovery of Stalin's Okhrana file is in David Shub's archive, deposited with Gene Sosin, an official of Radio Liberty in New York.

—— 'Stalin Was a Tsarist Agent'. Unpublished typewritten article for *The New Leader*, 1956. In I. D. Levine's and the author's archives.

Londonskii syezd rossiiskoi sotsial-democraticheskoy rabochei partii (1907 g), Paris, 1909.

Malaya sovetskaya entsiklopediya, Moscow, 1st ed., 1930–1931; 2nd ed., 1933-1947; 3rd ed., 1958–61.

Martynov, A. P. 'My Service in the Separate Corps of Gendarmes, 1898–1917', manuscript on file at the Hoover Institution.

Nazi–Soviet Relations 1939–1941, *Documents from the Archives of the German Foreign Office*, ed. Raymond J. Sonntag and James S. Beddie, Washington, 1948.

Nikolaevsky Collection at the Hoover Institution on War and Peace, Stanford University. Contains valuable clippings from newspapers of the Revolutionary period available nowhere else.

Not Guilty (Report of the John Dewey Commission), New York, 1937.

Okhrana Archive at the Hoover Institution, Stanford University. This is the Okhrana Foreign Agency Paris archive from the Russian Imperial Embassy in Paris brought to the United States by the Russian ambassador of the Provisional Government, V. Maklakov.

Orlov, Boris, 'Fania Kaplan'. Research paper at Jerusalem University.

'Osnovnye vekhi zhizni i deyatelnosti I.V. Stalina', *Propaganda i agitatsiya*, no. 23, 1939.

'Ot ministerstva yustitsii', *Vestnik vremennogo pravitelstva*, 16 June 1917.

Padenie tsarskogo rezhima (Stenograficheskie otchety doprosov i pokazanii, dannykh v 1917 g. v Chrezvychainoy Sledstvennoy Komissii Vremennogo Pravitelstva) ed. by P. E. Shchegolev, 7 vols, Moscow/Leningrad, 1925.

Piatakov Trial. 'Report of the Court Proceedings: The Case of the Anti-Soviet Trotskyite Center', English edn, Moscow, 1936. Referred to as 'Piatakov Trial'.

Pis'ma P. B. Akselroda i Yu. O. Martova 1902–1916, Berlin, 1924.

Proletarskii prigovor nad vrediteliami-interventami, record of court proceedings, Moscow, 1930.

Radio Libery Archive, Washington DC, and Prague, Czechoslovakia.

Rybin, A. T. (recollections of Stalin's bodyguard), 'Vremia, Idei, Sudby', *Sotsialisticheskie issledovaniya*, no. 3, 1988.

Sacardy, Paul. 'Lenin's Deputy: The Story of a Double Agent.' Manuscript on R. Malinovsky, dated October 1967, on file at Radio Liberty Committee Research Library. Copy in the author's archive.

Sarkisov, A. 'Sud'ba Marshala', *Kommunist*, no. 147, 22 June 1988.

Senate Internal Security Subcommittee Report, dated 10 January 1958, of hearings held on 8 February, 7 June, and 1 October 1957, designated part 66, exposing Martin K. Tytell as perjurer.

Shaginian, Margorita. On Lenin's Jewish grandfather, in Radio Liberty Committee broadcast from New York on Program no. 103/72.

Shumsky, S. Manuscript in Nikolaevsky Collection, file 132, box 4, no. 27. Relates Beletsky's testimony before the Muraviev Commission in 1917 about the Rozmirovich provocations.

Slusser, Robert M. 'Lenin's Deal with Stalin, April 1917'. Lecture at Yale University on 26 January 1978.

Smith, Edward Ellis. Letter to the author, dated 19 August 1974.

Spiridovich, General Alexander. Letter to I. D. Levine, dated 19 July 1949.

Spiridovich, General Alexander. Letter to Vadim Makarov, dated 13 January 1950. Russian original text and English translation in the author's archive.

'Spisok obschego sostava chinov otdelnogo korpusa zhandarmov', 1911.

Tytell, Martin. 'Exposing a Documentary Hoax', Paper presented to the American Association for the Advancement of Science', 29 December 1956. Copy in Levine's and the author's archives.

Uratadze, G. I. 'Moi vospominaniya'. Manuscript on file at the Hoover Institution, Stanford University.

'V komissii Politburo TK KPSS', *Izvestia TK KPSS*, January, 1989. Protokol no. 7, 29 December 1988.

Veselago, N. V. Former Okhrana officer and a relative of S. P. Beletsky, director of the Department of Police 1909–12), Veselago's letter to I. D. Levine, dated 25 June 1956, with his analysis of the Eremin Letter forgery. Copies in Levine's and the author's archives.

—— 'The Department of Police, 1911–1913'. From the recollections of Nikolay

Vladimirovich Veselago, unpublished taped interview with Edward Ellis Smith, on file at the Hoover Institution (Ms. HV 8225/S646). Copies in Smith's and the author's archives.

Zinoviev Trial. 'Report of Court Proceedings: the Case of the Trotskyite–Zinovievite Terrorist Center', English edn, Moscow, 1936. Referred to as 'Zinoviev Trial'.

INTERVIEWS

Agursky, Melik. Historian. Jerusalem, 1975.

Avigur, Saul. Head of the Russian Desk in the Israeli Intelligence. 1969.

Ben-Gurion, David. Prime Minister of Israel. Sde-Boker, 24 April 1969 and Tel-Aviv, 3 May 1969.

Berger, Iosif. Israel, 1969.

Chaplia, Alexander. Former Soviet officer and Gulag inmate related his recollections about the 'General Dubrovsky case', of which he had been one of the defendants. Miami, 1 June 1974.

Cohen, Aaron. Member of Mapam, arrested as a Soviet agent. Haifa, 1969.

Drapkina, Sara. Story on Poskrebyshev and Itskov, Tel-Aviv, 18 August 1975.

Fedoseev, Victor. Telephone interview from London, 16 June 1971.

Finegold, Nathan. Dissident, present at Stalin's funeral procession. New York, Hotel Tudor, 13 June 1974.

Gerbov, Tikhon Vasilievich. Tsarist army general. Testimony on Golovachev, Nayak, New York, February 14 1975.

Glick, Anna and Boris. New York City, 1967

Guriel, Boris. Head of the Weizman Archive. Tel-Aviv, 1969.

Gutkin, Vladimir. New York City, 1993.

Itskov, I. P. New York, 1989.

Kalik, Mikhail. Former Soviet movie director and Gulag inmate who is presently in Israel. 1971.

Kennan, George. Interview in his office at the Smithsonian Institution, Washington, DC, May 1979.

Kogan, Yura. Son of an executed high official in Minsk, on arrest of a general with a copy of the Eremin report. Mikhail Meerson taped this interview in Jerusalem, 1978.

Krotkov, Yury. New York City, 1972.

Levine, I. D. Chappaqua, New York, 19 June 1976.

Lifshitz, David. Head of Israeli bank. Tel-Aviv, 1969.

Litvinov, Pavel. Grandson of Maxim Litvinov. Chappaqua, New York, 1975.

Marshak, Beni. Former Political 'commissar' of Palmakh. Israel, 6 July 1969.

Meerson-Aksenov, Mikhail. New York City, 1969.

Mikunis, Samuel. Israeli M. P. and the leader of the Israeli Communist Party. Jerusalem, 12 May 1969.

Oren, Mordekhai. Member of Mapam, arrested in 1951 as defendant in Slansky trial. Israel, 1969.

Osinina, Rosa Solomonovna. Vitaly Svechinsky's aunt and the widow of the high-ranking NKVD officer Grigory Osinin-Vinnitsky and herself a secretary of NKVD chiefs Balitsky and Katznelson. Haifa, 18 August 1975.

Rodovsky, Alexander. Haifa, Israel, 1990.

Rodovsky, Natalia and Alexander. Haifa, Israel, 1979.

Rudich, Vasily. Yale University lecturer. Several taped interviews, starting 15 September 1975 at Brookline, MA, and ending in 1979 in Chappaqua, New York.

Selman, Abraham. Tel-Aviv, Israel, 1969.

Semenov, Yulian. Soviet writer. 1968 and 1988.

Sevela, Efim. Soviet movie director and writer, on Stalin's role in several movies. Chappaqua, 30 November 1974, 13 December 1975 and 15 February 1976.

Sharia, Nugzar. Honorary Actor of the Georgian SSR, presently at Radio Liberty Georgian Desk in Munich. A nephew of Stalin's assistant Peter Sharia. Sag Harbor, July 1971 to August 1973.

Shatunovskaya, Lidia, a Kremlin insider and Gulag inmate, and Tumerman, Lev. Weizman Institute, Rehavot, Israel, 18 August 1975.

Shatunovskaya, Olga. An Old Bolshevik. Unpublished memoirs related in taped interviews with V. Rudich and A. Tamarchenko.

Shmulevich, Matetiahu. Lehi terrorist. Yaffa, 1969.

Shragin, Boris. Leading dissident. Chappaqua, New York, 11 November 1979.

Spivakovsky, Efim. Dissident and former Gulag inmate. On the 'Kremlin Doctors' case, Chappaqua, 5 May 1974.

Svechinsky, Vitaly. Former Gulag inmate and author's co-defendant. Haifa and New York, 1971.

Svetlov, Felix. New York City, 1990 and 1991.

Tornopoler, Samuel. Editor of *Al-Hamishmar*. Tel-Aviv, Israel, February 1969.

Tumerman, Alexey. Son of Lidia and Alexander Tumerman, co-defendants in 1947–53 'Zionist Plot' case. Chappaqua, 5 October 1974.

Ulanovskaya, Maya. Daughter of Soviet intelligence officer. On Soviet intelligence in the USA in the 1930s and on the Alger Hiss–Chambers story. Jerusalem, 20 February 1979.

Vinkovetsky, Yakov and Diana. Chappaqua, 1975.

Volkovich, Samuel. Polish officer sent to Palestine in 1942. Tel-Aviv, Israel, 1969.

Yanai, Yakov. Israeli diplomat. Tel-Aviv, Israel, 1971.

Zubok, Boris. On barracks for Jews in Novaya Zemlia. Chappaqua, New York 1 March 1975.

Index

DISCARD